Swarm Robotics

Swarm Robotics

Special Issue Editor

Giandomenico Spezzano

MDPI • Basel • Beijing • Wuhan • Barcelona • Belgrade

MDPI

Special Issue Editor
Giandomenico Spezzano
CNR-ICAR
Italy

Editorial Office
MDPI
St. Alban-Anlage 66
4052 Basel, Switzerland

This is a reprint of articles from the Special Issue published online in the open access journal *Applied Sciences* (ISSN 2076-3417) from 2017 to 2019 (available at: https://www.mdpi.com/journal/applsci/special_issues/LAI_Swarm_Robotics).

For citation purposes, cite each article independently as indicated on the article page online and as indicated below:

LastName, A.A.; LastName, B.B.; LastName, C.C. Article Title. *Journal Name* **Year**, *Article Number*, Page Range.

ISBN 978-3-03897-922-7 (Pbk)
ISBN 978-3-03897-923-4 (PDF)

Contents

About the Special Issue Editor

Giandomenico Spezzano is Director of Research at the Institute of Computing and High-Performance Networks (ICAR) of the National Research Council (NRC) of Italy. He is head of the 'Distributed and Pervasive Intelligent Systems' laboratory at CNR-ICAR. Dr. Spezzano is also an Adjunct Professor at the Faculty of Engineering of the University of Calabria. He is a member of the teaching faculty of the PhD in 'Systems and Computer Engineering' at the DIMES Department of the University of Calabria. He worked as a senior researcher at the Consortium for Research and Applications of Computer Science (CRAI), where he was in charge of the research group 'distributed and parallel systems' of CRAI, carrying out numerous research projects at the national and international level in the field of parallel and distributed computing.

His research activities to date concern: the study of the methods and techniques of parallel processing for the definition of environments and programming tools to facilitate the programmability of parallel machines, GPU computing, cloud computing and peer-to-peer systems, autonomic and self-adaptive cloud workflows, models with cellular automata for scientific computations concerning the simulation of complex phenomena of the real world (landslides, soil restoration, infiltration, etc.), parallel data mining algorithms for the classification and clustering of large amounts of data, tools for parallel evolutionary programming, high-performance enabling platforms, multiagent systems with collective behavior (swarm intelligence), large-scale cyber-physical systems, middleware for smart object management, and smart cities based on the Internet of Things.

Dr. Spezzano is a member of the program committee of numerous international conferences in the field of distributed and parallel systems and complex adaptive systems. He is the author of four books and more than 200 scientific articles published in books, conference proceedings, and international journals. He is a member of the ACM and IEEE–CS, and is also a member of the IEEE Technical Committee on Self-Organized Distributed and Pervasive Systems and the IEEE Computer Society Technical Committee on Parallel Processing.

applied sciences

MDPI

Editorial

Editorial: Special Issue "Swarm Robotics"

Giandomenico Spezzano

Institute for High Performance Computing and Networking (ICAR), National Research Council of Italy (CNR), Via Pietro Bucci, 8-9C, 87036 Rende (CS), Italy; giandomenico.spezzano@icar.cnr.it

Received: 1 April 2019; Accepted: 2 April 2019; Published: 9 April 2019

Swarm robotics is the study of how to coordinate large groups of relatively simple robots through the use of local rules so that a desired collective behavior emerges from their interaction. The group behavior emerging in the swarms takes its inspiration from societies of insects that can perform tasks that are beyond the capabilities of the individuals. The swarm robotics inspired from nature is a combination of swarm intelligence and robotics [1], which shows a great potential in several aspects. The activities of social insects are often based on a self-organizing process that relies on the combination of the following four basic rules: Positive feedback, negative feedback, randomness, and multiple interactions [2,3].

Collectively working robot teams can solve a problem more efficiently than a single robot while also providing robustness and flexibility to the group. The swarm robotics model is a key component of a cooperative algorithm that controls the behaviors and interactions of all individuals. In the model, the robots in the swarm should have some basic functions, such as sensing, communicating, motioning, and satisfy the following properties:

1. *Autonomy*—individuals that create the swarm-robotic system are autonomous robots. They are independent and can interact with each other and the environment.
2. *Large number*—they are in large number so they can cooperate with each other.
3. *Scalability and robustness*—a new unit can be easily added to the system so the system is easily scalable. More number of units improve the performance of the system. The system is quite robust to the losing of some units, as there still exists some units left to perform. However, in this instance, the system will not perform up to its maximum capabilities.
4. *Decentralized coordination*—the robots communicate with each other and with environment to take the final decision.
5. *Flexibility*—it requires the swarm robotic system to have the ability to generate modularized solutions to different tasks.

Potential applications for swarm robotics are many. They include tasks that demand miniaturization (nanorobotics, microbotics), like distributed sensing tasks in micromachinery or the human body [4]. They are also useful for autonomous surveillance and environment monitoring to investigate environmental parameters, search for survivors, and locate sources of hazards such as chemical or gas spills, toxic pollution, pipe leaks, and radioactivity. Swarm robots can perform tasks in which the main goal is to cover a wide region. The robots can disperse and perform monitoring tasks, for example, in forests. They can be useful for detecting hazardous events, like a leakage of a chemical substance. Robotics is expected to play a major role in the agricultural/farming domain. Swarm robotics, in particular, is considered extremely relevant for precision farming and large-scale agricultural applications [5]. Swarm robots are also useful in solving problems encountered in IoT (Internet of Things) systems, such as co-adaptation, distributed control and self-organization, and resource planning management [6].

This special issue on Swarm Robotics focuses on new developments that swarm intelligence techniques provide for the coordination distributed and decentralized of a large numbers of robots in multiple application fields. A collection of 15 papers has been selected to illustrate the research work and the experimental results of the future swarm robotics in real world applications. The papers of this special issue can be classified into the following three research areas:

Formation control and self-assembly methods: The papers belonging to this area present control algorithms to allow a fleet of robots to follow a predefined trajectory while maintaining a desired spatial pattern. Jian Yang and their colleagues introduce a limited visual field constrained formation control strategy inspired by flying geese coordinated motion [7]. Additionally, the methods proposed in [8,9] can reconfigure the group of robots into different formation patterns by coordinating, also in a decentralized way, the joint angles in the corresponding mechanical linkage. A self-reconfigurable robotic system that is capable of autonomous movement and self-assembly is introduced in [10]. The formation problem of multiple robots based on the leader–follower mechanism is investigated in [11]. A model based on Swarm Chemistry is used in [12] to investigate as interesting patterns can be detected. Finally, a three-dimensional (3D) model identification method based on weighted implicit shape representation (WISR) is proposed in [13].

Localization and search methods for UAV and drone swarms: This special issue presents papers to define the position information of the robot members in the system and real-time search to cover a broad search space. In [14], an algorithm for UAV path planning based on time-difference-of-arrival (TDOA) is proposed. In [15], the authors propose a decision-control approach with the event-triggered communication scheme for the problem of signal source localization. The authors of [16] present a novel search method for a swarm of drones—a PSO algorithm is used as mechanism to update the position. Furthermore, in [17], an integrated algorithm combining the potential field and the three degrees (the dispersion degree, the homodromous degree, and the district-difference degree) is proposed to deal with cooperative target hunting by multi-AUV team in a surface-water environment. Another search algorithm based on a multi-agent system with a behavioral network made up by six different behaviors, whose parameters are optimized by a genetic algorithm and adapt to the scenario, is present in [18].

Intelligence techniques for solving optimization problems. An algorithm inspired by the process of migration and reproduction of flora is proposed in [19] to solve some complex, non-linear, and discrete optimization problems. An additional parallel technique for meta-heuristic algorithms designed for optimization purposes is presented in [20]. The idea was based primarily on the action of multi-threading, which allowed placing individuals of a given population in specific places where an extreme can be located. Finally, a distributed hybrid fish swarm optimization algorithm (DHFSOA) designed in order to optimize the deployment of underwater acoustic sensor nodes has been proposed in [21].

Acknowledgments: We would like to thank all authors, the many dedicated referees, the editor team of Applied Sciences, and especially Daria Shi (Assistant Managing Editor) for their valuable contributions, making this special issue a success.

Conflicts of Interest: The author declares no conflicts of interest.

References

1. Beni, G. From swarm intelligence to swarm robotics. In *Swarm Robotics Workshop: State-of-the-Art Survey*; Şahin, E., Spears, W., Eds.; Springer: Berlin, Germany, 2005; pp. 1–9.
2. Camazine, S.; Deneubourg, J.-L.; Franks, N.; Sneyd, J.; Theraulaz, G.; Bonabeau, E. *Self-Organization in Biological Systems*; Princeton University Press: Princeton, NJ, USA, 2001.
3. Bonabeau, E.; Dorigo, M.; Theraulaz, G. *Swarm Intelligence: From Natural to Artificial Systems*; Oxford University Press: New York, NY, USA, 1999.
4. Ceraso, D.; Spezzano, G. Controlling swarms of medical nanorobots using CPPSO on a GPU. In Proceedings of the 2016 International Conference on High Performance Computing & Simulation (HPCS), Innsbruck, Austria, 18–22 July 2016; pp. 58–65.

5. Albani, D.; IJsselmuiden, J.; Haken, R.; Trianni, V. Monitoring and mapping with robot swarms for agricultural applications. In Proceedings of the 2017 14th IEEE International Conference on Advanced Video and Signal Based Surveillance (AVSS), Lecce, Italy, 29 August–1 September 2017; pp. 1–6.

6. Zedadra, O.; Guerrieri, A.; Jouandeau, N.; Spezzano, G.; Seridi, H.; Fortino, G. Swarm intelligence-based algorithms within IoT-based systems: A review. *J. Parallel Distrib. Comput.* **2018**, *122*, 173–187. [CrossRef]

7. Yang, J.; Wang, X.; Bauer, P. V-Shaped Formation Control for Robotic Swarms Constrained by Field of View. *Appl. Sci.* **2018**, *8*, 2120. [CrossRef]

8. Liu, Y.; Gao, J.; Shi, X.; Jiang, C. Decentralization of Virtual Linkage in Formation Control of Multi-Agents via Consensus Strategies. *Appl. Sci.* **2018**, *8*, 2020. [CrossRef]

9. Liu, Y.; Gao, J.; Liu, C.; Zhao, F.; Zhao, J. Reconfigurable Formation Control of Multi-Agents Using Virtual Linkage Approach. *Appl. Sci.* **2018**, *8*, 1109. [CrossRef]

10. Tan, W.; Wei, H.; Yang, B. SambotII: A New Self-Assembly Modular Robot Platform Based on Sambot. *Appl. Sci.* **2018**, *8*, 1719. [CrossRef]

11. Wang, H.; Li, Y.; Qian, D.; Xi, Y. Leader–Follower Formation Maneuvers for Multi-Robot Systems via Derivative and Integral Terminal Sliding Mode. *Appl. Sci.* **2018**, *8*, 1045.

12. Nishikawa, N.; Suzuki, R.; Arita, T. Exploration of Swarm Dynamics Emerging from Asymmetry. *Appl. Sci.* **2018**, *8*, 729. [CrossRef]

13. Garcia-Aunon, P.; Barrientos Cruz, A. Comparison of Heuristic Algorithms in Discrete Search and Surveillance Tasks Using Aerial Swarms. *Appl. Sci.* **2018**, *8*, 711. [CrossRef]

14. Wang, W.; Bai, P.; Li, H.; Liang, X. Optimal Configuration and Path Planning for UAV Swarms Using a Novel Localization Approach. *Appl. Sci.* **2018**, *8*, 1001. [CrossRef]

15. Pan, L.; Lu, Q.; Yin, K.; Zhang, B. Signal Source Localization of Multiple Robots Using an Event-Triggered Communication Scheme. *Appl. Sci.* **2018**, *8*, 977. [CrossRef]

16. Lee, K.-B.; Kim, Y.-J.; Hong, Y.-D. Real-Time Swarm Search Method for Real-World Quadcopter Drones. *Appl. Sci.* **2018**, *8*, 1169. [CrossRef]

17. Ge, H.; Chen, G.; Xu, G. Multi-AUV Cooperative Target Hunting Based on Improved Potential Field in a Surface-Water Environment. *Appl. Sci.* **2018**, *8*, 973. [CrossRef]

18. Jin, X.; Kim, J. 3D Model Identification Using Weighted Implicit Shape Representation and Panoramic View. *Appl. Sci.* **2017**, *7*, 764. [CrossRef]

19. Cheng, L.; Wu, X.-H.; Wang, Y. Artificial Flora (AF) Optimization Algorithm. *Appl. Sci.* **2018**, *8*, 329. [CrossRef]

20. Połap, D.; Kęsik, K.; Woźniak, M.; Damaševičius, R. Parallel Technique for the Metaheuristic Algorithms Using Devoted Local Search and Manipulating the Solutions Space. *Appl. Sci.* **2018**, *8*, 293. [CrossRef]

21. Chang, T.; Chang, S.; Fan, Y. Event-Driven Sensor Deployment in an Underwater Environment Using a Distributed Hybrid Fish Swarm Optimization Algorithm. *Appl. Sci.* **2018**, *8*, 1638.

applied sciences

MDPI

Article

V-Shaped Formation Control for Robotic Swarms Constrained by Field of View

Jian Yang [1,†,‡] (ORCID), Xin Wang [1,*,†,‡] and Peter Bauer [2,‡]

1   Department of Mechanical and Automation Engineering, Harbin Institute of Technology Shenzhen, Shenzhen 518055, China; jyang10.hit@gmail.com
2   Department of Electrical Engineering, University of Notre Dame, Notre Dame, IN 46656, USA; pbauer@nd.edu
*   Correspondence: wangxinsz@hit.edu.cn; Tel.: +86-755-2603-3286
†   Current address: D414, HIT Campus, University Town, Shenzhen 518055, China.
‡   These authors contributed equally to this work.

Received: 31 August 2018; Accepted: 2 October 2018; Published: 1 November 2018

Featured Application: The proposed formation control method has the potential to be applied in swarm robotics relevant to collaborative searching tasks.

Abstract: By forming a specific formation during motion, the robotic swarm is a good candidate for unknown region exploration applications. The members of this kind of system are generally low complexity, which limits the communication and perception capacities of the agents. How to merge to the desired formation under those constraints is essential for performing relevant tasks. In this paper, a limited visual field constrained formation control strategy inspired by flying geese coordinated motion is introduced. Usually, they flock together in a V-shape formations, which is a well-studied phenomenon in biology and bionics. This paper illustrates the proposed methods by taking the research results from the above subjects and mapping them from the swarm engineering point of view. The formation control is achieved by applying a behavior-based formation forming method with the finite state machine while considering anti-collision and obstacle avoidance. Furthermore, a cascade leader–follower structure is adopted to achieve the large-scale formations. The simulation results from several scenarios indicate the presented method is robust with high scalability and flexibility.

Keywords: swarm robotics; formation control; coordinate motion; obstacle avoidance

1. Introduction

Swarm robotics is a research field of the multi-robot system inspired by the self-organizing behavior of social animals such as birds, bees, fish, and so forth [1]. Formation control is one of the essential topics of the cooperative behavior of those systems [2]. The goal is to deploy robots regularly and repeatedly within a specific distance from each other to obtain the desired pattern, and then maintain it during movement. The members in the swarm are usually homogeneous with low complexity, only equipped with local sensing and communication devices with decentralized architecture. Swarms can be used for missions such as virgin territories exploration [3], contamination detection or tracking, and disaster search and rescue [4]. We have shown a formation-based distributed processing paradigm for collaborative searching of swarms in a scanner-like manner with a moving line formation [5]. We also extended this paradigm to more general cases not only for line formation but also for V-shaped formations [6]. In those works, the moving formations are treated as a sensor network with dynamically changing positions, so that multi-dimensional based algorithms could be applied in a distributed way. In this paper, we deal with how to get those formations under the constraints of limited visual sensing and communication abilities of each swarm member.

Formation forming problem is a well-studied problem in swarm robotics field. There are many state-of-the-art methods to deal with this problem. There are macroscopic collective behavior-inspired methods such as structured approaches (leader–follower [7], virtual structure [8]), behavior-based methods (finite state machine [9], potential fields [10], and consensus-based control [11]. In addition, multicellular mechanism-inspired formation control has also been developed, such as morphogen diffusion [12], reaction-diffusion model [13], chemotaxis [14], gene regulatory networks [15], etc. A more detailed review was published by Oh et al. [16]. However, sensors equipped in swarms are limited not only by the sensing range but also by the field of view (FOV) [17]. Under the condition of limited FOV, the connectivity of the members cannot be maintained if the omnidirectional sensing model is still applied, thus the above formation control strategies might be invalid under this constraint.

In biological research, the way geese or other big birds fly together in formations is a widely studied phenomenon [18]. Many researchers believe that those species flying in such a way can reduce the flight power demands and energy expenditure, as well as improve orientation abilities by communication within groups [19,20]. Some other works hold the different opinion that this phenomenon is constrained by the visual factors and the formations might be a by-product of the limited field of view of the following birds during flying [21]. The members of the team are communicating indirectly based on their sensed information, which means the communication is also constrained by the FOV [22]. According to Heppner's research on flying geese [23], the visual field for each eye of a flying goose is $135°$ with a binocular overlap of $20°$, as shown in Figure 1. This means the members in a swarm could only follow others in this visual field, which causes the line or V-shape formations during moving.

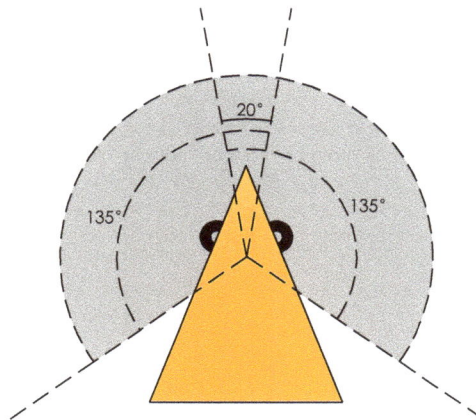

Figure 1. Geese visual field in biological research.

This paper illustrates a formation forming control strategy inspired by flying geese. This work studies the V-shape formation forming control problem with limited visual field constraints of sensing and communication inspired by flying geese. The leader broadcasts the heading angle directly to the members in a specific range, while each member in this range also broadcasts the heading with some other simple statuses. Members in the so-called visual field limited Time-varying Characteristic Swarm (v-TVCS, which represents sub-swarms with members in the communication range of an agent) receive that information and combine it with the distances and bearing angles observed by itself to reach the motion decisions. Anti-collision and obstacle avoidance are also considered in the proposed method. The main contributions of this paper are the adoption of geese visual field constraint mechanism of formation flying. A behavior-based control strategy for line and V-shape formation forming is also presented combined with a cascade leader–follower structure.

The rest of this paper is organized as follows. In Section 2, we first state the problem of line and V-shape formation control along with the concept of v-TVCS. Section 3 introduces a modified leader–follower structure with behavior-based finite state machine design of proposed formation control strategy. Simulations under different situations are implemented to evaluate our method, and the results are given in Section 4. Section 5 is the dicussion. The conclusion is reached in Section 6.

2. Problem Statement

We suppose each member in the swarm works in the same 2-D Cartesian coordinate system with the following assumptions:

- Limited visual field: The members in the swarm only have a specific visual field in front of them; the visual angle θ is set to 250°, i.e., $(-35° \leq \theta \leq 235°)$.
- Limited perception and communication range: An agent can only communicate with members or sense others or obstacles in a certain local range (R) within the visual field.
- GPS-free: The swarm system is not equipped with GPS, i.e., no member has the global position information to perform formations.

2.1. Kinematic Model of Members

The agent in the swarm uses the following non-holonomic motion model [24], which means the agent is only able to move forward with heading changes.

$$\begin{bmatrix} x_i(t+\Delta t) \\ y_i(t+\Delta t) \\ \alpha_i(t+\Delta t) \end{bmatrix} = \begin{bmatrix} x_i(t) \\ y_i(t) \\ \alpha_i(t) \end{bmatrix} + \begin{bmatrix} \cos\alpha_i(t) & 0 \\ \sin\alpha_i(t) & 0 \\ 0 & 1 \end{bmatrix} \begin{bmatrix} v \\ \omega \end{bmatrix} \tag{1}$$

where (x_i, y_i, α_i) are the Cartesian position and heading of agent i, v is the linear velocity in each agent's coordinates $x_i o y_i$, and ω is the angular velocity. Suppose each member in the swarm is able to detect relative distances and angles of others in visual field respective to its own coordinates. l_{ij} and φ_{ij} are the measured distance and angle of agent j in agent i's sensing range. We have:

$$\begin{cases} x_{ij} = l_{ij}\cos\varphi_{ij} \\ y_{ij} = l_{ij}\sin\varphi_{ij} \end{cases} \tag{2}$$

where $-35° \leq \varphi_{ij} \leq 235°$ is the visual angle constraint, $l_{ij} \in [0, R]$. Now, for every agent in the swarm, the formation forming problem translates to finding a pose that make the agent keep the distance and bearings of the nearest neighbor, as well as the same heading angle relative to the reference agent. Furthermore, anti-collision with each other and obstacle avoidance must be considered.

2.2. Visual Field Limited Time-Varying Characteristic Swarm

Under the communication constraint, members in a swarm are not required to connect with other agents outside of some proximity, which defines the notation of communication-based neighborhood first presented by Pugh et al. [25]. The communication-based neighborhood of agent i is a set of teammates within a fixed radius R to the position of agent i, which can be written as:

$$\mathcal{N}(r_i) = \{r_{j\in N, j\neq i}, \| p_i - p_j \| \leq R\} \tag{3}$$

where $\mathcal{N}$ is the communication-based neighborhood; N is the number of members in the swarm; r_i denotes agent i; p_i and p_j are spacial positions of i and j agents, respectively; and R is the maximum communication radius. While the swarm is moving, the neighborhoods may change over time, which causes the whole swarm to be divided into several dynamically changing sub-swarms. Xue et al. defined those sub-swarms with the concept of Time-varying Characteristic Swarm (TVCS) [26]. The TVCS of agent i at time t can be represented as follows:

$$\mathcal{S}^t(r_i) = r_i \cup \{r_{j \in N, j \neq i}, \| p_i^t - p_j^t \| \leq R\} \tag{4}$$

where $\mathcal{S}^t(r_i)$ represents the TVCS of agent i. The number of members in one TVCS is obviously dynamically changing. At time t, r_i is only able to communicate with other agents in $\mathcal{S}^t(r_i)$. In our case, the perception-based communication range is also limited by the visual field of each member, thus the definition of above TVCS changes to:

$$\mathcal{S}_v^t(r_i) = r_i \cup \{r_{j \in N, j \neq i}, \| p_i^t - p_j^t \| \leq R \wedge \varphi_{ij} \in \mathcal{V}\} \tag{5}$$

where $\mathcal{S}_v^t(r_i)$ is visual field limited TVCS (v-TVCS), φ_{ij} is the bearing angle of r_j in r_i's frame, and $\mathcal{V}_i$ is the visual field of agent i. The illustration of v-TVCS is shown in Figure 2.

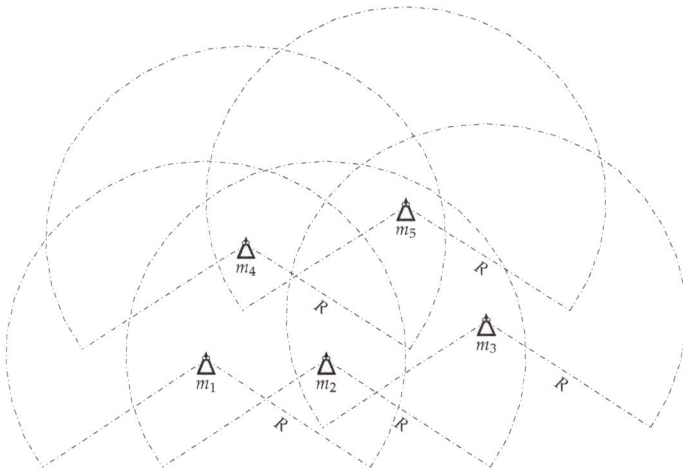

Figure 2. Visual field limited Time-varying Characteristic Swarm (v-TVCS).

3. Methods

Based on some previous works [7,9,17,26], here, we employ a modified leader–follower structure combined with a behavioral finite state machine to achieve the V-shaped formation control under the constraints we assumed above.

3.1. Behavior Based Approach

Behavior-based method is one of the common choices for swarm robotics, since it is typically decentralized and can be realized with less communication compared to the others [1]. It usually defines some simple rules and actions for members in a swarm to guide them to take particular actions when conditions change; finite state machines (FSM) can realize this. For every swarm member, a finite state machine could be defined as a triple $T = (S, I, F)$ where $S = \{S_1, S_2, \cdots, S_n\}$ is a finite non-empty set of states, $I = \{I_1, I_2, \cdots, I_n\}$ is a finite non-empty set of inputs, and $F : I \times S \to S$ is the state-transition function set, which describes how inputs I affect states S. Since the member has some blind zone in the back, one cannot see any other member in the case of no individual in its visual field. Furthermore, the members need to fly together in V-shape formation without collision with each other or hit the obstacles. The states in S can be defined as $S = \{S_1, S_2, S_3\}$ where S_1 is searching team members, S_2 is anti-collision with other member or obstacle avoidance, and S_3 is forming the formation. $S_v^t(r_i)$ is the TVCS of agent i at time t; l_c^t and l_o^t are the measured distance of the nearest member and the closest obstacle, respectively; and d_s is the safe distance. The input set now can be represented as $I = \{I_1, I_2, I_3\}$, where:

$$
\begin{cases}
I_1 : S_v^t(r_i) - \{r_i\} = \phi \\
I_2 : l_c < d_s \vee l_o < d_s \\
I_3 : \text{Others}
\end{cases}
\tag{6}
$$

The state-transition functions could be listed as follows and are represented in Figure 3.

$$
\begin{aligned}
&F(I_1, S_1) = S_1, F(I_2, S_1) = S_2, F(I_3, S_1) = S_3, \\
&F(I_1, S_2) = S_1, F(I_2, S_2) = S_2, F(I_3, S_2) = S_3, \\
&F(I_1, S_3) = S_1, F(I_2, S_3) = S_2, F(I_3, S_3) = S_3.
\end{aligned}
$$

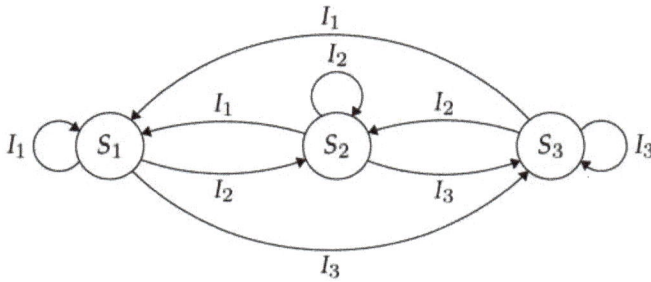

Figure 3. Finite state machine of designed behavior based approach.

3.2. Cascade Leader–Follower Structure

The leader–follower structure is a frequently used method for formation control for groups of robots. The $l - \varphi$ method, which controls the followers to keep desired distances and bearing angles to the leader, can be represented as:

$$
\begin{cases}
\lim_{t \to \infty}[l(t) - l^d] & = 0 \\
\lim_{t \to \infty}[\varphi(t) - \varphi^d] & = 0
\end{cases}
\tag{7}
$$

where l^d and $l(t)$ are desired and current distances to the leader respectively; and φ^d and $\varphi(t)$ are the desired and current bearing angles to the leader, respectively. In our case, one cannot see the leader all the time. Consequently, instead of following the leader, we make the members form the desired formation by following a particular agent in the v-TVCS with the assistance of simple communications.

To cope with this task, the swarm leader, which defines the reference frame for the others, must first broadcast its heading direction. Other members in leader's v-TVCS will receive this message, combine it with other state messages and then rebroadcast it in their v-TVCS again. Since we aim at building a V-shape formation, this means the leader will divide the swarm into two parts: the left part and the right part. As shown in Figure 4, the desired bearings for the two parts are different. The angle of the formatted V-shape formation is γ, members of the left part will keep the relative bearing angle to the leader or closest right top member with the same role of $-\gamma/2$, while the right part will keep the desired bearing between the leader or closest left top member with the same role of $\gamma/2$. Because the desired bearings are different for the two parts, the messages communicated between swarm members should be the received leader's heading, the agent's own heading, and the role of which part it belongs. At the initial stage, if one can see the leader, it is able to determine the part role by evaluating the initial leader bearing minus the heading error with the leader. Otherwise, if the leader is not in one's field of view, it will synchronize its role from the broadcasting of the closest member in its v-TVCS.

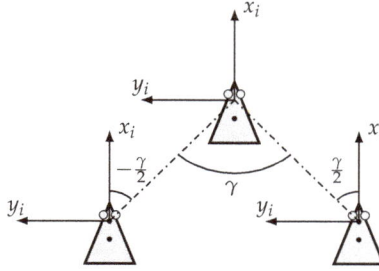

Figure 4. Desired bearing angle of two parts.

In the case a member cannot see anyone in its visual field, it will search others by rotating with a certain forward speed with turning. Thus, the actions in S_1 can be simply defined as:

$$\begin{cases} v = v_r \\ \omega = \omega_r \end{cases} \tag{8}$$

where $v_r \in (0, v_{max})$ and $\omega_r \in (0, \omega_{max})$ are random forward speed and turn speed, respectively.

Figure 5 shows the relationship with leader and follower. According to Equation (1), the kinematic equations for follower i are established:

$$\begin{cases} \Delta l = v_i \cos(\theta) - v_l \cos\varphi + d\omega_i \sin(\theta) \\ \Delta\varphi = \frac{1}{l}(v_l \sin\varphi - v_i \sin(\theta) + d\omega_i \cos(\theta) - l\omega_l) \\ \Delta\alpha_i = \omega_i \end{cases} \tag{9}$$

where α_i is the heading error with the leader, $\theta = \varphi + \alpha_i$. On the other hand, according to the feedback control law, we have:

$$\begin{cases} \Delta l = k_l(l_d - l) \\ \Delta\varphi = k_\varphi(\varphi_d - \varphi) \end{cases} \tag{10}$$

where k_l and k_φ are feedback coefficients.

By combining Equations (9) and (10), we can get the control inputs for formation:

$$\begin{cases} \omega_i = \frac{\cos\theta}{d}[k_\varphi l(\varphi_d - \varphi) - v_l \sin\varphi + l\omega_l + p\sin\theta] \\ v_i = p - d\omega_i \tan\theta \end{cases} \tag{11}$$

where $p = v_l \cos\varphi + k_l(l_d - l)/\cos\theta$.

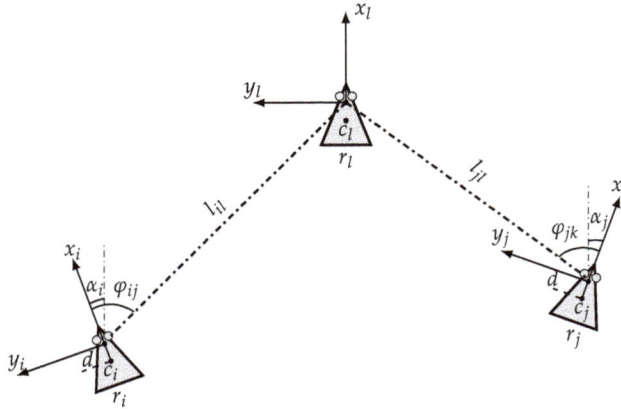

Figure 5. Configurations of swarm members.

3.3. Anti-Collision and Obstacle Avoidance

Anti-collision and obstacle avoidance is essential for task implementation. It ensures the agents avoid hitting others in the swarm or obstacles in the environment. With the low-complexity swarm in mind, here we use a simplified Vector Field Histogram (VFH) algorithm to achieve this goal. VFH algorithm determines the movement direction by constructing vector field histogram to represent polar obstacle density (POD). First, it divides sensing field of an agent into n sectors and each sector's cover angle is $360°/n$. Then, the following equation is used to calculate the corresponding POD in the histogram for each sector [27]:

$$h^k(\mathbf{q_i}) = \int_{\Omega_k} P(\mathbf{p})^n \cdot \left(1 - \frac{d(\mathbf{q}_{t_i}, \mathbf{p})}{d_{max}}\right)^m d\mathbf{p} \tag{12}$$

where $h^k(\mathbf{q_i})$ is the polar obstacle density in sector k, $P(\mathbf{p})$ is the probability a point is occupied by an obstacle, $d(\mathbf{q}_{t_i}, \mathbf{p})$ is the distance from the center of the agent to point $\mathbf{p}$, d_{max} is the maximum detection range of the sensor, and the dominion of integration Ω_k is defined as

$$\Omega_k = \{\mathbf{p} \in k \wedge d(\mathbf{q}_{t_i}, \mathbf{p}) < d_s\} \tag{13}$$

By applying a threshold to the polar histogram, a set of candidate directions that are closest to the target direction can be obtained. In the next step, the strategy to choose a direction of this set depends on the relationships between the selected sectors and the target sector. It has been proven that this method is effective for obstacle avoidance of mobile robots. In our case, since the simple swarm members need to keep the formation during moving, we have to consider the low computational complexity as well as the velocity constraints. By adopting the fundamental principle of VHF algorithm, we can design our actions in state S_2 for anti-collision and obstacle avoidance as follows.

As shown in Figure 6, it is assumed that the robot can detect the ranges in $2a + 1$ sectors ($a > 0$) in its visual field, i.e., $-125°$ to $125°$, where $0°$ is the heading direction of an agent. By considering the effects of neighbor sectors, the smoothed polar obstacle density on kth direction can be represented as:

$$\rho_k = \sum_{i=-l}^{l} w(i) f(k + i) \tag{14}$$

$$f(k + i) = (1 - \frac{\min\{d_s, d(k + i)\}}{d_s})^2 \tag{15}$$

where l is a positive number that represents the compute window of each direction $k \in [-a, a]$, $d(k+i)$ is the distance from the center of the agent to the obstacle in direction $k + i$, d_s is the predefined safe distance, and $w(i)$ is the weight of the corresponding neighbor directions, which can be determined by:

$$w(i) = \begin{cases} \frac{l-|i|+1}{\sum_{i=-l}^{l}(l-|i|+1)}, & -a \leq k+i \leq a \\ 0, & \text{others} \end{cases} \tag{16}$$

This choice of $w(i)$ ensures that the farther the neighbor direction from k is, the smaller the weight is as well as that the current heading direction k ($i = 0$) has the largest one.

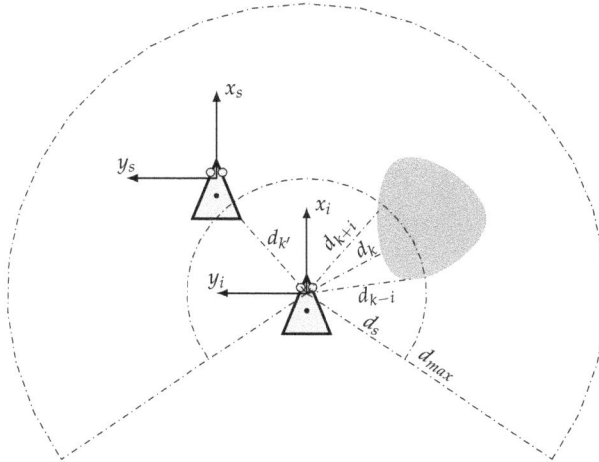

Figure 6. Sensing sectors with obstacles.

Consequently, denote $\hat{k} = \text{argmin}\{\rho_k\}$ as the potential direction(s); we can choose the solution direction by:

$$k_s = \begin{cases} \hat{k}, & \hat{k} \text{ is unique} \\ \text{argmin}(||k_t - \hat{k}||), & \text{others} \end{cases} \tag{17}$$

where k_s is the solution direction, and k_t is a direction that contains a target determined by formation control strategy. Furthermore, the safe distance d_s is related to the turning radius at maximum speed and the update cycle T of the agent, i.e.,

$$d_s = K_s \left(\frac{v_{max}}{\omega_{max}} + v_{max}T \right) \tag{18}$$

where $K_s > 1$ is the safety coefficient. We can use the following equations to determine the final inputs for anti-collision and obstacle avoidance.

$$v(n+1) = \rho_{min} \cos(k_s \beta), \qquad \text{others} \tag{19}$$

$$\omega(n+1) = \begin{cases} \omega_{max}, & |k_s \beta| > \omega_{max} \\ -k_s \beta, & \text{others} \end{cases} \tag{20}$$

where ρ_{min} is the minimal ranges to the obstacles and β is the angular resolution of the ranger sensor, i.e., the width of each sector.

3.4. Proposed Formation Control Algorithm

In summary, the computation procedure of each member in the proposed method is as shown in Algorithm 1. The programs are identical for each member, which ensures the high scalability of the system. The agent detects the neighbor members and obstacles, and uses the transfer functions to switch to corresponding actions described above. The complexity of the algorithm is $O(n)$, which is equivalent to most state-of-the-art strategies.

Algorithm 1: Cascade leader–follower formation control with limited field of view

---

    Input: Input set refer to Equation (6)
    Output: Forward and Turn Speeds of an Agent
1 **switch** I **do**
2   **case** I_1 **do**
3        $v = v_r, \omega = \omega_r$;   `// Action in S`$_1$`, refer to Equation (8)`
4   **case** I_2 **do**
5   Compute safe direction k_s ;   `// Actions in S`$_2$`, refer to Equation (14)-(17)`
6   Compute v and ω for anti-collision ;   `// Refer to Equations (19)-(20)`
7   **case** I_3 **do**
8   Synchronize role with leader or closest Member;
9   Determine desired bearing to target member;
10   Compute v and ω for formation forming ;   `// Actions in S`$_3$`, refer to`
          Equation (11)
11 **Set Speed** v, ω ;   `// Set forward and turn speeds`
12 **end**

---

4. Results

We evaluated the proposed method using simulations in the stage simulator [28]. We studied the proposed method under the condition of obstacle avoidance, formation with turns, and large populations. The safe distance d_s is set to 5 m while the desired distance l_d is set to $1.2d_s = 6$ m, the desired formation angle is set to $\gamma = 100°$, and the target forward speed of the swarm leader is set to 1 m/s. Figure 7 shows the configuration of each member. The large sector with field of view 250° is its communication range. The agent is able to exchange simple data to others in this area. This radius is set to 30 m for simulations with swarms of fewer than 50 members, and 100 m for larger swarms ($N = 200$). The small sector is the coverage of nine ranger sensors with 30° FOV spread on the 250° with some overlaps for anti-collision and obstacle avoidance. With those configurations, the simulation process and other details are given in following subsections.

Figure 7. Member configurations in stage simulator.

4.1. Formation Control with Obstacle Avoidance

As mentioned above, the anti-collision strategy of the proposed method includes keep away from each other and obstacle avoidance. Anti-collision is considered for all simulations. The experiment in this section aims to test the strategy in an environment with obstacles. Initially, we put seven swarm members in the bottom part of a 100 m × 200 m environment, with random position and headings. The target direction of the swarm leader is set to the north. Some obstacles are placed on the way to the north, as shown in Figure 8a. The sector around the agent indicates the visual field of each member. Figure 8b shows the swarm leader starts to move to the north, and the other members are adjusting their positions and headings according to the proposed strategy. Each member chooses the corresponding target leader to achieve the cascaded leader–follower structure, and calculates control inputs according to predefined l_d and φ_d, as shown in Figure 8c. Figure 8d shows that the formation is formed at around 57.4 s.

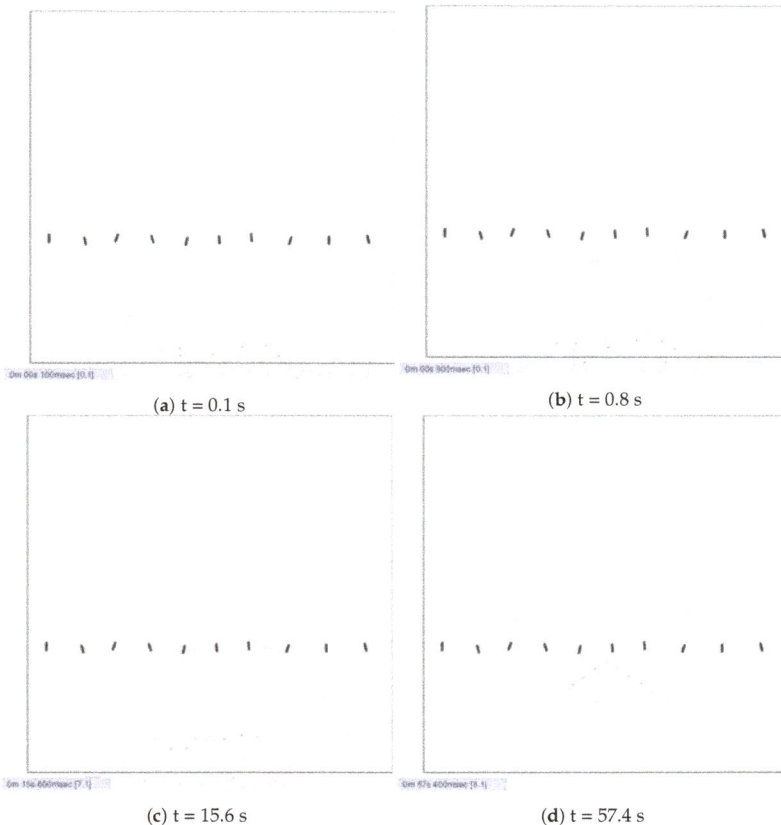

(**a**) t = 0.1 s

(**b**) t = 0.8 s

(**c**) t = 15.6 s

(**d**) t = 57.4 s

Figure 8. Formation before encounter obstacles.

When the moving formation encounters obstacles, as shown in Figure 9a,b, the members adjust their forward and turning speeds to obey the defined anti-collision rules to avoid obstacles. Meanwhile, they also keep away from each other during the adjustments. When they pass the barrier region, they start to reform the shape, as shown in Figure 9c. The formation is reshaped at 2 min 6.6 s, as shown in Figure 9d. The trajectories of this simulation are shown in Figure 10. In the figure, we can see the adjustments of the anti-collision movements of each members.

(a) t = 1 min 1.7 s

(b) t = 1 min 15.9 s

(c) t = 1 min 53.4 s

(d) t = 2 min 6.6 s

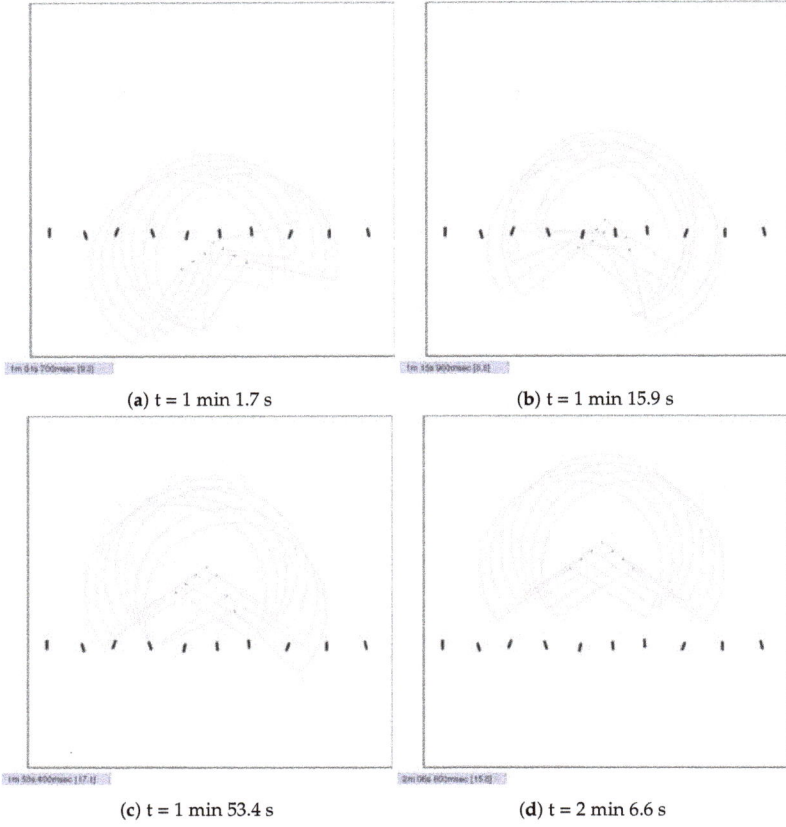

Figure 9. Formation after encounter obstacles.

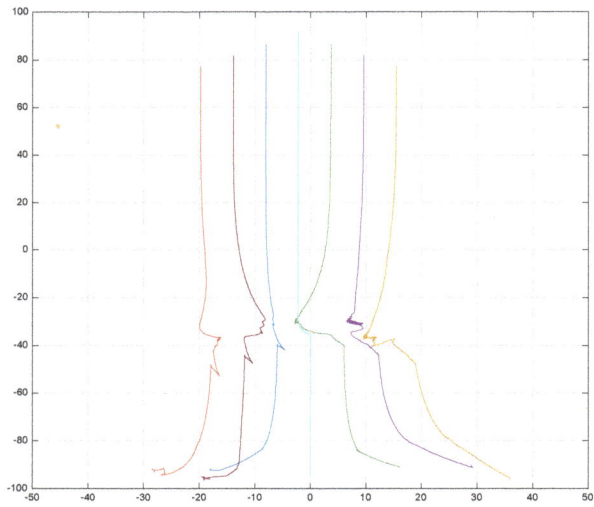

Figure 10. The trajectories of member movements.

4.2. Flexibility Evaluation

In many searching tasks, the entire swarm may need to do more maneuvers than just moving in one direction. Members in a swarm are required to follow the leader's trajectory change after forming the formation. We test this problem in a swarm with 31 members (1 swarm leader and 30 other members). The swarm leader is set to make a left turn at the position of $(0, 600)$ with the turning speed of 0.1 rad/s. The simulation results are as shown in Figures 11 and 12.

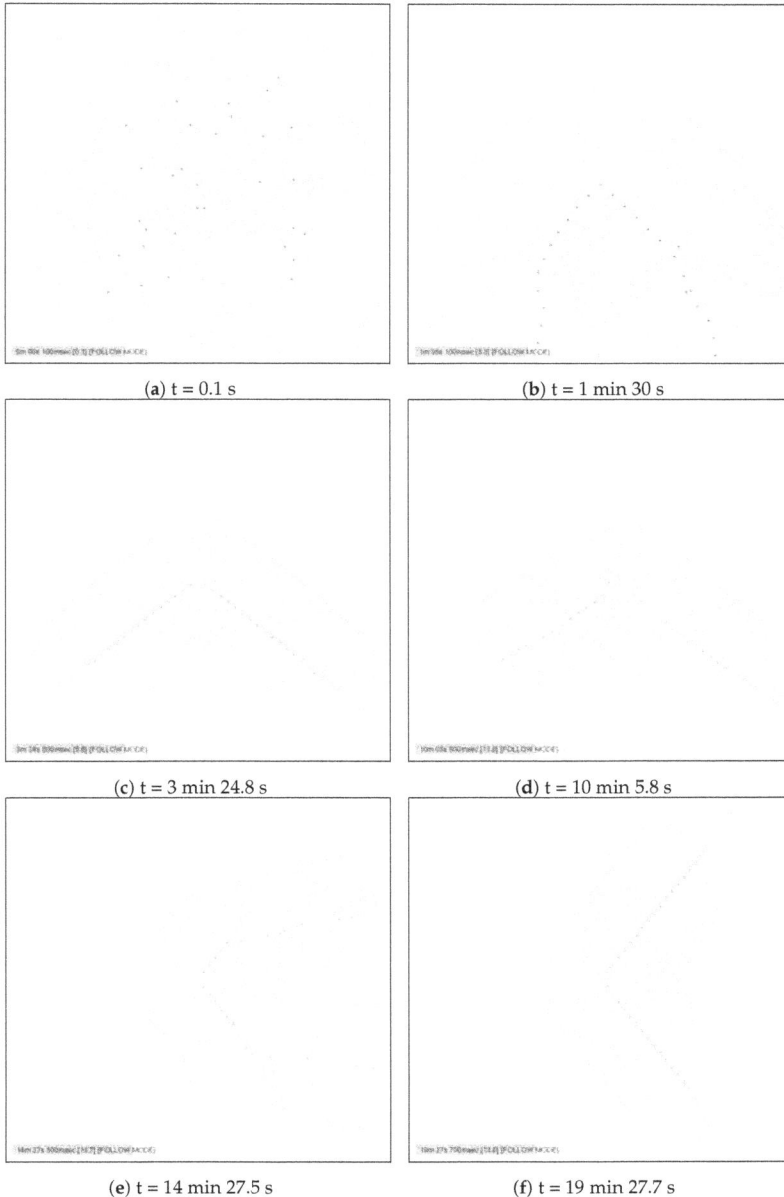

(a) t = 0.1 s

(b) t = 1 min 30 s

(c) t = 3 min 24.8 s

(d) t = 10 min 5.8 s

(e) t = 14 min 27.5 s

(f) t = 19 min 27.7 s

Figure 11. Formation with turns.

Initially, we put the leader at point $(0, 0)$, and the other 30 members are distributed in a certain range $(x, y) \in [-50, 50]$ m around the leader with random positions and headings. Figure 11a shows the initial status of this simulation. After the swarm leader starts to move, the whole group forms the desired V-shape (Figure 11b), and the formation is formed at 3 min 24.8 s (Figure 11c). The formed shape continues to move forward until the swarm leader begins to turn, as indicated in Figure 11d. The swarm then reshapes after the disorder caused by the turn, as shown in Figure 11e. We can see in Figure 11f that the formation reformed at 19 min 27.7 s. The trajectories of this process are shown in Figure 12.

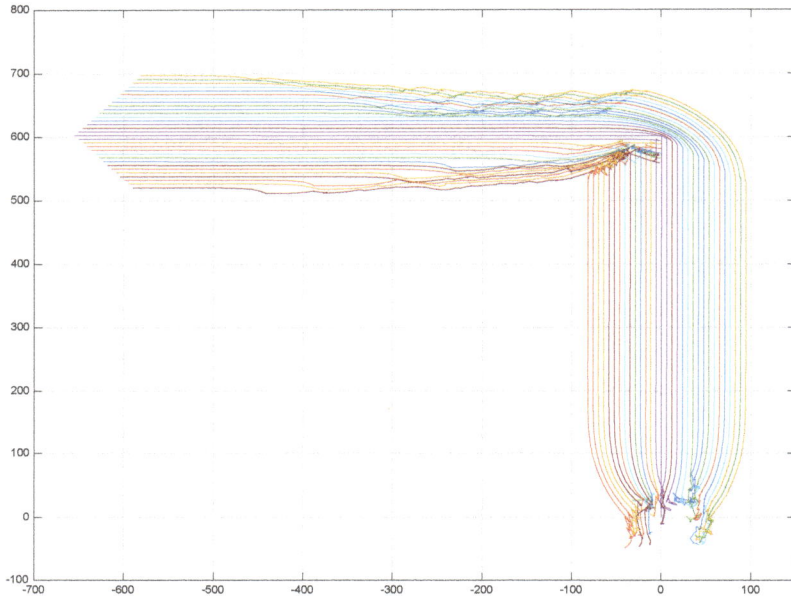

Figure 12. The trajectories of member movements.

4.3. Large Swarm

One of the distinguishing characteristics of swarm robotics compared to the traditional multi-robot system is low-complexity with robust organization rules, which can be realized in large-scale applications. To evaluate our proposed method in a large swarm, in stage, we use a population of 201 (1 leader and 200 members) for the formation forming test. Similar to the flexibility evaluation, we put the leader at position $(0, 0)$, and the other 200 members are distributed in the range of $(x, y) \in [-100, 100]$ m around the leader with random positions and headings, as shown in Figure 13a. The sensing radius is set to 100 m to avoid possible disconnections between different sub-swarms. The target direction of the leader is set to the north with anti-collision, i.e., the swarm leader keeps away from the others, as shown in Figure 13b. After the leader moves be the north most member of the swarm, the remaining simulation processes are shown in Figure 13c–f. It can be seen that the proposed method can form the formation under the condition of large populations of swarm members. The trajectories for this simulation is given in Figure 14.

16

(a) t = 0.1 s

(b) t = 1 min 57.8 s

(c) t = 3 min 26.3 s

(d) t = 4 min 24.4 s

(e) t = 10 min 39.5 s

(f) t = 21 min 11.6 s

Figure 13. Large-scale formation control simulation.

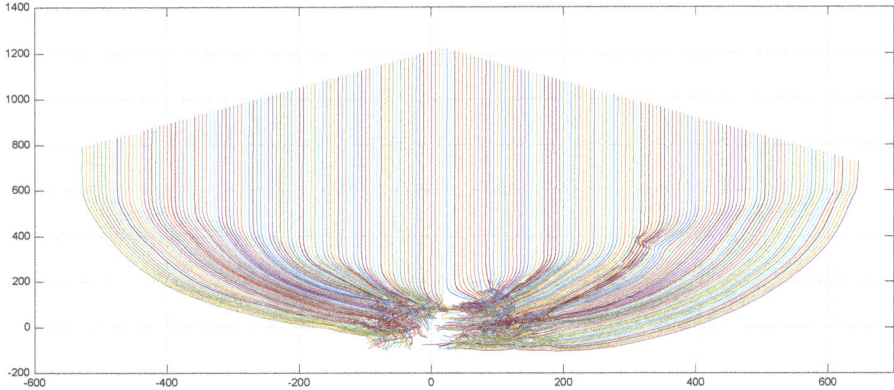

Figure 14. The trajectories of member movements.

4.4. Statistical Results

We tested the above simulations under each condition several times to get the statistical results. In particular, for the large-scale formation problem, we set a different sensing radius to get the impact of this parameter. As shown in Table 1, the success rates with seven agents in the environment with obstacles and 31 agents in an open environment are both 100%. The sensing radius of those situations is all set to 30 m. For the large-scale test, we set this value to 30 m, 50 m, 70 m and 100 m. The corresponding success rates are 0%, 10%, 50% and 100%, respectively. The sensing radius obviously affects the results of large-scale simulations.

Table 1. Statistical results of the proposed method.

No. of Agents	Obstacles	Sensing Radius	Succ. Rates (%)	Avg. Time (s)	No. of Tests
7	Yes	30	100	130.4	20
31	No	30	100	232.7	20
201	No	30	0	/	10
		50	10	1801.3	10
		70	50	1405.8	10
		100	100	1283.6	10

5. Discussion

It can be seen from the listed results above that the presented formation forming strategy for robotic swarms is proven to be effective with different populations. The following subsections are some more considerations worth discussing.

5.1. The Local Minimal

Formation control strategies with obstacle avoidance often suffer from local minima problems. They are usually caused by the conflicts between the formation control inputs and the anti-collision calculations. In Figure 10, the traces of the last two agents have vibration near the position of $(10, -30)$, which indicates those two agents have the risk of falling into the local optimum. Fortunately, According to Equation (8), our strategy for formation control has random inputs in the state of S_1. Furthermore, we only calculate nine directions of range sensors for anti-collision. These two points ensure our method can jump out from the risk. Figure 8c indicates the right two members have some delay in reforming the formation due to the time consumed by getting out of the trouble; however, they can still catch up to move with the formation.

5.2. Unbalanced Formations

Since we do not assign the roles for each member before the task, each member gets its role during the simulation. The final results might be unbalanced V-shaped formations, which will affect the coverage of the swarm. As shown in Figure 13f, the number of agents on the left-hand side is never equal to the number on the right-hand side. When this kind of swarm formation is used in some spatially relevant tasks, the coverage area differences should be carefully considered. We also mentioned this issue in one of our previous works, which utilized unbalanced formations for collaborative target searching tasks [6].

5.3. Robustness and Scalability

Robustness and scalability are typical characteristics of swarm systems. Robustness means the system could operate normally in the case of disturbance or individual failure. Since the designed system is fully distributed with high redundancy, some members failing will be compensated by others. The distributed scheme also resists disturbance from surroundings.

Scalability is another essential property of swarm robotics, which implies the system has the ability to work under arbitrary populations. As shown in the simulations with different populations and circumstances, the proposed method is identical for every member of the swarm, so it has high robustness and scalability.

6. Conclusions

This paper introduces a flying geese-inspired V-shaped formation control strategy, which is constrained by the limited field of view. A behavior-based method combined with a cascade leader–follower structure is adapted to get the desired formation. The anti-collision issue including keep away from other members and obstacle avoidance is also achieved with a simplified polar vector field histogram method. Comparing with other methods, we have shown the introduced method is able to form the formations under the condition of the field-of-view constrained sensing and communication. Furthermore, the proposed strategy is fully distributed with robustness and scalability, which has the potential to be utilized in large-scale swarms. Although we have verified the effectiveness of the method through simulation, utilizing it in physical system still has challenges, such as the sensor based communication protocols, the kinematics of different types of robots and so forth. The future work of our research will be focused on implementing the method to physical swarm systems such as mobile robots, UAVs and underwater vehicles.

Author Contributions: Conceptualization, J.Y. and P.B.; Methodology, J.Y.; Software, J.Y.; Validation, X.W., P.B. and J.Y.; Investigation, J.Y., X.W. and P.B.; Resources, X.W.; Data Curation, J.Y.; Writing—Original Draft Preparation, J.Y.; Writing—Review and Editing, P.B.; Visualization, J.Y.; Supervision, X.W.; Project Administration, X.W.; and Funding Acquisition, X.W.

Funding: This research was funded by Shenzhen Science and Technology Innovation Commission grant number JCYJ20170413110656460 and JCYJ20150403161923545.

Conflicts of Interest: The authors declare no conflict of interest.

References

1. Brambilla, M.; Ferrante, E.; Birattari, M.; Dorigo, M. Swarm robotics: A review from the swarm engineering perspective. *Swarm Intell.* **2013**, *7*, 1–41. [CrossRef]
2. Trianni, V.; Campo, A. Fundamental collective behaviors in swarm robotics. In *Springer Handbook of Computational Intelligence*; Springer: Berlin/Heidelberg, Germany, 2015; pp. 1377–1394.
3. Taraglio, S.; Fratichini, F. Swarm underwater acoustic 3D localization: Kalman vs Monte Carlo. *Int. J. Adv. Robot. Syst.* **2015**, *12*, 102. [CrossRef]
4. Scheutz, M.; Bauer, P. Ultra-low complexity control mechanisms for sensor networks and robotic swarms. *Int. J. New Comput. Archit. Appl.* **2013**, *3*, 86–119.

5. Yang, J.; Wang, X.; Bauer, P. Formation forming based low-complexity swarms with distributed processing for decision making and resource allocation. In Proceedings of the 2016 14th International Conference on Control, Automation, Robotics and Vision (ICARCV), Phuket, Thailand, 13–15 November 2016; pp. 1–6.

6. Yang, J.; Wang, X.; Bauer, P. Line and V-Shape Formation Based Distributed Processing for Robotic Swarms. *Sensors* **2018**, *18*, 2543. [CrossRef] [PubMed]

7. Panagou, D.; Kumar, V. Cooperative visibility maintenance for leader–follower formations in obstacle environments. *IEEE Trans. Robot.* **2014**, *30*, 831–844. [CrossRef]

8. Askari, A.; Mortazavi, M.; Talebi, H. UAV formation control via the virtual structure approach. *J. Aerosp. Eng.* **2013**, *28*, 04014047. [CrossRef]

9. Balch, T.; Arkin, R.C. Behavior-based formation control for multirobot teams. *IEEE Trans. Robot. Autom.* **1998**, *14*, 926–939. [CrossRef]

10. Spears, W.M.; Spears, D.F. *Physicomimetics: Physics-Based Swarm Intelligence*; Springer Science & Business Media: Cham, Switzerland, 2012.

11. Tanner, H.G.; Jadbabaie, A.; Pappas, G.J. Flocking in teams of nonholonomic agents. In *Cooperative Control*; Springer: Cham, Switzerland, 2005; pp. 229–239.

12. Foty, R.A.; Steinberg, M.S. The differential adhesion hypothesis: A direct evaluation. *Dev. Biol.* **2005**, *278*, 255–263. [CrossRef] [PubMed]

13. Meinhardt, H.; Gierer, A. Pattern formation by local self-activation and lateral inhibition. *Bioessays* **2000**, *22*, 753–760. [CrossRef]

14. Bai, L.; Eyiyurekli, M.; Lelkes, P.I.; Breen, D.E. Self-organized sorting of heterotypic agents via a chemotaxis paradigm. *Sci. Comput. Program.* **2013**, *78*, 594–611. [CrossRef]

15. Oh, H.; Jin, Y. Evolving hierarchical gene regulatory networks for morphogenetic pattern formation of swarm robots. In Proceedings of the 2014 IEEE Congress on Evolutionary Computation (CEC), Beijing, China, 6–11 July 2014; pp. 776–783.

16. Oh, H.; Shirazi, A.R.; Sun, C.; Jin, Y. Bio-inspired self-organising multi-robot pattern formation: A review. *Robot. Auton. Syst.* **2017**, *91*, 83–100. [CrossRef]

17. Maeda, R.; Endo, T.; Matsuno, F. Decentralized navigation for heterogeneous swarm robots with limited field of view. *IEEE Robot. Autom. Lett.* **2017**, *2*, 904–911. [CrossRef]

18. Pennycuick, C.J. The Flight of Birds and Other Animals. *Aerospace* **2015**, *2*, 505–523. [CrossRef]

19. Weimerskirch, H.; Martin, J.; Clerquin, Y.; Alexandre, P.; Jiraskova, S. Energy saving in flight formation. *Nature* **2001**, *413*, 697–698. [CrossRef] [PubMed]

20. Galler, S.R.; Schmidt-Koenig, K.; Jacob, G.J.; Belleville, R.E. *Animal Orientation and Navigation. NASA SP-262*; NASA Special Publication: Washington, DC, USA, 1972.

21. Bajec, I.L.; Heppner, F.H. Organized flight in birds. *Anim. Behav.* **2009**, *78*, 777–789. [CrossRef]

22. Strandburg-Peshkin, A.; Twomey, C.R.; Bode, N.W.; Kao, A.B.; Katz, Y.; Ioannou, C.C.; Rosenthal, S.B.; Torney, C.J.; Wu, H.S.; Levin, S.A.; et al. Visual sensory networks and effective information transfer in animal groups. *Curr. Biol.* **2013**, *23*, R709–R711. [CrossRef] [PubMed]

23. Heppner, F.H.; Convissar, J.L.; Moonan, D.E., Jr.; Anderson, J.G. Visual angle and formation flight in Canada Geese (Branta canadensis). *Auk* **1985**, *102*, 195–198. [CrossRef]

24. Qu, Z. *Cooperative Control of Dynamical Systems: Applications To Autonomous Vehicles*; Springer Science & Business Media: London, UK, 2009.

25. Pugh, J.; Martinoli, A. Multi-robot learning with particle swarm optimization. In Proceedings of the Fifth International Joint Conference on Autonomous Agents and Multiagent Systems, Hakodate, Japan, 8–12 May 2006; pp. 441–448.

26. Xue, S.; Zhang, J.; Zeng, J. Parallel asynchronous control strategy for target search with swarm robots. *Int. J. Bio-Inspired Comput.* **2009**, *1*, 151–163. [CrossRef]

27. Siciliano, B.; Khatib, O. *Springer Handbook of Robotics*; Springer: Berlin/Heidelberg, Germany, 2016.

28. Vaughan, R. Massively multi-robot simulation in stage. *Swarm Intell.* **2008**, *2*, 189–208. [CrossRef]

applied
sciences

MDPI

Article

Decentralization of Virtual Linkage in Formation Control of Multi-Agents via Consensus Strategies

Yi Liu [1,2], Junyao Gao [1,*], Xuanyang Shi [1,3] and Chunyu Jiang [1]

[1] Intelligent Robotics Institute, School of Mechatronical Engineering, Beijing Institute of Technology, Beijing 100081, China; YiLiu@bit.edu.cn (Y.L.); 3120170111@bit.edu.cn (X.S.); jiangchunyu@bit.edu.cn (C.J.)
[2] Key Laboratory of Biomimetic Robots and Systems, Ministry of Education, Beijing 100081, China
[3] Beijing Advanced Innovation Center for Intelligent Robots and Systems, Beijing 100081, China
* Correspondence: gaojunyao@bit.edu.cn

Received: 28 September 2018; Accepted: 20 October 2018; Published: 23 October 2018

Featured Application: The method proposed in this paper can be used for formation control autonomous robots, such as nonholonomic mobile robots, unmanned aerial vehicles and has potential applications in search and rescue missions, area coverage and reconnaissance, etc.

Abstract: Featured Application: This paper addresses the formation control of a team of agents based on the decentralized control and the recently introduced reconfigurable virtual linkage approach. Following a decentralized control architecture, a decentralized virtual linkage approach is introduced. As compared to the original virtual linkage approach, the proposed approach uses decentralized architecture rather than hierarchical architecture, which does not require role assignments in each virtual link. In addition, each agent can completely decide its movement with only exchanging states with part of the team members, which makes this approach more suitable for situations when a large number of agents and/or limited communication are involved. Furthermore, the reconfiguration ability is enhanced in this approach by introducing the scale factor of each virtual link. Finally, the effectiveness of the proposed method is demonstrated through simulation results.

Keywords: formation control; virtual linkage; virtual structure; formation reconfiguration; mobile robots; robotics

1. Introduction

Formation control is one of the most leading research areas in robotics. It has been extensively studied by researchers around the world on different platforms: mobile robots, aerial robots, spacecraft, and autonomous surface and underwater vehicles [1–8].

In the literature, formation control approaches can be classified into three basic strategies: leader-following, behavior-based, and virtual structure. In the leader–follower approach [9–11], some agents are considered as leaders, while others act as followers which track the leaders with predefined offset. However, the leader's motion is independent of the followers. When a follower fails, the leader will keep on moving as predefined and results in the break of the formation shape. In the behavior approach [12–14], several reactive behaviors are prescribed (e.g., move-to-goal, avoid-robot, avoid-static-obstacles, and maintain-formation). The action of each agent is derived by a weighted sum of all the behaviors. The main problem with this approach is that it is difficult to formalize the group mathematically and the team of agents is not guaranteed to converge to the desired formation configuration. The virtual linkage approach considers the entire formation as a single rigid body and is able to maintain the formation shape in high precision during manoeuvers [15–17]. Perhaps the main criticism of the virtual structure approach is that it has poor reconfiguration ability and needs to refresh the relative positions of all the team members when a different formation pattern changes.

Although these three approaches have been used in many applications, they focus more on maintaining a specified formation pattern throughout a task and few studies address the effects of formation reconfiguration. However, situations also exist where different formation patterns are needed, for example, a group of agents might need to reconfigure into different patterns to go through a gallery. A reconfigurable formation control method named virtual linkage is proposed by the authors in Reference [18]. Instead of treating the whole formation as a single rigid body, as in the virtual structure, the virtual linkage approach considers the formation as a mechanical linkage which is a collection of rigid bodies connected by joints. A virtual linkage is defined as an assembly of virtual structures (named "virtual link") connected by virtual joints. By coordinating the value of each virtual joint, the virtual linkage approach is able to reconfigure a group of agents into different formation shapes.

Currently, the virtual linkage approach uses hierarchical architecture. In detail, the states of the virtual linkage are implemented in a virtual linkage server and broadcast to all the virtual link servers. Each virtual link's state is in turn calculated in the corresponding virtual link server and transmits to all its virtual link members. The principal limitation of this hierarchical architecture is that it does not scale well with the number of agents in the team. In addition, due to the communication range limitations, the virtual linkage server might lose communication with some virtual link servers when the agent group covers a large area. A possible way to solve these drawbacks is to use decentralized architecture in which each agent runs a consensus strategy and totally decides its moving action with communication with parts of the members.

The concept of consensus is an important idea in control and information theory, and it has been applied to the formation control of multiple agents [2,16,19–21]. The basic idea of a consensus algorithm is that each agent updates its state's information only based on its neighbors' state's information and finally enable the convergence of all the agent's state's information.

The main contribution of this paper is the decentralization of the virtual linkage approach via consensus strategies. Motivated by the pros and cons of the virtual linkage approach and consensus algorithm, a decentralized virtual linkage approach is presented in this paper. Instead of using hierarchical architecture, the proposed method instantiates a local copy of the virtual linkage's state implements the same consensus algorithm on each agent to facilitate the reconfigurable formation control of a team of agents. The decentralized virtual linkage approach has several advantages as compared to the original virtual linkage approach. First, the decentralized architecture overcomes the limitations of the hierarchical architecture. In details, this approach scales well with the number of agents in the group and only requires each agent to communicate with its local neighbors. Second, with the introduction of expansion/contraction rates for each virtual link, this approach has a stronger reconfiguration ability than the traditional virtual linkage approach.

The paper is organized as follows. In Section 2, the preliminary knowledge is presented. Section 3 illustrates the control strategy for the formation movement. Simulation results are in Section 4. Finally, in Section 5, some concluding remarks of this paper are given.

2. Problem Statement

2.1. Virtual Linkage

The virtual linkage is a reconfigurable formation control method proposed by the authors in Reference [18]. The main idea of virtual linkage is to consider the entire formation as a mechanical linkage which is a collection of rigid bodies connected by joints. It can be defined as a collection of virtual structures connected by virtual joints. Instead of specifying each agent's desired position relative to a single reference frame, as in the virtual structure, the virtual linkage approach tells each agent the virtual link it belongs to and the relative position in the corresponding virtual link. In this way, the designed virtual linkage can be reconfigured into different formation patterns by coordinating the value of each virtual joint.

Definition 1 (Virtual Joints [18]). *A virtual joint is a connection between two virtual structures and imposes constraints on their relative movement.*

Definition 2 (Virtual Linkage (VL) [18]). *A virtual linkage is an assembly of virtual structures (named "virtual link") connected by virtual joints.*

Figure 1 shows the comparison of an intuitive example of a virtual linkage. Three agents are designed into a virtual linkage composed of two virtual links. They are able to be configured into line formation and arrow formation by only changing the virtual joint angle.

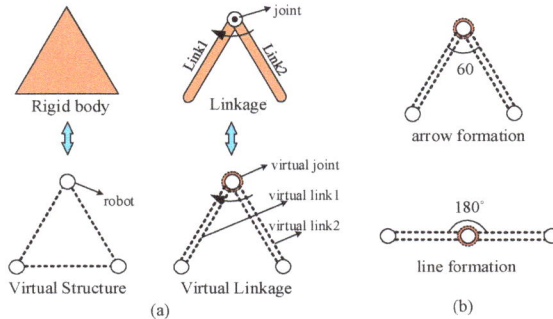

Figure 1. (**a**) Principle of virtual structure and virtual linkage. (**b**) Different formation using a specified virtual linkage.

2.2. Architecture of the Previous Virtual Linkage

Figure 2 shows the hierarchical architecture of the original virtual linkage approach proposed in Reference [18]. The states of the virtual linkage are implemented in a virtual linkage server and broadcast to all the virtual link servers. Each virtual link's state is in turn calculated in the corresponding virtual link server and transmits to all the virtual link members. As can be seen in Figure 2, there is a demand for the virtual link server F_{vli} to exchange message with all the agents which belong to the corresponding virtual link. Meanwhile, the virtual linkage server F also has to communicate with all the virtual link servers. The disadvantages of this hierarchical architecture lie in two aspects. First, it does not scale well with the number of agents in the team with limited communication bandwidth. Second, the virtual linkage server might lose communication with some virtual link servers when the agent group covers a large area.

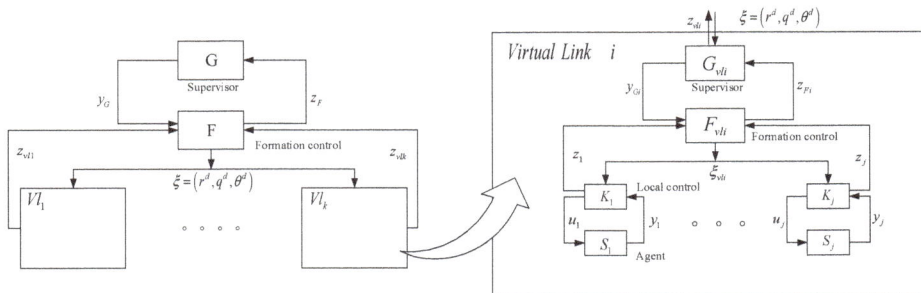

Figure 2. Hierarchical architecture of the previous virtual linkage.

2.3. Preliminaries of Digraphs and Consensus

To implement the decentralized formation control, the communication topology among a group of agents is represented as a diagraph $G = (R, \varepsilon)$. In detail, $R = \{R_i | i = \{1, 2, \ldots n \}\}$ is a set of agents and are called as *nodes*. $\varepsilon \in R \times R = \{(R_i, R_j)\}$ is a set of unordered pair of nodes and called as *edge*. If (R_i, R_j) is an edge of the diagraph, then information flow from R_i to R_j is allowed and R_i, R_j are neighbors. Especially, self-loop edges in the form (R_i, R_i) are not allowed. Another way to represent G is called the adjacency matrix $A = [a_{i,j}] \in R^{n \times n}$. The elements a_{ij} equals 1 if there exists an edge $(R_i, R_j) \in \varepsilon$, otherwise $a_{ij} = 0$.

Theorem 1 (Consensus algorithm [22]). *Let $A = [a_{i,j}] \in R^{n+1 \times n+1}$ be the adjacency matrix, where $a_{ij} = 1, \forall i, j \in \{1, \ldots, n\}$ once the agent j's formation state estimate is available to agent i and 0 otherwise. $a_{i(n+1)} = 1$ if agent i has knowledge of reference value ξ_{contr} and 0 otherwise, and $a_{(n+1)k} = 0, \forall k \in \{1 \ldots n+1\}$ 0. Then the consensus algorithm*

$$\dot{\xi}_i = \frac{1}{\eta_i} \sum_{j=1}^{n} a_{ij} \left[\dot{\xi}_j - \kappa (\xi_i - \xi_j) \right] + \frac{1}{\eta_i} a_{i(n+1)} \left[\dot{\xi}^r_{contr} - \kappa (\xi_i - \xi_{contr}) \right] \tag{1}$$

guarantees that $\xi_i \to \xi_d, \forall i$, asymptotically if and only if the graph of A has a directed spanning tree.

2.4. Agent Model

In this paper, a group of n fully actuated agents is considered. The agents are assumed to know their position in a global coordinate frame and can move in any direction with any specified velocity. The model of the agent is considered as follows:

$$\begin{aligned} \dot{x}_k &= u_{xk} \\ \dot{y}_k &= u_{yk} \end{aligned} \tag{2}$$

where $p_k = [x_k, y_k]$ and $u_k = (u_{xk}, u_{yk})$ are the position coordinate and control input of the *k*th agent respectively.

3. Decentralization of Virtual Linkage Approach

This section illustrates the decentralization of virtual linkage approach. First, the decentralized architecture is introduced to illustrate the advantages as compared to the hierarchical architecture. Then the consensus formation control is presented to enable each agent to decide its movement independently with only exchanging state information with its local neighbors.

3.1. Decentralized Coordination Architecture

In this paper, instead of using hierarchical architecture in which the desired destination of each agent is informed by the corresponding virtual link server, a decentralized architecture is adopted in the proposed approach. As compared to the hierarchical architecture, there does not exist virtual linkage and virtual link servers, each agent only needs to exchange information with its local neighbors.

Figure 3 shows the architecture diagram of the proposed decentralized virtual linkage approach. Each agent instantiates a local copy of consensus module, denoted as F_i. The consensus module F_i is responsible for calculating the instantiation of virtual linkage states $\xi_i = (r_i, q_i, \Theta_i, \lambda_i)$ for the *i*th agent, with the inputs of instantiations of virtual linkage states $\xi_j = (r_j, q_j, \Theta_j, \lambda_j)$ produced by its local neighbors. The main aim of consensus module is to drive each instantiation of virtual linkage state to converge into the desired states $\xi^d = (r^d, q^d, \Theta^d, \lambda^d)$.

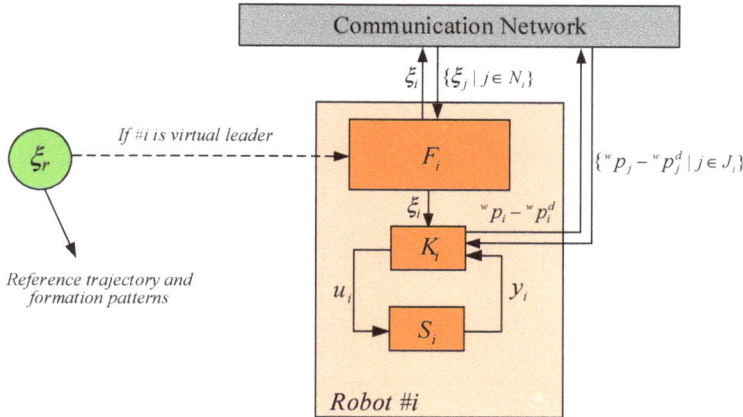

Figure 3. Decentralized virtual linkage architecture.

The states of the virtual linkage are defined as a coordination variable $\xi = (r, q, \Theta, \lambda)$, where r and q are the desired position and attitude of the virtual linkage's reference frame, respectively, $\Theta = (\theta_1, \theta_2, \ldots, \theta_{k-1}, \theta_k)$ is the desired virtual joint angles, where k is the number of virtual links in the virtual linkage. In addition, $\lambda = \left(\lambda_{1x}, \lambda_{1y}, \lambda_{1z}, \ldots, \lambda_{kx}, \lambda_{ky}, \lambda_{kz}\right)$ is a vector which represents the expansion rates of all virtual links. The benefit of introducing λ lies that a group of agents is able to reconfigure into more formation shapes since the length and width of each virtual link can be specified now.

3.2. Consensus Control

3.2.1. Implication of Consensus of Virtual Linkage's State ξ_i

As mentioned above, each agent has an instantiation of virtual linkage states $\xi_i = (r_i, q_i, \theta_i, \lambda_i)$ and the consensus module implement consensus strategies to ensure each instantiation converge into the desired value. In this part, the implication of ξ_i is illustrated.

In the virtual linkage approach, each agent is specified with a vector $\chi = \left(l_i, {}^{vj}p_i^{Ini}\right)$ before task. The l_i is the ID number of virtual link which the ith agent belongs to, and ${}^{vj}p_i^{Ini}$ is the ith agent's relative position in the jth unit virtual link. Meanwhile, each agent is randomly initialized with a $\xi_i = (r_i, q_i, \Theta_i, \lambda_i)$. With knowing the χ and ξ_i, each agent now is able to calculate its global position in the world.

Note that each ξ_i corresponds to a state of the virtual linkage (See Figure 4). The consensus module will ensure all the ξ_i converge into a common value

$$\xi_1 = \xi_2 = \ldots = \xi_n = {}^r\xi_{contr}. \tag{3}$$

The team of agents forms virtual linkages and moves in desired formation shapes along a specified path. Note that the formation pattern can be easily reconfigured by reconfiguring the coordinate variable ${}^r\xi_{contr} = ({}^rr_{contr}, {}^rq_{contr}, {}^r\Theta_{contr}, {}^r\lambda_{contr})$.

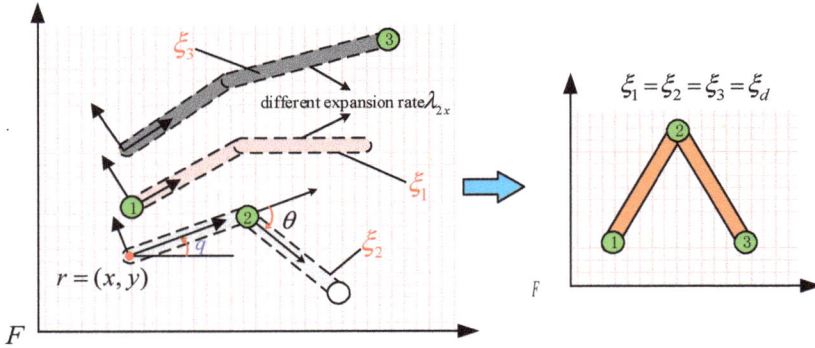

Figure 4. Implication of virtual linkage states ξ_i.

3.2.2. Consensus Module

With the previous section, each agent now is initialized with a $\xi_i = (r_i, q_i, \theta_i, \lambda_i)$. This part aims to design a consensus law and drive ξ_i to the desired value $^r\xi_{contr}$. Here, the consensus tracking algorithm in Reference [22]

$$\dot{\xi_i} = \frac{1}{\eta_i}\sum_{j=1}^{n} a_{ij}\left[\dot{\xi_j} - \kappa(\xi_i - \xi_j)\right] + \frac{1}{\eta_i}a_{i(n+1)}\left[\dot{\xi}^r_{contr} - \kappa(\xi_i - \xi_{contr})\right] \tag{4}$$

is directly used, where a_{ij} are the elements of the adjacency matrix $A^c = \left[a_{ij}^c\right] \in R^{n+1 \times n+1}$ and $\eta_i = \sum_{j=1}^{n+1} a_{ij}^c$. The consensus law consists of two parts. The first term uses the information of its neighbors to make all the ξ_i converge into a common value which leads to the desired formation shape. The existence of the second term is to make formation move along the desired path ξ_{contr}. For a connected graph, consensus to the reference value is guaranteed [22].

3.3. Local Control of Each Agent

After each agent has calculated the $\dot{\xi_i}$, then each agent is able to update the value of ξ_i using Equation (5). Note that $\lambda = [\lambda_{1x}, \lambda_{1y}, \ldots \lambda_{kx}, \lambda_{ky}]$ represents the expansion/contraction rates of each virtual link along their coordinate frame's axis (See Equation (6)). Figure 5 shows the geometry definition of the virtual linkage. The position of a specified agent can be calculated using manipulation kinematics in Equation (7). Here, $^{vj}p_i$ is the relative position of Agent i in the corresponding virtual link j which it belongs to

$$\xi_i(r_i, q_i, \Theta_i, \lambda_i) = \xi_i + \dot{\xi_i} \cdot dt \tag{5}$$

$$^{vj}p_i = \begin{bmatrix} \lambda_{iy} \cdot {}^{vj}p_{ix}^{Ini} \\ \lambda_{iy} \cdot {}^{vj}p_{iy}^{Ini} \\ 1 \end{bmatrix} \tag{6}$$

$$^wp_i^d = {}^wT_R(r_i, q_i) \cdot {}^RT_{vj}^d(\Theta_i, \lambda_i) \cdot {}^{vj}p_i \tag{7}$$

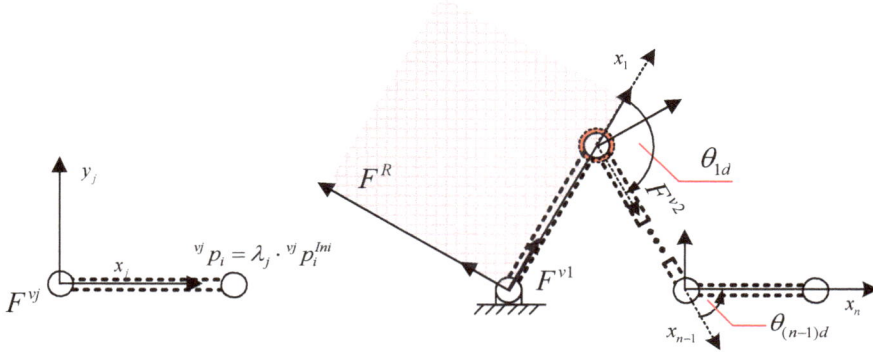

Figure 5. Geometry definition of the virtual linkage.

Finally, the desired absolute position is passed onto the local controller to position the vehicle. Each agent is supposed to know its own position $^w p_i$, and the consensus control algorithm in Reference [22]

$$u_i = {}^w \dot{p}_i^d - k_p \cdot \left({}^w p_i - {}^w p_i^d \right) - \sum_{j=1}^{n} a_{ij}^v [({}^w p_i - {}^w p_i^d) - ({}^w p_j - {}^w p_j^d)] \tag{8}$$

is used, where a_{ij}^v are the elements of the adjacency matrix $A^v = \left[a_{ij}^v \right] \in R^{n \times n}$. For a connected graph, consensus to the reference value is guaranteed.

4. Simulation and Results

In this section, the proposed decentralized virtual linkage approach is applied to a multi-agents' formation control scenario using MATLAB. In the scenarios, nine agents are required to move around a circle while maintaining line formation shapes with a uniform distance of 0.1 m or performing formation reconfigurations by coordinating the desired virtual joint angles Θ_d and the virtual linkage extract/expansion rates λ_d.

4.1. Simulation Setup

In the scenarios, nine agents are designed as a virtual linkage which consists of two virtual links (See Figure 6) and move around a circle with a radius of 1 m in 10 s. The states of $\chi = \left(l_i, {}^{vj} p_i^{Ini} \right)$ for each agent is predefined with Equations (9) and (10).

$$Virtual\, linkage = \begin{cases} virtual\, link1 = \{agent1, agent2, agent3, agent4, agent5\} \\ virtual\, link2 = \{agent5, agent6, agent7, agent8, agent9\} \end{cases} \tag{9}$$

Recall that $^{vj} p_i$ is the representation of the ith point in the jth virtual link coordinate frame. The nine agents are initialized with:

$$\begin{aligned} &{}^{v1} p_1^{Ini} = [0,0], {}^{v1} p_2^{Ini} = [0.2,0], {}^{v1} p_3^{Ini} = [0.4,0], {}^{v1} p_4^{Ini} = [0.6,0], {}^{v1} p_5^{Ini} = [1,0] \\ &{}^{v2} p_5^{Ini} = [0,0], {}^{v2} p_6^{Ini} = [0.2,0], {}^{v2} p_7^{Ini} = [0.4,0], {}^{v2} p_8^{Ini} = [0.6,0], {}^{v2} p_9^{Ini} = [1,0] \end{aligned} \tag{10}$$

Meanwhile, each agent has an instantiation of virtual linkage states $\xi_i = (r_i, q_i, \Theta_i, \lambda_i)$ and is initialized as:

$$\xi_i = randn(6,1) \tag{11}$$

Moreover, there does not exist leader selection for each virtual link. Figure 7 shows the communication topologies used for these two simulations. Notice that apart from agent 2, each agent only needs to exchange ξ_i and its own position $^w p_i$ with its two neighbors.

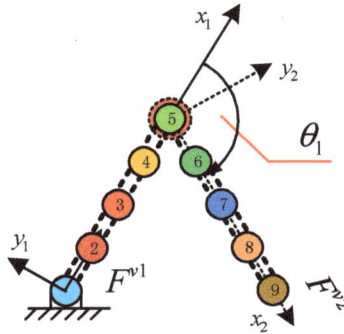

Figure 6. Predefined virtual linkage used in these two simulations.

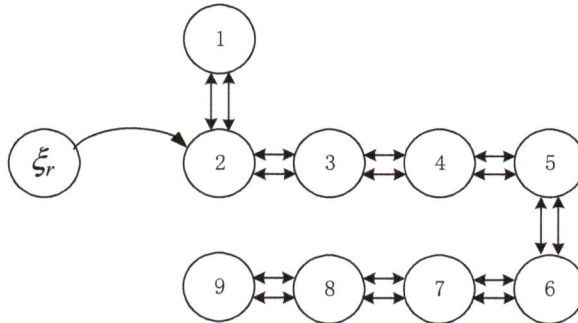

Figure 7. Information-exchange topologies.

Initially, the nine agents are required to align in a line formation with a uniform distance of 0.1 m. Then different formation shapes are reconfigured by coordinating the virtual joint angles Θ_d and the virtual linkage extract expansion rates λ_d. It is worth mentioning that instead of refreshing the relative positions of all the agents, the virtual linkage approach can be reconfigured into different shapes by only changing Θ_d and λ_d.

In the following simulations, the required trajectory and formation shapes are specified by:

$$\xi_{contr} = (r_d, q_d, \Theta_d, \lambda_d) \tag{12}$$

4.2. Formation Moving Using Decentralized Virtual Linkage

In this section, the nine agents are required to align in a line formation with a uniform distance of 0.1 m and move around a circle with a radius of 1 m in 100 s. To perform such tasks, the trajectory of the virtual linkage is specified:

$$r_d = \left(-\frac{9\pi}{500} \cos(\frac{\pi}{50} t), \frac{9\pi}{500} \sin(\frac{\pi}{50} t) \right) \tag{13}$$

Meanwhile, the attitude of the virtual linkage can be expressed as the angle from the x direction of the virtual link1 to the world coordination frame x direction and is also specified as a function of time

$$q_d = \frac{\pi}{50}t + \frac{\pi}{2} \tag{14}$$

Using the virtual linkage approach, the nine agents are able to maintain a line formation with a uniform distance of 0.1 m by specifying:

$$\Theta_d = \theta_1 = 0° \tag{15}$$

$$\lambda_d = [\lambda_{1x}, \lambda_{1y}, \lambda_{2x}, \lambda_{2y}] = [0.4, 1, 0.4, 1] \tag{16}$$

Figure 8 shows the snapshots during the simulation for 100 s.

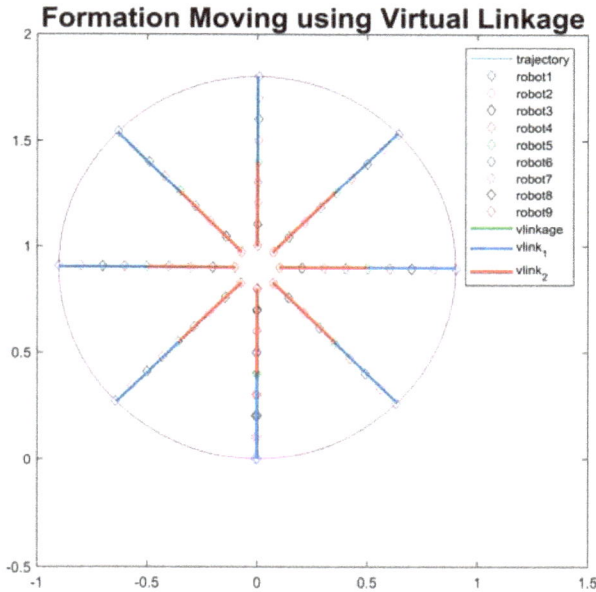

Figure 8. Snapshot of the formation moving using virtual linkage.

Figure 9a,b show the reference state and desired trajectory of the virtual linkage defined in Equations (13)–(16). The individual elements of each ξ_i are plotted in Figure 9c–h respectively. As can be seen from the figures, the nine random initialized $\xi_i (i = 1, 2, \ldots, 9)$ finally converge into reference state defined in Equations (13)–(16). Recall the implication of virtual linkage states ξ_i illustrated in Section 3.2.1 in which the convergence of ξ_i indicates that the nine agents finally forms a specified virtual linkage and moves in desired formation shapes along the specified path. Therefore, the simulation results indicate the effectiveness of moving in formation using the virtual linkage approach.

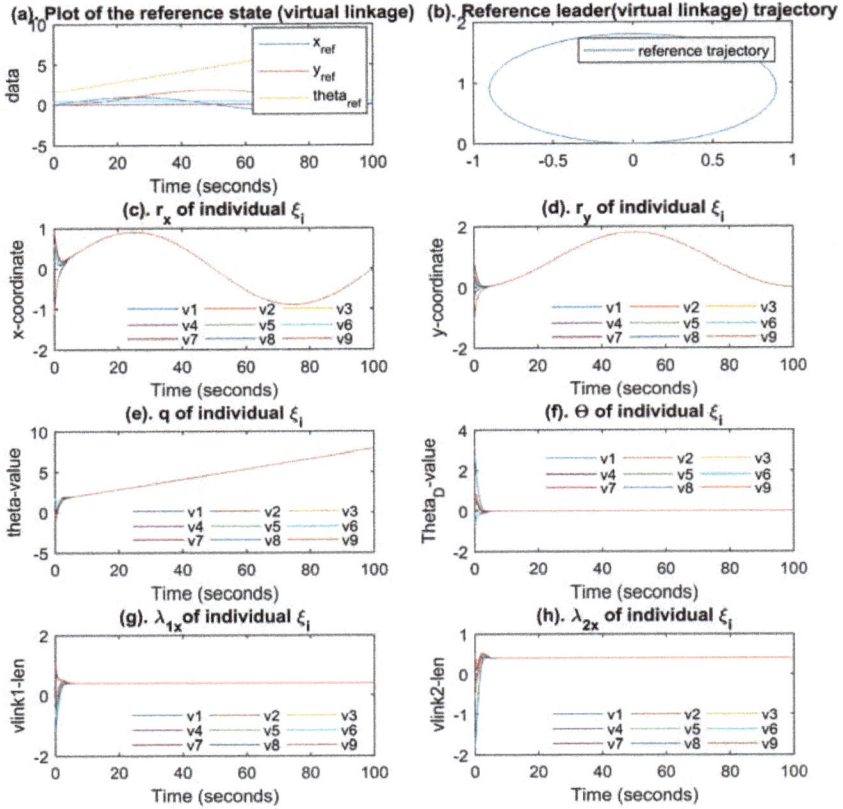

Figure 9. Simulation results of nine agents move around a circle in line formation.

4.3. Formation Reconfiguration Using Decentralized Virtual Linkage Approach

In this part, formation reconfiguration simulation is performed to show the virtual linkage approach's reconfiguration ability by coordinating the desired virtual joint angle Θ_d and expansion/contraction vector λ_d.

In the original virtual linkage approach [18], the designed virtual linkage is able to present different formation shapes by coordinating the desired virtual joint angle Θ_d. Moreover, an expansion/contraction vector λ_d is introduced in this decentralized virtual linkage approach to enable the designed virtual linkage to be reconfigured into more formation patterns, as compared to the hierarchical virtual linkage approach. In this simulation, the group of agents is designed as the virtual linkage defined in Equations (9) and (10) and move along the trajectory in Equations (13) and (14). The Θ_d and λ_d are specified as Equations (17) and (18) to illustrate the formation reconfiguration ability.

$$\Theta_d = \theta_1 = \begin{cases} \frac{\pi}{100}t & t \leq 50 \\ -\frac{\pi}{100}t + \frac{\pi}{2} & 50 < t < 100 \end{cases} \tag{17}$$

$$\lambda_d = [\lambda_{1x}, \lambda_{1y}, \lambda_{2x}, \lambda_{2y}] = [0.4 - 0.002t, 1, 0.4 - 0.002t, 1] \tag{18}$$

Figure 10 shows the snapshots during the simulation for 100 s. As can be seen, the team of agents move around a circle with varying formation patterns. It is worth noting that the two virtual links have different lengths at each moment during the simulation, which indicates that the introduction of λ_d has provided a stronger reconfiguration ability to the virtual linkage approach.

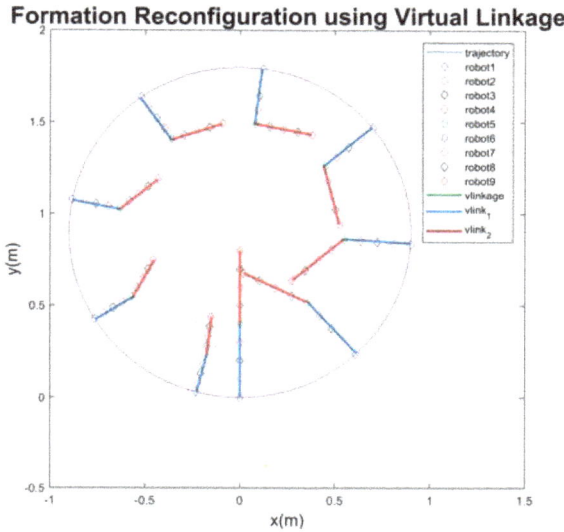

Figure 10. Snapshot of the formation reconfiguration using virtual linkage.

Figure 11a,b report the reference state and desired trajectory of the virtual linkage defined in Equations (13), (14), (17) and (18). The individual elements of each ξ_i are plotted in Figure 11c–h, respectively. As can be seen from the figures, the nine random initialized ξ_i finally converge into the same value, which indicates that the nine agents finally form a specified virtual linkage and move in desired formation shapes along the specified path. Notice that $\lambda_{1x}, \lambda_{2x}$ and Θ of each ξ_i track well with the varying function. Recall that a virtual linkage can reconfigure into different formation patterns by changing the joint anglesand extracting/expanding each link with the scale factor λ_d. Thus, the simulation results indicate the effectiveness of formation reconfiguration using the proposed decentralized virtual linkage approach. What is important for us to recognize here, is the coordinate variable $\xi_r = (r_d, q_d, \Theta_d, \lambda_d)$ in the proposed approach can be arbitrarily set, which provides great potential to perform complicated tasks. For example, when a group of agents is required to go through a gallery, the desired trajectory and varying formation shapes ($\xi_r = (r_d, q_d, \Theta_d, \lambda_d)$) can be solved by plan method.

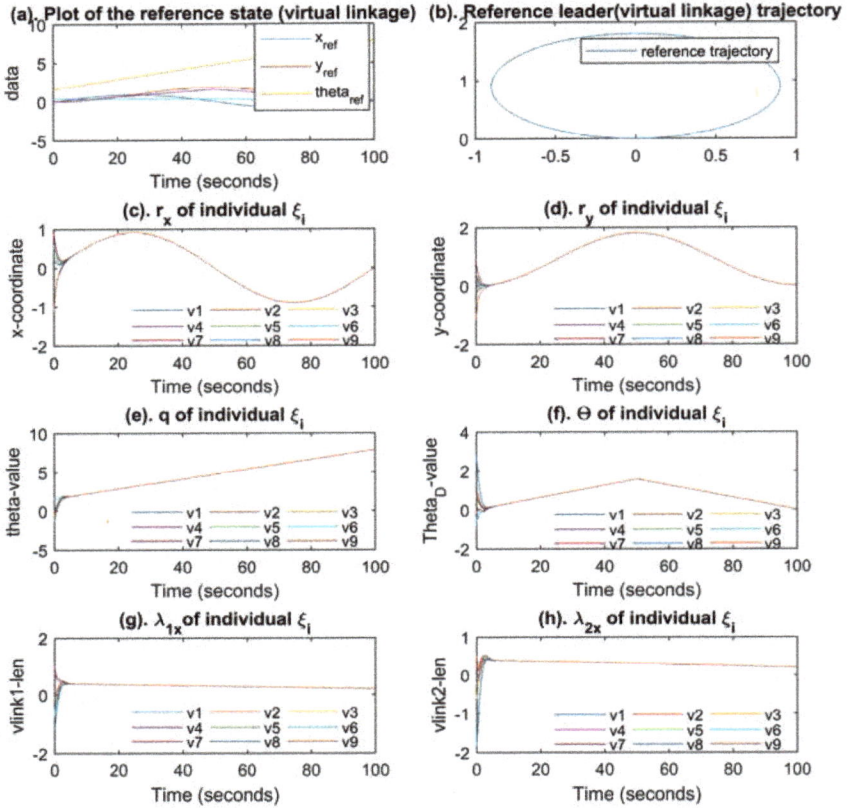

Figure 11. Simulation results formation reconfiguration using virtual linkage.

5. Comparison with Hierarchical Virtual Linkage Approach

In this section, the advantages of the proposed decentralized virtual linkage approach are illustrated through the comparison with the hierarchical virtual linkage approach and the performance is discussed.

5.1. Role Assignments

The detailed architecture of the hierarchical virtual linkage approach when performing the same simulation in Section 4.2 are presented in Figure 12. In the hierarchical virtual linkage approach, there exist virtual link/linkage servers which handle part of the formation control and communicate with part of agents. In reality, the virtual link/linkage server can be implemented in a specified agent, which implies there exist some agents (virtual link/linkage server) which need to perform the formation control computations. However, other agents only need to communicate with their corresponding virtual link server and move according to the states of the corresponding virtual link. In conclusion, there exist different kinds of agents which play different roles and need extra role assignments in the previous approach.

In the decentralized virtual linkage approach, there does not need to be extra role assignment in Figure 3 since all the agents run the same formation control algorithm in Equations (4) and (8).

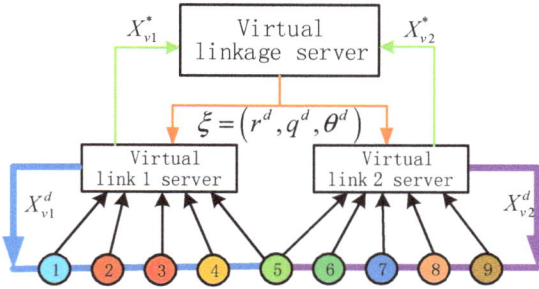

Figure 12. Detailed architecture of the hierarchical virtual linkage approach for simulation.

5.2. Scalability

As described in Section 3.1, each agent can completely decide its movement and only exchange states with its local neighbors. To verify the scalability of the proposed approach, five agents are required to align in a line formation with a uniform distance of 0.1 m and perform the same simulation task in Section 4.2 using the proposed decentralized virtual linkage approach.

To perform such a task, a virtual linkage which also consists of two virtual links is designed as follows:

$$Virtuallinkage\_B = \begin{cases} virtuallink1 = \{agent1, agent2, agent3\} \\ virtuallink2 = \{agent3, agent4, agent5\} \end{cases} \tag{19}$$

$$\begin{aligned} {}^{v1}p_1^{Ini} = [0,0], {}^{v1}p_2^{Ini} = [0.1,0], {}^{v1}p_3^{Ini} = [0.2,0], \\ {}^{v2}p_3^{Ini} = [0,0], {}^{v2}p_4^{Ini} = [0.1,0], {}^{v2}p_5^{Ini} = [0.2,0] \end{aligned} \tag{20}$$

The extract/expansion rate is set as $\lambda_d = [\lambda_{1x}, \lambda_{1y}, \lambda_{2x}, \lambda_{2y}] = [1,1,1,1]$. Figure 13 shows the designed virtual linkage and communication topologies used for this simulation. Figure 14 shows the snapshot during the simulation.

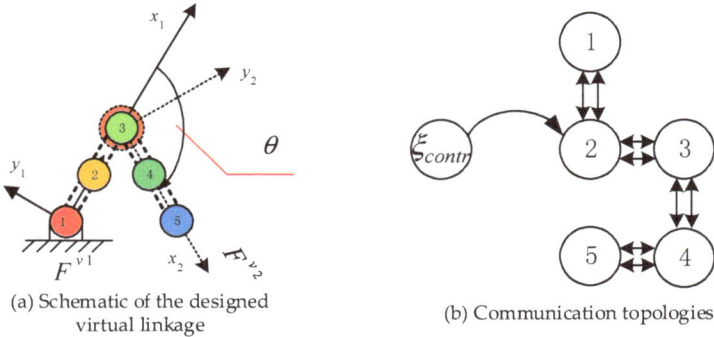

(a) Schematic of the designed
virtual linkage

(b) Communication topologies

Figure 13. Schematic of designed virtual linkage and communication topologies.

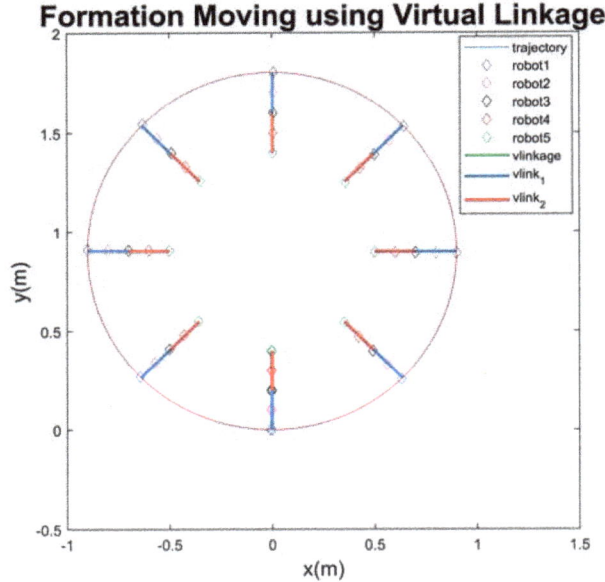

Figure 14. Snapshot of the formation moving of five agents.

Recall that in Figure 3, each agent exchanges its own understanding of virtual linkage states $\xi_i = (r_i, q_i, \Theta_i, \lambda_i)$ and the individual tracking error ${}^w p_i - {}^w p_i^d$ with its neighbors. Supposing $6K$ bits are required to encode each instantiation of virtual linkage ξ_i, $2K$ bits for individual tracking error ${}^w p_i - {}^w p_i^d$, then each agent only needs exchange these $8K$ bits message with its neighbors. If an agent has M neighbors and communicates with them for every period of time T and then the required bandwidth in units of bits per second is:

$$BW = 8K \cdot M/T \tag{21}$$

The maximum communication bandwidth BW_1 in this five agents involved simulation occurs in agent 2, since it has three neighbors (See Figure 13b):

$$BW_1 = 8K \cdot 3/T = 24K/T \tag{22}$$

Meanwhile, nine agents are involved in the simulation in Section 4.2, the maximum communication bandwidth also occurs in agent 2:

$$BW_2 = 8K \cdot 3/T = 24K/T = BW_1 \tag{23}$$

It is worth noting that, the maximum communication bandwidth in the team is determined by the maximum number of agents' neighbors and does not increase with the number of agents in the group.

In contrast to the decentralized virtual linkage approach, the hierarchical virtual linkage approach does not scale well with the number of agents. As illustrated in Reference [18], the maximum communication bandwidth increases with the number of agents in the team. The results indicate that the proposed decentralized virtual linkage approach is more suitable for situations when a large number of agents and/or limited communication are involved.

5.3. Reconfiguration Ability

As compared to the virtual structure approach, an important property of the hierarchical virtual linkage approach is that it can reconfigure the group of agents into different formation patterns by coordinating the value of virtual joint angles. To evaluate the reconfiguration ability of the virtual linkage approach, the definition of reconfiguration space is proposed:

Definition 3 (Reconfiguration Space). *In virtual linkage approach, the reconfiguration space is defined as the set of formation configuration that can be realized by the designed virtual linkage model. In other words, it corresponds to the formation patterns to which the designed virtual linkage can be reconfigured.*

To compare the reconfiguration ability between the original and proposed approach, the reconfiguration spaces of these two approaches are evaluated. In the proposed approach, instead of using $\xi^d = (r^d, q^d, \Theta^d)$ to control the designed behavior of the team like the hierarchical virtual linkage approach (See Figure 12), $\xi^d = (r^d, q^d, \Theta^d, \lambda^d)$ is used as the coordinate variable. Meanwhile, each agent i record its relative percentage position $^{vj}p_i^{Ini}$ in the corresponding virtual link j rather than the relative position $^{vj}p_i$. The benefit of this is that the virtual linkage is now able to extract/expansion the virtual link using Equation (6), which facilitates the reconfiguration ability of the proposed virtual linkage.

In detail, the reconfiguration spaces of the hierarchical and decentralized approaches are denoted as RS_{hier} and RS_{dec} respectively. Recall that $^d r, ^d q$ are the predefined trajectory and attitude of the virtual linkage, the formation pattern is only determined by the vectors $^d\Theta = (\theta_1, \ldots, \theta_n)$ and $\lambda_d = [\lambda_{1x}, \lambda_{1y}, \ldots, \lambda_{nx}, \lambda_{ny}]$. Then the RS_{hier} and RS_{dec} can be expressed as vector spaces:

$$RS_{hier} = \left(^d\Theta, ^d\lambda_{const}\right) = (\theta_1, \ldots \theta_n, 1, 1, \ldots 1, 1) \tag{24}$$

$$RS_{dec} = \left(^d\Theta, ^d\lambda\right) = (\theta_1, \ldots \theta_n, \lambda_{1x}, \lambda_{1y}, \ldots, \lambda_{nx}, \lambda_{ny}) \tag{25}$$

It is worth noting that RS_{hier} can be seen a special case of RS_{dec} when

$$\lambda_d = [\lambda_{1x}, \lambda_{1y}, \ldots, \lambda_{nx}, \lambda_{ny}] = [1, 1, \ldots, 1, 1] \tag{26}$$

and the decentralized approach has stronger reconfiguration ability than the hierarchical approach since

$$RS_{hier} \subset RS_{dec} \tag{27}$$

Figure 15 shows an intuitive way of illustrating the stronger reconfiguration ability by introducing the scale factor λ_d. In the original approach, the designed virtual linkage corresponds to a mechanical linkage which has fixed length and width and is only able to reconfigure into different shapes by coordinating the joint angles. However, proposed approach enables each virtual link to extract/expansion its length and width by introducing the scale factor λ_d, which allows the mechanical linkage to reconfigure into more shapes by extracting/expanding each link and changing the joint angles simultaneously.

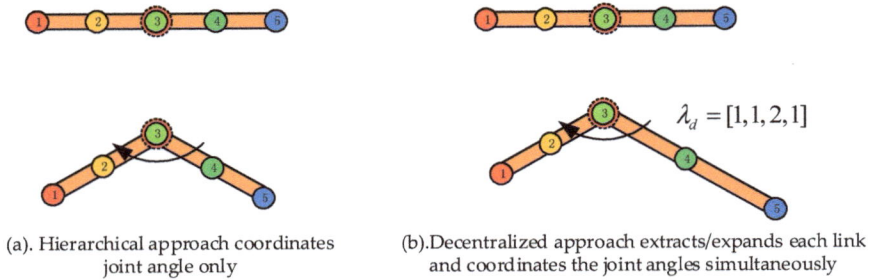

(a). Hierarchical approach coordinates joint angle only

(b).Decentralized approach extracts/expands each link and coordinates the joint angles simultaneously

Figure 15. Reconfiguration ability of hierarchical and decentralized virtual linkage approach.

6. Conclusions

In this paper, the decentralized virtual linkage approach is presented. Instead of using a hierarchical architecture, as with the original virtual linkage approach, the proposed approach uses decentralized architecture in which each agent can independently determine its movement with only the exchange of state information with its local neighbors. The simulation results show the effectiveness of the decentralized virtual linkage approach. There are several advantages as compared with the original virtual linkage approach. First, the proposed approach uses decentralized architecture rather than hierarchical architecture, which does not require role assignments in each virtual link. In detail, there does not exist an agent which needs to exchange with all the agent members in the same virtual link. Meanwhile, each agent can completely decide its movement with only the exchange of states with its local neighbors, which makes this approach more suitable for situations when a large number of agents and/or limited communication are involved. Last but not least, the reconfiguration ability is enhanced in this approach by introducing the scale factor λ_d.

In future work, more attention will be paid to the formation feedback of the virtual linkage approach. Furthermore, the dynamical formation pattern generation and route planning for unknown environments is also an attractive direction and is worth researching.

Author Contributions: Y.L. conceived of the presented idea. Y.L. and J.G. developed the theoretical formalism. Y.L. and J.G. designed the simulation experiments and analyzed the data. Y.L., J.G., X.S. and C.J. discussed the results and wrote the paper.

Acknowledgments: This work is based on work supported in part by the National Key Technology R&D Program of China under Grant 2013BAK03B03 and National Defense Basic Research Project under Grant B2220132014.

Conflicts of Interest: The authors declare no conflict of interest.

References

1. Van den Broek, T.H.A. Formation Control of Unicycle Mobile Robots: A Virtual Structure Approach. In Proceedings of the 48th IEEE Conference on Decision and Control and 28th Chinese Control Conference (International Conference), Shanghai, China, 15–18 December 2009; pp. 8328–8333.
2. Wang, W.; Huang, J.; Wen, C.; Fan, H. Distributed adaptive control for consensus tracking with application to formation control of nonholonomic mobile robots. *Automatica* **2014**, *50*, 1254–1263. [CrossRef]
3. Rezaee, H.; Abdollahi, F. A decentralized cooperative control scheme with obstacle avoidance for a team of mobile robots. *IEEE Trans. Ind. Electron.* **2014**, *61*, 347–354. [CrossRef]
4. Dong, X.; Yu, B.; Shi, Z.; Zhong, Y. Time-varying formation control for unmanned aerial vehicles: Theories and applications. *IEEE Trans. Control Syst. Technol.* **2015**, *23*, 340–348. [CrossRef]
5. Abbasi, Y.; Moosavian, S.A.A.; Novinzadeh, A.B. Formation control of aerial robots using virtual structure and new fuzzy-based self-tuning synchronization. *Trans. Inst. Meas. Control* **2017**, *39*, 1906–1919. [CrossRef]
6. Ren, W.; Beard, R. Decentralized Scheme for Spacecraft Formation Flying via the Virtual Structure Approach. *J. Guid. Control Dyn.* **2004**, *27*, 73–82. [CrossRef]

7. Qian, D.; Xi, Y. Leader–Follower Formation Maneuvers for Multi-Robot Systems via Derivative and Integral Terminal Sliding Mode. *Appl. Sci.* **2018**, *8*, 1045. [CrossRef]
8. Cui, R.; Ge, S.S.; How, B.V.E.; Choo, Y.S. Leader–follower formation control of underactuated autonomous underwater vehicles. *Ocean Eng.* **2010**, *37*, 1491–1502. [CrossRef]
9. Consolini, L.; Morbidi, F.; Prattichizzo, D.; Tosques, M. Leader-follower formation control of nonholonomic mobile robots with input constraints. *Automatica* **2008**, *44*, 1343–1349. [CrossRef]
10. Chen, J.; Sun, D.; Yang, J.; Chen, H. Leader-follower formation control of multiple non-holonomic mobile robots incorporating a receding-horizon scheme. *Int. J. Rob. Res.* **2010**, *29*, 727–747. [CrossRef]
11. Das, A.K.; Fierro, R.; Kumar, V.; Ostrowski, J.P.; Spletzer, J.; Taylor, C.J. A Vision-Based Formation Control Framework. *IEEE Trans. Robot. Autom.* **2002**, *18*, 813–825.
12. Balch, T.; Arkin, R.C. Behavior Based Formation Control for Multirobot Teams. *IEEE Trans. Robot. Autom.* **1998**, *14*, 926–939. [CrossRef]
13. Antonelli, G.; Arrichiello, F.; Chiaverini, S. Flocking for multi-robot systems via the Null-space-based behavioral control. *Swarm Intell.* **2010**, *4*, 37–56. [CrossRef]
14. Xu, D.; Zhang, X.; Zhu, Z.; Chen, C.; Yang, P. Behavior-based formation control of swarm robots. *Math. Probl. Eng.* **2014**, *2014*. [CrossRef]
15. Lewis, M.A.; Tan, K.H. High Precision Formation Control of Mobile Robots Using Virtual Structures. *Auton. Robots* **1997**, *4*, 387–403. [CrossRef]
16. Dong, L.; Chen, Y.; Qu, X. Formation Control Strategy for Nonholonomic Intelligent Vehicles Based on Virtual Structure and Consensus Approach. *Procedia Eng.* **2016**, *137*, 415–424. [CrossRef]
17. Chen, L.; Baoli, M. A nonlinear formation control of wheeled mobile robots with virtual structure approach. In Proceedings of the 2015 34th Chinese Control Conference (CCC), Hangzhou, China, 28–30 July 2015; pp. 1080–1085.
18. Liu, Y.; Gao, J.; Liu, C.; Zhao, F.; Zhao, J. Reconfigurable Formation Control of Multi-Agents Using Virtual Linkage Approach. *Appl. Sci.* **2018**, *8*, 1109. [CrossRef]
19. Ren, W.; Randal, B. *Distributed Consensus in Multi-Vehicle Cooperative Control*; Springer: London, UK, 2008.
20. Ren, W. Decentralization of Virtual Structures in Formation Control of Multiple Vehicle Systems via Consensus Strategies. *Eur. J. Control* **2008**, *14*, 93–103. [CrossRef]
21. Ren, W. *Consensus Seeking, Formation Keeping, and Trajectory Tracking in Multiple Vehicle Cooperative Controlconsensus Seeking, Formation Keeping, and Trajectory Tracking in Multiple Vehicle Cooperative Control*; Brigham Young University: Provo, UT, USA, 2004.
22. Ren, W.; Sorensen, N. Distributed coordination architecture for multi-robot formation control. *Rob. Auton. Syst.* **2008**, *56*, 324–333. [CrossRef]

applied sciences

MDPI

Article

Reconfigurable Formation Control of Multi-Agents Using Virtual Linkage Approach

Yi Liu [1], Junyao Gao [1,2,*], Cunqiu Liu [1], Fangzhou Zhao [1,3] and Jingchao Zhao [1]

[1] Intelligent Robotics Institute, School of Mechatronical Engineering, Beijing Institute of Technology, Beijing 100081, China; YiLiu@bit.edu.cn (Y.L.); 2120160164@bit.edu.cn (C.L.); fzzhao@bit.edu.cn (F.Z.); jch_zhao@bit.edu.cn (J.Z.)

[2] Key Laboratory of Biomimetic Robots and Systems, Ministry of Education, Beijing 100081, China

[3] Beijing Advanced Innovation Center for Intelligent Robots and Systems, Beijing 100081, China

* Correspondence: gaojunyao@bit.edu.cn; Tel.: +86-010-68917611

Received: 10 April 2018; Accepted: 4 July 2018; Published: 9 July 2018

Abstract: Formation control is an important problem in cooperative robotics due to its broad applications. To address this problem, the concept of a virtual linkage is introduced. Using this idea, a group of robots is designed and controlled to behave as particles embedded in a mechanical linkage instead of as a single rigid body as with the virtual structure approach. As compared to the virtual structure approach, the method proposed here can reconfigure the group of robots into different formation patterns by coordinating the joint angles in the corresponding mechanical linkage. Meanwhile, there is no need to transmit all the robots' state information to a single location and implement all of the computation on it, due to virtual linkage's hierarchical architecture. Finally, the effectiveness of the proposed method is demonstrated using two simulations with nine robots: moving around a circle in line formation, and moving through a gallery with varying formation patterns.

Keywords: formation control; virtual structure; formation reconfiguration; multi-agents; robotics

---

1. Introduction

Formation control is an important and fundamental problem in the coordinated control of multi-agent systems. In many applications, a group of agents is expected to move around while maintaining a specified spatial pattern. For example, aircraft flying in V-shaped formation could reduce the fuel consumption required for propulsion [1]. As for the box pushing problem, formation control of a team of identical robots provides the ability to move heavy boxes, which is difficult for a single robot [2]. In military and security patrol missions, formations allow each member of the team to monitor only a small part of the environment for full area coverage and surveillance [3–6].

In the literature, there are roughly three formation control approaches, namely leader-following, behavioral, and virtual structure approaches. In the leader-following approaches [7–10], some agents are considered as leaders, while others act as followers. The formation control problem is converted into two tracking problems: the leaders track the predefined trajectories, and the followers track the transformed coordinates of the leader with some prescribed offsets. The primary advantage of this approach is that the formation stability can be analyzed as tracking stabilities through standard control theories. In addition, the analysis is easy to understand and implement using a vision system equipped on the robot [11,12]. The disadvantage is that the leader has no information about the followers' states. If a follower fails, the leader will still move as predefined, and the formation cannot be maintained.

In the behavioral approaches [13–16], a set of reactive behaviors are designed for the individual agent, such as move-to-goal, avoid-static-obstacle, avoid-robot and maintain-formation. The control action of each agent is generated as a weighted sum of all the behaviors accordingly. One advantage of this approach is that it provides a natural solution for each agent when it has to maintain formation and avoid obstacles. Learning-based methods can also be used to determine agents' behavior to improve the formation performance [17,18]. Furthermore, the formation feedback is implicitly induced through control action, which partly depends on the states of neighboring agents. However, the mathematical analysis of this approach is difficult, and the group stability is not guaranteed.

In the virtual structures approach [19–21], the entire formation is treated as a single rigid body. The desired position of each agent in the team is derived from the virtual particles embedded in the virtual structure. One advantage of the virtual structure approach is that it is straightforward to prescribe the desired behavior for the whole group. Another advantage of this approach is that the group is able to keep a geometric pattern in high precision during movement. Nevertheless, most approaches based on the virtual structure are designed to hold the same shape during the whole task [22–25], and tend to have poor performance when the formation shape needs to be reconfigured frequently.

When talking about formation control, it is desirable to have a group of agents moving in formation with high precision when a specified shape needs to be preserved. Nevertheless, the formation stability is not guaranteed using behavioral approaches. In leader-following approaches, the formation shape also cannot be maintained when a follower fails. Therefore, it is a suitable choice to have all the agents move as a single rigid body by using a virtual structure, out of the three approaches mentioned above. However, the virtual structure approach has limited formation reconfiguration ability for the group of agents.

The main aim of this paper is to provide high precision formation control with some reconfiguration ability for a group of agents. Motivated by the advantages and disadvantages of the virtual structure approach, a novel idea named virtual linkage (VL) is proposed in this paper. Instead of considering the entire formation as a single rigid body, as in the virtual structure approach, the formation is treated as a mechanical linkage which is an assembly of rigid bodies connected by joints. As compared to a single rigid body, a mechanical linkage is able to change its geometric shape by coordinating the angles between each link. Figure 1 illustrates that, instead of remaining the same shape, different geometric shapes can be presented using a mechanical linkage. In other words, the formation shape can be reconfigured if the individual agents are controlled as particles in a mechanical linkage.

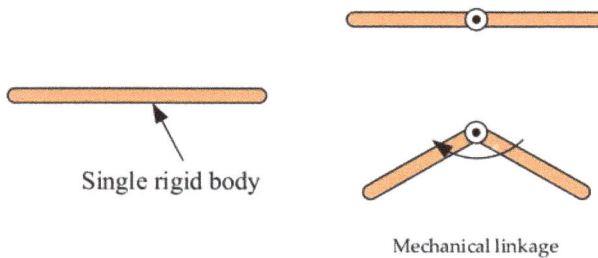

Single rigid body

Mechanical linkage

Figure 1. Example of a single rigid body and a mechanical linkage.

The main advantage of the virtual linkage approach is that it can maintain the formation shape in high precision and is able to reconfigure the geometric shape when needed. On the one hand, if the angles between each link are kept at a constant value, the multi-link mechanism is expected to behave like a single rigid body and has high precision formation control. On the other hand, the formation shape can be reconfigured by varying the angle value between links. Another advantage is that there is no need to transmit all the agents' state information into a central location as in [19] due to the hierarchical architecture of the virtual linkage approach.

The remainder of this paper is organized as follows. In Section 2, the definition of virtual linkage is presented. Section 3 illustrates the control strategy for the formation movement. Simulation results are in Section 4. Finally, in Section 5, some concluding remarks of this paper are given.

2. Problem Statement

2.1. Virtual Linkage

A mechanical linkage is an assembly of rigid bodies connected by joints. Meanwhile, a rigid body is defined as a group of point masses fixed by the constraint that the distances between every pair of points must be constant [26]. A joint is a connection between two bodies and imposes constraints on their relative movement. In other words, a linkage is also a collection of points which belong to different rigid bodies.

Prior to analyzing a linkage directly, each rigid body component is discussed first. In a single rigid body, particles can be thought of as stationary with respect to a certain frame of reference. If the particles in a rigid body are replaced with movable elements, we obtain the definition of virtual structure proposed in [19], which can be seen below.

Definition 1: *Virtual Structure*

A virtual structure is a collection of elements, e.g., robots, which maintain a (semi-) rigid geometric relationship to each other and to a frame of reference [19].

The definition of virtual linkage also can be given by replacing particles of a linkage with movable elements and controlling them to act as the original linkage. An intuitive solution to this problem is to model each link as a virtual structure and define a virtual linkage as a collection of virtual structures connected by virtual joints.

Definition 2: *Virtual Joints*

A virtual joint is a connection between two virtual structures and imposes constraints on their relative movement.

Definition 3: *Virtual Linkage (VL)*

A virtual linkage is an assembly of virtual structures (named "virtual link") connected by virtual joints.

The principle of the virtual structure and virtual linkage is illustrated in Figure 2. In the generation of a virtual linkage, the existence of the virtual joints has enabled relative movement between cascaded virtual structures. Therefore, different geometric shapes are possible to be presented using the same virtual linkage by controlling each virtual joint at different values.

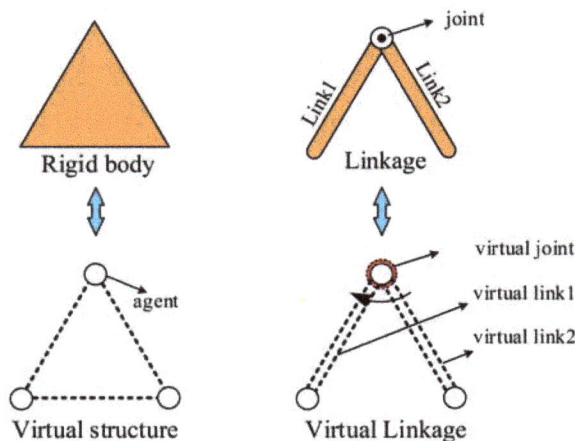

Figure 2. Principle of virtual structure and virtual linkage.

2.2. Moving in Formation

When talking about formation control, it is a fundamental problem to enable a group of agents to move along a predefined trajectory while maintaining a rigid geometric relationship. The virtual structure approach is an intuitive idea to solve this problem by considering the formation as a single rigid body, enabling the movement of the virtual structure. In contrast to a virtual structure, the geometric relationship is maintained by controlling virtual joints at predefined constant values in the virtual linkage approach (see Figure 2).

Another way to illustrate the formation ability of the virtual linkage exists in the relationship between the virtual linkage and virtual structure. In mechanical engineering, a linkage designed to be stationary is called a structure and can be regarded as a single rigid body. Similarly, a virtual linkage also degenerates to a virtual structure when it is designed to be stationary by controlling the virtual joint at a fixed value. In this way, the formation problem of using a virtual linkage can be solved by controlling the virtual joints at fixed angles and enabling the movement of the virtual linkage.

The geometry of the problem statement is illustrated in Figure 3. Formalizing these ideas, the problem is stated as follows:

1. Given n agents labeled $1, \ldots, n$, and the position of the ith agent in the world, the coordinate frame is represented as $^w r_i$.

2. Imagining there is a virtual linkage consisting of k virtual links and n points, the position of the ith point in the jth virtual link coordinate frame is represented as $^{vj} p_i$.

3. Let $^w T_{vj}$ be the transformation that maps $^{vj} p_i$ to $^w p_i$ and the position of the ith point of the virtual linkage in the world coordinate frame.

4. Say the agents are moving in the desired formation if the agents satisfy the constraints $^w r_i = {}^w p_i$ in time by controlling the virtual joints at specified angles and fitting each agent into the corresponding virtual link.

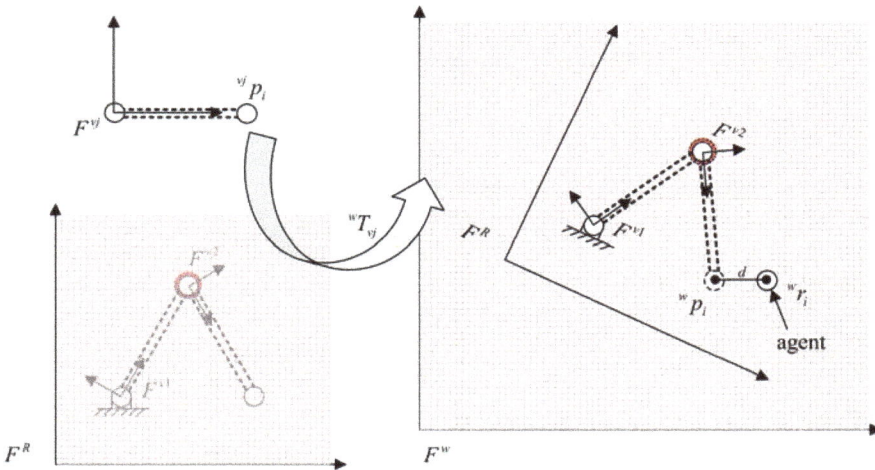

Figure 3. Geometry of the virtual linkage definition: F^{vj}, F^R, F^w are the reference coordinate frames of the jth virtual link, virtual linkage and world, respectively. The point p_i belongs to the jth virtual link and is mapped from $^{vj} p_i$ to $^w p_i$ through the transformation $^w T_{vj}$. The agents act as a whole mechanical linkage when all $^w r_i = {}^w p_i$.

2.3. Formation Reconfiguration

In some situations, such as aircraft flying in a V-shaped formation, agents are only required to maintain a specified spatial pattern throughout the whole task. However, there also exist situations where the formation pattern should be reconfigured in order to perform a complex task. Figure 4 shows an example of formation reconfiguration. The three agents initially move in a line formation in order to have a broad view, and the formation pattern needs to be reconfigured as an arrow shape in order to go through obstacles.

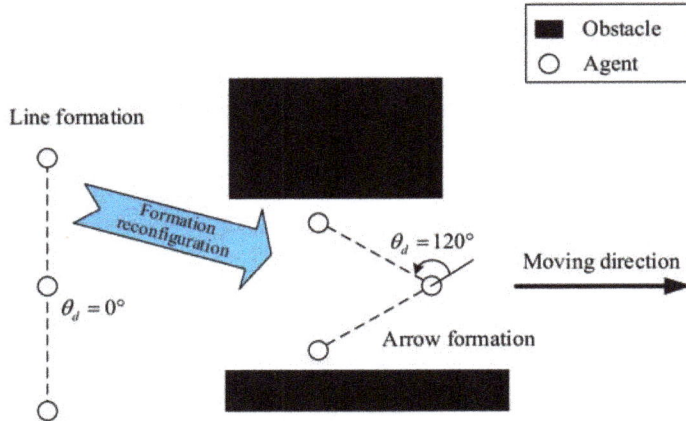

Figure 4. Formation reconfiguration example.

In the virtual structure approach, each virtual structure corresponds to a unique rigid body. Therefore, it should be redesigned if different formation patterns are required. A solution to this problem is to model the group of agents as a virtual linkage and set the desired virtual joint angle θ_d to different values. For example, in Figure 4, the three agents are in line formation when $\theta_d = 0$, and can be reconfigured into a regular triangle shape when θ_{id} is set to 120°.

2.4. Agent Model Definition

This paper considers a group of n fully actuated agents without motion constraints. The agents are assumed to know their position in a global coordinate frame. The model of the agent is considered as follows:

$$\dot{x}_k = u_{xk}$$
$$\dot{y}_k = u_{yk}$$

where $p_k = [x_k, y_k]$ is the coordinate of the kth agent, and $u_k = \left(u_{xk}, u_{yk}\right)$ is the control input to control the movement of the agent. In other words, the agent is able to track a specified trajectory by designing u_k property.

3. Formation Control: Virtual Linkage Approach

The idea of using a virtual linkage to solve the problem of moving in formation is much the same as virtual structures: the agents are controlled to fit the virtual linkage and then the virtual linkage tracks the predefined trajectory. The real position and orientation of the virtual linkage are determined by the individual virtual links, which in turns are determined by the agents' position. In this paper, each agent is assumed to know its position in a global coordinate frame. In real robotic systems, this assumption can be realized by "localization" technics such as using global position systems, motion capture system or other perception methods. With knowing the position of virtual linkage, the desired position for each agent is given. In other words, there exists a hierarchical architecture and bi-directional control as shown in Figure 5.

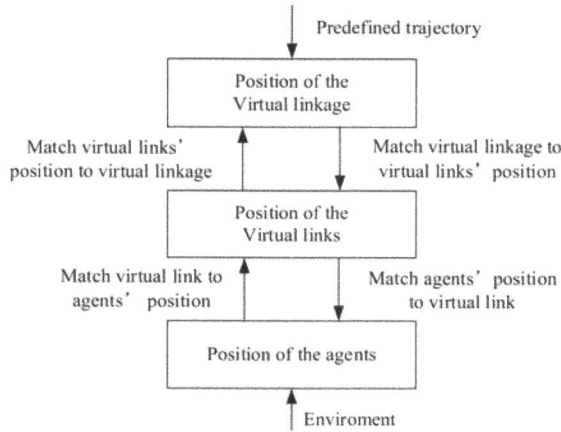

Figure 5. Bi-direction flow control of the virtual linkage.

In this section, the virtual linkage approach will be carefully illustrated to solve the formation control problem. Firstly, the overall control architecture of the virtual linkage approach and its advantages are derived. Then, the state representation of the virtual link and virtual linkage is illustrated. Finally, the detailed method is introduced to enable a group of agents to move in formation and facilitate formation reconfiguration ability.

3.1. Architecture of the Virtual Linkage

As defined in Section 2.1, a virtual linkage consists of a set of virtual links, and each virtual link in turns consists of a set of agents. Hence, it is natural to apply the hierarchical architecture to the control of a virtual linkage. In this architecture, each virtual link oversees the performance of the other virtual links. Each agent of a virtual link in turn oversees the other agents in the same links.

The architecture block diagram of the virtual linkage is shown in Figure 6. The module Vl_i is the ith virtual link in the virtual linkage, with the coordination input ξ, and output vector v_i representing the state information of the ith virtual link. The system F represents the formation control in the virtual linkage. The inputs to F are the performance of each virtual link z_{vli}, and the outputs y_G of the supervisor. Also, a formation feedback from F to G can be induced by the performance measure z_F. In reality, the module G and F can be implemented in a specified agent or a server computer outside of the agent.

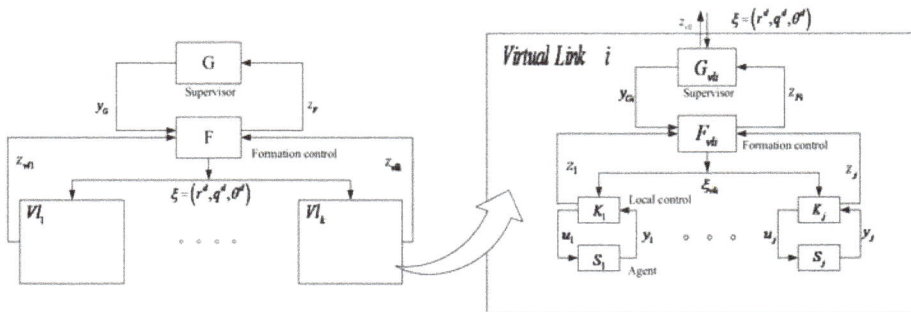

Figure 6. Architecture of the virtual linkage.

43

The second layer of the architecture is the coordination of each virtual link module Vl_i. Here, the coordination architecture proposed in [27] is directly used because each Vl_i is a small virtual structure, as stated in the Definition 3. The systems S_i and K_i are the agent and corresponding local controller. Meanwhile, u_i and y_i represent the control variable to the agent and measurable outputs, respectively. The rest of the modules and variables are much the same as the first layer. In practical applications, a specified agent is responsible for running the G_{vli} and F_{vli} module, including receiving the state of the agents that participate in the same link, handling the control algorithm and sending desired information ξ_{vli} to the agents.

Figure 7 shows the scheme of the centralized architecture based on the virtual structure approach [28]. In contrast to the centralized formation control [19,24,29], the virtual linkage architecture has several advantages. Firstly, the hierarchical architecture does not need to exchange all agents' state information to a central location, which reduces the burden of communication bandwidth, and scales much better than the centralized approaches. Secondly, the heavy computation of fitting agents into the virtual linkage also has been distributed to several low-level controllers F_{vli} and can be calculated simultaneously. This makes the proposed algorithm faster and more suitable for real-time control. Finally, by varying virtual joint angle θ_d in the coordination input $\xi = \left(r^d, q^d, \theta^d \right)$ different formation patterns can be achieved without the need to re-plan the whole formation procedure. In other words, the virtual linkage approach provides the formation reconfiguration ability that is not provided by the virtual structure approach.

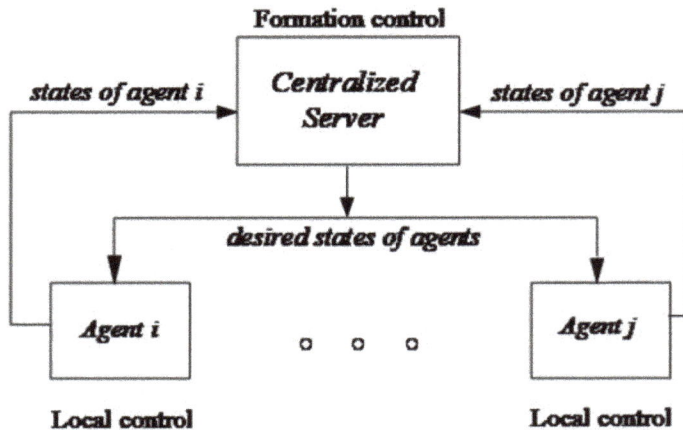

Figure 7. Centralized architecture based on the virtual structure approach.

3.2. State Representations of Virtual Linkage and Virtual Link

In mechanical engineering, the state of a rigid body can be represented as a vector (r, q), where r and q are the position and attitude of the rigid body. In order to describe the state of each link, a frame attached to each link is defined. That is, F^{vj} is attached rigidly to link j. Following the Denavit–Hartenberg convention [30], which is used for selecting the reference frame and analyzing the state of a linkage, the reference frames of links are laid out as follows:

1. The z-axis lies in the direction of the joint axis.
2. The x-axis is parallel to common normal: $x_i = z_i \times z_{i-1}$ points from joint $i-1$ to i.
3. The y-axis is formed by the right-hand rule to complete the jth frame.

Meanwhile, the virtual joint angle θ_i is defined as the angle from axis x_{i-1} to x_i measured about z_{i-1}.

The coordinate frame F^{vj} corresponding to the jth virtual link is shown in Figure 8. The state of the jth virtual link is represented as a vector (r_{vj}, q_{vj}), where r_{vj} and q_{vj} are the real position and attitude of the jth virtual link. In reality, only a parameter θ_{1d} besides the length of the two links is required to describe the shape of the virtual linkage. Thus, the F^R is chosen to be the same with F^{v1} and the state of the virtual linkage can also be denoted as (r_R, q_R), where r_R and q_R are the position and orientation of the reference coordinate frame F^R (See Figure 8).

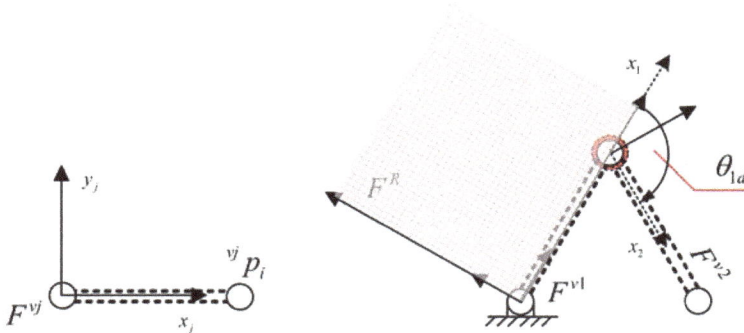

Figure 8. Definition of a virtual link's coordinate frame and virtual joint angle.

3.3. Moving in Formation Using Virtual Linkage

In order to illustrate the bi-directional flow and hierarchical architecture presented in Figures 5 and 6, the detailed virtual linkage approach is illustrated to enable a group of agents to move in formation.

Table 1 shows the moving-in-formation algorithm using a virtual linkage. In step 1, the virtual linkage is aligned with the agents. The virtual linkage then moves to track the predefined trajectory in step 2. In step 3, the agents update their destinations which enable them to move like a mechanical linkage. In step 4, individual agent is controlled to move to the desired position using a local controller. The individual steps will be explained in more details in the following section.

Table 1. Moving-in-formation algorithm using virtual linkage.

(1). Align the virtual linkage with the current agents' position.
a. Calculate each virtual links' state with each group of agents' position.
b. Align the virtual linkage with the virtual links' state calculated from the above step.
(2). Move the virtual linkage to the desired position along the predefined trajectory
(3). Calculate individual agent's positions to track the moving virtual linkage.
a. Calculate the desired state for each virtual link to track the moving linkage.
b. Calculate individual agent's positions track the corresponding virtual link.
(4). Move the agents to the desired position using agents' local controller.
(5). Go to step (1).

3.3.1. Fitting the Virtual Linkage

A virtual linkage is made up of several cascaded virtual links, where a virtual link is an assembly of agents. In order to align the virtual linkage to a group of agents, we break the fitting process into two steps. Firstly, each virtual links' state is calculated using the corresponding group of agents. Secondly, the virtual linkage is aligned with all virtual links' states. The advantages of doing so lie in two aspects: on the one hand, there is no need to transmit all the agents' state information into a central location. On the other hand, each virtual link can calculate its individual state simultaneously which accelerates the whole fitting process.

A.   Fitting the Virtual Link

In the first step, an objective function is created to measure the fitness of the virtual link to corresponding agents. Here, the objective function proposed in [19] to fit virtual structure with a group of agents is adopted since a virtual link is a virtual structure. It is defined as the sum error between all the agents' position and its assigned point in the virtual link:

$$f(X_{vj}) = \sum_{i \in vj} d\left({}^w r_i, {}^w T_{vj}(X_{vj}) \cdot {}^{vj} p_i \right) \tag{1}$$

where $i \in vj$ refers to the agents belonging to the jth virtual link, and d is the distance between the agent and its assigned point in virtual link (See Figure 3). Recall that, as defined in Section 2.2, the ${}^w r_i$ is the position of the ith agent in the world coordinate frame and ${}^{vj} p_i$ is the assigned position of agent i in the frame of the jth virtual link. The function ${}^w T_{vj}$ is a transformation that maps ${}^{vj} p_i$ to ${}^w p_i$, the position of the ith point of the virtual linkage in the world coordinate frame.

In detail, the ${}^w T_{vj}$ is a homogeneous transform and takes the form

$$ {}^w T_{vj}(X_{vj}) = \begin{bmatrix} R & P \\ 0 & 1 \end{bmatrix} \tag{2}$$

$R \in SO(3)$ and $P \in R^3$ are parameterized by the element of $X_{vj} = [r_{vj}, q_{vj}]$ which is the attitude and position of F^{vj} in the world coordinate frame. The objective of this step is to find X_{vj}^* which enables $f\left(X_{vj}^* \right) \leq f(X_{vj})$ for all X_{vj} and treat it as the position and attitude of the jth virtual link.

B. Fitting the Virtual Linkage

In the second step, the "best" position and attitude of the whole virtual linkage is required to be determined using the X_{vj}^* obtained from the above step. The alignment of the virtual linkage is performed by minimizing the error between calculated position and altitude of virtual links X_{vj}^* and their corresponding state derived from the virtual linkage. The objective function is of the form:

$$F(X_R) = \sum_{vj=1}^{k} D\left({}^w T_{vj}(X_{vj}^*), {}^w T_R(X_R) \cdot {}^R T_{vj}^d(\theta_d) \right) \tag{3}$$

where k is the number of the virtual links, $D(\cdot)$ is the norm which measures the cost between the calculated state of the jth virtual links X_{vj}^* and its assigned state in virtual linkage. ${}^R T_{vj}^d$ is a fixed homogeneous transform from the coordinate frame of jth virtual link $\{vj\}$ to the virtual linkage's reference coordinate frame $\{R\}$. It is determined when the formation shape is configured with θ_d.

In order to implement $D(\cdot)$, the error between ${}^w T_{vj}(X_{vj}^*)$ and ${}^w T_R(X_R) \cdot {}^R T_{vj}^d(\theta_d)$ are transformed into the distance between four pair of points. In details, a homogeneous transform is a moving coordinate frame $\{vj\}$, and the position and orientation error between two coordinate frames can be calculated by moving and rotating a tetrahedron. Here the shape of the tetrahedron is determined by four vertices in the $\{vj\}$ coordinate frame: $\left\{ {}^{vj} r_{p1} = (1,0,0,1)^T, {}^{vj} r_{p2} = (0,1,0,1)^T, {}^{vj} r_{p3} = (0,0,1,1)^T, {}^{vj} r_{p4} = (0,0,0,1)^T \right\}$ (See Figure 9). Hence, the objective function $D(\cdot)$ is converted into the distance between four pairs of points:

$$F(X_R) = \sum_{vj=1}^{k} \sum_{i=1}^{4} d\left({}^w T_{vj}(X_{vj}^*) \cdot {}^{vj} r_{pi}, {}^w T_R(X_R) \cdot {}^R T_{vj}(\theta_d) \cdot {}^{vj} r_{pi} \right) \tag{4}$$

The objective of this step is to find X_R^* which enables $f(X_R^*) \leq f(X_R)$ for all X_R and treat it as the position and attitude of virtual linkage.

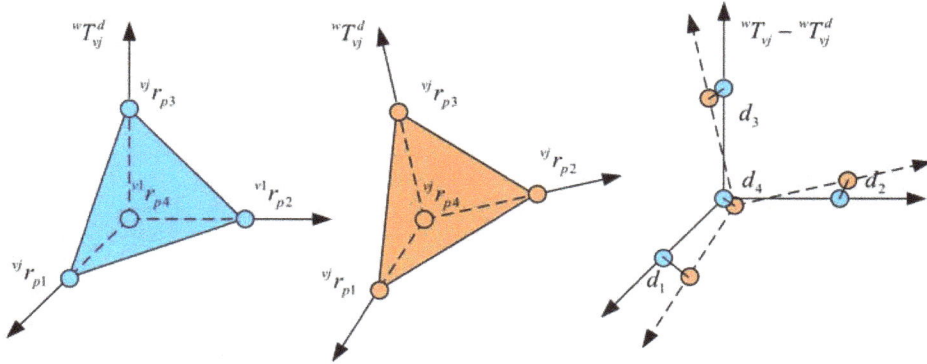

Figure 9. Calculating differences between two homogeneous transforms.

3.3.2. Moving the Virtual Linkage

This involves simply moving the virtual linkage's coordinate frame $\{R\}$ along the predefined reference trajectory $r_R^d = \zeta_R(t)$ with attitude $q_R^d = q(t)$. Then, the coordinate frame of the jth virtual link $\{vj\}$ will follow its desired trajectory, X_{vj}^d, given by:

$$^wT_{vj}\left(X_{vj}^d\right) = {}^wT_R\left(X_R^d\right) \cdot {}^RT_{vj}(\theta_d) \tag{5}$$

where ${}^RT_{vj}(\theta_d)$ is determined by the predefined formation shape and can be expressed using the Denavit–Hartenberg convention [30]. The desired trajectory and attitude of the jth link is illustrated using ${}^wT_{vj}\left(X_{vj}^d\right)$ when the virtual linkage $\{R\}$ follows the trajectory and attitude $X_R^d = \left(r_R^d, q_R^d\right)$.

Hence, the desired position of the agent i which belongs to the jth virtual link can be represented as follows:

$$^wr_i^d = {}^wT_{vj}(X_{vj}^d) \cdot {}^{vj}p_i \tag{6}$$

3.3.3. Moving the Agents to the Desired Position

The next step in the formation algorithm is to move the agent i to the desired point ${}^wr_i^d$ at each iteration step. Each agent is supposed to known its own position ${}^wr_i$, and the control input to the agent model is given by:

$$u = {}^w\dot{r}_i^d + k_p \cdot \left({}^wr_i^d - {}^wr_i\right) \tag{7}$$

3.4. Formation Reconfiguration Using Virtual Linkage

As described in Section 2.3, virtual structure approaches should be redesigned if different formation patterns are required, as each virtual structure corresponds to a unique rigid body. In detail, the agents have to be recalled back and refresh their relative position in the virtual structure ${}^Rr_i$ which is saved in each local agent. Another way to update the ${}^Rr_i$ for all agents can be implemented by informing all the agents through communication. If a group of agents needs to be reconfigured for every period of time T, and 3*K bits are needed to record the relative position ${}^Rr_i$ in the virtual structure, then the required bandwidth in units of bits per second is

$$BW_1 = 3 \cdot N \cdot K/T \tag{8}$$

This turns out to be a heavy burden to the communication network and is not suitable for real-time control, especially when the number of agents N increases.

Differently to the virtual structure, each virtual linkage corresponds to a linkage (or manipulator) rather than a unique rigid body. In mechanical engineering, a linkage (or manipulator) is a kinematic configuration which is able to change its state configuration by changing the value of joints. Therefore, a virtual linkage is able to be reconfigured as different formation shapes by changing the virtual joint angle θ_d without need to recall back and refresh all the agents' relative position in the *j*th virtual link $^{vj}r_i$.

In detail, by changing the θ_d in Figure 8, a different formation shape is able to be presented. It is worth mentioning that the θ_d is only necessary to broadcast to *k* locations which handle the individual formation control of the *k* virtual links. Supposing *K* bits are required to encode each virtual joint angle, then the communication bandwidth reduces to

$$BW_2 = K \cdot k / T \tag{9}$$

Here, the number of virtual links is not bigger than the number of agents ($k \le N$) since each virtual link is a collection of agents. Hence, the bandwidth ratio is

$$\frac{BW_2}{BW_1} = \frac{k}{3 \cdot N} \le \frac{1}{3} \tag{10}$$

Figure 10 shows the bandwidth ratio increases linearly with the number of virtual links k when the number of agents is fixed. The maximum value, $1/3$, is reached when $k = N$. This indicates that the virtual linkage requires less than 33.3% bandwidth to reconfigure a formation shape as compared to the virtual structure approach.

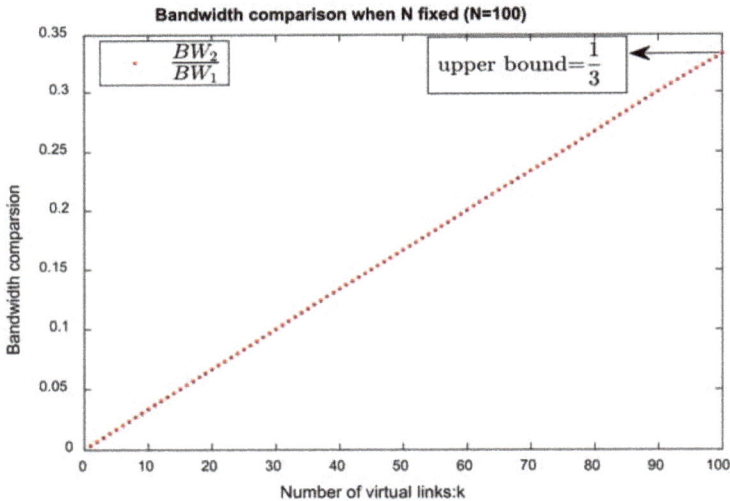

Figure 10. Bandwidth ratio $\frac{BW_2}{BW_1}$ increases linearly with the number of virtual links.

4. Simulation and Results

In this section, numerical simulations including formation moving and formation reconfiguration are presented using Matlab to validate the effectiveness of the proposed virtual linkage approach. To illustrate the formation moving ability, the commonly used scenario of moving around a circle is selected in Section 4.1 [7,31]. In the first simulation, nine agents are required to move around a circle in line formation with uniform spacing of 0.1 m. As for the second parts, moving through a gallery is a practical scenario where formation reconfiguration ability is needed and has been adopted by related researchers [32,33]. Therefore, nine agents are reconfigured into predefined formation shape to go through a knowing obstacle gallery in the second simulation. In Section 4.3, parameter analysis is conducted to illustrate function of the number of agents and number of virtual links and shape transformations. Finally, the comparison between the virtual structure approach and the proposed virtual linkage approach is presented in Section 4.4.

4.1. Formation Moving Using Virtual Linkage

To illustrate the formation moving ability of the proposed virtual linkage approach, a simulation is carried out. In this simulation task, nine agents are required to align in a line formation with a uniform distance of 0.1 m and move around a circle with a radius of 1 m in 10 s. Therefore, the velocity and angle velocity $v = \pi/5\,m/s, \omega = \pi/5\,rad/s$ are specified to enable this task. The uniform distance of 0.1 m is specified to make the simulation results more easily comprehensible to readers.

4.1.1. Simulation Setup

In order to complete this task and illustrate the effectiveness of the proposed approach, a virtual linkage which consists of two virtual links is designed (See Figure 11). It is worth mentioning that a virtual linkage with only one virtual link degenerates into a virtual structure with no reconfiguration ability. Therefore, a virtual linkage consisting of two virtual links can be considered as the smallest unit to illustrate the standard validity of the proposed approach. In this simulation, the configuration of the virtual linkage is predefined:

$$\text{virtual linkage} = \begin{cases} \text{virtual link1} = \{\text{agent1, agent2, agent3, agent4, agent5}\} \\ \text{virtual link2} = \{\text{agent5, agent6, agent7, agent8, agent9}\} \end{cases} \tag{11}$$

By controlling the virtual joint at $180°$, the nine agents are able to maintain a line formation. Since the nine agents are required to align in a line formation with uniform distance 0.1 m, each virtual link then holds a length of 0.4 m in Figure 11.

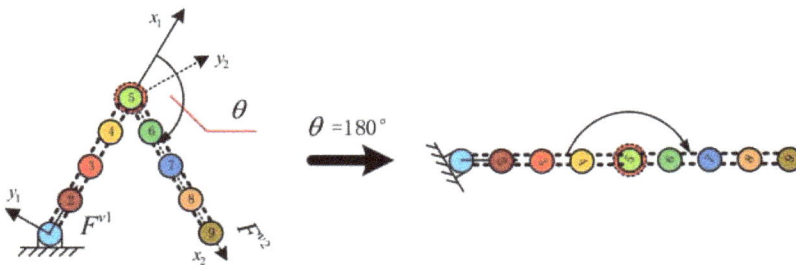

Figure 11. Predefined virtual linkage used in these two simulations.

Recall that the position of the ith point in the jth virtual link coordinate frame is represented as $^{vj}p_i$, and the designed virtual linkage has the following points.

$$^{v1}p_1 = [0,0], ^{v1}p_2 = [0.1,0], ^{v1}p_3 = [0.2,0], ^{v1}p_4 = [0.3,0], ^{v1}p_5 = [0.4,0] \\ ^{v2}p_5 = [0,0], ^{v2}p_6 = [0.1,0], ^{v2}p_7 = [0.2,0], ^{v2}p_8 = [0.3,0], ^{v2}p_9 = [0.4,0] \tag{12}$$

The nine agents are randomly initialized at the region $\{(x_i, y_i) | x_i \in [0,1], y_i \in [0,1]\}$.

4.1.2. Simulation Results

The trajectories of the individual agents and snapshots during the simulation for 10 s are plotted in Figures 12 and 13, respectively.

Formation moving using Virtual Linkage

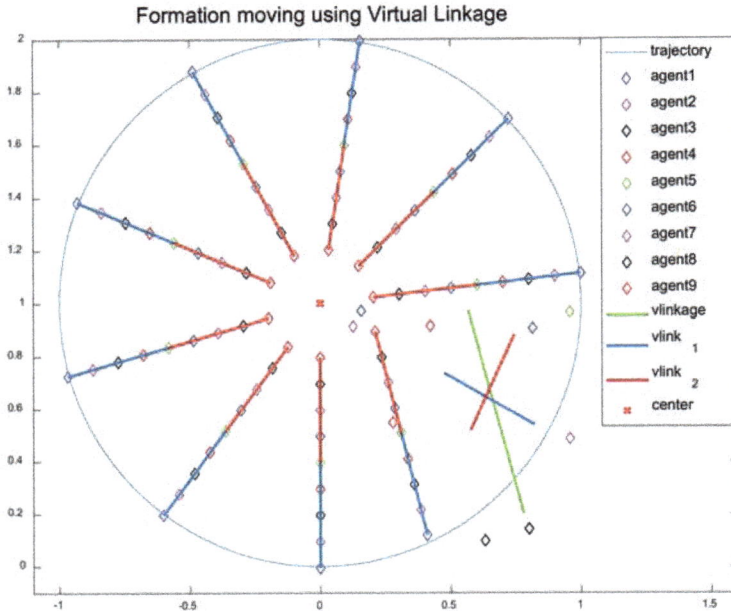

Figure 12. Snapshots of the formation moving.

Trajectory of individual agent

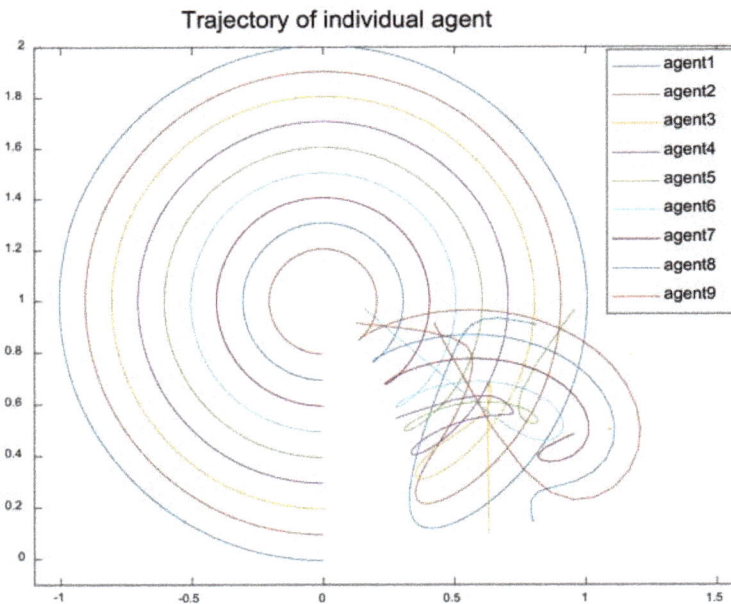

Figure 13. Trajectory of individual agents.

Notice how the agents fit themselves into the defined virtual linkage at the beginning when the agents are randomly initialized. This can be explained as follows. During the first few seconds, the agents 1, 2, 3, 4, 5 fit themselves into virtual link1, shown by the blue line, and the agents 5, 6, 7, 8, 9 fit themselves into virtual link2, shown by the red line (See Figure 12). Then, the two virtual links fit themselves into the whole virtual linkage shown by the green line and determine the 'best' position and orientation of it. Once the states of the virtual linkage are determined, the agents quickly move to their corresponding placeholder in the virtual linkage to reach formation. Meanwhile, the whole virtual linkage moves along the circle; each agent then adjusts its velocity according to its position and the placeholder in the fitting virtual linkage.

Figure 13 shows that the trajectory of each individual agent and indicates the effectiveness of moving in formation using the virtual linkage approach.

4.2. Formation Reconfiguration Using Virtual Linkage

An important property of the proposed virtual linkage approach is that it is easy to be reconfigured into some different formation patterns by coordinating the virtual joint angles. To show the formation reconfiguration ability of the proposed virtual linkage approach a simulation is conducted for the following scenario. Knowing the map of the environment, the agents are given the predefined trajectory and varying formation shapes (shown in Figure 14) to pass through the gallery, which is surrounded by obstacles.

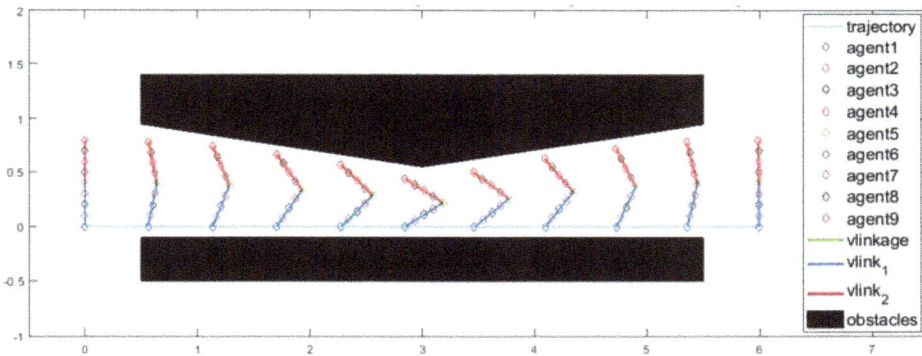

Figure 14. Reconfiguring nine agents into varying formation shapes to go through the gallery.

4.2.1. Simulation Setup

In order to pass through the gallery, a team of nine agents is initially moving in a vertical line formation with a uniform distance 0.1 m, and then reconfigured into arrow formations with varying angles to pass through the gallery. In this scenario, nine agents are designed as the same virtual linkage in Figure 11 using Equations (11) and (12).

The required trajectory and varying formation shapes to pass through the gallery are predefined as Equations (13)–(15), which can also be provided using planning algorithms [34]. In details, the agents are initialized as a line formation at position $r_R = (0, 0)$ with orientation $q_R = 0$. The virtual linkage is specified to move with a velocity $v_x = 0.3\ m/s$, $v_y = 0\ m/s$ to pass through the gallery in 20 s according to the task. That is the position of the virtual linkage holds:

$$r_R = (0.3t, 0) \tag{13}$$

Meanwhile, the attitude of the virtual linkage can be expressed as the angle from the x direction of the virtual link1 to the world coordination frame x direction and is also specified as a function of time

$$q_R = \begin{cases} -\frac{\pi}{30}t + \frac{\pi}{2} & t \le 10 \\ \frac{\pi}{30} + \frac{\pi}{6} & 10 < t < 20 \end{cases} \tag{14}$$

The virtual joint angle $\theta_d = \theta_1$ also obeys the function

$$\theta_1 = \begin{cases} \frac{\pi}{15}t & t \le 10 \\ -\frac{\pi}{15}t + \frac{2\pi}{3} & 10 < t < 20 \end{cases} \tag{15}$$

4.2.2. Simulation Result

Figure 14 shows the simulation solution to this problem. The path tracking errors between the real position and the desired place holder in virtual linkage $^w r^d_{ix} - {}^w r_{ix}$, $^w r^d_{iy} - {}^w r_{iy}$ are shown in Figure 15. These errors are at the magnitude of 10^{-3}, which also indicates that the group of agents are able to move in varying formation patterns determined by Equation (15). Figure 16 reports the real attitude of the virtual linkage and the reference attitude defined in Equation (14). The attitude error $q^r_R - q^d_R$ is also presented in Figure 16. The real, reference virtual joint angle θ_r, θ_d and their error $\theta_r - \theta_d$ are plotted in Figures 16 and 17, respectively. These show that the virtual linkage is able to track the planed varying q^d_R and θ_d to pass through the gallery.

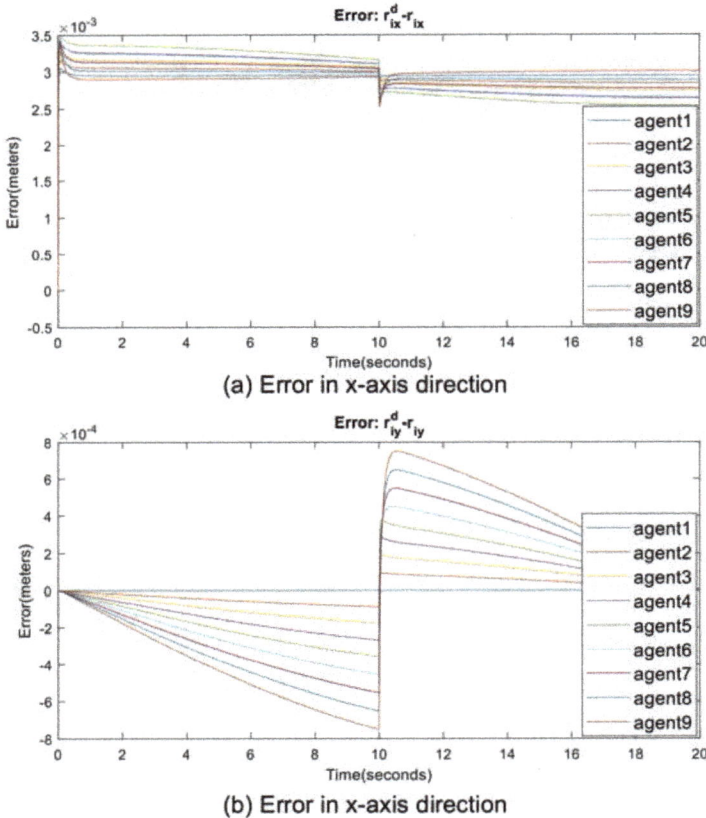

(a) Error in x-axis direction

(b) Error in x-axis direction

Figure 15. Errors between the real position and the desired position of the agents.

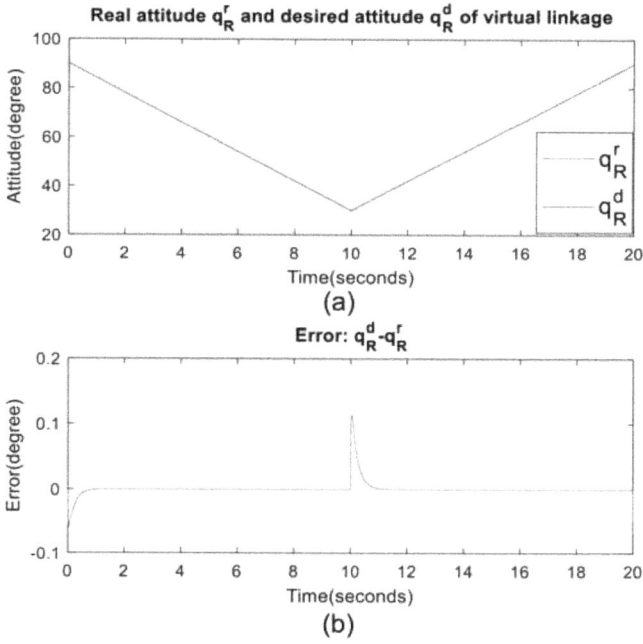

Figure 16. (**a**) Real and desired attitude of the virtual linkage; (**b**) error between real and desired attitude.

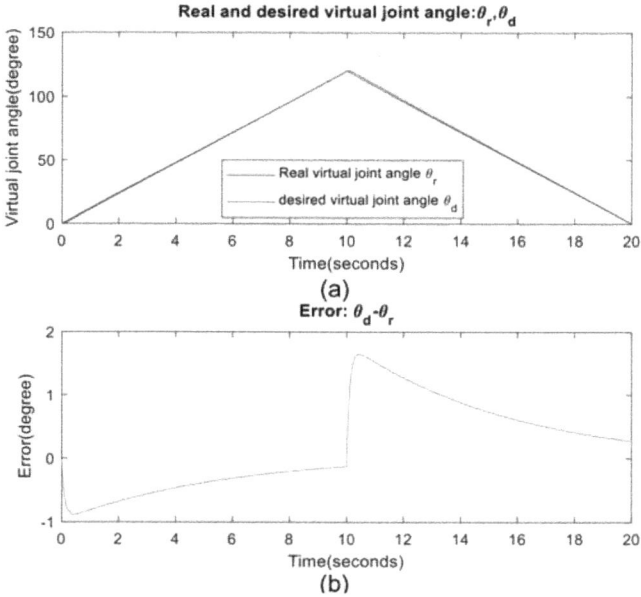

Figure 17. (**a**) Real and desired virtual joint angle; (**b**) error between real and desired virtual joint angle.

4.3. Parameters Analysis

In this section, two simulations are presented to illustrate the effects of the number of agents and number of virtual links. In the first part, five agents are required to perform the same formation moving task as in Section 4.1. In the second parts, nine agents are designed as a virtual linkage which consists of three virtual links to perform the same simulation task as in Section 4.2.

4.3.1. Number of Agents

In order to analyze the performance of a different number of agents, five agents are required to perform the same task as in Section 4.1: aligning in a line formation with a uniform distance of 0.1 m and moving around a circle with a radius of 1 m in 10 s. With the consideration of only changing the number of agents, a virtual linkage which also consists of two virtual links is designed:

$$\text{virtual linkage\_B} = \begin{cases} \text{virtual link1} = \{\text{agent1, agent2, agent3}\} \\ \text{virtual link2} = \{\text{agent3, agent4, agent5}\} \end{cases} \tag{16}$$

Similar to Section 4.1.1, each virtual link then holds a length of 0.2 m (See Figure 18) and has the following points:

$$\begin{aligned} {}^{v1}p_1 &= [0,0], {}^{v1}p_2 = [0.1,0], {}^{v1}p_3 = [0.2,0], \\ {}^{v2}p_3 &= [0,0], {}^{v2}p_4 = [0.1,0], {}^{v2}p_5 = [0.2,0] \end{aligned} \tag{17}$$

The trajectories of the individual agents and snapshots during the simulation for 10 s are plotted in Figures 19 and 20. These results indicate that the proposed virtual linkage approach is able to be applied to groups with different numbers of agents.

The influence of the agents' number is analyzed by comparing the two simulations conducted in Sections 4.1 and 4.3.1. As can be seen from Figure 21, each virtual link server needs to communicate with five agents when nine agents are involved in the formation moving simulation (See Section 4.1). In the simulation presented in this section, the communication burden has been reduced, as each virtual link server needs to communicate with three agents.

Therefore, the influence of the agents' number can be concluded. With the growing number of agents, the largest bandwidth of the communication equipment in the system increases.

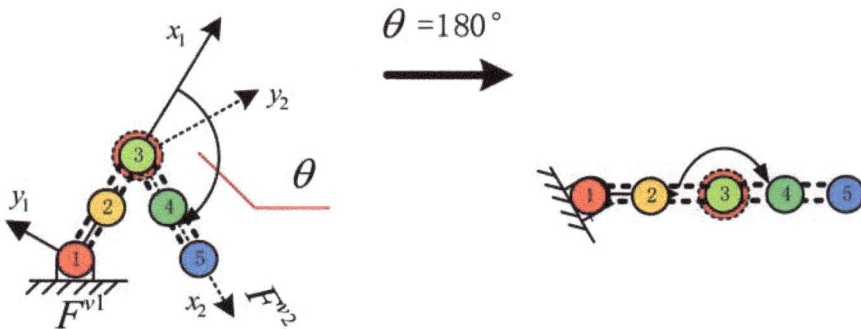

Figure 18. Predefined virtual linkage used in these two simulations.

Formation moving using Virtual Linkage

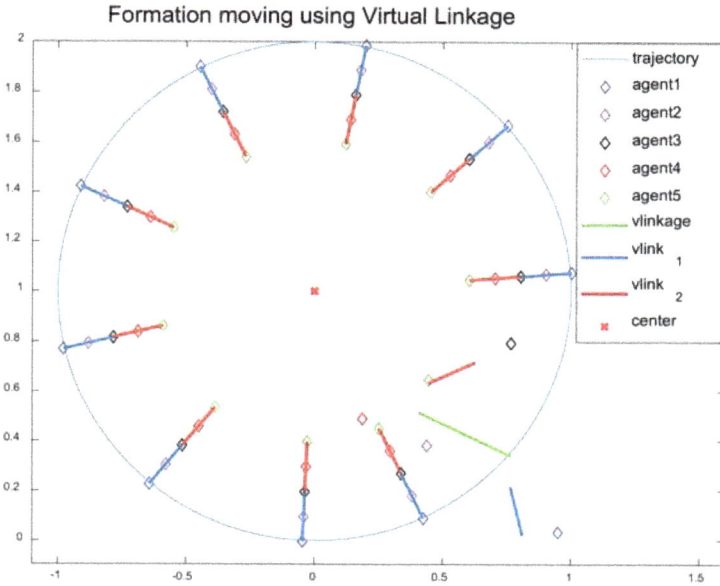

Figure 19. Snapshots of the formation moving.

Trajectory of individual agent

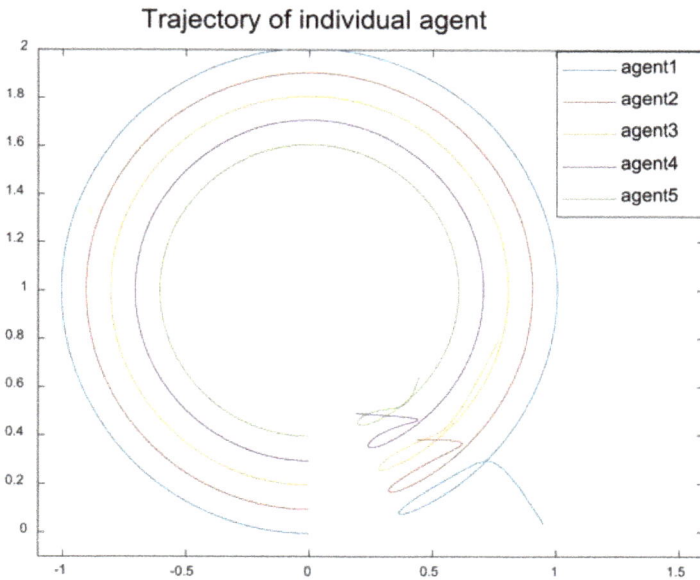

Figure 20. Trajectory of individual agents.

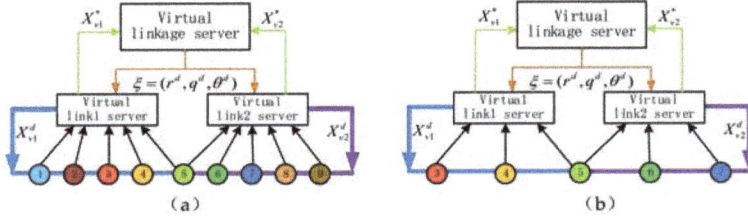

Figure 21. Comparison between virtual linkages with different number of agents: (**a**) the virtual linkage defined in Equation (11); (**b**) the virtual linkage defined in Equation (16).

4.3.2. Number of Virtual Links and Shape Transformations

In order to analyze the performance using a different number of virtual links, nine agents are designed as a virtual linkage with three virtual links to perform the same task in Section 4.2. In detail, the configuration of the virtual linkage is predefined:

$$Virtuallinkage\_C = \begin{cases} virtuallink1 = \{agent1, agent2, agent3, agent4, agent5\} \\ virtuallink2 = \{agent5, agent6, agent7\} \\ virtuallink3 = \{agent7, agent8, agent9\} \end{cases} \tag{18}$$

Recall that the position of the ith point in the jth virtual link coordinate frame is represented as $^{vj}p_i$, and the designed virtual linkage has the following points.

$$\begin{aligned} ^{v1}p_1 &= [0,0], \quad ^{v1}p_2 = [0.1,0], ^{v1}p_3 = [0.2,0], ^{v1}p_4 = [0.3,0], ^{v1}p_5 = [0.4,0]; \\ ^{v2}p_5 &= [0,0], ^{v2}p_6 = [0.1,0], ^{v2}p_7 = [0.2,0]; \\ ^{v3}p_7 &= [0,0], ^{v3}p_8 = [0.1,0], ^{v3}p_9 = [0.2,0]; \end{aligned} \tag{19}$$

The schematic of the designed virtual linkage is presented as Figure 22. It is worth mentioning that two virtual joint angles,

$$\theta_d = [\theta_1, \theta_2], \tag{20}$$

are needed to specify the formation pattern. The significance of this property is that we are able to have more reconfiguration ability. In detail, the virtual linkage here is able to behave as the virtual linkage defined as Equations (11) and (12) by letting $\theta_2 = 0$. Meanwhile, the nine agents are able to form some additional formation shapes and transformations by setting θ_2 into different values.

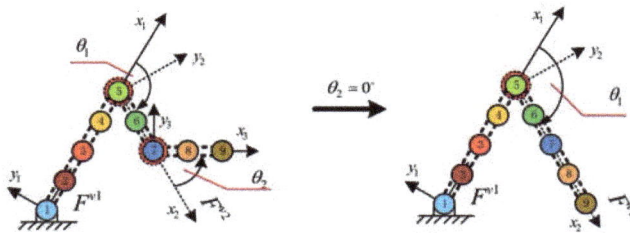

Figure 22. Schematic of the designed virtual linkage.

The nine agents are designed to pass through the gallery with a predefined trajectory and formation transformation using Equations (13)–(15) and (21).

$$\theta_2 = \begin{cases} 0 & t \leq 10 \\ \frac{\pi}{20}t & 10 < t < 20 \end{cases} \tag{21}$$

Figure 23 shows the simulation solution to this problem. The path tracking errors between the real position and the desired place holder in the virtual linkage ${}^{w}r_{ix}^{d} - {}^{w}r_{ix}, {}^{w}r_{iy}^{d} - {}^{w}r_{iy}$ are shown in Figure 24. These errors are at the magnitude of 10^{-3}, which also indicates that the group of agents are able to move in varying formation patterns determined by Equation (15). Figure 25 reports the real attitude of the virtual linkage and the reference attitude defined in Equation (14). The attitude error $q_R^r - q_R^d$ is also presented in Figure 25. The real, reference virtual joint angle $\theta_{r1}, \theta_{r2}, \theta_{d1}, \theta_{d2}$ and their error $\theta_{r1} - \theta_{d1}, \theta_{r2} - \theta_{d2}$ are plotted in Figures 25 and 26 respectively. These show that the virtual linkage approach is able to be applied to virtual linkage with different numbers of virtual links.

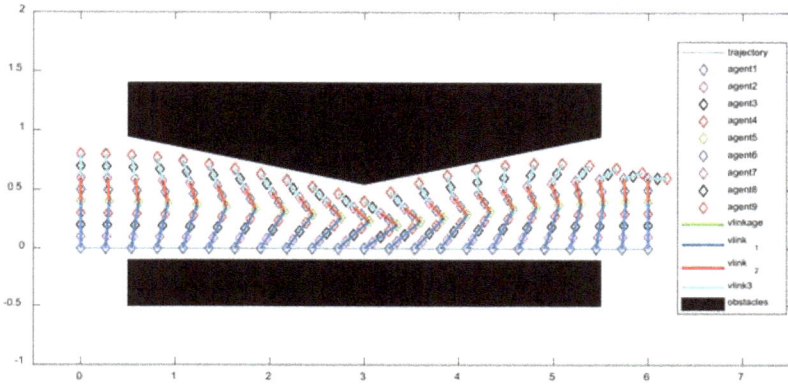

Figure 23. Formation reconfiguration using a virtual linkage with three virtual links.

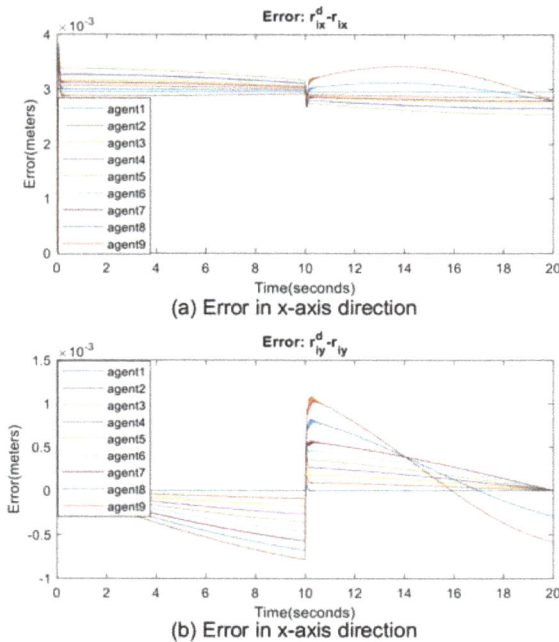

Figure 24. Errors between the real position and the desired position of the agents.

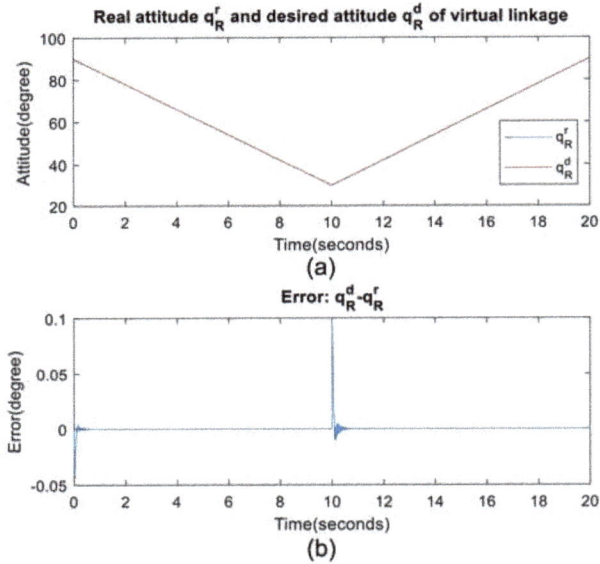

Figure 25. (**a**) Real and desired attitude of the virtual linkage; (**b**) error between real and desired attitude.

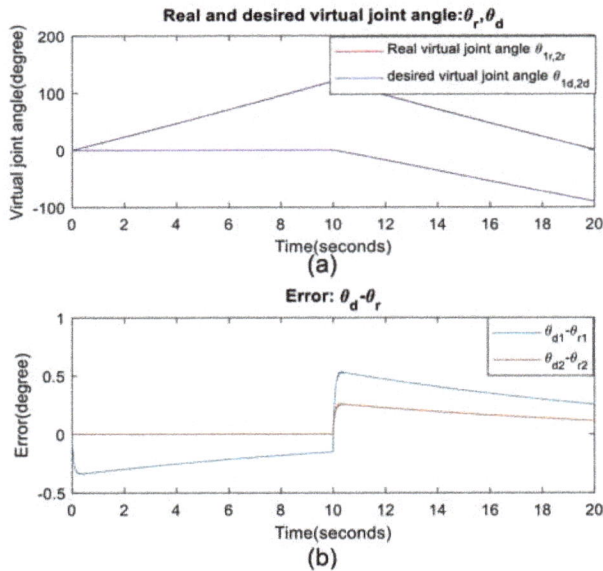

Figure 26. (**a**) Real and desired virtual joint angle; (**b**) error between real and desired virtual joint angle.

As it can be seen from the results, the virtual linkage here behaves as the virtual linkage defined in Figure 11 when $\theta_2 = 0$. Meanwhile, the virtual linkage can transform into more formation shapes when $\theta_2 \neq 0$. In fact, this phenomenon can be illustrated with the principle of DOF (degrees of freedom). In mechanical engineering, DOF is the number of independent parameters that define its configuration. This implies that the more DOF there are, the more formation shapes the virtual linkage can be configured to. When the virtual linkage is designed as a series of virtual links connected by virtual joints that extend from a base to an end, the DOF has the form:

$$DOF = number of virtual joints = number of virtual links - 1 \tag{22}$$

In such situations, the reconfiguration ability of the virtual linkage increases with the growing number of virtual links.

4.4. Comparison with Virtual Structure Approach (k = 1)

According to the Definition 3, a virtual linkage degenerates into a virtual structure because a virtual linkage is a collection of virtual structures (virtual links). Therefore, the centralized virtual structure approach can be seen as a special case of the virtual linkage approach, where the number of the virtual links $k = 1$. In this section, the same simulation task in Section 4.2 is conducted using the virtual structure approach [19]. Then, the comparison between the centralized virtual structure and the proposed virtual linkage approach is discussed.

Since virtual structure approaches treat each formation as a single rigid body, the whole virtual structure should be redesigned once the formation shape changes. Therefore, a different virtual structure should be redesigned each time to achieve the formation shape defined in Equation (15). Figure 27 shows some virtual structures when different formation shape involves. Each time the nine desired place holders should be refreshed by communication. Figure 28 shows simulation solution to this problem using virtual structure approach [19]. Although the formation reconfiguration simulation can be successfully performed, the virtual structure has been redesigned during the whole simulation.

Figure 29 shows that, in the centralized virtual structure, the position information of all the nine agents is sent into the single virtual structure server to implement the formation control algorithm.

In contrast, in the virtual linkage defined in Equations (11) and (12), there is no need to transmit all the agents' position information into a single localization. The virtual link1 server only needs to receive the position information of agents 1, 2, 3, 4, 5. The virtual link2 server also only needs to communicate with part of the agents, namely agents 5, 6, 7, 8, 9. The significance of this property is that the largest bandwidth of communication equipment in the system is reduced.

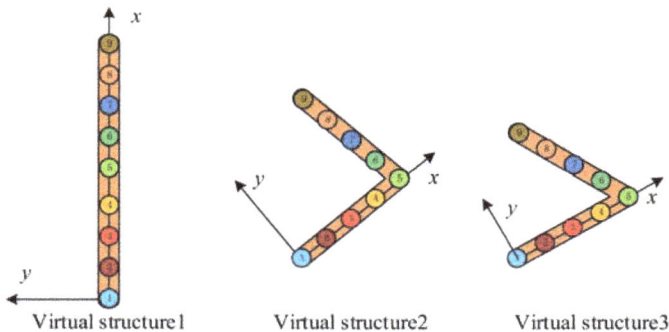

Virtual structure 1   Virtual structure 2   Virtual structure 3

Figure 27. (**a**) Real and desired attitude of the virtual linkage; (**b**) error between real and desired attitude.

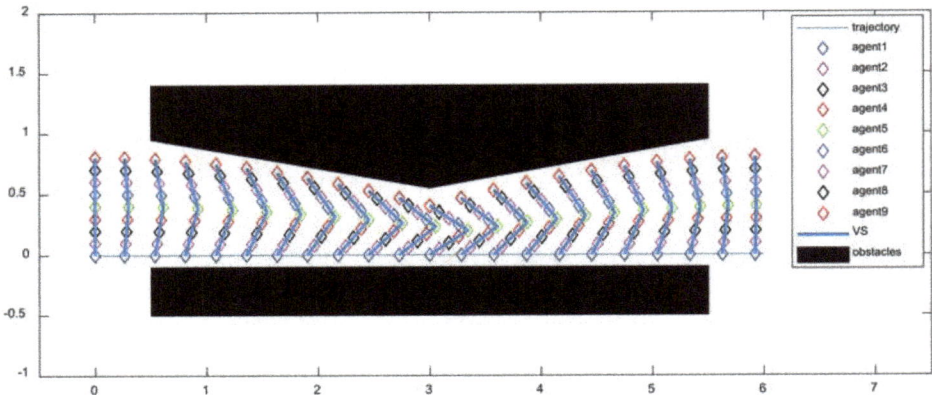

Figure 28. Formation reconfiguration using virtual structure approach.

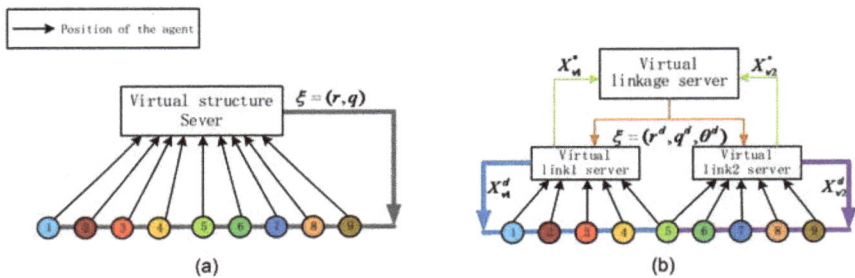

Figure 29. Comparison between (**a**) centralized virtual structure and (**b**) virtual linkage approach.

Another advantage of virtual linkage lies in the time complexity as compared to the centralized virtual structure approach. Using the virtual structure approach [19], the optimal position and attitude of the virtual structure X_v^* is calculated using Equation (1) with nine agents' positions. Nevertheless, the whole fitting process presented in Section 3.3.1 is broken into individual parts. The X_{v1}^*, X_{v2}^* can be simultaneously calculated using only five corresponding agents' position on the two virtual link severs. This allows the virtual linkage approach can be implemented faster and to be more suitable for real-time control. Roughly speaking, if a virtual linkage consists of k virtual links and each virtual link has the same number of agents, the virtual linkage approach runs k times faster than centralized virtual structure.

It is worth mentioning that this particular task shows the novelty of the virtual linkage approach. A virtual linkage is able to be reconfigured as different formation shapes by changing the virtual joint angle θ_d. Using Equations (8) and (9), it can be seen that the proposed virtual linkage only needs a communication bandwidth of

$$BW_2 = K \cdot k / T = \frac{2K}{T} \qquad (23)$$

bits per second to realize formation reconfiguration. In contrast, for the virtual structure approach, a bandwidth of

$$BW_1 = 3 \cdot N \cdot K / T = 3 \cdot 9 \cdot K / T = \frac{27K}{T} \qquad (24)$$

bits per second is needed. The bandwidth ratio is as follows:

$$\frac{BW_2}{BW_1} = \frac{k}{3 \cdot N} = \frac{2}{27} \approx 7.4\% \qquad (25)$$

This implies that only 7.4% communication bandwidth is required to reconfigure the formation shape using the virtual linkage approach. This makes it suitable for situations when formation patterns need to be reconfigured frequently.

5. Conclusions

In this paper, the virtual linkage approach is presented to solve the formation control problem. Instead of treating the group of agents as a single rigid body, as with the virtual structure, the whole formation is designed to be a mechanical linkage in the proposed approach. The simulation results show the effectiveness of the virtual linkage approach. There are several advantages as compared to the virtual structure approach. Firstly, the hierarchical architecture does not require the transmission of all the agents' state information into a single location, as compared to centralized virtual structure approaches. In detail, the information of each agent is reported to the corresponding virtual link's controller, respectively, and the calculated state information of the virtual link is then transmitted to the virtual linkage formation controller. Meanwhile, the time complexity of the proposed algorithm is reduced since the fitting process is broken into individual parts which can be calculated simultaneously, which makes it faster and more suitable for real-time control. Last but not least, the virtual linkage is able to be configured into different formation patterns by only changing the virtual joint angle, which makes it suitable for situations when formation patterns need to be reconfigured frequently.

In future work, more attention will be paid to the decentralization and formation feedback of the virtual linkage approach. Furthermore, the dynamical formation pattern generation and route planning for unknown environments is also an attractive direction and is worth researching.

Author Contributions: Y.L. conceived of the presented idea. Y.L. and J.G. developed the theoretical formalism. Y.L. and J.G. designed the simulation experiments and analyzed the data. Y.L., J.G., C.L., F.Z. and J.Z. discussed the results and wrote the paper.

Acknowledgments: This work is based on work supported in part by the National Key Technology R&D Program of China under Grant 2013BAK03B03 and National Defense Basic Research Project under Grant B2220132014.

Conflicts of Interest: The authors declare no conflict of interest.

References

1. Cutts, C.J.; Speakman, J.R. Energy savings in formation flight of pink-footed geese. *J. Exp. Biol.* **1994**, *189*, 251–261. [PubMed]
2. Kube, C.R.; Zhang, H. The Use of Perceptual Cues in Multi-Robot Box-Pushing. In Proceedings of the IEEE International Conference on Robotics and Automation, Minneapolis, MN, USA, 22–28 April 1996; pp. 2085–2090.
3. Stilwell, D.J.; Bishop, B.E. Platoons of underwater vehicles. *IEEE Control Syst.* **2000**, *20*, 45–52. [CrossRef]
4. Xiang, X.; Jouvencel, B.; Parodi, O. Coordinated formation control of multiple autonomous underwater vehicles for pipeline inspection. *Int. J. Adv. Robot. Syst.* **2010**, *7*, 3. [CrossRef]
5. Robertson, A.; Robertson, A.; Inalhan, G.; How, J.P. Formation control strategies for a separated spacecraft interferometer. In Proceedings of the 1999 American Control Conference, San Diego, CA, USA, 2–4 June 1999; Volume 6, pp. 4142–4147.
6. Scharf, D.P.; Hadaegh, F.Y.; Ploen, S.R. A survey of spacecraft formation flying guidance and control. Part II: Control. In Proceedings of the 2004 American Control Conference, Boston, MA, USA, 30 June–2 July 2004; Volume 4, pp. 2976–2985.
7. Consolini, L.; Morbidi, F.; Prattichizzo, D.; Tosques, M. Leader-follower formation control of nonholonomic mobile robots with input constraints. *Automatica* **2008**, *44*, 1343–1349. [CrossRef]
8. Chen, J.; Sun, D.; Yang, J.; Chen, H. Leader-follower formation control of multiple non-holonomic mobile robots incorporating a receding-horizon scheme. *Int. J. Robot. Res.* **2010**, *29*, 727–747. [CrossRef]
9. Das, A.K.; Fierro, R.; Kumar, V.; Ostrowski, J.P.; Spletzer, J.; Taylor, C.J. A Vision-Based Formation Control Framework. *IEEE Trans. Robot. Autom.* **2002**, *18*, 813–825. [CrossRef]

10. Wang, P.K.C. Navigation strategies for multiple autonomous mobile robots moving in formation. *J. Robot. Syst.* **1991**, *8*, 177–195. [CrossRef]
11. Wang, H.; Guo, D.; Liang, X.; Chen, W.; Hu, G.; Leang, K.K. Adaptive Vision-Based Leader-Follower Formation Control of Mobile Robots. *IEEE Trans. Ind. Electron.* **2017**, *64*, 2893–2902. [CrossRef]
12. Liu, X.; Ge, S.S.; Goh, C.H. Vision-Based Leader-Follower Formation Control of Multiagents with Visibility Constraints. *IEEE Trans. Control Syst. Technol.* **2018**, *99*, 1–8. [CrossRef]
13. Balch, T.; Arkin, R.C. Behavior Based Formation Control for Multirobot Teams. *IEEE Trans. Robot. Autom.* **1998**, *14*, 926–939. [CrossRef]
14. Sugihara, K.; Suzuki, I. Distributed algorithms for formation of geometric patterns with many mobile robots. *J. Robot. Syst.* **1996**, *13*, 127–139. [CrossRef]
15. Rezaee, H.; Abdollahi, F. A decentralized cooperative control scheme with obstacle avoidance for a team of mobile robots. *IEEE Trans. Ind. Electron.* **2014**, *61*, 347–354. [CrossRef]
16. Antonelli, G.; Arrichiello, F.; Chiaverini, S. Flocking for multi-robot systems via the Null-space-based behavioral control. *Swarm Intell.* **2010**, *4*, 37–56. [CrossRef]
17. Wen, G.; Chen, C.L.P.; Liu, Y.-J. Formation Control with Obstacle Avoidance for a Class of Stochastic Multiagent Systems. *IEEE Trans. Ind. Electron.* **2018**, *65*, 5847–5855. [CrossRef]
18. Ugur, E.; Nagai, Y.; Sahin, E.; Oztop, E. Staged development of robot skills: Behavior formation, affordance learning and imitation with motionese. *IEEE Trans. Auton. Ment. Dev.* **2015**, *7*, 119–139. [CrossRef]
19. Lewis, M.A.; Tan, K.H. High Precision Formation Control of Mobile Robots Using Virtual Structures. *Auton. Robots* **1997**, *4*, 387–403. [CrossRef]
20. Dong, L.; Chen, Y.; Qu, X. Formation Control Strategy for Nonholonomic Intelligent Vehicles Based on Virtual Structure and Consensus Approach. *Procedia Eng.* **2016**, *137*, 415–424. [CrossRef]
21. Chen, L.; Baoli, M. A nonlinear formation control of wheeled mobile robots with virtual structure approach. In Proceedings of the 2015 34th Chinese Control Conference (CCC), Hangzhou, China, 28–30 July 2015; pp. 1080–1085.
22. Ghommam, J.; Mehrjerdi, H.; Saad, M.; Mnif, F. Formation path following control of unicycle-type mobile robots. *Robot. Auton. Syst.* **2010**, *58*, 727–736. [CrossRef]
23. Van den Broek, T.H.A. Formation Control of Unicycle Mobile Robots: A Virtual Structure Approach. In Proceedings of the 48h IEEE Conference on Decision and Control (CDC) held jointly with 2009 28th Chinese Control Conference, Shanghai, China, 15–18 December 2009; pp. 8328–8333.
24. Ren, W.; Beard, R.W. Formation feedback control for multiple spacecraft via virtual structures. *IEE Proc. Control Theory Appl.* **2004**, *151*, 357–368. [CrossRef]
25. Do, K.D.; Pan, J. Nonlinear formation control of unicycle-type mobile robots. *Robot. Auton. Syst.* **2007**, *55*, 191–204. [CrossRef]
26. Arnold, V. *Mathematical Methods of Classical Mechanics*; Springer: Berlin, Germany, 1989; pp. 1–536.
27. Beard, R.W.; Lawton, J.; Hadaegh, F.Y. A coordination architecture for spacecraft formation control. *IEEE Trans. Control Syst. Technol.* **2001**, *9*, 777–790. [CrossRef]
28. Ren, W.; Beard, R. Decentralized Scheme for Spacecraft Formation Flying via the Virtual Structure Approach. *J. Guid. Control Dyn.* **2004**, *27*, 73–82. [CrossRef]
29. Belta, C.; Kumar, V. Abstraction and control for groups of robots. *IEEE Trans. Robot.* **2004**, *20*, 865–875. [CrossRef]
30. Hartenberg, R.S.; Denavit, J. *Kinematic Synthesis of Linkages*; McGraw-Hill: New York, NY, USA, 1964.
31. Ren, W. Decentralization of Virtual Structures in Formation Control of Multiple Vehicle Systems via Consensus Strategies. *Eur. J. Control* **2008**, *14*, 93–103. [CrossRef]
32. Desai, J.P.; Ostrowski, J.P.; Kumar, V. Modeling and control of formations of nonholonomic mobile robots. *IEEE Trans. Robot. Autom.* **2001**, *17*, 905–908. [CrossRef]
33. Desai, J.P.; Kumar, V.; Ostrowski, J.P. Control of changes in formation for a team of mobile robots. In Proceedings of the 1999 IEEE International Conference on Robotics and Automation (Cat. No.99CH36288C), 10–15 May 1999; Volume 2, pp. 1556–1561.
34. LaValle, S.M. *Planning Algorithms*; Cambridge University Press: Cambridge, UK, 2006; ISBN 1139455176.

applied
sciences

MDPI

Article

SambotII: A New Self-Assembly Modular Robot Platform Based on Sambot

Wenshuai Tan, Hongxing Wei and Bo Yang *

School of Mechanical Engineering & Automation, BeiHang University, Beijing 100083, China;
sebastian_tan@163.com (W.T.); whx1630@163.com (H.W.)
* Correspondence: yangkkb@aliyun.com; Tel.: +86-186-1199-6961

Received: 31 July 2018; Accepted: 17 September 2018; Published: 21 September 2018

Featured Application: This manuscript developed a new self-assembly modular robot (SMR) system SambotII and provided a new vision-based method for efficient and accurate autonomous docking of SMRs. The present work lays a foundation for the future research of modular and swarm robots. Based on the present hardware and software platforms, complex behaviors and various tasks can be achieved on SambotII in the future, such as environment exploration, path planning, robotic swarm control, morphology control and, etc.

Abstract: A new self-assembly modular robot (SMR) SambotII is developed based on SambotI, which is a previously-built hybird type SMR that is capable of autonomous movement and self-assembly. As is known, SambotI only has limited abilities of environmental perception and target recognition, because its STM-32 processor cannot handle heavy work, like image processing and path planning. To improve the computing ability, an x86 dual-core CPU is applied and a hierarchical software architecture with five layers is designed. In addition, to enhance its perception abilities, a laser-camera unit and a LED-camera unit are employed to obtain the distance and angle information, respectively, and the color-changeable LED lights are used to identify different passive docking surfaces during the docking process. Finally, the performances of SambotII are verified by docking experiments.

Keywords: modular robots; self-assembly robots; environmental perception; target recognition; autonomous docking

---

1. Introduction

1.1. Background

A self-assembly or self-reconfiguration modular robot (SMR) system is composed of a collection of connected modules with certain degrees of locomotion, sensing, and intercommunication [1–3]. When compared with robots that have fixed topologies, SMR systems have some advantages, such as versatility, robustness, and low cost [4].

The concept of dynamically self-reconfigurable robotic system was firstly proposed by Toshio Fukuda in 1988 [5]. Since then, many interesting robot systems have been proposed. In spite of the significant advances of SMRs, researchers in this field believe that there is a gap between the state-of-art research on modular robots and their real-world applications [3]. As Stoy and Kurokawa [6] stated, the applications of self-reconfigurable robots are still elusive.

One main challenge in this field is how to achieve autonomous docking among modules, especially with higher efficiency and accuracy. Autonomous docking is an essential capability for the system to realize self-reconfiguration and self-repairing in completing operational tasks under complex environments. Various methods, such as the infrared-red (IR) ranging, vision-based ranging, ultrasonic ranging, etc., have been employed to guide the autonomous docking process.

The IR-based methods generally have high accuracy, simple structure and small size. Thus, they are suitable for self-reconfigurable robotic systems with the shapes of chain, tree or lattices. They were applied in many SMR systems, like PolyBot [7], ATRON [8], ModeRED [9], SYMBRION [10], etc. However, the IR-based methods are unsuitable for mobile robotic systems due to the limited detection ranges.

The vision-based methods can provide more information than IR-based method do. Some SMR systems like CKBot [11], M-TRAN [12], and UBot [13] utilize the vision-based methods in their autonomous docking process. However, these methods generally involve large-scale and complex image processing and information extraction. This restricts their applications in SMR systems, to some extent.

Except the IR and vision-based methods, ultrasonic sensors are also used in the docking process. For example, the JL-2 [14] conducts autonomous docking under the guidance of several ultrasonic sensors. In addition, the eddy-current sensors, hall-effect sensors and capacitance meters are occasionally applied in the docking navigation. However, they are easy to be interfered by motors and metallic objects.

1.2. Related Works

For SMRs that utilize the vision-based methods in autonomous docking, it is important to set proper target features, such as LEDs, special shapes, etc. Not only should the target features make the target robot module easily recognizable, but also it should provide enough information for distance/orientation measurement. Additionally, each docking module should have target features that can provide unique identification.

As showed in Table 1 and Figure 1a, M-TRAN have five LEDs (two on its front face and three on its side face) as its target features. Depending on those LEDs, M-TRAN can determine the distance and orientation of the target-robot group, which consists of three M-TRAN modules and a camera module. However, this method cannot be used to simultaneously identify different robot groups, which means only one docking robot group can be recognized during the docking process. In each M-TRAN system, the captured images are processed by a host PC (personal computer). Because of the limitation in accuracy, the robot group has to form a special configuration to tolerate the docking error (see Figure 1b).

Table 1. Existing self-assembly modular robot (SMR) systems that utilize the vision-based method.

Name	Target Features	Capable of Identifying Different Module	Image Processor (Type)	Location of the Image Processor
M-TRAN	5 white-colored LEDs	No	X86 CPU (PC)	Outside robot
CKBot	LED blink sequences	Yes	PIC18F2680 (MCU)	Camera module of robot
UBot	Cross label on robot	No	X86 CPU (PC)	Outside robot
SambotII	Combination of color-changeable LEDs	Yes	X86 CPU (Edison module)	Inside robot

The CKBot can achieve an autonomous docking process after the robot system exploded into three parts, each of which consists of four CKBot modules and one camera module. Some specific LED blink sequences are used as target features for the distance and orientation measurements. In this way, different disassembled parts of the robot system can be identified (see Figure 1c). However, this method costs too much time, because of the large number of images to be processed and the limited computing power of its PIC18F2680 MCU.

For UBot, a yellow cross label is chosen as the target feature (see Figure 1d), by which the distance and orientation between the active and passive docking robot can be determined. Nevertheless, when the distance between the two docking surface is small enough, the UBot will use Hall sensors instead to guide the final docking process. In addition, the UBots are similar to the M-TRANs in two aspects: The images are processed by a host PC; and, different modules cannot be simultaneously distinguished.

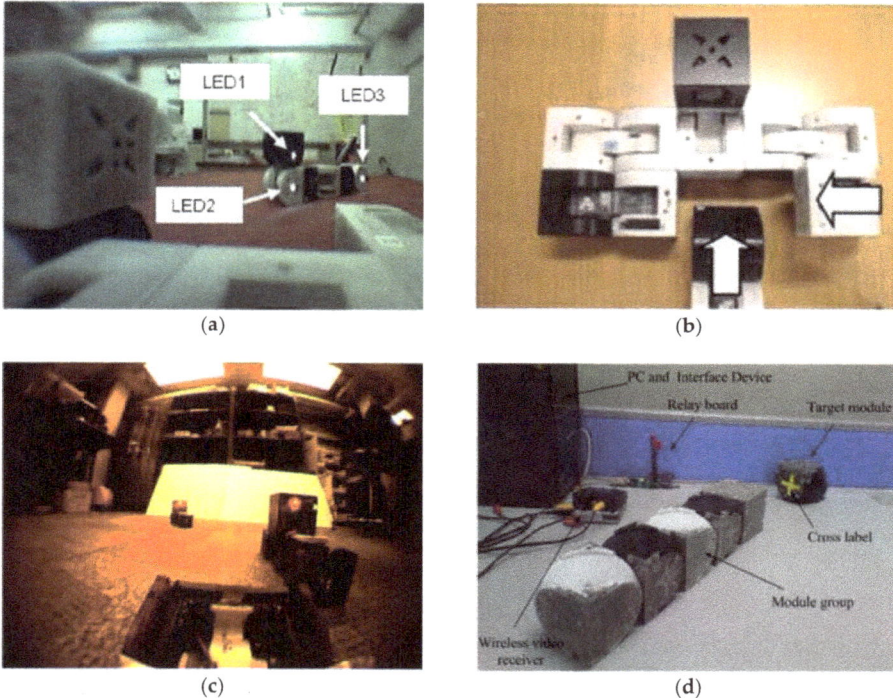

Figure 1. The docking processes of existing SMR systems. (**a**) The docking process of M-TRAN and three white LEDs in its side face [12], reproduced with permission from Murata et al. [12]; (**b**) Special configuration of M-TRAN used for error tolerance [12], reproduced with permission from Murata et al. [12]; (**c**) The docking process of CKBot [11], reproduced with permission from Yim et al. [11]; and, (**d**) The docking process of UBot [13], reproduced with permission from Liu et al. [13].

1.3. The Present Work

In the present work, a new SMR SambotII is developed based on SambotI [15], a previously-built SMR (Figure 2a), In SambotII (Figure 2b), the original IR-based docking guidance method is replaced by a vision-based method. A laser-camera unit and a LED-camera unit are applied to determine the distance and angle between the two docking surfaces, respectively. Besides, a group of color-changeable LEDs are taken as a novel target feature. With the help of these units and the new target feature, the autonomous docking can be achieved with higher efficiency and accuracy.

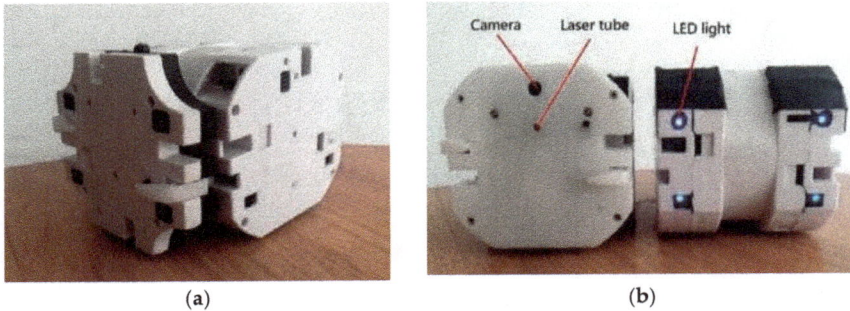

Figure 2. SambotI and SambotII. (a) SambotI, the last generation; and, (b) SambotII: the left is active docking surface with camera and laser tube, the right is a passive docking surface with four LED lights.

An Intel x86 dual-core CPU is applied to improve the computing ability for image processing, information extraction, and other tasks with large computing consumption in the future. Besides, a five-layer hierarchical software architecture is proposed for better programming performances and it is a universal platform for our future research.

Compared with existing SMRs utilizing the vision-based method, the SambotII has three main advantages: (1) The autonomous docking process is more independent, because the whole procedure, including image process and information extraction, is controlled by the SambotII system itself. (2) Apart from distance and orientation measurement, the target feature can be used to identify different modules simultaneously. (3) The docking process is more accurate and efficient, because it costs less than a minute and no extra sensors or procedures are needed to eliminate the docking error.

In the remaining parts, a brief description is given at first for the mechanical structure, electronic system, and software architecture. Then, a detailed introduction is made on the principle of the laser-camera unit, LED-camera unit and docking strategy. Finally, docking experiments are preformed to verify the new docking process.

2. Mechanical Structure of SambotII

As displayed in Table 2, each SambotII is an independent mobile robot containing a control system, a vision module, a driving module, a power module, and a communication system.

Table 2. Main parameters of SambotII.

Content	Parameters
Overall sizes	120 mm × 80 mm × 80 mm
Weight	Approx. 355 g
DOFs	4 (1 neck rotation + 2 wheels + 1 hook)
Connector	A pair of mechanical hooks
Torque of neck	1.3 Nm (max)
Motion method	A pair of wheels
Power source	Inner 7.4V Lithium battery
Battery capacity	Approx. 1200 mAh (8.88 Wh)
Assistant peripherals	Laser tube, LEDs, switches and, etc.
Vision module	HD CMOS camera
Camera resolution	640 × 480 mode (currently used) or 1920 × 1080 mode (maximum resolution)
Wireless system	Wi-Fi 2.4 G/5.8 G + Bluetooth 4.0
Coprocessor	ARM Cortex-M3 STM32
Central Processing Unit	Intel Atom dual-core x86 CPU

The mechanical structure of SambotII includes an autonomous mobile body and an active docking surface. They are connected by a neck (the green part in Figure 3). Each active docking surface has a pair of hooks.

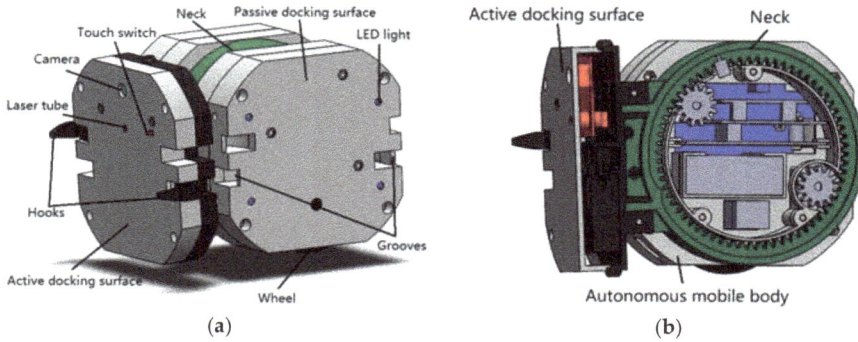

Figure 3. Main parts of SambotII. (**a**) The overall view; and, (**b**) The cutaway view.

2.1. Autonomous Mobile Body

The autonomous mobile body of SambotII is a cube with four passive docking surfaces (except for the top and the bottom surfaces). Each passive docking surface contains four RGB LED lights and a pair of grooves. The hooks on the active docking surface of a SambotII robot can stick into the grooves of a passive docking surface of another SambotII robot to form stable mechanical connection between them. The LED lights are used to guide the active docking robot during the self-assembly process. Also, they are used to identify different passive docking surfaces by multiple combinations of colors. In addition, two wheels on the bottom surface of the main body provide mobility for SambotII.

2.2. Active Docking Surface

Actuated by a DC motor, the active docking surface could rotate about the autonomous mobile body by ±90°. It contains a pair of hooks, a touch switch, a camera, and a laser tube. As mentioned above, the hooks are used to form a mechanical connection with a passive docking surfaces of another SambotII. The touch switch is used to confirm whether the two docking surfaces are touched or not. The camera and laser tube are used for distance measurement and docking guidance, and they will be described in detail in the following parts.

2.3. Permissible Errors of the Docking Mechanism

It is necessary to mention that there are multiple acceptable error ranges during the docking process of two robots (see Figure 4 and Table 3), which can enhance the success rate of docking. The analysis of permissible errors is given in [16].

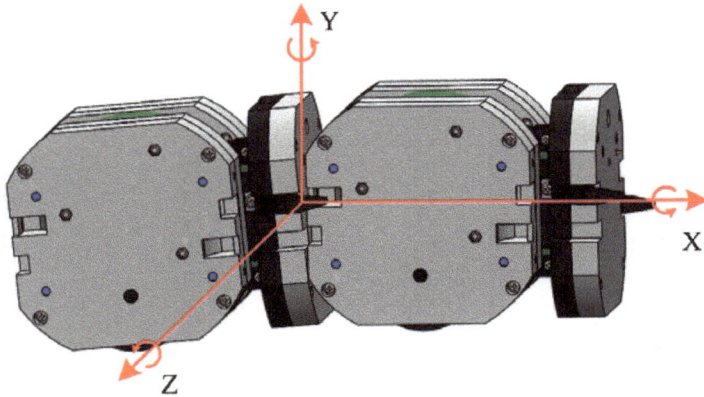

Figure 4. The schematic of docking deviation of two SambotII.

Table 3. The acceptable docking deviation between two SambotIIs.

Direction	Permission Deviation/mm	Direction	Permission Deviation/(°)
Movement along X	13	Rotation around X	±5
Movement along Y	±4.5	Rotation around Y	10
Movement along Z	±19.5	Rotation around Z	±5

3. Information System of SambotII

One noticeable improvement of SambotII, as compared with SambotI, is the information system (see Figure 5). The perception, computing, and communication abilities are enhanced by integrating a camera, a MCU (i.e., a microprocessor unit that serves as a coprocessor), a powerful x86 dual-core CPU, and some other sensors into a cell robot. Figure 6 shows the major PCBs (Printed Circuit Board) of SambotII.

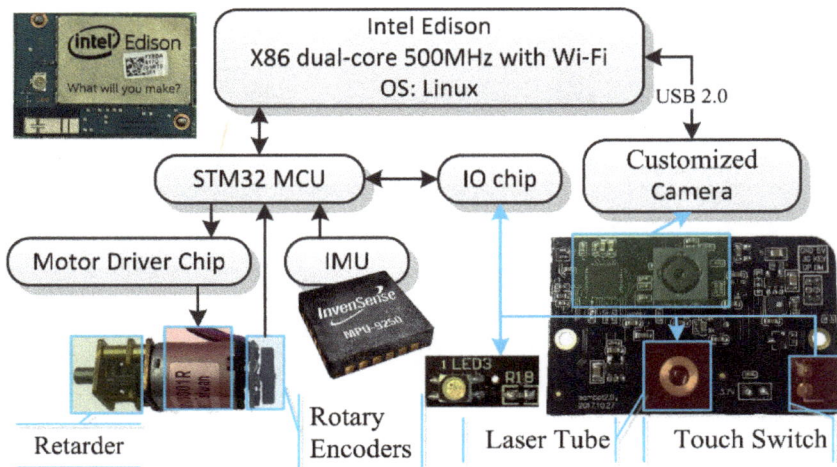

Figure 5. Structure of the information system.

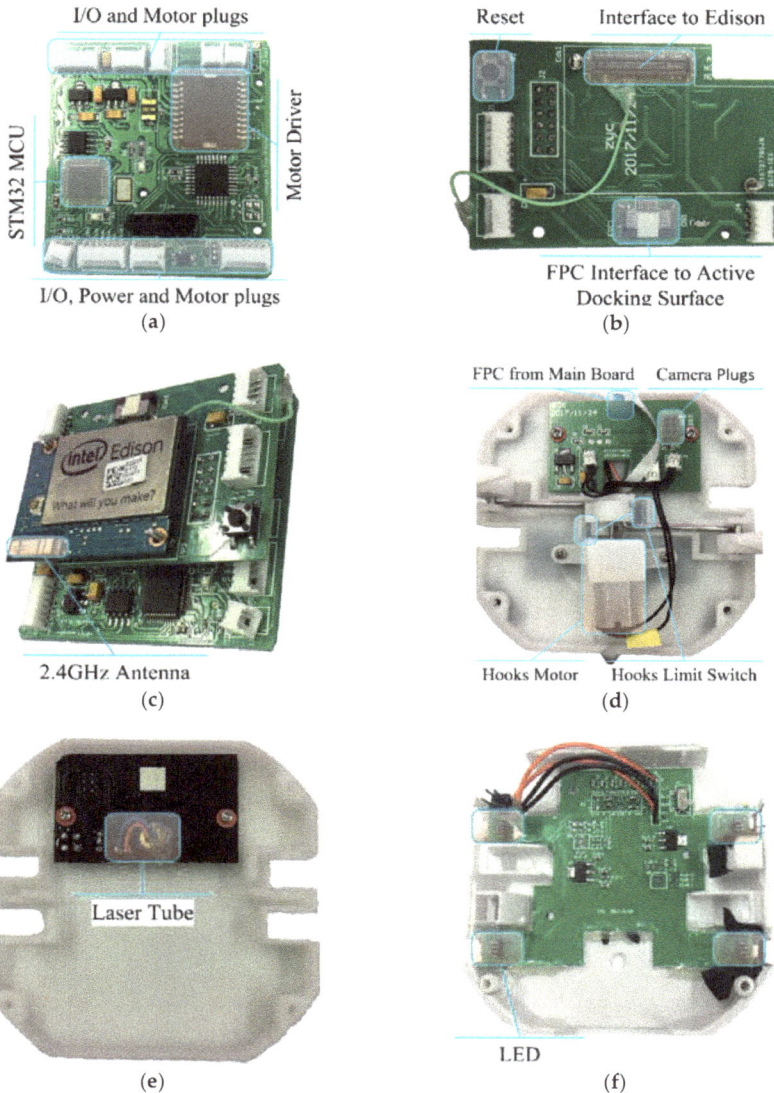

Figure 6. The major PCBs (Printed Circuit Board) of SambotII. (**a**) Top view of main board 1, which contains motor drivers, MCU, plugs, etc.; (**b**) Top view of main board 2 with some level translation and I/O chips on its back; (**c**) Assembly of main board 1, main board 2 and Intel Edison module; (**d**) Mechanisms of the hooks and its PCB in the active docking surface; (**e**) Camera and laser tube in the active docking surface; and,(**f**) PCB of LEDs in both left and right sides of SambotII with the I/O chip on the back of PCB.

The information system consists of three subsystems: The actuator controlling system, the sensor system, and the central processing system.

The actuator controlling system controls motors, which determine the movement and operations of SambotII. The PWM signals are generated by a MCU at first, and then they are transmitted into the driver chip to be amplified. Those amplified analog signals are eventually used to drive the customized motors. Each motor is integrated with a Hall effect rotary encoder, which converts angular velocity into pulse frequency and then feed back into MCU, forming a closed-loop control system. When combining with limit switches, the MCU can open or close the hooks and rotate the neck. By controlling the I/O chip, the MCU can change the colors of LED lights, read the states of switches and turn on or off the laser.

The sensor system includes the encoders, switches, an IMU (Inertial Measurement Unit used to measure orientation and rotation) and a customized HD CMOS camera. Combined with laser tube and LED lights, the sensor system can measure the distance and angle between two docking robots. By identifying the combination of color-changeable LED lights, the robot can locate the specific surface it should connect with during the self-assembly procedure.

The central processing system is a high-density integrated module [17] (see Figure 5) that contains an Intel Atom CPU, a storage, a wireless, etc. (see Table 4). It supports Linux Operation System (OS) and can run multiple softwares concurrently, capture pictures from the camera through USB, and communicate with other robots through Wi-Fi. Moreover, it is binary compatible with PC.

Table 4. Features of the Intel Edison CPU module.

Components	Description
Processor	Dual-core, dual-threaded Intel Atom CPU at 500 MHz with 1MB cache. Supporting SIMD SSE2, SSE3, SSE4.1/4.2
RAM memory	1 GB
Storage	4 GB eMMC
Wireless	2.4 and 5 GHz IEEE 802.11a/b/g/n
Bluetooth	BT4.0
USB	USB2.0 OTG
Sizes	$35.5 \times 25.0 \times 3.9$ mm

4. Software Architecture and Task Functions of SambotII

A hierarchical architecture is proposed for the software system. As shown in Figure 7, the hardware and software are decoupled from each other in the architecture. It improves the software reusability and simplifies programming by using the uniform abstract interfaces between different layers and programs.

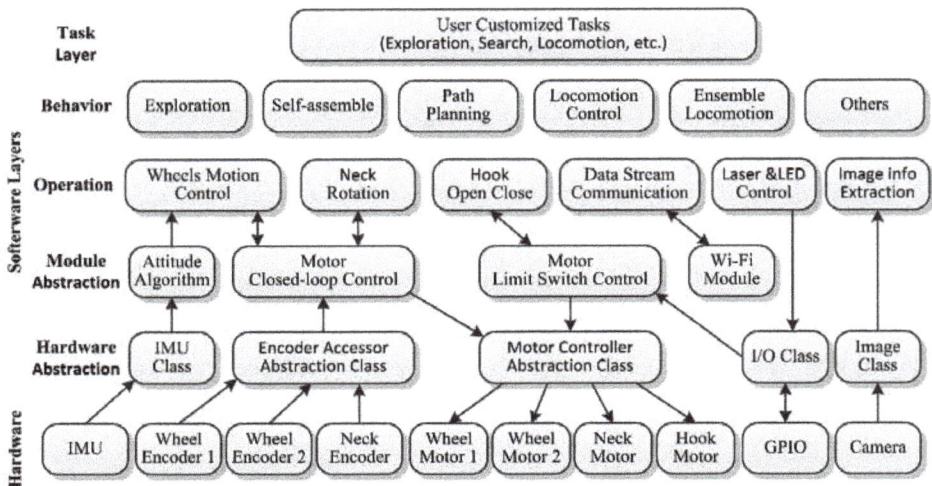

Figure 7. Software architecture.

There are five main layers in the software system: (1) hardware abstract layer; (2) module abstract layer; (3) operation layer; (4) behavior layer; and, (5) task layer. Different layer consists of different blocks, which are designed for particular functions and offer implementation-irrelevant interfaces to upper layers.

The hardware abstract layer acts as an abstract interconnection between the hardware and the software. All the control details of the hardware are hidden in this layer. For instance, the "motor controller abstraction class" controls four motors and offers an interface for upper layer to adjust motor speed. The "encoder accessor abstraction class" processes pulse signals generated by the encoder and converts them into velocity and positional data. The I/O class reads and sets GPIO through I/O chip. The "IMU class" reads the rotation and acceleration data from IMU. These four classes are built in MCU to meet real-time requirements. Besides, the "image class" captures images from the camera by utilizing the OpenCV library in Intel Edison module.

The module abstract layer offers higher level module abstractions by integrating the blocks of the hardware abstract layer into modules. For instance, the "motor closed-loop control class" reads velocity and positional data from the "encoder accessor abstraction class" and sends speed commands to the "motor controller abstraction class". With the inner control algorithms, it can control speed and position, making it easier for the operation layer to control robot's motion, and so does the "motor limit control class". The "attitude algorithm class" reads data from the "IMU class" and calculates the orientation after data filtering and fusion. Finally, the Wi-Fi module is used to establish the wireless network environment for data communication.

The operation layer contains operation blocks, which control the specific operations of the robot. For example, the "wheels motion control block" in the operation layer combines the "motor closed-loop control block" and the "attitude algorithm block", and so it can control the movement operations of the robot. In this way, we can just focus on designing the behavior and task algorithms, rather than the details of motor driving, control, or wheels movement. Similarly, the blocks, "neck rotation", "hooks open close", "laser control", and "LED control", are used to control the corresponding operations of the robot, respectively. The "image info extraction block" is designed to extract the useful information we care about from images. Through the "data stream communication block", robots can coordinate with each other by exchanging information and commands.

The behavior layer is a kind of command-level abstraction designed for executing practical behaviors. A behavior can utilize operation blocks and other behavior blocks when executing. For instance, if the robot needs to move to a certain place, the "locomotion control behavior block" first performs path planning behavior after it receives the goal command, and then it continuously interacts with the "wheels motion control block" until the robot reaches the target position. In the docking behavior, the "Self-assembly block" will invoke the "hooks open close block", "locomotion block", "image info extraction block", and so on. Also, the "exploration block" can achieve information collection and map generation by combing the "locomotion block", "data stream communication block", and "image processing block".

The task layer consists of tasks, the ultimate targets that user wants robots to achieve. Each task can be decomposed into behaviors. For example, if the robots are assigned with a task to find something, they will perform the "exploration behavior" for environmental perception, the "locomotion-control behavior" for movement, as well as the "self-assembly and ensemble locomotion behaviors" for obstacle crossing.

5. Self-Assembly of SambotII

During the self-assembly process of SambotII, it is necessary to obtain the information of distance and angle between the two docking robots. For this purpose, a laser-camera unit and a LED-camera unit are employed to gain the distance and angle, respectively. The position of the camera, laser tube, and LED lights are shown in Figure 8.

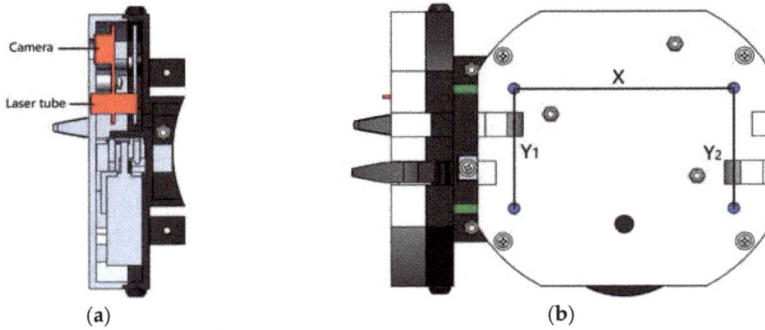

Figure 8. The positions of camera, laser tube and LED lights. (**a**) The relative position of camera and laser tube; and, (**b**) The relative distances of four LED lights on a passive docking surface. X = 60 mm and $Y_1 = Y_2 = 35$ mm.

5.1. Laser-Camera Unit

As is known, the idea of laser triangulation means the formation of a triangle by using a laser beam, a camera and a targeted point. The laser-camera unit consists of a laser tube and a camera, both of which are installed parallel on the vertical middle line of the active docking surface (see Figures 3a and 8a). Due to the actual machining and installation errors, the optical axes of the camera and laser may be inclined to some extent (see α and β showed in Figure 9). Here, α indicates the angle between the central axis of the laser beam and the horizontal line, while β represents the angle between the camera and the horizontal line. Theoretically speaking, the position of the laser spot that is projected in the camera image (x) changes with the distance between the object and the active docking surface.

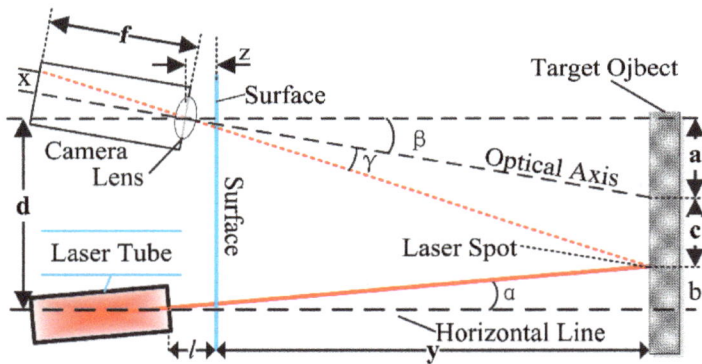

Figure 9. Principle of distance measurement.

In Figure 9, the 'Surface' denotes the active docking surface and the right panel refers to a target object. The parameter x stands for the distance between the laser projection spot and the central point of the captured image. The x is calculated by the number of pixels, y denotes the actual distance between the active docking surface and the measured object, and z is the distance between the camera lens and the active docking surface. The parameter d is the vertical distance between the center of camera lens and the emitting point of the laser beam. f represents the focal distance of camera and l is the distance between the laser tube and surface.

According to the principle of similar triangles and the perspective projection theory, one can get:

$$b = \tan \alpha (l + y) \tag{1}$$

$$a + c = d - b \tag{2}$$

$$\tan(\gamma + \beta) = \frac{a + c}{z + y} = \frac{(x + f \tan \beta) \sin(90° - \beta)}{f \frac{1}{\cos \beta} - (x + f \tan \beta) \cos(90° - \beta)} \tag{3}$$

From Formulas (1)–(3), one can obtain:

$$Axy + Bx + Cy + D = 0 \tag{4}$$

where

$$A = \cos \beta - \tan \alpha \sin \beta \tag{5}$$

$$B = z \cos \beta + d \sin \beta - \tan \alpha \sin \beta \cdot l \tag{6}$$

$$C = f \left[\sin \beta + \tan \alpha \left(\frac{1}{\cos \beta} - \tan \beta \sin \beta \right) \right] \tag{7}$$

$$D = f \left[\sin \beta(z + d \tan \alpha) - d \frac{1}{\cos \beta} + l \tan \alpha \left(\frac{1}{\cos \beta} - \tan \beta \sin \beta \right) \right] \tag{8}$$

Based on Formulas (4)–(8), one can determine the relationship between x and y. The values of coefficients A, B, C, and D can be obtained by using the methods of experimental calibration and the least square estimation algorithm.

Figure 10 shows the calibration process of the laser-camera unite. The distance between the camera and target is marked as y_i (e.g., In Figure 10 y_i = 0.2 m), and the vertical distance between the laser point and the center of image shown in camera was marked as x_i. In the calibration process, n pairs of x_i and $y_i(1 \le i \le n)$ can be obtained by putting the camera at different distances from 50 mm to 300 mm for several turns.

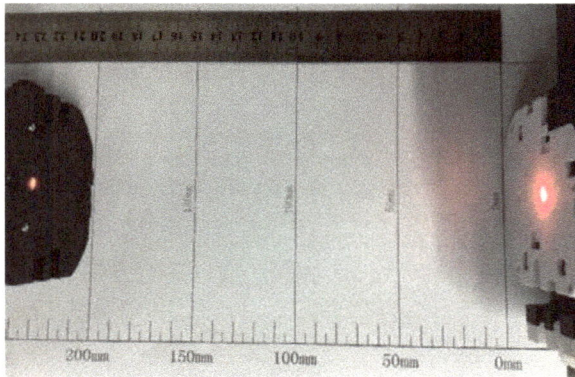

Figure 10. The calibration process of the laser-camera unit.

The sum of the squared-residual is defined as:

$$S = \sum_{i=1}^{n} (Ax_iy_i + Bx_i + Cy_i + D)^2 \tag{9}$$

In order to estimate the optimal values of A, B, C and D, S must be minimized. So, the following equations should be simultaneously satisfied:

$$\frac{\partial S}{\partial A} = 2 \left[A \sum_{i=1}^{n} (x_iy_i)^2 + B \sum_{i=1}^{n} \left(x_i^2 y_i \right) + C \sum_{i=1}^{n} \left(x_i y_i^2 \right) + D \sum_{i=1}^{n} (x_iy_i) \right] = 0 \tag{10}$$

$$\frac{\partial S}{\partial B} = 0 \tag{11}$$

$$\frac{\partial S}{\partial C} = 0 \tag{12}$$

Then, a system of linear equations can be derived, as below:

$$\begin{bmatrix} \sum_{i=1}^{n}(x_iy_i)^2 & \sum_{i=1}^{n}(x_i^2y_i) & \sum_{i=1}^{n}(x_iy_i^2) & \sum_{i=1}^{n}(x_iy_i) \\ \sum_{i=1}^{n}(x_i^2y_i) & \sum_{i=1}^{n}x_i^2 & \sum_{i=1}^{n}(x_iy_i) & \sum_{i=1}^{n}x_i \\ \sum_{i=1}^{n}(x_iy_i^2) & \sum_{i=1}^{n}(x_iy_i) & \sum_{i=1}^{n}y_i^2 & \sum_{i=1}^{n}y_i \end{bmatrix} \begin{bmatrix} A \\ B \\ C \\ D \end{bmatrix} = 0 \tag{13}$$

Formula (13) is a singular matrix equation, so let D = 1. Here, are:

$$\zeta = \left(X^TX\right)^{-1}\left(X^TY\right) \tag{14}$$

Where Y is a n × 3 matrix with all elements being 1 and ζ and X are defined as:

$$\zeta = \begin{bmatrix} A & B & C \end{bmatrix}^T \tag{15}$$

$$X = \begin{bmatrix} x_1y_1 & x_1 & y_1 \\ \vdots & \vdots & \vdots \\ x_ny_n & x_n & y_n \end{bmatrix} \tag{16}$$

From Formulas (14)–(16), the value of coefficients A, B, and C can be determined. Finally, the relationship between x and y can be expressed as:

$$y = \frac{-D - Bx}{Ax + C} \tag{17}$$

According to the measurement principle, the accuracy will reduce dramatically with the increasing distance, because the resolution of camera is limited. In actual experiments, it is found that the error is ±5 mm, when the distance between the target and the active docking surface is within 50 cm. If the distance is more than 50 cm and less than 150 cm, the maximum error may reach 15 mm. Under this condition, the value of measured distance is useless. Therefore, the actual docking process should be performed within 50 cm.

5.2. LED-Camera Unit

In order to determine the angle between two docking surfaces, a LED-camera unit is designed and a three-step measurement method is proposed.

The first step is to determine the relationship between the horizontal distance x of the adjacent LED lights showed in captured image and the actual distance L between the two docking surfaces. The LED identification algorithms can be used to find out the LEDs in complex backgrounds and determine their positions in the image, as shown in Figure 11, where each LED is marked by a red rectangle. Then, one can work out the value of x.

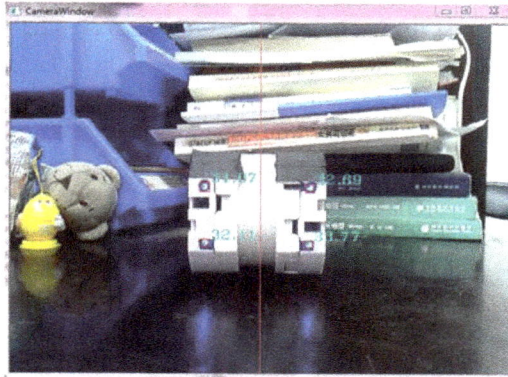

Figure 11. Results of the LED-identification algorithms.

In this step, it is assumed that the two docking surfaces are parallel to each other. The measurement principle is shown in Figure 12a.

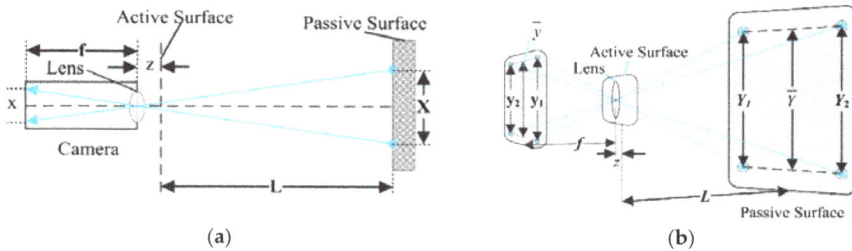

(a)   (b)

Figure 12. Principles of the LED measurement method. (**a**) Top view that shows the measurement principle in the horizontal direction; and, (**b**) A side view that shows the measurement principle in the vertical direction.

In Figure 12, L represents the distance between the passive and active docking surfaces, f denotes the focal distance of the camera, and z is the distance between the camera lens and the active docking surface. In Figure 12a, X is the horizontal distance between the two upper adjacent LED lights on the passive docking surface (also see Figure 8b), and x is the distance calculated from the pixel length that X showed in camera image

According to the principles of similar triangles and perspective projection, one can get:

$$\frac{x}{f} = \frac{X}{L+z} \tag{18}$$

It can be rewritten as:

$$(L + B_1)x + D_1 = 0 \tag{19}$$

Where:

$$B_1 = z, \; D_1 = -fX \tag{20}$$

Similar to the case of laser-camera unit, the two unknown coefficients B and D can be determined by experimental calibration. From Formula (19), x can be expressed as:

$$x = \frac{-D_1}{L + B_1} \tag{21}$$

75

The second step is to determine the average vertical distance of the two adjacent LED lights shown in the image at distance L. Here, L is obtained by the LED-camera unit rather than the laser-camera unit. The laser-camera unit can obtain the distance between the camera and the laser spot, however, the distance between the camera and the horizontal center of LEDs (middle of Y_1 and Y_2) is required. It is hard to assure that the laser spot just locates at the center of LEDs. Thus, if the distance that is obtained by laser is used, it may cause unpredictable error in the result of angle measurement.

As shown in Figure 12b, Y_1 and Y_2 are the vertical distances of the adjacent LED lights and $\overline{Y}$ is their average value, i.e., $\overline{Y} = (Y_1 + Y_2)/2$. While, y_1 and y_2 are the images of Y_1 and Y_2 projected in the camera. The average value of y_1 and y_2 is $\overline{y}$, i.e., $\overline{y} = (y_1 + y_2)/2$.

Similarly, one can get:

$$\frac{\overline{y}}{f} = \frac{\overline{Y}}{L + z} \tag{22}$$

It can be rewritten as:

$$(L + B_2)\overline{y} + D_2 = 0 \tag{23}$$

where

$$B_2 = z, \ D_2 = -f\overline{Y} \tag{24}$$

Using the same calibration method, one can obtain the relationship between $\overline{y}$ and L as:

$$L = \frac{-D_2 - B_2\overline{y}}{\overline{y}} \tag{25}$$

The last step is to determine the angle θ between the two docking surfaces. As shown in Figure 13, the two docking surfaces are not parallel to each other in a practical situation. Therefore, the horizontal distance X shown in the image is actually its projection ($\widetilde{X}$) in the direction of the active docking surface.

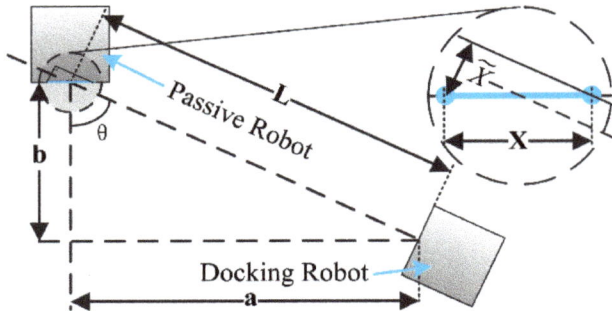

Figure 13. Top view of the actual position of the two docking robots.

From Figure 13, it can be obtained that:

$$\widetilde{X} = X \cos \theta \tag{26}$$

When considering the distance showed in the captured image, one has:

$$\widetilde{x} = x \cos \theta \tag{27}$$

Contrarily, the average vertical distance y only depends on the distance L between the two docking surfaces and it is not affected by θ.

By combining Formulas (21), (25), and (27), angle θ could be expressed as:

$$\theta = cos^{-1}\left\{\frac{\tilde{x}[(B_1 - B_2)\bar{y} - D_2]}{-D_1\bar{y}}\right\} \tag{28}$$

5.3. Experimental Verification of the Angle Measurement Method

When the angle between two docking surfaces is too large, the adjacent LED lights in the same horizontal surface will become too close to be identified in the image. Thus, four group of data are measured at the angles of 15°, 30°, 45°, and 60°. When the distance between two docking surfaces are too small, the camera cannot capture all of the LED lights. When the distance is too far, the measurement accuracy will reduce dramatically because of the limited resolution of the camera. Therefore, the distance is restricted between 15–50 cm in the angle measurement experiments and its variation step is prescribed as 5 cm. Based on our previous work [18] and the additional supplementary experiment, the measurement results of the angle θ are shown in Figure 14.

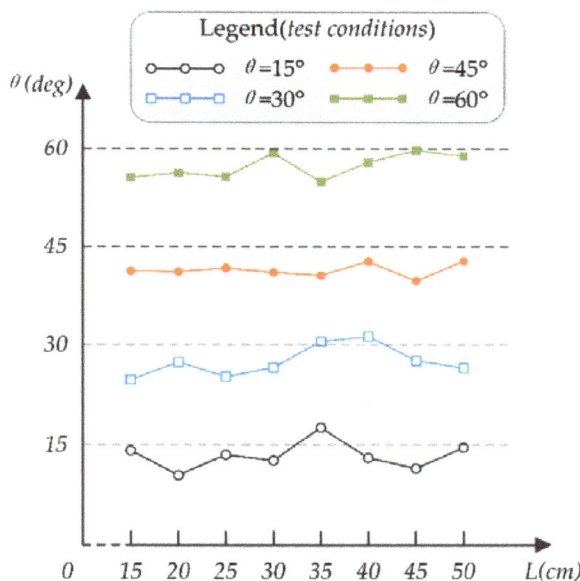

Figure 14. Experimental results of angle measurement. L is the distance, the θ axis is the angle in degree. Four types of lines with different color represent the measurement results under different test conditions.

From Figure 14, it is seen that the maximum angle error approaches 6°. Except for few data, the overall measurement results are smaller than the actual angle. The error mainly comes from two aspects:

1. The error of Formula (21) and (25).
2. The error caused by the LED identification algorithm, because the point that is found by the algorithm may not be the center of the LEDs.

Because the mechanical structure of SambotII allows a range of measurement error in the docking process and the maximum error of angle measurement is in that range, the angle information that was obtained by the present LED algorithm can be used in the docking process.

5.4. Outlines of the Docking Strategy

The docking procedure (see Figure 15) is divided into three phases:

1.   wandering and searching phase;
2.   position and angle adjustment phase; and,
3.   docking phase

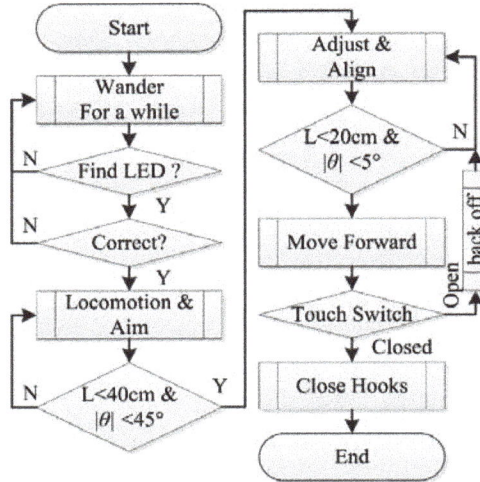

Figure 15. The docking procedure.

5.4.1. Wandering and Searching Phase

In this step, the active robot wanders under a certain strategy to explore and search for the correct passive docking surface whose LED lights formed a specific pattern. After finding the target passive docking surface, the robot will enter the next phase.

5.4.2. Position and Angle Adjustment Phase

Because the active robot just move forward directly to complete the docking without extra measurement in the third phase, it should make position and angle adjustment in this step so as to assure that the distance and angle are within specific ranges.

During this phase, a series of adjusting movements need to be performed. In each adjusting movement, the active robot rotates at first to adjust its orientation and then moves forward to adjust its position, because SambotII is a differential wheeled robot. After each adjusting movement, it has to rotate again to face the passive docking surface to check if the specific tolerance condition has been met. Each move-and-check operation generally costs much time. In order to enhance the efficiency, this procedure is further divided into two steps: the rough aiming step and the accurate alignment step.

In the rough aiming step (Locomotion & Aim), the active robot moves a relatively larger distance in each adjusting movement under a loose tolerance condition: L (distance) < 40 cm and θ (deviation degree) < 45°. When this condition is met, the active robot will stop in front of the passive docking surface and face it.

The laser-camera unit has its best performance when L < 40 cm and LED-camera unit has better accuracy when θ < 45°. That is why L < 40 cm and θ < 45° is chosen as the finish condition of this phase.

In the accurate alignment step (Adjust & Align), robot moves a smaller distance in each adjusting movement under a strict tolerance condition: L < 20 and θ < 5°. This condition ensures that the robot can just move forward for docking without check L and θ for a second time, due to the permissible errors of docking mechanism.

The laser-camera is used to get distance during the whole phase, because it is more accurate than the LED-camera. Moreover, when the four LEDs are too far or the angle θ is too large, LEDs may not be clearly recognized for measuring.

5.4.3. Docking Phase

In this phase, the robot opens its hooks and moves forward until it contacts the passive docking surface (when the touch switch is triggered). Then, it closes its hooks to form mechanical connection with the passive docking surface. If failed, it will move backward and restart the position and angle adjustment phase.

6. Docking Experiments

In this section, docking experiments are performed between two robots to verify the entire hardware and software system.

Before the final structure was fixed, two prototypes (see Figure 16) of SambotII are built by adding the camera, laser tube, LED lights, and other components into SambotI. Due to the limitation of size, the hooks in the active docking surface are removed from these prototypes. The coincidence degree of the the two docking surfaces is chosen as the evaluation index. In the final structure of SambotII, after the customized camera has been delivered, the hooks are equipped (as shown in Figure 2b).

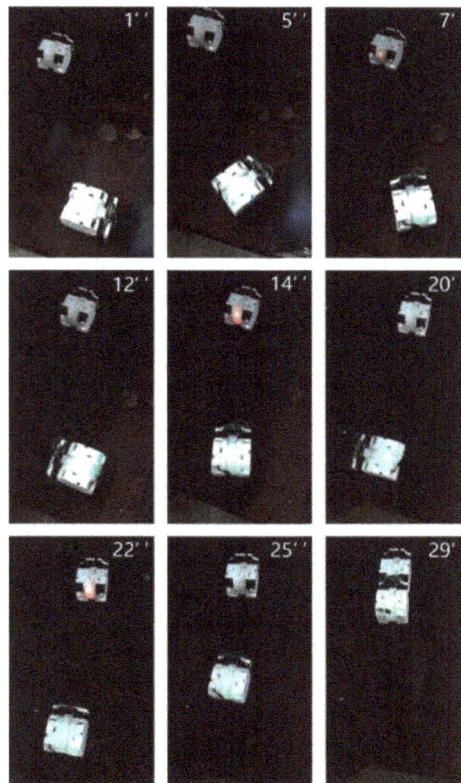

Figure 16. A docking process experiment. It takes 29 s in total.

In Figure 17, L = 80 mm is the width of each surface, C is the coincident width of the two surfaces and E is the docking error. The coincidence degree η is defined as $\eta = (C/L) \times 100\%$. As shown in Table 2, the permission deviation along the Z axis is ± 19.5 mm. Thus, when E is less than 19.5 mm or $\eta \geq [(L - 19.5mm)/L] \times 100\% \approx 75\%$, the docking process can be regarded as successful.

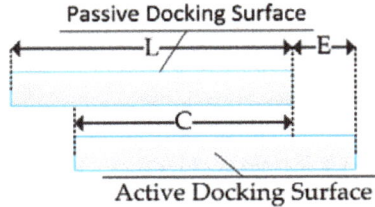

Passive Docking Surface

Active Docking Surface

Figure 17. Diagram of the coincidence degree from the top view of the two docking surfaces.

The experiment was carried out on a 60×60 cm platform with an enclosure being 40 cm high. Because the enclosure surface is rough, the reflection of light is so weak that the recognition of the laser and LED lights cannot be affected. Because only two robots are applied in the experiments, only the LEDs on one passive docking surfaces are turned on.

The passive robot is placed on one side of the platform and stay still, while the active docking robot is placed on the other side. The docking process is repeated 10 times to evaluate the success rate of the first docking. In each time, if the active robots misses the passive docking surface, the docking process will end, and this experiment is then counted as a failure.

Experiment indicate that the success rate of the first docking is approximately 80%. Thus, the feasibility and validity of the docking algorithm is verified. The experimental results are shown in Table 5 [18].

Table 5. Result of autonomous docking experiment.

Coincidence Degree	Times
0~64%	1
65~74%	1
75~84%	1
85~94%	4
95~100%	3

There are two failed dockings in the experiments. One failure occurs due to compound errors. When the accurate alignment step ends, the angle that was calculated by the active robot is less than 5°, but the actual angle might be 6° or 7°. Besides, the speed difference between the two wheels may also lead to angle error. Influenced by these two errors, the final coincidence degree is between 65% and 75%. Another failure may be caused by incorrect LED recognition. When the accurate alignment step ends, the angle between the two robots exceeds the expected value. So, the active robot misses the passive docking surface finally.

The failure caused by errors are inevitable. They can be reduced by improving the measurement accuracy and decreasing the speed difference between the two wheels. The failure cause by LED misrecognition may occur of the light reflected by LED is incorrectly identified as a LED's light. So, the algorithm should be further optimized to deal with the problem of reflection.

When compared with SambotI, SambotII has higher efficiency and a larger range (it is 50 cm, but for SambotI it is just 20 cm).

Appl. Sci. **2018**, *8*, 1719

7. Conclusions and Future Works

A new self-assembly modular robot (SambotII) is developed in this manuscript. It is an upgraded version of SambotI. The original electronic system is redesigned. An Intel x86 CPU, a memory, a storage, a Wi-Fi module, a camera, a laser tube, and LEDs are integrated into robot for the purpose of improving the computing performance, the communication ability, and the perception capability. Meanwhile, a five-layer hierarchical software architecture is proposed and thus the reliability and reusability of programs are enhanced. By using this architecture, a large application program can be well organized and built efficiently.

Moreover, a laser-camera unit and a LED-camera unit are employed to perform distance and angle measurements, respectively. Besides, by identifying different color combinations of LED-lights, the active robot can find the specific passive docking surface clearly and precisely so that the traditional random try is effectively avoided. Finally, two prototype SambotII robots are used to perform docking experiments, by which the effectiveness of the entire system and docking strategy have been verified.

In general, SambotII can serve as a fundamental platform for the further research of swarm and modular robots. In the future, three major aspects of work can be done for further improvement:

1. Hardware optimization, including the increase of battery capacity, the enhancement of the motor's torque, the improvement of the LEDs' brightness, the addition of a rotational DOF, the addition of a FPGA chip in robot, and etc.
2. Optimization of the LED-identification algorithms so as to improve the angle measurement accuracy.
3. Enhancement of the software functions in behavior layer, such as the exploring and path planning.

Author Contributions: Conceptualization, B.Y. and H.W.; Funding Acquisition, H.W.; Project Administration, B.Y.; Software, B.Y.; Supervision, H.W.; Validation, W.T.; Writing-Original Draft, W.T. and B.Y.

Funding: This research was funded by the National Natural Science Foundation of China grant number [No. 61673031] and the APC was funded by the National Natural Science Foundation of China grant number [No. 61673031].

Conflicts of Interest: The authors declare no conflict of interest.

References

1. Rus, D.; Butler, Z.; Kotay, K.; Vona, M. Self-reconfiguring robots. *Commun. ACM* **2002**, *45*, 39–45. [CrossRef]
2. Christensen, D.J.; Schultz, U.P.; Stoy, K. A distributed and morphology-independent strategy for adaptive locomotion in self-reconfigurable modular robots. *Robot. Autom. Syst.* **2013**, *61*, 1021–1035. [CrossRef]
3. Ahmadzadeh, H.; Masehian, E.; Asadpour, M. Modular robotic systems: Characteristics and applications. *J. Intell. Robot. Syst.* **2016**, *81*, 317–357. [CrossRef]
4. Yim, M.; Shen, W.M.; Salemi, B.; Rus, D.; Moll, M.; Lipson, H.; Klavins, E.; Chirikjian, G.S. Modular self-reconfigurable robot systems. *IEEE Robot. Autom. Mag.* **2007**, *14*, 43–52. [CrossRef]
5. Fukuda, T.; Nakagawa, S. Dynamically reconfigurable robotic system. In Proceedings of the IEEE International Conference on Robotics and Automation, Philadelphia, PA, USA, 24–29 April 1988; pp. 1581–1586.
6. Stoy, K.; Kurokawa, H. Current topics in classic self-reconfigurable robot research. In Proceedings of the IROS Workshop on Reconfigurable Modular Robotics: Challenges of Mechatronic and Bio-Chemo-Hybrid Systems, San Francisco, CA, USA; 2011. Available online: https://www.researchgate.net/publication/265179113_Current_Topics_in_Classic_Self-reconfigurable_Robot_Research (accessed on 20 September 2018).
7. Yim, M.; Zhang, Y.; Roufas, K.; Duff, D.; Eldershaw, D. Connecting and disconnecting for chain self-reconfiguration with PolyBot. *IEEE/ASME Trans. Mechatron.* **2002**, *7*, 442–451. [CrossRef]
8. Stoy, K.; Christensen, D.J.; Brandt, D.; Bordignon, M.; Schultz, U.P. Exploit morphology to simplify docking of self-reconfigurable robots. In *Distributed Autonomous Robotic Systems 8*; Asama, H., Kurokawa, H., Ota, J., Sekiyama, K., Eds.; Springer: Berlin/Heidelberg, Germany, 2009; pp. 441–452.

9.   Baca, J.; Hossain, S.G.M.; Dasgupta, P.; Nelson, C.A.; Dutta, A. ModRED: Hardware design and reconfiguration planning for a high dexterity modular self-reconfigurable robot for extra-terrestrial exploration. *Robot. Autom. Syst.* **2014**, *6*, 1002–1015. [CrossRef]

10. Liu, W.; Winfield, A.F.T. Implementation of an IR approach for autonomous docking in a self-configurable robotics system. In *Proceedings of the Towards Autonomous Robotic Systems*; Kyriacou, T., Nehmzow, U., Melhuish, C., Witkowski, M., Eds.; 2009; pp. 251–258. Available online: http://eprints.uwe.ac.uk/13252/ (accessed on 20 September 2018).

11. Yim, M.; Shirmohammadi, B.; Sastra, J.; Park, M.; Dugan, M.; Taylor, C.J. Towards robotic self-reassembly after explosion. In Proceedings of the IEEE/RSJ International Conference on Intelligent Robots and Systems, San Diego, CA, USA, 29 October–2 Novermber 2007; pp. 2767–2772.

12. Murata, S.; Kakomura, K.; Kurokawa, H. Docking experiments of a modular robot by visual feedback. In Proceedings of the IEEE/RSJ International Conference on Intelligent Robots and Systems, Beijing, China, 9–15 October 2006; pp. 625–630.

13. Liu, P.; Zhu, Y.; Cui, X.; Wang, X.; Yan, J.; Zhao, J. Multisensor-based autonomous docking for UBot modular reconfigurable robot. In Proceedings of the IEEE International Conference on Mechatronics and Automation, Chengdu, China, 5–8 August 2012; pp. 772–776.

14. Wang, W.; Li, Z.L.; Yu, W.P.; Zhang, J.W. An autonomous docking method based on ultrasonic sensors for self-reconfigurable mobile robot. In Proceedings of the IEEE International Conference on Robotics and Biomimetics (ROBIO), Guilin, China, 19–23 December 2009; pp. 1744–1749.

15. Wei, H.X.; Chen, Y.D.; Tan, J.D.; Wang, T.M. Sambot: A Self-Assembly Modular Robot System. *IEEE/ASME Trans. Mechatron.* **2011**, *16*, 745–757. [CrossRef]

16. Wei, H.X.; Liu, M.; Li, D.; Wang, T.M. A novel self-assembly modular swarm robot: Docking mechanism design and self-assembly control. *Robot* **2010**, *32*, 614–621.

17. Intel Edison Compute Module. Available online: https://software.intel.com/node/696745?wapkw=edison (accessed on 22 May 2018).

18. Zhang, Y.C.; Wei, H.X.; Yang, B.; Jiang, C.C. Sambot II: A self-assembly modular swarm robot. *AIP Conf. Proc.* **2018**, *1955*, 040156. [CrossRef]

applied
sciences

MDPI

Article

Leader–Follower Formation Maneuvers for Multi-Robot Systems via Derivative and Integral Terminal Sliding Mode

Dianwei Qian and Yafei Xi *

School of Control and Computer Engineering, North China Electric Power University, Beijing 102206, China; dianwei.qian@gmail.com
* Correspondence: xi_yafei@163.com; Tel.: +86-10-6177-2755

Received: 10 May 2018; Accepted: 11 June 2018; Published: 27 June 2018

Featured Application: The presented control design can enrich the multi-robot technologies and can benefit the coordination of multi-robot systems.

Abstract: This paper investigates the formation problem of multiple robots based on the leader–follower mechanism. At first, the dynamics of such a leader–follower framework are modeled. The input–output equations are depicted by calculating the relative degree of a leader–follower formation system. Furthermore, the derivative and integral terminal sliding mode controller is designed based on the relative degree. Since the formation system suffers from uncertainties, the nonlinear disturbance observer is adopted to deal with the uncertainties. The stability of the closed-loop control system is proven in the sense of Lyapunov. Finally, some numerical simulations are displayed to verify the feasibility and effectiveness by the designed controller and observer.

Keywords: multiple robots; formation; sliding mode controller; nonlinear disturbance observer; system stability

---

1. Introduction

In recent years, the coordination control scheme of multiple robots has drawn considerable attention in various fields [1]. Multiple robots can be applied in many dangerous places to free the human being, including the earthquake rescue, the warehouse translations, and some tasks at nuclear power plants. A multi-robot system can be treated as a coupling network of some robots, where the robots communicate with each other to achieve some complex duties [2,3]. Various investigations have been explored to achieve the coordination control of multiple robots. These investigations can be roughly classified into leader–follower formations [4–8], virtual structure mechanisms [9–12], graph-based approaches [13,14], and behavior-based methods [15,16].

The leader–follower formations are attractive in the coordination control of multi-robot systems. Partly, such formations benefit multiple robots because the formations can have guaranteed formation stability via control design [17]. The basic control idea of the leader–follower mechanism is that multiple robots are divided into several leader–follower pairs. In the leader–follower mechanism, all follower robots share the same leader. In each pair, the leader robot moves along the predefined trajectory, while the follower robots track the leader with desired relative distance and angle. In the leader–follower system of multiple robots, only partial followers can obtain the state of the leader, and the interaction between follower robots and leader robot is local [18]. Many control methods have been applied in the leader–follower multi-robot systems, such as sliding mode control (SMC) based on nonlinear disturbance observer [18], SMC [19], second-order SMC [20], adaptive control [21,22], predictive control [23], integral terminal SMC [24], and terminal SMC [25].

In actuality, it is unavoidable for any robots to be affected by uncertainties such as external disturbances, unmodeled dynamics, and parameter perturbations [26]. The dynamics of multi-robot systems becomes uncertain, due to these uncertainties [27]. These uncertainties can be categorized into unmatched uncertainties and matched uncertainties [28]. However, the SMC method, as a strong robust tool, has invariant nature to the matched uncertainties when an SMC system enters into the sliding mode. Unfortunately, the effects of unmatched uncertainties cannot be suppressed by the SMC methods [29]. The unmatched uncertainties can challenge the performance of the SMC system seriously. The characteristic of terminal SMC (T-SMC) has its nonlinear sliding surface. Compared with those traditional SMC approaches, the T-SMC method has faster convergence speed and higher accuracy. However, the T-SMC method has the singular problem due to its fractional function. Therefore, the derivative and integral T-SMC (DIT-SMC) method is proposed [30]. The DIT-SMC method is of merit. Due to the existence of the integral term, the sliding mode of the DIT-SMC method starts on the derivative and integral terminal sliding mode surface. Moreover, the DIT-SMC method can guarantee the exact estimation of finite error convergence time, and resolve the singular problem of the T-SMC. On the other hand, the derivative term of the DIT-SMC method can reduce the nonlinear effects to the stability of a DIT-SMC system.

In the previous works [21–30], the assumption that the uncertainties have a known boundary is assumed. Concerning the formation maneuvers of multi-robot systems, the assumption is not mild. In fact, the boundary of uncertainties in multiple robots is hard to be known exactly in advance. In case of the lack of the important information, several serious problems may be raised in reality, for example, the decrease of the formation robustness, the deterioration of the formation performance, as far as the deficiency of the formation stability. In order to resolve the problem of the uncertainties, the nonlinear disturbance observer is adopted. The unknown unmatched uncertainties are estimated by the nonlinear disturbance observer. The technique of nonlinear disturbance observer (NDOB) can handle the unmatched uncertainties problem and improve the robustness of the formation control system.

This paper deals with the formation problem of multiple robots with uncertainties. The control scheme combining derivative and integral terminal sliding mode and nonlinear disturbance observer is investigated. The derivative and integral terminal sliding mode method allows the system start on the sliding surface. The reaching time of sliding surface is eliminated. The matched uncertainties in formation system are suppressed by the DIT-SMC method. Under the mild assumption that the uncertainties have an unknown boundary, the NDOB is designed to estimate the unmatched uncertainties in the formation system. The estimate errors will converge to zero in the limited time by setting the parameter of NDOB. In the sense of Lyapunov, the system stability is guaranteed in spite of uncertainties. Finally, some numerical simulations are displayed to illustrate the feasibility and effectiveness.

2. Problem Formulation

2.1. Modeling of Single Robot

Shown by Figure 1, a unicycle-like robot is taken into account. The robot is round, with r in radius, and has two parallel wheels controlled independently by two DC motors. Because the robot is capable of simultaneous arbitrary rotation and translation in the horizontal plane, a three dimensional vector $q = [x, y, \theta]^T$ is used to describe the robot. In Figure 1, (x, y) represents the translational coordinates of the robot, and is the center of the robot. The rotational coordinate is depicted by the variable θ.

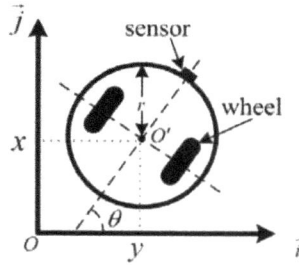

Figure 1. Sketches of the mobile robot.

There are n robots in the formation system of multi-robot. Provided the pure rolling and no-slipping condition, the ideal dynamic models of the nth robot are described by

$$\dot{q}_n = \begin{bmatrix} \dot{x}_n \\ \dot{y}_n \\ \dot{\theta}_n \end{bmatrix} = \begin{bmatrix} \cos\theta_n & 0 \\ \sin\theta_n & 0 \\ 0 & 1 \end{bmatrix} \cdot \begin{bmatrix} v_n \\ \omega_n \end{bmatrix}, \tag{1}$$

where v_n, ω_n are the linear velocities and angular velocities, respectively.

Differentiate (1) with respect to time t. Considering the parameter fluctuations, model uncertainties, and external disturbances, such as slipping and skidding effects in the formation system, the dynamic model of the nth robot is obtained by

$$\begin{bmatrix} \ddot{x}_n \\ \ddot{y}_n \\ \ddot{\theta}_n \end{bmatrix} = \begin{bmatrix} -\dot{y}_n\dot{\theta}_n \\ \dot{x}_n\dot{\theta}_n \\ 0 \end{bmatrix} + \begin{bmatrix} \cos\theta_n & 0 \\ \sin\theta_n & 0 \\ 0 & 1 \end{bmatrix} \times u_n + \begin{bmatrix} \cos\theta_n & 0 \\ \sin\theta_n & 0 \\ 0 & 1 \end{bmatrix} \times \Delta u_n + \pi_n(q_n, \dot{q}_n), \tag{2}$$

where $u_n = [\alpha_n\ \beta_n]^T$ is the control input of nth robot. α_n, β_n are the acceleration and angular acceleration respectively, which are described by $\alpha_n = F_n/m_n$, $\beta_n = \tau_n/J_n$. Here, F_n, m_n, τ_n, and J_n donate the force, the nominal mass, the torque of the robot, and the nominal moment of inertia, respectively. Δ_n represents the parameter fluctuations, written by

$$\Delta_n = \begin{bmatrix} \varepsilon_n & 0 \\ 0 & \varepsilon'_n \end{bmatrix},$$

where ε_n, ε'_n represent the variant on the mass and the inertia. $\pi_n(q_n, \dot{q}_n)$ is described by $[\pi_{nx}\ \pi_{ny}\ \pi_{n\theta}]^T$, meaning the uncertainties and external disturbances in the lumped model.

2.2. Leader–Follower Formation Framework

In this section, the kinematics model of the leader–follower formation system is given. The leader–follower formation mechanism is displayed in Figure 2. In the leader–follower formation system, there is a leader robot, and others are selected as follower robots. The ith robot is set as the leader robot, and the kth robot is picked up as the representative of all follower robots. The relative distance l_{ik} and relative bearing angle φ_{ik} between the leader robot and follower robot are defined in Figure 2. The relative distance l_{ik} means the distance between the center of the leader robot ith and the front castor of the follower robot kth, described by

$$l_{ik} = \sqrt{(x_i - \bar{x}_k)^2 + (y_i - \bar{y}_k)^2}. \tag{3}$$

Here, (x_i, y_i) denotes the center of the leader robot i, and $(\bar{x}_k, \bar{y}_k)$ represents the caster position of the follower robot k. The calculation of $\bar{x}_k, \bar{y}_k$ has the following form

$$\begin{aligned} \bar{x}_k &= x_k + r\cos\theta \\ \bar{y}_k &= y_k + r\sin\theta \end{aligned}.$$

(4)

Here, r is the radius of the round robot, and (x_k, y_k) denotes the center of the follower robot k. Simultaneously, ψ_{ik} is formulated by

$$\psi_{ik} = \pi + \zeta_{ik} - \theta_i.$$

(5)

Here, θ_i denotes the orientation angle of the leader robot i, $\zeta_{ik} = \arctan\frac{y_i - y_k - r\sin\theta_k}{x_i - x_k - r\cos\theta_k}$.

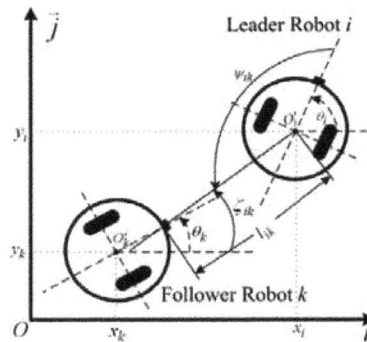

Figure 2. Sketches of the leader–follower coordinated framework.

In this paper, the derivative and integral terminal sliding mode controller is designed so that the follower robots can follow the leader robot with desired relative distance and angler. Therefore, the following conditions are satisfied: The collisions between the robots are avoided. There is no communication delay between the leader robot and the follower robot. Each follower robot knows its position, velocity, and corresponding information of the leader robot.

According to leader–follower formation mechanism, the robots move along a specified trajectory with desired relative distance and bearing angle. It is necessary to shape the dynamics of the leader–follower formation system. Differentiate (3) and (5) twice with the respect to time t, and substitute (2) into the second derivative of (3) and (5). Define the state variable $x_{ik} = [x_1\ x_2\ x_3\ x_4]^T$, where $x_1 = l_{ik}$, $x_2 = \psi_{ik}$, $x_3 = \dot{l}_{ik}$, $x_4 = \dot{\psi}_{ik}$. The dynamic model of the formation system has the form of

$$\begin{aligned} \dot{x}_{ik} &= f(x_{ik}, d_{ik}(t)) + B_{ik,1}u_k \\ y_{ik} &= h(x_{ik}) \end{aligned}.$$

(6)

Here, $B_{ik,1}$ is a 2×2 matrix whose columns are smooth vector fields $B_{ik,1K}$. $h(x_{ik})$ is the output equation of formation system. Here,

$$f(x_{ik}, d_{ik}(t)) = A_{ik}x_{ik} + B_{ik,2}\tilde{d}_{ik}(t) + B_{ik,1}\Delta_k u_k$$

$A_{ik}, B_{ik,1}, B_{ik,2}, h(x_{ik})$ are described by

$$A_{ik} = \begin{bmatrix} 0 & 1 & 0 & 0 \\ 0 & 0 & 0 & 0 \\ 0 & 0 & 0 & 1 \\ 0 & 0 & 0 & 0 \end{bmatrix}, B_{ik,2} = \begin{bmatrix} 0 & 0 \\ 1 & 0 \\ 0 & 0 \\ 0 & 1 \end{bmatrix}, B_{ik,1} = \begin{bmatrix} 0 & 0 \\ \cos\varphi_{ik} & r\sin\varphi_{ik} \\ 0 & 0 \\ \frac{-\sin\varphi_{ik}}{l_{ik}} & \frac{d\cos\varphi_{ik}}{l_{ik}} \end{bmatrix}, h(x_{ik}) = \begin{bmatrix} x_1 \\ x_3 \end{bmatrix}.$$

Here, $\varphi_{ik} = \psi_{ik} + \theta_{ik}$, $\tilde{d}_{ik}(t)$ denotes the uncertainties of the leader–follower formation system (6), written by

$$\tilde{d}_{ik}(t) = L_{ik}(I_2 + \Delta_i)u_i + F_{ik} + P_{ik} \tag{7}$$

$$L_{ik} = \begin{bmatrix} 0 & 0 \\ -\cos\psi_{ik} & 0 \\ 0 & 0 \\ \frac{\sin\psi_{ik}}{l_{ik}} & -1 \end{bmatrix}, F_{ik} = \begin{bmatrix} 0 \\ F_1 \\ 0 \\ F_2 \end{bmatrix}, P_{ik} = \begin{bmatrix} 0 \\ P_1 \\ 0 \\ P_2 \end{bmatrix}.$$

F_1, F_2, P_1, P_2 are depicted respectively by

$$F_1 = (\dot{\psi}_{ik})^2 l_{ik} + 2\dot{\psi}_{ik}\dot{\theta}_i l_{ik} + (\dot{\theta}_i)^2 l_{ik} - r\cos\varphi_{ik}(\dot{\theta}_k)^2$$
$$-(\dot{y}_k\dot{\theta}_k - \dot{y}_i\dot{\theta}_i)\cos(\psi_{ik} + \dot{\theta}_i) - (\dot{x}_i\dot{\theta}_i - \dot{x}_k\dot{\theta}_k)\sin(\psi_{ik} + \theta_i)$$
$$F_2 = \frac{-(\dot{y}_k\varphi_{ik} - \dot{\psi}_{ik}\dot{y}_i)\sin(\psi_{ik} + \theta_i) - r\dot{\theta}_k\dot{\varphi}_{ik}\sin\varphi_{ik}}{l_{ik}}$$
$$\frac{-(\dot{x}_k\dot{\varphi}_{ik} - \dot{\psi}_{ik}\dot{x}_i)\cos(\psi_{ik} + \theta_i) + i_{ik}((\dot{y}_i - \dot{y}_k)\cos(\psi_{ik} + \theta_i)}{l_{ik}}$$
$$-\frac{(\dot{x}_i - \dot{x}_k)\sin(\psi_{ik} + \theta_i) - r\dot{\theta}_k\dot{\varphi}_{ik}\cos\varphi_{ik})}{l_{ik}}$$
$$P_1 = -(\pi_{ix} - \pi_{kx})\cos(\psi_{ik} + \theta_i) - (\pi_{iy} - \pi_{ky})\sin(\psi_{ik} + \theta_i)$$
$$+r\pi_{k\theta}\sin\varphi_{ik}$$
$$P_2 = \frac{(\pi_{ix} - \pi_{kx})\sin(\psi_{ik} + \theta_i) - (\pi_{iy} - \pi_{ky})\cos(\psi_{ik} + \theta_i)}{l_{ik}}$$
$$\frac{+r\pi_{k\theta}\sin\varphi_{ik} - l_{ik}\pi_{i\theta}}{l_{ik}}$$

2.3. Control Problem Formulation

Considering the dynamic mode (6) of the leader–follower formation system, a relative-degree is calculated by

$$L_f h_1(x_{ik}) = \frac{\partial h_1(x_{ik})}{\partial x} f(x_{ik}, d_{ik}) \tag{8}$$

$$L_f h_2(x_{ik}) = \frac{\partial h_2(x_{ik})}{\partial x} f(x_{ik}, d_{ik}) \tag{9}$$

$$L_{B_{ik,1}K} L_f h_1(x_{ik}, d_{ik}) = L_{B_{ik,1K}}\left(L_f h_1(x_{ik}, d_{ik})\right) = \frac{\partial\left(L_f h_1(x_{ik}, d_{ik})\right)}{\partial x_{ik}} \cdot B_{ik,1K} \tag{10}$$

$$L_{B_{ik,1K}} L_f h_2(x_{ik}, d_{ik}) = L_{B_{ik,1K}}\left(L_f h_2(x_{ik}, d_{ik})\right) = \frac{\partial\left(L_f h_2(x_{ik}, d_{ik})\right)}{\partial x_{ik}} \cdot B_{ik,1K}. \tag{11}$$

Here, r_K ($K = 1, 2$) is the smallest integer so that the least one of the control inputs appears in $y_K^{r_K}$ ($K = 1$, 2), then

$$\begin{bmatrix} y_1^{r_1} \\ y_2^{r_2} \end{bmatrix} = \begin{bmatrix} L_f^{r_1} h_1(x_{ik}) + \sum\limits_{K=1}^{m} L_{B_{ik,1}K} L_f h_1(x_{ik}, d_{ik})u_k \\ L_f^{r_2} h_2(x_{ik}) + \sum\limits_{K=1}^{m} L_{B_{ik,1}K} L_f h_2(x_{ik}, d_{ik})u_k \end{bmatrix}. \tag{12}$$

Here, $r_1 = r_2 = 2$, $m = 2$. $L_{B_{ik,1K}}$, L_f are lie derivatives. Further, the input–output dynamic equation is depicted by

$$\ddot{y}_{ik} = d_{ik} + H(x_{ik}, d_{ik})u_k. \tag{13}$$

Here, $d_{ik} = \tilde{L}_{ik}(I_3 + \Delta_i)u_i + \tilde{P}_{ik} + \tilde{F}_{ik}$, $H(x_{ik}, d_{ik}) = G_{ik}(I_4 + \Delta_k)$. Here, I_3, I_4 are 2×2 matrices, u_i is the control input of ith robot, and other matrices are described by

$$G_{ik} = \begin{bmatrix} \cos\varphi_{ik} & r\sin\varphi_{ik} \\ -\frac{\sin\varphi_{ik}}{l_{ik}} & \frac{r\cos\varphi_{ik}}{l_{ik}} \end{bmatrix}, \tilde{L}_{ik} = \begin{bmatrix} -\cos\psi_{ik} & 0 \\ \frac{\sin\psi_{ik}}{l_{ik}} & -1 \end{bmatrix}, \tilde{F}_{ik} = \begin{bmatrix} F_1 \\ F_2 \end{bmatrix}, \tilde{P}_{ik} = \begin{bmatrix} P_1 \\ P_2 \end{bmatrix}.$$

Hypothesis 1. *$H(x_{ik}, d_{ik})$ has the normal part G_{ik} and nonlinear part $G_{ik}\Delta_k$, and meets the following in equation*

$$\delta_{ik}I \leq H(x_{ik})H_{dik}^{-1} \leq \delta_{ik}^{-1}I. \tag{14}$$

Here, $\delta_{ik} > 1$, $H_{dik} = H\left(x_{ik}^d\right)$, I is the 2 × 2 square matrix, x_{ik}^d denotes the desired state vector in (6).

Remark 1. *$G_{ik}\Delta_k u_k$ is the matched uncertainties in (13), meaning the parameter fluctuations of the follower robot k. The term d_{ik} depicts the unmatched uncertainties in the leader–follower formation system, and consists of three parts. Due to the formation, framework (13) is applied to the follower robot, and the information of leader robot u_i can't be matched.*

The terms $\widetilde{F}_{ik}$, $\widetilde{P}_{ik}$ denote the model uncertainties and external disturbances caused by slipping, friction, and obstacles etc., which are also hard to be matched.

3. Control Design

Due to the inherent characteristics of centralization, the scheme mainly depends on the leader robots and exists as the "single point of failure" problem. In order to develop derivative and integral terminal sliding mode approach to coordinate the leader robot i and follower robot k, a recursive structure of the terminal sliding function for high relative-degree MIMO systems (with r_1, $r_2 > 1$) is designed as

$$e_{ik,DO1} = y_{ik,1} - y_{ik,1}^d, \quad e_{ik,DO2} = y_{ik,2} - y_{ik,2}^d, \tag{15}$$

$$e_{ik,D11} = \dot{e}_{ik,DO1}^{p_{11}/q_{11}} + \gamma_{ik,1}e_{ik,DO1}, \quad e_{ik,D12} = \dot{e}_{ik,DO2}^{p_{12}/q_{12}} + \gamma_{ik,2}e_{ik,DO2}, \tag{16}$$

$$s_{ik} = \begin{bmatrix} s_{ik,1} \\ s_{ik,2} \end{bmatrix} = \begin{bmatrix} e_{ik,D11} + \lambda_{ik,1}e_{ik,I1} \\ e_{ik,D12} + \lambda_{ik,2}e_{ik,I2} \end{bmatrix}, \tag{17}$$

where $\dot{e}_{ik,I1} = e_{ik,D11}^{q_{21}/p_{21}}$, $e_{ik,I2} = e_{ik,D12}^{q_{22}/p_{22}}$. $\gamma_{ik,1}$, $\gamma_{ik,2}$, $\lambda_{ik,1}$, $\lambda_{ik,2}$ are all positive constants. $p_{Kj} > q_{Kj}$, here K, $j = 1, 2$. p_{Kj} and q_{Kj} are all odd positive constants.

Theorem 1. *Considering the derivative and integral terminal sliding mode surface $S_{ik}(t)$ with the fractional function, the state error of formation system can reach the equilibrium point $e = 0$ at the limited time*

$$T = \max_{K=1,2} \left(\frac{|e_{D1K}(0)|^{1-q_{2K}/q_{2K}}}{\alpha_K(1 - q_{2K}/q_{2K})} + \frac{|e_{DOK}(t_{1K})|^{1-q_{1K}/q_{1K}}}{\beta_K(1 - q_{1K}/q_{1K})} \right). \tag{18}$$

Here, t_{1K} (K = 1, 2) is the reaching time of terminal slide mode e_{D1K}.

Proof. From (17), the sliding mode s_{ik} starts on $t = 0$. Then, the equations $e_{ik,D11} = -\lambda_{ik,1}e_{ik,I1}$ and $e_{ik,D12} = -\lambda_{ik,2}e_{ik,I2}$ can always hold true by control design. Subsequently, substituting $e_{ik,D11} = -\lambda_{ik,1}e_{ik,I1}$, $e_{ik,D12} = -\lambda_{ik,2}e_{ik,I2}$ into $\dot{e}_{ik,I1} = e_{ik,D11}^{q_{21}/p_{21}}$ and $e_{ik,I2} = e_{ik,D12}^{q_{22}/p_{22}}$, respectively, yields

$$\dot{e}_{ik,I1}(t) = -\lambda_{ik,1}^{q_{21}/p_{21}} e_{ik,I1}^{q_{21}/p_{21}}, \quad \dot{e}_{ik,I2}(t) = -\lambda_{ik,2}^{q_{22}/p_{22}} e_{ik,I2}^{q_{22}/p_{22}}. \tag{19}$$

□

The converge time of sliding mode $e_{ik,I1}$ and $e_{ik,I2}$ can obtained by solving (19).

$$t_{11} = \frac{|e_{ik,D11}(0)|^{1-q_{21}/p_{21}}}{\lambda_{ik,1}(1 - q_{21}/p_{21})}, \quad t_{12} = \frac{|e_{ik,D12}(0)|^{1-q_{22}/p_{22}}}{\lambda_{ik,2}(1 - q_{22}/p_{22})} \tag{20}$$

In sliding mode $s_{ik} = 0$, $e_{ik,D_{11}} = -\lambda_{ik,1}e_{ik,I1}$, and $e_{ik,D_{12}} = -\lambda_{ik,2}e_{ik,I2}$ can always hold true. Therefore, the reaching time of $e_{ik,D_{11}}$ and $e_{ik,D_{12}}$ are the same as the convergence time of $e_{ik,I1}$ and $e_{ik,I2}$, respectively. When $e_{ik,D_{11}} = e_{ik,D_{12}} = 0$, $e_{ik,I1}$ and $e_{ik,I2}$ will converge to zero successfully. At $t = t_{1K}$ (K = 1, 2), the $e_{ik,I1}$ and $e_{ik,I2}$ are formulated by

$$\dot{e}_{ik,D01}(t_{11}) = -\gamma_{ik,1}^{q_{11}/p_{11}}e_{ik,D01}^{q_{11}/p_{11}}(t_{11}), \quad \dot{e}_{ik,D02}(t_{12}) = -\gamma_{ik,2}^{q_{12}/p_{12}}e_{ik,D02}^{q_{12}/p_{12}}(t_{12}). \tag{21}$$

Solving (21), the $\dot{e}_{ik,D01}$, $\dot{e}_{ik,D02}$ from $\dot{e}_{ik,D01}(t_{11})$, $\dot{e}_{ik,D02}(t_{12})$ to $\dot{e}_{ik,D01} = \dot{e}_{ik,D01} = 0$ will spend the time

$$t_{01} = \frac{\left|e_{ik,D01}(0)\right|^{1-q_{11}/p_{11}}}{\gamma_{ik,1}(1-q_{11}/p_{11})}, \quad t_{02} = \frac{\left|e_{ik,D02}(0)\right|^{1-q_{12}/p_{12}}}{\gamma_{ik,2}(1-q_{12}/p_{12})}. \tag{22}$$

Since the sliding mode $s_{ik} = 0$ consists of the derivative term and integral term, the time T_K spending from $s_{ik,K} = 0$ (K = 1, 2) to $e_{ik,K} = 0$ (K = 1, 2) is the summation of the two terms. Since the fact that each sliding mode $s_{ik,1}$, $s_{ik,2}$ is independent, the time spent for equilibrium point is the max of the T_K.

Hypothesis 2. $\| d_{ik} \|_\infty \leq \overline{d}_{ik}$. *It means that the unmatched uncertainties of formation system (13) have a boundary.*

Differentiating the sliding function s_{ik} with the respect to time t, and substituting (13) into the derivative of s_{ik} can get

$$\dot{s}_{ik} = diag\left[\frac{p_{11}}{q_{11}}\dot{e}_{D01}^{(P_{11}/q_{11}-1)}, \frac{p_{12}}{q_{12}}\dot{e}_{D02}^{(P_{12}/q_{12}-1)}\right]\left[d_{ik} + H(x_{ik}, d_{ik})u_k - \ddot{y}_{ik}^d\right] + \phi_{ik}, \tag{23}$$

where $y_{ik}^d = \begin{bmatrix} y_{ik,1}^d & y_{ik,2}^d \end{bmatrix}^T$ denotes the desired distance and angle between the leader robot and follower robots. $\phi_{ik} = \begin{bmatrix} \phi_{ik,1} & \phi_{ik,2} \end{bmatrix}^T$. $\phi_{ik,1}$ and $\phi_{ik,2}$ are depicted respectively by

$$\phi_{ik,1} = \gamma_{ik,1}\dot{e}_{D01} + \lambda_{ik,1}e_{D11}^{q_{21}/p_{21}}, \quad \phi_{ik,2} = \gamma_{ik,2}\dot{e}_{D02} + \lambda_{ik,2}e_{D12}^{q_{22}/p_{22}}. \tag{24}$$

The derivative and integral terminal sliding mode control law is set as

$$\begin{aligned} u &= \hat{H}_{dik}^{-1}\left[\ddot{y}_{ik}^d - k_{eik}\| \phi_{ik} \|diag\left[\frac{q_{11}}{p_{11}}, \frac{q_{12}}{p_{12}}\right]A_{\pi ik}^{-1}\frac{s_{ik}}{\|s_{ik}\|_1}\right] \\ &\quad -H_{ik}^{-1}\left(\overline{d}_{ik}(t) - k_{ik}sign(s_{ik}) - \eta_{ik}s_{ik}\right) \end{aligned}, \tag{25}$$

where $sign(s_{ik}) = sign\begin{bmatrix} s_{ik,1} & s_{ik,2} \end{bmatrix}^T$, k_{eik}, η_{ik} are all the positive constant set by designer. $\overline{d}_{ik}(t)$ is the upper bound of the unmatched uncertainties.

$A_{\pi ik} = \begin{bmatrix} A_{\pi ik,1} & A_{\pi ik,2} \end{bmatrix}^T$, $A_{\pi ik,K}$ (K = 1, 2) are written as

$$A_{\pi ik,K} = \begin{cases} \dot{e}_{ik,0K}^{(p_{1K}/q_{1K}-1)}, for\left|\dot{e}_{ik,0K}^{(p_{1K}/q_{1K}-1)}\right| \geq \varepsilon_{ik} \\ \varepsilon_{ik}, otherwise \end{cases}. \tag{26}$$

Here, $\varepsilon_{ik} > 0$, χ_{ik} and k_{eik} meet the following conditions

$$\left\| \left(A_{\pi ik} - diag\left[\dot{e}_{ik,D01}^{(P_{11}/q_{11}-1)}, \dot{e}_{ik,D02}^{(P_{12}/q_{12}-1)}\right]\right)A_{\pi ik}^{-1} \right\| \leq \chi_{ik} < 1, \tag{27}$$

$$k_{eik} > 1/(1-\chi_{ik}). \tag{28}$$

Substitute the control law (25) into (23), considering the conditions (26). Then, $\dot{V}_{ik} < 0$ can be guaranteed when $k_{iek} > \bar{d}_{ik}$ holds true. However, apart from Hypothesis 2, the unmatched uncertainties d_{ik} in (13) are unknown, which means that the upper bound is also unknown. Therefore, it cannot select an appropriate parameter k_{iek} to guarantee $\dot{V}_{ik} < 0$. Therefore, the stability of control system cannot be guaranteed.

DIT-SMC Design Based NDOB

In order to resolve the above problem, the nonlinear disturbance is proposed to estimate the uncertainties d_{ik} in the leader–follower formation system (13). At first, the following assumption is taken into account.

Hypothesis 3. *The unmatched uncertainties possess a slow change rate, meaning that $\dot{d}_{ik} \approx 0_{2\times1}$, where* $0_{2\times1} = \begin{bmatrix} 0 & 0 \end{bmatrix}^T$.

Considering the formation dynamic model (6), the nonlinear disturbance observer is formulated by

$$\begin{cases} \dot{z}_{ik} = -L_{ik}B_{ik,2}p_{ik} - L_{ik}(B_{ik,2}L_{ik}x_{ik} + A_{ik}x_{ik} + B_{ik,1}(1+\Delta_k)u_k) \\ \hat{d}_{ik} = z_{ik} + L_{ik}x_{ik} \end{cases}. \tag{29}$$

Here $z_{ik} \in R^{2\times1}$, $L_{ik} \in R^{2\times1}$, $\hat{d}_{ik} \in R^{2\times1}$ are the state vector of nonlinear disturbance observer, the observer gain matrix set by designer, and the estimated value of unmatched uncertainties respectively.

Define the estimate error vector as

$$e_{dik} = d_{ik} - \hat{d}_{ik}.$$

Differentiate e_{dik} with respect to time t and take the Hypothesis 3 into account. Furthermore, the dynamics of e_{dik} is presented as

$$\begin{aligned} \dot{e}_{dik} &= \dot{d}_{ik} - \dot{\hat{d}}_{ik} \\ &= -\dot{p}_{ik} - L_{ik}\dot{x}_{ik} \\ &= L_{ik}B_{ik,2}p_{ik} + L_{ik}(B_{ik,2}L_{ik}x_{ik} + A_{ik}x_{ik} + B_{ik,1}(I+\Delta_k)u_k) \\ &\quad -L_{ik}(A_{ik}x_{ik} + B_{ik,1}(I+\Delta_k)u_k + B_{ik,2}d_{ik}) \\ &= L_{ik}B_{ik,2}\left(\hat{d}_{ik} - L_{ik}x_{ik}\right) + L_{ik}(B_{ik,2}L_{ik}x_{ik} + A_{ik}x_{ik} + B_{ik,1}(I+\Delta_k)u_k) \\ &\quad -L_{ik}(B_{ik,2}d_{ik} + A_{ik}x_{ik} + B_{ik,1}(I+\Delta_k)u_k) \\ &= L_{ik}B_{ik,2}\left(\hat{d}_{ik} - d_{ik}\right) = -L_{ik}B_{ik,2}e_{dik} \end{aligned}. \tag{30}$$

The solution of (30) is $e_{dik} = \exp(-L_{ik}B_{ik,2}t)e_{dik}(0)$, which indicates the estimate error will exponentially converge to zero as $t \to \infty$ if $L_{ik}B_{ik,2}$ is set as a positive constant. Here, $e_{dik}(0)$ is the initial state of e_{dik}.

Considering input–output dynamics (13) and observer (29), the control law based on NDOB is determined by

$$\begin{aligned} u &= \hat{H}_{dik}^{-1}\left[\ddot{y}_{ik}^d - k_{eik}\| \phi_{ik} \|diag\left[\frac{q_{11}}{p_{11}}, \frac{q_{12}}{p_{12}}\right]A_{\pi ik}^{-1}\frac{s_{ik}}{\|s_{ik}\|_1}\right] \\ &\quad -H_{ik}^{-1}\left(\hat{d}_{ik}(t) - k_{ik}sign(s_{ik}) - \eta_{ik}s_{ik}\right) \end{aligned}. \tag{31}$$

Theorem 2. *Consider the dynamic model of leader–follower formation system (6), take the assumption 1, 2, 3, 4 into account, adopt the input–output model (13), design the derivative and integral terminal sliding mode surface (17) and nonlinear disturbance observer (29). If the derivative and integral terminal control law is* set as (31), the leader–follower formation system with unmatched uncertainties is asymptotically stable when $k_{iek} > e_d^*$.

Proof. Selecting the Lyapunov function as $V_{ik} = \frac{1}{2}s\dot{s}$, differentiating V_{ik} with the respect to time t and substituting the $\dot{s}_{ik}$ into the derivative of V_{ik} yields

$$
\dot{V}_{ik} = \frac{s_{ik}^T}{\|s_{ik}\|_2} diag\left[\frac{p_{11}}{q_{11}}, \frac{p_{12}}{q_{12}}\right] J_{ik}\left\{ \begin{array}{c} d_{ik} - \hat{d}_{ik} - \eta_{ik}s_{ik} \\ -k_{ik}\text{sgn}(s_{ik}) \end{array} \right\} \\
+ \frac{s_{ik}^T}{\|s_{ik}\|_2}\phi_{ik} - \delta_{ik}k_{eik}\| \phi_{ik} \|s_{ik}^T H \hat{H}_{dik}^{-1} J_{ik} A_{\pi ik}^{-1} \frac{s_{ik}}{\|s_{ik}\|_1 \|s_{ik}\|_2}
\tag{32}
$$

Here, $J_{ik} = diag\left[\dot{e}_{D01}^{(P_{11}/q_{11}-1)}, \dot{e}_{D02}^{(P_{12}/q_{12}-1)}\right]$. Since $p_{1K} > 0$, $q_{1K} > 0$, $p_{2K} > 0$, $q_{2K} > 0$, $p_{1K} > q_{1K}$, $p_{2k} > q_{2K}$ exist in the controller, $\dot{e}_{D01}^{(P_{11}/q_{11}-1)}$ and $\dot{e}_{D02}^{(P_{12}/q_{12}-1)}$ hold true for all $\dot{e}_{D01}^{(P_{11}/q_{11}-1)} \neq 0$, $\dot{e}_{D02}^{(P_{12}/q_{12}-1)} \neq 0$. According to the Hypothesis 1, (27), the second term and the third term can be deduced by

$$
s_{ik}^T\phi_{ik} - \delta_{ik}k_{eik}\| \phi_{ik} \|s_{ik}^T J_{ik} H \hat{H}_{dik}^{-1} A_{\pi ik}^{-1} \frac{s_{ik}}{\|s_{ik}\|} \\
\leq \| \phi_{ik} \|\| s_{ik}^T \| - k_{eik}\| \phi_{ik} \|\| s_{ik}^T \| \\
+k_e\| \phi_{ik} \|\| (A_{\pi ik} - J_{ik})A_{\pi ik}^{-1} \|\| s_{ik} \| \\
\leq \| \phi_{ik} \|\| s_{ik} \| - k_{eik}(1 - \chi_{ik})\| \phi_{ik} \|\| s_{ik} \| \\
\leq 0
\tag{33}
$$

□

In (33), the condition $k_{eik} > 1/(1 - \chi_{ik})$ can be picked up so that the $\| \phi_{ik} \|\| s_{ik} \| - k_{eik}(1 - \chi_{ik})\| \phi_{ik} \|\| s_{ik} \| \leq 0$ holds true.

The first term of $\dot{V}_{ik}$ has the following form of

$$
\frac{s_{ik}^T}{\|s_{ik}\|_2} diag\left[\frac{p_{11}}{q_{11}}, \frac{p_{12}}{q_{12}}\right] J_{ik}\left\{ Z(x_{ik}, d_{ik}) - \hat{d}_{ik} - k_{ik}\text{sgn}(s_{ik}) - \eta_{ik}s_{ik} \right\} \\
\leq \min\left\{ diag\left[\frac{p_{11}}{q_{11}}, \frac{p_{12}}{q_{12}}\right] J_{ik}\right\}\left(-k_{ik}\frac{\|s_{ik}\|_1}{\|s_{ik}\|_2} - \eta_{ik}\frac{\|s_{ik}\|_2^2}{\|s_{ik}\|_2} + \frac{s^T}{\|s_{ik}\|_2}\left[\begin{array}{c} \| e_{dik} \|_\infty \\ \| e_{dik} \|_\infty \end{array} \right] \right) \\
\leq \min\left\{ diag\left[\frac{p_{11}}{q_{11}}, \frac{p_{12}}{q_{12}}\right] J_{ik}\right\}\left(-k_{ik}\frac{\|s_{ik}\|_1}{\|s_{ik}\|_2} - \eta_{ik}\frac{\|s_{ik}\|_2^2}{\|s_{ik}\|_2} + \frac{\|s_{ik}\|_1}{\|s_{ik}\|_2}\| e_{dik} \|_\infty \right) \\
= \min\left\{ diag\left[\frac{p_{11}}{q_{11}}, \frac{p_{12}}{q_{12}}\right] J_{ik}\right\}\left(-(k_{ik} - \| e_{dik} \|_\infty)\frac{\|s_{ik}\|_1}{\|s_{ik}\|_2} - \eta_{ik}\frac{\|s_{ik}\|_2^2}{\|s_{ik}\|_2} \right)
\tag{34}
$$

$\eta_{ik} > 0$, $k_{ik} > \| e_{dik} \|_\infty$ can be selected in the control design in order to ensure $\frac{s_{ik}^T}{\|s_{ik}\|_2} diag\left[\frac{p_{11}}{q_{11}}, \frac{p_{12}}{q_{12}}\right] J_{ik}\left\{ \begin{array}{c} Z(x_{ik}, d_{ik}) - \hat{d}_{ik} \\ -k_{ik}\text{sgn}(s_{ik}) \\ -\eta_{ik}s_{ik} \end{array} \right\} \leq 0$ is held true.

$\dot{V}_{ik} < 0$ can be picked up by deducing from (32)–(34). That illustrates the control law can asymptotically stabilize the leader–follower formation system by the derivative and integral terminal sliding mode. Therefore, the follower robots can trace the leader robot with the desired distance and angle steadily. The characteristics of DIT-SMC method are as follows: (1) the convergence time T_k can be adjusted by the parameters of the control law; (2) the formation system starts on the derivative and integral terminal sliding surface; (3) the singular problem of T-SMC is avoided; (4) the derivative term can weaken the nonlinear effect.

In (31), the parameter must be assigned as a conservative value to guarantee the formation system stability. From (30), e_{dik} can be exponentially convergent to $0_{2\times1}$ by selecting L_{ik}, meaning that κ_{ik} can be very small. Even if κ_{ik} is assigned from a conservative perspective, its value may not be very large. That illustrates the DIT-SMC based NDOB control law protects the formation from the high switching frequency problem, and can substantially alleviate the chattering problem.

4. Numerical Simulations

Considering the dynamic model of the leader–follower formation system (6), the derivative and integral terminal sliding mode controller is proposed. There are three robots in the leader–follower framework, where the two follower robots track along with the leader robot. The radius of each robot is 0.05 m. The parameter fluctuations in formation system are determined by

$$\Delta_i = \Delta_k = \begin{bmatrix} 0.3rand() - 0.15 & 0 \\ 0 & 0.3rand() - 0.15 \end{bmatrix}, \tag{35}$$

where $i = 1$ denotes the leader robot, and $k = 2, 3$ represent the two follower robots. The uncertainties and external disturbances in lumped model (6) are depicted by

$$\begin{aligned} \pi_{ix} = \pi_{iy} = \pi_{i\theta} = 0.5\sin(2\pi t) \\ \pi_{kx} = \pi_{ky} = \pi_{k\theta} = 0.2\sin(\pi t) \end{aligned} \tag{36}$$

The parameters in control design are set as $\gamma_{12,1} = \gamma_{12,2} = \gamma_{13,1} = \gamma_{13,2} = 4$, $\lambda_{12,1} = \lambda_{12,2} = \lambda_{13,1} = \lambda_{13,2} = 1$, $p_{11} = p_{12} = 9$, $q_{11} = q_{12} = 7$, $q_{21} = 3$, $p_{21} = 5$, $q_{22} = 7$, $p_{22} = 9$, $k_{e12} = k_{e13} = 20$, $\varepsilon_{12} = \varepsilon_{13} = 4$, $k_{12} = k_{13} = 2$, $\delta_{12} = \delta_{13} = 4$, $\eta_{12} = \eta_{13} = 0.2$.

Considering the circle trajectory for the formation system in Figure 3, the initial state vector is respectively set as $x_{12}^0 = [0.5 \text{ m } 0 \text{ m/s}^{-1} 3.2\pi/4 \text{ rad } 0 \text{ rad/s}]$, $x_{13}^0 = [0.707 \text{ m } 0 \text{ m/s}^{-1} 3\pi/4 \text{ rad } 0 \text{ rad/s}]$. The desired state vectors are respectively designated as $x_{12}^d = [0.13 \text{ m } 0 \text{ m/s}^{-1} \pi/2 \text{ rad } 0 \text{ rad/s}]$, $x_{13}^d = [0.26 \text{ m } 0 \text{ m/s}^{-1} \pi/2 \text{ rad } 0 \text{ rad/s}]$. The desired linear and angular velocities of leader robot are designated as $v_1^d = 0.5 \text{ m}$, $w_1^d = 1 \text{ rad/s}$. The simulation results are shown in Figures 4–6.

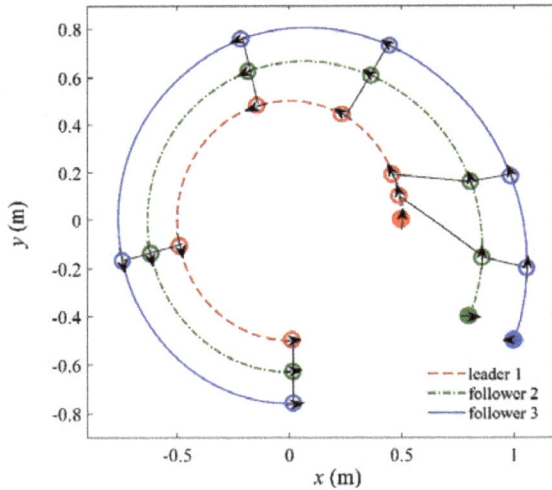

Figure 3. Moving trajectory of leader–follower formation system.

Figure 3 displays the moving curve of the formation system, which shows the robots are in a line while moving along the circular trajectory. In Figure 3, the solid point denotes the initial position of the formation robots. The arrows are the moving directions of the three robots. It is seen form the Figure 3 that the follower can track the leader robot with the desired distance and angle, while the leader robot tracks the circular trajectory.

In order to provide more insight into the system performance, some comparisons among the SMC method, the second-order SMC, the SMC based NDOB [18], and the DIT-SMC based NDOB are shown in Figures 4–6. The parameters of the sole SMC and SMC based NDOB method are presented in [18], and the parameters of second-order SMC are same as paper [20]. The relative distance and relative angular between the leader robot 1 and the two follower robots 2, 3 are displayed in Figure 4. Comparing with the SMC method, the second-order SMC and the SMC based NDOB, the DIT-SMC based NDOB method has shorter convergence time and smoother than the other methods.

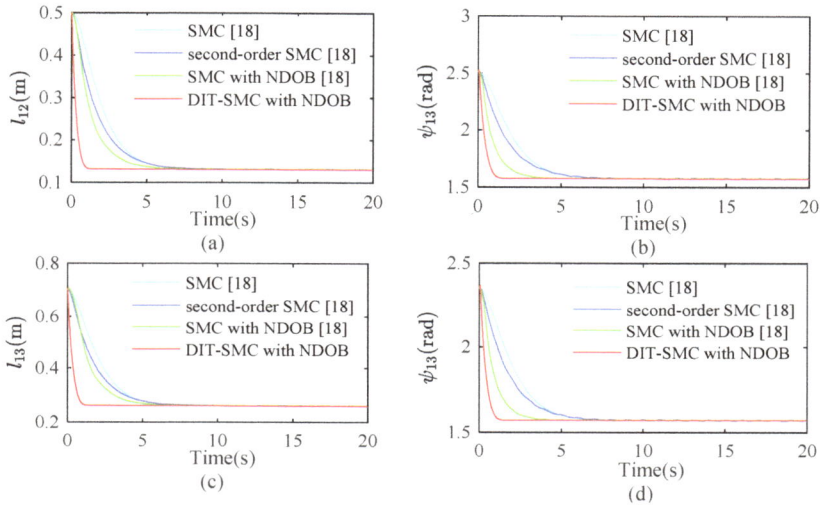

Figure 4. Relative distance and anger of leader–follower framework; (a) l_{12}; (b) ψ_{12}; (c) l_{13}; (d) ψ_{13}.

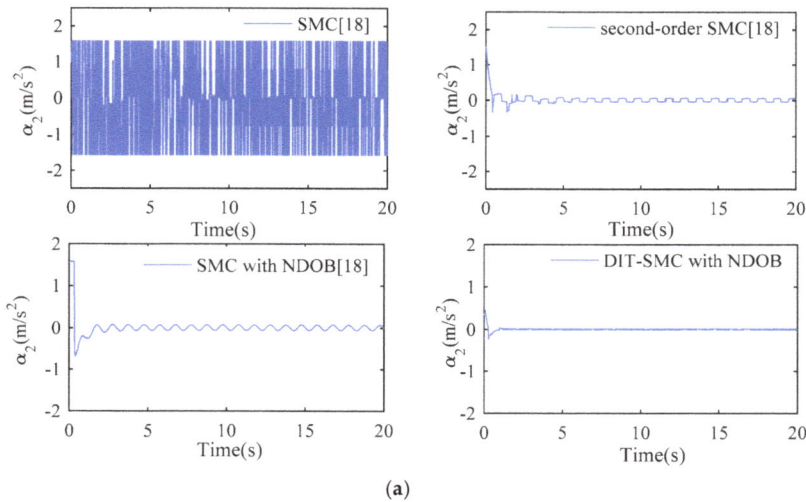

(a)

Figure 5. *Cont.*

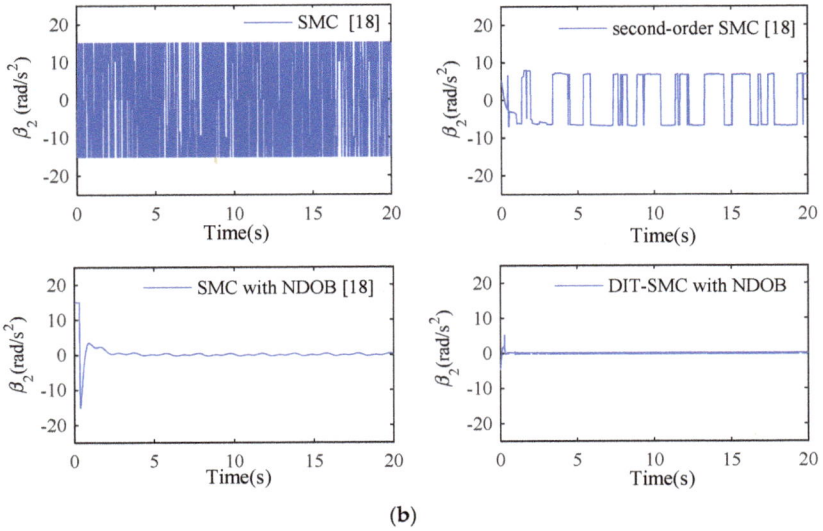

(b)

Figure 5. The acceleration and angular acceleration of follower robot 2; (**a**) α_2; (**b**) β_2.

Figure 5 denotes the control input of follower robot 2 using different control method. In Figure 5a, the acceleration of follower robot 2 are shown, while the angular accelerations of follower robot 2 are displayed in Figure 5b. From Figure 5a,b, the control input of DIT-SMC based NDOB is smoother than other control methods, which denotes the acceleration and angular acceleration are more stable.

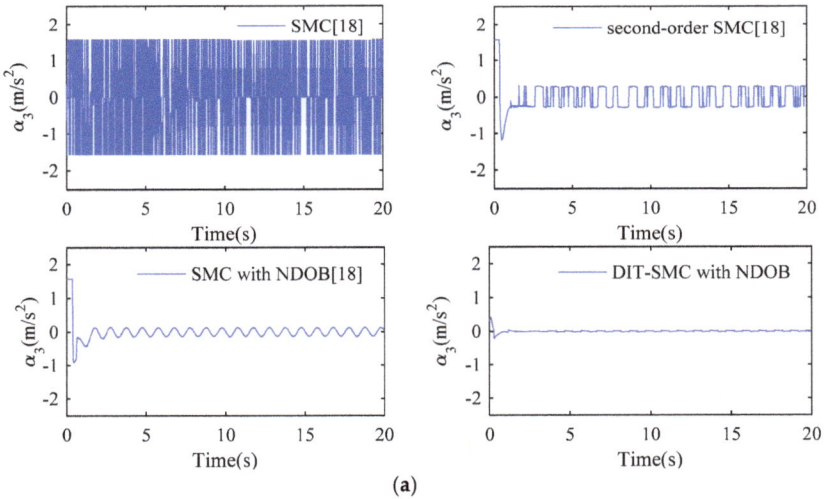

(a)

Figure 6. *Cont.*

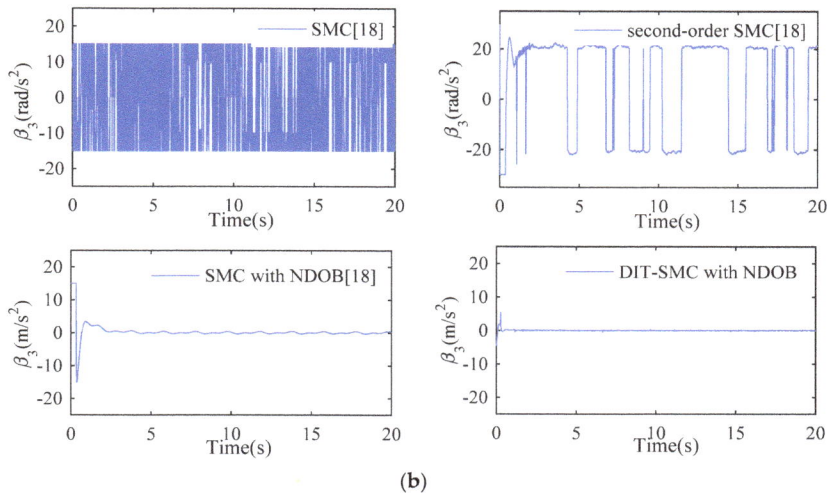

Figure 6. The acceleration and angular acceleration of follower robot 3; (a) α_3; (b) β_3.

The control inputs of follower robot 3 are shown in the Figure 6, which denotes the acceleration and angular acceleration of follower robot 3. The accelerations of follower robot of follower robot using the three control methods are displayed in Figure 6a, while the angular acceleration using three methods are shown in Figure 6b. From Figures 5 and 6, the combination of the DIT-SMC and NDOB can benefit the decrease of the chattering phenomenon that is an inherent drawback of the SMC methodology.

Figure 7 denotes the sliding mode vectors of two follower robots. As proven in the Theorem 1, the reaching time of sliding surface will be eliminated, and the error of formation system will reach to the equilibrium point in the finite time. From Figure 7, the formation system can enter the sliding mode in the beginning, which can guarantee the system stability.

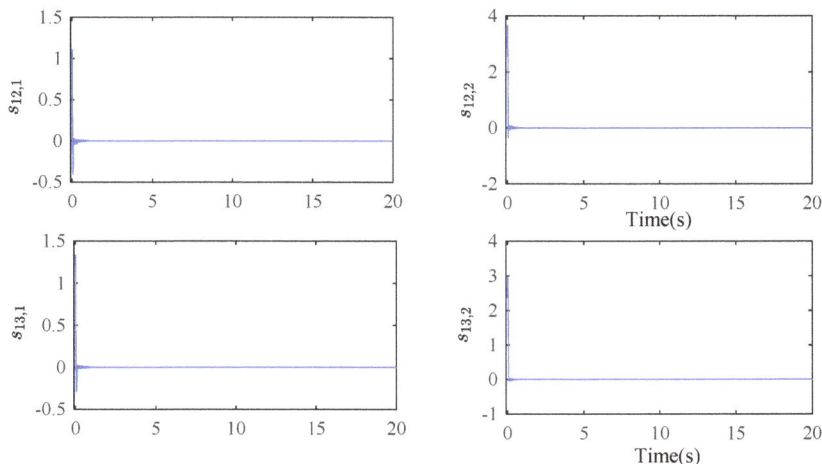

Figure 7. The sliding surface.

Figure 8 illustrates the elements of the estimate-error vectors, where the vectors ed_{12} are shown in the Figure 8a, and the vectors ed_{13} are shown in the Figure 8b. From the Figure 8, the estimate-error can converge to zero in the finite time. The value of estimate-error is max when $t = 0$, that is, the maximum is less than 0.5. However, the value of k_{ik} is selected 2. Therefore, the system stability can be guaranteed.

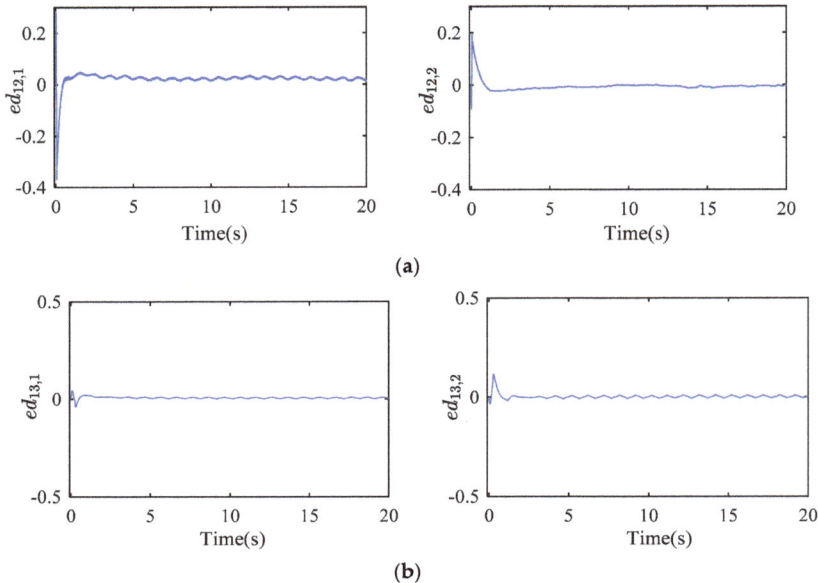

(a)

(b)

Figure 8. Estimate-error (**a**) ed_{12}; (**b**) ed_{13}.

5. Conclusions

This paper investigates the formation control problem of multi-robot systems based on the leader–follower mechanism. The leader–follower formation system becomes uncertain because of some adverse effects, such as the parameter fluctuations, external disturbances, and so on. In order to estimate the uncertainties, a control scheme, combining the DIT-SMC and the NDOB, is proposed under the assumption that the uncertainties have an unknown boundary. The stability of the control scheme is proven in the light of Lyapunov theorem. Some simulation results are demonstrated to show the feasibility of the control scheme.

Author Contributions: Methodology, D.Q.; Software, Y.X.; D.Q. contributed theoretical analysis and Y.X. performed the numerical experiments.

Funding: The work is supported by the National Natural Science Foundation of China (61473176) and the Fundamental Research Funds for the Central Universities (2018MS025).

Conflicts of Interest: The authors declare no conflict of interest.

References

1. Dai, Y.; Kim, Y.; Wee, S.; Lee, D.; Lee, S. Symmetric caging formation for convex polygonal object transportation by multiple mobile robots based on fuzzy sliding mode control. *ISA Trans.* **2016**, *60*, 321–332. [CrossRef] [PubMed]
2. Li, C.D.; Gao, J.L.; Yi, J.Q.; Zhang, G.Q. Analysis and design of functionally weighted single-input-rule-modules connected fuzzy inference systems. *IEEE Trans. Fuzzy Syst.* **2018**, *26*, 56–71. [CrossRef]

3. Qian, D.W.; Li, C.D. Formation control for uncertain multiple robots by adaptive integral sliding mode. *J. Intell. Fuzzy Syst.* **2016**, *31*, 3021–3028. [CrossRef]

4. Loria, A.; Dasdemir, J.; Jarquin, N.A. Leader-follower formation and tracking control of mobile robots along straight paths. *IEEE Trans. Control Syst. Technol.* **2016**, *24*, 727–732. [CrossRef]

5. Li, C.D.; Ding, Z.X.; Zhao, D.B.; Yi, J.Q.; Zhang, G.Q. Building energy consumption prediction: An extreme deep learning approach. *Energies* **2017**, *10*, 1525. [CrossRef]

6. Li, C.D.; Ding, Z.X.; Yi, J.Q.; Lv, Y.S.; Zhang, G.Q. Deep belief network based hybrid model for building energy consumption prediction. *Energies* **2018**, *11*, 242. [CrossRef]

7. Biglarbegian, M. A novel robust leader-following control design for mobile robots. *J. Intell. Robot. Syst.* **2013**, *71*, 391–402. [CrossRef]

8. Dai, Y.; Lee, S.G. The leader-follower formation control of nonholonomic mobile robots. *Int. J. Control Autom. Syst.* **2012**, *10*, 350–361. [CrossRef]

9. Mehrjerdi, H.; Ghommam, J.; Saad, M. Nonlinear coordination control for a group of mobile robots using a virtual structure. *Mechatronics* **2011**, *21*, 1147–1155. [CrossRef]

10. Li, J.; Wang, J.; Pan, Q.; Duan, P.; Sang, H.; Gao, K.; Xue, Y. A hybrid artificial bee colony for optimizing a reverse logistics network system. *Soft Comput.* **2017**, *21*, 6001–6018. [CrossRef]

11. Qian, D.W.; Tong, S.W.; Li, C.D. Observer-based leader-following formation control of uncertain multiple agents by integral sliding mode. *Bull. Pol. Acad. Sci. Tech. Sci.* **2017**, *65*, 35–44. [CrossRef]

12. Qian, D.W.; Tong, S.W.; Lee, S.G. Fuzzy-Logic-based control of payloads subjected to double-pendulum motion in overhead cranes. *Autom. Constr.* **2016**, *65*, 133–143. [CrossRef]

13. Fax, J.A.; Murray, R.M. Information flow and cooperative control of vehicle formations. *IEEE Trans. Autom. Control* **2004**, *49*, 1465–1476. [CrossRef]

14. Lin, Z.Y.; Francis, B.; Maggiore, M. Necessary and sufficient graphical conditions for formation control of unicycles. *IEEE Trans. Autom. Control* **2005**, *50*, 121–127.

15. Lawton, J.T.; Beard, R.W.; Young, B.J. A decentralized approach to formation maneuvers. *IEEE Trans. Robot. Autom.* **2003**, *19*, 933–941. [CrossRef]

16. Liang, H.Z.; Sun, Z.W.; Wang, J.Y. Finite-time attitude synchronization controllers design for spacecraft formations via behaviour based approach. *Proc. Inst. Mech. Eng. Part G J. Aerosp. Eng.* **2013**, *227*, 1737–1753. [CrossRef]

17. Li, J.; Sang, H.; Han, Y.; Wang, C.; Gao, K. Efficient multi-objective optimization algorithm for hybrid flow shop scheduling problems with setup energy consumptions. *J. Clean. Prod.* **2018**, *181*, 584–598. [CrossRef]

18. Qian, D.W.; Tong, S.W.; Li, C.D. Leader-following formation control of multiple robots with uncertainties through sliding mode and nonlinear disturbance observer. *ETRI J.* **2016**, *38*, 1008–1018. [CrossRef]

19. Park, B.S.; Park, J.B.; Choi, Y.H. Robust formation control of electrically driven nonholonomic mobile robots via sliding mode technique. *Int. J. Control Autom. Syst.* **2011**, *9*, 888–894. [CrossRef]

20. Defoort, M.; Floquet, T.; Kokosy, A.; Perruquetti, W. Sliding-mode formation control for cooperative autonomous mobile robots. *IEEE Trans. Ind. Electron.* **2008**, *55*, 3944–3953. [CrossRef]

21. Chen, X.; Jia, Y. Adaptive Leader-follower formation control of non-holonomic mobile robots using active vision. *IET Control Theory Appl.* **2014**, *9*, 1302–1311. [CrossRef]

22. Park, B.S.; Park, J.B.; Choi, Y.H. Adaptive formation control of electrically driven non-holonomic mobile robots with Limited Information. *IEEE Trans. Syst. Man Cybern. B Cybern.* **2011**, *41*, 1061–1075. [CrossRef] [PubMed]

23. Howard, T. Model-predictive motion planning several key developments for autonomous mobile robots. *IEEE Robot Autom. Mag.* **2014**, *21*, 64–73. [CrossRef]

24. Muhammad, A.; Muhammad, J.K.; Attaullah, Y.M. Integral terminal sliding mode formation control of non-holonomic robots using leader follower approach. *Robotica* **2017**, *35*, 1473–1487.

25. Nair, R.R.; Karki, H.; Shukla, A.; Behera, L.; Jamshidi, M. Fault-tolerant formation control of nonholonomic robots using fast adaptive gain nonsingular terminal sliding mode control. *IEEE Syst. J.* **2018**. [CrossRef]

26. Qian, D.W.; Tong, S.W.; Liu, H.; Liu, X.J. Load frequency control by neural-network-based integral sliding mode for nonlinear power systems with wind turbines. *Neurocomputing* **2016**, *173*, 875–885. [CrossRef]

27. Zhao, L.; Jia, Y.M. Neural network-based distributed adaptive attitude synchronization control of spacecraft formation under modified fast terminal sliding mode. *Neurocomputing* **2016**, *171*, 230–241. [CrossRef]

28. Qian, D.W.; Tong, S.W.; Guo, J.R.; Lee, S.G. Leader-follower-based formation control of non-holonomic mobile robots with mismatched uncertainties via integral sliding mode. *Proc. Inst. Mech. Eng. Part I J. Syst. Control Eng.* **2015**, *229*, 559–569. [CrossRef]
29. Nair, R.R. Multi-satellite formation control for remote sensing applications using artificial potential field and adaptive fuzzy sliding mode control. *IEEE Syst. J.* **2015**, *9*, 508–518. [CrossRef]
30. Chiu, C.S. Derivative and integral terminal sliding mode control for a class of MIMO nonlinear systems. *Automatica* **2012**, *48*, 316–326. [CrossRef]

Article

Exploration of Swarm Dynamics Emerging from Asymmetry

Naoki Nishikawa * [ID]**, Reiji Suzuki and Takaya Arita**

Department of Complex Systems Science, Graduate School of Information Science, Nagoya University, Furo-cho, Chikusa-ku, Nagoya 464-0814, Japan; reiji@nagoya-u.jp (R.S.); arita@nagoya-u.jp (T.A.)
* Correspondence: nishikawa@alife.cs.is.nagoya-u.ac.jp; Tel.: +81-52-789-3503

Received: 5 March 2018; Accepted: 27 April 2018; Published: 5 May 2018

Abstract: A swarm might exhibit interesting motions or structures when it includes different types of agents. On a swarm model named Swarm Chemistry, some interesting patterns can appear if the parameters are well-tuned. However, there is a hurdle for us to get capable of tuning the parameters by automatic searching methods like a genetic algorithm, particularly because defining interestingness itself is a challenging issue. This paper aims to investigate how interesting patterns can be detected, comparing seven measures from an aspect of system asymmetries. Based on numerical experiments, the effects of changing kinetic parameters are discussed, finding that: (1) segregating patterns, which are frequently observed but uninteresting, tend to appear when the perception range is small and normal (ideal) speed is large or when cohesive force is weak and separating force is strong; (2) asymmetry of information transfer represented by topological connectivity is an effective way to characterize the interestingness; (3) pulsation-like patterns can be captured well by using time-derivative of state variables like network-degrees; (4) it helps capture a gradual structural deformation when fitness function adopts the mean over min-max differences of state variables. The findings will help the efficient search of already-discovered or undiscovered interesting swarm dynamics.

Keywords: swarm behavior; Swarm Chemistry; self-organization; asymmetrical interaction; genetic algorithm

1. Introduction

Collective behaviors of swarms can be seen in nature, e.g., ant swarms, birds flocks and fish schools, as well as in human society around us. It is an interesting fact that, without having either a very sophisticated intelligence in each component, nor a centralized mechanism to control them, unexpected patterns or dynamics sometimes appear if once they gather in numbers. Each component member in such swarms usually acts based on some simple recognition, decision and action rules. In this paper, we call such a component an agent.

1.1. Swarm Robotics

There have been a lot of work to simulate and analyze swarming behaviors or structures using computational models (e.g., [1–3]). One of the best-known swarm models is Reynolds' Boids [4]. The motions of agents are governed only by three simple interaction rules among agents: cohesion, separation and alignment. In spite of its simplicity of interaction, agents can self-organize into some interesting formation patterns like bird swarms.

From an engineering perspective, there have been many studies in the field of swarm robotics to promote practical applications of swarm behaviors. For example, swarm models can be applied to control design of autonomous robots like unmanned ground vehicles (UGVs), aerial vehicles (UAVs) and marine vehicles (UMVs) exploited in disaster situations [5].

1.2. Heterogeneity of Swarm

What happens if a swarm includes different types of agents within it? It is expected that a swarm might exhibit or form much more interesting behaviors than when it is composed of agents all with the same character. Based on the Boids rules, Sayama introduced some extensions and established a swarm model called Swarm Chemistry (SC) [6–13]. Its most notable feature is that it allows the coexistence of different types of agents in the same swarm. The self-organized patterns or behaviors emerging in this model are pretty attractive. An example of heterogeneous swarm appearing in SC simulator, is shown in Figure 1, which is composed of three different types. In addition, a useful interactive graphical user interface (GUI) tool of SC is open to everyone on Sayama's website [14], where one can try to "design" swarms of his/her own preference. This tool helps users create swarms and adjust parameters. Charming swarm patterns appear when the parameters could be well-adjusted. Some of them are listed in Figure 2. To support the readers' visual understanding, animations of these swarms are prepared as a Supplementary Material, Video S1. The details of Swarm Chemistry will be described in the next section.

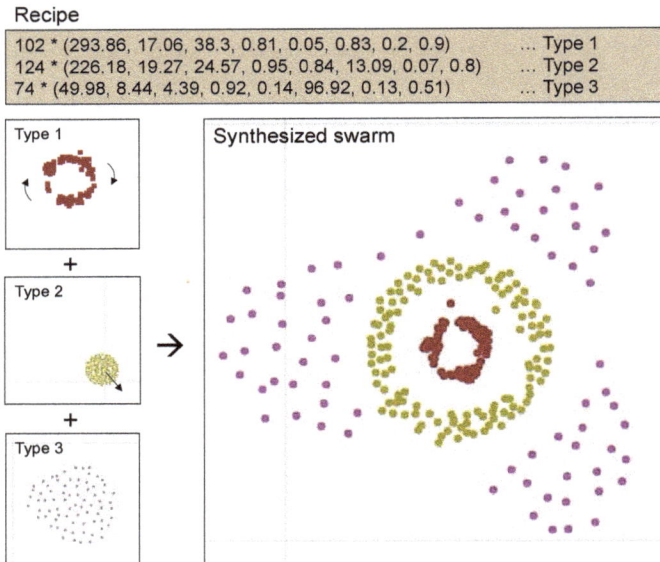

Recipe

102 * (293.86, 17.06, 38.3, 0.81, 0.05, 0.83, 0.2, 0.9)	... Type 1
124 * (226.18, 19.27, 24.57, 0.95, 0.84, 13.09, 0.07, 0.8)	... Type 2
74 * (49.98, 8.44, 4.39, 0.92, 0.14, 96.92, 0.13, 0.51)	... Type 3

Figure 1. Example recipe of a swarm composed of three different types of agent.

No.	Recipe name	Recipe	Snapshot	Classification of motion
1	Linear Oscillator	133 * (214.41, 17.93, 35.14, 0.64, 0.13, 0.29, 0.08, 0.97) 24 * (253.6, 7.19, 15.51, 0.82, 0.33, 32.65, 0.34, 0.56)		Reciprocating
2	Blobs	300 * (20.8, 1.95, 20.75, 0.95, 0.99, 9.31, 0.05, 0.68)		Clustered
3	Turbulent Runner	131 * (177.1, 9.71, 30.06, 0.8, 0.43, 19.65, 0.45, 0.91) 169 * (277.3, 14.67, 37.71, 0.68, 0.23, 77.01, 0.02, 0.31)		Tracting
4	Wedding Ring	24 * (220.51, 13.88, 3.47, 0.46, 0.38, 6.23, 0.19, 0.68) 13 * (64.07, 1.4, 19.7, 0.88, 0.27, 0.36, 0.47, 0.72) 35 * (117.53, 7.31, 21.72, 0.3, 0.5, 98.69, 0.03, 0.29)		Tracting
5	Rotary	29 * (122.13, 19.19, 17.98, 0.65, 0.44, 19.88, 0.46, 0.2) 51 * (299.13, 0.79, 38.71, 0.25, 0.18, 86.49, 0.38, 0.43) 10 * (252.92, 19.99, 10.21, 0.23, 0.17, 1.22, 0.28, 0.92)		Rotating
6	Swinger	48 * (150.39, 15.89, 23.54, 0.74, 0.45, 62.65, 0.33, 0.13) 152 * (217.14, 12.13, 12.42, 0.59, 0.98, 14.06, 0.04, 0.65) 14 * (248.54, 5.85, 22.26, 0.43, 0.11, 17.14, 0.06, 0.68) 31 * (141.53, 2.91, 4.86, 0.92, 0.03, 21.87, 0.28, 0.2)		Tracting
7	Fast Walker, Slow Follower	67 * (216.35, 11.75, 7.7, 0.83, 0.97, 97.31, 0.02, 0.38) 29 * (254.64, 7.28, 7.0, 0.95, 0.11, 22.41, 0.43, 0.31) 13 * (105.4, 3.55, 5.24, 0.34, 0.18, 23.53, 0.39, 0.24)		Tracting
8	Aggressive Predetor	18 * (211.92, 12.59, 19.37, 0.09, 0.21, 57.92, 0.0, 0.95) 41 * (257.27, 14.96, 35.66, 0.2, 0.8, 47.81, 0.13, 0.13) 35 * (262.68, 2.82, 38.32, 0.21, 0.01, 54.93, 0.11, 0.19) 31 * (78.58, 5.7, 33.23, 0.89, 0.18, 45.44, 0.04, 0.05) 7 * (194.21, 12.88, 21.68, 0.97, 0.19, 99.21, 0.5, 0.13)		Reciprocating
9	Chaos Cells	144 * (109.03, 6.71, 12.7, 0.47, 0.6, 61.43, 0.02, 0.21) 89 * (117.15, 16.33, 31.88, 0.39, 0.13, 12.96, 0.48, 0.8) 67 * (76.3, 8.59, 26.57, 0.7, 0.64, 28.39, 0.3, 0.35)		Clustered
10	Pulsating Eye	102 * (293.86, 17.06, 38.3, 0.81, 0.05, 0.83, 0.2, 0.9) 124 * (226.18, 19.27, 24.57, 0.95, 0.84, 13.09, 0.07, 0.8) 74 * (49.98, 8.44, 4.39, 0.92, 0.14, 96.92, 0.13, 0.51)		Pulsating
11	Playing Catch	76 * (84.06, 0.09, 9.89, 0.33, 0.32, 15.66, 0.22, 0.68) 100 * (158.86, 18.4, 24.98, 0.3, 0.3, 1.72, 0.06, 0.37)		Rotating
12	Recombining Blobs	132 * (45.91, 10.82, 21.11, 0.86, 0.13, 42.48, 0.32, 0.74) 84 * (113.26, 3.41, 25.71, 0.4, 0.39, 49.53, 0.13, 0.24)		Clustered
13	No Wait This Way	60 * (262.68, 2.82, 38.32, 0.21, 0.01, 54.93, 0.11, 0.19) 40 * (78.58, 5.7, 33.23, 0.89, 0.18, 45.44, 0.04, 0.05) 40 * (257.27, 14.96, 35.66, 0.2, 0.8, 47.81, 0.13, 0.13)		Reciprocating
14	Jelly Fish	134 * (262.65, 12.01, 25.87, 0.97, 1.0, 56.35, 0.26, 0.61) 67 * (288.17, 6.19, 23.37, 0.95, 1.0, 1.31, 0.1, 0.9) 68 * (150.5, 12.97, 15.87, 0.46, 0.39, 57.95, 0.17, 0.48)		Tracting
15	Muliticellularity	99 * (19.8, 15.73, 2.61, 0.85, 0.64, 10.51, 0.17, 0.06) 48 * (300.0, 14.63, 0.0, 0.48, 0.81, 90.27, 0.25, 0.78) 37 * (275.18, 16.9, 7.05, 0.48, 0.81, 90.27, 0.17, 0.85) 8 * (159.59, 2.09, 24.19, 0.96, 0.59, 76.03, 0.01, 0.07) 42 * (73.07, 1.82, 2.36, 0.27, 0.61, 40.55, 0.22, 0.86)		Cell-like
16	Cell With Two Nuclei	41 * (249.84, 4.85, 28.73, 0.34, 0.45, 14.44, 0.09, 0.82) 26 * (277.87, 15.02, 35.48, 0.68, 0.05, 82.96, 0.46, 0.9) 30 * (277.87, 15.02, 24.44, 0.68, 0.05, 82.96, 0.43, 0.9) 28 * (110.8, 16.12, 38.6, 0.18, 0.34, 14.3, 0.01, 0.01) 48 * (83.79, 13.29, 7.54, 0.08, 0.79, 1.07, 0.15, 0.45) 74 * (269.64, 6.62, 34.69, 0.36, 0.5, 30.2, 0.03, 0.23)		Cell-like
17	Insurmountable Wall	42 * (52.57, 9.91, 20.42, 0.32, 0.76, 1.8, 0.01, 0.64) 25 * (84.87, 8.82, 24.98, 0.91, 0.44, 40.97, 0.18, 0.6) 45 * (220.42, 4.65, 7.53, 0.96, 0.35, 46.18, 0.25, 1.0) 49 * (279.64, 10.29, 35.95, 0.37, 0.49, 38.09, 0.32, 0.89)		Rotating

Figure 2. Already found interesting patterns (recipe names and values were taken from [14] and snapshots were reproduced by the authors). Classification of motions, which will appear again in Table 3, has been added originally in this paper. For animations of these swarms, see Supplementary Material, Video S1.

1.3. Issues to be Addressed

As stated above, SC is an excellent model. Yet, the potential of the emergence of interesting patterns in SC has not been totally revealed and leveraged. For a more comprehensive exploration of this model, an automated way of searching is necessary because the parameter space is so large that finding patterns manually almost impossible. However, another problem arises. Automatic searching such as genetic algorithm (GA) requires a quantitative measure (a fitness function). As of now, such parameters need to be searched through manual try-and-error depending on user's sense without any objective measures. It is not easy to identify the parameters to create interesting patterns systematically. The main reason is that defining "interestingness" itself is a quite difficult problem.

1.4. Past Approaches

Sayama also tried an evolutionary and automated way of letting interesting patterns appear [13,15,16], by introducing additional rules to the original version of SC, which is called the evolutionary SC (ESC). The major points of ESC model include that [13]:

- an agent has either active or inactive (passive) state, meaning it is moving and has a recipe in it, or it is staying still and has no recipe, respectively.
- a recipe is transmitted from an active agent to another passive agent when these two agents collide, making the latter active.
- the active agent differentiates at random into either type defined in the recipe.
- the direction of recipe transmission is determined by some competition mechanisms.

As a result, in ESC model, the recipe of a swarm can change dynamically and continuously, enabling interesting swarms can appear here and there within the simulation space. This means, a swarm can "evolve" in a single simulation run. However, this method aims to reproduce the evolution process in the natural world, principally for scientific purposes. A comprehensive search using explicit fitness functions is not carried out.

To enable systematic search, Nishikawa et al. proposed a GA-based framework to optimize parameters based on SC [17]. It is for the real-world tasks to be realized by the swarm robots and the fitness functions are comparatively objective. For the case of the present paper, however, we need to quantify how interesting the self-organized swarm is, as a fitness function, which is quite challenging because the recognition, creation and designing of these patterns depend on subjective senses of a human.

Regarding how to measure the interestingness, Sayama has tried to measure the interestingness of swarm using 24 different metrics based on the average or the variation of kinetic outcomes (including agent positions and velocities). and topological outcomes (including number of connected components, average size of connected components, clustering coefficient, and link density) [18,19]. From the Monte Carlo simulation results he demonstrated that the interaction between different types of agents (heterogeneity) helped produce dynamic behaviors. Also, statistically significant differences were detected for most of the outcome variables, especially for topological variables. However, it is still challenging to make a complete answer what is the effective metric.

1.5. Structure of This Paper

This paper aims to investigate how an interesting pattern can be detected, introducing seven explicit metrics from an aspect of system asymmetries. Parameter search is done using GA. Based on numerical experiments, the effects of kinetic parameters and major points to capture characteristic dynamics are discussed.

This paper is composed as follows. In Section 2, the basic description of Swarm Chemistry will be provided. Then Section 3 will present an optimization scheme to search such recipes to generate interesting structures or motion. Next, in Section 4, several possible measures to quantify the swarm structure or dynamics will be presented. Subsequently, Section 5 will show the optimization results obtained from the experiments. After that, Section 6 will give a brief overview on the results and analysis of the especially interesting patterns obtained. Finally, Section 7 will conclude the whole paper.

2. Basic Algorithm of Swarm Chemistry

SC is an extended version of one of the best-known swarm models, Boids [4], in which the motions of agents are controlled only by three simple interaction rules among agents: cohesion, separation and alignment. The entire set of kinetic rules in Boids are:

- Straying If there are no other agents within its local perception range, steer randomly.
- Cohesion (c_1) Steer to move toward the average position of nearby agents.
- Alignment (c_2) Steer toward the average velocity of nearby agents.
- Separation (c_3) Steer to avoid collision with nearby agents.
- Randomness (c_4) Steer randomly with a given probability.
- Self-propulsion (c_5) Approximate its speed to its own normal speed.

Algorithm 1 describes the kinetic rules to govern the movement of agents in SC in more detail [9]. $\vec{x}_i$, $\vec{v}_i$, $\vec{v}'_i$ and $\vec{a}_i$ are the location, the current velocity, the next velocity, and the acceleration of the i-th agent, respectively. r and $r_{\pm p}$ are random numbers in $[0, 1)$ and $[-p, +p)$, respectively. The interaction properties of an agent are described by 8 kinetic parameters (KPs) denoted as follows.

$$(R, \ V_n, \ V_m, \ c_1, \ c_2, \ c_3, \ c_4, \ c_5) \tag{1}$$

The definitions, units and their possible values are summarized in Table 1. Especially, KP4, KP5 and KP6 are the coefficients for the three effects: cohesion, alignment and separation, respectively. They are used to calculate the acceleration of the agent. So their units should be consistent with that of acceleration, i.e., (Pixel · Step^{-2}). For example, KP4 has a unit of (Step^{-2}), because the first term on the right on Line 8 of Algorithm 1,

$$(\langle \vec{x} \rangle - \vec{x}_i) \, , \tag{2}$$

has a unit of position, i.e., (Pixel).

Table 1. Kinetic parameters (KP) in a recipe to control agent behaviors [9]. Each agent is assigned unique values in its recipe.

KP	Name	Min	Max	Definition	Unit
KP1 (β_1)	R^i	0	300	Radius of local perception range	Pixel
KP2 (β_2)	V_n^i	0	20	Normal speed	Pixel Step^{-1}
KP3 (β_3)	V_m^i	0	40	Maximum speed	Pixel Step^{-1}
KP4 (β_4)	c_1^i	0	1	Coefficient for cohesive effect	Step^{-2}
KP5 (β_5)	c_2^i	0	1	Coefficient for aligning effect	Step^{-1}
KP6 (β_6)	c_3^i	0	100	Coefficient for separating effect	Pixel^2 Step^{-2}
KP7 (β_7)	c_4^i	0	0.5	Probability of random steering	–
KP8 (β_8)	c_5^i	0	1	Tendency of self-propulsion	–

In Boids, all the parameters are shared over all the agents. In SC, unlike Boids, each agent is assigned a unique set of kinetic parameters, which represents its "character". Therefore, a swarm is allowed to have two or more different types of agents. A design parameter of a swarm is described by a recipe (i.e., some sets of KPs). If there are multiple types in a swarm, then it is said to be heterogeneous (otherwise homogeneous). When a swarm has M types agents, the recipe $\mathcal{R}$ for it is written as follows.

$$
\mathcal{R} =
\begin{cases}
N_1 & * (R, V_n, V_m, c_1, c_2, c_3, c_4, c_5)_1 \\
N_2 & * (R, V_n, V_m, c_1, c_2, c_3, c_4, c_5)_2 \\
\quad \vdots & \\
N_M & * (R, V_n, V_m, c_1, c_2, c_3, c_4, c_5)_M,
\end{cases}
\tag{3}
$$

where N_j ($j = 1, \ldots, M$) at the beginning of each row denotes the number of agents that share the same set of KPs. The parameters newly introduced in SC are:

- R: the perception range to define the size of the neighborhood
- V_n: the ideal speed
- V_m: the maximum speed

It should be noted that the perception range R is a particularly important parameter deciding whether an interaction occurs between an agent and another. Figure 3 illustrates the perception ranges of the agents. Each one of them has its perception range R_i. An agent i ($i = 1, \cdots, N$) perceives and communicates locally with its neighbors when they come within the perception range of agent i. Figure 3b represents the "cohesion" effect, i.e., every agent makes its orientation towards the center position among its neighboring agents. Figure 3c represents the "aligning" effect, i.e., every agent adjusts its velocity (orientation) to the velocity averaged over those of its neighboring agents. Figure 3d represents the "separation" effect to avoid collisions between the agents. The smaller the distance between the agents i and j becomes, the greater the separating (repulsion) force becomes. These effects are involved together and used to determine the acceleration of the agent i as indicated in Line 8 of Algorithm 1.

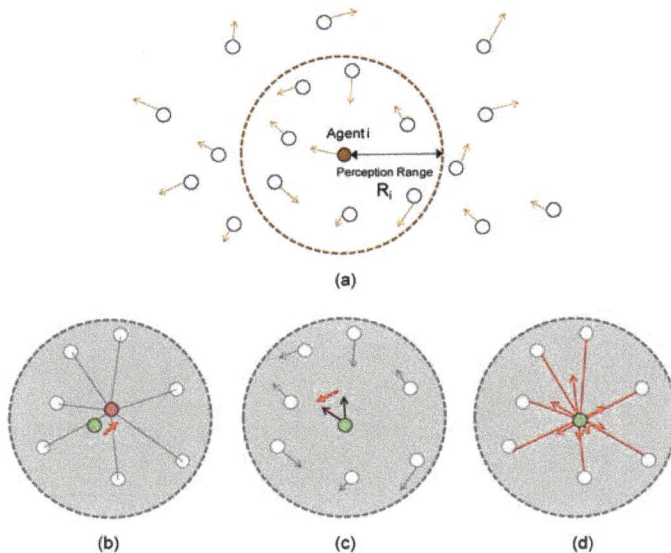

Figure 3. Kinetic interaction between agents (drawn based on [9]). (**a**) Agent i perceives the positions and the velocities of neighboring agents within its perception range, R_i; (**b**) Cohesion; (**c**) Alignment and (**d**) Separation.

Algorithm 1 Kinetic Rules in Swarm Chemistry [9]. Line 2: The set of neighboring agents (i.e., other agents within the local perception range), $\mathcal{N}$ of agent i is found. Lines 3–4: The number of neighboring agents, $|\mathcal{N}|$, is then calculated. If the set $\mathcal{N}$ is empty, i.e., if there is no agent within its perception range, a random acceleration is set, which means a random straying by the agent. Lines 6–7: Otherwise, the average positions and velocities of nearby particles are calculated, respectively. Line 8: A tentative acceleration is calculated according to the three Boids rules (cohesion, alignment and separation). Lines 9–11: At a given probability c_4, a random perturbation is applied to the tentative acceleration. Line 13: A tentative velocity is calculated by time-integrating the acceleration. Line 14: The tentative velocity is limited to prevent overspeed. Line 15: The speed is approximated to its own normal speed (self-propulsion). Lines 17–20: After the above calculation is complete for all the agents, the velocities and then the locations are updated by time-integration.

1: **for all** $i \in$ agents **do**

2:     $\mathcal{N} \leftarrow \{j \neq i\}$ that satisfies $\left| \vec{x}_j - \vec{x}_i \right| < R^i$

3:     **if** $|\mathcal{N}| = 0$ **then**

4:       $\vec{a} \leftarrow (r_{\pm 0.5}, r_{\pm 0.5})$ // Random steering

5:     **else**

6:       $\langle \vec{x} \rangle \leftarrow \sum_{j \in \mathcal{N}} \vec{x}_j / |\mathcal{N}|$

7:       $\langle \vec{v} \rangle \leftarrow \sum_{j \in \mathcal{N}} \vec{v}_j / |\mathcal{N}|$

8:       $\vec{a} \leftarrow c_1^i (\langle \vec{x} \rangle - \vec{x}_i) + c_2^i (\langle \vec{v} \rangle - \vec{v}_i) + c_3^i \sum_{j \in \mathcal{N}} (\vec{x}_i - \vec{x}_j) / |\vec{x}_i - \vec{x}_j|^2$ // Cohesion, alignment and

      separation

9:       **if** $r < c_4^i$ **then**

10:         $\vec{a} \leftarrow \vec{a} + (r_{\pm 5}, r_{\pm 5})$ // Random perturbation

11:       **end if**

12:     **end if**

13:     $\vec{v}_i' \leftarrow \vec{v}_i + \vec{a}$

14:     $\vec{v}_i' \leftarrow \min(V_m^i / |\vec{v}_i|, 1) \cdot \vec{v}_i'$ // Limiting overspeed

15:     $\vec{v}_i' \leftarrow c_5^i (V_n^i / |\vec{v}_i| \cdot \vec{v}_i) + (1 - c_5^i) \vec{v}_i'$ // Self-propulsion

16: **end for**

17: **for all** $i \in$ agents **do**

18:     $\vec{v}_i \leftarrow \vec{v}_i'$ // Update velocity

19:     $\vec{x}_i \leftarrow \vec{x}_i + \vec{v}_i$ // Update position

20: **end for**

---

3. Methods

3.1. Parameter Optimization

We used a genetic algorithm, known as one of the most widely used parameter optimization techniques, in order to find recipes from which interesting and life-like patterns or behaviors evolutionarily. Specifically, a real-coded genetic algorithm (RCGA) [20] was used because the parameters under optimization take continuous values. The flow of optimization is depicted in Figure 4a. For crossover operation, the blend crossover (BLX-α) method, which is commonly used in RCGA was applied. Figure 4b depicts the concept of BLX-α method. The figure is for the case of having only two parameters to be optimized, for simplicity. Actually, however, the dimension is the same as the number of parameters of the problem, which is 24 in this paper. The parameters of child individual are randomly generated within the domain, indicated with a rectangle surrounded by chain lines, determined from the domain the parameter values of the parent individuals A and B. α is the coefficient for the extent of domain expansion. No mutation was applied since BLX-α itself can control randomness. The magnification rate α is an important parameter to control the optimization. So we have conducted parameter search after tuning this parameter carefully for each fitness function.

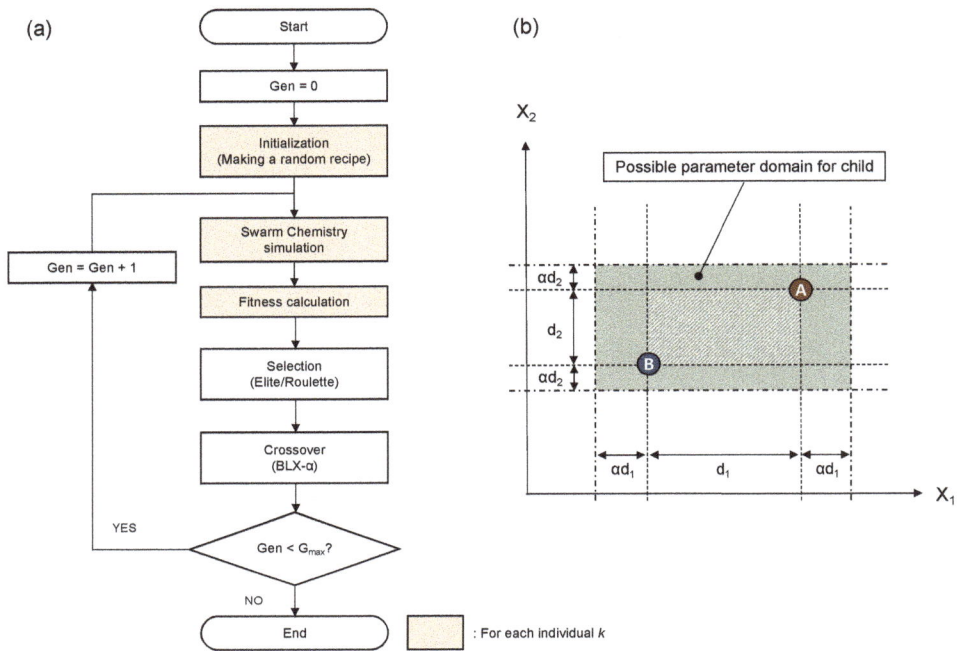

Figure 4. (**a**) The optimization flow with genetic algorithm (GA); (**b**) The conceptual drawing of blend crossover (BLX-α) method.

3.2. Optimization Flow

In each GA iteration (g), each individual (k) has a recipe $\mathcal{R}(g, k)$ input to its Swarm Chemistry simulation. The initial recipes of the individuals are randomly given.

At the beginning of a simulation, agents are placed at random positions within $[0 : 300] \times [0 : 300]$ [pixel] on an infinite continuous plane and then move according to the rules shown in Algorithm 1. Thus the system is time-evolved. The simulation is conducted in discrete time steps and finally outputs the history of agent positions, $\vec{x}_i(t) = [x_i(t), y_i(t)]$. Simulation is done for 1000 time steps then the fitness is calculated using the history for the final 500 time steps.

Based on fitness calculated for each individual, blending crossover is applied. In selecting parents, r_E [%] of the highest scoring individuals are chosen and preserved. For the rest of seats, random individuals are chosen by roulette selection, i.e., in proportion to the fitness values.

For simplicity, we set the total number of individuals (n_I) was 100, with the fraction of elite individuals $r_E = 0.2$; $n_E = r_E n_I$. Also, we fixed the number of agent types M to 3 and the number of agents of each type N_j to $300/M = 300/3 = 100, \forall j$, respectively. Overall, we had therefore 24 (8×3) parameters to be optimized. The methods of designing effective functions are not limited to the heterogeneous swarms; they can also be applied to the swarms of single type as well. In this case, the model is equivalent to Boids model, whose basic behaviors have already been studied. In Swarm Chemistry, though there are some exceptional cases like "Blobs" shown in No. 2 of Figure 2, the possibility of emergence of "interesting" patterns basically seems to be limited with a single type, compared to the swarms of heterogeneous agents. The interestingness of the emerging behavior depends on the number of types in general. If the number of types is 1, the diversity of the emerging behavior will be limited. On the other hand, for example, it is thought that if the type number is too large, the minimum structure or order does not emerge, as is apparent from the case that the type is different for each particle. In this study, as it is at the primary stage, we have decided to set it to 3. In addition, if the types with different size interact, there is a possibility that some different roles emerge according to the size, which are different from the case where all the types have the same number of agents. We believe it is a promising direction for the future.

4. Measures to Quantify the Swarm Dynamics

4.1. What is an Interesting Pattern?

Before defining the measures, let us discuss what a visually interesting pattern is. It is a premise that providing a strict definition of interestingness is principally impossible since interestingness can be diverse: it can vary from person to person. On the other hand, we believe that there should be certain universal patterns which look interesting to everyone. Some possible conditions, which we have empirically found, in which a swarm looks at least somewhat interesting include:

- A certain regular shape or motion pattern is self-organized
- An organism-like pattern is self-organized
- The swarm pattern is deformed as time evolves
- The role of a type alters as time evolves
- Fission and fusion continuously occur

Of course, there might be some other features to let a swarm look interesting.

On the other hand, it is relatively easy to say what patterns are NOT interesting. Here we show two typical patterns that are uninteresting. One possibility is that it is a necessary condition that the swarm pattern continues to change in time, not falling into a fixed pattern. We consider two typical extreme swarm patterns, which may be uninteresting, illustrated by Figure 5. The first pattern (a) is a simple aggregation, where the agents only gather into a sphere-like structure without changing its shape. Such a motion can be obtained from a recipe, for example:

$$100 \times (244.19, 4.19, 8.74, 0.63, 0.35, 54.69, 0.08, 0.66) \tag{4}$$

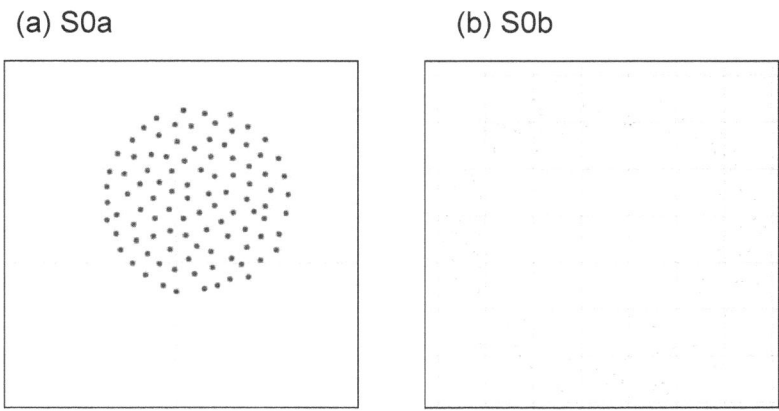

(a) S0a   **(b) S0b**

Figure 5. Two extreme swarm patterns we consider as example swarms which seem uninteresting. (**a**) The first pattern "S0a" is a simple aggregating pattern, where the agents only gather into a sphere-like structure without changing its shape. (**b**) Another pattern "S0b" is a simply segregating pattern, where the agents just wander randomly and go far from each other without interacting with any others.

In this paper we call it "S0a". Another pattern is a simply segregating pattern (We use the words "segregation" or "dissipation" to avoid confusion with "separation" in context of original rule of Boids.), where the agents just wander randomly and go far from each other without interacting with any others. Such a motion can be obtained from a recipe, for example:

$$100 \times (9.05, 10.09, 37.8, 0.98, 0.24, 79.97, 0.22, 0.3) \tag{5}$$

In this paper we call it "S0b". These patterns are also included shown later in Table 3.

4.2. Importance of Asymmetry

In biology, for decades (left-right) morphological asymmetries have evoked curiosity and wonder, which is one of those exceedingly rare characteristics of animals that has evolved independently many times [21,22].

In physics, the symmetry principle proposed by Pierre Curie has become the object of renewed philosophical discussion in connection with the growing interest in the role of symmetry and symmetry breaking in recent decades [23], stating that "When certain causes produce certain effects, the elements of asymmetry of the causes must be found in the effects produced" [24].

Although the meanings of asymmetry in both fields are significantly different, inspired by these recent discussions, we assume that asymmetry, which might be in the causes or effects, plays an important role in creating interesting swarm patterns, as a working hypothesis.

4.3. Fitness Function Candidates

Upon the above discussion, we define seven fitness function (FF) candidates from the aspect of asymmetry of some kinds. Table 2 summarizes the features of the fitness functions. FF-A and FF-B treat asymmetries in macroscopic positions. FF-C to FF-F are based on asymmetries related to microscopic interactions. While these six FFs measure explicit asymmetry, the final one, FF-G, measures the system asymmetry implicitly by using chaoticity index. In this context, "implicit" means measuring directly the appeared (resultant) asymmetry. On the other hand, "explicit" means measuring asymmetry by computing the consequent complexity arising from inherent asymmetry of system.

Another classification can also be made according to dynamicity. The functions are classified into either static or dynamic. Here, "static" means that the FF measures the instance arrangement or state whereas "dynamic" means that the FF focuses on the change of arrangement or state in time. From this point of view, FF-A to FF-C are regarded static and the remainders dynamic, respectively.

The detailed description for each function will be provided in more detail in the following subsections.

Table 2. Fitness functions (FF) proposed in this paper.

FF	Meaning	Explicity of Aymmetry	Asymmetry Type	Dynamicity
A	Typewise centroid deviation		Positional	Static
B	Variation of pairwise distance		Positional	Static
C	In-/out-degree difference	Explicit		
D	Derivative of in-/out-degree difference	Explicit	Topological	Dynamic
E	Sum of derivatives of in-/out-degrees		Topological	Dynamic
F	Fluctuation of in-/out-degree difference			
G	Max. Lyapunov exponent λ_{max}	Implicit		

4.3.1. Fitness Function A

One straightforward way to characterize the swarm structure can be the geometrical asymmetry of a swarm. We have defined a fitness function which represents the positional deviation of the centroid of each type from the global centroid. This measure is computed from the snapshots of the swarm.

In this sense, it is a metric of the static structure of swarm. In a mathematical form, this fitness function could be written as:

$$\phi = \frac{1}{M} \sum_{t=1}^{T} \sum_{j=1}^{M} \left\| \vec{x}_{jC} - \vec{x}_{GC} \right\| \tag{6}$$

$$\vec{x}_{jC} = (x_{jC}, y_{jC}) \tag{7}$$

$$\vec{x}_{GC} = (x_{GC}, y_{GC}), \tag{8}$$

where M is the number of types, $\vec{x}_{jC}$ is the centroid coordinate of j-th type, and $\vec{x}_{GC}$ is the centroid coordinate of all agents. T denotes the whole duration of the simulation. The centroid coordinate of j-th type equals to the (x, y) positions averaged over the set of agents belonging to that type j. Similarly, the global centroid coordinate equals to the (x, y) positions averaged over all the agents. When the emerged swarm has a unique shape like ones shown in Figure 2, there are cases where the type-wise centroid does not overlap the global centroid while achieving balances between the different types. There is a possibility that maximizing this function leads to an interesting pattern.

4.3.2. Fitness Function B

Another possibility of characterizing the swarm pattern from the asymmetry of static structure can be based on the variation of the pair-wise distance between two agents. We define the fitness function as:

$$\phi = \frac{1}{T} \sum_{t=1}^{T} \sigma \left[D_{ij}(t) \right], \tag{9}$$

where $D_{ij}(t) = \left\| \vec{x}_i(t) - \vec{x}_j(t) \right\|$ is the distance between agent i and agent j at the time step t. This function is the standard deviation σ of the pair-wise distances, measured by the snapshots of the swarm, too. If the structure is a simple ball-like pattern or just dispersing, the pair-wise distances will be uniform. As it is suggested that the distance between two agents at the equilibrium state depends on the ratio of kinetic parameters c_1/c_3 (c_1: cohesion coefficient, c_3: separating coefficient) of these agents [7,10].

4.3.3. Fitness Function C

As one of the most important features of SC, different types of agents are allowed to exist in a swarm, implying the interactions among agents can be asymmetrical. Unlike other swarm system models, the perception ranges R are not always consistent between any pair of agents (i, j), making such a situation possible to occur that the motion of one of them (agent i) is affected by the other (agent j), but not necessarily vice versa. The topological connectivity could be relevant to the emergence of a life-like behavior of agents. From terminology of graph theory, the network topology of interactions can be modeled as a directed graph, whose adjacency matrix is asymmetrical. In preparation, we need to define the in-degree and out-degree functions.

- In-degree (K^-): The number of agents that agent i perceives. In other words, how many agents affect the motion of agent i.
- Out-degree (K^+): The number of agents that perceive agent i. In other words, how many agents are affected by agent i.

A numerical example is illustrated in Figure 6. Consider a swarm heterogeneous of 4 agents. In the case shown in (a), agent 1 is perceived from only agent 3, which means the in-degree of agent 1 is 1. By contrast, agent 1 perceives agent 2, 3 and 4. This means the out-degree of agent 1 is 3. The relationship of perception is visualized in (b). The degrees for the other agents can be computed in the same way. The result is shown in (c).

In addition, as the degrees K^+ and K^- are dependent on both time (t) and agent ID (i), they can be formally written as:

$$K^-(t, i) \text{ and } K^+(t, i), \tag{10}$$

respectively. After every simulation, an adjacency matrix $A = [a_{ij}]$ was computed for each timestep. Let $a_{ij} = 1$ if agent i "perceives" agent j, otherwise $a_{ij} = 1$, and vice versa.

Based on the above preparation, a fitness function could be defined as follows.

$$\Delta K(t, i) = \left| K^+(t, i) - K^-(t, i) \right| \tag{11}$$

$$\phi = \frac{1}{TN^2} \sum_{t=1}^{T} \sum_{i=1}^{N} \Delta K(t, i) \tag{12}$$

(a)

(b)

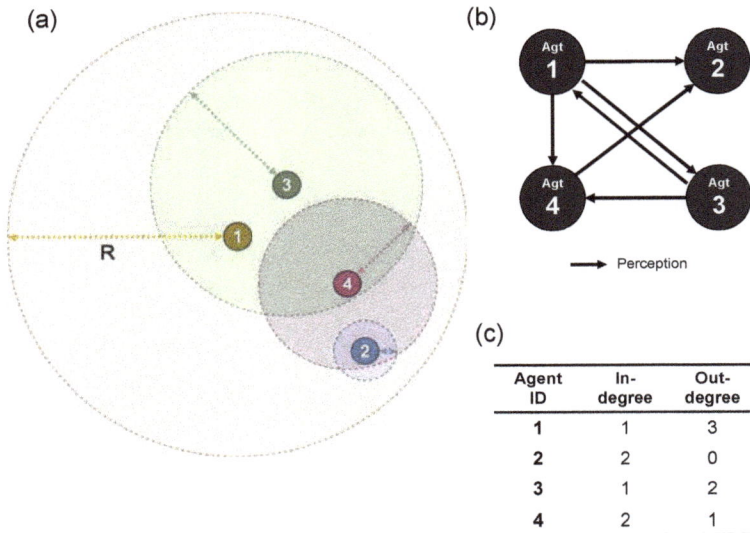

Agt 1   Agt 2

Agt 4   Agt 3

→ Perception

(c)

Agent ID	In-degree	Out-degree
1	1	3
2	2	0
3	1	2
4	2	1

Figure 6. Definition of in- and out-degrees. (a) An example swarm consisting of 4 agents; (b) Its perception relationship; (c) The in- and out- degrees.

4.3.4. Fitness Function D

$$\phi = \frac{1}{TN^2} \sum_{t=2}^{T} \sum_{i=1}^{N} \left| \Delta K(t, i) - \Delta K(t - 1, i) \right| \tag{13}$$

This function means the time derivative of in/out difference. Using not only ΔK itself, we assumed that it could make it possible to detect the dynamic structural change.

4.3.5. Fitness Function E

We introduce another function similar to FF-D.

$$\Delta K(t,i) \quad = \quad \left| K^+(t,i) - K^-(t,i) \right| \tag{14}$$

$$\phi \quad = \quad \frac{1}{2TN} \sum_{t=2}^{T} \sum_{i=1}^{N} \left[\left| K^+(t,i) - K^+(t-1,i) \right| + \left| K^-(t,i) - K^-(t-1,i) \right| \right] \tag{15}$$

As will be shown later in the result section, the optimization result from FF-D looked interesting. Therefore we came to a hypothesis that a derivative operation could help capture a pulsating or alternating motion. We investigate whether it is still possible to get a similar kind of motion as well by this fitness function.

What this function differs from FF-D is that the derivatives are taken for K^+ and K^-, respectively.

4.3.6. Fitness Function F

Another approach based on the topological connectivity could be defined as:

$$\Delta K(t,i) \quad = \quad \left| K^+(t,i) - K^-(t,i) \right| \tag{16}$$

$$\phi \quad = \quad \frac{1}{N} \sum_{i=1}^{N} \left[\max_t \left(\Delta K(t,i) \right) - \min_t \left(\Delta K(t,i) \right) \right]. \tag{17}$$

This function measures the average of the amplitude of in/out difference over all time range. By this function we expected to get more gradual structural formation and deformation, while the previous function in Equation (13) measures the temporal variation between two successive time steps, leading to a snappy motion, as described in the result section.

4.3.7. Fitness Function G

The behaviors of swarms in SC can be seen as a kind of nonlinear dynamic system. We assume inherent asymmetry might exist in the system dynamics. Therefore, this concept was woven into a form of fitness function. The FF is related to the instability or the unpredictiveness.

Let the state of system be denoted using a vector $\vec{x}$, which represents the agent positions in the two-dimension:

$$\vec{x}_i = [x_{1i}, x_{2i}]^T. \tag{18}$$

Hence, the system state vector is defined as:

$$\vec{X} = \left[\vec{x}_1^T \; \vec{x}_2^T \ldots \vec{x}_N^T \right]^T. \tag{19}$$

Namely, $\vec{X} \in R^m$, $m = 2N$, N is the number of agents. As $\vec{X}$ time-evolves, it can be written as $\vec{X}(t)$.

A Lyapunov exponent λ is often used to determine if a dynamical system is chaotic. Lyapunov exponent is defined as:

$$\lambda = \frac{1}{T} \sum_{t=1}^{T} \log_{10} \left| \frac{\Delta X(t)}{\Delta X(t-1)} \right| \tag{20}$$

A Lyapunov exponent indicates the slope λ when the expansion of system state locus is approximated by an exponential function $e^{\lambda t}$. Thus the stability of the system can be determined by the following expressions.

$$\lambda \;>\; 0 \Rightarrow \text{unstable (chaotic)} \tag{21}$$

$$\lambda \;=\; 0 \Rightarrow \text{critical} \tag{22}$$

$$\lambda \;<\; 0 \Rightarrow \text{stable} \tag{23}$$

As Lyapunov exponent is computed for each dimension of the state vector $\vec{X}$, m Lyapunov exponents $\{\lambda_1, \lambda_2, \ldots, \lambda_m\}$ (Lyapunov spectrum) are obtained for m dimensions. We used the maximum λ_{max} as a measuring index because it determines the convergence of solution locus along time evolution of system.

From this, the fitness function is

$$\phi = c\left(e^{\lambda_{max}} - b\right) \tag{24}$$

Here, an exponential function is used so that the fitness function only takes positive values. In addition, the constants c and b were introduced as a magnification coefficient and an offset constant, respectively, and set $c = 1000$ and $b = 1$ empirically because the expression $e^{\lambda_{max}}$ itself gives values around 1 and the difference is small (the order of 10^{-3}). We have introduced these correcting constants because if these parameters were not involved (i.e., $c = 1$ and $b = 0$) in the beginning, the difference in fitness values between the individuals was too small to be discriminated in optimization process. If the magnification factor c is larger, it may be easier to discriminate the fitness difference between individuals. On the other hand, when it is too large, the probability that the individuals with low fitness cannot be selected. So we have chosen a moderate value whose order is similar to that of the averaged fitness values from the case these parameters were not involved. The constant b has been introduced to remove the offset before magnifying by c. This value should be positive but not exceed the averaged offset value, from the case these parameters were not involved, in order to keep fitness values greater than zero.

4.4. Numerical Examples

Using the proposed fitness functions, the fitness values have been computed for already found interesting patterns shown in Table 2. The results are plotted in Figure 7. We can see from this figure that the FFs can be classified roughly into two groups. For the first group (FFs-A, B and G), the variation is small and every swarm takes similar fitness scores. For the other group (FFs-C, D, E and F), only some swarms take a high fitness score. Next, looking at the swarm, some swarms take a specifically high score for the latter group of FF. For example, the swarm No. 10 takes a preeminently high score in FFs-D and E. It is thought that the reason is that the derivative function could capture intensively alternating motion. Overall, we have found that each FF has a diverse individuality and could produce quite different distributions of fitness scores.

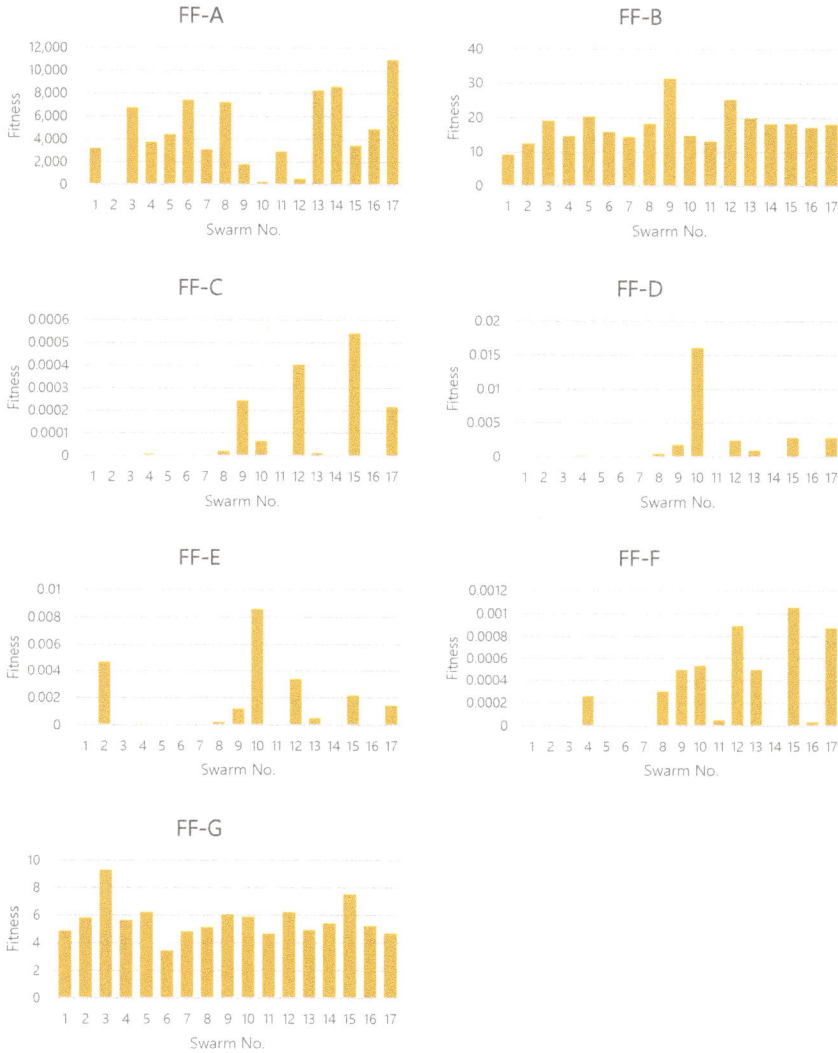

Figure 7. The fitness values computed for already found patterns shown in Table 2, according to the proposed fitness functions.

5. Results

5.1. Summary of Optimization Results and Obtained Recipes

We have carried out parameter searches by means of the GA. The evolutionary change in fitness for fitness functions FF-A to FF-G are shown in Figure A1a–g, respectively. The best recipes $\mathcal{R}$ gained through optimization for each FF are summarized in Figure 8. Note that the KPs in recipes here are normalized with the upper limit of each KP. The result will be discussed later in the next section.

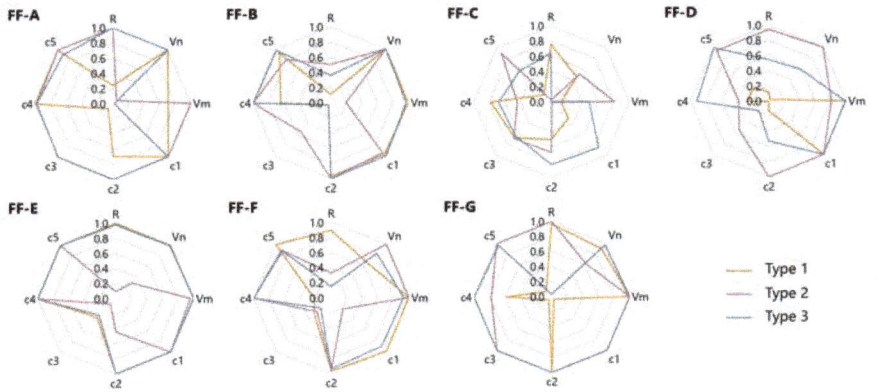

Figure 8. Optimization results: the recipes gained using the proposed fitness functions. Each KP is normalized with its upper limit value.

Statistics	N_j	R	V_n	V_m	c_1	c_2	c_3	c_4	c_5
	# of agents (fixed)	Radius of local perception range	Normal speed	Maximum speed	Cohesive force	Aligning force	Separating force	Probability of random steering	Tendency of self-propulsion
Min	0.333	0.023	0.005	0.016	0.010	0.130	0.002	0.220	0.100
Max	0.333	1.000	1.000	1.000	1.000	1.000	1.000	1.000	1.000
Mean	0.333	0.557	0.710	0.809	0.821	0.840	0.428	0.793	0.823
Standard Deviation	0.000	0.385	0.357	0.320	0.344	0.249	0.356	0.268	0.293

5.2. Evolved Swarm Behaviors

This subsection presents the evolved swarming behaviors obtained through optimization. The snapshots for each fitness function are also shown in Figures A2–A8, respectively. The different types of agents are shown in different colors. The semi-transparent dots behind the agents also show their past positions at the recent 60 time steps, allowing us to understand the direction of movement of each agent. Animated versions of swarm motions are also available as Supplementary Materials, Videos S2–S8.

5.2.1. Fitness Function A

Type 1 agents (colored in green) quickly got apart of the other types and no interesting pattern was formed. In this sense, it seemed this fitness function itself was not well defined.

Although, we could find an interesting motion appearing from this recipe. Beginning simulations with several different initial conditions (i.e., agent positions), it was found that two distinctive patterns appear from this recipe (see Figure 9): while the aggregation size of yellow agents is small, they are captured within the "gel-structure" composed of the grey agents. But once the yellow aggregation of agents gathers in number, the aggregation gets out of the gel and goes away. Such a behavior might happen near a critical condition. Whether the yellow agents could escape from the gel or not depends on the sensitive balance of forces applied to the agents. The number of aggregations was occasionally two or three.

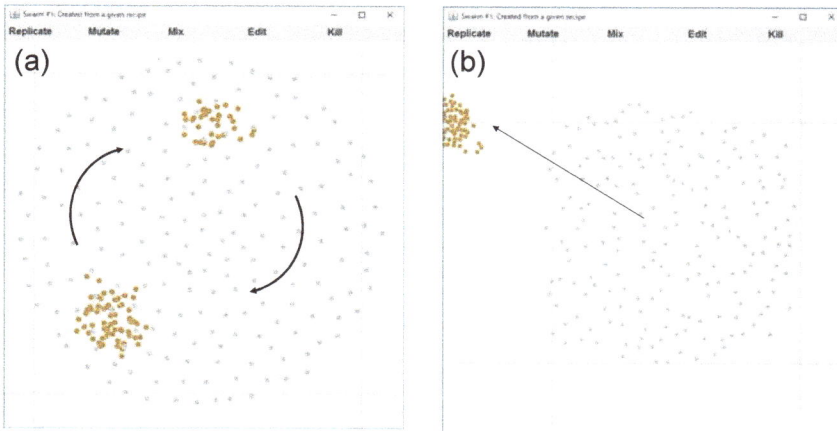

Figure 9. Different motions observed in the FF-A. (**a**) While the aggregation size of yellow agents is small, they are captured within the "gel-structure" of the grey agents; (**b**) As soon as the yellow aggregation of agents gathers in number, the aggregation gets out of the gel and goes away.

5.2.2. Fitness Function B

One type (Type 1) of agents quickly go far and segregate from others and the interaction connection is soon broken off. Here, Type 1 has a small perception range R and a relatively high speed. This will lead the Type 1 agents to quick segregation.

5.2.3. Fitness Function C

This FF resulted in a dispersing pattern, a little different from the results in FFs-A and B. In those FFs, one type get out quickly in aggregation, while in this FF, one type (Type 2) dispersed outwards. Type 2 has a small perception range R and a relatively high speed.

5.2.4. Fitness Function D

A shell-like structure and a snappy motion like convulsion, blinking or pulsation can be observed. This kind of motion seems to be in the same category of "pulsating eye", shown in Figure 2 (No. 10). Figure 10 shows its representative dynamics extracted , with the snapshots over 4 successive timesteps: (a) is the snapshot at a timestep t, (b) at $t + 1$, (c) at $t + 2$, and (d) at $t + 3$, respectively. We can see that the radii of the outer and inner shells increase and decrease in odd and even steps alternately. This is due to the attraction and repulsion forces (i.e., cohesion and separation, respectively). This can be seen as that contraction and relaxation are repeated, as we can also see by looking at the shadows of the Type 3 agents (colored in red) in e.g., Figure A5e–i. This swarm successfully sustained its self-organized structure without segregation. Even though the perception range of Type 1 is relatively small, the speed is also small. So the Type 1 can keep staying in the structure.

(a) (b)

(c) (d)

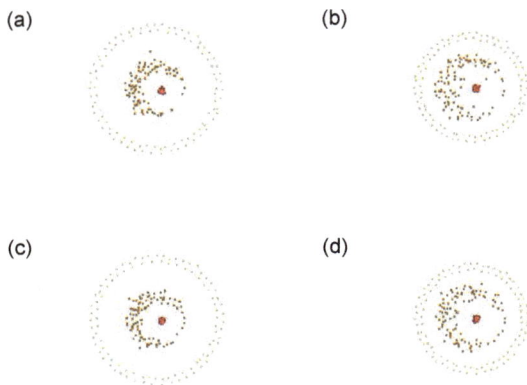

Figure 10. Representative dynamics of the swarm obtained from FF-D. (**a**) The snapshot at a timestep t; (**b**) at $t + 1$; (**c**) at $t + 2$; and (**d**) at $t + 3$, respectively. We can observe a blinking motion: the radii of outer and inner shells increase and decrease in odd and even steps alternately. This is due to the attraction and repulsion forces (i.e., cohesion and separation, respectively) are acting.

5.2.5. Fitness Function E

Figure 11 shows its representative dynamics. This motion looks like a pulsation, blinking or hiccup, like the one appearing in the previous FF-D. The same arrangements appear every 2 time steps alternately, and the agents of yellow type go back and forth. Again, Type 2, which has a small perception range and a low speed, is able to stay in a structure. And Types 1 and 3 are almost the same type.

(a) (b)

(c) (d)

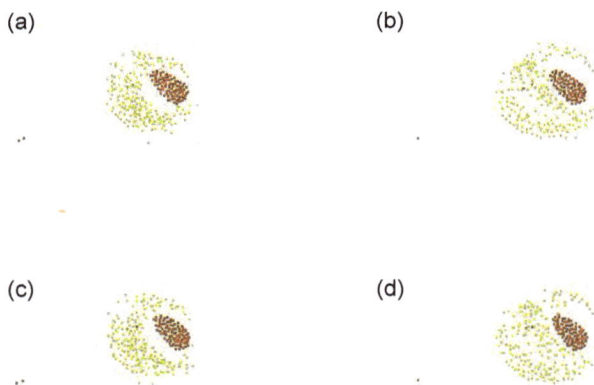

Figure 11. Representative dynamics of the swarm obtained from FF-E. (**a**) The snapshot at a timestep t; (**b**) at $t + 1$; (**c**) at $t + 2$; and (**d**) at $t + 3$. Similar to the result from FF-D, the same arrangements appear every 2 time steps alternately. The agents of yellow type go back and forth.

5.2.6. Fitness Function F

Figure A7 illustrates the agent trajectories and its characteristic dynamics is depicted in Figure 12. This recipe led us to a dynamics exhibiting a kind of motion like oviposition. The shape continues to deform during the transient from an egg-like structure to eventually fission into several aggregations.

It looks interesting also because the three types temporarily composed a three-layer structure and experienced a two-stage segregation. In the first segregation was that Type 2 agents (blue) created an elastic tube-like structure and the other types (Types 1 and 3) created an egg-like structure flowing down the tube. The subsequent segregation was that of Type 1 (red) agents as an egg from Type 3 agents (green) as a tube. Finally, each type grew into isolated eggs. This FF led to a life-like or lively change of shape: some types experienced both roles as a tube and as an egg in the transient history. While observing the motion, we can also feel something viscous during the fission process above. This viscosity is thought to be due to some complex forces around the interface between the types.

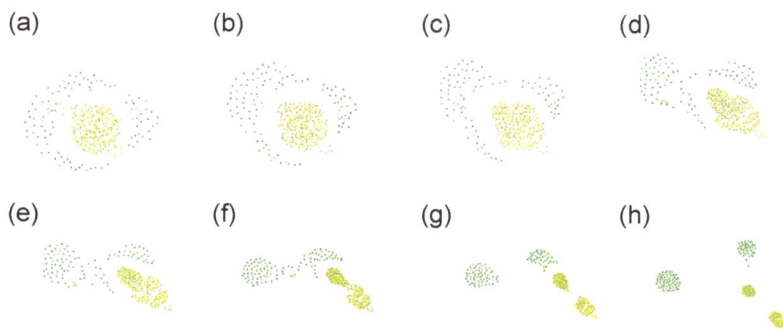

Figure 12. Representative dynamics of the swarm obtained from FF-F. (**a**) The snapshot at a timestep t; (**b**) at $t + 10$; (**c**) at $t + 15$; (**d**) at $t + 35$; (**e**) at $t + 40$; (**f**) at $t + 60$; (**g**) at $t + 75$; and (**h**) at $t + 105$. The shape continues to deform from an egg-like structure to eventually fission into several aggregations.

5.2.7. Fitness Function G

This recipe also results in a swarm like FF-C, undergoing segregation and not interesting pattern can be formed. The main reason for the segregation is the perception range R of Type 3 which is too small to keep the connection, because if this value 10.82 is replaced by 200, then a structure is retained.

6. Discussion

6.1. Overview of Results

According to their dynamical motions, we have roughly classified the patterns including already found ones (S1 to S17) shown in Figure 2 and uninteresting ones (S0a and S0b), into several categories. This classification is shown in Table 3. The results from the seven fitness functions proposed in this paper are also in this table.

Defining a good measure was found to be not easy: there are not few cases where even uninteresting patterns could get a high fitness score. A swarm tends to result in a segregating pattern, which is frequently observed but uninteresting, when one or more types have a too small perception range and a too large speed. Therefore, introducing some terms of limiting into the fitness functions may be effective to prevent an easy breaking of the structure.

The recipes gained through the optimization are shown in Figure 8. We can see from this table that:

1. Some types have a small perception range R and a large normal speed V_n (e.g., Type 1 in FF-A, Type 1 in FF-B, Type 2 in FF-C, Types 2 and 3 in FF-F and Type 3 in FF-G). On the contrary, some other types have a large R and a small V_n (e.g., Type 1 in FF-C, Types 1 and 3 in FF-D, Type 1 in FF-F, Types 1 and 2 in FF-G).
2. Similarly, some types have a small cohesion coefficient c_1 and a large separation coefficient c_3 (e.g., Types 1 and 2 in FF-C), and vice versa.
3. In FF-E, Types 1 and 3 share the almost identical KPs.

Especially, as can be seen in items 1 and 2 above, the relationships between the perception range R and the normal speed V_n as well as between the cohesion coefficient c_1 and the separation coefficient c_3 seem important to control the dispersion behaviors.

From the above results together with the dynamics obtained, we discuss the relationship between the recipe (KPs) and the resultant swarm patterns. Dispersive motions like FFs-A, B, C and G are observed when: the swarm has one or more types whose perception range R is small whereas normal speed V_n is large; and/or separation coefficient c_3 is large whereas cohesion coefficient c_1 is small. Therefore, it seems better to keep c_1 large and c_3 small, as well as to keep R large and V_n small, in order to create a linked formation preventing from a dispersion.

Figure 8 also summarizes the statistical tendency, telling us that:

1. As the standard deviations are small and the mean values are relatively high (approximately 0.8) in c_2 (aligning coefficient), c_4 (randomness) and c_5 (tendency of self-propulsion), implying that these parameters are almost common and less sensitive to the definition of fitness functions than the other ones.
2. On the other hand, diversity is large for R (perception range), V_n (normal speed), V_m (maximum speed), c_1 (cohesive coefficient) and c_3 (separating coefficient), implying that these parameters are sensitive to the definition of fitness functions.
3. In addition, the mean values of c_1 tends to be large and that of c_3 is small.

Table 3. Classification of typical motions observed in Swarm Chemistry (SC).

Category	Kind of Motion	Swarm No.
G1	Aggregating	S0a
G2	Segregating	S0b, **FF-A, FF-B, FF-C, FF-G**
G3	Reciprocating	S1, S8, S13
G4	Rotating	S5, S11, S17
G5	Tracting	S3, S4, S6, S7, S14
G6	Pulsating	S10, **FF-D, FF-E**
G7	Clustered	S2, S9, S12
G8	Cell-like	S15, S16
G9	Viscous interfacing	**FF-F**

6.2. Analysis of Especially Interesting Patterns

In this subsection we would like to get into a little more detailed discussion especially on the most interesting swarm patterns shown in the previous subsection, analyzing how such a motion could be obtained. From the classification above, let us pick up the result from FF-D, FF-E and FF-F. Notable dynamical patterns have been yielded from FFs-D, E and F. FFs-D and E have delivered some motion like a pulsation. Their corresponding swarm patterns keep alternating motion and its formation without dissipating. FF-F has delivered a gradually changing structure. It is also interesting that the type could experience different roles in the same transient history. The other FFs resulted in simply segregating motions, where agents tend to go far and the interactions between them are broken off.

We can see that the asymmetry of information transfer, which is represented by the asymmetrical topological connectivity, is an effective way to characterize the interestingness of heterogeneous swarm patterns. As indicated by FFs-D and E, the usage of derivative function can be seen as it helps detect a pulsating motion. The differential operation seems to facilitate the sustainment of quick transitions between high-degree and low-degree states over two successive time steps. The reason is if the degree monotonically increased or decreased, the fitness value would have been low. This argument may not be limited only to the case of using the degrees, but applicable also to some other measuring indices representing the state of system. The difference in the definition of the fitness functions between FF-D and FF-E is that FF-D uses the time-derivative for the in-/out-degree difference ΔK, whereas FF-E uses the sum of time-derivatives for each of in and out degrees, calculated separately. The optimization results from both FFs have converged into a very similar pattern: a pulsating pattern. However, as shown in the new Figure 5 (fitness functions calculated for Sayama's 17 swarms), a difference to be addressed is that FF-D excludes the swarm of a single type because ΔK is always zero for such swarms, whereas FF-E includes the swarm of a single type.

FF-F could lead to a gradual structural deformation, which looks lively. The contributing factor is supposed to be the long evaluation period which starts at a sufficiently time-elapsed point. If a swarm quickly segregates in the early time steps of the simulation, the min-max difference at the period of evaluation will not be so large. Therefore, it is suggested that the combination of a measuring function and an evaluation period might help detect a slowly deforming swarm pattern.

7. Conclusions

The present study has been motivated by the practical needs to the potential of the emergence of interesting patterns in SC has not been totally revealed and leveraged. It is better to be able to detect measure the interestingness of the static structures of the swarms or the dynamic changes in them, in an objective manner, e.g., by GA.

This paper has studied an effective way of quantifying the interestingness of swarm patterns that emerge in SC and then to detect such interesting patterns automatically. We have defined several quantitative measures, focusing particularly on the asymmetry of some kinds. While swarms tend to result in a segregating pattern, which is not interesting, several notable dynamical patterns have been yielded from the proposed FFs. FFs-D and E have delivered some motion like a pulsation, and FF-F has delivered a gradually changing structure. It is also interesting that the a type could experience different roles in the same transient history.

The contributions of this paper are summarized as follows.

1. We have constructed a framework to search higher-scoring swarms using a genetic algorithm. Experimental results showed the possibility of detecting several characteristic and attractive patterns using the proposed quantitative measures and optimization framework.
2. Discussing the relationship between the fitness functions and the corresponding swarm behaviors or structures gained by them, we have derived some key points of designing a good function to detect interesting patterns.

The results provide some clue to what kind of fitness function should be used to obtain a specific type of structure or motion. Numerical study using seven different fitness functions has given a brief overview and general knowledge about the quantification of interestingness. As a general conclusion on how we can define the interestingness, the geometrical (positional) asymmetry of structures and topological asymmetry of information transfer have possibilities to let interesting swarm patterns emerge. Major findings are summarized as below.

1. A swarm tends to result in a segregating pattern, which is frequently observed but uninteresting, when one or more type has a too small perception range and a too high speed. Therefore, it is better to choose values for a recipe with a large perception range, a speed which does not overwhelm the perception range. Introducing some terms of limiting into the fitness functions may be effective to prevent an easy breaking of structure.
2. Another possibility of avoiding a segregating patterns is making the cohesion force large and the separation force small.
3. The asymmetry of information transfer, which is represented by the topological connectivity (used in FFs-D, E and F), is an effective way to characterize the interestingness of heterogeneous swarm patterns.
4. The usage of derivative function can help detect a pulsating motion (finding from FFs-D and E). The differential operation is believed to be facilitating quick transitions between high-degree and

Appl. Sci. **2018**, *8*, 729

low-degree states over two successive time steps to be sustained, while preventing from tendency of breaking off. The fitness value would have been low if the degree monotonically increased or decreased. The same discussion might be applied only to the case of using the degrees, but also to some other measuring indices representing the state of system.

5. A gradual deformation, which looks lively or like an organism, can be captured by a function form like FF-F, in combination with a long evaluation period which starts at a sufficiently time-elapsed point, because a swarm with quick segregation occurring in the early time steps will not have so large min-max difference at the period of evaluation and eventually its fitness score will be low.

Recently, Kano and others have presented a minimal model of swarming behavior, inspired from friendship formation in human society [25]. Simulation results showed that emerged patterns can be classified into 6 categories by introducing two macroscopic variables. Comparative study of this and our models would be fruitful.

The proposal may also have applications to the more practical situations. For instance, the pulsating pattern could be applied to the formation control of excavating robots as its motion pattern seems to be able to shatter the rock walls. Swarm robots, with controlling recipes like the ones presented in this paper, could be introduced to such tasks, where every single robot is inexpensive and easily replaceable because the robots have a self-repairing ability. Of course, in order to realize it in the real-world robots, we require further considerations such as the mass (volume) effects, the strength of materials of the body and the delays of operating commands.

Additionally, we have chosen 2D for the first step of the study, since 3D is more computationally intensive task. However, the extension to 3D version should be one of the most important directions because we can expect to observe much more complex swarm behavior including twisting movement.

Though it is still a challenging problem to fully define the interestingness, our results have presented some part of possible answers. The achievement will help the design of swarms that one desires. Of course, the fitness functions or measures appeared in this paper are just a few examples and there might still be other possible ways to find further interesting patterns. They await to be revealed in the future.

Supplementary Materials: To support the readers' visual understanding of the swarm dynamics we have uploaded the animation files online. Video S1: Animation of already reported swarm dynamics listed in Table 2 (https://youtu.be/eLJwa0jz5GQ), Video S2: Swarm dynamics obtained for FF-A (https://youtu.be/QSyZHCI-ffo), Video S3: Swarm dynamics obtained for FF-B (https://youtu.be/3byzpQqtcpU), Video S4: Swarm dynamics obtained for FF-C (https://youtu.be/cCreYJUASoQ), Video S5: Swarm dynamics obtained for FF-D (https://youtu.be/QuGpkG5mI4I), Video S6: Swarm dynamics obtained for FF-E (https://youtu.be/gz5Nk98sRLQ), Video S7: Swarm dynamics obtained for FF-F (https://youtu.be/B888eKL400Q), Video S8: Swarm dynamics obtained for FF-G (https://youtu.be/Dr1RDinc4AU), Video S9: Swarm dynamics of S0a (https://youtu.be/hImZelcStVE), Video S10: Swarm dynamics of S0b (https://youtu.be/02qQYx4cxQ0).

Author Contributions: Naoki Nishikawa, Reiji Suzuki and Takaya Arita conceived and designed the experiments; Naoki Nishikawa performed the experiments, analyzed the data and wrote the paper.

Acknowledgments: This work was supported by MEXT/JSPS Grant-in-Aid for Scientific Research on Innovative Areas #4903 (Evolinguistics), Grant Number JP17H06383.

Conflicts of Interest: The authors declare no conflict of interest.

Abbreviations

The following abbreviations appeared in this manuscript:

SC   Swarm Chemistry
ESC   Evolutionary Swarm Chemistry
KP   kinetic parameter
GA   genetic algorithm
FF   fitness function

Appendix A   Whole Dynamics for Each Fitness Function

The snapshots for each fitness function are also shown in Figures A2–A8, respectively.

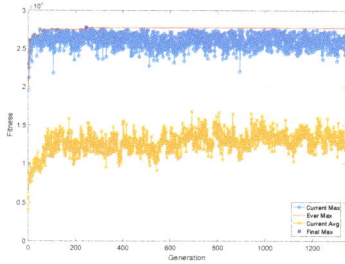

(a) FF-A

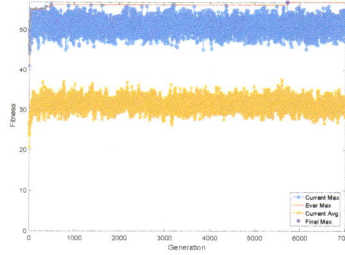

(b) FF-B

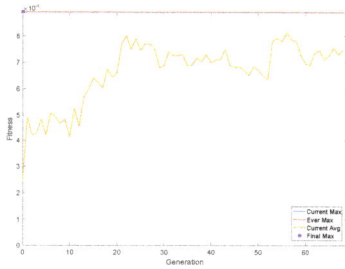

(c) FF-C

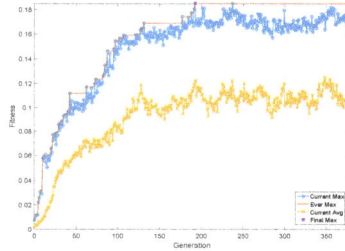

(d) FF-D

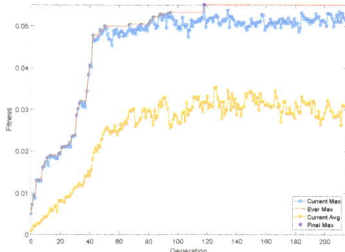

(e) FF-E

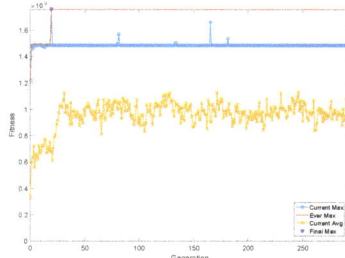

(f) FF-F

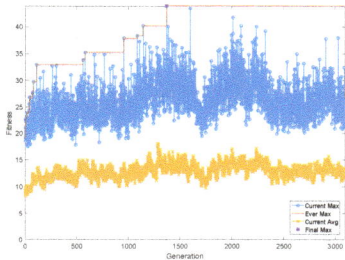

(g) FF-G

Figure A1. Evolutionary change in fitness for each fitness function.

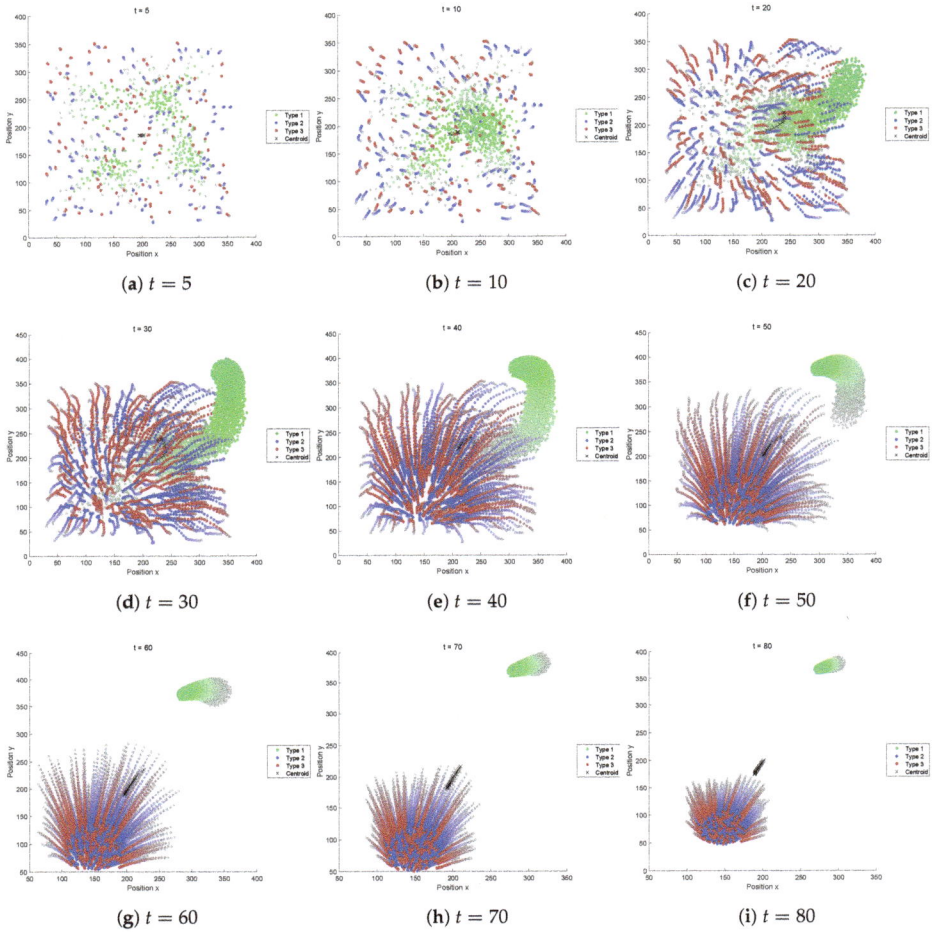

Figure A2. Trajectory of agents (FF-A). The semi-transparent dots behind the agents indicate their past positions at the recent 60 time steps. The "×" mark traces the trajectory of swarm centroid.

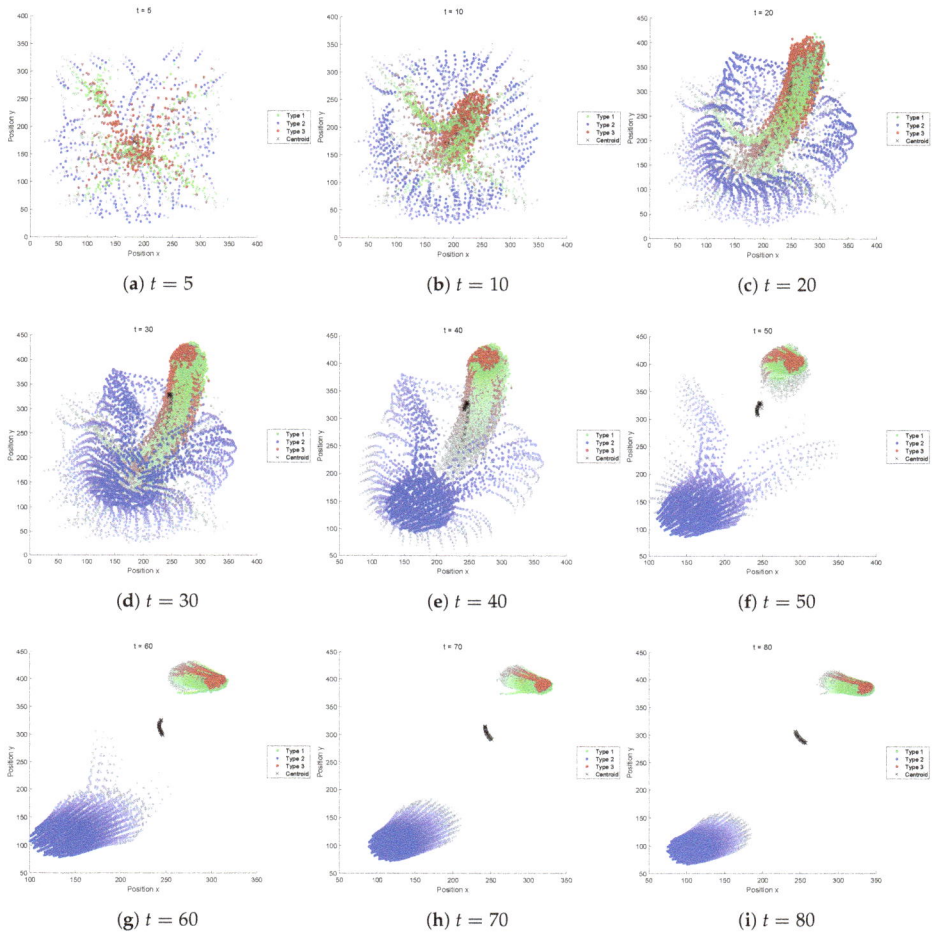

Figure A3. Trajectory of agents (FF-B). The semi-transparent dots behind the agents indicate their past positions at the recent 60 time steps. The "×" mark traces the trajectory of swarm centroid.

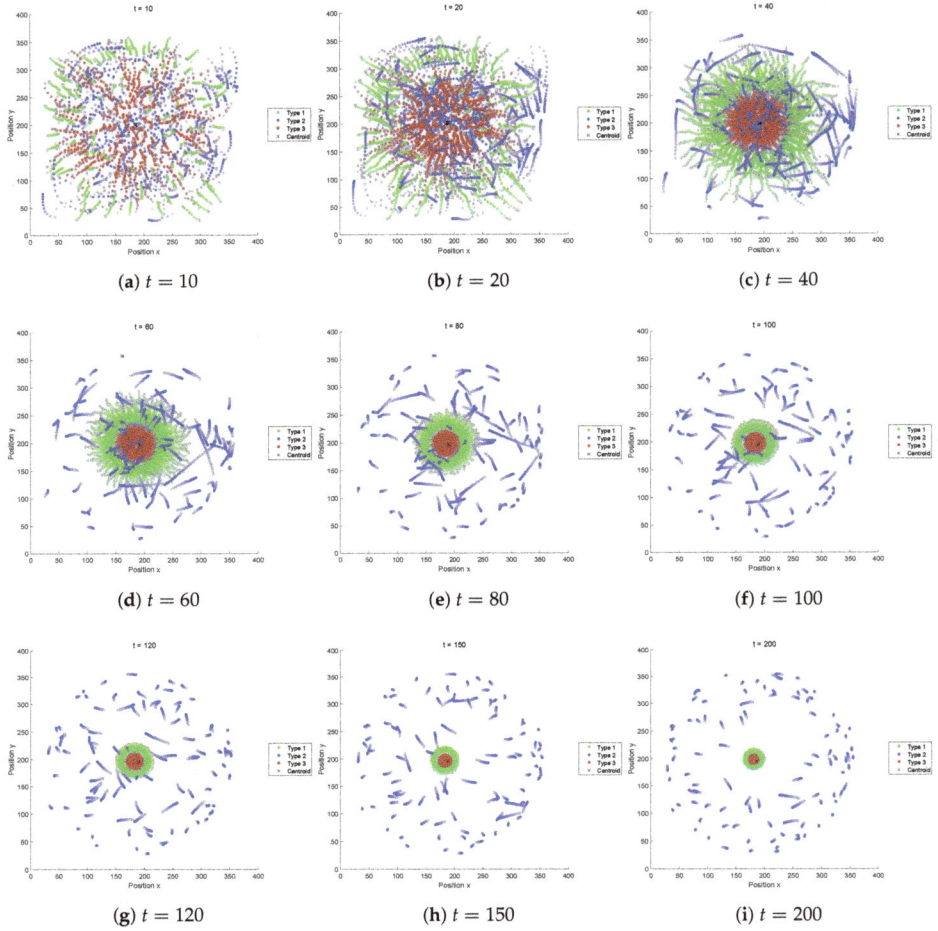

Figure A4. Trajectory of agents (FF-C). The semi-transparent dots behind the agents indicate their past positions at the recent 60 time steps. The "×" mark traces the trajectory of swarm centroid.

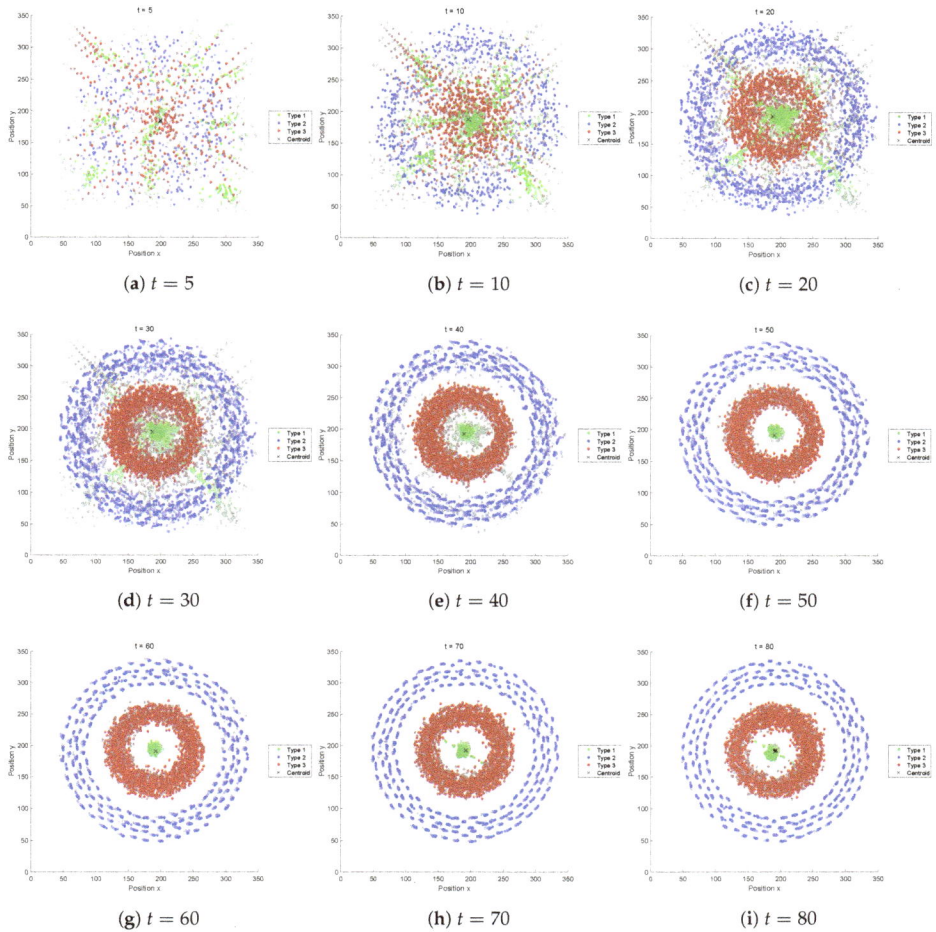

Figure A5. Trajectory of agents (FF-D). The semi-transparent dots behind the agents indicate their past positions at the recent 60 time steps. The "×" mark traces the trajectory of swarm centroid.

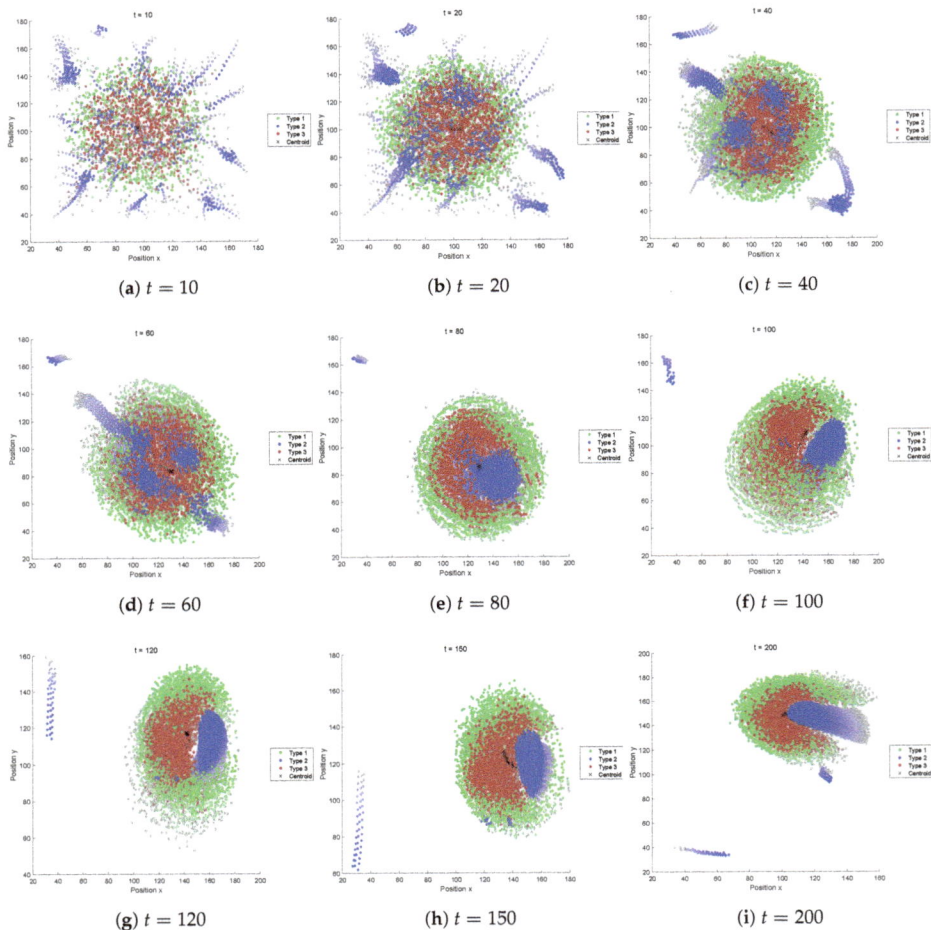

(a) $t = 10$

(b) $t = 20$

(c) $t = 40$

(d) $t = 60$

(e) $t = 80$

(f) $t = 100$

(g) $t = 120$

(h) $t = 150$

(i) $t = 200$

Figure A6. Trajectory of agents (FF-E). The semi-transparent dots behind the agents indicate their past positions at the recent 60 time steps. The "×" mark traces the trajectory of swarm centroid.

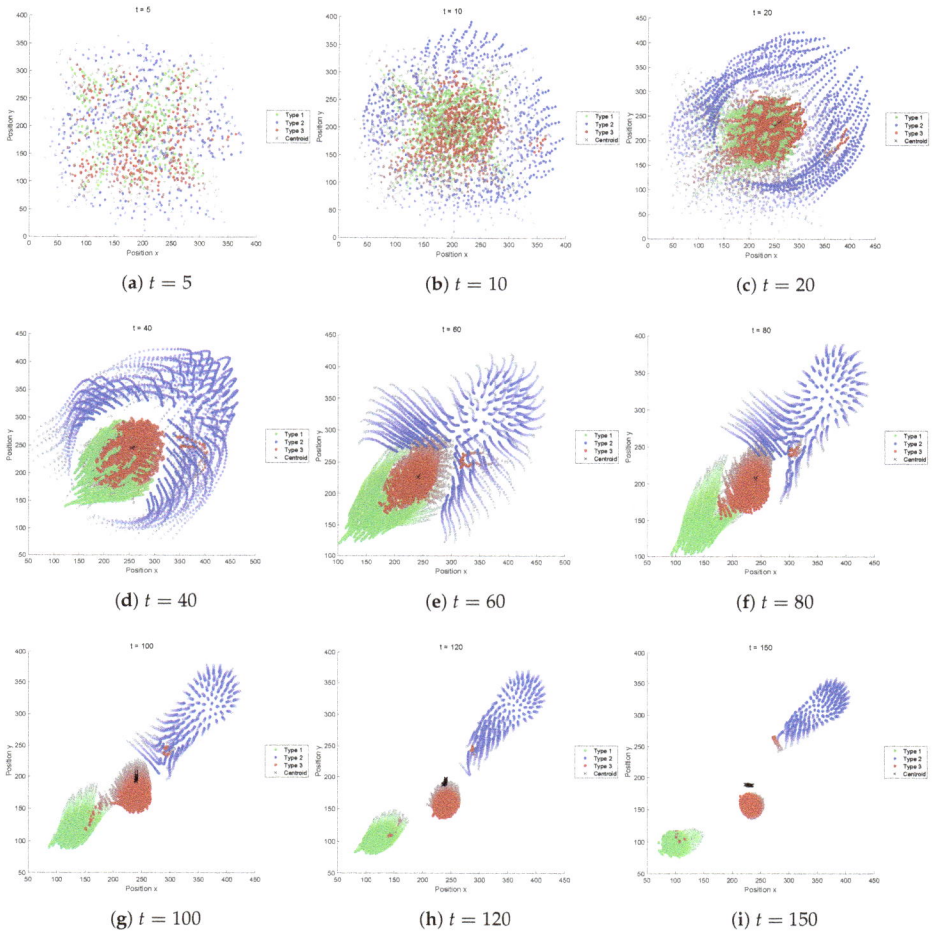

Figure A7. Trajectory of agents (FF-F). The semi-transparent dots behind the agents indicate their past positions at the recent 60 time steps. The "×" mark traces the trajectory of swarm centroid.

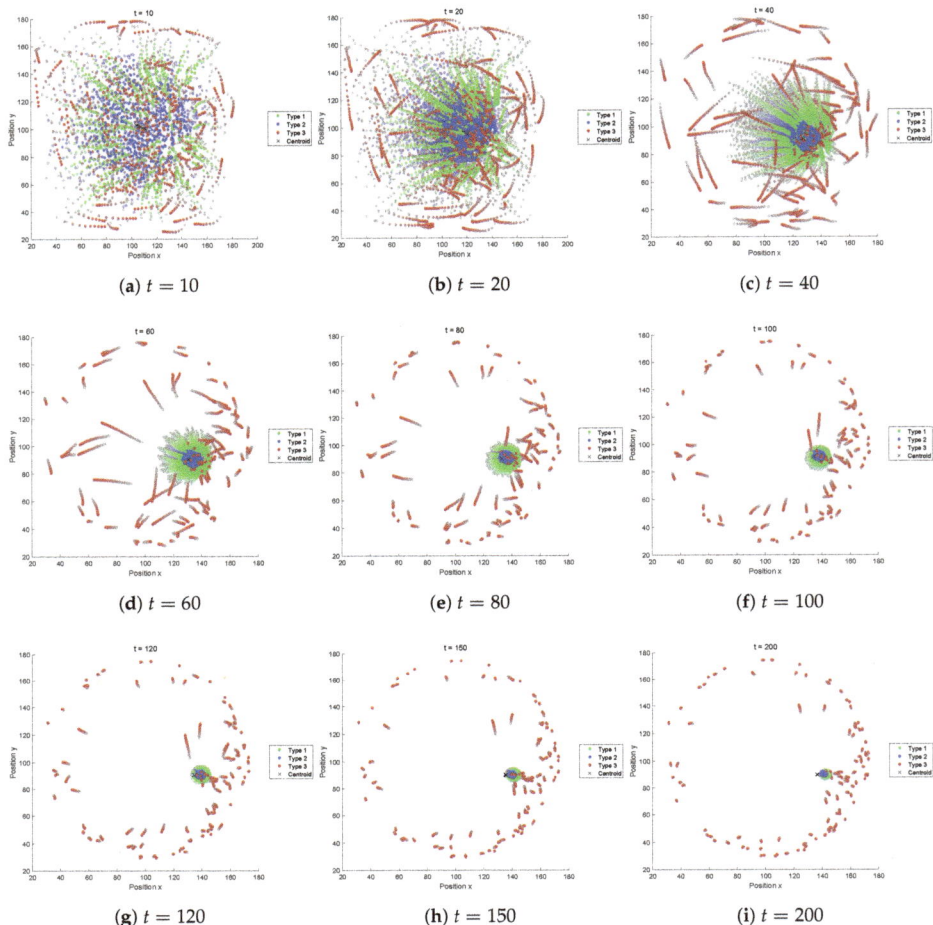

(a) $t = 10$ **(b)** $t = 20$ **(c)** $t = 40$

(d) $t = 60$ **(e)** $t = 80$ **(f)** $t = 100$

(g) $t = 120$ **(h)** $t = 150$ **(i)** $t = 200$

Figure A8. Trajectory of agents (FF-G). The semi-transparent dots behind the agents indicate their past positions at the recent 60 time steps. The "×" mark traces the trajectory of swarm centroid.

References

1. Vicsek, T.; Czirok, A.; Ben-Jacob, E.; Cohen, I.; Shochet, O. Novel Type of Phase Transition in a System of Self-Driven agents. *Phys. Rev. Lett.* **1995**, *75*, 1226–1229. [CrossRef] [PubMed]
2. Vicsek, T. A question of scale. *Nature* **2001**, *411*, 421.
3. Schmickl, T.; Stefanec, M.; Crailsheim, K. How a life-like system emerges from a simple particle motion law. *Sci. Rep.* **2016**, *6*, 37969. [CrossRef] [PubMed]
4. Reynolds, C. Flocks, Herds, and Schools: A Distributed Behavioral Model. *Comput. Graph.* **1987**, *25*, 25–34. [CrossRef]
5. Murphy, R.R. *Disaster Robotics*; MIT Press: Cambridge, MA, USA, 2014.
6. Doursat, R.; Sayama, H.; Michel, O. *Morphogenetic Engineering*; Springer: Berlin/Heidelberg, Germany, 2013; pp. 191–208.
7. Sayama, H. Analysis and design of self-organizing heterogeneous swarm systems. In Proceedings of the 2016 Conference on Complex Systems, Amsterdam, The Netherlands, 19–22 September 2016.

8. Doursat, R.; Sayama, H.; Michel, O. A review of morphogenetic engineering. *Nat. Comput.* **1987**, *12*, 517–535. [CrossRef]

9. Sayama, H. Robust Morphogenesis of Robotic Swarms. *IEEE Comput. Intell. Mag.* **2010**, *5*, 43–49.

10. Sayama, H. Swarm chemistry. *Artif. Life* **2009**, *15*, 105–114. [CrossRef] [PubMed]

11. Sayama, H.; Wong, C. Quantifying evolutionary dynamics of Swarm Chemistry. In Proceedings of the Eleventh European Conference on Artificial Life (ECAL 2011), Paris, France, 8–12 August 2011; pp. 729–730.

12. Sayama, H. Morphologies of self-organizing swarms in 3D swarm chemistry. In Proceedings of the Fourteenth InternationAl Conference on Genetic and Evolutionary Computation Conference, Philadelphia, PA, USA, 7–11 July 2012; pp. 577–584.

13. Sayama, H. Swarm Chemistry Evolving. In Proceedings of the Alife XII Conference, Odense, Denmark, 19–23 August 2010; pp. 32–33.

14. Sayama, H. Swarm Chemistry Homepage. Available online: http://bingweb.binghamton.edu/~sayama/SwarmChemistry/ (accessed on Apr. 29, 2018).

15. Sayama, H. Seeking Open-Ended Evolution in Swarm Chemistry. In Proceedings of the IEEE ALIFE 2011, Paris, France, 11–15 April 2011; pp. 186–193.

16. Sayama, H. Guiding Designs of Self-Organizing Swarms: Interactive and Automated Approaches. In *Guided Self-Organization: Inception*; Springer: Berlin/Heidelberg, Germany, 2014; pp. 365–387.

17. Nishikawa, N.; Suzuki, R.; Arita, A. Coordination Control Design of Heterogeneous Swarm Robots by means of Task-Oriented Optimization. *Artif. Life Robot.* **2016**, *21*, 57–68. [CrossRef]

18. Sayama, H. Four Classes of Morphogenetic Collective Systems. In Proceedings of the Fourteenth International Conference on the Synthesis and Simulation of Living Systems (ALIFE 14), New York, NY, USA, 31 July–2August 2014.

19. Sayama, H. Behavioral Diversities of Morphogenetic Collective Systems. In Proceedings of the European Conference on Artificial Life 2015, New York, NY, USA, 20–24 July 2015.

20. Eshelman, L.J.; Schaffer, J.D. Real-coded Genetic Algorithms and Interval-Schemata. *Found. Genet. Algorithms* **1993**, *2*, 187–202.

21. Palmer, A.R. Animal Asymmetry. *Curr. Biol.* **2009**, *19*, 473–477. [CrossRef] [PubMed]

22. Palmer, A.R. Symmetry breaking and the evolution of development. *Science*, **2004**, *306*, 828–833. [CrossRef] [PubMed]

23. Castellani, E.; Ismael, J. Which Curie's Principle? *Philos. Sci.* **2016**, *83*, 1002–1013. [CrossRef]

24. Chalmers, A.F. Curie's Principle. *Br. J. Philos. Sci.* **1970**, *21*, 133–148. [CrossRef]

25. Kano, T.; Osuka, K.; Kawakatsu, T.; Matsui, N.; Ishiguro, A. A Minimal Model of Collective Behaviour Based on Non-reciprocal Interactions. In Proceedings of the fourteenth European Conference on Artificial Life (ECAL 2017), Lyon, France, 4–8 September 2017; pp. 237–244.

applied
sciences

MDPI

Article

Comparison of Heuristic Algorithms in Discrete Search and Surveillance Tasks Using Aerial Swarms

Pablo Garcia-Aunon *,† [ID] and **Antonio Barrientos Cruz** [ID]

Centre for Automation and Robotics (CAR), Technical University of Madrid (UPM), 28006 Madrid , Spain;
antonio.barrientos@upm.es
* Correspondence: pablo.garcia.aunon@upm.es; Tel.: +34-620-402-032
† Current address: C/ José Gutiérrez Abascal, 2, 28006 Madrid, Spain.

Received: 24 March 2018; Accepted: 2 May 2018; Published: 3 May 2018

Abstract: The search of a given area is one of the most studied tasks in swarm robotics. Different heuristic methods have been studied in the past taking into account the peculiarities of these systems (number of robots, limited communications and sensing and computational capacities). In this work, we introduce a behavioral network made up of different well-known behaviors that act together to achieve a good performance, while adapting to different scenarios. The algorithm is compared with six strategies based on movement patterns in terms of three performance models. For the comparison, four scenario types are considered: plain, with obstacles, with the target location probability distribution and a combination of obstacles and the target location probability distribution. For each scenario type, different variations are considered, such as the number of agents and area size. Results show that although simplistic solutions may be convenient for the simplest scenario type, for the more complex ones, the proposed algorithm achieves better results.

Keywords: swarm robotics; search; surveillance; behaviors; patterns; comparison

1. Introduction

1.1. Multi-Agent and Swarm Robotics

In nature, as well as in our societies, it is easy to find individuals that act together to achieve a specific goal. In some cases, a good performance cannot be achieved without a coordinated action of various agents. In some other cases, it may be even mandatory to use more than one agent. With the development of robotics, it has been possible to cover increasingly complex tasks by using groups of intelligent agents that coordinately act as a team. In many circumstances, subdividing those tasks not only speeds up their fulfillment, but also allows specialization by allocating specific tasks to agents designed for those purposes. On the other hand, multi-agent systems present important complexities that must be correctly addressed, among which we can highlight the coordination of the agents, the communications between them and how to make the team learn in order to improve the performance.

There are several cases in which the use of multi-agent systems may be desirable. In [1], three types of tasks are considered: tasks that require multiple agents (for example, a task that needs the simultaneous presence of an agent in two places separated by a great distance); tasks that are traditionally multi-agent (e.g., because they can be naturally divided); and tasks that might benefit from the use of multiple agents. Search, surveillance and exploration belong to this last group. Some other tasks might not benefit from the use of more than one robot, either because they are simple or because the development of the coordination and the communication between the members is a barrier not worth overcoming.

Some examples in nature show that individually, simple animals have been capable of surviving during millions of years all over the Earth. Consider for example the most well known of these animals, ants. Ants have a very simple nervous system made up by 250,000 neurons and very limited sensing and communication capabilities. Communications are achieved mostly by pheromones [2], chemicals spread in the environment used to mark trails, warn other members of the nest and confuse enemies. It is obvious how difficult it would be for them if they had to survive individually. However, acting as a coordinated group, they have survived for 130 million years and form around 15–25% of the terrestrial animal biomass. The reason why such a simple creature has been so successful is because of their collective behavior. Every ant acts in a very simple way that turns out to be very inefficient individually. However, collectively, because of the high number of members, an efficient behavior emerges. Similar social structures and interactions may be found in other species, such as bees, termites, fishes (forming schools), ungulates and birds (flocks).

Swarm behaviors are a particular case of collective behavior, in which a large number of members is involved, requiring very limited communications between them and being individually simple. Some researches started bringing the ideas of swarms in nature to the robotics field. Goals are achieved using a high number of homogeneous robots, which behave following simple and mostly reactive rules. The pioneers of swarm robotics appeared in the late 1980s and the beginning of the 1990s [3–5]. Swarm robotic systems present some well-known advantages such as robustness, simplicity, scalability and flexibility, while it is difficult to achieve a good global performance [6]. More recently, many researchers have used the term swarm robotics to name or classify these works. Hardware miniaturization and cost reduction have made possible new research lines in this direction, and hundreds of papers developing all sorts of algorithms have been published.

1.2. Search with Swarms

From the very beginning of the development of swarm robotics, researches have focused on implementing behaviors in robots to solve simple tasks [7]. Those behaviors are mainly inspired by how natural swarms act, and the missions may be used as test beds for more complex and useful tasks. Typical examples of them are aggregation (gathering in a common place), flocking, foraging (collecting items scattered in the space), path formation (establishing a path of robots between two points) and deployment (expanding and occupying the available space). Note that all of these behaviors are very common in animal swarms such as fish schools, bird flocks, ants and bees.

Besides those basic tasks, more complex missions have been also studied in the past. Exploration of unknown areas, search, surveillance, patrolling, collaborative manipulation and self-assembly are only some examples of missions that have been carried out with robotic swarms. In this work, the focus is on the search task, where multiple and different solutions have been proposed over the years. Most of these methods may be assigned to one of the following categories:

- Virtual pheromones: Inspired by the chemicals dropped by some insects, the search is led using them in their virtual version [8,9]. They are conveniently created and eliminated, and in many cases, their transportation in the area of interest is calculated by means of the diffusion equation.
- Potential fields: The agents are subjected to virtual potential fields created by them or by other objects (such as obstacles) and react to them [10].
- Flocking techniques: Mimicking flocks of birds and schools of fishes, the agents move coordinately, keeping appropriate distances between them [11].
- Probabilistic maps: Making use of prior knowledge of the locations of the targets, the robots search according to it [12]. Adapting the decisions depending on the data acquired during the process is also possible [13].
- Patterns: These comprise a wide range of methods and techniques that try to organize the search to achieve high efficiencies [14–16].

As can be seen, all the previous solutions are heuristic methods, since they do not guarantee optimal solutions. There have been approaches trying to optimally solve the search, although they require high computational loads, and the calculations only reach reduced time horizons. Note that the number of solutions increase exponentially with the number of agents, making the finding of optimal solutions almost intractable. Some of these methods will be briefly reviewed in Section 1.4.

In this paper, we propose an algorithm based on a behavioral network, made up by different behaviors that act together to obtain a common decision in order to lead each agent. On the one hand, this type of control responds quickly to changes in the environment (which is a typical property of reactive systems). On the other hand, the behaviors are capable of constructing representations of the world (they have memory, a typical property of the deliberative controls). Decisions are taken as a result of the interactions between the behaviors and the environment and between the behaviors. All this results in a good trade-off between reactive and mid-term decisions [17]. Behavior-based architectures turn out to be adequate for changing and stochastic environments, and therefore, they are also very suitable for multi-agent systems. Note that if each agent makes its own decisions (there is no central planning), the state of the task changes rapidly, and planning at the individual level becomes likely unfeasible.

The search task is an interesting challenge not only because of its direct application in real-world situations, but also because it may be extended to similar, but more complex tasks such as surveillance, exploration, patrolling, area coverage and the so-called traveling salesman problem:

- Exploration: This differs from search in that there does not exist a previous map of the area.
- Surveillance: This is basically persistently searching a given area. Each zone must be re-visited frequently enough to ensure up-to-date information.
- Patrolling: Similar to surveillance, the area of interest is restricted to singular points or lines (for instance, corridors inside a building).
- Probabilistic maps and obstacles: Another extension of the search task in its simplest form is the inclusion of probabilistic maps, which consider prior knowledge about where it is more likely that a target is located in the area. Moreover, obstacles may be included, it being impossible for the agents to go through them.

Authors frequently define area coverage as deploying the agents until they reach certain fixed positions so that the covered area (by either the sensor or the communication footprint) is maximized. However, some other authors use the word coverage to define a task similar to search. For instance, in [18], the search area is covered by subdividing it into k regions, which are individually assigned to k robots. Each robot searches then in its assigned area following regular patterns. Another example can be found in [19], where the coverage task is addressed using the spanning tree coverage method. In any case, the strategies proposed in these works do not differ from the strategies listed above.

1.3. Search Patterns

In order to organize the search, most of the past works based on patterns have made use of dividing the area into cells, taking into account if they have been visited or not. The sensed area is frequently restricted to those cells, and therefore, the search implies visiting all the existing cells. The agent's movement is restricted, and they are only allowed to travel between the centers of adjacent cells. With these assumptions, the search is simplified since it becomes a discrete problem. In the following, the main works addressing this kind of mission by implementing movement patterns are analyzed.

In [20], the task is addressed with an algorithm made up by four behaviors that act together:

- Contour following: This leads the agent along boundaries, i.e., cells that have at least one non-visited cell surrounding them. This is the behavior with the highest priority.

- Avoidance: When two agents are within a given range, this behavior is triggered. The velocity command is perpendicular to their mutual collision course, and it is added to the contour following the behavior output.
- Gradient descend: Having defined a distance field, computed at each cell as the distance to the closest non-visited cell, when this behavior is active, it leads the agent along the gradient. It is activated when an agent is completely surrounded by visited cells.
- Random movement: The agent decides randomly which cell to visit next. It is activated when none of the other behaviors are active.

The distance matrix is treated here as a pheromone field. The members of the swarm share information with the agents within a communication range, updating the distance matrix (i.e., which cells have been visited). Assuming a constant velocity and considering that traveling diagonally requires the same time as traveling in the other directions, the minimum needed time is then $O\left(\frac{m \cdot n}{l}\right)$, where $m \cdot n$ is the number of cells and l is the number of agents. The algorithm is tested for different numbers of agents, as well as for different avoidance and communication ranges. The needed time to accomplish the mission is used as the performance measurement. The influence of implementing a central communication point, which distributes the state of the search grid among the agents, is analyzed. Having distributed the agents randomly, the results show that the time needed to finish the mission is higher than the theoretical lower bound, even with the centralization of the information. However, even with short communication ranges, the overtime to complete the search is less than 50%, with a standard deviation of 6% on average due to the variability in the initial conditions. With only one agent, the time needed is close to the minimum bound. Furthermore, another performance measurement criterion is proposed:

$$E = \frac{1}{1 + \frac{N_m}{N}} \tag{1}$$

where N_m are the number of cells visited more than once and N is the total number of cells. Again, for only one member, this ratio is close to one, whereas for the higher number of agents, this figure decreases. If the communication range increases, the solution converges to the centralized map, as expected.

In another work [21], three search strategies are compared in a mission in which the agents are deployed in an area that contains targets to be localized and destroyed, forming coalitions. The three studied strategies are:

- Random search: Each agent follows its current heading until one boundary is reached. At that moment, it changes its direction to re-enter the search area.
- Search lanes: The area is organized into lanes, and each agent is assigned to a unique one. Once a lane has been traveled, a new one is assigned.
- Grid-based search: The agents go to the closest non-visited cell.

Since in this work, targets to be destroyed are considered, the search task stops to pursue and destroy them. Therefore, no absolute search performance metric is provided, and these behaviors are compared by only considering the time needed to complete the mission. Monte Carlo simulations are run varying the number of agents and targets.

There have been many works in which the task is solved by partitioning the area and assigning individually those partitions to the agents. For instance, in [22], each partition is filled with zig-zag lanes, computed to be energetically efficient. However, the algorithm requires that the area is a polygon on whose boundaries the UAVs must be initially placed, restricting the initial positions.

Making use of the probability that a target is located in a specific cell in [23], scores are assigned to each one, taking also into account forbidden flying zones and areas that should be avoided if possible. The scores are updated either externally or because of the findings of the agents. The agents select the cell to visit depending on that score. In this work, the area is partitioned using a Voronoi diagram, and the results are compared with other algorithms:

- Lawn mower: Each agent moves in a straight line, and when it encounters an obstacle, it turns to head in a clear direction.
- Raster scan: The agents move in parallel lanes north/south or east/west.
- Gradient climb: This is a greedy algorithm based on the surrounding cell scores.
- Randomized Voronoi: The area is partitioned with the Voronoi diagram using the agent's position as the generators.
- Full algorithm: This is the same algorithm, developed in previous works, but without the Voronoi partitioning.

The algorithms are compared using as a performance measurement the mean cell scores, computed along 20 runs, the most efficient algorithm being the one proposed in the work. This result seems reasonable, since the performance is measured using the same score on which the algorithm is based.

1.4. Optimal Methods in Discrete Search Tasks

Although the discrete search task using teams of agents has been shown to be a hard problem to solve optimally, there have been some works addressing the problem by looking for optimal solutions. For instance, in [24], an exact mixed-integer linear programing formulation to solve in an optimal way the search of a discretized area is proposed. Given a mission state defined by the position of the agents and the cells already visited, the best sequence of movements is calculated for a specific time horizon. While the found path is being followed, a new sequence is generated over a receding horizon. Eight possible movements are considered at each decision instant, as well as a prior belief about where the targets are possibly located. The authors remark that the number of possible solutions for n agents and a time horizon of T movements is 8^{nT}, which reaches prohibitive values quickly. Using a six-core processor, for a grid of 10×10 cells and considering two and five agents, with time horizons of 10 and 20 steps, optimal solutions are found within one minute (except for one of the cases studied, which needed 142 s). Bigger scenarios and/or more agents are unfeasible to solve.

In [25], a receding time horizon is also used to optimize on-line the trajectories of a group of UAVs in a discrete bi-dimensional search area. Based on the current state of the agents, the optimizer tries to maximize the reward of finding a target and of exploring the area, while it keeps the energy consumption low. The optimization problem is broken down into local ones assuming communications between the agents, so that it can be solved in a decentralized way. For this procedure, Nash optimality is considered and a particle swarm optimization used as the optimizer tool. Simulations are carried out in a search area of 50 km × 50 km (a grid of 500 × 500 units), and the results show that although the decentralized optimization does not reach the performance of the centralized one, it requires half of the computational time.

1.5. Organization of This Paper

This paper is organized as follows: In Section 2, the problem is presented, defining the search area and its grid, the agent's dynamics and the measurement of the algorithms' performance. Furthermore, the four different types of scenarios used to compare the algorithms are shown; in Section 3, the proposed algorithm based on a set of behaviors is explained in detail, as well as how it is configured for any scenario. In Section 5, the algorithms are compared measuring their performance for the four scenarios types; also, the communications needed by each algorithm and their adaptation to surveillance missions are analyzed. Finally, in Section 6, the conclusions of this work are depicted, as well as the proposed future developments.

The main contributions of this papers are: (i) the proposal of a behavioral network made up by six behaviors; (ii) systematical comparison with six search patterns in four different scenario types, considering the wide variations of the parameters that define each scenario; (iii) a performance model for this type of mission.

2. Problem Formulation

2.1. Scenario

The task proposed consists of observing a given two-dimensional search space, which is a rectangular area subdivided into cells of fixed size. The movement of the agents is restricted to those cells, so that each agent is allowed to move from the center of each cell to the center of any of the eight adjacent cells. As already mentioned, this assumption is convenient, since it converts the search into a discrete problem, simplifying it.

We consider that the search is carried out by flying robots, more specifically, multicopters. The agents are capable of flying at a constant altitude and at given commanded velocity v_n and are equipped with a camera capable of detecting targets within a circular area of radius R_f. This area is called the sensor footprint. The team of robots is made up by N_a of equal multicopters, initially deployed randomly in non-coincident positions in the search area. Each agent will be configured equally, i.e., the control parameters will be the same for each one.

Having divided the search space into a grid, with a total area of A_s (m^2), we allow the robots to move to any adjacent cell. In order to ensure that the cells are completely observed by the sensor footprint, they must be inscribed in it. Therefore, the number of cells in each direction is:

$$n_x = \lceil \frac{L_x}{\sqrt{2}R_f} \rceil \tag{2a}$$

$$n_y = \lceil \frac{L_y}{\sqrt{2}R_f} \rceil \tag{2b}$$

where $\lceil \; \rceil$ indicates the ceil function, and the dimensions of each search cell are:

$$\Delta L_x = \frac{L_x}{n_x} \tag{3a}$$

$$\Delta L_y = \frac{L_y}{n_y} \tag{3b}$$

When flying in any direction, part of the adjacent cells is observed; see Figure 1. Those cells, which we will denominate from now on search cells, should be then subdivided into thinner cells to take into account whether those portions of space have been observed or not. We will refer to these other cells as discretization cells. Therefore, the movement will be restricted to the search cells, but not the search task itself, since a search cell can be completely observed without visiting it. We consider for the rest of the work a size of the discretization cells of 2×2 m, i.e., $\Delta l_x = \Delta l_y = \Delta l = 2$ m.

In Figure 1, both types of cells have been represented. We define observing a cell as placing an agent so that at least half of that discretization cell is inside the sensor footprint. We also define visiting a cell as placing an agent in the center of that search cell. Since the search cells are inscribed in the sensor footprint, visiting a search cell implies observing the discretization cells inside it.

In Table 1, the parameters that define the scenarios with their considered range of values have been presented. Note that instead of limiting the total search area A_s, it is more sensible to limit the search area per agent, A_s / N_a. On the other hand, we define the aspect ratio f_A of the search space as:

$$f_A = \frac{L_x}{L_y} \tag{4}$$

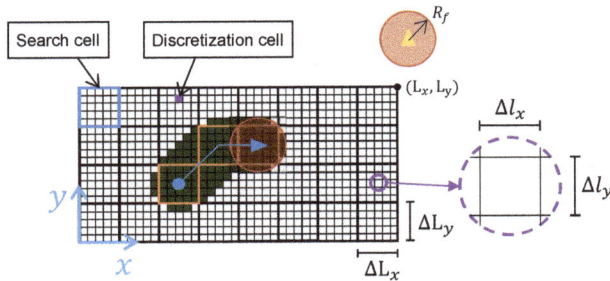

Figure 1. Search area example. A search and a discretization cell have been highlighted. The agent, represented as a triangle, has moved in the diagonal and in the horizontal directions. The three visited search cells by the agent have been highlighted. The observed discretization cells have been marked in dark green. Note that the footprint area circumscribes the search cells.

Table 1. List of parameters that define the scenario.

Parameter	Description	Range of Values
A_s/N_a	Search area per agent	$[2, 15] \times 10^3$ m^2
N_a	Number of agents	$[2, 30]$
v_n	Nominal velocity of the agents	$[2, 20]$ m/s
R_f	Radius of the sensor footprint	$[5, 20]$ m
f_A	Aspect ratio of the search area	$[0.25, 1]$

2.2. Plain, Obstacles and Probability Scenarios

Given the scenario above described, four different types of scenarios are considered:

- Plain scenario: In the simplest scenario type, every cell is flyable, and all the discretization cells must be observed at least once to finish the mission (see Figure 2a).
- Probability distribution scenario: We assume prior knowledge about the possible location of targets to be found. According to this distribution, $N_t = \frac{5}{2000} \cdot \frac{A_s}{N_a}$ targets are generated. The search is finished when all the targets have been observed. The probability distribution is generated using the midpoint displacement method, normally used as a terrain generator method. The initial distribution is generated randomly with a roughness $r \in [0, 0.5]$ and its derivative $r_r \in [0, 0.1]$. Seven iterations are applied. In Figure 2b, an example of this scenario type is shown.
- Obstacles scenario: Some of the search cells are occupied, and the agents cannot fly through them. The search is completed when all the discrete cells that are not inside the obstacles have been observed at least once. The map is generated using the Schelling segregation model, fixing the tolerance limit to 0.3 and the percentage of the population that look for new houses to 0.7. The percentage of non-flyable search cells is drawn from a normal distribution $\mathcal{N}(0.75, 0.1^2)$, while the percentage of empty cells (cells that may be occupied by obstacles) is drawn from $\mathcal{N}(0.25, 0.1^2)$. Once the equilibrium has been reached, the empty cells are transformed into flyable cells. It is checked that every flyable cell can be reached (i.e., there are no cells completely surrounded by obstacles). An example of the result of this procedure has been shown in Figure 2c.
- Probability distribution and obstacles scenario: Both the probability distribution of target locations and obstacles are considered; see Figure 2d.

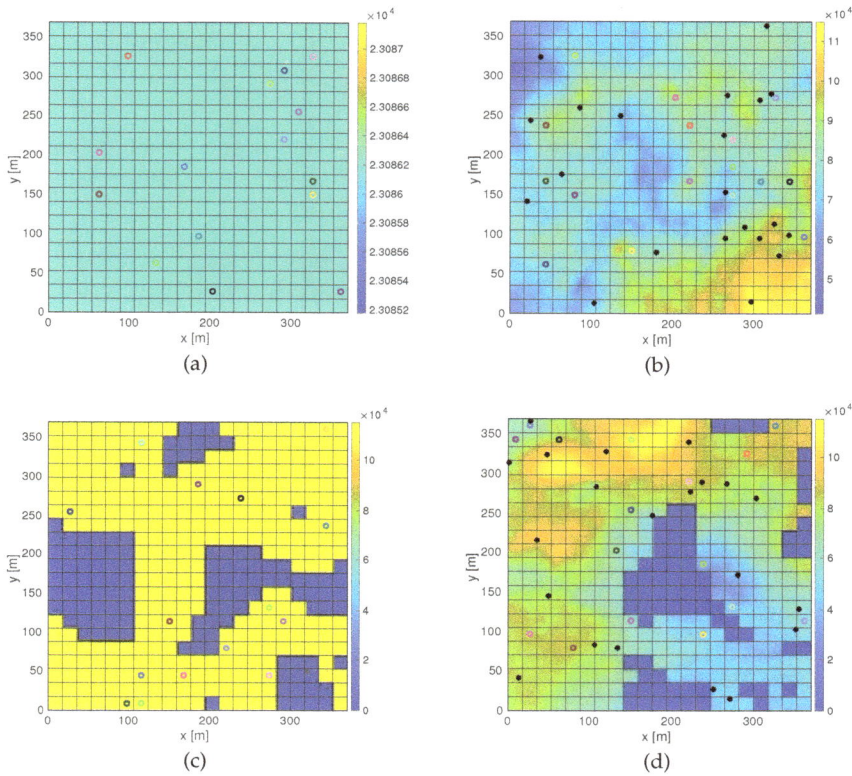

Figure 2. (**a**) Plain scenario; (**b**) probability distribution scenario; (**c**) obstacles scenario; (**d**) probability distribution and obstacles scenario. Examples of scenarios with the four types considered. The color bar represents the concentration of pheromones (see Section 3), proportional to the probability distribution of the targets' location. The colored circles represent the initial position of the agents. The black dots are the targets to be detected. Obstacles have been colored in dark blue.

2.3. Model of the Agent

2.3.1. Dynamics

The agent considered here is a multicopter, i.e., a holonomic UAV capable of flying in any direction and keeping a fixed position. The high level control generates a commanded velocity in the $\{x, y\}$ plane, defined by two variables, a reference velocity v_n and its heading ψ_c. The actual velocity vector is modeled as:

$$\mathbf{v}(t) = v(t) \left(\sin(\psi_c(t)), \cos(\psi_c(t)) \right) \tag{5}$$

where $v(t)$ is assumed to be dependent on the change of the flying direction:

$$\frac{v(t)}{v_n} = \begin{cases} 1 - \frac{|\Delta\psi|}{2\pi} \left(1 - \cos\left(2\pi \frac{t-t_d}{t_v} \right) \right) & \text{if } t - t_d \leq t_v \\ 1 & \text{if } t - t_d > t_v \end{cases} \tag{6}$$

where t_d is the time instant at which the agent changes its direction and t_v is the characteristic time for the velocity reduction due to the change in the flying direction ($\Delta\psi$).

2.3.2. Energy Consumption

The agents are considered to have an energy consumption proportionally to the flown distance:

$$E_d = \alpha_{E_d} d \tag{7}$$

where E_d is the dimensionless energy needed to fly a distance d (m) and α_{E_d} is a coefficient. Furthermore, if a quadcopter changes its flying direction, an extra energy consumption is considered:

$$E_{\Delta\psi} = \alpha_{\Delta\psi} \frac{|\Delta\psi|}{\pi} \tag{8}$$

where $E_{\Delta\psi}$ is the dimensionless energy needed to change the flying direction in $\Delta\psi$ radians and $\alpha_{\Delta\psi}$ is a coefficient. The remaining energy in each quadcopter will be then calculated as:

$$E_a = E_{max} - E_d - E_{\Delta\psi} \tag{9}$$

being E_{max} the maximum energy in the quadcopter's batteries. In Table 2, the chosen values for the parameters that define the model have been presented.

Table 2. List of parameters that define the model of the agent.

Parameter	Description	Equation	Value
t_v	Velocity reduction time due to $\Delta\psi$	(6)	5 s
α_{E_d}	Energy-distance coefficient	(7)	0.1 m^{-1}
$\alpha_{\Delta\psi}$	Energy-change-of-heading coefficient	(8)	2
E_{max}	Max available energy	(9)	180

2.4. Measuring the Performance

As already seen, in past works, several different ways of measuring the performance of a search task have been proposed. Some of them are not absolute metrics, i.e., they have been created ad hoc for specific missions or situations and cannot be translated in a general way to other search missions. The best way to measure the efficiency would be comparing the performance with a solution whose optimality is ensured. However, as we have seen, only partial optimal solutions (with limited time horizons) have been achieved. Therefore, we will make use of three different models or methods to measure the efficiency.

2.4.1. Model 1

The first model we consider is the one presented in [23]. The efficiency is measured with a coefficient between the total number of search cells and the number of search cells that have been visited more than once:

$$E_1 = \frac{1}{1 + \frac{N_m}{N}} \tag{10}$$

where N_m is the number of search cells visited more than once and N is the total number of search cells. Note that if every cell is visited only once, the efficiency reaches the maximum value, equal to one.

2.4.2. Model 2

In the first model of the efficiency, the search cells have been considered to measure it, counting whether they have been visited more than once or not. However, when traveling diagonally, parts of the surrounding cells are observed, as well. In order to take this into account, in this second model, Equation (10) is used, but considering the discretization cells:

$$E_2 = \frac{1}{1 + \frac{n_m}{n}} \tag{11}$$

being n_m the discretization cells that have been observed more than once and n the total number of discretization cells. With this approach, a result closer to the reality is expected.

2.4.3. Model 3

A final third model of the efficiency is proposed, and it is based on the time the team of agents need to complete the search. The ideal performance would be reached if the search area was completely observed without observing any of the discretization cells more than once and if during the search process, no part of the agent's footprint is outside the search area. If this were the case, the time needed to observe a specific area would be:

$$t_i = \frac{A_o - A_i}{2R_f v_n N_a} \tag{12}$$

where A_i is the observed area at $t = 0$ and A_o is the actual observed area at the end of the mission. Note that in some missions, depending on the search area per agent, the footprint sensor radius and the configuration of the algorithm, it may be $A_o < A_s$ if the available energy is limited. If this is the case, we consider that the search is not completed. If a group of N_a agents needs a time t_n to completely observe that area, we can define the efficiency as:

$$E_3 = \frac{t_i}{t_n} \tag{13}$$

where $E_3 \in (0, 1)$. Note that reaching an efficiency equal to one, i.e., $t_n = t_i$, is not possible since the footprint invades part of the adjacent cells, and therefore, when flying over the cells at the boundaries, part of the sensor footprint would be outside the search area, implying a loss of efficiency. It is also very likely that some of the discretization cells are observed more than once. Probably if we chose the search cells so that the footprint is inscribed inside them, the efficiency would increase. However, the corners of the search area would never be observed.

2.4.4. Fitness Function

In Section 2.3.2, we have assumed that each agent accounts for a specific amount of available energy; once it is consumed, it stops flying, and therefore, it stops observing the scenario. Depending on how efficient the configuration of the algorithm is and on the scenario characteristics, it may happen that the search area is not completely observed. In those cases, the efficiency will be penalized by only considering 25% of the efficiency. Note that it may happen that for the same scenario, with the same configuration of the algorithm, the task may be completed or not depending on the initial conditions. In those cases, the efficiency penalization will be only applied for the trials in which the search has not been completed.

We assume that the efficiency depends on the initial conditions, for a given configuration Ω and scenario Y. We consider that a configuration is robust if for different initial conditions, it achieves efficiencies with a small standard deviation, since it is capable of carrying out the task within similar periods of time, independently of the initial positions. Therefore, instead of evaluating the goodness of the configuration with the efficiency, we define a fitness function that accounts for this:

$$f = E \cdot \beta_f \cdot \beta_e \tag{14a}$$

$$\beta_f = \frac{1}{3}\left(2 + \frac{\tanh\left(50(\sigma_c - \sigma)\right) + 1}{\tanh\left(50\sigma_c\right) + 1}\right) \tag{14b}$$

$$\beta_e = \begin{cases} 1 & \text{if search completed} \\ 0.25 & \text{if search not completed} \end{cases} \tag{14c}$$

where $\beta_f \in [2/3, 1]$ is a correction factor that penalizes high standard deviations, being $\beta_f(\sigma = 0) = 1$; β_e is the penalization in the case that the search is not completed. Based on experience, it has been chosen $\sigma_c = E/10$, considering this value as reachable if the algorithm is properly configured. In Figure 3, the correction factor has been represented for $\sigma_c = 0.03$ as a function of the standard deviation.

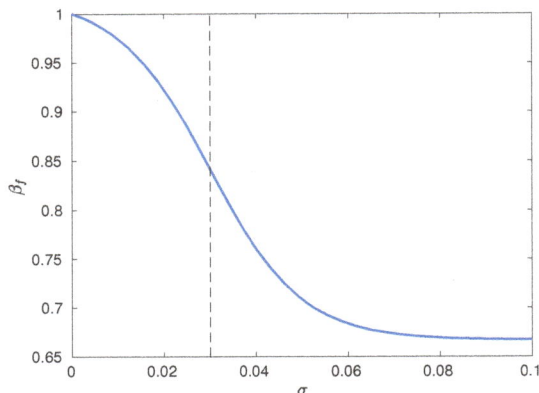

Figure 3. Correction factor β_f of the efficiency as a function of its standard deviation. For the dashed line, the value of $\sigma_c = 0.03$.

For each of the models of the efficiency already presented, Equations (10), (11) and (13), the fitness value will be calculated as well in order to estimate the variance of the algorithm, taking also into account whether the search has been completed or not.

3. Proposed Search Algorithm, a Set of Behaviors: A1

3.1. Search Behavior

This first behavior is the main one and leads the multicopter to search unexplored areas. It is based on the presence of virtual pheromones, whose dynamics and different classes are explained in the next subsections. The virtual pheromones are created on the search space and are absorbed by the robots as the area is observed. The robots are then attracted to unobserved zones, where the concentration of the pheromones is higher.

3.1.1. Pheromone Dynamics

The dynamics of the virtual pheromones have been implemented following the bi-dimensional heat flow (or gas diffusion) equation:

$$\frac{\partial \phi(\mathbf{r}, t)}{\partial t} = -\nabla \mathbf{F} + S \tag{15a}$$

$$\mathbf{F} = -D(\mathbf{r}, t) \nabla \phi(\mathbf{r}, t) \tag{15b}$$

where ϕ is the concentration of the virtual pheromones, ∇ is the divergence operator, $\mathbf{F}$ is the pheromone flux and D is the diffusion coefficient and represents how well the pheromones are transported. S is the source of pheromones, i.e., the creation of pheromones at each discretization cell.

Using the divergence theorem in Equation (15) and considering as volumes of control the discretization cells, we can solve the obtained integral equation with an explicit scheme, forward in time and centered in space (FTCS). We consider therefore mean values of ϕ and S inside those cells and mean values of **F** and D along their boundaries. The problem is then properly posed by finally defining the initial and the boundary conditions:

$$\phi(x, y, t = 0) = \phi_0(x, y) \tag{16a}$$

$$\phi_x(0, y, t) = \phi_x(L_x, y, t) = 0 \tag{16b}$$

$$\phi_y(x, 0, t) = \phi_y(x, L_y, t) = 0 \tag{16c}$$

The first equation represents the initial concentration of pheromones over the search space, whereas the next four are von Neumann conditions, which state that the pheromone's flux through the boundaries must always be zero. Obstacles inside the scenario are impermeable to the pheromones flux, similarly to the boundaries of the area.

3.1.2. Cell Types and Properties

The properties of each discretization cell, i.e., the concentration, creation and diffusion of pheromones, variables $\phi_{i,j}^k$, $D_{i,j}^k$ and $S_{P_{i,j}}^k$ associated with the cell (i, j) at moment k, depend on three types of cells:

- Non-observed cells: cells that have not been observed yet:

$$S_{i,j}^k = S_{no} \tag{17a}$$

$$D_{i,j}^k = D_{no} \tag{17b}$$

- Observed cells: cells already observed by any agent:

$$S_{i,j}^k = S_o \tag{18a}$$

$$D_{i,j}^k = D_o \tag{18b}$$

- Recently-observed cells: if a cell has just been observed, there is n instantaneous drop of its pheromone concentration of:

$$\Delta_{ro}\phi_{i,j}^{k+1} = \delta_{ro} \cdot \phi_{i,j}^k \tag{19}$$

where Δ_{ro} indicates variation due to the fact that the cell has recently been observed and $\delta_{ro} \in [-1, 0]$. This drop is accounted only once, so that at the next time step, a recently-visited cell becomes a regularly-visited cell.

- Isolated cells: Each non-observed cell has associated a so-called isolation index, $\theta_{i,j}^k$, which is the number of observed cells surrounding it. If the cell has already been observed, its isolating index is forced to be equal to zero. Every time step the isolation index changes, there is an increment in the pheromone concentration of:

$$\Delta_\theta\phi_{i,j}^{k+1} = \rho_{\Delta\theta} \cdot \Delta\theta_{i,j}^{k+1} \cdot \phi_{i,j}^k \tag{20}$$

where $\Delta\theta_{i,j}^{k+1} \geq 0$ is the variation of the isolation index from time k to $k+1$:

$$\Delta\theta_{i,j}^{k+1} = \theta_{i,j}^{k+1} - \theta_{i,j}^k \tag{21}$$

The parameter $\rho_{\Delta\theta} \geq 0$ makes the concentration increase when its isolation index changes. Moreover, there is an extra pheromone creation proportional to the isolation index in these cells:

$$\Delta_\theta S_{i,j}^k = \rho_\theta \cdot \theta_{i,j}^k \tag{22}$$

In Figure 4, the above-mentioned cells have been represented. The white discretization cells have not been observed yet. At each time step, the cells that have just been observed become recently-observed cells, in dark green. In the next step, those cells become regular observed cells, in light green. Note that even though there may be a variation in the isolation index at position (w, h), the variation of the isolation index is forced to be zero, since the cell becomes observed. In the example shown in the figure, the pheromone concentration in those four cells will suffer a variation, exclusively due to the type of the cell (Δ_{tc}), of:

$$\Delta_{tc}\phi_{i,j}^{k+1} = S_o \cdot \Delta t$$

$$\Delta_{tc}\phi_{i-1,j+1}^{k+1} = S_{no} \cdot \Delta t + \Delta_\theta \phi_{i-1,j+1}^{k+1} = (S_{no} + \Delta_\theta S_{i,j}^{k+1})\Delta t = (S_{no} + \rho_\theta \cdot \theta_{i,j}^{k+1})\Delta t$$

$$\Delta_{tc}\phi_{w,h}^{k+1} = S_o \cdot \Delta t + \delta_{ro} \cdot \phi_{w,h}^k$$

$$\Delta_{tc}\phi_{w+1,h+1}^{k+1} = S_{no} \cdot \Delta t + \rho_{\Delta\theta} \cdot \Delta\theta_{w+1,h+1}^{k+1} \cdot \phi_{w+1,h+1}^k$$

(23)

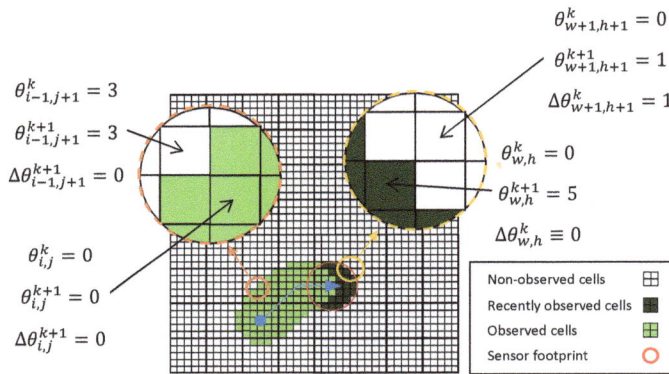

$$\theta_{w+1,h+1}^k = 0$$
$$\theta_{w+1,h+1}^{k+1} = 1$$
$$\Delta\theta_{w+1,h+1}^k = 1$$

$$\theta_{i-1,j+1}^k = 3$$
$$\theta_{i-1,j+1}^{k+1} = 3$$
$$\Delta\theta_{i-1,j+1}^{k+1} = 0$$

$$\theta_{w,h}^k = 0$$
$$\theta_{w,h}^{k+1} = 5$$
$$\Delta\theta_{w,h}^k \equiv 0$$

$$\theta_{i,j}^k = 0$$
$$\theta_{i,j}^{k+1} = 0$$
$$\Delta\theta_{i,j}^{k+1} = 0$$

Non-observed cells	⊞
Recently observed cells	■
Observed cells	⊞
Sensor footprint	○

Figure 4. Types of cells in the search behavior. The white cells have not been already observed. The light green cells are the already observed cells, whereas the darker green are the cells just observed.

Besides these changes in the concentration of pheromones, the natural diffusion, Equation (15), will also apply during each time step.

If there is a prior probability distribution of the possible location of the targets, it can be easily implemented in the algorithm. Given a probability distribution $q_t(x, y)$, each discretization cell (i, j) is assigned a probability value $p_{t_{i,j}}$:

$$p'_{t_{i,j}} = q_t(x_i, y_j) \tag{24a}$$

$$p_{t_{i,j}} = \frac{p'_{t_{i,j}}}{\sum_{i=1}^{n_x} \sum_{j=1}^{n_y} p'_{t_{i,j}}} \tag{24b}$$

being therefore:

$$\sum_{i=1}^{n_x} \sum_{j=1}^{n_y} p_{t_{i,j}} = 1 \tag{25}$$

and this probability distribution is finally normalized with the maximum value:

$$\bar{p}_{t_{i,j}} = \frac{p_{t_{i,j}}}{\max_{i,j} p_{t_{i,j}}} \tag{26}$$

and therefore, $0 \leq p_{t_{i,j}} \leq 1$. The sources of pheromones, as well as the initial value of the pheromones (see Equations (15a) and (16a)) are then multiplied by the associated normalized probability $\bar{p}_{t_{i,j}}$. In this way, the regions where it is more probable to find a target generate more pheromones, and the agents are more attracted to them.

3.1.3. Layers of Pheromones

The actual usefulness of pheromones is to transmit information about observed and non-observed cells along the search area, so that the agents are aimed at zones with more unobserved cells. This way, it is expected that the observed cells generate and transmit less pheromone levels than the unobserved ones. However, if there exist unobserved cells, surrounded by observed cells, it is possible that these last ones act like a barrier, avoiding an effective transmission of the information by the pheromones. On the other hand, it is our experience that it is useful to try to organize the search by prioritizing the observation of isolated (i.e., with high θ values) cells surrounding each agent. In order to address these issues, we propose a multi-layer pheromone system made up by three independent layers:

- Standard layer (L1): There is no impact of the isolation index on this layer, and it has different diffusion coefficients for observed and unobserved cells.
- Long-range layer (L2): Intended to transmit information from unobserved cells along the entire search area. The diffusion coefficients of observed and unobserved cells are equal, and the observed cells do not produce pheromones.
- Isolation layer (L3): This mainly considers pheromone creation due to the isolation index. Once the cells are observed, they lose their pheromone concentration at this layer.

In Table 3, the parameters for the three layers are summarized. Each parameter has been named with a super-index to indicate the layer to which they belong, except for $\rho_{\Delta\theta}$ and ρ_θ, which only apply to Layer 3.

Table 3. Parameters related to the search behavior for each of the three layers.

	ϕ_0	S_{no}	S_o	D_{no}	D_o	δ_{ro}	$\rho_{\Delta\theta}$	ρ_θ
L1	ϕ_0^{L1}	S_{no}^{L1}	S_o^{L1}	D_{no}^{L1}	D_o^{L1}	δ_{ro}^{L1}	0	0
L2	ϕ_0^{L2}	S_{no}^{L2}	0	D^{L2}	D^{L2}	δ_{ro}^{L2}	0	0
L3	ϕ_0^{L3}	S_{no}^{L3}	0	0	0	-1	$\rho_{\Delta\theta}$	ρ_θ

3.1.4. Evaluating Modes

Each time an agent reaches the center of a search cell, it makes the decision of which search cell to visit next, and the search behavior will be taken into account, depending on the concentration of pheromones on the surrounding cells at each layer.

At each time step, each discretization cell G_{D_c} has associated a concentration of pheromones $\phi_c^l = \phi^l(G_{D_c})$ at each layer l. The total quantity of the pheromones concentration is then:

$$\phi_c = \phi(G_{D_c}) = \sum_{l=1}^{3} \phi^l(G_{D_c}) \tag{27}$$

Each search cell G_{S_g} has associated a set of discretization cells, so that their centers lie inside it. Furthermore, if the final search cell g is in a diagonal position (with respect to the agent), half of the contiguous cells will be observed (see Figure 1), and therefore, the discretization cells inside these halves will be accounted for.

We propose two methods for accounting for the pheromone level at each search cell, for candidates to be visited next:

- Mean values: The mean values of the pheromone concentration of the cells inside each search cell are considered. The income for each surrounding cell is then calculated:

$$I_{\phi mm_g} = \frac{\sum\limits_{\forall c | G_{D_c} \in G_{S_g}} \phi(G_{D_c})}{\sum\limits_{\forall c | G_{D_c} \in G_{S_g}} c} \tag{28}$$

- Maximum values: The maximum value of the concentration inside each search cell is considered.

$$I_{\phi max_g} = \max_{c | G_{D_c} \in G_{S_g}} \phi(G_{D_c}) \tag{29}$$

To consider both solutions, the total income of each surrounding cell g will be calculated as a weighted sum of both:

$$I_{\phi_g} = \beta_\phi I_{\phi mm_g} + (1 - \beta_\phi) I_{\phi max_g} \tag{30}$$

where $\beta_\phi \in [0, 1]$ is the weighting parameter, to be set.

3.2. Energy Saving Behavior

As already mentioned in Section 2.3.2, there is a need for extra energy to change the direction of flight, besides the energy needed to continue flying. This increment in the consumption depends on how much the direction of flight changes. Moreover, there is a reduction of velocity when the agent changes its flight direction (see Equation (6)), which will have an impact on the performance. In Figure 5a, the energy costs C_{E_g} for each cell g considered has been shown. As we will see, since those values will be multiplied by a coefficient, their absolute values are not relevant, but only the relationship between them.

3.3. Diagonal Movement Behavior

Moving in the diagonal might improve the performance of the search since there is potentially less overlap between the sensor footprints. Therefore, a behavior is proposed to encourage the movement in these directions, equal to the pheromone concentration in those cells:

$$I_{DM_g} = \delta(g - g_d) I_{\phi_g} \tag{31}$$

where $\delta(g - g_d)$ is the Dirac delta centered in each diagonal cell $g_d = [2, 4, 6, 8]$ and I_{ϕ_g} is the input due to the pheromone concentration; see Equation (30).

3.4. Collision Avoidance Behavior

To avoid collisions between the agents, this behavior is considered. Every time an agent makes the decision about which cell to visit next, it advises the other agents.

It is important to remark that this behavior does not prevent the collision itself, since two agents may head to two different cells and collide anyway. However, this is an assumed simplification, considering that there will be also a collision avoidance system to take over the control in those situations. The cost of $C_{C_g} = -10^9$ is considered; see Figure 5b.

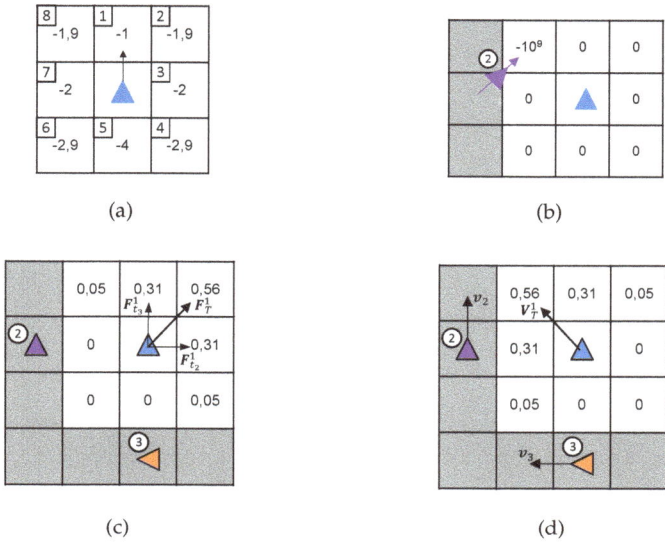

(a)

(b)

(c)

(d)

Figure 5. In (**a**), energy costs considered in the energy saving behavior. The arrow indicates the current flight direction. In the upper left corner of each search cell, the cell number has been indicated. In (**b**) collision avoidance costs. Agent 2 is already heading to a cell, so that traveling to that one would imply a cost of -10^9 for the agent. In Figure (**c**), an example of the keep distance behavior has been represented; Agents 2 and 3 apply a total force $F_T^1 = 1$, being $\psi_F = \pi/4$, over the agent. The incomes I_{D_g} have been calculated using Equation (42). In (**d**), an example of income due to the keep velocity behavior is; see Equation (47). In this example, $V_T^1 = 1$ m/s.

3.5. Keep Distance Behavior

Imitating several animal species in nature, such as bird flocks, fish schools and ungulate herds, this behavior is proposed. Each agent tries to keep a stable distance with the surrounding agents, by means of the result of attractive and repulsive forces. These are normally implemented similarly to the attractive-repulsive forces presented in the molecules' interactions. The total force over an agent i due to the presence of an agent j is made up of two forces:

$$\mathbf{F}_{tj}^i = \mathbf{F}_{aj}^i + \mathbf{F}_{rj}^i = \left(\frac{A_a}{|\mathbf{d}_j^i|^{m_a}} - \frac{A_r}{|\mathbf{d}_j^i|^{m_r}} \right) \frac{\mathbf{d}_j^i}{|\mathbf{d}_j^i|} \tag{32}$$

where $\mathbf{F}_{aj}^i$ is the attractive force, $\mathbf{F}_{rj}^i$ is the repulsive force and $\mathbf{d}_j^i$ is the vector from the position of agent i to the position of agent j, $\mathbf{d}_j^i = \mathbf{r}_j - \mathbf{r}_i$. $A_a > 0$, $A_r > 0$ and $m_r > m_a > 0$ are parameters to be set.

Since the configuration is expected to be valid no matter how many agents are carrying out the task or the size of the search area, it is convenient to adimensionalize the distance $\mathbf{d}_j^i$. There are two candidates for this purpose, the footprint radius:

$$d_{c_1} = R_f \tag{33}$$

and a distance representing the size of the search area:

$$d_{c_2} = \sqrt{L_x^2 + L_y^2} \tag{34}$$

If one takes the first option, the keep distance behavior will be related to the covered area at each moment, and it will lead the agents to behave more as a flock. On the other hand, if the second option is chosen, the agents will tend to cover bigger zones, spreading out themselves across the search area. In order to let the optimization choose any combination of these characteristic distances, a weighted distance is considered:

$$d_c = \beta_d d_{c_1} + (1 - \beta_d) d_{c_2} \tag{35}$$

where β_d is a coefficient to be chosen. The adimensionalized distance $\tilde{\mathbf{d}}_j^i$ is then obtained by:

$$\tilde{\mathbf{d}}_j^i = \frac{\mathbf{d}_j^i}{d_c} \tag{36}$$

Making $\mathbf{F}_{t_j}^i = 0$ in Equation (32), we get the equilibrium distance, whereas differentiating that equation and equaling it to zero, we get the distance at which the attractive force is maximum:

$$\tilde{d}_0 = \left(\frac{A_r}{A_a}\right)^{\frac{1}{m_r - m_a}} \tag{37a}$$

$$\tilde{d}_{max} = \left(\frac{A_r m_r}{A_a m_a}\right)^{\frac{1}{m_r - m_a}} \tag{37b}$$

where $\tilde{d}_{max} > \tilde{d}_0$. To reduce the number of parameters, we consider, as well:

$$m_r = m_a + 1 \tag{38}$$

so that Equation (37a) becomes:

$$\tilde{d}_0 = \frac{A_r}{A_a} \tag{39}$$

With this assumption, we finally get the relationship:

$$m_r = \frac{\tilde{d}_{max}/\tilde{d}_0}{\tilde{d}_{max}/\tilde{d}_0 - 1} \tag{40a}$$

$$A_a = \frac{F_{t_{max}} \left(\tilde{d}_0\right)^{m_a}}{\left(\frac{m_r}{m_a}\right)^{m_a} - \left(\frac{m_r}{m_a}\right)^{m_r}} \tag{40b}$$

Again, since this behavior will be multiplied by a coefficient, the actual value of the total force is irrelevant, and therefore, we can take $F_{t_{max}} = 1$. The behavior so posed depends only on three variables, the adimensionalized distance at which the forces are at equilibrium, $\tilde{d}_0$, the adimensionalized distance at which the attractive force is maximum, $\tilde{d}_{max}$, and the characteristic distance, d_c. Once these distances are set, m_r and m_a are calculated with Equations (40a) and (38), respectively. A_a is calculated with Equation (40b), and finally, with Equation (39), we get A_r. In Figure 6a, the resultant forces have been represented for $\tilde{d}_0 = 1/3$ and $\tilde{d}_{max} = 0.5$. Having N_a the number of agents, the total force on agent i will be:

$$\mathbf{F}_T^i = \sum_{\substack{j=1 \\ \forall j \neq i}}^{N_a} \mathbf{F}_{t_j}^i \tag{41}$$

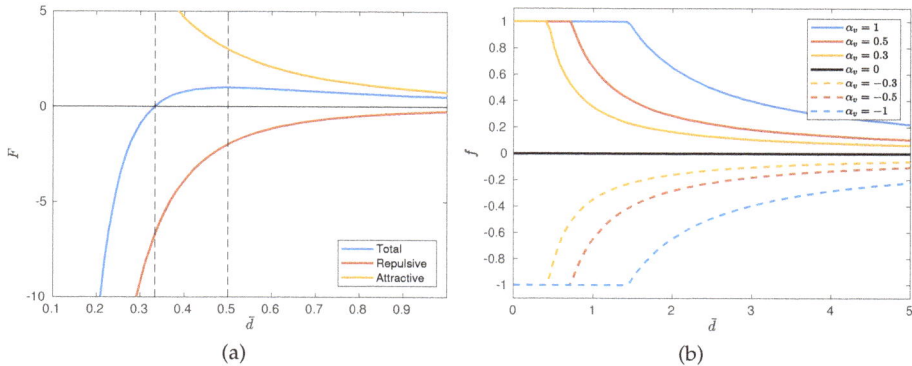

Figure 6. In (**a**) attractive, repulsive and total forces with $\tilde{d}_0 = 1/3$ and $\tilde{d}_{max} = 0.5$. In (**b**) function f of the keep velocity behavior (see Equation (45)) depending on the dimensionless distance $\tilde{d}$ and for different values of α_v.

Once the total force vector $\mathbf{F}_T$ over an agent has been calculated, an income value must be assigned to each surrounding cell. Given the direction ψ_F of $\mathbf{F}_T$ and its modulus F_T, a normal distribution is used along the different headings of the surrounding cells:

$$I_{D_g} = \frac{F_T}{\sqrt{2\pi\sigma^2}}e^{-\frac{\left(\Delta\psi_F^g\right)^2}{2\sigma^2}} \tag{42}$$

where I_{D_g} is the income corresponding to the surrounding cell g, σ is the variance of the normal distribution, and it has been chosen as $\sigma^2 = 0.5$; $\Delta\psi_F^g$ is the difference of the heading of $\mathbf{F}_T$ and the heading of each surrounding cell g. In Figure 5c, an example of the keep distance behavior has been represented. Agents 2 and 3 apply two repulsive forces $\mathbf{F}_{t_2}^1$ and $\mathbf{F}_{t_3}^1$ on Agent 1. The total force in this example is $F_T^i = 1$. The incomes I_{D_g} for each surrounding cell have been calculated with Equation (42). In this case, since the heading of the total force is $\pi/4$, we have:

$$\Delta\psi_{1...8}^{F_T} = [-\frac{\pi}{4}, 0, \frac{\pi}{4}, \frac{\pi}{2}, \frac{3\pi}{4}, \pi, -\frac{3\pi}{4}, -\frac{\pi}{2}] \tag{43}$$

3.6. Keep Velocity Behavior

Similar to the keep distance behavior, and mimicking flocks and schools, a behavior aimed at keeping the velocity of the other agents is also implemented. Most of these sorts of behaviors are proportional to a certain function of the distance between the agents; see, for instance, [26]. Here, a similar law is proposed. The total velocity effect over an agent i is calculated as:

$$\mathbf{V}_T^i = \sum_{\substack{j=1 \\ \forall j \neq i}}^{N_a} \mathbf{v}_j f_j^i \tag{44}$$

where $\mathbf{v}_j$ is the velocity vector of agent j, different from agent i, and f_j^i is a function of the distance between both agents:

$$f_j^i = \text{sign}\left(\alpha_v\right) \cdot \min\left\{e^{|\alpha_v|/\tilde{d}_j^i} - 1, 1\right\} \tag{45}$$

where $\tilde{d}_j^i$ is the adimensional distance between agents i and j and α_v is the coefficient to be configured. In this case, the characteristic distance is taken equal to the sensor footprint:

$$\tilde{d}_j^i = \frac{|\mathbf{d}_j^i|}{R_f} \tag{46}$$

In Figure 6b, the function f_j^i, Equation (45), has been represented depending on the adimensional distance $\tilde{d}$ for three values of α_v. Once the total velocity $\mathbf{V}_T$ over agent i has been calculated, the incomes of each surrounding cell are calculated similarly to Equation (42):

$$I_{V_g} = \frac{V_T}{\sqrt{2\pi\sigma^2}} e^{-\frac{\left(\Delta\psi_V^g\right)^2}{2\sigma^2}} \tag{47}$$

where $V_T = |\mathbf{V}_T|$ and $\sigma^2 = 0.5$. An example of incomes for each cell has been presented in Figure 6b, where it has been assumed $V_T^1 = 1$ m/s.

3.7. Final Decision

Once every income for each behavior has been calculated, a final decision process takes place. For each surrounding cell g, a final decision income is calculated as follows:

$$I_{f_g} = I_{\phi_g} + \alpha_E C_{E_g} + \alpha_{DM} I_{DM_g} + C_{C_g} + \alpha_D I_{D_g} + \alpha_V I_{V_g} \tag{48}$$

where I_{f_g} is the total income of cell g, I_{ϕ_g} is the income due to the pheromone concentration, C_{E_g} is the energy cost, I_{DM_g} is the income due to the diagonal movement behavior, C_{C_g} is the collision cost, I_{D_g} is the income due to the keep distance behavior and I_{V_g} is finally the income due to the keep velocity behavior. Note that the above Equation (48) is a weighted linear sum of all costs and incomes, where α_E, α_{DM}, α_D and α_V are the weights to be set. The next cell to visit is then chosen so that the total income is maximum.

3.8. Configuration of the Algorithm

As we have shown, the algorithm consists of six different behaviors with a total of 23 parameters to be selected. Moreover, the optimum values of these parameters presumably depend on the scenario, i.e., on the values of the variables shown in Table 1. To solve this optimization problem, the following procedure was carried out.

Given any plain scenario i (the scenario shown in Figure 2a) defined by the tuple $Y_i = \{A_s/N_a, N_a, v_n, R_f, f_A\}_i$, the algorithm parameters must be configured accordantly to achieve an appropriate performance. If we have a big-enough dataset of $i = 1, ..., N$ scenarios with N suboptimal configurations Ω_i^*, i.e., with N suboptimal values for each of the 23 parameters of the algorithm, we can model them individually as a function of the scenario, using Y as predictors. As a result, for any scenario Y_j, a suboptimal estimation $\hat{\Omega}_j$ is obtained, and the algorithm can then configured. The model selected to predict the suboptimal values is a Gaussian process (see [27]). To generate the dataset of suboptimal configurations, a genetic algorithm is used, whose main characteristics are:

- Chain of genes: a vector made up by the 23 parameters of the algorithm. Each of the genes is normalized with a range of possible values.
- Population: 100 members.
- Initial population: Half of the initial population is taken from the two closest scenarios already optimized, 25 from each one. To select those members, a trade-off between fitness and genetic diversity is considered. The other half is taken as a prediction of the model. Since the model is probabilistic, these 50 member are drawn from the normal distribution of the Gaussian process.
- Fitness function: To evaluate each member, Equation (14) is used. In order to measure the noise due to the variability of the initial conditions, each member is tested 100 times.

- Crossover: The members will be combined using the roulette-wheel technique, with a probability proportional to the fitness value. Two pairs made up by the same two members is forbidden. Two members being selected for the crossover, a new member will be created by applying a weighted sum of each gene individually. The weighting coefficient is a random number between zero and one. The offspring is made up of 50 new individuals.
- Next generation selection: After evaluating the new individuals, elitism is used to select the 100 best members for the next generation from the 150 available members.
- Stopping criteria: The optimization is stopped when one of these criteria is met:

  - Maximum number of generations (30) has been reached.
  - Maximum time for each optimization (24 h) has been reached.
  - Maximum number of generations (10) without an improvement higher than 10% of the best member has been reached.
  - Maximum number of generations (3) without an improvement higher than 10% of the mean fitness of the population has been reached.

Having obtained $k < N$ suboptimal configurations for k scenarios, the next scenario $k + 1$ is obtained so that the mean uncertainty of the GPs of the 23 parameters is most reduced, i.e., the scenario with the highest uncertainty is selected. A total of $N = 100$ scenarios is optimized and used as the dataset. In Figure 7, the complete modeling process has been schematically depicted.

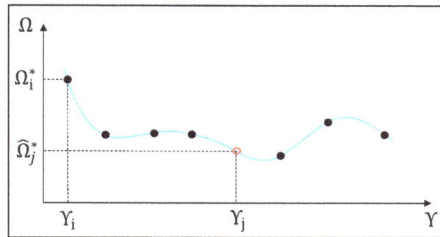

Figure 7. Schematic representation of the modeling process. Y represents the scenario parameter space, while Ω is the configuration space of the algorithm (the value of the 23 parameters). The black points represent the dataset, i.e., the suboptimal configurations Ω^* found with the genetic algorithm for each of the scenarios Y_i, with $i = 1, ..., 100$. The blue line represents the model of the suboptimal configurations based on GPs. Each parameter has been modeled independently (one GP for each parameter). For any new scenario j, the suboptimal configuration $\hat{Y}_j^*$ is predicted (red circle).

4. Search Patterns

In this section, six search patterns are proposed, which will be compared with the above explained set of behaviors.

4.1. Random Walk: A2

The simplest solution to explore the area is to walk randomly. Every time an agent reaches the center of a search cell, it randomly decides which surrounding cell to visit next. Given a present heading ψ_i, the next course will be then $\psi_{i+1} = \psi_i + \Delta\psi_i$, being:

$$\Delta\psi_i \sim \mathcal{N}\left(0, \sigma_{rw}^2\right) \tag{49}$$

where $\mathcal{N}$ indicates normal distribution and σ_{rw} is its standard deviation, which has been chosen as $\sigma_{rw} = \pi/2$. Since the movement is restricted to the surrounding eight cells, ψ_{i+1} is rounded to the closest possible heading pointing to any of those cells. In addition to this behavior, the collision avoidance is also implemented as explained in Section 3.4. In Figure 8, an example of a random walk has been represented for two agents.

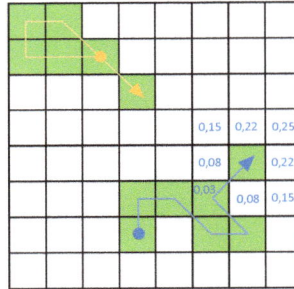

Figure 8. Example of random walk with two agents. The agents deviate from their current heading as per Equation (49). Surrounding the blue agent, the probability distribution of selecting each cell has been written.

4.2. Go to the Closest Non-Visited Cell: A3

The next pattern to be compared is heading to the closest cell that has not been already visited. The distance is computed as the Euclidean norm, and once the target cell is selected, the needed heading is obtained. Depending on that course, utility values are assigned to the surrounding cells as per:

$$I_{CC_g} = \frac{1}{\sqrt{2\pi\sigma^2}} e^{-\frac{\left(\Delta\psi_E^g\right)^2}{2\sigma^2}} \tag{50}$$

where it has been chosen $\sigma = \pi/10$. Note that this utility assignment is similar to the one used in the keep distance and keep velocity behaviors; see Equations (42) and (48). If there is more than one cell at the same distance, the utilities for each surrounding cell are calculated and summed up. In addition to this behavior, the energy saving and the collision behaviors are implemented; see Sections 3.2 and 3.4. This implies that if more than one cell is situated at a similar Euclidean distance, the agent will head to the one that implies lower energy consumption. The utility of each surrounding cell g is therefore calculated as:

$$I_g = 10 \cdot I_{CC_g} + C_{C_g} \tag{51}$$

where C_{C_g} is the energy cost. In Figure 9, an example of this algorithm has been represented.

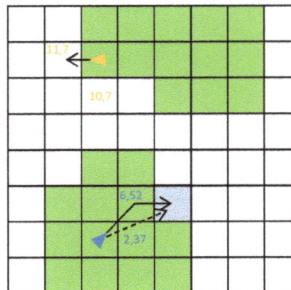

Figure 9. Example of going to the closest non-visited cell behavior. For the cell candidates, the utility values have been written. The yellow agent has two choices at the same distance, but due to the energy saving behavior, one of them is preferred (see energy cost in Figure 5a).

4.3. Boundary Following: A4

As proposed in [20], an effective way of traveling along the search area is selecting the next cell to visit depending on if they are surrounded by already-visited cells or not. This way, the task is organized in a compact way.

In order to implement such a behavior, we make use of the isolation index $\theta_{i,j}^k$ as defined in Section 3.1.2, but instead of applying it on the discretization cells, it will be referred to as the search cells. Each surrounding cell will have a utility equal to its isolation index. Moreover, the energy saving behavior is also implemented, so that for equally-isolated cells, the one that needs less energy is preferred. The utility of each surrounding cell g is therefore calculated as:

$$I_g = 10 \cdot \theta_g + C_{C_g} \tag{52}$$

Finally, if there is not any surrounding unvisited cell, the behavior go to closest non-visited cell takes over the control. In Figure 10, an example of this behavior has been shown.

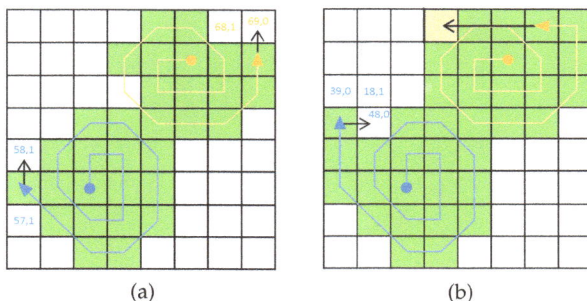

Figure 10. Example of the boundary following behavior with the associated utilities for each cell. In (**a**), instant a; for cells with equal isolation index, the one that requires less energy is selected. In (**b**), instant b; the yellow agent activates the go to closest non-visited cell behavior.

4.4. Energy Saving: A5

The energy saving behavior, depicted in Section 3.2, can be implemented separately so that each agent keeps its current course unless a collision may take place, or in case the agent is going to fly outside the search area. In those cases, the safe heading that requires less energy is chosen. In Figure 11, an example of this behavior is represented.

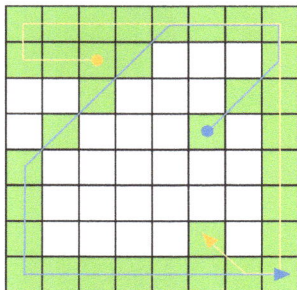

Figure 11. Example of energy saving behavior. The agents keep their headings unless they run into the borders or if a collision may occur.

4.5. Billiard Random Movement: A6

Similarly to the lawn mower behavior proposed in [23], the billiard random movement behavior directs the agents to go straight until they encounter any border. Then, they select randomly any other free direction. This behavior differs from the energy saving in the way the next course is selected (randomly here, the most energy convenient in the other). The collision avoidance behavior is also active in this algorithm. In Figure 12, an example of this behavior is shown.

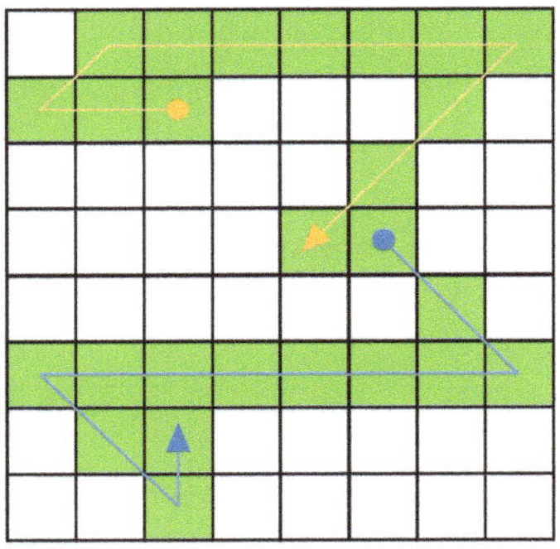

Figure 12. Example of billiard random movement behavior. When an agent encounters a boundary, it redirects its heading randomly. Otherwise, the course is kept constant (unless a collision may occur).

4.6. Lanes Following: A7

Finally, the lanes following algorithm is considered. Similar to the raster scan behavior depicted in [23], a lane is assigned for each agent. The direction of the lanes (north-south or east-west) is selected so that the minimum number of lanes is created; if that number is lower than the number of agents, the other direction is selected. When a lane is assigned to an agent, it goes first to the closest extreme cell of the lane, and after, it starts traveling along it. When the lane is completely observed, the closest non-observed lane is assigned. If there are no available lanes, the go to closest unvisited cell behavior is activated. In Figure 13, an example of this behavior is shown.

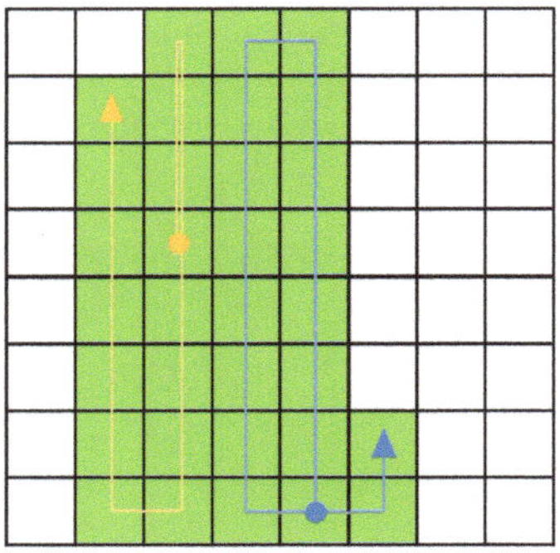

Figure 13. Example of the lanes following behavior. In the first lane assigned to the yellow agent, it travels first to the closest extreme cell. When each lane is completely observed, a new one is assigned.

5. Comparison of the Algorithms

In order to compare all the search algorithms considered in this work, random scenarios are generated considering the parameters (and their valid ranges) shown in Table 1 for each of the four scenario types. Recall that each scenario is defined by the area per agent, A_s/N_a, the number of agents, N_a, the nominal velocity of the robots, v_n, the sensor footprint radius, R_f, and the aspect ratio of the area, f_a. For each scenario, 100 different initial conditions are generated, and each algorithm is tested having considered them. The mean values of the efficiencies as per Models 1, 2 and 3 (see Equations (10), (11) and (13)) are calculated and considering the standard deviations among the 100 trials, the fitness value is obtained according to Equation (14). For this last figure, whether the search has been completed or not is also taken into account.

First, we carry out a quantitative comparison based on the measurement of the efficiency and fitness values for each scenario type. Secondly, we present a qualitative analysis discussing the complexity of the communications needed and how appropriate each algorithm could be for a surveillance mission.

5.1. Quantitative Comparison

5.1.1. Plain Scenarios

In Table 4, the results of the simulations have been presented for the plain scenario. For each of the three models, the mean efficiency among 200 scenarios and the mean fitness value are shown. Notice that in turn for each of the scenarios, the efficiency and the fitness is the result of the mean of 100 trials.

For Model 1, the best algorithms turn out to be A4, A3, A7 and A1, with an efficiency between 70 and 78%. In any case, the efficiencies of all algorithms lie above 78% of the maximum efficiency ($0.61/0.78 = 0.78$), which may indicate a bad representation of the real performance of the algorithm. Note that even a random movement, which a priori is considered as very inefficient, achieves mean absolute efficiency values of 61%. The fitness values based on this model indicate that the algorithms A3, A7, A4 and A1 combine good efficiencies with low noises due to the initial conditions. We should underline the important drop in the fitness values compared with the efficiency for algorithms A2, A5 and A6, which indicates a high variance in the efficiency depending on the initial conditions.

The case of Model 2 is similar, although the values are in general lower. The best algorithms based on it are A3 and A7. However, in this case, the differences between the algorithms are lower, all the efficiencies lying between 0.57 and 0.61. Again, there are remarkable drops in the fitness for algorithms A2, A5 and A6.

Table 4. Efficiencies and fitness values for each algorithm, based on the three models depicted in Section 2.4.

	Model 1		Model 2		Model 3	
	Eff	**Fit**	**Eff**	**Fit**	**Eff**	**Fit**
A1: Behaviors set	0.70	0.58	0.57	0.49	0.39	0.29
A2: Random	0.61	0.21	0.57	0.20	0.09	0.03
A3: Closest	0.75	0.68	0.62	0.57	0.36	0.27
A4: Boundary	0.78	0.67	0.59	0.53	0.31	0.22
A5: Energy	0.66	0.21	0.59	0.19	0.16	0.04
A6: Billiard	0.61	0.23	0.55	0.22	0.16	0.05
A7: Lanes	0.73	0.68	0.61	0.57	0.35	0.28

In Figure 14, the efficiencies distributions as per Models 1 and 2 for the 200 scenarios have been represented, in descending order of mean efficiency. Note the high variance in the efficiency of A5 for both models, which indicates that the algorithm is very sensitive to the scenario.

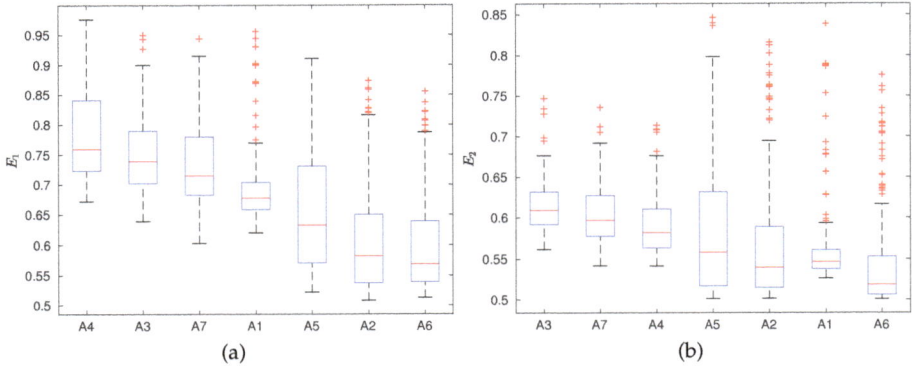

Figure 14. (a) Efficiency Model 1; (b) Efficiency Model 2; efficiency based on Models 1 and 2 for each proposed algorithm. The distribution corresponds to 200 scenarios, tested with 100 random initial conditions.

In the case of Model 3, the results are different. First, the efficiencies are in general lower, with their average between 9 and 39%. We can distinguish two groups of algorithms: the first group, composed by A1, A3, A7 and A4, achieves high efficiencies, higher than 0.31. The second group, made up of A6, A5 and A2, reaches efficiencies between 0.09 and 0.16. Note that with this model, the worst algorithm (A2, random movement) is four-times less efficient than any of the first group, which may be a sensible result. Regarding the fitness, the same drop from the efficiency values shows up again in A2, A5 and A6. A1 reaches the highest fitness value, indicating robustness against the initial conditions. In Figure 15, the efficiencies based on Model 3 and the associated fitness values have been represented for each algorithm, for all the scenarios. Note that A3 and A7, although reaching high efficiencies, present a high variance depending on the scenario. In 75% of the scenarios, both algorithms reach an efficiency that lies between 0.17 and 0.55, which is a wide interval compared with A1, with the interval from 0.35 to 0.40 comparatively narrow. A similar situation takes place regarding the fitness, in Figure 15b. Although A7 may reach up to 0.50 of fitness in some scenarios, it is also possible that it drops to 0.10 in some other. A similar behavior is present in A3. On the other hand, A1 only reaches maximum fitness values of 0.4; however, the values among the scenarios are more stable.

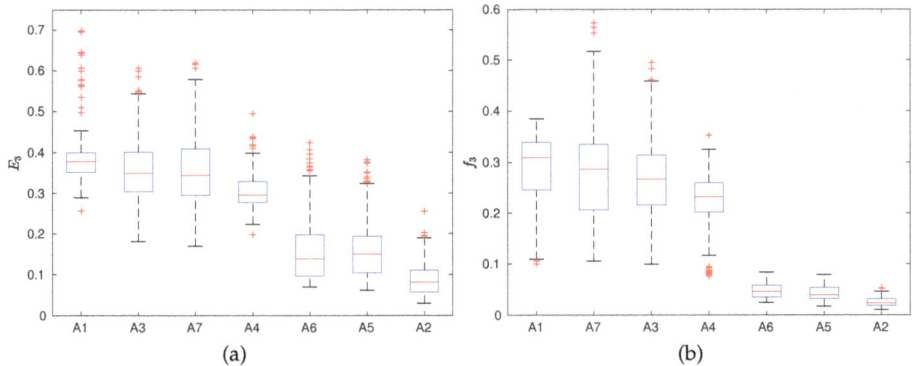

Figure 15. Efficiency (**a**) and fitness (**b**) based on Model 3.

5.1.2. Scenarios with the Probability Distribution

In the second scenario type, a probability distribution of the possible locations of the targets is considered; see Figure 2b. Note that as the search mission in this case ends when all the targets having been seen, it is likely that not every discretization cell is finally observed. Therefore, since the task may end prematurely, the efficiency and the fitness measured as per Equations (13) and (14) are not absolute metrics anymore. For the comparison, 50 scenarios are generated; for each scenario, five different probability distributions are analyzed, considering 100 different initial conditions for each one.

In Figure 16a, the distributions of the efficiency have been represented, considering Model 3. Again, A1 turns out to be the best, followed by A3, A7 and A4. However, in this scenario type, A1 is clearly above the others, reaching a mean efficiency of 0.54. The second best algorithm, A3, reaches a mean efficiency of 0.44. A similar situation occurs when the fitness is compared; see Figure 16b. Note that also for this scenario type, A7 presents a high variability in both efficiency and fitness among the scenarios.

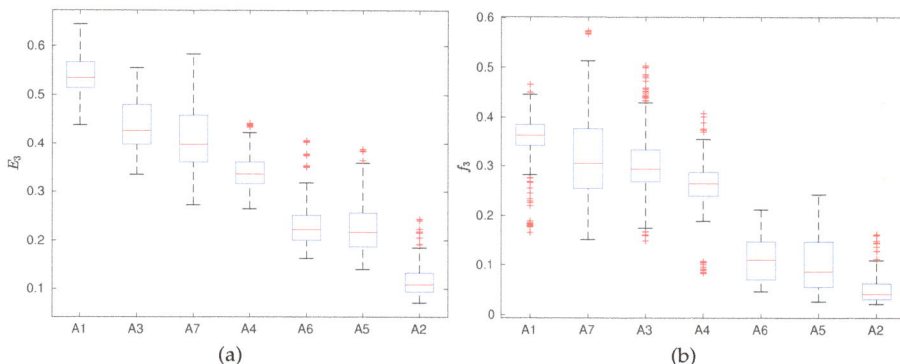

Figure 16. Efficiency (**a**) and fitness (**b**) for the scenario with the probability distribution of the location of the targets.

5.1.3. Scenarios with Obstacles

The next type of scenario to be analyzed is the scenario with non-flyable obstacles. In this comparison, 50 scenarios have been generated, and for each one, five different obstacle arrangements are created. Each algorithm is tested 100 times, varying randomly the initial positions of the agents.

The efficiency and fitness distributions are represented in Figure 17a,b, respectively. The A1 performs better than the others, considering both efficiency and fitness, although the difference in this case is lower. For algorithm A7, which in other cases is a competitive solution, in this scenario type, its performance lies between the two groups of algorithms.

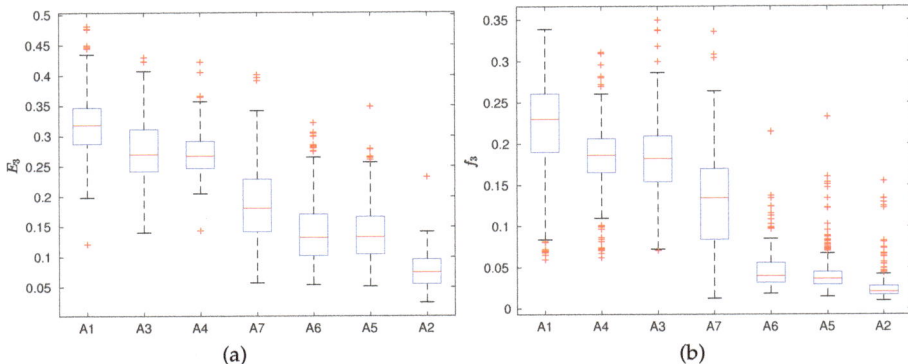

Figure 17. Efficiency (**a**) and fitness (**b**) for the scenario with obstacles inside the area.

5.1.4. Scenarios with Probability Distribution and Obstacles

Finally, the last scenario type is analyzed. Similarly to the previous ones, 50 scenarios are generated, and for each one, five different combinations of probability distribution and obstacle arrangements are created. Again, each algorithm is tested for 100 initial conditions. In Figure 18a,b, the efficiency and fitness distribution have been represented. For both performance measurements, A1 clearly outperforms the other algorithms.

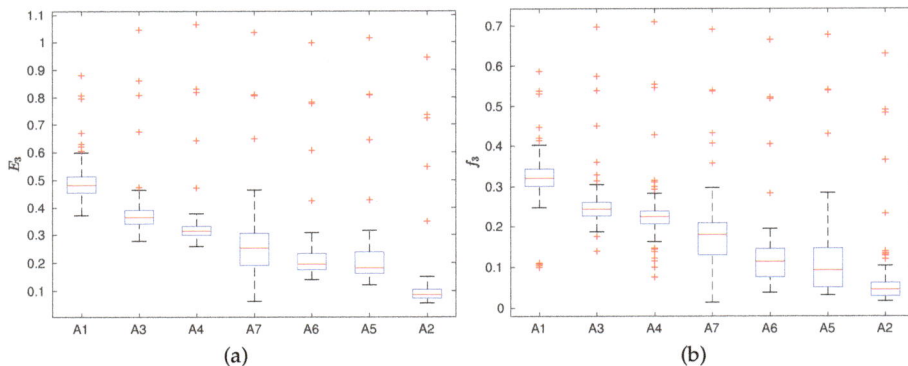

Figure 18. Efficiency (**a**) and fitness (**b**) for the scenario with the probability distribution of the location of the targets and obstacles inside the area.

5.2. Communication Needs and Adaptation to Surveillance

As we have seen in the previous section, the proposed algorithms can be classified attending to objective measurements depending on the type of scenario. However, some of the algorithms make use of intensive communications between the agents, whereas others only need sharing information in specific moments. This may be a drawback when using them in real systems. On the other hand, these algorithms can be used in similar missions, such as surveillance and patrolling, although some modifications might need to be done. The algorithms are qualitatively analyzed hereafter regarding these two issues.

- A1, behaviors set: This algorithm requires a demanding communication system because the behaviors implemented need up-to-date information in order to update the individual map of pheromones, calculate the resulting forces, etc. Surveillance and patrolling are easy to implement: L3 may be eliminated, and visited and non-visited cells may be equally treated; this way, once a zone is visited and its level of pheromones is reduced, it will gradually create pheromones. After some time, it will become a tractor for the agents, which will then return periodically to it.
- A2, random: The random movement only needs communication between agents when they are close and a collision may take place, not needing to share information with other agents. Surveillance and patrolling missions are already covered, since a random walk will statistically revisit the areas with some frequency.
- A3, closest: The requires updated information to know which cells have not been visited yet, besides short-range communication in case a collision may occur. Although the transmitted information is less than for A1, it is also considered as heavy. For surveillance and patrolling, the "age" of the cell (measured as time passed since it was last observed) may be used similarly as the probability map.
- A4, boundary: This algorithm needs the same information as A3, which is considered as high. The surveillance task can only be carried out if the essence of the behavior is lost; if for instance, the decision is made as a weighted sum of the isolation index and the age of the cell, the compaction of the search, which is the main value of the algorithm, will be probably lost. Note that the algorithm makes heavy use of the distinction between visited and non-visited cells, which cannot be easily overridden in persistent missions.
- A5, energy: this algorithm is basically similar to the random movement regarding the communication complexity and its use in surveillance and patrolling.
- A6, billiard: similarly to A2 and A5, the billiard movement only needs the agents to share information if a collision may take place. The surveillance task is already included in the algorithm, since it recursively visits the cells.
- A7, lanes: This requires only medium communications because the agents must only share the lanes they are visiting, which happens with low frequency. The surveillance mission is fulfilled if the visited lanes are marked with incremental numbers (instead of visited and non-visited). The proximity of the lanes and their visit index (i.e., the number of times the lane has been observed) may be then considered together. To do this, a weighted decision may be made.

6. Conclusions and Future Works

In this work, we have first presented an algorithm that is a behavioral network made up by six different behaviors, whose parameters are optimized by a genetic algorithm and adapt to the scenario. Furthermore, based on the literature, six additional algorithms have been proposed, some of which have been combined to improve their efficiency. Additionally, three models to measure the efficiency are suggested, and a fitness function, which takes into account the robustness of the algorithm against the variability of the initial conditions. The algorithms have been compared making use of the models of the efficiency and the fitness for four scenario types. Finally, the communication complexity and the possibility of adapting the algorithms to surveillance and patrolling tasks have been analyzed, as well. All the algorithms compared fulfill robustness and scalability.

Taking a look at the results, our opinion is that Models 1 and 2 to measure the efficiency do not represent correctly the performance of each algorithm. Note that if a cell is visited twice, the efficiency suffers a drop. However, subsequent visits to the same cell do not have an impact on the efficiency, although those visits could have been used potentially to visit new unvisited cells. This situation would affect the efficiency if Model 3 is considered, since the time to finish the search would increase. As has been already pointed out, the random movement achieves efficiencies of 61% with Model 1 for the plain scenario (whose performance is expected to be low a priori), whereas the best algorithm reaches 78%, which also indicates that the model may not be a good indicator of the performance. Therefore, we consider Model 3 as the one that more faithfully represents the efficiency.

Comparing the efficiency and fitness values, we have seen that there are four algorithms that are competitive: behaviors set (A1), go to the closest unvisited cell (A3), travel along lanes (A7) and boundary following (A4). The other three achieve much lower values. In Table 5, a final comparison has been shown; for each scenario type, the efficiency and fitness have been divided by the maximum value achieved. As can be seen, A1's performance is the highest for all scenario types, although for the plain scenario and the scenario with the probability distribution, the difference is not high. In those cases, A3 and A7 could reach a good performance in terms of fitness. However, for scenarios with obstacles, the difference is higher. The second best algorithms, which are A3 and A4, achieve 87% and 84% of the maximum efficiency and fitness. Finally, if the scenario considered has obstacles and a probability distribution, A1 outperforms the other algorithm more significantly; again, the second best algorithm is A3, only reaching 76% and 77% of the maximum efficiency and fitness.

Table 5. Relative efficiencies and fitness values for each algorithm and each scenario type.

	Plain		Probability		Obstacles		Prob. + Obs.	
	Eff	Fit	Eff	Fit	Eff	Fit	Eff	Fit
A1: Behaviors set	1	1	1	1	1	1	1	1
A2: Random	0.23	0.09	0.22	0.14	0.24	0.13	0.21	0.18
A3: Closest	0.91	0.93	0.81	0.86	0.87	0.84	0.76	0.77
A4: Boundary	0.78	0.78	0.63	0.72	0.86	0.84	0.66	0.71
A5: Energy	0.41	0.15	0.42	0.28	0.44	0.20	0.43	0.34
A6: Billiard	0.42	0.17	0.43	0.31	0.45	0.22	0.44	0.37
A7: Lanes	0.90	0.99	0.76	0.90	0.59	0.60	0.52	0.53

If the task at hand is just searching in an area, probably the preferred algorithm would be separating the search space into lanes (A7) or that each agent heads to the closest non-visited cell (A3), because they are easy to implement, do not need any optimization process and perform well. However, if we want to make use of a map of probabilities or there are non-flyable obstacles in the area, algorithm A1 should be considered. Similarly, if the task is surveillance or patrolling, A1 may be also convenient, although this is only an intuition, and simulations need to be carried out to ground this assertion.

In future works, the search patterns should be modified to adapt to all the scenario types, trying to achieve better results; this way, the comparison with A1 would be more fair. If in these modifications, parameters have to be included, an optimization process may need to be performed. In a similar way, the surveillance task may be analyzed with these algorithms (modifications will also need to be included, with the corresponding tuning). For this mission, objective functions to evaluate the efficiency are easier to implement (see for instance [28], where the maximum age of the cells is used).

Author Contributions: P.G.-A. has developed the proposed algorithm, implemented the algorithms for the simulations and analyzed the results. A.B.C. has supervised the complete process of the work and reviewed the document.

Acknowledgments: We would like to thank the SAVIER (Situational Awareness Virtual EnviRonment) Project, which is both supported and funded by Airbus Defence & Space. The research leading to these results has received funding from the RoboCity2030-III-CM project (Robótica aplicada a la mejora de la calidad de vida de los ciudadanos. Fase III; S2013/MIT-2748), funded by Programas de Actividades I+Den la Comunidad de Madrid and co-funded by Structural Funds of the EU, and from the DPI2014-56985-R project (Protección Robotizada de Infraestructuras Críticas (PRIC)) funded by the Ministerio de Economía y Competitividad of Gobierno de España.

References

1. Dudek, G.; Jenkin, M.R.M.; Milios, E.; Wilkes, D. A taxonomy for multi-agent robotics. *Auton. Robot.* **1996**, *3*, 375–397. [CrossRef]
2. Jackson, D.E.; Ratnieks, F.L.W. Communication in ants. *Curr. Biol.* **2006**, *16*, R570–R574. [CrossRef] [PubMed]
3. Deneubourg, J. *Self-organizing Collection and Transport of Objects in Unpredictable Environments. Japan–USA Symposium on Flexible Automation*; American Society of Mechanical Engineers: New York, NY, USA, 1990; pp. 1093–1098.
4. Kube, C.R.; Zhang, H. Collective robotics: From social insects to robots. *Adapt. Behav.* **1993**, *2*, 189–218. [CrossRef]
5. Mataric, M.J. Designing emergent behaviors: From local interactions to collective intelligence. In Proceedings of the Second International Conference on Simulation of Adaptive Behavior, Honolulu, HI, USA, 13 April 1993; pp. 432–441.
6. Şahin, E. Swarm Robotics: From Sources of Inspiration to Domains of Application. In *Swarm Robotics*; Şahin, E., Spears, W.M., Eds.; Number 3342 in Lecture Notes in Computer Science; Springer: Berlin/Heidelberg, 2004; pp. 10–20.
7. Bayındır, L. A review of swarm robotics tasks. *Neurocomputing* **2016**, *172*, 292–321. [CrossRef]
8. Sauter, J.A.; Matthews, R.; Van Dyke Parunak, H.; Brueckner, S.A. Performance of digital pheromones for swarming vehicle control. In *Proceedings of the Fourth International Joint Conference on Autonomous Agents and Multiagent Systems, Utrecht, Netherlands, 25–29 July 2005*; ACM: New York, NY, USA, 2005; pp. 903–910.
9. McCune, R.R.; Madey, G.R. Control of artificial swarms with DDDAS. *Proc. Comput. Sci.* **2014**, *29*, 1171–1181. [CrossRef]
10. Sutantyo, D.K.; Kernbach, S.; Levi, P.; Nepomnyashchikh, V.A. Multi-robot searching algorithm using lévy flight and artificial potential field. In Proceedings of the 2010 IEEE International Workshop on Safety Security and Rescue Robotics (SSRR), Bremen, Germany, 26–30 July 2010; pp. 1–6.
11. Liu, W.; Taima, Y.E.; Short, M.B.; Bertozzi, A.L. Multi-scale Collaborative Searching through Swarming. In Proceedings of the International Conference on Informatics in Control, Automation and Robotics (ICINCO), Funchal, Portugal, 15–18 June 2010; pp. 222–231.
12. Waharte, S.; Symington, A.C.; Trigoni, N. Probabilistic search with agile UAVs. In Proceedings of the International Conference on Robotics and Automation (ICRA), Anchorage, AK, USA, 3–7 May 2010; pp. 2840–2845.
13. Pastor, I.; Valente, J. Adaptive sampling in robotics: A survey. *Revista Iberoamericana de Automática e Informática Industrial (RIAI)* **2017**, *14*, 123–132. [CrossRef]
14. Altshuler, Y.; Yanovsky, V.; Wagner, I.A.; Bruckstein, A.M. Efficient cooperative search of smart targets using uav swarms. *Robotica* **2008**, *26*, 551–557. [CrossRef]
15. Stirling, T.; Wischmann, S.; Floreano, D. Energy-efficient indoor search by swarms of simulated flying robots without global information. *Swarm Intell.* **2010**, *4*, 117–143. [CrossRef]
16. Jevtić, A.; Gutiérrez, A. Distributed bees algorithm parameters optimization for a cost efficient target allocation in swarms of robots. *Sensors* **2011**, *11*, 10880–10893. [CrossRef] [PubMed]
17. Siciliano, B.; Khatib, O. *Springer Handbook of Robotics*; Springer Science & Business Media: Berlin, Germany, 2008.
18. Karapetyan, N.; Benson, K.; McKinney, C.; Taslakian, P.; Rekleitis, I. Efficient multi-robot coverage of a known environment. In Proceedings of the IEEE Intelligent Robots and Systems (IROS), Vancouver, BC, Canada, 24–28 September 2017; pp. 1846–1852.
19. Senthilkumar, K.; Bharadwaj, K. Multi-robot exploration and terrain coverage in an unknown environment. *Robot. Auton. Syst.* **2012**, *60*, 123–132. [CrossRef]
20. Erignac, C. An exhaustive swarming search strategy based on distributed pheromone maps. In Proceedings of the AIAA Infotech@Aerospace 2007 Conference and Exhibit, Rohnert Park, CA, USA, 7–10 May 2007; p. 2822.
21. George, J.; Sujit, P.; Sousa, J.B. Search strategies for multiple UAV search and destroy missions. *J. Intell. Robot. Syst.* **2011**, *61*, 355–367. [CrossRef]
22. Maza, I.; Ollero, A. Multiple UAV Cooperative Searching Operation Using Polygon Area Decomposition and Efficient Coverage Algorithms. In *Distributed Autonomous Robotic Systems 6*; Springer: Berlin, Germany, 2007; pp. 221–230.

23. Lum, C.; Vagners, J.; Jang, J.S.; Vian, J. Partitioned searching and deconfliction: Analysis and flight tests. In Proceedings of the IEEE American Control Conference (ACC), Baltimore, MD, USA, 30 June–2 July 2010; pp. 6409–6416.

24. Berger, J.; Lo, N. An innovative multi-agent search-and-rescue path planning approach. *Comp. Op. Res.* **2015**, *53*, 24–31. [CrossRef]

25. Peng, H.; Su, F.; Bu, Y.; Zhang, G.; Shen, L. Cooperative area search for multiple UAVs based on RRT and decentralized receding horizon optimization. In Proceedings of the IEEE Asian Control Conference (ASCC), Hong Kong, China, 27–29 August 2009; pp. 298–303.

26. Saska, M.; Vakula, J.; Přeućil, L. Swarms of micro aerial vehicles stabilized under a visual relative localization. In Proceedings of the IEEE International Conference on Robotics and Automation (ICRA), Hong Kong, China, 31 May–5 June 2014; pp. 3570–3575.

27. Rasmussen, C.E.; Williams, C.K. *Gaussian Processes for Machine Learning*; MIT Press Cambridge: Cambridge, MA, USA, 2006; Volume 1.

28. Nigam, N.; Bieniawski, S.; Kroo, I.; Vian, J. Control of multiple UAVs for persistent surveillance: Algorithm and flight test results. *IEEE Trans. Control Syst. Technol.* **2012**, *20*, 1236–1251. [CrossRef]

*applied
sciences*

MDPI

Article

Optimal Configuration and Path Planning for UAV Swarms Using a Novel Localization Approach

Weijia Wang [1] **, Peng Bai** [1]**, Hao Li** [1,2,***] **and Xiaolong Liang** [1]

1   Air Traffic Control and Navigation College, Air Force Engineering University, Xi'an 710051, China;
    visionwng@foxmail.com (W.W.); baipeng@126.com (P.B.); afeu_wwj@126.com (X.L.)
2   Air Force Early Warning Academy, Wuhan 430065, China
*   Correspondence: snk.poison@163.com; Tel.: +1-512-924-8091

Received: 18 April 2018; Accepted: 11 June 2018; Published: 19 June 2018

Abstract: In localization estimation systems, it is well known that the sensor-emitter geometry can seriously impact the accuracy of the location estimate. In this paper, time-difference-of-arrival (TDOA) localization is applied to locate the emitter using unmanned aerial vehicle (UAV) swarms equipped with TDOA-based sensors. Different from existing studies where the variance of measurement noises is assumed to be independent and changeless, we consider a more realistic model where the variance is sensor-emitter distance-dependent. First, the measurements model and variance model based on signal-to-noise ratio (SNR) are considered. Then the Cramer–Rao low bound (CRLB) is calculated and the optimal configuration is analyzed via the distance rule and angle rule. The sensor management problem of optimizing UAVs trajectories is studied by generating a sequence of waypoints based on CRLB. Simulation results show that path optimization enhances the localization accuracy and stability.

Keywords: time-difference-of-arrival (TDOA); Cramer–Rao low bound (CRLB); optimal configuration; UAV swarms; path optimization

---

1. Introduction

Passive localization of an emitter from its radio frequency (RF) transmissions has many applications such as search and rescue, electronic surveillance, cognitive radio networks, and wireless sensor networks. The receiving platform can employ sensors measuring angle of arrival (AOA) [1], time difference of arrival (TDOA) [2], and received signal strength (RSS) [3]. TDOA measurements construct a time difference observation equation by measuring the time difference of the emitter signal arriving at different sensors. Therefore, each time difference, corresponding to one hyperboloid, and the emitter can be obtained from two or more hyperbolas. With its high accuracy and simplicity, the TDOA localization technique is widely applied [4].

The equations of the TDOA technique are quadratic and the goal is to find the position of an emitter by solving a set of nonlinear equations obtained from TDOA measurements. The TDOA measurements can be calculated by a simple closed form, e.g., spherical intersection (SX) and spherical interpolation (SI) [5], which usually uses nonlinear least-square solutions. Furthermore, the maximum likelihood method, like the Chan algorithm, was also proposed in [6] and semidefinite programming (SDP) methods in [7]. It is well known that location accuracy depends not only on the localization algorithm but also on the sensor-emitter geometry. Therefore, the selection of an optimal configuration can further improve the location accuracy. Yang et al. [8] initially performed a theoretical analysis of the sensor-emitter geometry based on CRLB with uncorrelated TDOA measurements. Lui [9] discussed optimal sensor deployment considering the correlated TDOA measurement, which makes the configuration rule more applicable. Meng et al. [10,11] formulated an optimal configuration in centralized and decentralized types of TDOA localization and further research focused on the heterogeneous sensor network. Francisco et al. [4] applied a multi-objective optimization in sensor placement. Kim et al. [12] studied the optimal configuration of sensors with the assumption that the emitter was located far from the sensors, while the sensors were relatively close to each other. In recent years, more realistic distance-dependent noise for TOA and AOA measurements was also considered [4,13,14]. In this paper, the CRLB in TDOA localization with distance-dependent noise is calculated in both static and movable scenarios; the distance rule and angle rule of the optimal configuration are extracted, which can provide guidance in optimal sensor-emitter geometries.

The application of unmanned aerial vehicle (UAV) swarms can provide unique platforms for TDOA localization. Their characteristics of flexible movement and cooperation enable them to rapidly change current geometries to achieve higher location accuracy [15,16]. Therefore, the sensor management of real-time UAV path optimization has been a heated research issue in recent years [17]. Frew [18] presented the signal strength measurement to control the UAVs movement. Soltanizadeh et al. applied the determinant of Fisher information matrix (FIM) as the control objective function in RSS localization. Wang [19] investigated UAV path planning for tracking a target using bearing-only sensors. Alomari et al. [20] provided a path planning algorithm based on the dynamic fuzzy-logic method for a movable anchor node. Kaune [21,22] preliminarily considered the path optimization method when there was only one sensor moving platform during TDOA localization. In this paper, UAVs' trajectories are optimized by generating a sequence of waypoints based on CRLB. The CRLB of TDOA location is not only taken as a performance estimator but also as the rule of UAV path optimization. The emitter position is solved by combining the SDP methods and an extended Kalman filter (EKF) estimator. Meanwhile, the constraints of UAV swarms are considered, such as motion and communication constraints. Therefore, the real-time path planning of UAVs is converted to nonlinear optimization with constraints. The interior penalty function method is adopted to convert the nonlinear optimization to simple unconstrained optimization so as to get the flight path of each UAV for the next time.

The rest of the paper is structured as follows. Section 2 introduces the TDOA measurement model and distance-dependent noise model. In Section 3, the optimal configuration is analyzed in both static and movable emitter scenarios based on the CRLB. Section 4 presents the optimal UAV path optimization method. Simulations and conclusions are given in Sections 5 and 6, respectively.

2. Problem Formulation

2.1. Measurement Model

Consider that M time-synchronized UAVs are applied to receive the emitted signals and measure the TOAs with the state vector of each UAV $\chi_i(k) = (x_i(k), y_i(k))^T$, $i = 1, 2, \cdots M$. Let $\mathbf{x}_t = (x_t, y_t) \in \mathbb{R}^2$ be the location of an unknown emitter. The TDOA measurement can be obtained by the difference between any two TOA measurements, eliminating the unknown time of emission. By multiplication of the TDOA measurements by the electromagnetic wave transmission speed, the measurement function in the range domain is obtained:

$$z_{ij} = r_i - r_j, \, i, j \in \{1, \ldots, M\} \wedge j \neq i, \tag{1}$$

with $r_i = \sqrt{(x_t - x_i)^2 + (y_t - y_i)^2}$ being the distance between the emitter and receiver. Let v_i denote the TOA estimation error, which is assumed to be Gaussian. Then the TDOA measurement equation can be expressed as

$$\hat{\mathbf{z}}_{ij} = \mathbf{z}_{ij}(\mathbf{x}_t) + v_{ij}, i, j \in \{1, \ldots, M\} \wedge i \neq j, \, v_{ij} \sim \mathcal{N}(0, \sigma_i^2 + \sigma_j^2), \tag{2}$$

where σ_i^2 is the measurement variance of the i-th receiver of the UAV platform, the measurement noise $v_{ij} = v_i + v_j$ is composed of the noise at the two associated receivers and has the covariance $\sigma_i^2 + \sigma_j^2$.

Without loss of generality, let the 1st receiver be the reference receiver and the others be auxiliary receivers. The variance matrix of measurement matrix $\hat{\mathbf{z}}_{1j}$ consisting of $M-1$ measurements can be represented as:

$$\boldsymbol{\Sigma}_{r1} = \begin{bmatrix} \sigma_1^2 + \sigma_2^2 & \sigma_1^2 & \cdots & \sigma_1^2 \\ \sigma_1^2 & \sigma_1^2 + \sigma_3^2 & \cdots & \sigma_1^2 \\ \vdots & \vdots & \ddots & \vdots \\ \sigma_1^2 & \sigma_1^2 & \cdots & \sigma_1^2 + \sigma_M^2 \end{bmatrix}. \tag{3}$$

Therefore, the measurement vector is given by

$$\hat{\mathbf{z}} = \mathbf{z}(\mathbf{x}_t) + \mathbf{w}, \mathbf{w} \sim \mathcal{N}(0, \boldsymbol{\Sigma}_{r1}). \tag{4}$$

2.2. Measurement Variance Model with Distance-Dependent Noise

Considering the influence of signal frequency, bandwidth, response time, and SNR, the CRLB of the TOA measurement error variance σ_i^2 can be represented as [23]:

$$\sigma_i^2 = \frac{c}{\tau \cdot SNR_i \cdot F(f_0, B)}, \tag{5}$$

where, τ is the observation time, f_0 is the center frequency, B is the bandwidth of the received signal, and c is some constant. High accuracy can be achieved by utilizing high-precision time of arrival measurement techniques at reasonable SNR levels. With constant emitter power and constant frequency, the variance of time-delay measurement is inversely proportional to the SNR, and the SNR is inversely proportional to r^2. Therefore, the relationship of the i-th receiver error and distance can be expressed as [24]:

$$\sigma_i^2(r) = \begin{cases} \frac{a}{SNR_0} \cdot \frac{r_i^2}{r_0^2} & r_i > r_0 \\ \frac{a}{SNR_0} & r_i \leq r_0 \end{cases}, \tag{6}$$

where r_0 is the lower bound of the distance corresponding to the minimum of TOA error variance and SNR_0 is the corresponding optimal SNR at the shortest distance.

The parameter-dependent standard deviation is more complex compared with the constant deviation, so the CRLB and field of view is changing in TDOA localization. Hence, the parameter-dependent standard deviation must be taken into account for accuracy analysis.

The problem of emitter localization is to estimate the location more precisely. In this paper, we mainly study the optimal sensor configuration, which can provide two basic rules to understand the rules to improve the localization performance. Then the online sensor management problem of optimal UAVs trajectories is explored.

3. Optimal Configuration Analysis

In this section, a theoretical analysis of optimal sensor-emitter geometry in TDOA localization is given without considering any constraints. Analytic solutions are derived in both the static and movable emitter scenarios.

3.1. Static Emitter Scenario

The relative sensor-emitter geometry is closely related to the location accuracy, which can be reflected by CRLB, and the configuration corresponding to the minimum CRLB is the optimal configuration.

For unbiased estimator $\hat{\mathbf{x}}$ of $\mathbf{x}$, its Cramer–Rao bound can be expressed as:

$$E\left[(\mathbf{x} - \hat{\mathbf{x}})(\mathbf{x} - \hat{\mathbf{x}})^T\right] \geq \mathbf{J}^{-1} \triangleq \mathbf{CRLB}(\mathbf{x}), \tag{7}$$

where **J** is the Fisher information matrix (FIM).

Then the FIM for TDOA localization with distance-dependent noise is given by [25]

$$\mathbf{J}_{i,j} = \left[\frac{\partial}{\partial x_i} \ln(f_{\mathbf{\hat{z}}}(\mathbf{\hat{z}};\mathbf{x})) \frac{\partial}{\partial x_j} \ln(f_{\mathbf{\hat{z}}}(\mathbf{\hat{z}};\mathbf{x})) \right], \tag{8}$$

where $i, j \in \{1, 2\}$. This FIM can be divided into two parts; as for the first part,

$$\mathbf{J}_{1,(i,j)} = \frac{\partial \mathbf{z}(\mathbf{x})}{\partial x_i} \mathbf{\Sigma}_{r1}^{-1}(\mathbf{x}) \left(\frac{\partial \mathbf{z}(\mathbf{x})}{\partial x_j} \right)^T. \tag{9}$$

The Jacobian matrix of the measurement set with receiver 1 as the reference receiver is

$$\begin{aligned}
\frac{\partial \mathbf{z}(\mathbf{x})}{\partial x_1} &= \left[\frac{\partial z_{12}(\mathbf{x})}{\partial x_1}, \frac{\partial z_{13}(\mathbf{x})}{\partial x_1}, \cdots, \frac{\partial z_{1M}(\mathbf{x})}{\partial x_1} \right]^T \\
&= [\cos(\theta_2) - \cos(\theta_1), \cos(\theta_3) - \cos(\theta_1), \cdots, \cos(\theta_M) - \cos(\theta_1)]^T
\end{aligned} \tag{10}$$

$$\frac{\partial \mathbf{z}(\mathbf{x})}{\partial x_2} = [\sin(\theta_2) - \sin(\theta_1), \sin(\theta_3) - \sin(\theta_1), \cdots, \sin(\theta_M) - \sin(\theta_1)]^T, \tag{11}$$

with θ_i is the angle of arrival measurement of the i-th sensor and the emitter.

For the second part, when $r_i > r_0$,

$$\mathbf{J}_{2,(i,j)} = \frac{1}{2} Tr \left(\mathbf{\Sigma}_{r1}^{-1}(\mathbf{x}) \frac{\partial \mathbf{\Sigma}_{r1}(\mathbf{x})}{\partial x_i} \mathbf{\Sigma}_{r1}^{-1}(\mathbf{x}) \frac{\partial \mathbf{\Sigma}_{r1}(\mathbf{x})}{\partial x_j} \right), \tag{12}$$

where the Jacobian matrix for computing the distance dependent FIM is expressed by

$$\frac{\partial \mathbf{\Sigma}_{r1}(\mathbf{x})}{\partial x_1} = 2\beta \begin{bmatrix} r_1 \cos\theta_1 + r_2 \cos\theta_2 & r_1 \cos\theta_1 & \cdots & r_1 \cos\theta_1 \\ r_1 \cos\theta_1 & r_1 \cos\theta_1 + r_3 \cos\theta_3 & \cdots & r_1 \cos\theta_1 \\ \vdots & \vdots & \ddots & \vdots \\ r_1 \cos\theta_1 & r_1 \cos\theta_1 & \cdots & r_1 \cos\theta_1 + r_{(M-1)} \cos\theta_{(M-1)} \end{bmatrix} \tag{13}$$

$$\frac{\partial \mathbf{\Sigma}_{r1}(\mathbf{x})}{\partial x_2} = 2\beta \begin{bmatrix} r_1 \sin\theta_1 + r_2 \sin\theta_2 & r_1 \sin\theta_1 & \cdots & r_1 \sin\theta_1 \\ r_1 \sin\theta_1 & r_1 \sin\theta_1 + r_3 \sin\theta_3 & \cdots & r_1 \sin\theta_1 \\ \vdots & \vdots & \ddots & \vdots \\ r_1 \sin\theta_1 & r_1 \sin\theta_1 & \cdots & r_1 \sin\theta_1 + r_{(M-1)} \sin\theta_{(M-1)} \end{bmatrix}, \tag{14}$$

where $\beta = \frac{a}{SNR_0 r_0^2}$.

Based on the characteristics of the FIM, the optimal configuration is analyzed via distance rule and angle rule.

(1) Distance rule

As pointed out in [26], arbitrarily selecting a reference sensor does not change the CRLB for TDOA-based source localization with distance-independent noises. Here, we extend it to the distance-dependent noise model.

Theorem 1. *Given the positions of the receivers and emitter, i.e., given distance r_i and angle θ_i the election of reference receiver has no impact on the CRLB with distance-dependent noise.*

Proof. Without loss of generality, receivers 1 and 2 are taken as the reference receivers. Then the TDOA measurement with different reference receivers can be represented by

$$\hat{\mathbf{z}}_{r1} = \begin{bmatrix} \hat{z}_{21} & \hat{z}_{31} & \cdots & \hat{z}_{M1} \end{bmatrix}^T = \mathbf{T}_1 \begin{bmatrix} \hat{z}_1 & \hat{z}_2 & \cdots & \hat{z}_M \end{bmatrix}^T \tag{15}$$

$$\hat{\mathbf{z}}_{r2} = \begin{bmatrix} \hat{z}_{12} & \hat{z}_{32} & \cdots & \hat{z}_{M2} \end{bmatrix}^T = \mathbf{T}_2 \begin{bmatrix} \hat{z}_1 & \hat{z}_2 & \cdots & \hat{z}_M \end{bmatrix}^T, \tag{16}$$

where $\mathbf{T}_1$ and $\mathbf{T}_2$ are transformation matrices and are all of dimension $(M-1) \times M$. $\mathbf{T}_1$ and $\mathbf{T}_2$ can be represented by

$$\mathbf{T}_1 = \begin{bmatrix} -1 & 1 & 0 & \cdots & 0 \\ -1 & 0 & \ddots & \ddots & \vdots \\ \vdots & \vdots & \ddots & \ddots & 0 \\ -1 & 0 & \cdots & 0 & 1 \end{bmatrix} \quad \mathbf{T}_2 = \begin{bmatrix} 1 & -1 & 0 & \cdots & 0 \\ 0 & -1 & 1 & 0 & \vdots \\ \vdots & \vdots & 0 & \ddots & 0 \\ 0 & -1 & 0 & 0 & 1 \end{bmatrix}.$$

It can be seen that through an element transformation matrix, $\mathbf{T}_2$ can be transformed to $\mathbf{T}_1$, i.e.,

$$\mathbf{T}_2 = \mathbf{U}_{21}\mathbf{T}_1, \tag{17}$$

where $\mathbf{U}_{21}$ is a $(M-1) \times (M-1)$ elementary transformation matrix. It is easy to obtain

$$\frac{\partial \mathbf{z}_{r2}(\mathbf{x})}{\partial x_i} = \frac{\partial \mathbf{z}_{r1}(\mathbf{x})}{\partial x_i} \mathbf{U}_{21}^T \tag{18}$$

$$\mathbf{\Sigma}_{r2} = \mathbf{U}_{21}\mathbf{\Sigma}_{r1}\mathbf{U}_{21}^T. \tag{19}$$

Then $\mathbf{J}_{1,(i,j)}^{r2}$ can be written as

$$\begin{aligned} \mathbf{J}_{1,(i,j)}^{r2} &= \frac{\partial \mathbf{z}_{r2}(\mathbf{x})}{\partial x_i} \mathbf{\Sigma}_{r2}^{-1}(\mathbf{x}) \left(\frac{\partial \mathbf{z}_{r2}(\mathbf{x})}{\partial x_j} \right)^T \\ &= \frac{\partial \mathbf{z}_{r1}(\mathbf{x})}{\partial x_i} \mathbf{U}_{21}^T \left(\mathbf{U}_{21}\mathbf{\Sigma}_{r1}(\mathbf{x})\mathbf{U}_{21}^T \right)^{-1} \left(\frac{\partial \mathbf{z}_{r1}(\mathbf{x})}{\partial x_i} \mathbf{U}_{21}^T \right)^T \\ &= \frac{\partial \mathbf{z}_{r1}(\mathbf{x})}{\partial x_i} \left(\mathbf{U}_{21}^T \left(\mathbf{U}_{21}^T \right)^{-1} \right) \mathbf{\Sigma}_{r1}^{-1}(\mathbf{x}) \left(\left(\mathbf{U}_{21}^T \right)^{-1} \mathbf{U}_{21}^T \right) \frac{\partial \mathbf{z}_{r1}(\mathbf{x})}{\partial x_i} \\ &= \frac{\partial \mathbf{z}_{r1}(\mathbf{x})}{\partial x_i} \mathbf{\Sigma}_{r1}^{-1}(\mathbf{x}) \frac{\partial \mathbf{z}_{r1}(\mathbf{x})}{\partial x_i} \\ &= \mathbf{J}_{1,(i,j)}^{r1} \end{aligned} \tag{20}$$

Similarly, we can get $\mathbf{J}_{2,(i,j)}^{r2} = \mathbf{J}_{2,(i,j)}^{r1}$. This completes the proof. □

Therefore, the selection of a reference receiver does not influence the CRLB with distance-dependent noise.

Theorem 2. *Given the angle θ_i, $i = 1, 2, \cdots M$, the smaller the distance between receiver and the source, the less the localization error is.*

Proof. Due to the meaning of $\mathbf{J}$ and the fact that the receiver measurement noise becomes larger as the range increases, $\mathbf{J}^{-1}$ increases. A similar proof can be found in [27], but is omitted here. This distance rule can guide UAVs to fly as close to the emitter as possible. □

(2) Angle rule

Assuming the distance between the emitter and each receiver is identical, i.e., $r_1 = r_2 = \cdots = r$, which means the receivers have equal noise variances, we get [6,9]

$$\mathbf{J}_1 = \mathbf{G}\mathbf{\Sigma}^{-1}(x)\mathbf{G}^T, \tag{21}$$

with

$$\mathbf{G} = [\mathbf{g}_{ij}, \cdots]_{\{i,j\} \in \mathcal{I}_0} \tag{22}$$

$$\mathbf{g}_{ij} = \mathbf{g}_i - \mathbf{g}_j \tag{23}$$

$$\mathbf{g}_i = \begin{bmatrix} \frac{x_t - x_i}{\sqrt{(x_t - x_i)^2 + (y_t - y_i)^2}} \\ \frac{y_t - y_i}{\sqrt{(x_t - x_i)^2 + (y_t - y_i)^2}} \end{bmatrix} = \begin{bmatrix} \cos(\theta_i) \\ \sin(\theta_i) \end{bmatrix}. \tag{24}$$

Take 1st receiver as the reference receiver and $\mathcal{I}_0 = [\{21\}, \{31\}, \cdots, \{M1\}]$ is as corresponding subset of sensor pairs, then we get

$$\mathbf{G} = [\mathbf{g}_{21}, \mathbf{g}_{31}, \cdots, \mathbf{g}_{M1}] \tag{25}$$

$$\boldsymbol{\Sigma}_{r1}(x) = 2 \frac{a}{SNR_0} \cdot \frac{r^2}{r_0^2} \begin{bmatrix} 1 & 1/2 & \cdots & 1/2 \\ 1/2 & \ddots & \ddots & \vdots \\ \vdots & \ddots & \ddots & 1/2 \\ 1/2 & \cdots & 1/2 & 1 \end{bmatrix}. \tag{26}$$

Substitute it into Equation (23), with $\mathbf{J}_1$ given by

$$\mathbf{J}_1 = \frac{r^2}{\beta} \begin{bmatrix} \sum\limits_{i=1}^{M} \cos^2(\theta_i) - \frac{1}{M} \left(\sum\limits_{i=1}^{M} \cos(\theta_i) \right)^2 & \sum\limits_{i=1}^{M} \cos(\theta_i)\sin(\theta_i) - \frac{1}{M} \sum\limits_{i=1}^{M} \cos(\theta_i) \sum\limits_{i=1}^{M} \sin(\theta_i) \\ \sum\limits_{i=1}^{M} \cos(\theta_i)\sin(\theta_i) - \frac{1}{M} \sum\limits_{i=1}^{M} \cos(\theta_i) \sum\limits_{i=1}^{M} \sin(\theta_i) & \sum\limits_{i=1}^{M} \sin^2(\theta_i) - \frac{1}{M} \left(\sum\limits_{i=1}^{M} \sin(\theta_i) \right)^2 \end{bmatrix}. \tag{27}$$

For the second part, after the algebraic simplification in Equation (12), $\mathbf{J}_2$ can be simplified as

$$\mathbf{J}_2 = \begin{bmatrix} \frac{2(M-1)^2-4}{M^2} \sum\limits_{i=1}^{M} \cos^2(\theta_i) + \frac{4}{M^2} \sum\limits_{i=1}^{M} \sum\limits_{j=1}^{M} \cos(\theta_i)\cos(\theta_j) & \frac{(M-1)^2}{M^2} \sum\limits_{i=1}^{M} \sin(2\theta_i) + \frac{2}{M^2} \sum\limits_{i=1}^{M} \sum\limits_{j>i}^{M} \sin(\theta_i + \theta_j) \\ \frac{(M-1)^2}{M^2} \sum\limits_{i=1}^{M} \sin(2\theta_i) + \frac{2}{M^2} \sum\limits_{i=1}^{M} \sum\limits_{j>i}^{M} \sin(\theta_i + \theta_j) & \frac{2(M-1)^2-4}{M^2} \sum\limits_{i=1}^{M} \sin^2(\theta_i) + \frac{4}{M^2} \sum\limits_{i=1}^{M} \sum\limits_{j=1}^{M} \sin(\theta_i)\sin(\theta_j) \end{bmatrix}. \tag{28}$$

Combine $\mathbf{J}_1$ and $\mathbf{J}_2$, the FIM can be expressed as

$$\mathbf{J} = \begin{bmatrix} \eta_1 \sum\limits_{i=1}^{M} \cos^2(\theta_i) - \eta_2 \left(\sum\limits_{i=1}^{M} \cos(\theta_i) \right)^2 & \eta_1 \sum\limits_{i=1}^{M} \cos(\theta_i)\sin(\theta_i) - \eta_2 \sum\limits_{i=1}^{M} \cos(\theta_i) \sum\limits_{i=1}^{M} \sin(\theta_i) \\ \eta_1 \sum\limits_{i=1}^{M} \cos(\theta_i)\sin(\theta_i) - \eta_2 \sum\limits_{i=1}^{M} \cos(\theta_i) \sum\limits_{i=1}^{M} \sin(\theta_i) & \eta_1 \sum\limits_{i=1}^{M} \sin^2(\theta_i) - \eta_2 \left(\sum\limits_{i=1}^{M} \sin(\theta_i) \right)^2 \end{bmatrix}, \tag{29}$$

where $\eta_1 = \left(\frac{2(M-1)^2-2}{M^2} + \frac{r^2}{\beta} \right)$, $\eta_2 = \left(\frac{r^2}{M\beta} - \frac{2}{M^2} \right)$.

Theorem 3. *Given the ranges $r_i = r_j$, $\forall i, j \in \{1, 2, \cdots N\}$ from each receiver to the emitter, we have*

$$Tr(\mathbf{J}^{-1}) \geq \frac{\eta_1}{4}; \tag{30}$$

the equality holds if and only if

$$\begin{aligned} \sum\limits_{i=1}^{M} \cos(\theta_i) = 0, \ \sum\limits_{i=1}^{M} \sin(\theta_i) = 0 \\ \sum\limits_{i=1}^{M} \cos(2\theta_i) = 0, \ \sum\limits_{i=1}^{M} \sin(2\theta_i) = 0 \end{aligned}. \tag{31}$$

Proof. Let $\lambda_i, i = 1, 2$ be the eigenvalues of **J**, which is a positive definite. Then the eigenvalues of $\mathbf{J}^{-1}$ are $1/\lambda_i$, It is obvious that

$$2 \leq \sqrt{(1/\lambda_1 + 1/\lambda_2)(\lambda_1 + \lambda_2)} = \left(Tr(\mathbf{J})Tr(\mathbf{J}^{-1})\right)^{1/2}, \tag{32}$$

implying that

$$Tr(\mathbf{J}^{-1}) \geq 4/Tr(\mathbf{J}). \tag{33}$$

The equality holds if and only if $\lambda_1 = \lambda_2 = \lambda$. Since **J** is a two-dimensional symmetric positive definite matrix, according to the Courant–Fischer–Weyl principle, the equation holds when **J** is diagonal and has equal eigenvalues. Hence it implies that

$$\mathbf{J} = \lambda \mathbf{I}. \tag{34}$$

As for the $Tr(\mathbf{J})$, we can obtain

$$Tr(\mathbf{J}) = \eta_1 - \eta_2 \left[\left(\sum_{i=1}^{M} \cos(\theta_i) \right)^2 + \left(\sum_{i=1}^{M} \sin(\theta_i) \right)^2 \right] \leq \eta_1. \tag{35}$$

Combining Equations (34) and (35), we get

$$\begin{array}{ll} \sum_{i=1}^{M} \cos(\theta_i) = 0, & \sum_{i=1}^{M} \sin(\theta_i) = 0 \\ \sum_{i=1}^{M} \cos(2\theta_i) = 0, & \sum_{i=1}^{M} \sin(2\theta_i) = 0 \end{array}. \tag{36}$$

As is known from the formulas above, when the distance between each receiver is identical, the measurement accuracy depends on the included angle θ_i between each receiver and the emitter. Therefore, it can be called the angle rule for the optimal configuration. □

Figure 1 shows $Tr(\mathbf{J})$ when $M = 3$ and $\eta_1 = 7$, where $A = \theta_2 - \theta_1$, $B = \theta_3 - \theta_1$ and $A + B \leq 2\pi$. At this time, when $A = 2\pi/3$ and $B = 2\pi/3$, $Tr(\mathbf{J})$ has the only maximum value.

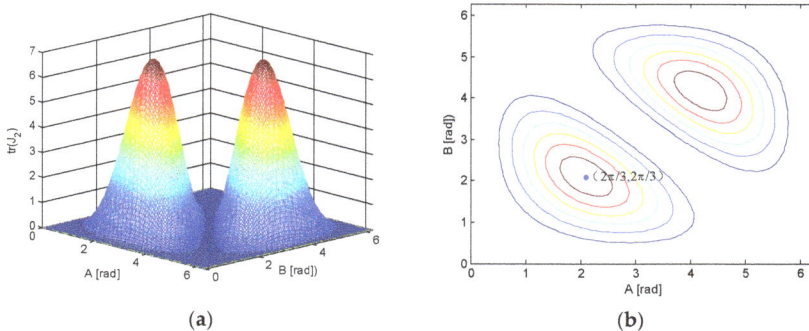

(a)   (b)

Figure 1. 3D plot of the information function $Tr(\mathbf{J})$ for three sensors. (**a**) The value of $Tr(\mathbf{J})$; (**b**) The contour plot of $Tr(\mathbf{J})$.

When $M \geq 3$, it is proven that the receiver distribution with uniform angular arrays (UAAs) can meet the above conditions [9]:

$$\theta_i = \theta_0 + \frac{2\pi}{M}(i-1), \ i = 1, 2, \ldots, M, \tag{37}$$

where θ_i is any constant given on $[0, 2\pi M / (M - 1))$. Figure 2 shows the optimal receiver geometries for $M = 3$, $M = 4$, and $M = 5$. When $M = 4, 5$, UAAs distribution method is the unique solution of Equation (38). For $M \geq 6$, even though the optimal deployment is still given by partitions of appropriate angle each with UAA distribution, the UAAs distribution method is an optimal solution.

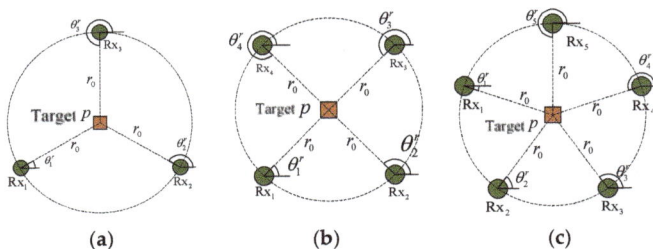

(a)   (b)   (c)

Figure 2. Optimal receiver geometries for (a) $M = 3$, (b) $M = 3$, (c) $M = 5$.

Remark 1. *The Cramer–Rao bound $\mathbf{J}^{-1}$ under different distribution methods is a function of the receiver–emitter distance and angle. The optimal distribution method is to approach the distance lower bound r_0, according to the distance rule and select a good angular separation according to the angle rule.*

For the case of arbitrary distances and angles, getting an analytic solution for the receiver–emitter geometry problem may be impossible. Some optimization algorithms can be applied to acquire a local solution.

3.2. Movable Emitter Scenario

Semidefinite programming methods [6] are applied in this paper to estimate the emitter location. Then the estimator value, calculated by SDP methods each time, can further improve the result estimated by the EKF estimator [28]. In actual applications, the SDP methods can provide initialization information for EKF. The process of the EKF filter is given by:

(1) Predict:

$$\hat{\mathbf{x}}_{k+1|k} = f_k(\hat{\mathbf{x}}_{k|k}) \tag{38}$$

$$\mathbf{P}_{k+1|k} = f_k^x \mathbf{P}_{k|k}(f_k^x)^T + f_k^w \mathbf{Q}_{k|k}(f_k^w)^T. \tag{39}$$

(2) Update:

$$\mathbf{K}_{k+1|k} = \mathbf{P}_{k+1|k}[\mathbf{P}_{k+1|k} + \mathbf{J}_{k+1}^{-1}]^{-1} \tag{40}$$

$$\mathbf{P}_{k+1|k+1} = (\mathbf{I} - \mathbf{K}_{k+1|k})\mathbf{P}_{k+1|k} \tag{41}$$

$$\hat{\mathbf{x}}_{k+1|k+1} = \hat{\mathbf{x}}_{k+1|k} + \mathbf{K}_{k+1|k}\left[\mathbf{z}_{k+1} - h_{k+1}(\hat{\mathbf{x}}_{k+1|k})\right], \tag{42}$$

where the Jacobian matrix of the emitter movement model and the measurement model is:

$$f_k^x = \left.\frac{\partial f_k(x_k, w_k)}{\partial x_k}\right|_{\substack{x_k = \hat{x}_{k|k} \\ w_k = 0}}, \quad f_k^w = \left.\frac{\partial f_k(x_k, w_k)}{\partial w_k}\right|_{\substack{x_k = \hat{x}_{k|k} \\ w_k = 0}}.$$

Here, we mainly focus on analyzing the optimal receiver–emitter geometry, which will enable optimal localization in terms of the posterior error covariance matrix $\mathbf{p}_{k+1|k}$. In order to establish a relationship between $\mathbf{J}^{-1}$ and the predicted value, Equation (43) can be expressed as follows [29]:

$$\mathbf{p}_{k+1|k+1} = \left((\mathbf{p}_{k+1|k})^{-1} + \mathbf{J}_{k+1} \right)^{-1}. \tag{43}$$

Define $\mathbf{p}_{k+1|k} = \begin{bmatrix} p_{11} & p_{12} \\ p_{12} & p_{22} \end{bmatrix}$, $\mathbf{S} = (\mathbf{p}_{k+1|k})^{-1} + \mathbf{J}_{k+1}$ which is positive definite. Then $\mathbf{S}$ is given by

$$\mathbf{S} = \begin{bmatrix} \mathbf{J}_{(1,1)} + \frac{p_{22}}{p_{11}p_{22}-p_{12}^2} & \mathbf{J}_{(1,2)} - \frac{p_{12}}{p_{11}p_{22}-p_{12}^2} \\ \mathbf{J}_{(1,2)} - \frac{p_{12}}{p_{11}p_{22}-p_{12}^2} & \mathbf{J}_{(2,2)} + \frac{p_{11}}{p_{11}p_{22}-p_{12}^2} \end{bmatrix}. \tag{44}$$

For the moveable emitter scenario, the objective is to minimize the mean square error (MSE), i.e., $Tr(\mathbf{p}_{k+1|k+1})$, then the following results can be obtained.

Theorem 4. *For* $M \geq 3$, *we have*

$$Tr(\mathbf{p}_{k+1|k+1}) \geq \frac{4}{\mathbf{J}_{(1,1)} + \mathbf{J}_{(2,2)} + \frac{p_{11}+p_{22}}{p_{11}p_{22}-p_{12}^2}}. \tag{45}$$

The equality holds if and only if

$$\begin{cases} \mathbf{J}_{(1,1)} - \mathbf{J}_{(2,2)} = \frac{(p_{11}-p_{22})}{p_{11}p_{22}-p_{12}^2} \\ \mathbf{J}_{(1,1)} = \frac{2p_{12}}{p_{11}p_{22}-p_{12}^2}. \end{cases} \tag{46}$$

Proof. The proof is similar to that of Corollary 3 and is omitted here. $\square$

The explicit solutions of the optimal configuration can be acquired when the ranges are identical. Given $r_i = r_j$, $\forall i, j \in \{1, \cdots, M\}$, $\mathbf{S}$ can be written as follows [10,11]:

$$\mathbf{S} = \begin{bmatrix} \eta_1 \sum\limits_{i=1}^{M} \cos^2(\theta_i) - \eta_2 \left(\sum\limits_{i=1}^{M} \cos(\theta_i) \right)^2 + \frac{p_{22}}{p_{11}p_{22}-p_{12}^2} & \eta_1 \sum\limits_{i=1}^{M} \cos(\theta_i)\sin(\theta_i) - \eta_2 \sum\limits_{i=1}^{M} \cos(\theta_i) \sum\limits_{i=1}^{M} \sin(\theta_i) - \frac{p_{12}}{p_{11}p_{22}-p_{12}^2} \\ \eta_1 \sum\limits_{i=1}^{M} \cos(\theta_i)\sin(\theta_i) - \eta_2 \sum\limits_{i=1}^{M} \cos(\theta_i) \sum\limits_{i=1}^{M} \sin(\theta_i) - \frac{p_{12}}{p_{11}p_{22}-p_{12}^2} & \eta_1 \sum\limits_{i=1}^{M} \sin^2(\theta_i) - \eta_2 \left(\sum\limits_{i=1}^{M} \sin(\theta_i) \right)^2 + \frac{p_{11}}{p_{11}p_{22}-p_{12}^2} \end{bmatrix}. \tag{47}$$

Then the optimal configuration can be acquired if and only if

$$\sum\limits_{i=1}^{M} \cos(\theta_i) = 0, \quad \sum\limits_{i=1}^{M} \sin(\theta_i) = 0$$
$$\sum\limits_{i=1}^{M} \cos(2\theta_i) = \frac{p_{11}-p_{22}}{\eta_1(p_{11}p_{22}-p_{12}^2)}, \quad \sum\limits_{i=1}^{M} \sin(2\theta_i) = \frac{p_{12}}{\eta_1(p_{11}p_{22}-p_{12}^2)}. \tag{48}$$

If $\left| \frac{p_{11}-p_{22}}{\eta_1(p_{11}p_{22}-p_{12}^2)} \right| > M$, $\left| \frac{p_{12}}{\eta_1(p_{11}p_{22}-p_{12}^2)} \right| > M$, or r_i is an arbitrary value, it is hard to find the explicit solution for optimal configuration. What can be done is to apply the results in Theorem 4 for the expression of the determinant of the CRLB, and then solve an optimization problem.

4. UAV Path Optimization

Section 3 provides the optimal configuration, without considering receiver constraints. However, in general, the UAV receiving platform is affected by its movement constraints and cannot achieve the conditions for optimal configuration within a short time [30]. Usually, the UAVs are far from the emitter; also, they are affected by the communication constraint and collision avoidance constraint. Therefore, it takes some time before reaching the optimal localization configuration.

The UAV path planning problem is a constrained optimization problem [31] that involves the calculation of UAVs waypoints at discrete time instants. The optimal trajectory is generated by minimizing the trace of the CRLB, which is analyzed in Section 3. The receiver measurements are assumed to be synchronized with waypoint updates. In addition, UAVs are assumed to be equipped with a Global Positioning System (GPS) and robust line-of-sight (LOS) datalinks [32].

Assuming the systematic UAV discrete dynamic model is [15,33]:

$$\mathbf{X}_{k+1} = f(\mathbf{X}_k, \mathbf{u}_k), k = 1, 2, \cdots, M, \tag{49}$$

where $\mathbf{X}_k$ is the system status value $\mathbf{X}_k = [\chi_1(k), \cdots, \chi_M(k)]^T$ at the time k, and $\mathbf{u}_k$ is the control vector $\mathbf{u}_k = [u_1(k), u_2(k), \cdots u_M(k)]$ of UAV at each moment. Without loss of generality, UAV1 is assigned as the reference node, and the proposed waypoint update equation of the UAV is:

$$\mathbf{x}_i(k+1) = \begin{bmatrix} x_i(k) \\ y_i(k) \end{bmatrix} + v_0 T \begin{bmatrix} \cos u_i(k) \\ \sin u_i(k) \end{bmatrix}, \tag{50}$$

where v_0 is the UAV flight speed and T is the time interval between waypoint updates. The UAVs path can be optimized by taking the CRLB as the optimization rule. Within each time interval, SDP methods and EKF are used to update emitter localization and tracking estimations.

Therefore, the objective function can be expressed as:

$$\begin{cases} \operatorname{argmin} f(\mathbf{u}_{k+1}) = Tr(\mathbf{J}_{k+1}^{-1}(r_i, \theta_i)), \ k \leq 3 \\ \operatorname{argmin} f(\mathbf{u}_{k+1}) = Tr(\mathbf{P}_{k+1|k+1}(r_i, \theta_i)), k > 3 \end{cases} \tag{51}$$

$$s.t. \|u_i(k+1) - u_i(k)\| \leq u_{\max} \tag{52}$$

$$g_{1ij}(\mathbf{u}_k) = R_h - \|\mathbf{x}_i(k+1) - \hat{\mathbf{x}}_t(k)\| \geq 0 \tag{53}$$

$$g_{2ij}(\mathbf{u}_k) = \|\mathbf{x}_i(k+1) - \hat{\mathbf{x}}_t(k)\| - R_l \geq 0 \tag{54}$$

$$g_{3ij}(\mathbf{u}_k) = c_h - \|\mathbf{x}_i(k+1) - \mathbf{x}_j(k+1)\| \geq 0 \tag{55}$$

$$g_{4ij}(\mathbf{u}_k) = \|\mathbf{x}_i(k+1) - \mathbf{x}_j(k+1)\| - c_l \geq 0, \tag{56}$$

where Equation (52) is the turn rate constraint of the UAV. Equations (53) and (54) represent the distance constraint from the UAV to the emitter. Equations (55) and (56) are the UAV communication constraint and collision avoidance constraint, respectively.

Therefore, the path optimization can be converted to non-linear optimization [34]. This problem is solved by directly configuring the non-linear programming method (DCNLP) or sequential quadratic programming (SQP) [35]. Considering that only the inequality constraint is included in this constraint, the interior penalty function is adopted in this paper to convert this non-linear constraint to an unconstrained problem of minimization auxiliary function. A small calculation amount guarantees the real-time performance of the calculation. The calculation steps are as follows:

Step 1: Give the system status $\mathbf{X}_k = [\chi_1(k), \cdots, \chi_M(k)]^T$ of each UAV at the time k, TDOA measurement $\hat{\mathbf{z}}$ and Equations (52)–(56).

Step 2: Use the SDP methods to calculate the emitter location value $\hat{\mathbf{x}}_t(k)$ and the estimated value $\mathbf{x}_t(k|k)$ by using EKF estimator.

Step 3: The feasible region of non-linear Equations (53)–(56) in the constraints can be defined as:

$$S = \{\mathbf{u}_k | g_{1ij}(\mathbf{u}_k) \geq 0, g_{2ij}(\mathbf{u}_k) \geq 0, g_{3ij}(\mathbf{u}_k) \geq 0, g_{4ij}(\mathbf{u}_k) \geq 0\}. \tag{57}$$

The logarithmic barrier function can be obtained as:

$$G(\mathbf{u}_k, \gamma) = f(\mathbf{u}_k) + \gamma B(\mathbf{u}_k), \gamma > 0, \tag{58}$$

where γ is a logarithmic barrier function, $\gamma \to 0$,

$$B(\mathbf{u}_k) = -\sum_{i=1}^{M} \ln(g_{1ij}(\mathbf{u}_k)) - \sum_{i=1}^{M} \ln(g_{2ij}(\mathbf{u}_k)) - \sum_{i=1}^{M-1} \sum_{j=i+1}^{M} \ln(g_{3ij}(\mathbf{u}_k)) - \sum_{i=1}^{M-1} \sum_{j=i+1}^{M} \ln(g_{4ij}(\mathbf{u}_k)). \tag{59}$$

Therefore, the non-linear constraint is converted to an unconstrained problem. The minimum value of $G(\mathbf{u}_k, \gamma)$ can be solved by setting the initial internal point.

Step 4: As for linear Equation (52), for the convenience of calculation, the $\mathbf{u}_k$ solved in Step 3 can be substituted into the constrained inequality. When the constraint conditions are satisfied, it is the final output result; otherwise, the boundary value $u_{\max}$ is selected.

Step 5: The control amount $\mathbf{u}_k$ of the UAV for the next waypoint.

Figure 3 demonstrates the steps of the algorithm for UAV path planning based on CRLB. In this figure, $\mathbf{u}_k$ is the output of the algorithm at time step k. When UAVs arrive at new waypoints, new measurements are collected and new estimations are acquired.

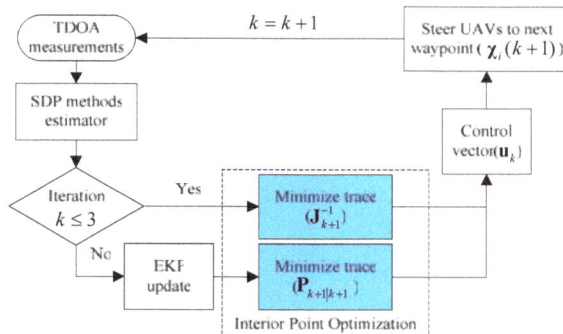

Figure 3. UAV path planning for localization based on CRLB (TDOA: time-difference-of-arrival; SDP: semidefinite programming; EKF: extended Kalman filter).

5. Simulation Results

In this section, four UAVs are considered to locate the static and movable emitter to verify the sensor-emitter geometries, respectively. MATLAB simulations are implemented with a 2.7 GHz Intel core processor with 8 GB of memory. The initial UAVs state vectors are $\chi_1(1) = [-9600, -5000]^T$, $\chi_2(1) = [-10000, -5000]^T$, $\chi_3(1) = [-10000, -5400]^T$ and $\chi_4(1) = [-9600, -5400]^T$. The headings for UAVs are all equal to $\pi/2$(north) at the initial moment and other key parameters are listed in Table 1.

Table 1. Parameters used in simulations.

Parameters	Symbols	Values
Initial emitter position	$\mathbf{x}_t$	$[0,0]^T$
Fixed flight velocity	v_0	150 m/s
Sampling time interval	T	1 s
Signal to noise ratio	SNR_0	30 dB
Control vector	u_{max}	15°
Maximum distance from the UAV platform to the emitter	R_h	30 km
Minimum distance from the UAV platform to the emitter	R_l	1000 m
Safe distance between the UAV platform	c_l	200 m
Communication maximum distance	c_h	15 km
Barrier parameter for interior point optimization	γ	10^{-8}

5.1. Angle Rule

Firstly, the UAVs path optimization with only a turn rate constraint is investigated to verify the angle rule. The true emitter location is $\mathbf{x}_t = [0,0]^T$. Here we assume that σ_i^2 is irrelevant to distance r_i. Figure 4a,c show the optimal UAV path, taking CRLB as the rule and the straight-line UAV trajectories, respectively. The red triangle in the figure denotes the true emitter location; the small blue circles denote the estimated value of the emitter position with SDP methods and EKF estimator within each time step.

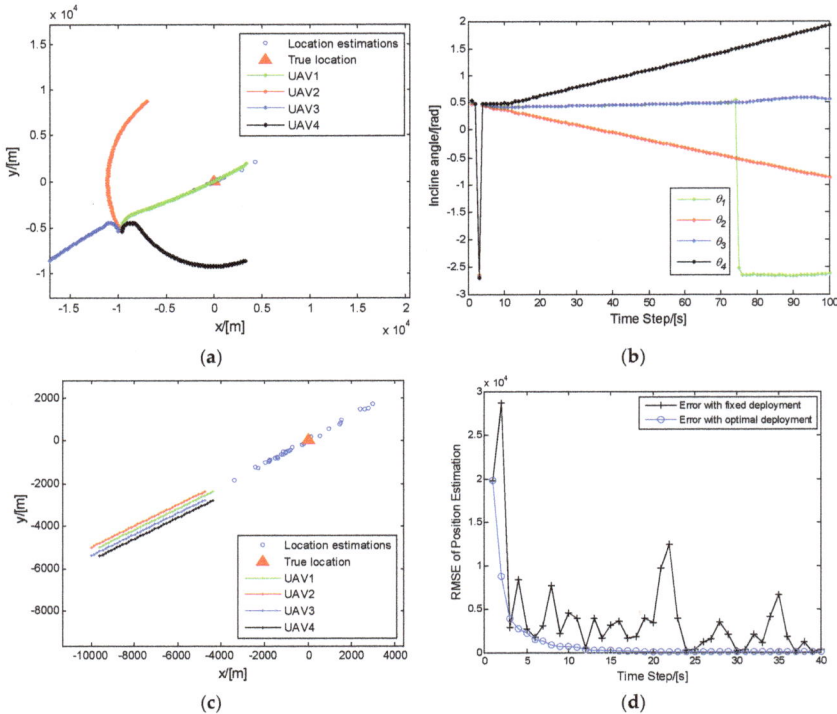

Figure 4. (**a**) Optimal paths without constraints. (**b**) Evolution of angle changes. (**c**) Straight-line paths. (**d**) Comparison of localization performance: optimal deployment and fixed deployment.

From Figure 4a,b, it can be seen that the UAVs try to fly away from each other and obtain the evolution of angle θ_i. Meanwhile, it is noted that each UAV does not obtain effective emitter information due to the initial deployment, and the localization errors is high. After the 10th time step, the localization error drops sharply with changes in the θ_i, emitter, as is shown in Figure 4d. Figure 4c shows the straight-line UAV trajectories, whereby each UAV is steered directly towards the estimated emitter position.

To demonstrate the effectiveness of the proposed path planning algorithm, Figure 4d shows the RMSE of optimal trajectories compared with straight-line trajectories after 50 Monte Carlo simulations. This shows that the application of the angle rule is capable of reducing the location error, while the location error with straight-line trajectories is large and apparently uncertain. However, even after all constraints are considered, it can be seen that minimizing the localization could result in baseline expansion. UAVs fly away from each other only within the constrained scope, which is not desirable in actual situations. Hence, it is impractical to reach the optimal location by relying only on the angle rule.

5.2. Combination of Angle Rule and Distance Rule

The optimal paths considering the noise variance change with distance and all constraints are included in the optimization problem. The simulation results are shown in Figure 5.

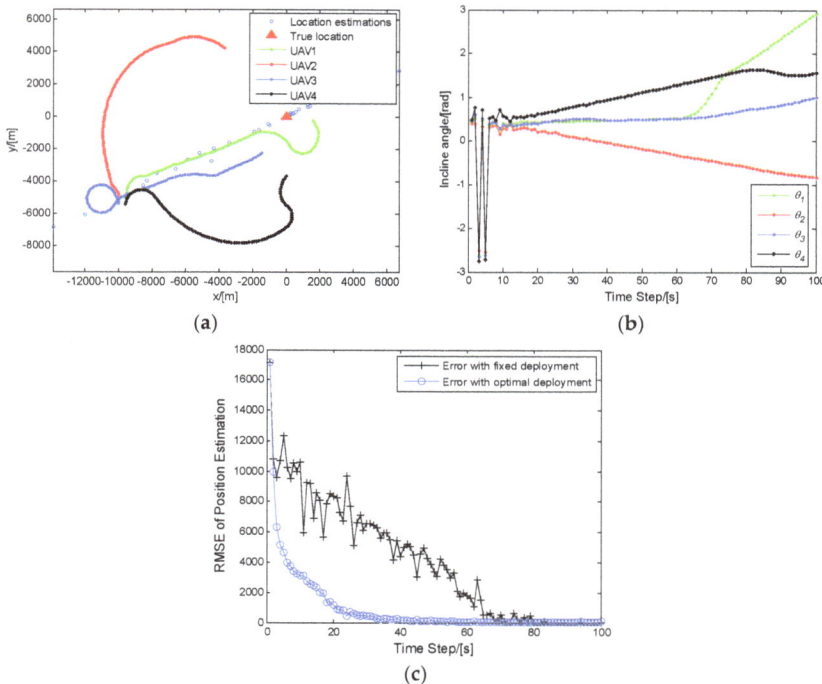

Figure 5. (a) Optimal paths with constraints. (b) Evolution of angle changes. (c) Comparison of localization performance: optimal deployment and fixed deployment.

According to Figure 5a,b, the distance between each UAV and the emitter in the initial stage is nearly the same in the initial time step, so it is similar to the angle rule case: Each UAV tends to expand the detection angles to have a better view of the emitter. The initial flight direction of UAV3 is basically the same as the path in Section 5.1. After about the 10th time step, UAV3 begins to make a turn and fly toward the emitter, which is mainly caused by the distance rule. The flight path of UAV2 and UAV4 is mainly affected by the angle rule during the first several steps and they fly away from the UAV1. When large angles are obtained, they start to be affected by the distance rule and fly towards the emitter so that a balance between the angle rule and distance rule is eventually reached. UAV1 flies towards the emitter and starts to rotate around the emitter since it is affected by a lower limit R_l of distance at about $t = 63$ s. Figure 5c shows a comparison of the optimal UAV paths and straight-line paths. The RMSE of UAVs flying with straight-line trajectories generally tends to decrease, mainly because of the distance rule. However, its location accuracy is still unstable as the relative deployment of UAVs and the emitter at certain moments are rather inappropriate for the emitter localization. Similar to the angle rule case, the localization performance using path optimization is much better than the straight-line paths. If there is a requirement to the lower RMSE, UAVs will rotate around the estimated emitter location in a fixed distance according to the angle rule.

5.3. Effect of the Number of UAVs on TDOA Localization Performance

The purpose of this simulation is to compare the localization performance with different numbers of UAVs (i.e., $M = 3, 4, 5$).

Figure 6 shows the evolution of RMSE corresponding to varying values of M. As can be expected, as M becomes larger, a lower and more stable RMSE is obtained.

We also notice that the objective function has a growing number of local parameters causing sensitivities to initialization with M increases. This may lead to suboptimal solutions if not initialized properly. Hence, the initialization of the target plays an important role in SDP methods. The results in Section 3 can be helpful for a proper choice of the initial measurements.

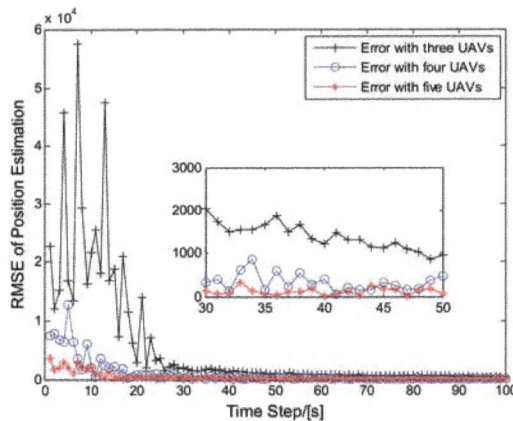

Figure 6. Evolution of RMSE with different numbers of UAVs.

5.4. Dynamic Emitter

As for dynamic emitter, it is assumed that the emitter is uniform linear motion and the dynamic behavior of the state is described by:

$$\mathbf{x}_t(k) = \mathbf{F}\mathbf{x}_t(k-1) + \mathbf{v}(k). \tag{60}$$

The initial state is $\mathbf{x}_t(1) = \begin{bmatrix} 0, & 50/\sqrt{2}, & 0, & 50/\sqrt{2} \end{bmatrix}^T$, with the state transition matrix given by:

$$\mathbf{F} = \begin{bmatrix} 1 & \Delta T & 0 & 0 \\ 0 & 1 & 0 & 0 \\ 0 & 0 & 1 & \Delta T \\ 0 & 0 & 0 & 1 \end{bmatrix}, \tag{61}$$

where $\Delta T = 1s$. In order to simplify the calculation, it is assumed that the emitter flies at a speed of 50 m/s along the straight line and other constraints are the same as in the static emitter situation.

Figure 7a shows the results of location and tracking for a dynamic emitter. Different from static emitters, each UAV starts to fly towards the estimated emitter position after obtaining a certain angle. Since the distance between the emitter and the UAV changes significantly at each moment, the distance rule exerts more influence on the UAV path at this time as compared with the static emitter localization. According to Figure 7b, the location accuracy after path optimization is still high and stable as compared with a location with straight-line paths.

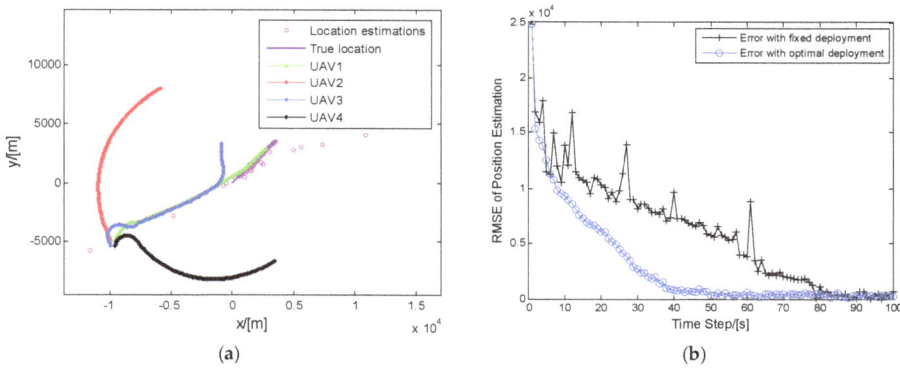

Figure 7. (**a**) Optimal paths for dynamic emitter location and tracking. (**b**) Comparison of localization performance: optimal deployment and fixed deployment.

6. Conclusions

In this paper, we have provided an algorithm for UAV path planning based on TDOA localization. The receiver measurement model and distance-dependent noise were presented, and optimal geometry based on CRLB was investigated in both static and movable scenarios. A hybrid SDP method and EKF estimator were applied to locate the emitter and the online sensor management presented here was particularly useful for TDOA measurements. The knowledge of optimal sensor-emitter geometries provided useful tactical information and revealed important insights into the impact of sensor-emitter geometries on the performance of emitter localization and tracking. Simulation results showed that the UAV complied with distance and angle rules when looking for an optimal path. The optimized path was able to provide accurate and stable localization.

For future work, we will consider the long-term optimization, i.e., multi-step optimization, which may bring burdens for the reference receiver. Future work will also include obstacle avoidance in real applications, which may affect the localization accuracy.

Author Contributions: Both authors contributed to the research work. W.W. and P.B. designed the new method. H.L. and X.L. mainly planned the experiments. W.W. performed experiments and wrote the paper.

Acknowledgments: This research was funded by the National Natural Science Foundation of China (Nos. 61472443, 61502522) and Shaanxi Province Lab of Meta-synthesis for Electronic & Information systems. The authors sincerely thank the anonymous reviewers for their valuable and constructive comments.

Conflicts of Interest: The authors declare no conflict of interest.

References

1. Jin, Y.; Liu, X.; Hu, Z.; Li, S. DOA estimation of moving sound sources in the context of nonuniform spatial noise using acoustic vector sensor. *Multidimens. Syst. Signal Process.* **2015**, *26*, 321–336. [CrossRef]
2. Compagnoni, M.; Canclini, A.; Bestagini, P. Source localization and denoising: A perspective from the TDOA space. *Multidimens. Syst. Signal Process.* **2016**, 1–26. [CrossRef]
3. Chang, S.; Li, Y.; He, Y.; Wang, H. Target Localization in Underwater Acoustic Sensor Networks Using RSS Measurements. *Appl. Sci.* **2018**, *8*, 225. [CrossRef]
4. Domingo-Perez, F.; Lazaro-Galilea, J.L.; Wieser, A. Sensor placement determination for range-difference positioning using evolutionary multi-objective optimization. *Exp. Syst. Appl.* **2016**, *47*, 95–105. [CrossRef]
5. Malanowski, M. Two Methods for Target Localization in Multistatic Passive Radar. *IEEE Trans. Aerosp. Electr. Syst.* **2012**, *48*, 572–580. [CrossRef]
6. Chan, Y.T.; Ho, K.C. A Simple and Efficient Estimator for Hyperbolic Location. *IEEE Trans. Signal Process.* **1994**, *42*, 1905–1915. [CrossRef]
7. Zou, Y.; Liu, H.; Xie, W.; Wan, Q. Semidefinite Programming Methods for Alleviating Sensor Position Error in TDOA Localization. *IEEE Access* **2017**, *5*, 23111–23120. [CrossRef]
8. Yang, B. Different Sensor Placement Strategies for TDOA Based Localization. In Proceedings of the ICASSP, Honolulu, HI, USA, 15–20 April 2007; pp. 1093–1096.
9. Lui, K.W.K.; So, H.C. A Study of Two-Dimensional Sensor Placement Using Time-Difference-of-Arrival Measurements. *Dig. Signal Process.* **2009**, *19*, 650–659. [CrossRef]
10. Meng, W.; Xie, L.; Xiao, W. Optimality Analysis of Sensor-Source Geometries in Heterogeneous Sensor Networks. *IEEE Trans. Wirel. Commun.* **2013**, *12*, 1958–1967. [CrossRef]
11. Meng, W.; Xie, L.; Xiao, W. Optimal TDOA Sensor-Pair Placement With Uncertainty in Source Location. *IEEE Trans. Veh. Technol.* **2016**, *65*, 9260–9271. [CrossRef]
12. Kim, S.-H.; Park, J.H.; Yoon, W.; Ra, W.-S. A note on sensor arrangement for long-distance target localization. *Signal Process.* **2017**, *133*, 18–31. [CrossRef]
13. Fang, X.; Yan, W.; Zhang, F. Optimal Sensor Placement for Range-Based Dynamic Random Localization. *IEEE Geosci. Remote Sens. Lett.* **2015**, *12*, 2393–2397. [CrossRef]
14. Herath, S.C.K.; Pathirana, P.N. Optimal Sensor Arrangements in Angle of Arrival (AoA) and Range Based Localization with Linear Sensor Arrays. *Sensors* **2013**, *13*, 12277–12294. [CrossRef] [PubMed]
15. Sarunic, P.; Evans, R. Hierarchical Model Predictive Control of UAVs Performing Multitarget-Multisensor Tracking. *IEEE Trans. Aeros. Electr. Syst.* **2014**, *50*, 2253–2268. [CrossRef]
16. Tripathi, A.; Saxena, N.; Mishra, K.K. A nature inspired hybrid optimisation algorithm for dynamic environment with real parameter encoding. *Int. J. Bio-Inspir. Comput.* **2017**, *10*, 24–32. [CrossRef]
17. Dogancay, K. UAV Path Planning for Passive Emitter Localization. *IEEE Trans. Aerosp. Electr. Syst.* **2012**, *48*, 1150–1166. [CrossRef]
18. Frew, E.; Dixon, C.; Argrow, B. Radio source localization by a cooperating UAV team. In Proceedings of the AIAA Infotech@Aerospace, Arlington, TX, USA, 26–29 September 2005.
19. Wang, X.; Ristic, B.; Himed, B.; Moran, B. Joint Passive Sensor Scheduling for Target Tracking. In Proceedings of the 20th International Conference on Information Fusion, Xi'an, China, 10–13 July 2017; pp. 1671–1677.
20. Alomari, A.; Phillips, W.; Aslam, N.; comeau, F. Dynamic Fuzzy-Logic Based Path Planning for Mobility-Assisted Localization in Wireless Sensor Networks. *Sensors* **2017**, *17*, 1904. [CrossRef] [PubMed]
21. Kaune, R. Finding Sensor Trajectories for TDOA Based Localization—Preliminary Considerations. In Proceedings of the Workshop Sensor Data Fusion: Trends, Solutions, Applications, Bonn, Germany, 4–6 September 2012.
22. Kaune, R.; Charlish, A. Online Optimization of Sensor Trajectories for Localization using TDOA Measurements. In Proceedings of the International Conference on Information Fusion, Istanbul, Turkey, 9–12 July 2013; pp. 484–491.

23. Li, X.; Deng, Z.D.; Rauchenstein, L.T.; Carlson, T.J. Contributed Review: Source-localization algorithms and applications using time of arrival and time difference of arrival measurements. *Rev. Sci. Instrum.* **2016**, *87*, 041502. [CrossRef] [PubMed]

24. Kaune, R.; Horst, J.; Koch, W. Accuracy Analysis for TDOA Localization in Sensor Networks. In Proceedings of the 14th International Conference on Information Fusion, Chicago, IL, USA, 5–8 July 2011; pp. 1647–1654.

25. Huang, B.; Xie, L.; Yang, Z. TDOA-based Source Localization with Distance-dependent Noises. *IEEE Trans. Wirel. Commun.* **2015**, *14*, 468–480. [CrossRef]

26. So, H.C.; Chan, Y.T.; Chan, F.K.W. Closed-form formulae for time-difference-of-arrival estimation. *IEEE Trans. Signal Process.* **2008**, *56*, 2614–2620. [CrossRef]

27. Yan, W.; Fang, X.; Li, J. Formation Optimization for AUV Localization with Range-Dependent Measurements Noise. *IEEE Commun. Lett.* **2014**, *18*, 1579–1582. [CrossRef]

28. Fanaei, M.; Valenti, M.C.; Schmid, N.A.; Alkhweldi, M.M. Distributed parameter estimation in wireless sensor networks using fused local observations. In Proceedings of the SPIE Defense, Security, and Sensing, Baltimore, MD, USA, 9 May 2012; p. 17.

29. Bar-Shalom, Y.; Li, X.; Kirubarajan, T. *Estimation with Applications to Track and Navigation*; Wiley: New York, NY, USA, 2001.

30. Duan, K.; Wang, Z.; Xie, W. Sparsity-based STAP algorithm with multiple measurement vectors via sparse Bayesian learning strategy for airborne radar. *IET Signal Process.* **2017**, *11*, 544–553. [CrossRef]

31. Yahya, N.M.; Tokhi, M.O. A modified bats echolocation-based algorithm for solving constrained optimisation problems. *Int. J. Bio-Inspir. Comput.* **2017**, *10*, 12–23. [CrossRef]

32. Nikolakopoulos, K.G.; Koukouvelas, I.; Argyropoulos, N.; Megalooikonomou, V. Quarry monitoring using GPS measurements and UAV photogrammetry. In Proceedings of the SPIE Remote Sensing, Toulouse, France, 10 October 2015; p. 8.

33. Lai, Y.-C.; Ting, W.O. Design and Implementation of an Optimal Energy Control System for Fixed-Wing Unmanned Aerial Vehicles. *Appl. Sci.* **2016**, *6*, 369. [CrossRef]

34. Rajput, U.; Kumari, M. Mobile robot path planning with modified ant colony optimisation. *Int. J. Bio-Inspir. Comput.* **2017**, *9*, 106–113. [CrossRef]

35. Xu, D.; Xiao, R. An improved genetic clustering algorithm for the multi-depot vehicle routing problem. *Int. J. Wirel. Mob. Comput.* **2015**, *9*, 1–7. [CrossRef]

applied
sciences

MDPI

Article

Signal Source Localization of Multiple Robots Using an Event-Triggered Communication Scheme

Ligang Pan [1], Qiang Lu [1,*] , Ke Yin [1,2] and Botao Zhang [1]

[1] School of Automation, Hangzhou Dianzi University, Hangzhou 310018, China;
    161060037@hdu.edu.cn (L.P.); yinke@hdu.edu.cn (K.Y.); billow@hdu.edu.cn (B.Z.)
[2] College of Electrical Engineering, Zhejiang University, Hangzhou 310027, China
* Correspondence: lvqiang@hdu.edu.cn; Tel.: +86-138-1913-9153

Received: 16 May 2018; Accepted: 8 June 2018; Published: 14 June 2018

check for
updates

Abstract: This paper deals with the problem of signal source localization using a group of autonomous robots by designing and analyzing a decision-control approach with an event-triggered communication scheme. The proposed decision-control approach includes two levels: a decision level and a control level. In the decision level, a particle filter is used to estimate the possible positions of the signal source. The estimated position of the signal source gradually approaches the real position of signal source with the movement of robots. In the control level, a consensus controller is proposed to control multiple robots to seek a signal source based on the estimated signal source position. At the same time, an event-triggered communication scheme is designed such that the burden of communication can be lightened. Finally, simulation and experimental results show the effectiveness of the proposed decision-control approach with the event-triggered communication scheme for the problem of signal source localization.

Keywords: signal source localization; multi-robot system; event-triggered communication; consensus control

1. Introduction

Signal source localization can be widely found in nature and society [1–7]. For example, some bacteria are able to find chemical or light sources through the perception of the external environment [1]. Moreover, reproducing this kind of behavior in mobile robots can be used to perform some complex missions such as monitoring environments [2,3,8,9], searching and rescuing victims [10], and so on. How to deal with the problem of signal source localization has attracted increasing interest from scientists and engineers and involves two aspects of study. One aspect is to estimate the possible positions of signal sources, while the other aspect is to control robots to locate signal sources based on the estimated positions [2,3]. For a single robot, some approaches have been proposed for the problem of signal source localization. For example, in [11], the SPSA (Simultaneous Perturbation Stochastic Approximation) method was designed to control the mobile robot to locate a signal source. In [12,13], the extremum seeking technique, originally developed for adaptive control, was also applied in signal source localization. In [14], a source probability estimation approach was proposed to control the robot to locate the signal source by using the information on signal strength and direction angle. However, the aforementioned approaches need the robot to take more time to collect measurements at different locations. Moreover, some search trajectories generated by these approaches are usually unnecessary.

Compared with the single robot, due to the wide detection range and simultaneous sampling, multi-robot systems have received much attention for the problem of signal source localization (see Figure 1) [15–21]. Usually, the integrated gradient estimation of the signal strength distribution is a common method to estimate the possible position of the signal source, which means that multiple robots simultaneously obtain the measurements at different locations and give the movement direction such that some unnecessary trajectories are neglected [18,22,23]. For example, in [18], Nikolay approximated the signal strength gradient at the formation centroid via a Finite-Difference (FD) scheme and proposed distributed control strategies for localizing a noisy signal source. In [2], Lu used a radial basis function network to model the search environment and guided the robots to move toward the signal source based on gradient information provided by the environment model. Correspondingly, some cooperative control approaches [2,3] have been developed in terms of consensus control theory [23–26]. Moreover, the idea of cooperative control is further extended to deal with the management of crisis situations [27]. For example, in [28], Garca-Magariño proposed a coordination approach among citizens for locating the sources of problems by using peer-to-peer communication and a global map.

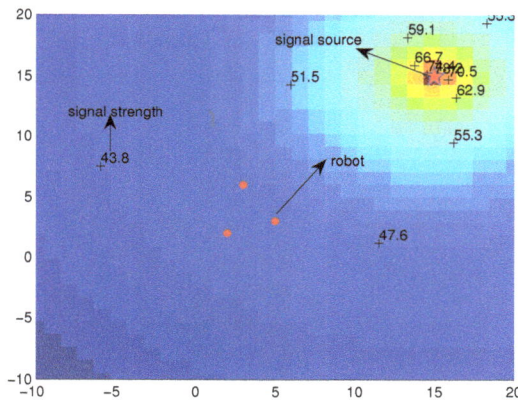

Figure 1. Search environment where the red point denotes the robot, and the red star is the signal source. The colors of the background represent the signal strength and are also labeled by the numbers.

It should be pointed out that two issues may arise in the aforementioned approaches for the problem of signal source localization. One issue is that the gradient estimation method is easily influenced by noises so as to fall into local optima [29]. For this issue, a particle filter approach can be employed to deal with the uncertainty problem raised by noises. The other issue is that the communication resources in multi-robot systems are constrained, i.e., each robot has a limited communication bandwidth. For this issue, an event-triggered scheme can be used to reduce communication times for each robot. It is worth mentioning that there are some event-triggered rules that have been proposed [2,30–32] for multi-robot systems. However, these kinds of event-triggered rules only save computational resources. For multi-robot systems, continuous communication schemes still need to be used to hold system stability. In order to reduce both computational resources and communication burden, several event-triggered communication schemes have been designed [33–36] such that communication resources can be saved. However, there is no result available for the problem of signal source localization, which can combine the particle filter approach with the cooperative control approach with an event-triggered communication scheme. One challenge is how to design event-triggered communication rules based on the given cooperative control approach. The other challenge is how to derive stability conditions for the multi-robot systems with the proposed cooperative control approach using an event-triggered communication rule. Therefore, how to develop the decision-control approach for the problem of signal source localization in the face of the aforementioned challenges motivates the present study.

The proposed decision-control approach has two advantages. One advantage is that the use of the event-triggered communication scheme can effectively decrease the communication times and lower the updating frequency of control input such that the communication and chip resources are saved. The other advantage is that the detection information from the multi-robot system can be well used to estimate the position of the signal source by the particle filter and cooperative controller. The remainder of this paper is arranged as follows. In Section 2, we will briefly give the preliminaries on the dynamics of mobile robots and communication topologies. In Section 3, we will use a particle filter to estimate the position of the signal source and propose a cooperative control approach with an event-triggered communication scheme to coordinate the mobile robots to locate the signal source. In Sections 4 and 5, we will show the effectiveness of the proposed decision-control approach with the event-triggered communication scheme by simulation and experimental results, respectively. Finally, we will conclude this paper in Section 6.

2. Preliminaries

2.1. Dynamics of Mobile Robots

For mobile robots, such as Qbot in Figure 2, the dynamics can be described by:

$$
\begin{pmatrix} \dot{r}_{xi} \\ \dot{r}_{yi} \\ \dot{\theta}_i \\ \dot{v}_i \\ \dot{\omega}_i \end{pmatrix} = \begin{pmatrix} v_i\cos\theta_i \\ v_i\sin\theta_i \\ \omega_i \\ 0 \\ 0 \end{pmatrix} + \begin{pmatrix} 0 & 0 \\ 0 & 0 \\ 0 & 0 \\ \frac{1}{m_i} & 0 \\ 0 & \frac{1}{J_i} \end{pmatrix} \begin{pmatrix} F_i \\ \tau_i \end{pmatrix}
\tag{1}
$$

where $r_i = (r_{xi}, r_{yi})^T$ is the position of the $i-$th robot; θ_i denotes the orientation; v_i is the linear velocity; ω_i is the angular velocity; τ_i is the torque; F_i is the force; m_i is the mass; and J_i is the moment of inertia. Let $y_i = (r_i, \theta_i, v_i, \omega_i)^T$ be the state of the $i-$th robot and $I_i = (F_i, \tau_i)^T$ be the control input.

Figure 2. The Qbot robot.

Because the nonholonomic systems cannot be stabilized with continuous static state feedback, we use the "hand position" instead of "center position" of the robot [37]. It should be pointed out that "hand position" is a position and lies a fixed offset L_i from the "center position". The line between between "hand position" and "center position" is perpendicular to the wheel axis (see [37]). Let (2) be the dynamics of the "hand position" of the robot.

$$
\begin{cases}
\dot{x}_i = v_i \\
\dot{v}_i = u_i \quad i \in \{1, 2, \ldots, n\}
\end{cases}
\tag{2}
$$

where x_i and v_i, respectively, denote the position and the velocity for the robot i at the "hand position" and n is the number of robots. The relationship between the "hand position" and the "center position" can be described by:

$$
x_i = r_i + L_i \begin{pmatrix} \cos\theta_i \\ \sin\theta_i \end{pmatrix}
\tag{3}
$$

$$
v_i = \begin{pmatrix} \cos\theta_i & -L_i\sin\theta \\ \sin\theta_i & L_i\cos\theta_i \end{pmatrix} \begin{pmatrix} v_i \\ \omega_i \end{pmatrix}
\tag{4}
$$

According to (3) and (4), we can obtain the position and the velocity of the "hand position" of the robot and then calculate the control law u_i for the double-integrator system (2). Finally, we can obtain the control input (5) for the system (1) [37]:

$$
I_i = \begin{pmatrix} \frac{1}{m_i}\cos\theta_i & -\frac{L_i}{J_i}\sin\theta_i \\ \frac{1}{m_i}\sin\theta_i & \frac{L_i}{J_i}\cos\theta_i \end{pmatrix}^{-1} \left[u_i - \begin{pmatrix} -v_i\omega_i\sin\theta_i - L_i\omega_i^2\cos\theta_i \\ v_i\omega_i\cos\theta_i - L_i\omega_i^2\sin\theta_i \end{pmatrix} \right]
\tag{5}
$$

Usually, the applied torques for the left wheel and the right wheel can be calculated by:

$$
\tau_l = \frac{J_{wheel}}{b} \left(\frac{F_i}{m_i} - \frac{\tau_i l}{2J_i} \right)
\tag{6}
$$

$$
\tau_r = \frac{J_{wheel}}{b} \left(\frac{F_i}{m_i} + \frac{\tau_i l}{2J_i} \right)
\tag{7}
$$

where b is the radius of the wheel; l denotes the axis length between two wheels; J_{wheel} is the moment of inertia of the wheel; τ_l and τ_r refer to the applied torques for the left wheel and the right wheel, respectively.

Furthermore, the virtual leader is designed, and its dynamics is given as:

$$
\dot{x}_0(t) = v_0(t)
\tag{8}
$$

where $v_0(t) = v_0$ is a constant.

Remark 1. *It should be pointed out that the virtual leader is introduced to help the robot reach velocity consensus, and one can also control the final convergence velocity by setting v_0.*

2.2. Communication Topologies

Communication is very important for the coordination of multiple robots. The robots can receive and send information by communication links. In order to describe the communication links at the mathematical level, one can usually employ graph theory to model communication topologies where the vertices denote the robot and the edges refer to communication links. The undirected and connected graph $G_n(X, E, A)$ is used to present the communication topology for mobile robots in this paper. An undirected graph is a set of vertices and a collection of edges that each connect a pair of vertices.

We suppose that $G_n(X, E, A)$ is an undirected graph, which includes a set of nodes $X = x_1, x_2, ..., x_n$, a set of edges $E \subseteq X \times X$ and an adjacency matrix $A = [a_{ij}]$. It should be pointed out that, if there exists an edge between the i−th node and the j−th node, then $a_{ij} = 1$; otherwise, $a_{ij} = 0$. In addition, $G_{n+1} = G_n \cup x_0$ is an extension of graph $G_n(X, E, A)$, where x_0 is a fictitious node, which can represent a virtual leader. When the virtual leader's information can be provided to the robot, there exists an edge between the virtual leader and the robot, i.e., $a_{i0} = 1(i = 1, \cdots, n)$; otherwise, $a_{i0} = 0$. The Laplacian matrix of the graph $G_n(X, E, A)$ is $L_{G_n} = [l_{ij}] \in \mathbb{R}^{n \times n}$, where l_{ij} is:

$$l_{ij} = \begin{cases} \sum_{j=1, j \neq i}^{n} a_{ij}, & i = j \\ -a_{ij}, & i \neq j \end{cases} \tag{9}$$

3. Decision-Control Approach with an Event-Triggered Communication Scheme

In this section, a particle filter is used to estimate the position of a signal source. Then, a cooperative control approach with an event-triggered communication scheme is proposed to control robots to locate the signal source. Finally, convergence analysis and velocity design of the virtual leader are given.

3.1. Decision-Making for the Position of the Signal Source

With the movement of robots, the real signal strength can be obtained by

$$o_r(i, t) = f(x_i(t), r(t)) \tag{10}$$

where $o_r(i, t)$ denotes the real measured value for the i-th robot at t time; $f(x_i(t), r(t))$ is the signal transmission model depending on the position $x_i(t)$ of the i-th robot and the real position $r(t)$ of the signal source. It should be noted that $o_r(i, t)$ can be directly detected by the robot based on the signal measurement sensor.

In order to estimate the position of the signal source, a particle filter is used in terms of the real signal strength $o_r(i, t)$ and has the following steps.

(i) We first generate N particles, which are uniformly distributed in the search range.
(ii) According to Equation (10), the prediction signal strength $o_m(i, t)$ $(m = 1, \ldots, N)$ of the m-th particle for the i-th robot at time t can be described by:

$$o_m(i, t) = f(x_i(t), p_m(i, t)) + \sqrt{R} \times rand \tag{11}$$

where $p_m(i, t)$ is the position of the m-th particle for the i-th robot at time t; R represents the variance of noise; *rand* is a random number in [0,1]; $f(x_i(t), p_m(t))$ can be obtained according to the real signal transmission model.

(iii) In terms of (10) and (11), the weight of each particle can be calculated in (12).

$$w_m(i, t) = \frac{1}{\sqrt{2\pi R}} \exp\left(-\frac{(o_r(i, t) - o_m(i, t))^2}{2R}\right) \tag{12}$$

Further, the normalizing weight is computed by:

$$w_m'(i, t) = \frac{w_m(i, t)}{\sum\limits_{m=1}^{N} w_m(i, t)} \tag{13}$$

(iv)   Based on the normalizing weight $w'_m(i,t)$, we conduct a resampling process for particles, that is we remove the low weight particles and copy the high weight particles. These resampled particles $p'_m(i,t)$ represent the probability distribution of the real state. Hence, the possible position of the signal source can be estimated by:

$$p_s(i,t) = \sum_{m=1}^{N} \frac{p'_m(i,t)}{N} \tag{14}$$

where $p_s(i,t)$ is the position of the estimated signal source for the i-th robot at time t. Further, considering the estimated positions from other robots, we have:

$$p'_s(i,t) = \frac{\sum\limits_{j=1}^{n} a_{ij}p_s(j,t)}{\sum\limits_{j=1}^{n} a_{ij}} \tag{15}$$

where a_{ij} is the element of the adjacency matrix A and $p'_s(i,t)$ as the estimated position of signal source is used in the following simulations and experiments.

3.2. Cooperative Control with an Event-Triggered Communication Scheme

An event-triggered communication scheme is proposed to lower the communication burden. The event-triggered time sequence is generated iteratively by the following formula.

$$t^i_{s+1} = \inf\{t|t > t^i_s, g_i(t) > 0\} \tag{16}$$

where $g_i(t)$ is described by:

$$g_i(t) = \|M\|\|\alpha(e_{xi}(t)) + \beta(e_{vi}(t))\| + a_{i0}\|\alpha(e_{xi0}(t)) + \beta(e_{vi0}(t))\| - \gamma(\|\alpha y_i(t^i_s)\| + \|\beta z_i(t^i_s)\|) \tag{17}$$

with:

$$
\begin{aligned}
e_{xi}(t) &= x_i(t^i_s) - x_i(t) \\
e_{vi}(t) &= v_i(t^i_s) - v_i(t) \\
e_{xi0}(t) &= x_0(t^i_s) - x_0(t) \\
e_{xi0}(t) &= v_0(t^i_s) - v_0(t) \\
y_i(t^i_s) &= \sum_{j=0}^{n} a_{ij}(x_j(t^j_s) - x_i(t^i_s)) \\
z_i(t^i_s) &= \sum_{j=0}^{n} a_{ij}(v_j(t^i_s) - v_j(t^i_s))
\end{aligned}
$$

where $M = L_{G_n} + diag\{a_{10}, \cdots, a_{n0}\}$; $\alpha > 0$, $\beta > 0$, $\gamma > 0$ are the positive constants; Since $y_i(t^i_s)$ and $z_i(t^i_s)$ only are calculated at the event-triggered time, the proposed event-triggered scheme can reduce communication burdens. The event-triggered communication condition (16) has one main feature, that is whether or not the states of robots should be transmitted is determined by the errors $y_i(t^i_s)$, $z_i(t^i_s)$ between the states of its neighbors at the latest event time and the latest transmitted states and the errors $e_{xi}(t), e_{vi}(t), e_{xi0}(t), e_{xi0}(t)$ between the current states and the latest transmitted states.

Remark 2. *It is worth mentioning that the control input is updated when $g_i(t) > 0$, that is the condition of the event triggering. At the same time, the new state of the i-th robot will be sent to the other robots that have communication links with the i-th robot. Besides, if the above inequality does not hold, the i-th robot does not need to send information to others while the values of $y_i(t_s^i)$ and $z_i(t_s^i)$ will not be changed. Hence, the communication resources are saved.*

According to the proposed event-triggered communication scheme, the controller of the *i*-th robot is designed by:

$$u_i(t) = \sum_{j=0}^{n} a_{ij}(\alpha(x_j(t_s^j) - x_i(t_s^i)) + \beta(v_j(t_s^j) - v_i(t_s^i))) \tag{18}$$

where a_{ij} is the element of the adjacency matrix A; $x_i(t_s^i)$ and $x_j(t_s^j)$ are the positions of the *i*-th and the *j*-th robots at the event-triggering time, respectively; $v_i(t_s^i)$ and $v_j(t_s^j)$ are the velocities of the *i*-th and the *j*-th robots at the event-triggering time, respectively. It should be pointed out that the control input in (18) is determined by the position errors and velocity errors between the *j*-th robot and the *i*-th robot at the event-triggering time.

3.3. Convergence Analysis

In order to illustrate the position and velocity consensus for the multi-robot system (2) under the controller (18) with the event-triggered communication scheme (16), we first transform the model (2) in the following. Let $\bar{x}_i(t) = x_i(t) - x_0(t)$ and $\bar{v}_i(t) = v_i(t) - v_0(t)$. Then, the system (2) with the controller (18) can be rewritten as:

$$
\begin{cases}
\dot{\bar{x}}_i(t) = \bar{v}_i(t) \\
\dot{\bar{v}}_i(t) = \sum_{j=0}^{n} a_{ij}\alpha(\bar{x}_j(t) - \bar{x}_i(t)) \\
\quad + \sum_{j=0}^{n} a_{ij}\alpha(e_{xj}(t) - e_{xi}(t)) \\
\quad + \sum_{j=0}^{n} a_{ij}\beta(\bar{v}_j(t) - \bar{v}_i(t)) \\
\quad + \sum_{j=0}^{n} a_{ij}\beta(e_{vj}(t) - e_{vi}(t))
\end{cases}
$$

Furthermore, set:

$$y_i(t) = \sum_{j=0}^{n} a_{ij}((\bar{x}_j(t) - \bar{x}_i(t))$$

$$z_i(t) = \sum_{j=0}^{n} a_{ij}((\bar{v}_j(t) - \bar{v}_i(t))$$

$$e_i^x(t) = \sum_{j=0}^{n} a_{ij}(e_{xj}(t) - e_{xi}(t))$$

$$e_i^v(t) = \sum_{j=0}^{n} a_{ij}(e_{vj}(t) - e_{vi}(t))$$

Hence, the dynamics of a multi-robot system can be deduced as:

$$
\begin{cases}
\dot{y}(t) = z(t) \\
\dot{z}(t) = -M\phi(t) \\
\phi(t) = \alpha y(t) + \beta z(t) + \alpha e^x(t) + \beta e^v(t)
\end{cases} \tag{19}
$$

where $y(t) = [y_1(t), y_2(t), \cdots y_n(t)]^T$ and $z(t)$, $e^x(t)$, $e^v(t)$ are similar. The following lemmas are given in order to illustrate the convergence proof.

Lemma 1. *For a multi-robot system* (19) *with an event-triggered communication scheme* (16)*, the following inequality is established.*

$$\|M\|^2\|\alpha(e_x(t)) + \beta(e_v(t))\|^2 + \|B(\alpha e_{x0}(t) + \beta e_{v0}(t))\|^2 \leq \frac{2\gamma^2}{k_1}\|\phi(t)\|^2 \tag{20}$$

where $B = diag\{a_{10}, \cdot sa_{n0}\}$ and k_1 is a positive constant.

Proof. The event-triggered communication scheme (16) is listed as:

$$\|M\|\|\alpha e_{xi}(t) + \beta e_{vi}(t)\| + a_{i0}\|\alpha e_{x0}(t) + \beta e_{v0}(t)\| \leq \gamma(\|\alpha y_i(t_s^i)\| + \|\beta z_i(t_s^i)\|) \quad for \quad t \in [t_s^i, t_{s+1}^i) \tag{21}$$

According to the inequalities $a_1^2 + b_1^2 \leq (a_1 + b_1)^2, a_1 > 0, b_1 > 0$ and $2a_1^2 + 2b_1^2 \geq (a_1 + b_1)^2$, the inequality (21) can be further changed as:

$$\|M\|^2\|\alpha(e_{xi}(t)) + \beta(e_{vi}(t))\|^2 + a_{i0}\|\alpha e_{x0}(t) + \beta e_{v0}(t)\|^2 \leq 2\gamma^2(\|\alpha y_i(t_s^i)\|^2 + \|\beta z_i(t_s^i)\|^2) \tag{22}$$

Notice the definition of $\phi_i(t)$. The variable $\phi_i(t)^2$ is rewritten using a matrix-vector form.

$$\phi_i(t)^2 = [\alpha y_i(t_s^i) \quad \beta z_i(t_s^i)]Q[\alpha y_i(t_s^i) \quad \beta z_i(t_s^i)]^T$$

where $Q = \begin{bmatrix} 1 & 1 \\ 1 & 1 \end{bmatrix}$ which is a semi-positive definite matrix. We consider the sum of $\phi_i(t)^2, i = 1, \ldots, n$.

$$\sum_{i=0}^{n} \phi_i(t)^2 = \sum_{i=0}^{n} [\alpha y_i(t_s^i) \quad \beta z_i(t_s^i)]Q[\alpha y_i(t_s^i) \quad \beta z_i(t_s^i)]^T \tag{23}$$
$$= \epsilon(t)^T I_n \otimes Q\epsilon(t)$$

where $\epsilon(t) = [[\alpha y_1(t_s^1) \quad \beta z_1(t_s^1)], \cdots, [\alpha y_n(t_s^n) \quad \beta z_n(t_s^n)]]$. For the set $U = \{\sigma \in \mathbb{R}^{2n} : \sigma^T\sigma = 1\}$, which is bounded and closed, one can know $\frac{\epsilon(t)}{\|\epsilon(t)\|_2} \in U$, and there exists a positive constant $k_1 > 0$ for $(\frac{\epsilon(t)}{\|\epsilon(t)\|_2})^T I_n \otimes Q\frac{\epsilon(t)}{\|\epsilon(t)\|_2}$.

$$k_1 = \min_{\frac{\epsilon(t)}{\|\epsilon(t)\|_2} \in U} \left(\frac{\epsilon(t)}{\|\epsilon(t)\|_2}\right)^T I_n \otimes Q\frac{\epsilon(t)}{\|\epsilon(t)\|_2}$$

Then, in terms of Equation (23) and the minimum value k_1, the following inequality is established.

$$\sum_{i=0}^{n} \phi_i(t)^2 \geq k_1\|\epsilon(t)\|_2^2 \quad = k_1\sum_{i=1}^{n}(\|\alpha y_i(t_s^i)\|^2 + \|\beta z_i(t_s^i)\|^2)) \tag{24}$$

Finally, by combining (22) with (24), the inequality (25) holds.

$$\|M\|^2\|\alpha(e_x(t)) + \beta(e_v(t))\|^2 + \|D(\alpha e_{x0}(t) + \beta e_{v0}(t))\|^2 \leq \frac{2\gamma^2}{k_1}\|\phi(t)\|^2 \tag{25}$$

□

Lemma 2. *For a multi-robot system (19) with an event-triggered communication scheme (16), the following inequality is established.*

$$\|\alpha e^x(t) + \beta e^v(t)\| \leq \sqrt{\frac{8\gamma^2}{k_1 - 8\gamma^2}} \|\alpha y(t) + \beta z(t)\|$$

where $k_1 > 8\gamma^2$ and is constant.

Proof. From the definitions of e^x, e^v and M, the following inequalities are derived.

$$\|\alpha e^x(t) + \beta e^v(t)\| \leq \|M(\alpha e_x(t) + \beta e_v(t))\| + \|B((\alpha e_{x0}(t) + \beta e_{v0}(t))\|$$
$$\leq \|M\|\|(\alpha e_x(t) + \beta e_v(t))\| + \|B((\alpha e_{x0}(t) + \beta e_{v0}(t))\| \tag{26}$$

Further, according to the definition of $\|\phi(t)\|$ in (19), we can establish a new inequality.

$$\|\phi(t)\|^2 = \sum_{i=1}^{n} (\alpha y_i(t) + \beta z_i(t) + \alpha e_i^x(t) + \beta e_i^v(t))^2$$
$$\leq \sum_{i=1}^{n} (2(\alpha y_i(t) + \beta z_i(t))^2 + 2(\alpha e_i^x(t) + \beta e_i^v(t))^2) \tag{27}$$
$$\leq 2\|\alpha y(t) + \beta z(t)\|^2 + 2\|\alpha e^x(t) + \beta e^v(t)\|^2$$
$$\leq 2\|\alpha y(t) + \beta z(t)\|^2 + 4(\|M\|^2\|\alpha e_x(t) + \beta e_v(t)\|^2$$
$$+ \|B(\alpha e_{x0}(t) + \beta e_{v0}(t))\|^2)$$

By Lemma 1 and the inequality (27), we obtain the inequality (28).

$$\|M\|^2\|\alpha(e_x(t)) + \beta(e_v(t))\|^2 + \|B(\alpha e_{x0}(t) + \beta e_{v0}(t))\|^2 \leq \frac{2\gamma^2}{k_1}\|\phi(t)\|^2$$
$$\leq \frac{4\gamma^2}{k_1}\|\alpha y(t) + \beta z(t)\|^2 + \frac{8\gamma^2}{k_1}(\|M\|^2\|\alpha e_x(t) + \beta e_v(t)\|^2 \tag{28}$$
$$+ \|B(\alpha e_{x0}(t) + \beta e_{v0}(t))\|^2)$$

Simplify the inequality (28) as:

$$\|M\|\|\alpha e_x(t) + \beta e_v(t))\| + \|B(\alpha e_{x0}(t) + \beta e_{v0}(t))\|$$
$$\leq \sqrt{\frac{8\gamma^2}{k_1 - 8\gamma^2}} \|\alpha y(t) + \beta z(t)\| \tag{29}$$

Since $k_1 > 8\gamma^2$, in terms of (26) and (29), the following inequality holds.

$$\|\alpha e^x(t) + \beta e^v(t)\| \leq \sqrt{\frac{8\gamma^2}{k_1 - 8\gamma^2}} \|\alpha y(t) + \beta z(t)\|$$

□

Finally, we can give the following theorem for the multi-robot system (2) with the proposed communication scheme and controller. In addition, Zeno-behaviors denote that there is an infinite number of discrete transitions in a finite period of time in the multi-robot system. The following theorem can guarantee that the multi-robot system (2) with the proposed communication scheme and controller does not show Zeno-behaviors before consensus is achieved.

Theorem 1. *Consider the event-triggered communication scheme* (16) *and the cooperative controller* (18) *for a multi-robot system* (2). *Suppose that the undirected communication topology* $G_n(W, E, A)$ *is connected with at least one* a_{i0} *not being zero. Let* $k = \frac{1}{2}(\sum_{j=1}^{n} a_{ij} - \sum_{j=1}^{n} a_{ji}) + a_{i0}$. *The variable* u_{min} *denotes the minimum eigenvalue of* $M + M^T$. *The positive constant* k_1 *can be found in Lemma* 1. *If the inequalities* $\beta > \sqrt{\alpha/u_{min}}, \gamma < \sqrt{k_1/8}, \delta < \frac{\beta^2 u_{min} - \alpha}{2\beta^2}$ *where* $\delta = \|M\| \sqrt{\frac{8\gamma^2}{k_1 - 8\gamma^2}}$ *hold, the cooperative controller* (18) *with the event-triggered communication scheme* (16) *can guarantee that* $x_i(t) \to x_0(t)$ *and* $v_i(t) \to v_0(t), \forall i \in 1, \cdots, n$. *In addition, the multi-robot system does not show Zeno-behaviors before consensus is achieved.*

Proof. We have three steps to prove the theorem. First, it is proven that the following function $V(t)$ in (30) is a Lyapunov function. Second, it is proven that the system (2) with the event-triggered communication scheme (16) and the cooperative controller (18) is asymptotically stable. Finally, it is proven that the multi-robot system does not show Zeno-behaviors before consensus is reached.

We construct a Lyapunov functional as:

$$V(t) = 0.5\xi(t)^T \begin{pmatrix} \alpha\beta(M + M^T) & \alpha I \\ \alpha I & \beta I \end{pmatrix} \xi(t) \tag{30}$$

where $\xi(t) = [y(t)^T, z(t)^T]$ and I is a unit matrix of n order. Let:

$$\Omega = \begin{pmatrix} \alpha\beta(M + M^T) & \alpha I \\ \alpha I & \beta I \end{pmatrix}$$

where $M + M^T$ is a real symmetric matrix, and we can diagonalize it as $\beta^{-1}\Lambda\beta$, where $\Lambda = diag\{u_1, u_2, \cdots, u_n\}$ is a diagonal matrix and u_i is the eigenvalue of $M + M^T$. Thus, Ω can be written as:

$$\Omega = \begin{pmatrix} \beta & 0 \\ 0 & \beta \end{pmatrix}^{-1} \bar{\Omega} \begin{pmatrix} \beta & 0 \\ 0 & \beta \end{pmatrix}$$

where:

$$\bar{\Omega} = \begin{pmatrix} \alpha\beta\Lambda & \alpha I \\ \alpha I & \beta I \end{pmatrix}$$

Then, we solve its eigenvalue by:

$$det(\lambda I_{2n} - \bar{\Omega}) = det \begin{pmatrix} \lambda I - \alpha\beta\Lambda & -\alpha I \\ -\alpha I & \lambda I - \beta I \end{pmatrix}$$

The eigenvalues of $\bar{\Omega}$ are:

$$\lambda_{i\pm} = \frac{\beta + \alpha\beta u_i \pm \sqrt{(\beta + \alpha\beta u_i)^2 - 4(\alpha\beta^2 u_i - \alpha^2)}}{2}$$

where λ_{i+} and λ_{i-} are the eigenvalues of $\bar{\Omega}$, which are associated with u_i. Thus, if the condition $\beta > \sqrt{\alpha/u_{min}}$ is satisfied, the matrix Ω is a positive definite matrix, that is the Lyapunov function $V(t) \geqslant 0$. The derivative of $\dot{V}(t)$ is as:

$$\dot{V}(t) = y(t)^T \alpha \beta (M + M^T) z(t) + z(t)^T \alpha I z(t)$$
$$+ y(t)^T \alpha I \dot{z}(t) + z(t)^T \beta I \dot{z}(t)$$
$$= -z(t)^T (\beta^2 M - \alpha I) z(t) - y(t)^T \alpha^2 M y(t)$$
$$- (\alpha y(t)^T + \beta z(t)^T) M(\alpha e^z(t) + \beta e^v(t))$$

We can get the following inequality as:

$$\dot{V}(t) \leq -z(t)^T (\beta^2 M - \alpha I) z(t) - y(t)^T \alpha^2 M y(t) \tag{31}$$
$$+ \|\alpha y(t)^T + \beta z(t)^T\| \|M\| \|\alpha e^z(t) + \beta e^v(t)\|$$

From Lemma 1 and (30), we can give the following result.

$$\dot{V}(t) \leq -z(t)^T (\beta^2 M - \alpha I) z(t) - y(t)^T \alpha^2 M y(t) + \delta \|\alpha y(t) + \beta z(t)\|^2$$
$$\leq -z(t)^T (\beta^2 M - \alpha I - 2\delta \beta^2 I) z(t) - y(t)^T (\alpha^2 M - 2\delta \alpha^2 I) y(t)$$

where $\delta = \|M\| \sqrt{\frac{8\gamma^2}{k_1 - 8\gamma^2}}$. Since $\beta > \sqrt{\alpha / u_{min}}$, $\gamma < \sqrt{k_1 / 8}$ and $\delta < \frac{\beta^2 u_{min} - \alpha}{2\beta^2}$, the inequality $\dot{V}(t) \leq 0$ holds. It shows that the system $(y(t), z(t))$ will asymptotically converge to $(0_n, 0_n)$.

It is assumed that the velocity and acceleration of the robot are bounded by s_v and s_a. The variable $e_{xi}(t_s^i)$ is zero, and $x_i(t_s^i)$ is constant for $t \in [t_s^i, t_{s+1}^i)$. Then, the following inequality is established.

$$|e_{xi}(t)| \leq \left| \int_{t_s^i}^t \dot{e}_{xi}(t) d\tau \right| \leq \int_{t_s^i}^t |\dot{e}_{xi}(t)| d\tau = \int_{t_s^i}^t |\dot{x}_i(t)| d\tau \leq s_v(t - t_s^i), t \in [t_s^i, t_{(s+1)}^i)$$

In the same way, the following inequality is established.

$$|e_{vi}(t)| \leq s_a(t - t_s^i)$$

Moreover, we have $\|M\| * |\alpha(e_{xi}(t)) + \beta(e_{vi}(t))| + a_{i0}|\alpha(x_0(t_s^i) - x_0(t)) + \beta(v_0(t_s^i) - v_0(t))| \leq ((\|M\| + 1)\alpha s_v + (\|M\| + 1)\beta s_a)(t - t_s^i)$. According to the event-triggered communication scheme, we obtain $\|M\| * |\alpha(e_{xi}(t)) + \beta(e_{vi}(t))| + a_{i0}|\alpha(x_0(t_s^i) - x_0(t)) + \beta(v_0(t_s^i) - v_0(t))| - \gamma(|\alpha y_i(t_s^i)| + |\beta z_i(t_s^i)|) > 0$ at $t = t_{s+1}^i$. Hence, we derive $(t_{s+1}^i - t_s^i) > \frac{\gamma(|\alpha y_i(t_s^i)| + |\beta z_i(t_s^i)|)}{(\|M\| + 1)\alpha s_v + (\|M\| + 1)\beta s_a} > 0$. We can draw the conclusion that Zeno-behaviors are excluded for the multi-robot system before consensus is reached. □

3.4. Velocity Design of the Virtual Leader

According to Theorem 1, one can see that how to design the velocity $v_0(t)$ of the virtual leader is important, since the velocity of the virtual leader has an impact on the movement direction of the multi-robot system. Hence, the velocity of the virtual leader is as:

$$v_0(t) = \lambda(p_s'(0, t) - x_0(t)) \tag{32}$$

where λ is a positive constant as a step factor. If the virtual leader is installed in the i-th robot, we have $p_s'(0, t) = p_s'(i, t)$. Therefore, we design Algorithm 1 for signal source localization.

Algorithm 1 Decision-control approach with an event-triggered communication scheme.

/*Initialization*/

Initialize the parameters of the particle filter N, R and $w_m(i,t)$, $(m = 1, 2, \ldots, N)$;

Initialize the parameters α, β and γ of the consensus control (18) and the event-triggered rule (16), the position $x_i(0)$ and the velocity $v_i(0)$ of the i-th robot;

/*Main Body*/

repeat

 Receive its neighbors' information;

 Detect the new signal strength $o_r(i,t)$ at the position $x_i(t)$;

 Calculate the prediction signal strength $o_m(i,t)$ $(m = 1, \ldots, N)$ based on (11);

 Give the normalizing weight in (13), and obtain the estimated position of signal source in terms of (15);

 Compute the event-triggered condition in (16) and (17);

 if $g_i(t) > 0$ **then**

  Send the estimated position of signal source $p'_s(i,t)$, the position of the robot $x_i(t)$ and the velocity of the robot $v_i(t)$ to its neighbors;

 end if

 if $g_i(t) \leq 0$ **then**

  Calculate the control input in (18);

  According to (5), obtain the force and torque I_i, and give the applied torques for the left wheel τ_l and the right wheel τ_r in (6) and (7), respectively.

 end if

until The termination condition is satisfied.

---

4. Simulation Results

In this section, we use two cases to show the effectiveness of the proposed decision-control approach for signal source localization.

4.1. Simulation Environment

This subsection briefly describes the simulation environment where a static electromagnetic signal field is used. Correspondingly, due to different noise errors, two cases are considered.

For Case 1, the electromagnetic signal field can be established by using the following function.

$$f_1(x,r) = 10 \times \log(0.001) - 1.96 \times \log(\|x - r\|) + \sqrt{5} \times rand \tag{33}$$

where x is any position in the search environment; r is the position of the signal source; $rand$ is a random number in $[0,1]$.

For Case 2, a big noise is considered where the electromagnetic signal field can be established by applying the following function.

$$f_2(x,r) = 10 \times \log(0.001) - 1.96 \times \log(\|x - r\|) + \sqrt{8} \times rand \tag{34}$$

The simulation environment is built in MATLAB, where the search space is a square area with 30 m $\times$ 30 m, and other parameters can be found in Table 1.

Table 1. Parameters of the simulation environment.

Parameters	Values
Sampling time	0.001 s
Noise variance R	5, 8
Total run time	20 s for two cases
Communication distance	5 m
The number of robots n	3
The velocity range of robots	$[-3\,\text{m/s}, 3\,\text{m/s}]$

4.2. Cooperative Control and Performance Metrics

In order to avoid collisions, we further extend the cooperative controller (18) as:

$$u_i(t) = \sum_{j=0}^{n} a_{ij}(\alpha((x_j(t_s^j) - d_j) - (x_i(t_s^i) - d_i)) + \beta(v_j(t_s^j) - v_i(t_s^i))) \tag{35}$$

where d_i and d_j are the given safety distances for the i-th and j-th robots, respectively. The controller can effectively coordinate multiple robots and hold formation. The parameters of the proposed decision-control approach can be found in Table 2. The position of signal source is [15 m, 15 m]. Moreover, the safety distances are:

$$d = \begin{bmatrix} 0 & 1 & 0 \\ 0 & 0 & 1 \end{bmatrix}^T$$

and $d_0 = [1/3, 1/3]$. The initial velocities of robots are:

$$v = \begin{bmatrix} 0.1 & 0.1 & 0.1 \\ 0.1 & 0.1 & 0.1 \end{bmatrix}^T$$

Table 2. The parameters of the proposed decision-control approach.

Parameters	Value
α	17
β	22
γ	0.1
λ	0.001
N	10,000

In order to evaluate the proposed decision-control approach, we use two performance metrics: one is the communication frequency, while the other is the localization error.

The communication frequency is calculated by:

$$fre_i = \frac{\text{Event-Triggered Number}}{\text{Total Sampling Number}} \times 100\% \tag{36}$$

where fre_i denotes the communication frequency of the i-th robot. "*Event-Triggered Number*" refers to the communication times of the i-th robot. Note that if the event-triggered rule (16) is violated, a new control input needs to be calculated; otherwise, the previous control input is unchanged. "*Total Sampling Number*" stands for the total sampling times in a run. Hence, fre_i is a quantitative evaluation metric that is used to evaluate communication burden.

The localization error (LE) is computed by:

$$LE_i = \|p_s'(i,t) - r(t)\| \tag{37}$$

where $p'_s(i, t)$ is the estimated position of the signal source for the *i*-th robot value at time t; $r(t)$ is the real position of the signal source. LE_i can be utilized to evaluate the localization accuracy.

4.3. Case 1: The Variance of Noise R = 5

For Case 1, we consider the situation, i.e., the noise variance error $R = 5$. Figure 3a–f shows the movement trajectories of robots in one run, from which one can see that the robots can locate the signal source. Moreover, one can see that the red points denote the initial positions; the black lines are the trajectories of three robots; the yellow small stars are the current positions; and the red big star refers to the signal source. Correspondingly, the localization errors LE are illustrated in Figure 4, where one can see that the localization errors LE gradually become small with the movement of robots. Finally, the statistical results for communication frequencies fre and localization errors LE can be found in Table 3, where 30 runs are conducted, and the corresponding results are small to reflect the effectiveness of the proposed decision-control approach.

Table 3. Mean (standard deviation) results in communication frequency (%) and localization error (m) based on 30 runs for Case 1.

Robots	fre_i	LE_i
Robot 1	1.81 (0.44)	0.22 (0.16)
Robot 2	8.50 (0.48)	0.25 (0.20)
Robot 3	7.52 (0.53)	0.64 (0.71)

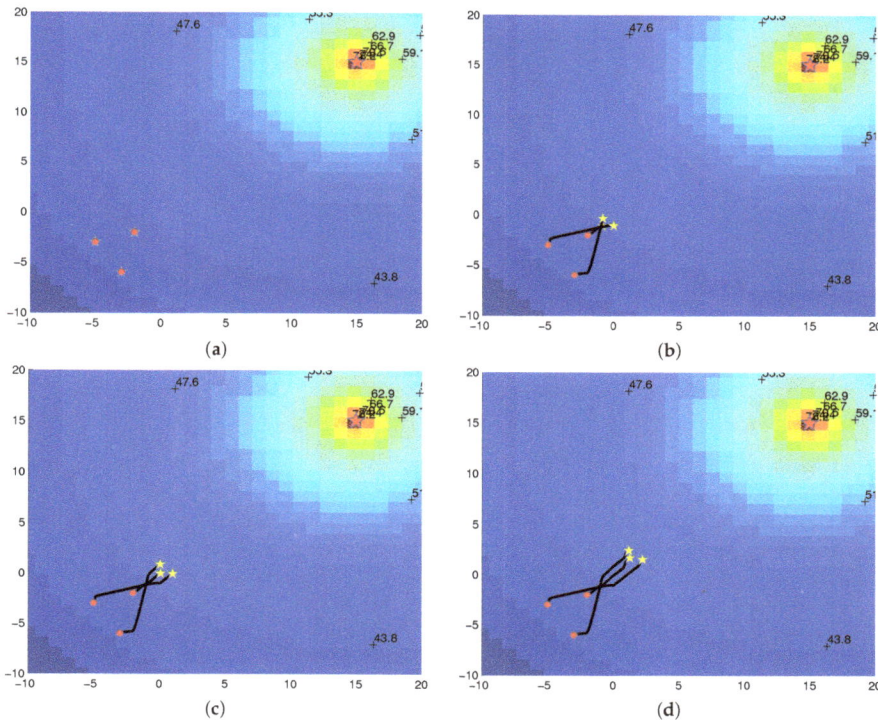

Figure 3. *Cont.*

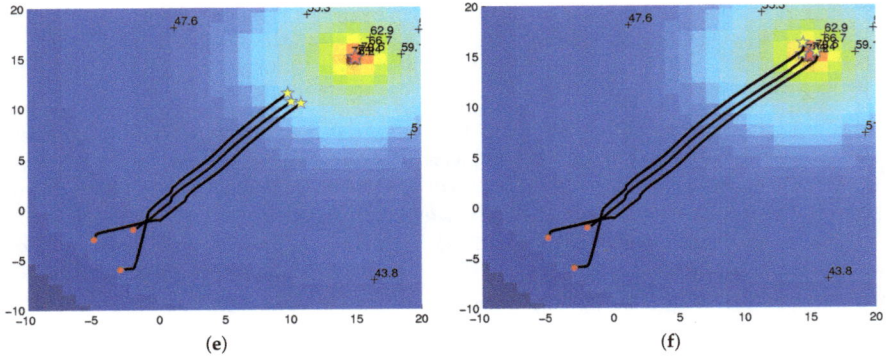

Figure 3. Movement trajectories of three robots for Case 1 where the red points denote the initial positions, the black lines are the trajectories of three robots, the yellow small stars are the current positions and the red big star refers to the signal source. The colors of the background represent the signal strength and are also labeled by the numbers. The signal strength increases with the decrease of the distance from the source. (**a**) $t = 0$ s; (**b**) $t = 5$ s; (**c**) $t = 10$ s; (**d**) $t = 15$ s; (**e**) $t = 20$ s; (**f**) $t = 30$ s.

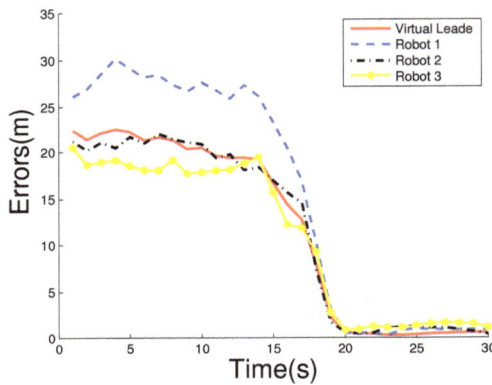

Figure 4. The curves for the localization errors for Case 1.

4.4. Case 2: The Variance of Noise $R = 8$

For Case 2, the noise variance error $R = 8$ is set in order to evaluate the noise influence on the proposed decision-control approach. The movement trajectories of three robots in one run are illustrated in Figure 5. From this figure, one can see that the three robots can coordinate their behaviors and locate the signal source. Correspondingly, Figure 6 shows the localization errors LE, where one can see that the localization errors LE quickly become small such that the signal source is found when the search time approaches 30 s. Finally, we conduct 30 runs and obtain the statistical results for communication frequencies fre_i and localization errors LE_i, shown in Table 4. From this table, one can see that the communication frequencies and the localization errors are small, which means that the communication burden is lightened and the proposed decision-control approach can predict the position of signal source under big noise well.

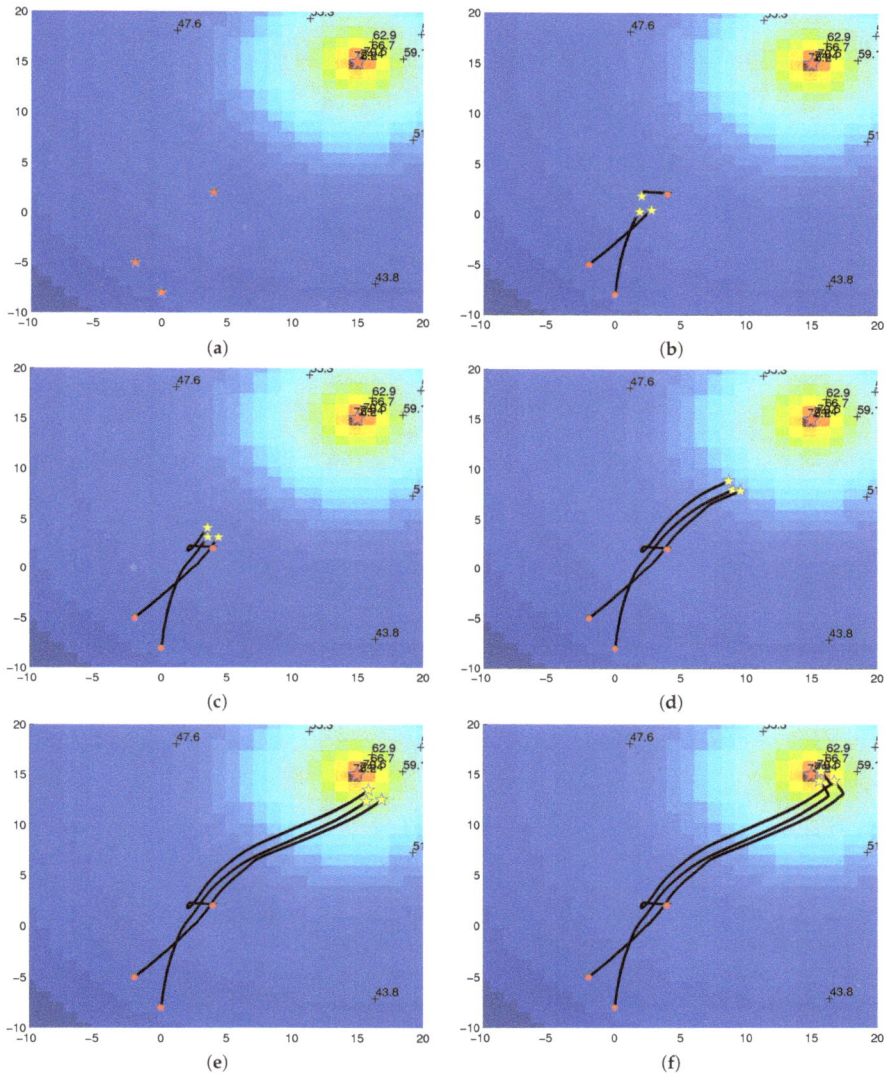

Figure 5. Movement trajectories of three robots for Case 2 where the red points denote the initial positions, the black lines are the trajectories of three robots, the yellow small stars are the current positions and the red big star refers to the signal source. The colors of the background represent the signal strength and are also labeled by the numbers. The signal strength increases with the decrease of the distance from the source. (**a**) $t = 0$ s; (**b**) $t = 5$ s; (**c**) $t = 10$ s; (**d**) $t = 15$ s; (**e**) $t = 20$ s; (**f**) $t = 30$ s.

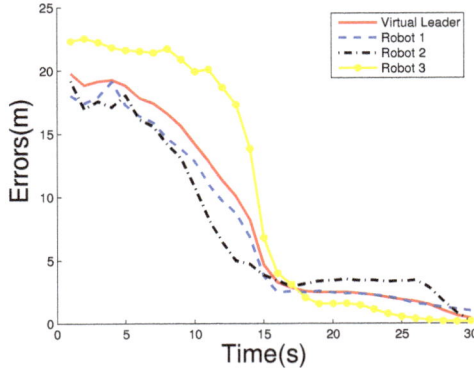

Figure 6. The curves for the localization errors for Case 2.

Table 4. Mean (standard deviation) results in communication frequency (%) and localization error (m) based on 30 runs for Case 2.

Robots	fre_i	LE_i
Robot 1	1.37 (0.54)	1.07 (0.44)
Robot 2	8.55 (0.50)	1.69 (1.08)
Robot 3	8.07 (0.59)	0.70 (0.71)

5. Experimental Results

In this section, the proposed decision-control approach is validated by the real experiments where the three Qbot robots are used to locate the signal source.

5.1. Experimental Setup

The real experimental environment is shown in Figure 7. Qbot is a differential drive wheeled mobile robot, equipped with two motors, a wireless communication module, an infrared and sonar sensor array and a Logitech Quickcam Pro 9000 USB camera. Moreover, the wireless modules use the ZigBee communication protocol. An electromagnetic module is used as a signal source, shown in Figure 8. At the same time, we employ the OptiTrack system to accurately locate the position of the Qbot. For the robot communication, the Qbots can build a local area network to communicate with each other and establish links with the computer host.

Figure 7. Experimental environment.

Figure 8. An electromagnetic signal source.

The following function is used to predict the position of the electromagnetic signal source.

$$f(x,r) = 10 \times \log(0.001) - 1.96 \times \log(\|(x-r)\|) \tag{38}$$

where r is the particle position for the particle filter. The parameters of Qbot robots are shown in Table 5. The parameters of the proposed decision-control approach can be found in Table 2.

Table 5. The parameters of Qbot mobile robots.

m_i (kg)	L_i (m)	J_i (kg m^2)	b (m)	l (m)	J_{wheel} (kg m^2)
2.92	0.126	0.05	0.03	0.252	0.002

5.2. Experimental Results

In this subsection, we control three robots to locate an electromagnetic signal source by employing the proposed decision-control approach. The experiments are conducted 30 times. Figures 9 and 10 show movement trajectories and localization errors in one run, respectively. In Figure 9, one can see that three robots can locate the electromagnetic signal source and hold a safe distance from each other, where the different colors denote the different trajectories of robots. Moreover, in Figure 10, the localization errors for three robots are shown, from which one can see that the localization errors are small. Finally, the statistical results for performance metrics are given in Table 6, where communication frequencies for three robots are low such that communication burden is well lightened. In addition, the location errors in Table 6 are also small, which implies that the proposed particle filter can predict the position of the electromagnetic signal source well and the proposed decision-control approach can control three robots to keep formation to detect signals well.

Table 6. Mean (standard deviation) results in communication frequency (%) and localization error (m) based on 30 runs.

Robots	fre_i	LE_i
Robot 1	6.21 (0.34)	0.30 (0.08)
Robot 2	12.56 (1.05)	0.46 (0.17)
Robot 3	11.64 (1.23)	0.27 (0.07)

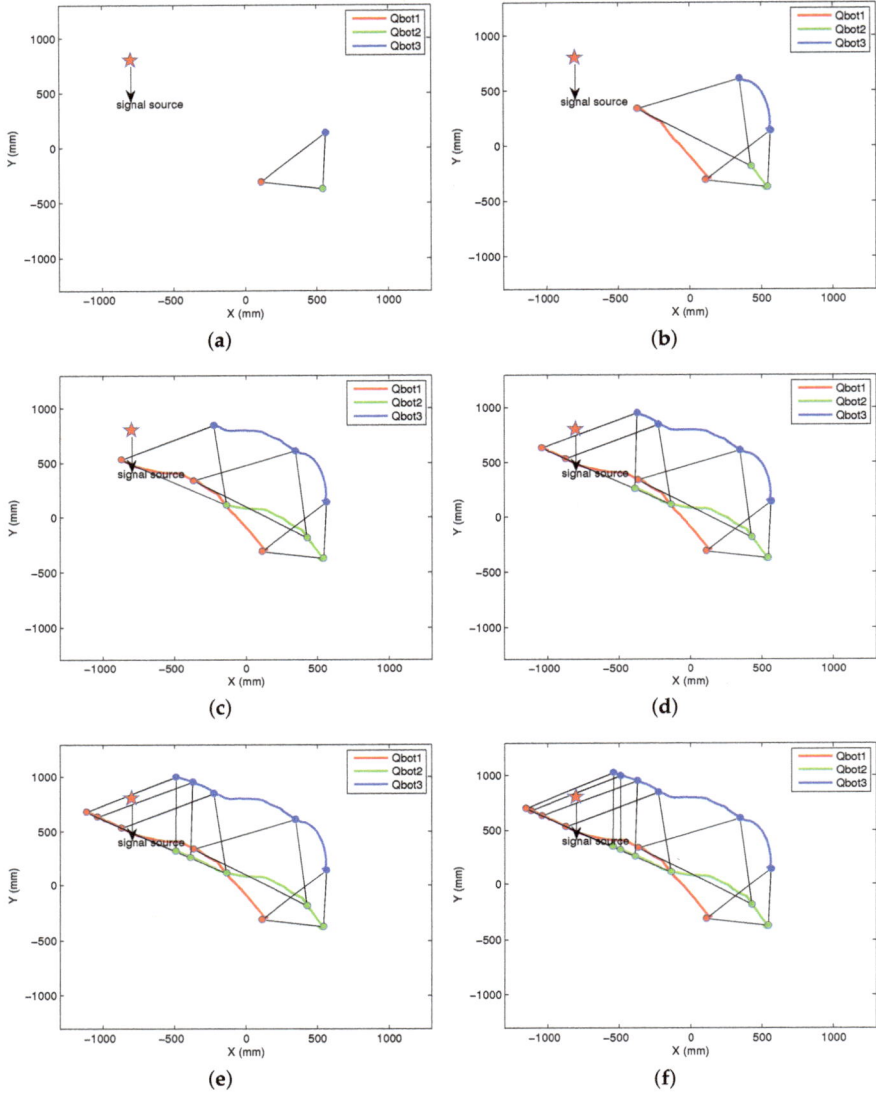

Figure 9. Movement trajectories of three robots where the red, blue and green lines denote the trajectories of three robots. (**a**) $t = 0$ s; (**b**) $t = 4$ s; (**c**) $t = 8$ s; (**d**) $t = 12$ s; (**e**) $t = 16$ s; (**f**) $t = 20$ s.

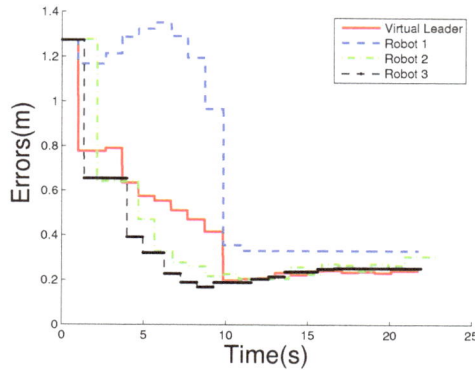

Figure 10. The curves for the localization errors.

6. Conclusions

We have proposed a decision-control approach with the event-triggered communication scheme for the problem of signal source localization. This proposed decision-control approach includes two levels. In the decision level, we have designed a particle filter approach, which is used to estimate the position of signal source. The designed particle filter can guide the movement of robots well under a search environment with big noises. At the control level, we have proposed a cooperative control approach with an event-triggered communication scheme. The proposed event-triggered communication scheme can save communication resources and lighten the communication burden. The simulation and experimental results have illustrated the effectiveness of the proposed decision-control approach.

Author Contributions: K.Y. performed the simulations and experiments. L.P. proposed the methods, analyzed the data and wrote the paper. Q.L. reviewed the paper and took on the task of project management. B.Z. revised the paper and took on the task of project supervision.

Acknowledgments: This work was supported in part by the Zhejiang Provincial Natural Science Foundation of China under Grant LY18F030008 and the National Natural Science Foundation of China under Grants 61503108 and 61375104.

Conflicts of Interest: The authors declare no conflict of interest.

Nomenclature

v_i	Linear velocity
ω_i	Angular velocity
τ_i	Torque
τ_l	Applied torques for the left wheel
τ_r	Applied torques for the right wheel
θ_i	Orientation angle
A	Adjacency matrix
a_{ij}	Element of an adjacency matrix
b	Radius of the wheel
e	State error
e_v	Velocity error
e_x	Position error
F	Force

f	Signal transmission model
fre	Communication frequency
g_i	Condition of event triggered
G_n	Undirected graph
G_{n+1}	Extension of graph $G_n(X, E, A)$
i	Serial number of robot
I_i	Control input of the i-th robot
J	Moment of inertia
J_{wheel}	Moment of inertia of the wheel
l	Axis length between two wheels
L_i	Distance between the hand position and the center position
L_{G_n}	Laplacian matrix of the graph
LE	Localization error
m	Mass
N	Number of particles
n	Number of robots
o_m	The m-th particle
o_r	Real measured value
p'_s	Final estimated position of signal source
p_m	Position of the m-th particle
p_s	Estimated position of signal source
R	Variance of noise
r	Real position of signal source
r_i^T	Position of the ith robot
$rand$	Random number in $[0,1]$
t_{s+1}^i	Event-triggered time sequence
u_i	Control law for the i-th robot
v_0	"Hand velocity" of virtual leader
w'_m	Normalizing weight of the m-th particle
w_m	Weight of the m-th particle
v_i	"Hand velocity" of the i-th robot
x_0	"Hand position" of virtual leader
x_i	"Hand position" of the i-th robot

References

1. Lux, R.; Shi, W. Chemotaxis-guided movements in bacteria. *Crit. Rev. Oral Biol. Med.* **2004**, *15*, 207–220. [CrossRef] [PubMed]
2. Lu, Q.; Han, Q.-L.; Zhang, B. Cooperative control of mobile sensor networks for environmental monitoring: An event-triggered finite-time control scheme. *IEEE Trans. Cybern.* **2017**, *47*, 4134–4147. [CrossRef] [PubMed]
3. Lu, Q.; Liu, S.; Xie, X.; Wang, J. Decision-making and finite-time motion control for a group of robots. *IEEE Trans. Cybern.* **2013**, *43*, 738–750. [PubMed]
4. Zhang, X.; Fang, Y.; Sun, N. Visual servoing of mobile robots for posture stabilization: From theory to experiments. *Int. J. Robust Nonlinear Control* **2015**, *25*, 1–15. [CrossRef]
5. Zhang, X.; Fang, Y.; Liu, X. Motion-estimation-based visual servoing of nonholonomic mobile robots. *IEEE Trans. Robot.* **2011**, *27*, 1167–1175. [CrossRef]
6. Wang, Y.-L.; Han, Q.-L. Network-based modeling and dynamic output feedback control for unmanned marine vehicles. *Automatica* **2018**, *91*, 43–53. [CrossRef]
7. Wang, Y.-L.; Han, Q.-L.; Fei, M.; Peng, C. Network-based T-S fuzzy dynamic positioning controller design for unmanned marine vehicles. *IEEE Trans. Cybern.* **2018**. [CrossRef]
8. Sukhatme, G.S.; Dhariwal, A.; Zhang, B. Design and development of a wireless robotic networked aquatic microbial observing system. *Environ. Eng. Sci.* **2007**, *24*, 205–215. [CrossRef]
9. Kumar, V.; Rus, D.; Singh, S. Robot and sensor networks for first responders. *IEEE Pervasive Comput.* **2004**, *3*, 24–33. [CrossRef]

10. Ferreira, N.L.; Couceiro, M.S.; Araujo, A. Multi-sensor fusion and classification with mobile robots for situation awareness in urban search and rescue using ROS. In Proceedings of the 2013 IEEE International Symposium on Safety, Security, and Rescue Robotics, Linkoping, Sweden, 21–26 October 2013; pp. 1–6.

11. Azuma, S.I.; Sakar, M.S.; Pappas, G.J. Stochastic source seeking by mobile robots. *IEEE Trans. Autom. Control* **2012**, *57*, 2308–2321. [CrossRef]

12. Zhang, C.; Arnold, D.; Ghods, N. Source seeking with non-holonomic unicycle without position measurement and with tuning of forward velocity. *Syst. Control Lett.* **2007**, *56*, 245–252. [CrossRef]

13. Liu, S.J.; Krstic, M. Stochastic source seeking for nonholonomic unicycle. *Automatica* **2012**, *46*, 1443–1453. [CrossRef]

14. Song, D.; Kim, C.Y.; Yi, J. Simultaneous localization of multiple unknown and transient radio sources using a mobile robot. *IEEE Trans. Robot.* **2012**, *28*, 668–680. [CrossRef]

15. Bachmayer, R.; Leonard, N.E. Vehicle networks for gradient descent in a sampled environment. In Proceedings of the 41st IEEE Conference on Decision and Control, Las Vegas, NV, USA, 10–13 December 2002; pp. 112–117.

16. Moore, B.J.; Canudas-De-Wit, C. Source seeking via collaborative measurements by a circular formation of agents. In Proceedings of the 2010 American Control Conference, Baltimore, MD, USA, 30 June–2 July 2010; pp. 1292–1302.

17. Ogren, P.; Fiorelli, E.; Leonard, N.E. Cooperative control of mobile sensor networks: Adaptive gradient climbing in a distributed environment. *IEEE Trans. Autom. Control* **2004**, *49*, 1292–1302. [CrossRef]

18. Atanasov, N.A.; Ny, J.L.; Pappas, G.J. Distributed algorithms for stochastic source seeking with mobile robot networks. *J. Dyn. Syst. Meas. Control* **2014**, *137*, 031004/1–031004/9. [CrossRef]

19. Li, S.; Kong, R.; Guo, Y. Cooperative distributed source seeking by multiple robots: Algorithms and experiments. *IEEE/ASME Trans. Mechatron.* **2014**, *19*, 1810–1820. [CrossRef]

20. Zhang, X.; Fang, Y.; Li, B.; Wang, J. Visual servoing of nonholonomic mobile robots with uncalibrated camera-to-robot parameters. *IEEE Trans. Ind. Electron.* **2017**, *64*, 390–400. [CrossRef]

21. Zhang, X.; Wang, R.; Fang, Y.; Li, B.; Ma, B. Acceleration-level pseudo-dynamic visual servoing of mobile robots with backstepping and dynamic surface control. *IEEE Trans. Syst. Man Cybern. Syst.* **2017**. [CrossRef]

22. Oyekan, J.; Gu, D.; Hu, H. Hazardous substance source seeking in a diffusion based noisy environment. In Proceedings of the 2012 International Conference on Mechatronics and Automation (ICMA), Chengdu, China, 5–8 August 2012; pp. 708–713.

23. Ge, X.; Han, Q.-L.; Yang, F. Event-based set-membership leader-following consensus of networked multi-agent systems subject to limited communication resources and unknown-but-bounded noise. *IEEE Trans. Ind. Electron.* **2017**, *64*, 5045–5054. [CrossRef]

24. Cao, Y.; Yu, W.; Ren, W.; Chen, G. An overview of recent progress in the study of distributed multi-agent coordination. *IEEE Trans. Ind. Inform.* **2013**, *9*, 427–438. [CrossRef]

25. Jiang, Y.; Zhang, H.; Chen, J. Sign-consensus of linear multi-agent systems over signed directed graphs. *IEEE Trans. Ind. Electron.* **2017**, *64*, 5075–5083. [CrossRef]

26. Valcher, M.E.; Zorzan, I. On the consensus of homogeneous multi-agent systems with positivity constraints. *IEEE Trans. Autom. Control* **2017**, *62*, 5096–5110. [CrossRef]

27. Garca-Magario, I.; Gutirrez, C.; Fuentes-Fernndez, R. The INGENIAS development kit: A practical application for crisis-management. In Proceedings of the 10th International Work-Conference on Artificial Neural Networks (IWANN 2009), Salamanca, Spain, 10–12 June 2009; Volume 5517, pp. 537–544.

28. Garca-Magario, I.; Gutirrez, C. Agent-oriented modeling and development of a system for crisis management. *Expert Syst. Appl.* **2013**, *40*, 6580–6592. [CrossRef]

29. Zou, R.; Kalivarapu, V.; Winer, E.; Oliver, J. Particle swarm optimization-based source seeking. *IEEE Trans. Autom. Sci. Eng.* **2015**, *12*, 865–875. [CrossRef]

30. Li, H.; Liao, X.; Huang, T. Event-triggering sampling based leader-following consensus in second-order multi-agent systems. *IEEE Trans. Autom. Control* **2015**, *60*, 1998–2003. [CrossRef]

31. Xie, D.; Xu, S.; Zhang, B. Consensus for multi-agent systems with distributed adaptive control and an event-triggered communication strategy. *IET Control Theory Appl.* **2016**, *10*, 1547–1555. [CrossRef]

32. Zhu, W.; Jiang, Z.P. Event-based leader-following consensus of multi-agent systems with input time delay. *IEEE Trans. Autom. Control* **2015**, *60*, 1362–1367. [CrossRef]

33. Dimarogonas, D.V.; Johansson, K.H. Event-triggered control for multi-agent systems. In Proceedings of the 48th Decision and Control, 2009 Held Jointly with the 2009 28th Chinese Control Conference, Shanghai, China, 15–18 December 2009; pp. 7131–7136.

34. Dimarogonas, D.V.; Frazzoli, E.; Johansson, K.H. Distributed event-triggered control for multi-agent systems. *IEEE Trans. Autom. Control* **2012**, *57*, 1291–1297. [CrossRef]

35. Fan, Y.; Feng, G.; Wang, Y. Distributed event-triggered control of multi-agent systems with combinational measurements. *Automatica* **2013**, *49*, 671–675. [CrossRef]

36. Zhang, H.; Feng, G.; Yan, H. Observer-Based Output Feedback Event-Triggered Control for Consensus of Multi-Agent Systems. *IEEE Trans. Ind. Electron.* **2014**, *61*, 4885–4894. [CrossRef]

37. Lawton, J.R.T.; Beard, R.W.; Young, B.J. A decentralized approach to formation maneuvers. *IEEE Trans. Robot. Autom.* **2003**, *19*, 933–941. [CrossRef]

applied
sciences

MDPI

Article

Real-Time Swarm Search Method for Real-World Quadcopter Drones

Ki-Baek Lee [1], Young-Joo Kim [2] and Young-Dae Hong [3,*]

[1]   Department Electrical Engineering, Kwangwoon University, Seoul 01897, Korea; kblee@kw.ac.kr
[2]   Korea Railroad Research Institute, Uiwang 437-757, Korea; osot@krri.re.kr
[3]   Department Electrical Engineering, Ajou University, Suwon 443-749, Korea
*   Correspondence: ydhong@ajou.ac.kr; Tel.: +82-10-9555-2654

Received: 9 June 2018; Accepted: 17 July 2018; Published: 18 July 2018

check for
updates

Featured Application: This work can be applied to the problem of autonomous search and rescue with a swarm of the drones.

Abstract: This paper proposes a novel search method for a swarm of quadcopter drones. In the proposed method, inspired by the phenomena of swarms in nature, drones effectively look for the search target by investigating the evidence from the surroundings and communicating with each other. The position update mechanism is implemented using the particle swarm optimization algorithm as the swarm intelligence (a well-known swarm-based optimization algorithm), as well as a dynamic model for the drones to take the real-world environment into account. In addition, the mechanism is processed in real-time along with the movements of the drones. The effectiveness of the proposed method was verified through repeated test simulations, including a benchmark function optimization and air pollutant search problems. The results show that the proposed method is highly practical, accurate, and robust.

Keywords: unmanned aerial vehicle; swarm intelligence; particle swarm optimization; search algorithm

1. Introduction

The demand for autonomous aerial vehicles, commonly called drones, has largely increased in recent years due to their compactness and mobility, which enable them to carry out various tasks that are economically inefficient or potentially dangerous to humans. For example, it is not easy for humans to explore rugged mountain terrains, flooded areas, or air pollution regions without drones. Consequently, they have been extensively employed in various search applications, such as industrial building inspections [1,2], search and rescue operations [3–5], and post-disaster area exploration [6–8].

The search applications have one important factor in common: search efficiency. Previous research has focused on improving the stand-alone performance of each drone, such as localization accuracy, communication robustness, and various sensors [9]. However, it is relatively expensive to employ a group of such high-end drones. Additionally, it takes a long time for a drone or a few drones to cover a broad search space. Thus, previous studies have tried to decompose the search space [10] or control a number of low-cost drones into several formation patterns [11,12].

Despite the previous research successfully demonstrating the feasibility of search-by-drones, there is still room for improvement. Most of all, considering time and cost, it is not the best strategy to thoroughly scan every available location in the search space. In other words, it is more effective for drones to conduct a brief survey first and successively progress to better locations by investigating the evidence of the surroundings and communicating with each other. We can easily find examples of this kind of strategy from nature, such as ants, bees, fish, birds, and so on. They show cooperative and intelligent behaviors to achieve complex goals, which is called swarm intelligence [13–16]. In fact, in the area of multi-robot path planning in 2-*D* space, there have been several studies of approaches based on swarm intelligence [17,18]. However, there is a crucial difference between mobile robots in 2-*D* space and drones in 3-*D* space. Whereas mobile robots can stand stably without any posture control and only need to be controlled by position feedback, the postures and positions of drones should be carefully controlled based on a certain dynamic model in order to hover stably.

Therefore, in this paper, a novel swarm search method for quadcopter drones is proposed by integrating the position update rule of the swarm intelligence algorithm and the motion controller using a dynamic model of the drones. In the proposed method, a swarm of more than 10 drones was employed for a search mission. The swarm was controlled by a position update mechanism which included the swarm intelligence inspired from a well-known swarm-based optimization algorithm. In addition, a dynamic model for the drones was applied to the mechanism since real-world drones, in contrast to the individuals in the optimization algorithm, have physical limitations such as maximum speed and maximum acceleration. Moreover, the overall mechanism was processed in real-time along with the movements of the drones.

To verify the effectiveness of the proposed method, the overall procedure was implemented as a simulation and repeatedly tested. As the test problems, Rosenbrock function optimization and air pollutant search problems were employed. The Rosenbrock function is a well-known benchmark function for numerical optimization. The air pollutant search problem was designed by modeling atmospheric dispersion though a Gaussian air pollutant dispersion equation. Additionally, the results of the proposed method were compared to those of a conventional grid search method.

This paper is organized as follows. Section 2 explains the proposed methodology in detail. In Section 3, the experimental results are demonstrated. Finally, Section 4 presents conclusions.

2. The Proposed Swarm Search Method

The main contribution of this paper is that a novel drone position update mechanism for the swarm search was designed to be specific enough to consider real-time control and the real-world environment. There are two important issues in the mechanism: the swarm intelligence and the dynamic model of the drones. The swarm intelligence calculates the next destinations of the drones at each iteration based on the particle swarm optimization algorithm, and the dynamic model determines how the drones approach the next destination based on the real-world environment. Note that, for simplicity, it is assumed that the drones are fully sharing their information, are able to predict the collisions between them, and can stop before the collision on their own. In other words, in the mechanism, the position commands of two or more drones can be the same at the same control period.

In this section, the drone position update mechanism is explained in detail, and then the entire search process is described step-by-step.

2.1. The Drone Position Update Mechanism

2.1.1. The Swarm Intelligence for the Mechanism

At each iteration of the proposed method, the update mechanism should calculate the next positions of the drones by obtaining the information of the current positions and sharing them with each other (i.e., swarm intelligence). To implement the swarm intelligence, as a backbone, a particle swarm optimization (PSO) scheme is employed [19,20]. In the PSO scheme, each drone decides where to go by combining the information of its previous displacement, the personal best position it has ever experienced, and the global best position the entire swarm has ever found. If we denote the displacement, the personal best position, and the global best position at iteration t as $\mathbf{v}_t$, $^P\mathbf{x}_t$, and $^g\mathbf{x}_t$, respectively, then the next displacement of a drone is determined as:

$$\mathbf{v}_{t+1} = w \cdot \mathbf{v}_t + c \cdot [\phi_1(^P\mathbf{x}_t - \mathbf{x}_t) + \phi_2(^g\mathbf{x}_t - \mathbf{x}_t)], \tag{1}$$

where $w = 0.7$ and $c = 0.6$ are constants and ϕ_1 and ϕ_2 are random real values uniformly distributed in $[0, 1]$. Note that the random values are newly generated at each iteration for each particle. Obviously, the next destination $\mathbf{x}_{t+1}^*$ is calculated as:

$$\mathbf{x}_{t+1}^* = \mathbf{x}_t + \mathbf{v}_{t+1}. \tag{2}$$

However, drones in the real world cannot teleport to their destinations. Instead, they gradually approach their destinations following control commands based on their dynamic model. Therefore, the next position $\mathbf{x}_{n+1}$ at the $(n+1)$-th control period is determined as:

$$\mathbf{x}_{t,n+1} = \mathbf{x}_{t,n} + \tilde{\mathbf{v}}(\mathbf{x}_{t+1}^*), \tag{3}$$

where $\tilde{\mathbf{v}}$ represents the control output according to the input. This control loop is repeated until $\mathbf{x}_{t,n} = \mathbf{x}_{t+1}^*$, and then t increases by 1.

2.1.2. The Dynamic Model of the Drones for the Mechanism

The update mechanism should reflect the way in which the drones approach the next destination based on the real-world environment (i.e., the dynamic model). To establish the dynamic model, first, the kinematic model of a drone is necessary, as shown in Figure 1.

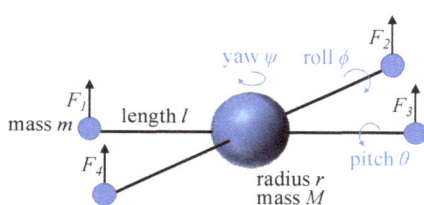

Figure 1. The physical model of a quadcopter drone.

From this kinematic model, the rotation matrix R for mapping the vector from the body frame to the inertial frame can be derived as

$$R = \begin{bmatrix} c_\phi c_\psi - c_\theta s_\phi s_\psi & -c_\psi s_\phi - c_\phi c_\theta s_\psi & s_\theta s_\psi \\ c_\theta c_\psi s_\phi + c_\phi s_\psi & c_\phi c_\theta c_\psi - s_\phi s_\psi & -c_\psi s_\theta \\ s_\phi s_\theta & c_\phi s_\theta & c_\theta \end{bmatrix}, \tag{4}$$

where c_ϕ and s_ϕ represent $cos(\phi)$ and $sin(\phi)$, respectively. Then, from Newton's equation, the linear motion can be derived as

$$m\ddot{x} = \begin{bmatrix} 0 \\ 0 \\ -mg \end{bmatrix} + RT_B + F_D, \tag{5}$$

where x is the position of the drone, g is the acceleration due to gravity, F_D is the drag force, and T_B is the thrust vector in the body frame. For simplicity, in this paper, the drag force is regarded as 0, and T_B is calculated based on [21]. Additionally, from Euler's equation, the angular motion can be derived as

$$I\dot{w} = \tau - w \times (Iw), \tag{6}$$

where w is the angular velocity vector, I is the inertia matrix, and τ is a vector of external torques. In this paper, I and τ are calculated based on [22,23]. Finally, based on these motion equations, the final state space equations for the dynamic model can be derived as

$$\dot{x}_1 = x_2,$$

$$\dot{x}_2 = \begin{bmatrix} 0 \\ 0 \\ -g \end{bmatrix} + \frac{RT_B}{m} + \frac{F_D}{m},$$

$$\dot{x}_3 = \begin{bmatrix} 1 & 0 & -s_\theta \\ 0 & c_\phi & c_\theta s_\phi \\ 0 & -s_\phi & c_\theta c_\phi \end{bmatrix}^{-1} \cdot x_4,$$

$$\dot{x}_4 = I^{-1} \cdot [\tau - x_3 \times (Ix_3)],$$

(7)

where x_1 is the velocity vector, x_2 is the acceleration vector, x_3 is the angular velocity vector, and x_4 is the angular acceleration vector. The model parameters used in this paper are listed in Table 1.

Table 1. Model parameters.

	Parameters	Values
Environment	Gravity acceleration g	9.81
	Draft coefficient b	0.02
Kinematic model	M	1.2
	m	0.1
	l	0.3
	r	0.1
Controller	Linear proportional (P) gain	[300, 300, 7000]
	Linear integral (I) gain	[0.04, 0.04, 4.50]
	Linear derivative (D) gain	[450, 450, 5000]
	Angular P gain	[22,000, 22,000, 1500]
	Angular I gain	[0.00, 0.00, 1.20]
	Angular D gain	[12,000, 12,000, 0.00]

As shown in Figure 2, the control system of the drone can be designed based on a well-known proportional-integral-derivative (PID) control scheme [24]. Note that the control system is not for the low-level motor actuation control, but for the high-level control of the commands transmitted to each drone. In addition, in simulation, the sensor system and the environment can be replaced by the dynamic model derived above.

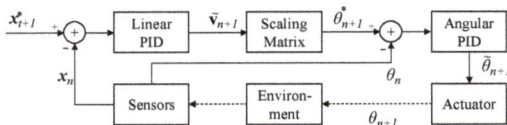

Figure 2. The control system of a quadcopter drone.

First, the position error at the n-th control period is calculated. Then, the linear PID system yields the desired displacement $\tilde{v}_{n+1}$, and the next destination posture θ^*_{n+1} can be calculated by multiplying a scaling matrix, since it is assumed that the drone is in a piecewise hovering state. Lastly, the angular PID system yields the posture displacement vector $\tilde{\theta}_{n+1}$, and the actuation system executes the corresponding throttle commands for the motors. As a result, the drone can gradually approach the next destination x^*_{t+1}.

Algorithm 1 Swarm search.

$\mathbb{S}$: The search space of the problem
S: The swarm of the drones
N_D: The number of drones in **S**
d^k: The k-th drone
$\mathbf{x}_t^k$: The position of d^k at iteration t
$\mathbf{v}_t^k$: The displacement of d^k at iteration t
$f(\mathbf{x}_t^k)$: The objective function value of $\mathbf{x}_t^k$
$^g\mathbf{x}_t$: The global best position of **S** at iteration t
$^p\mathbf{x}_t^k$: The personal best position of d^k at iteration t
$\mathbf{x}_{t,n}^k$: The position of d^k in the n-th control period at iteration t
$\mathbf{c}$: The command output of the controller

(1) Initialize **S**.
for $k = 1, 2, \ldots, N_D$ **do**
    $\mathbf{x}_0^k = \text{random vector} \in \mathbb{S}$
    $\mathbf{v}_0^k = \mathbf{0}$
    Evaluate $f(\mathbf{x}_0^k)$
    $^p\mathbf{x}_0^k = \mathbf{x}_0^k$
    Deploy d^k at $\mathbf{x}_0^k$
    if $f(^p\mathbf{x}_0^k)$ is better than $f(^g\mathbf{x}_0)$ **then**
        $^g\mathbf{x}_0 = {^p\mathbf{x}_0^k}$
    end if
end for
$t = 0$

(2) Update **S**.
for $k = 1, 2, \ldots, N_D$ **do**
    $\mathbf{v}_{t+1}^k = w \cdot \mathbf{v}_t^k + c \cdot [\phi_1(^p\mathbf{x}_t^k - \mathbf{x}_t^k) + \phi_2(^g\mathbf{x}_t - \mathbf{x}_t^k)]$
    $\mathbf{x}_{t+1}^{*k} = \mathbf{x}_t^k + \mathbf{v}_{t+1}^k$
    $\mathbf{x}_{t,0}^k = \mathbf{x}_t^k$
    $n = 0$
    while $\mathbf{x}_{t,n}^k \neq \mathbf{x}_{t+1}^{*k}$ or a collision is not predicted **do**
        $\mathbf{c} = \text{Controller}(\mathbf{x}_{t,n}^k, \mathbf{x}_{t+1}^{*k})$
        Actuate d^k with $\mathbf{c}$
        $(n = n + 1)$
        Evaluate $\mathbf{f}(\mathbf{x}_{t,n}^k)$
        if $f(\mathbf{x}_{t,n}^k)$ is better than $f(^p\mathbf{x}_t^k)$ **then**
            $^p\mathbf{x}_t^k = \mathbf{x}_{t,n}^k$
        end if
    end while
    if $f(^p\mathbf{x}_t^k)$ is better than $f(^g\mathbf{x}_t)$ **then**
        $^g\mathbf{x}_t = {^p\mathbf{x}_t^k}$
    end if
end for
$(t = t + 1)$

(3) Repeat (2) until a termination condition is met.

2.2. The Overall Procedure of the Swarm Search

The overall procedure of the proposed swarm search is summarized in Algorithm 1, and each step of the algorithm is explained in the following.

First, the swarm of the drones is initialized. For each drone in the swarm, the position is randomly initialized in the search space $\mathbb{S}$, and the displacement is initially set to a zero vector. The objective functions are initially calculated for each drone, and the initial personal best position of each drone $^{P}\mathbf{x}_0^k$ is set as the position of itself. Additionally, the initial global best position of the swarm $^{g}\mathbf{x}_0$ is set as $^{P}\mathbf{x}_0^1$.

Following this, the swarm of the drones is updated. For each drone in the swarm, the position is updated through the drone position update mechanism, as explained above. During the update process, the personal best positions and the global best position are also updated, and this update process is repeated until a termination condition is met. For example, a termination condition can be defined as a maximum number of iterations.

3. Experiment

In the experiment, first, the proposed swarm search method and, as a comparison, the conventional grid search method were implemented. Then, for each test problem, the objective function was designed and applied to both methods. Lastly, 100 simulations were run for each problem and method. Note that in the conventional method, it was assumed that the drones maintained a parallel formation and scanned every location of the search space unidirectionally along the axis in the order of x-, y-, and then z-axes. In addition, in the conventional method, since its position update process is independent of the objective function of the problem, the drones began the search mission at one corner of the search space and the goal was randomly set at each trial. To balance the different conditions of the two methods, in the comparison, one iteration for a drone was defined as one change of the searching direction instead of one visit to a point. Thus, for example, visiting all the grid points from $(-50, 0, 0)$ to $(50, 0, 0)$ along the x-axis direction was regarded as one iteration in the conventional method.

In this section, the detailed information about the environment settings is demonstrated, and then the experimental results and their analysis are provided.

3.1. Environment Settings

The proposed method was implemented as a software written in Python (Python software foundation, version 3.5.2) language with Numpy and Matplotlib libraries. The software was run on Linux OS (version 16.04) with Intel i7-6900K CPU, 128 GB DDR4 RAM, and NVIDIA Titan X Pascal GPU. The source code of the simulation engine was based on [25]. The update period of the drone dynamics was set to 0.01 s and the control period was set to 0.015 s.

The search mission based on the Rosenbrock function was adopted as Test Problem 1. In this problem, the drones obtained the sensor data at their positions virtually according to the mathematical model which was based on the Rosenbrock function, and the final goal was the position at which the function value was globally minimum. The Rosenbrock function is a well-known benchmark function for numerical optimization because it is hard to find the global minimum in its search space [26,27]. The following is the equation of the sensor data model:

$$f(\mathbf{x}) = \sum_{i=1}^{N-1} [100(\frac{x_{i+1}}{25} - \frac{x_i^2}{25^2})^2 + (1 - \frac{x_i}{25})^2], \tag{8}$$

where $\mathbf{x} = [x_1, ..., x_N] \in [-50.00, 50.00)$. In this problem, N was set to 3 since the real world is three-dimensional, and the number of drones was set to 25. The corresponding global minimum could be found at the position of $(25.00, 25.00, 25.00)$.

For Test Problem 2, an air pollutant search problem was employed. The mission of this problem was to find the origin of the air pollutant at which the pollution concentration was globally maximum.

The air pollutant search problem was designed by modeling atmospheric dispersion through a Gaussian air pollutant dispersion equation [28,29]. Figure 3 shows the visualization of the Gaussian air pollutant dispersion on x- and z-axes, which was originally from [30].

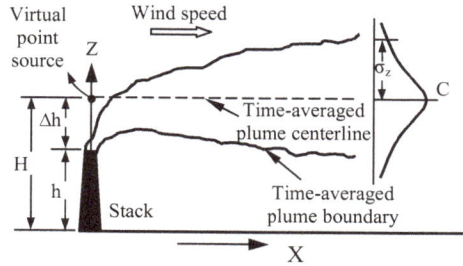

Figure 3. The visualization of the Gaussian air pollutant dispersion on x- and z-axes.

The Gaussian air pollutant dispersion equation can be written as:

$$
\begin{cases}
C(x,y,z) = \dfrac{Q}{u} \cdot \dfrac{f}{\sigma_y(x)\sqrt{2\pi}} \cdot \dfrac{g_1 + g_2}{\sigma_z(x)\sqrt{2\pi}} \\[2mm]
\quad = \dfrac{Q}{2\pi \cdot \sigma_y(x) \cdot \sigma_z(x) \cdot u} \cdot e^{-\frac{y^2}{2\sigma_y(x)^2}} \cdot \left[e^{-\frac{(z-H)^2}{2\sigma_z(x)^2}} + e^{-\frac{(z+H)^2}{2\sigma_z(x)^2}} \right], & \text{if } x \geq 0, \\[4mm]
C(x,y,z) = 0, & \text{otherwise,}
\end{cases}
\tag{9}
$$

where:

$$x,y \in [-50.00, 50.00), \quad z \in [0.00, 50.00)$$

$$f = \text{crosswind dispersion} = e^{-\frac{y^2}{2\sigma_y^2}}$$

$$g_1 = \text{vertical dispersion with no reflections} = e^{-\frac{(z-H)^2}{2\sigma_z^2}}$$

$$g_2 = \text{vertical dispersion for reflection from the ground} = e^{-\frac{(z+H)^2}{2\sigma_z^2}}$$

C = concentration of emissions, in g/m^3

Q = source pollutant emission rate, in g/s

u = horizontal wind velocity along the plume centerline, in m/s

H = height of emission plume centerline above ground level, in m

σ_z = vertical standard deviation of the emission distribution, in m

σ_y = horizontal standard deviation of the emission distribution, in m.

From [29], $\sigma_y(x)$ and $\sigma_z(x)$ can be determined as:

$$
\begin{aligned}
\sigma_y(x) &= e^{[I_y + J_y \cdot log(x+\epsilon) + K_y \cdot log(x+\epsilon)^2]}, \\
\sigma_z(x) &= e^{[I_z + J_z \cdot log(x+\epsilon) + K_z \cdot log(x+\epsilon)^2]},
\end{aligned}
\tag{10}
$$

where ϵ was set to 10^{-10} in this problem.

In this problem, the number of drones was set to 15. In addition, Q, u, and H were set to 10, 3, and 10, respectively. It was assumed that the atmosphere was in a neutral state, and, according to the classification of stability class proposed in [31,32], I_y, J_y, K_y, I_z, J_z, and K_z were set to -2.55, 1.04, -0.01, -3.19, 1.11, and -0.03, respectively. Based on these settings, the corresponding global maximum could be found at the position of $(0.00, 0.00, 10.00)$.

3.2. Experimental Results

The results demonstrate the effectiveness of the proposed method through the following figures describing the trajectories of the drones with the proposed method, as well as the tables representing the statistical comparisons between the proposed and conventional methods.

Figure 4 shows the simulation of Test Problem 1 through the proposed method at iterations 1, 10, 50, and 1500. As shown in the figure, the drones successfully found the target position at which the Rosenbrock function had the minimum value within 150 iterations. Note that the drones were unaware of the function as well as its derivatives.

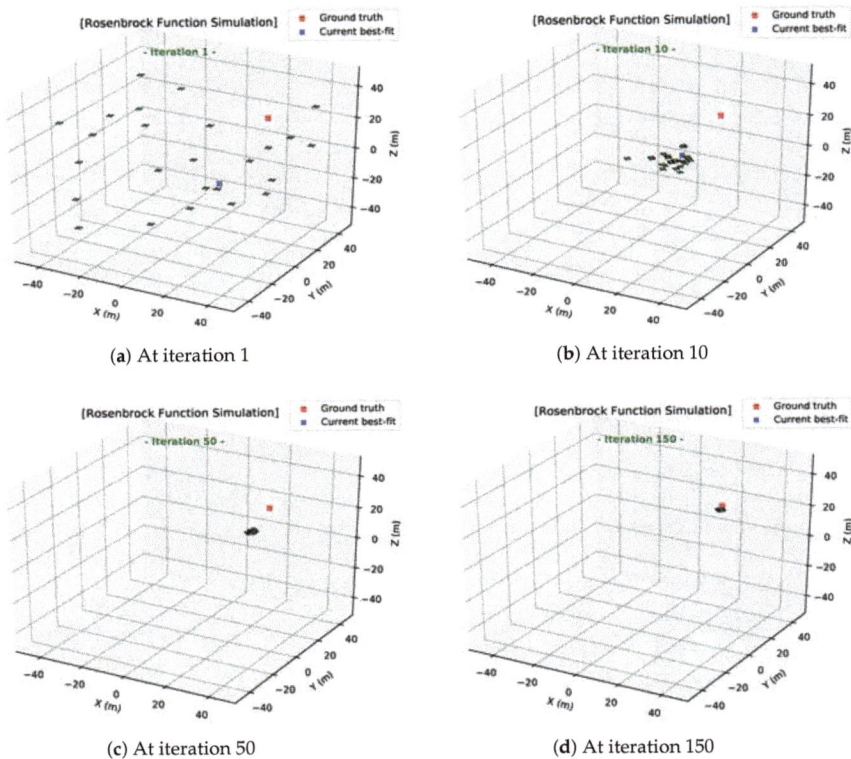

(a) At iteration 1

(b) At iteration 10

(c) At iteration 50

(d) At iteration 150

Figure 4. Screenshots of the simulation of Test Problem 1 by the proposed method.

Figure 5 shows the simulation of Test Problem 2 through the proposed method at iterations 1, 10, 20, and 30. As shown in the figure, the drones successfully found the target position at which the pollutant was being emitting within 30 iterations. Note that the drones had no knowledge of the dispersion model, and could simply measure the air pollution concentrations at their positions.

(a) At iteration 1

(b) At iteration 10

(c) At iteration 20

(d) At iteration 30

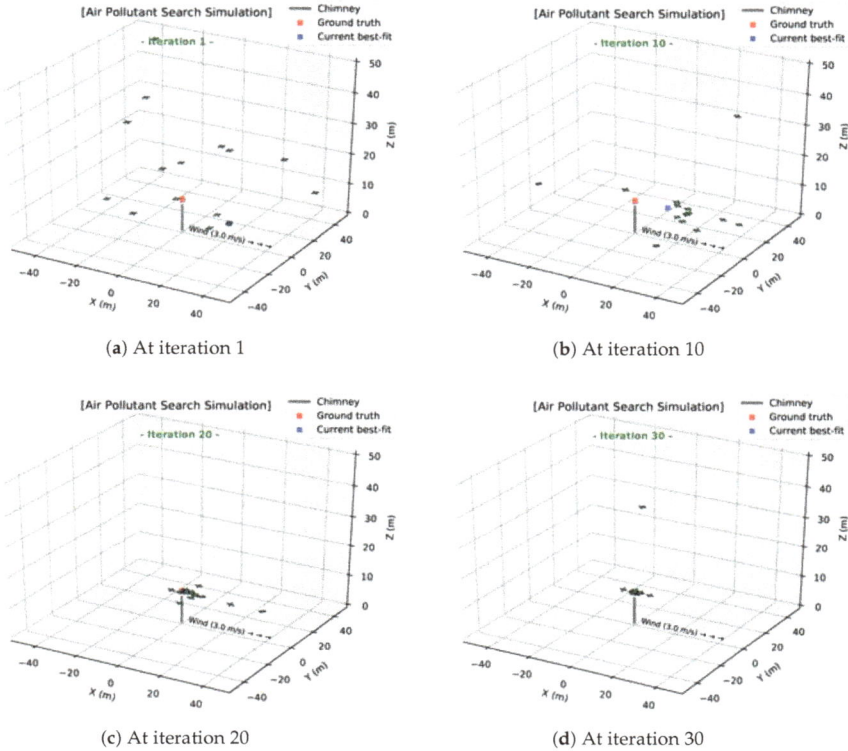

Figure 5. Screenshots of the simulation of Test Problem 2 by the proposed method.

The full simulation videos for Test Problems 1 and 2 are provided through the YouTube links "https://youtu.be/fIUmsO5B4CA" and "https://youtu.be/cdlCZQeN-Bo", respectively. The videos show that the drones could find the global minimum or maximum under non-convex or near non-convex environments. The videos also show that the drones could be controlled stably in real-time, and the dynamic model was well-applied considering the real-world environment.

Moreover, Table 2 shows the averages ($AVGs$) and standard deviations ($STDs$) of the number of iterations n for the proposed and conventional methods to satisfy the corresponding termination condition (TC) about error distance d_{err}. Since the search space was based on a real-world environment, the unit of distance was meters. If we consider the size of commonly-used drones (approximately 1.0 m), the minimum grid size for the conventional grid search should be greater than 1.0 m. Based on this condition, we can approve that the drone is close enough to the goal if d_{err} is less than 2.0, which is double the minimum grid size. Additionally, the $AVGs$ and $STDs$ of the final d_{err} for the proposed and conventional methods with the limited number of iterations n_{limit} are shown in Table 3. Smaller values of both n and d_{err} are desirable, where n and d_{err} imply the speed and the accuracy of the methods, respectively. As displayed in the tables, the proposed method could find the target more quickly and more accurately and robustly than the conventional method. Note that the proposed method showed a more powerful result in the real-world problem (e.g., Test Problem 2) than the virtual problem (e.g., Test Problem 1).

Table 2. The averages (*AVG*s) and standard deviations (*STD*s) of the number of iterations *n* for the methods to satisfy the termination condition (*TC*).

Problem	Proposed		Conventional		TC
	$AVG(n)$	$STD(n)$	$AVG(n)$	$STD(n)$	
1	141.72	37.73	409.68	244.95	$d_{err} < 2.0$
2	27.41	7.62	366.66	211.01	$d_{err} < 2.0$

Table 3. The *AVG*s and *STD*s of the error distance (d_{err}) for the methods with the limited number of iterations (n_{limit}).

Problem	Proposed		Conventional		n_{limit}
	$AVG(d_{err})$	$STD(d_{err})$	$AVG(d_{err})$	$STD(d_{err})$	
1	0.88	0.56	58.79	51.82	200
2	0.04	0.05	64.14	39.10	50

4. Conclusions

In this paper, a novel search method for a swarm of quadcopter drones was proposed. In the proposed method, inspired by the phenomena of swarms in nature, drones could effectively look for better locations by investigating the evidence from the surroundings and communicating with each other. The position update mechanism was implemented based on the particle swarm optimization algorithm (a well-known swarm-based optimization algorithm), as well as the dynamic model of the drones, which was used to take the real-world environment into account. In addition, the mechanism could be processed in real-time along with the movements of the drones. The experimental results showed that through the proposed method, the drones could find the target more quickly and accurately than by the conventional algorithm. Most importantly, the proposed method has high practical potential, considering that the drones were simulated in real-time and the dynamic model sufficiently reflected the real-world environment.

Author Contributions: K.-B.L. conceived and designed the methodology and experiments; K.-B.L. performed the experiments; Y.-D.H. analyzed the data; K.-B.L. wrote the paper; Y.-J.K. and Y.-D.H. reviewed and edited the paper.

Funding: This research received no external funding.

Acknowledgments: This work was supported by the "Research Grant of Kwangwoon University" in 2017 and "Human Resources Program in Energy Technology" of the Korea Institute of Energy Technology Evaluation and Planning (KETEP), granted financial resource from the Ministry of Trade, Industry&Energy, Republic of Korea (No. 20174010201620).

Conflicts of Interest: The authors declare no conflict of interest.

References

1. Cacace, J.; Finzi, A.; Lippiello, V.; Loianno, G.; Sanzone, D. Aerial service vehicles for industrial inspection: task decomposition and plan execution. *Appl. Intell.* **2015**, *42*, 49–62. [CrossRef]
2. Lippiello, V.; Siciliano, B. Wall inspection control of a VTOL unmanned aerial vehicle based on a stereo optical flow. In Proceedings of the IEEE/RSJ International Conference on Intelligent Robots and Systems (IROS), Vilamoura, Portugal, 7–12 October 2012; pp. 4296–4302.
3. Bevacqua, G.; Cacace, J.; Finzi, A.; Lippiello, V. Mixed-Initiative Planning and Execution for Multiple Drones in Search and Rescue Missions. In Proceedings of the Twenty-Fifth International Conference on Automated Planning and Scheduling, ICAPS, Jerusalem, Israel, 7–11 June 2015; pp. 315–323.

4.   Cacace, J.; Finzi, A.; Lippiello, V.; Furci, M.; Mimmo, N.; Marconi, L. A control architecture for multiple drones operated via multimodal interaction in search & rescue mission. In Proceedings of the IEEE International Symposium on Safety, Security, and Rescue Robotics (SSRR), Lausanne, Switzerland, 23–27 October 2016; pp. 233–239.

5.   Cacace, J.; Finzi, A.; Lippiello, V. Multimodal interaction with multiple co-located drones in search and rescue missions. *arXiv* **2016**, arXiv:1605.07316.

6.   Cui, J.Q.; Phang, S.K.; Ang, K.Z.; Wang, F.; Dong, X.; Ke, Y.; Lai, S.; Li, K.; Li, X.; Lin, F.; et al. Drones for cooperative search and rescue in post-disaster situation. In Proceedings of the IEEE 7th International Conference on Cybernetics and Intelligent Systems (CIS) and IEEE Conference on Robotics, Automation and Mechatronics (RAM), Angkor Wat, Cambodia, 15–17 July 2015; pp. 167–174.

7.   Rivera, A.; Villalobos, A.; Monje, J.; Mariñas, J.; Oppus, C. Post-disaster rescue facility: Human detection and geolocation using aerial drones. In Proceedings of the IEEE Region 10 Conference (TENCON), Singapore, 22–25 November 2016; pp. 384–386.

8.   Cui, J.Q.; Phang, S.K.; Ang, K.Z.; Wang, F.; Dong, X.; Ke, Y.; Lai, S.; Li, K.; Li, X.; Lin, J.; et al. Search and rescue using multiple drones in post-disaster situation. *Unmanned Syst.* **2016**, *4*, 83–96. [CrossRef]

9.   Bekhti, M.; Achir, N.; Boussetta, K. Swarm of Networked Drones for Video Detection of Intrusions. In Proceedings of the International Wireless Internet Conference, Tianjin, China, 16–17 December 2017; pp. 221–231.

10.   Šulák, V.; Kotuliak, I.; Čičák, P. Search using a swarm of unmanned aerial vehicles. In Proceedings of the 15th International Conference on Emerging eLearning Technologies and Applications (ICETA), Stary Smokovec, Slovakia, 26–27 October 2017; pp. 1–6.

11.   Gaynor, P.; Coore, D. Towards distributed wilderness search using a reliable distributed storage device built from a swarm of miniature UAVs. In Proceedings of the IEEE International Conference on Unmanned Aircraft Systems (ICUAS), Orlando, FL, USA, 27–30 May 2014; pp. 596–601.

12.   Altshuler, Y.; Pentland, A.; Bruckstein, A.M. *Swarms and Network Intelligence in Search*; Springer: Berlin, Germany, 2018.

13.   Leavitt, H.J. Some effects of certain communication patterns on group performance. *J. Abnorm. Soc. Psychol.* **1951**, *46*, 38. [CrossRef]

14.   Bandura, A. *Social Foundations of Thought and Action: A Social Cognitive Theory*; Prentice-Hall, Inc.: Englewood Cliffs, NJ, USA, 1986.

15.   Kennedy, J. The particle swarm: social adaptation of knowledge. In Proceedings of the IEEE International Congress on Evolutionary Computation, Indianapolis, IN, USA, 13–16 April 1997; pp. 303–308.

16.   Eberhart, R.C.; Shi, Y.; Kennedy, J. *Swarm Intelligence*; Elsevier: New York, NY, USA, 2001.

17.   Pugh, J.; Martinoli, A. Inspiring and modeling multi-robot search with particle swarm optimization. In Proceedings of the IEEE Swarm Intelligence Symposium, Honolulu, HI, USA, 1–5 April 2007; pp. 332–339.

18.   Couceiro, M.S.; Rocha, R.P.; Ferreira, N.M. A novel multi-robot exploration approach based on particle swarm optimization algorithms. In Proceedings of the IEEE International Symposium on Safety, Security, and Rescue Robotics (SSRR), Kyoto, Japan, 1–5 November 2011; pp. 327–332.

19.   Kennedy, J. Particle swarm optimization. In *Encyclopedia of Machine Learning*; Springer: Berlin, Germany, 2011; pp. 760–766.

20.   Du, K.L.; Swamy, M. Particle swarm optimization. In *Search and Optimization by Metaheuristics*; Springer: Berlin, Germany, 2016; pp. 153–173.

21.   Staples, G. Propeller Static & Dynamic Thrust Calculation. 2013. Available online: https://www. electricrcaircraftguy.com/2013/09/propeller-static-dynamic-thrust-equation.html (accessed on 13 April 2014).

22.   Beard, R. *Quadrotor Dynamics and Control Rev 0.1*; All Faculty Publications; Brigham Young University: Provo, UT, USA, 2008.

23.   Khan, M. Quadcopter flight dynamics. *Int. J. Sci. Technol. Res.* **2014**, *3*, 130–135.

24.   Praveen, V.; Pillai, S. A Modeling and simulation of quadcopter using PID controller. *Int. J. Control Theory Appl.* **2016**, *9*, 7151–7158.

25.   Majumdar, A. Quadcopter Simulator. 2017. Available online: https://github.com/abhijitmajumdar/ Quadcopter_simulatorl (accessed on 19 February 2018).

26.   Rosenbrock, H. An automatic method for finding the greatest or least value of a function. *Comput. J.* **1960**, *3*, 175–184. [CrossRef]

27. Shi, Y.; Eberhart, R.C. Empirical study of particle swarm optimization. In Proceedings of the IEEE International Congress on Evolutionary Computation, Washington, DC, USA, 6–9 July 1999; Volume 3, pp. 1945–1950.

28. Juan, S.; Jiong, S.; Bao, Q.; Yusen, D.; Qiang, W. An Industrid air pollution dispersion system based on Gauss dispersion model. *Environ. Pollut. Control* **2005**, *7*, 11.

29. Seinfeld, J.H.; Pandis, S.N. *Atmospheric Chemistry and Physics: From Air Pollution to Climate Change*; John Wiley & Sons: Hoboken, NJ, USA, 2016.

30. Abdel-Rahman, A.A. On the atmospheric dispersion and Gaussian plume model. In Proceedings of the 2nd International Conference on Waste Management, Water Pollution, Air Pollution, Indoor Climate, Corfu, Greece, 26–28 October 2008; pp. 31–39.

31. Pasquill, F. Atmospheric dispersion of pollution. *Q. J. R. Meteorol. Soc.* **1971**, *97*, 369–395. [CrossRef]

32. Hanna, S.R.; Briggs, G.A.; Hosker, R.P., Jr. *Handbook on Atmospheric Diffusion*; Technical Report; National Oceanic and Atmospheric Administration: Oak Ridge, TN, USA; Atmospheric Turbulence and Diffusion Lab.: Oak Ridge, TN, USA, 1982.

![applied sciences logo]

applied
sciences

MDPI

Article

Multi-AUV Cooperative Target Hunting Based on Improved Potential Field in a Surface-Water Environment

Hengqing Ge [1], Guibin Chen [1] and Guang Xu [2,*]

[1] School of Physics and Electronic Electrical Engineering, Huaiyin Normal University, Huaian 223001, China; ghq@hytc.edu.cn (H.G.); gbchen@hytc.edu.cn (G.C.)
[2] Western Australian School of Mines, Curtin University, Kalgoorlie 6430, Australia
* Correspondence: guang.xu@curtin.edu.au; Tel.: +61-890-886-113

Received: 7 May 2018; Accepted: 31 May 2018; Published: 14 June 2018

Abstract: In this paper, target hunting aims to detect target and surround the detected target in a surface-water using Multiple Autonomous Underwater Vehicles (multi-AUV) in a given area. The main challenge in multi-AUV target hunting is the design of AUV's motion path and coordination mechanism. To conduct the cooperative target hunting by multi-AUV in a surface-water environment, an integrated algorithm based on improved potential field (IPF) is proposed. First, a potential field function is established according to the information of the surface-water environment. Then, the dispersion degree, the homodromous degree, and district-difference degree are introduced to increase the cooperation of the multi-AUV system. Finally, the target hunting is solved by embedding the three kinds of degree into the potential field function. The simulation results show that the proposed approach is applicable and feasible for multi-AUV cooperative target hunting.

Keywords: cooperative target hunting; multi-AUV; improved potential field; surface-water environment

---

1. Introduction

To conduct the cooperative target hunting by multi-AUV in an underwater environment, the AUVs not only need to take into account basic problems (such as searching, path planning) but also need to cooperate in order to catch the targets efficiently [1]. The target hunting by multi-AUV has attracted much attention due to its complexity and significance [2,3]. Today, much research has been done on the multi-AUV hunting issue, and there are some approaches proposed that apply to this issue. Zhang et al. [4] presented a hunting approach derived from the virtual structure. The advantage of the virtual structure approach is that the formation can be maintained very well while maneuvering. Rezaee et al. [5] considered formation control of a team of mobile robots based on the virtual structure. The main advantage of this approach is that it is fairly easy to prescribe the coordinated behavior for the whole formation group and add a type of robustness to formation by using formation feedback.

However, the disadvantage of the virtual structure is that requiring the formation to act as a rigid virtual structure limits the class of potential applications.

Recently, some research has dealt the hunting process with simple obstacles. Yamaguchi [6] proposed a method based on making troop formations for enclosing the target and presented a smooth time-varying feedback control law for coordinating motions for multi-robots. Pan [7] has applied the improved reinforcement algorithm in the multi-robot hunting problem. However, in these studies, the hunting target is usually static.

For the shortcomings mentioned above, Ma [8] proposed a cooperative hunting strategy with dynamic alliance to chase moving target. This method can shorten the completion time to some extent. Wang [9] proposed a new hunting method with new definition concepts of occupy, overlapping angle and finally calculated an optimized path for hunting multi-robots, but the environment is too open, and the initial location of hunting robots is too close to a moving target.

Some work has been reported to adapt the leader-following algorithm to achieve target hunting. For example, Ni et al. [10] presented a bio-inspired neural network model with formation strategy to complete the hunting task. Liang et al. [11] proposed a leader-following formation control method for mobile robots with a directed tree topology. Qin et al. [12] have used leader-following formation algorithm to guide multi-agent cooperation for hunting task. These algorithms are easy to understand and implement, since the coordinated team members only need to maneuver according to the leader. However, the leader-following algorithm is no explicit feedback from the followers to leader, and the failure of the leader leads to the failure of the whole formation team.

There are many neural network approaches proposed for target hunting. For examples, Garcia et al. [13] proposed a simple ant colony optimization meta-heuristic (SACOdm) algorithm to solve the path planning problem of autonomous mobile robots. The SACOdm methods determine the robots' path based on the distance from the source to the target nodes, where the ants remember the visited nodes. Zhu et al. [14] proposed a hunting algorithm based on a bioinspired neural network. The hunting AUVs' paths are guided through the bio-inspired neural network and the results show that it can achieve the desired hunting result efficiency. Sheng [15] has proposed a method based on diffusion adaptation with network to research intelligent predators hunting for fish schools. Although neural networks can complete the hunting task, they often need to perform large amount of calculation, incurring prohibitive computational cost. Therefore, the neural network algorithm is not suitable for real-time system.

Potential field algorithms were proposed for real-time target hunting and became the most widely studied distributed control methods [16]. In the potential field methods, it is assumed that the robots combine attraction with the goal, and repulsion from obstacles [17,18]. Artificial potential field (APF) algorithms were proposed for real-time path planning for robots to solve obstacle avoidance problem and became the most widely studied distributed control methods [16–18]. In the APF methods, it is assumed that the robots combine attraction with the goal and repulsion from obstacles. Much work has been reported to adapt the APF algorithm to controlling swarm robots. Rasekhipour et al. [19] introduces a model predictive path-planning controller to potential functions along with the vehicle dynamics terms. Ge et al. [20] proposed formation tracking control based on potential field. However, the potential field algorithm is known for getting trapped easily in a local minimum.

This paper focuses on situation which the targets are intelligent and their motions are unpredicted and irregular. The multi-AUV hunting algorithm based on the improved potential field (IPF) is presented. The hunting AUVs' paths are guided through potential field function, and the three degrees (the dispersion degree, the homodromous degree, and district-difference degree) are used to solve the target search and capture of AUVs in the whole hunting process. The proposed algorithm can overcome local minimum problem. The simulation results show that the hunting efficiency can be as desired.

The rest paper is organized as follows. The proposed improved potential field based integrated hunting algorithm is presented in Section 2. The simulations for various situations are given in Section 3. Finally, the conclusion is given in Section 4.

2. The Improved Potential Field Approach

The potential field approach is a commonly used method for AUV path planning in a surface-water environment. However, the potential field approach is not cooperative when it is applied to target hunting. In this section, applying the cooperation method into potential field is a novel idea for multi-AUV cooperation target hunting. The flow of the target hunting task is shown in Figure 1. In this approach, when one AUV detects the targets, the multi-AUV system will calculate the distance between the each AUV and the target and request the proper AUVs to accomplish the hunting tasks. At the same time, the three degrees (the dispersion degree, the homodromous degree, and district-difference degree) are introduced to increase the collaboration of multi-robot system.

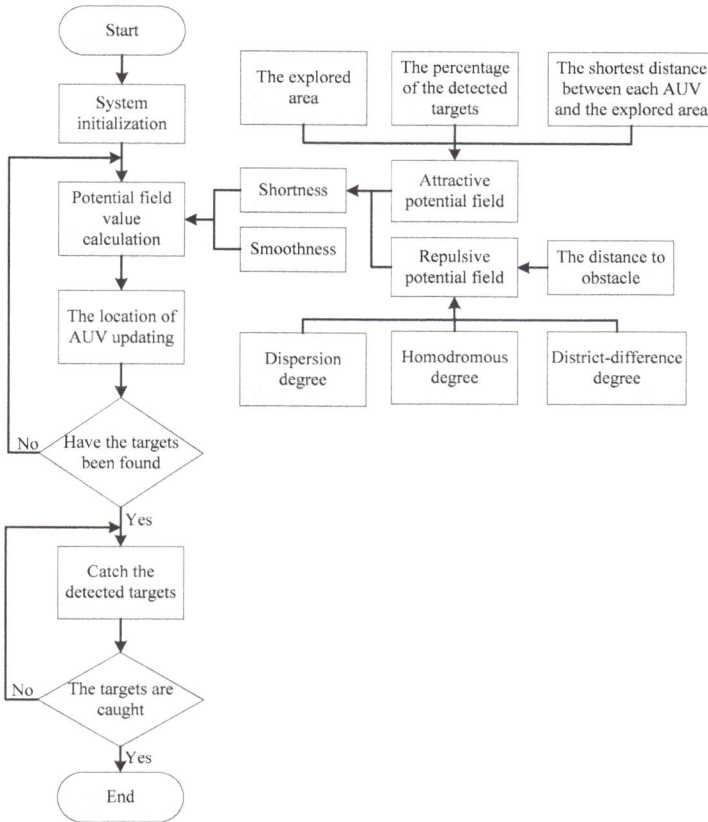

Figure 1. The flowchart for target hunting by Multiple Autonomous Underwater Vehicles (multi-AUV).

In the scheme, the whole potential value U of AUV R_i can be defined as

$$U = w_\alpha U_\alpha + w_\gamma U_\gamma \tag{1}$$

where U_α denotes the attractive potential value, U_γ represents the repellent potential value, and w_α and w_γ are weights in the distance potential. In static environments, w_α can be set within a limited range, while in dynamic environments, a linear increasing value of w_α is applied.

The attractive potential U_α at position X_{Ri} of AUV R_i is defined as [21]

$$U_\alpha = \begin{cases} \frac{1}{2} k_{\alpha 1} \frac{N_u/(N_u+N_\alpha)}{(A-A_\alpha)/A} d_0, & if\ R_i\ continues\ exploring, \\ \frac{1}{2} k_{\alpha 2} |X_{Ri} - X_{Tl}|^2, & if\ R_i\ moves\ to\ targets. \end{cases} \tag{2}$$

where $k_{\alpha 1}$ and $k_{\alpha 2}$ are the position gain coefficients, X_{Tl} is the position of target T_l, $l = 1, \ldots, N$, d_0 denotes the shortest distance from the AUV to the explored area, and the item $|X_{Ri} - X_{Tl}|$ is the relative distance between the AUV R_i and target T_l. The number of the detected targets is N_α while N_u is undetected targets number. The variable A denotes the area of the environment, while A_α represents the already explored area.

Because there are obstacles in the environment, the AUVs need to plan the collision-free paths to complete the task. In this case, the repulsive potential U_γ is given by [22]

$$U_\gamma = \begin{cases} \omega_{\gamma D}\frac{1}{H_D} + \omega_{\gamma H}\frac{1}{H_H} + \omega_{\gamma DD}\frac{1}{H_{DD}}, & if\ R_i\ continues\ exploring, \\ 0, & if\ R_i\ moves\ to\ targets, \\ \frac{1}{2}\eta\left(\frac{1}{d} - \frac{1}{d_1}\right)|X_{Ri} - X_{TI}|^2, & if\ R_i\ detects\ obstacles. \end{cases} \tag{3}$$

where $\omega_{\gamma D}$, $\omega_{\gamma H}$ and $\omega_{\gamma DD}$ are the density weights; and H_D, H_H and H_{DD} are the dispersion degree, homodromous degree and district-difference degree respectively. d is the nearest distance between the AUV and the detected obstacles. d_1 is the influence scope of obstacles. η is a position gain coefficient. The relative distance $|X_{Ri} - X_{TI}|$ between the AUV and target is added to the function, which ensures that the global minimum is only at the target in the entire potential field.

Dispersion degree H_D evaluates how close the robots are to each other by distance. If there are m AUVs in a M × N area, the parameter H_D is calculated by a Gaussian function as [23]

$$H_D = e^{-\frac{(\delta-\mu)^2}{2\sigma^2}} \tag{4}$$

where δ, μ and σ are calculated by [24]

$$\delta = \frac{\overline{D}}{\sqrt{M^2 + N^2}} \tag{5}$$

$$\mu = \frac{1}{t}\sum_{k=1}^{t}\delta_k \tag{6}$$

$$\sigma = \frac{1}{2}[\max(\delta_k) - \min(\delta_k)] \tag{7}$$

$$\overline{D} = \frac{\sum_{j=1}^{m}\sum_{f=j+1}^{m}D(j,f)}{C_m^2} = \frac{2}{m(m-1)}\sum_{j=1}^{m}\sum_{f=j+1}^{m}D(j,f) \tag{8}$$

where D is the real-time average distance between the AUVs; and $D(i,f)$ is the distance between AUV R_j and R_f.

Homodromous degree H_H evaluates how close the AUVs are to others by direction. If there are m AUVs and the AUV directions are $\{\theta_1, \theta_1, \ldots, \theta_{m0}\}$, where $0° \le \theta \le 360°$. The parameter H_H is calculated by [25]

$$H_H = \frac{\frac{2}{m(m-1)}\sum_{j=1}^{m}\sum_{f=j+1}^{m}abs\left(\theta_j, \theta_f\right)}{m_0} \tag{9}$$

where m_0 is the number of possible moving directions of the AUV. In this study, each possible direction area is regarded as a bound area of $45°$ angle. Therefore, there are eight possible direction areas in the simulations. The function abs() is absolute value function.

The district-difference degree is used to judge whether all the AUVs stay in the same area. Especially when both N_u and A_u are large, the district-difference degree is applied to provide a proper repulsive potential value to keep the AUVs from gathering. In the actual search task, the environment is usually divided into different parts based on the number of targets and search resources. If both the percentages of undetected targets (denoted as N_u/N) and unexplored area (denoted as A_u/A) are high, the district-difference degree can help the AUVs to explore separately rather than gather too close to each other. In other words, the density of the robots in a small part of the environment is supposed to be low under this situation. For the calculation, the environment is divided into N_d parts

$A_1, A_2, \ldots, A_{Nd}$, where N_d is a square number and $N_d < N$. The value of district-difference degree can be obtained by [26,27]

$$H_{DD} = \frac{\omega_{D1}\frac{A_u}{A} + \omega_{D2}\frac{N_u}{N} + \omega_{D3}\sum_{i=1}^{m} P(R_i, k)}{m} \tag{10}$$

where ω_{D1}, ω_{D2} and ω_{D3} are weights; $P(R_i, k)$ is the function to judge whether the AUV R_i is in the k-th part of the environment, which can be obtained by [26,27]

$$P(R_i, k) = \begin{cases} 1, & if \ in \ the \ part \\ 0, & otherwise \end{cases} \tag{11}$$

3. Simulation Studies

To demonstrate the effectiveness of the proposed approach for cooperative hunting by multi-AUV in surface-water environment, a simulation is conducted in MATLAB R2016a (The MathWorks, Inc., MA 01760-2098 UNITED STATES). In order to easy realization, the assumptions are as follows. (1) The turning radius of the AUV is ignorable in surface-water environment, thus the AUV is assumed to be able to move omni-directionally. (2) AUV is assumed to be able to recognize each other and identify their targets by the sonar. (3) The AUV velocity is set at a value more than the target velocity. (4) AUVs are capable of communicating with each other.

In this simulation, there are six AUVs, two targets, and several static obstacles of different size and shape. The area of the environment is 120×120 (m^2). AUVs and targets are allowed to move within the given space. Among them, targets move at random, and AUVs move at the proposed algorithm. When one target moves into any AUV's sensing range, this target is regarded as being found. Figure 2 shows the conditions where the target is successfully surrounded by hunting AUVs. When all targets have been surrounded by at least four AUVs, the targets are regarded as being caught, and the hunting task ends.

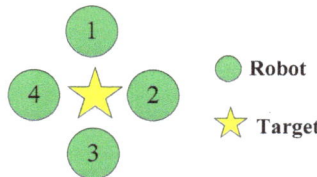

Figure 2. Target is hunted by AUVs.

3.1. One Target

The first simulation is conducted to test the cooperative hunting process without obstacles. It is assumed that there are four hunting AUVs with only one target. Figure 3a shows the initial locations and stage of hunting condition. At the beginning of the hunting task, AUVs search for targets in different directions based on the proposed algorithm. Targets move at random before being discovered. After a while, the target T1 is found by the AUV R2. Figure 3b shows AUVs' search trajectory for the target. Because the target has the same intelligence of AUV except the cooperation, target T1 will escape. The AUV R2 will track the target T1 and send the location information of the target to other AUVs. According to the location of the target T1, the proposed algorithm automatically plans a collision-free pursuing path for each hunter. Figure 3c shows R1, R2, R3, and R4 hunting trajectory for the target T1. Obviously, the simulation result shows that the proposed algorithm realizes cooperative hunting in surface-water experiments with obstacles.

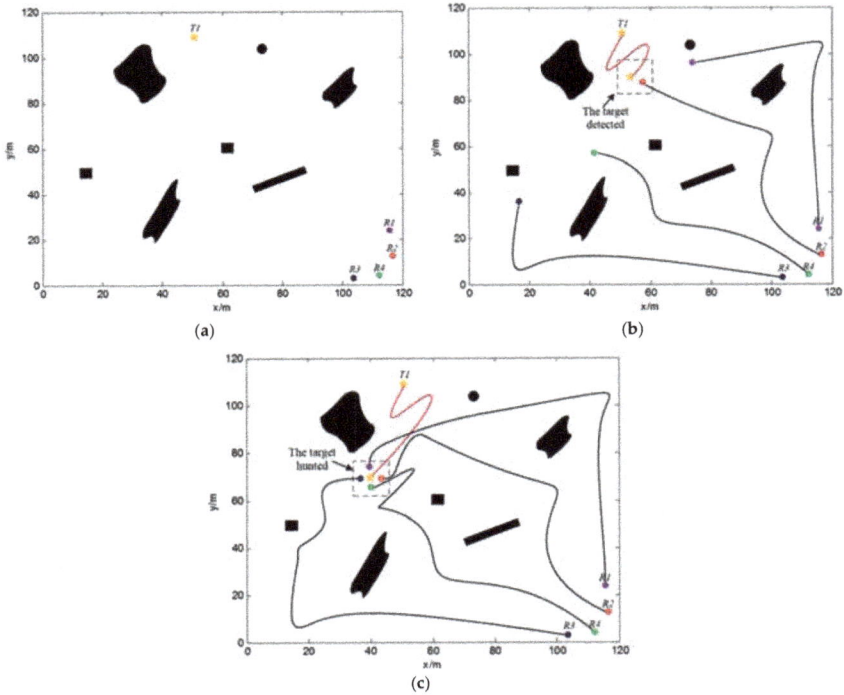

Figure 3. Simulation of hunting process with one target. (**a**) The initial state; (**b**) AUVs' search trajectory for the target; (**c**) Final trajectories of the AUVs.

In order to further validate the performance of the proposed algorithm, the Simulation of hunting process with dynamic obstacle is provided. Figure 4 shows this process of four AUVs hunting target and avoid dynamic obstacles clearly. The results show in the Figure 4, it validates that it is available to apply the proposed algorithm to the multi-AUV hunting task, and it can effectively avoid dynamic obstacle in path planning.

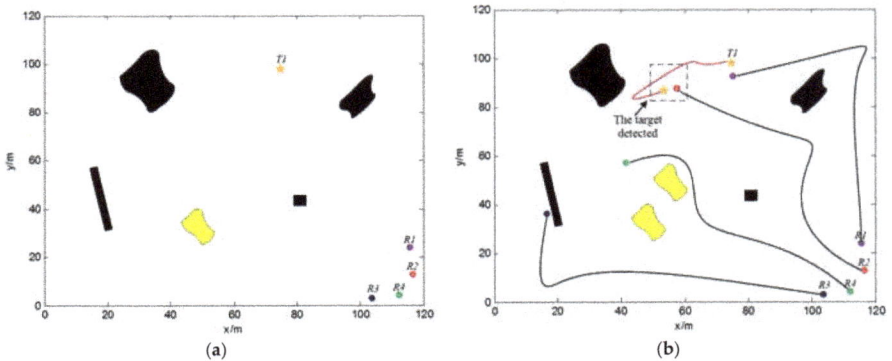

Figure 4. *Cont.*

(c)

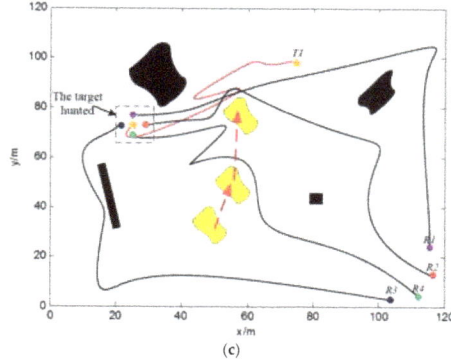

Figure 4. Simulation of hunting process with dynamic obstacle. (**a**) The initial state; (**b**) AUVs' search trajectory for the target; (**c**) Final trajectories of the AUVs.

3.2. Multiple Targets

The second simulation is conducted to test the dynamic cooperation when two targets need to be caught. It is assumed that there are two targets and six AUVs. Figure 5 shows this process of six AUVs hunting two targets clearly. Figure 5a shows the distribution of AUVs, targets, and obstacles. As well as hunting one target, six AUVs began searching the work area in different directions. Figure 5b shows AUVs' search trajectory for the first target. Because the target has the same intelligence of AUV except the cooperation, target *T1* will escape. The AUV *R1* will track the target *T1* and send the location information of the target to other AUVs. According to the location of the target *T1*. The multi-AUV system selects the four AUVs closest to the *T1*. *R1*, *R2*, *R3*, and *R4* are assigned to the target *T1*. Since *R5* and *R6* fail in the competition, they will not join in the pursuing task but keep search target. After the completion of the task assignment, the proposed algorithm automatically plans a collision-free pursuing path for each hunter. Figure 5c shows *R1*, *R2*, *R3*, and *R4* hunting trajectory for the first target *T1*. Same principle, the second target *T2* is found by the AUV *R5*, *R6*. The target *T2* is hunted by the AUV *R2*, *R4*, *R5*, and *R6*. Figure 5d shows final trajectories of the AUVs hunting targets. Obviously, the simulation result shows that the proposed algorithm realizes multi-AUV cooperative hunting for two dynamic targets. The results show in the Figure 5, it validates that it is available to apply the proposed algorithm to the multi-AUV hunting task, and it can effectively avoid AUV coordination conflict problem in path planning.

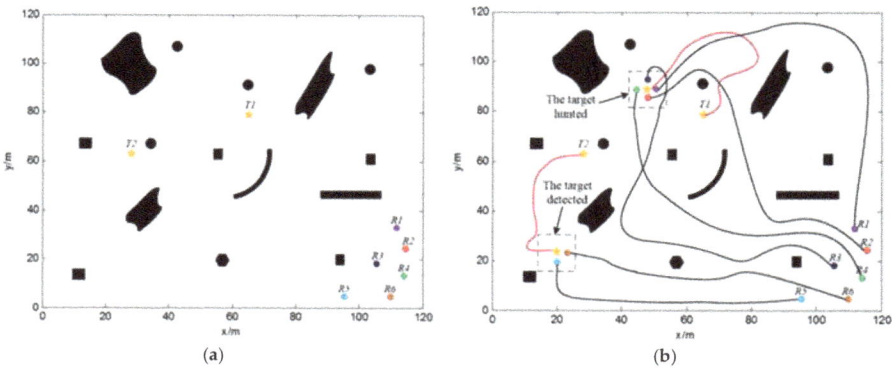

(a)

(b)

Figure 5. *Cont.*

(c)

(d)

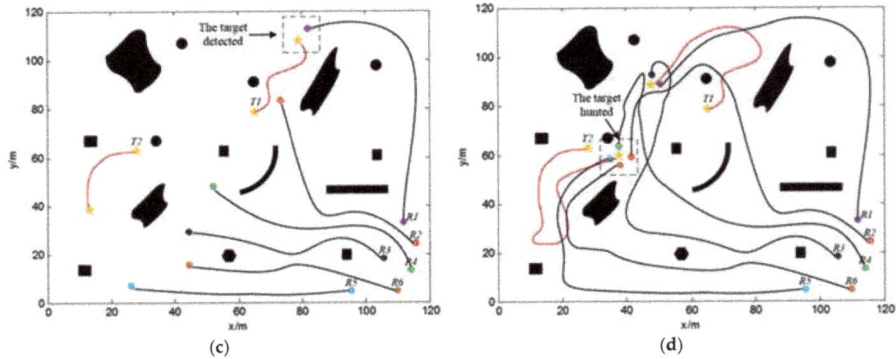

Figure 5. Simulation of hunting process with two targets. (**a**) The initial state; (**b**) AUVs' hunting trajectory for the first target; (**c**) AUVs' search trajectory for the first target; (**d**) Final trajectories of the AUVs.

3.3. Some AUVs Break Down

To prove the robustness of proposed approach, some AUV failures are added in this part of simulation. When search in real surface-water workspaces, it is likely that two AUVs suddenly break down due to mechanical problems. and then it is an important index for measuring the proposed algorithm's cooperation to see whether the multi-AUV work system could complete its search task through internal adjustment. In this case, the simulation deals with AUV failures in the same simulation environment as that in the Section 3.2. There are six AUVs involved in search task for one target. At the beginning, six AUVs are normal search target in the surface-water workspaces. After a period of time, the target *T1* is found by the AUV *R3*. The AUV *R3* will track the target *T1* and send the location information of the target to other AUVs. According to the location of the target *T1*, the multi-AUV system selects the four AUVs closest to the *T1*. *R1*, *R2*, *R3*, and *R6* are assigned to the target *T1*. Since *R4* and *R5* fail in the competition, they will not join in the pursuing task but keep search target. One of the AUVs, *R3*, breaks down in time, but the remaining AUV members still function properly (shown as in Figure 6a). Despite the breakdown of *R3*, AUV *R4* replaces AUV *R3* by reassigning tasks, the whole team is not paralyzed but keeps working on for their hunting task. When coming to the 40th second, the AUV *R6* also fails (shown as in Figure 6b). Since a distributed architecture is adopted, the rest one AUV *R5* will not be affected but go on with their hunt. And at last, the AUVs *R1*, *R2*, *R4*, and *R5* got the target *T1*. The final trajectories of the AUV team (see Figure 6c) show that the proposed algorithm can work satisfactorily in the case of unexpected events, and it does not need any added changes for different situations. From this simulation, it shows that the improved potential field algorithm has the ability to complete search task in the case of AUV mechanical failures through dynamical allocation. This also demonstrates an excellent cooperation of the proposed algorithm.

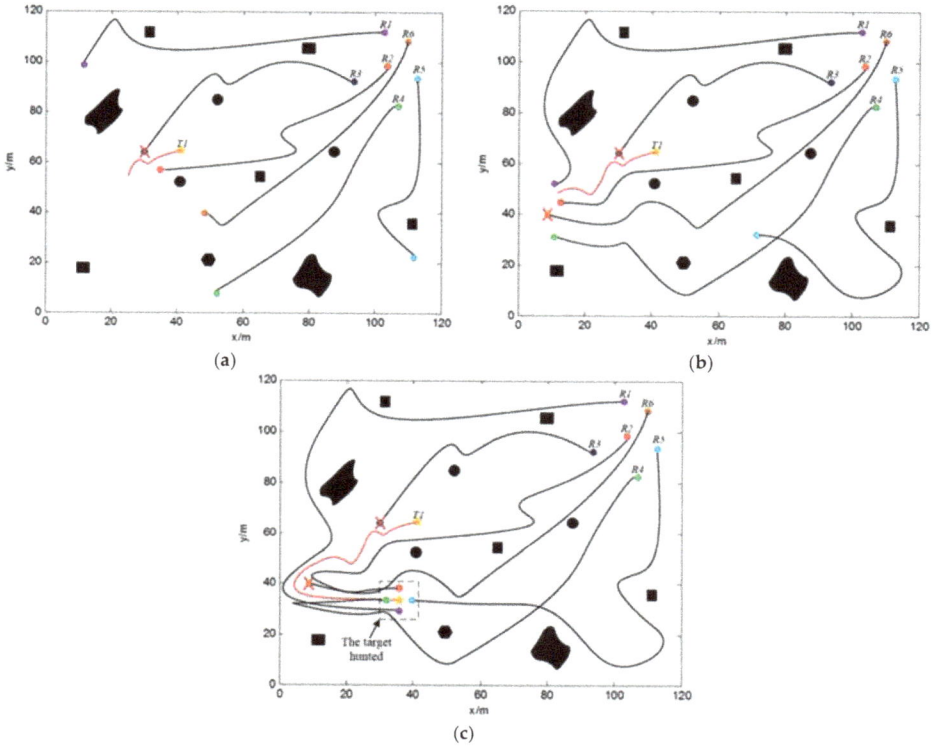

Figure 6. Search process when two AUVs break down. (**a**) The first AUV break down; (**b**) The second AUV breaks down; (**c**) Final trajectories of the whole hunting process.

3.4. Comparison of Different Algorithms

In order to further validate the performance of the proposed algorithm, it is compared with potential field (PF) algorithm. The comparison studies involve six AUVs, two targets, and some obstacles with environments scale of 120×120 (m^2). The target locations, AUVs and obstacles are randomly deployed. The both algorithms are applied to the multi-AUVs that are directed to hunt all the targets. In these conditions, the both algorithms simulation experiments of cooperative hunting were completed 50 times respectively. To make a clear distinction between the two algorithms, Table 1 lists the mean and standard deviation statistics of total path length and hunting time by both algorithms. It is reasonable to conclude that the integrated algorithm of IPF performs better than the PF in each item of simulation results. Hence, it distinguishes itself with the shorter path length and time. By analysis, the PF algorithm doesn't have the function of cooperation for AUVs. However, IPF can not only perform the target hunting, but also it can better complete the task in the environment filled with obstacles.

Table 1. Performance comparison between improved potential field (IPF) and potential field (PF).

Algorithm	Total Path Length (m)	Hunting Time (s)
IPF	845.3 ± 52.1	681.9 ± 30.5
PF	992.7 ± 75.6	807.6 ± 57.3

Appl. Sci. **2018**, *8*, 973

In order to further validate the performance of the proposed algorithm, comparison studies with the particle swarm optimization (PSO) algorithm will be carried out. The PSO algorithm plans a path by iteratively improving a candidate solution with regard to the fitness function. The comparison studies involve one target locations, four AUVs, and some obstacles with environments scale of 120×120 (m^2). The target locations, AUVs and obstacles are randomly deployed. Different algorithms are used to arrange the multi-AUVs to hunt target. Figure 7 shows the search process with four different algorithms. According to the result of Figure 7, the proposed algorithm completes the target hunting task. However, the PSO algorithm failed to hunt time the target because R1 hits an obstacle.

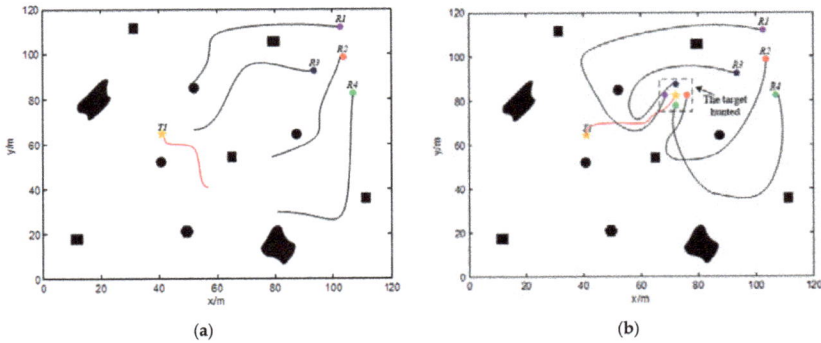

(a) (b)

Figure 7. Hunting path with two different algorithms. (**a**) PSO algorithm; (**b**) IPF algorithm.

In order to ensure the accuracy of the experiments, we conducted the experiments many times. In each experiment, the positions of the obstacles, targets, and AUVs are reset. The success rate of performing 50 times of target hunting using two different algorithms is depicted in Figure 7.

It is very clear to see that the proposed IPF algorithm reaches 100% success rate under a large number of experiments in Figure 8. It means that the most tasks are successfully executed. However, the PSO algorithm only reaches 100% success rate for a few experiments. In some special cases, the success rate of PSO algorithm is only 80%. By comparison, it is found that under certain circumstances, the success rate of the proposed IPF algorithm is below 100%, but it is still superior to the PSO algorithm. By analysis, the PSO algorithm only provides optimum solution under no obstacle conditions. However, IPF works properly for obstacle avoidance, therefore it deserves a high success rate in the environments filled with obstacles.

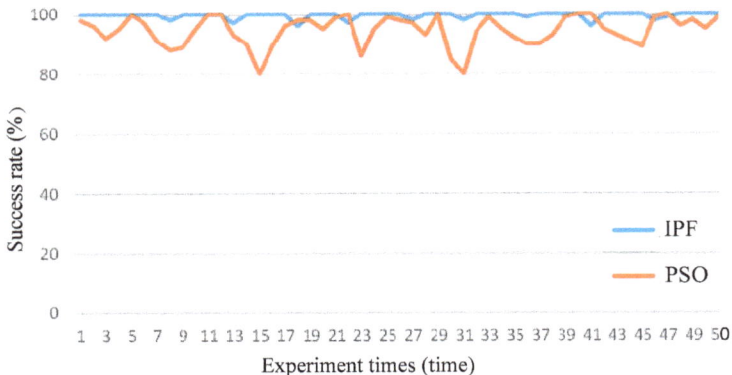

Figure 8. Success rate comparison between IPF and PSO algorithms.

4. Conclusions

In this paper, an integrated algorithm combining the potential field and the three degrees (the dispersion degree, the homodromous degree, and district-difference degree) is proposed to deal with cooperative target hunting by multi-AUV team in surface-water environment. On the one hand, it makes full use of the advantages of potential field, i.e., no pre-learning procedure and good real-time. On the other hand, the three degrees could improve the multi-AUV's cooperation and overcome local minimum problem. Despite these advantages, there are still practical problems to be researched further. For example, how should AUVs overcome the effects of ocean currents in a surface-water environment during their hunting process. The real surface-water environment is three-dimensional, while, in this paper, many factors are simplified into a two-dimensional simulation. There is still a necessity to carry on further studies on how to solve these problems.

Author Contributions: Conceptualization, H.G. and G.X.; Methodology, G.C.; Software, H.G.; Validation, H.G., G.C. and G.X.; Formal Analysis, H.G.; Investigation, G.C.; Resources, G.C.; Data Curation, H.G.; Writing-Original Draft Preparation, H.G.; Writing-Review & Editing, G.X.; Supervision, G.X.; Project Administration, H.G.; Funding Acquisition, H.G.

Funding: This work was supported by the University-industry cooperation prospective project of Jiangsu Province: Development of intelligent universal color-selecting and drying grain machine (BY2016062-01).

Conflicts of Interest: The authors declare no conflict of interest.

References

1. Cui, R.; Ge, S.S.; How, B.V.E.; Choo, Y. Leader-follower formation control of under actuated autonomous underwater vehicles. *Ocean Eng.* **2010**, *37*, 1491–1502. [CrossRef]
2. Huang, Z.R.; Zhu, D.Q.; Sun, B. A multi-AUV cooperative hunting method in 3-D underwater environment with obstacle. *Eng. Appl. Artif. Intell.* **2016**, *50*, 192–200. [CrossRef]
3. Cao, X.; Sun, C.Y. A potential field-based PSO approach to multi-robot cooperation for target search and hunting. *At-Automatisierungstechnik* **2017**, *65*, 878–887. [CrossRef]
4. Zhang, Q.; Lapoerre, L.; Xiang, X.B. Distributed control of coordinated path tracking for networked nonholonomic mobile vehicles. *IEEE Trans. Ind. Inform.* **2013**, *9*, 472–484. [CrossRef]
5. Rezaee, H.; Abdollahi, F. A decentralized cooperative control scheme with obstacle avoidance for a team of mobile robots. *IEEE Trans. Ind. Electron.* **2014**, *61*, 347–354. [CrossRef]
6. Yamaguchi, H. A distributed motion coordination strategy for multiple nonholonomic mobile robots in cooperative hunting operations. *Robot. Autom. Syst.* **2003**, *43*, 257–282. [CrossRef]
7. Pan, Y.; Li, D. Improvement with joint rewards on multi-agent cooperative reinforcement learning. In Proceedings of the International Conference on Computer Science and Software Engineering, Wuhan, China, 12–14 December 2008; pp. 536–539.
8. Ma, Y.; Cao, Z.; Dong, X.; Zhou, C.; Tan, M. A multi-robot coordinated hunting strategy with dynamic alliance. In Proceedings of the Control and Decision Conference, Guilin, China, 17–19 June 2009; pp. 2338–2342.
9. Wang, C.; Zhang, T.; Wang, K.; Lv, S.; Ma, H. A new approach of multi-robot cooperative pursuit. In Proceedings of the China Control Conference, Xi'an, China, 26–28 July 2013; pp. 7252–7256.
10. Ni, J.; Yang, S.X. Bioinspired neural network for real-time cooperative hunting by multirobots in unknown environments. *IEEE Trans. Neural Netw.* **2011**, *22*, 2062–2077. [PubMed]
11. Liang, X.W.; Liu, Y.H.; Wang, H.; Chen, W.D.; Xing, K.X.; Liu, T. Leader-following formation tracking control of mobile robots without direct position measurements. *IEEE Trans. Autom. Control* **2016**, *61*, 4131–4137. [CrossRef]
12. Qin, J.H.; Yu, C.B.; Gao, H.J. Coordination for linear multiagent systems with dynamic interaction topology in the leader-following framework. *IEEE Trans. Ind. Electron.* **2014**, *61*, 2412–2422. [CrossRef]
13. Garcia, M.A.P.; Montiel, O.; Castillo, O.; Sepulveda, R.; Melin, P. Path planning for autonomous mobile robot navigation with ant colony optimization and fuzzy cost function evaluation. *Appl. Soft Comput.* **2009**, *9*, 1102–1110. [CrossRef]
14. Zhu, D.Q.; Lv, R.F.; Cao, X.; Yang, S.X. Multi-AUV hunting algorithm based on bio-inspired neural network in unknown environments. *Int. J. Adv. Robot. Syst.* **2015**, *12*, 1–12. [CrossRef]

15. Sheng, Y.; Sayed, A.H. Cooperative prey herding based on diffusion adaptation. In Proceedings of the IEEE International Conference on Acoustics, Speech and Signal Processing, Prague, Czech Republic, 22–27 May 2011; pp. 3752–3755.

16. Cetin, O.; Zagli, I.; Yilmaz, G. Establishing obstacle and collision free communication relay for UAVs with artificial potential fields. *J. Intell. Robot. Syst.* **2013**, *69*, 361–372. [CrossRef]

17. Shi, W.R.; Huang, X.H.; Zhou, W. Path planning of mobile robot based on improved artificial potential field. *Int. J. Comput. Appl.* **2010**, *30*, 2021–2023. [CrossRef]

18. Couceiro, M.S.; Vargas, P.A.; Rocha, R.P.; Ferreira, N.M.F. Benchmark of swarm robotics distributed techniques in a search task. *Robot. Autom. Syst.* **2014**, *62*, 200–213. [CrossRef]

19. Rasekhipour, Y.; Khajepour, A.; Chen, S.K.; Litkouhi, B. A potential field-based model predictive path-planning controller for autonomous road vehicles. *IEEE Trans. Intell. Transp. Syst.* **2017**, *18*, 1255–1267. [CrossRef]

20. Ge, S.Z.S.; Liu, X.M.; Goh, C.H.; Xu, L.G. Formation tracking control of multiagents in constrained space. *IEEE Trans. Control Syst. Technol.* **2016**, *24*, 992–1003. [CrossRef]

21. Chen, H.; Xie, L. A novel artificial potential field-based reinforcement learning for mobile robotics in ambient intelligence. *Int. J. Robot. Autom.* **2009**, *24*, 245–254. [CrossRef]

22. Zhang, J.R.; Sun, C.; Mizutani, E. *Neuro-Fuzzy and Soft Computing: A Computational Approach to Learning and Machine Intelligence*; Prentice Hall: New York, NY, USA, 1997.

23. Wang, Z.X.; Chen, Z.T.; Zhao, Y.; Niu, Q. A novel local maximum potential point search algorithm for topology potential field. *Int. J. Hybrid Inf. Technol.* **2014**, *7*, 1–8. [CrossRef]

24. Kao, C.C.; Lin, C.M.; Juang, J.G. Application of potential field method and optimal path planning to mobile robot control. In Proceedings of the 2015 IEEE International Conference on Robotics and Automation Automation Science and Engineering (CASE), Gothenburg, Sweden, 24–28 August 2015; pp. 1552–1554.

25. Liu, X.; Ge, S.S.; Goh, C.H. Formation potential field for trajectory tracking control of multi-agents in constrained space. *Int. J. Control* **2017**, *90*, 2137–2151. [CrossRef]

26. Haumann, A.D.; Listmann, K.D.; Willert, V. DisCoverage: A new paradigm for multi-robot exploration. In Proceedings of the 2010 IEEE International Conference on Robotics and Automation, Anchorage, AK, USA, 3–7 May 2010; pp. 924–934.

27. Li, B.; Du, H.; Li, W. A Potential field approach-based trajectory control for autonomous electric vehicles with in-wheel motors. *IEEE Trans. Intell. Transp. Syst.* **2017**, *18*, 2044–2055. [CrossRef]

![applied sciences logo]

applied sciences

MDPI

Article

3D Model Identification Using Weighted Implicit Shape Representation and Panoramic View

Xun Jin [1] and Jongweon Kim [2],*

[1] Department of Copyright Protection, Sangmyung University, Seoul 03016, Korea; jinxun@cclabs.kr
[2] Department of Electronics Engineering, Sangmyung University, Seoul 03016, Korea
* Correspondence: jwkim@smu.ac.kr; Tel.: +82-222-875-410

Received: 7 July 2017; Accepted: 25 July 2017; Published: 27 July 2017

Abstract: In this paper, we propose a 3 dimensional (3D) model identification method based on weighted implicit shape representation (WISR) and panoramic view. The WISR is used for 3D shape normalization. The 3D shape normalization method normalizes a 3D model by scaling, translation, and rotation with respect to the scale factor, center, and principal axes. The major advantage of the WISR is reduction of the influences caused by shape deformation and partial removal. The well-known scale-invariant feature transform descriptors are extracted from the panoramic view of the 3D model for feature matching. The panoramic view is a range image obtained by projecting a 3D model to the surface of a cylinder which is parallel to a principal axis determined by the 3D shape normalization. Because of using only one range image, the proposed method can provide small size of features and fast matching speed. The precision of the identification is 92% with 1200 models that consist of 24 deformed versions of 50 classes. The average feature size and matching time are 4.1 KB and 1.9 s.

Keywords: 3D model identification; shape normalization; weighted implicit shape representation; panoramic view; scale-invariant feature transform

1. Introduction

Development of 3 dimensional (3D) printing technology has led to the explosive growth of 3D models recently. Hence the 3D printing services are increasing rapidly [1,2]. However, copyright infringement of 3D models has become an issue for 3D printing ecosystem of product distribution websites, 3D scanning and design-sharing [3,4]. To prevent the copyrighted 3D models from distributing and using illegally, the identification of 3D models remains.

2 dimensional (2D) view-based 3D model identification has a high discriminative property for 3D model representation [5–11]. Generally, a 2D view image is a range image obtained from a viewpoint located on a 3D model's bounding sphere. The identification is implemented by matching the features extracted from the range images. However, the existent approaches suffer from big size of features and slow matching speed. To overcome these problems, we propose an approach using only one range image, which means a panoramic view is used for identification. The panoramic view bridges the gaps between the range images rendered from multiple views. It is obtained by projecting a 3D model onto the surface of a cylinder, which is parallel to a principal axis determined by 3D shape normalization. The purpose of the 3D shape normalization is to normalize 3D models into a canonical coordinate frame to guarantee a unique representation [12–14]. Nevertheless, how to determine the principal axes is the keypoint. The most common method is principal component analysis (PCA). However, it is not preferable when 3D models have unobvious orientations or undergo large deformations. If the shape normalization cannot determine the principal axes of a query model as similar as those of original model in database, the identification needs many more range images to match them. Implicit shape

representation (ISR) was described in [13] for normalizing 3D articulated models. However, it has some limitations when some parts of a 3D model are removed or when a 3D model undergoes a large deformation. In this paper, the 3D shape normalization uses a weighted ISR (WISR) to reduce the influence caused by shape deformation and partial removal. It estimates the number of clusters based on rate distortion theory [15]. It also shows the most representative part for one viewpoint of the six degree of freedom.

After the shape normalization, the model is wrapped by the cylinder to generate a range image. The range image is used for providing features of the model. The feature used in our approach is the scale invariant feature transform (SIFT) descriptor [16]. The SIFT is generally used to extract geometric transformation invariant local features from images [17,18]. It detects interest points called keypoints and assigns orientation information to each keypoint based on local gradient directions. With the SIFT descriptor, object recognition approaches can achieve high performance in feature matching. In this paper, the 3D models are identified by matching the SIFT descriptors of the query model with those in database. In the section of experimental results, we show the comparisons between the precision of identification of the proposed method and those of other methods.

2. Related Work

Several researches have been conducted to group 3D models into corresponding categories by matching the features and comparing the similarities of the models [5–11,14,19–22]. The matching and comparison are implemented on a huge dataset containing various models of different poses and shapes. The models are mainly classified into two types: rigid models and non-rigid (deformable) models. Early works are rigid model-based approaches. In this paper, we focus on the identification of non-rigid models.

3D model identification methods are classified into two categories: view-based and model-based methods [6,7]. Model based methods include geometric moment [19], volumetric descriptor [20], surface distribution [21], surface geometry [22]. However, the geometry and topology based methods are generally computationally cost and are fragile to 3D model removal. View-based methods have a high discriminative property for 3D model representation [5–11]. A 2D view image is a range image obtained from a viewpoint located on a 3D model's bounding sphere. After the range image is obtained, image processing technologies are applied to the range image for extracting features. To be invariant against geometrical transformation, researchers proposed shape normalization methods to preprocess the 3D models before extracting the features.

Several view-based methods have been proposed. In Ref. [9], authors proposed a view based 3D model retrieval method using the SIFT and a bag-of-features approach. The bag-of-features was inspired by the bag-of-words in the text retrieval approach, which classifies documents by histograms of words in the text. The method extracted SIFT features from the range images of the model viewed from dozens of viewpoints located uniformly around the model. The bag-of-features was composed of the SIFT features. The well-known k-means clustering algorithm was applied to the bag-of-features to classify the features and generate visual words. The visual words are integrated in to a histogram and become a feature vector of the model. However, the large number of the range images leads to large capacity of features and slow matching speed.

In [10,11], authors proposed 3D model descriptors using the panoramic views which can describe the orientation and position of the model's surface. In [10], the panoramic views were obtained by projecting the model to surfaces of cylinders parallel to three principal axes. The principal axes were obtained by using continuous PCA and normal PCA. For each cylinder, the coefficients of 2D discrete Fourier transform and 2D discrete wavelet transform were extracted to generate the 3D shape descriptors. However, these descriptors are not suitable for distinguishing the 3D models well. In [11], the exes were perpendicular to the surfaces of a dodecahedron generated around the model. Three panoramic views were obtained from each axis. The other two panoramic views were obtained from additional two axes which are orthogonal to each other and to the principal axis. Then, the SIFT features were extracted to generate the 3D model descriptors. However, because of using dozens of panoramic views, the method leads to large capacity of features and slow matching speed.

In [8], authors normalized the model with the PCA and extracted 18 views from the vertices of a bounding 32-hedron of the model. The 3D model descriptors were composed of 2D Zernike moments, 2D Krawtchouk moments and coefficients of Fourier transform. However, the PCA is fragile to partial removed and deformed models, which means the PCA can't extract the same axes from the deformed and removed models as those of original models. Hence, the different axes lead to different views and descriptors. Eventually, the method can't identify the deformed and partial removed versions of the original models.

In [13], authors proposed a shape normalization method for 3D volumetric models using ISR. The ISR is a set of minimum Euclidean distance values between the surface of the model and the voxels inside the surface. It is invariant to translation and rotation. The method computed an initial center of the model with the ISR and voxels inside the model. It also computed an initial principal axis with the PCA. Then the center and three principal axes were iteratively upgraded based on implicit intensity value and principal axis dependent weight function. Finally, the method translated, rotated and scaled the model with the final center, principal axes and a scale factor which was computed with the ISR.

In [23], the competition results of SHREC 2015 range scans based 3D shape retrieval were presented. The best performance was achieved by a SIFT based cross-domain manifold ranking method. However the precision was about 70%. In [24], the results of the SHREC 2015 Track: Non-rigid 3D shape retrieval were presented. The best performance was achieved by a method of super vector-local statistical features. However, the local statistical feature extraction and matching is time consuming. The matching time is over 50 s for 907 models [25].

In [26], authors proposed a view-based 3D model retrieval method using bipartite graph matching and multi-feature collaboration. The complement descriptors were extracted from the interior region and contour of 3D models. The employed three types of features: Zernike moments, bag of visual words descriptor and Fourier descriptor to construct bipartite graphs. However, because of using various types of features, it is time consuming.

In [27], the discriminative information of 2D projective views were learned for 3D model retrieval. The dissimilarity between discriminative ability and view's semantic is investigated by classification performance. An effective and simple measurement is used to study the discriminative ability. The discriminative information is used for view set matching with a reverse distance metric. Various features were employed to boost the retrieval method. However, each model was represented by 216 views. The feature size is too large. The querying time is 1.7 s for 330 models. It is also time consuming.

In 2015, five leading feature extraction algorithms: SIFT, speeded-up robust features, binary robust independent elementary features, binary robust invariant scalable keypoints and Fast retina keypoint, were used to generate keypoint descriptors of radiographs for classification of bone age assessment [28]. After comparing the five algorithms, the SIFT was found to perform best based on precision. In 2016, a survey was presented to evaluate various object recognition methods based on local invariant features from a robotics perspective [29]. The evaluation results reported that the best performing keypoint descriptor is the SIFT and it is very robust to real-world conditions. Based on the previous research results on pattern recognition and computer vision, we decide to extract the SIFT descriptors as the features of 3D models.

3. 3D Shape Normalization Using WISR

3D shape normalization is a process of adjusting the orientation, location, and size of a given 3D model into a canonical coordinate frame. A 3D model is usually composed of a main body part and branch parts (e.g., arms and legs). To reduce the effect caused by the deformation or abscission of branch parts when determining the principal axes, we increase the weight of the main body part. The procedure of weight calculation requires three steps. The first step is automatically estimating the number of clusters based on rate distortion theory [15]. With the clustering method, we can distinguish the main body part and the branch parts. However, different 3D models have different shapes and topologies that lead to different main body and branch parts. Therefore, a method of automatically estimating the number of clusters is required. The second step is performing the k-means algorithm with the estimated number and calculating the distance among cluster centers. The third step is calculating the number of points inside each cluster sphere. Generally, the number of points inside a main body part is greater than that of a branch part. Thus the weight is obtained based on the number of points.

First of all, N random points $P = \{p_i | i = 1, \ldots, N\}$ are generated inside the surface of a model. A measure of cluster dispersion called distortion d is defined as Equation (1). It is derived from Mahalanobis distance.

$$d = \sum_{i=1}^{N} \left(p_i - c_{p_i}\right)^{\mathrm{T}} \Gamma^{-1} \left(p_i - c_{p_i}\right) \tag{1}$$

where Γ is the covariance and c_{p_i} is the closest center to a given point p_i. The cluster centers are obtained by using the k-means algorithm. We iteratively fit $k \in \{1, K\}$ clusters to the points P. Therefore, there are K distortions d_k corresponding to K clusters. Each d_k denotes cluster dispersion of k clusters. After evaluating the distortions with 1 to K partitions, the d_k is transformed as follows

$$J_k = d_k^{-\frac{m}{2}} - d_{k-1}^{-\frac{m}{2}} \tag{2}$$

where m is the dimension of the points, thus m is equal to 3. The $-\frac{m}{2}$ is a transform power motivated by asymptotic reasoning. The number of clusters is set to be $k' = \mathrm{argmax}_k\{J_k\}$. The k' is the ideal number of clusters. Then the k-means algorithm is performed to partition the P into k' clusters. The points near the boundaries of clusters interfere with the relation between the points and the main body and branch parts. Therefore, we only consider the points inside a sphere with a specific radius. First we compute a distance cd between two cluster centers as follows:

$$cd_{a,b} = \sqrt{(c_a - c_b)^2}, \, a, b = 1, \ldots, k' \tag{3}$$

Then we can obtain $C = k' - 1 + k' - 2 +, \ldots, + k' - (k' - 1)$ distances. The radius is defined as $r = \min\{cd_{a,b}\}/2$. The weight of each cluster is the number of nearest points within the radius from each center. The nearest points set of the jth cluster center c_j is defined as $S_j = \left\{i \middle| \sqrt{(c_j - p_i)^2} \leq r\right\}$.

The weight w_j of cluster j is the the number of the elements in the S_j. The ISR is defined as $f(p) = \min\{||p - q||\}$, which is the minimum Euclidean distance from p to vertices q on the surface of the model. The w_j is applied to the ISR of nearest points of cluster center j to produce WISR as follows

$$f'(p_i) = \begin{cases} f(p_i) \cdot w_j, \, if \, i \in S_j. \\ f(p_i), \, otherwise. \end{cases} \tag{4}$$

The points nearest to the cluster center inside a main body are much more than those inside a branch. Therefore, the weight of the main body will be increased, whereas that of the branch will be decreased. To reduce the influence of surface deformation of main body, we quantize the WISR and delete some values which are less than a specified threshold. We use search-based optimization of Otsu's criterion to find 5 thresholds $T = \{t_i | i = 1, \ldots, 5\}$. We delete the values of $f'(p_i)$ by setting them to be 0, if they are less than t_2. The ISR and WISR of a mouse model are shown in Figure 1. To illustrate their salient characteristic more clearly, the figures are shown in xy-plane.

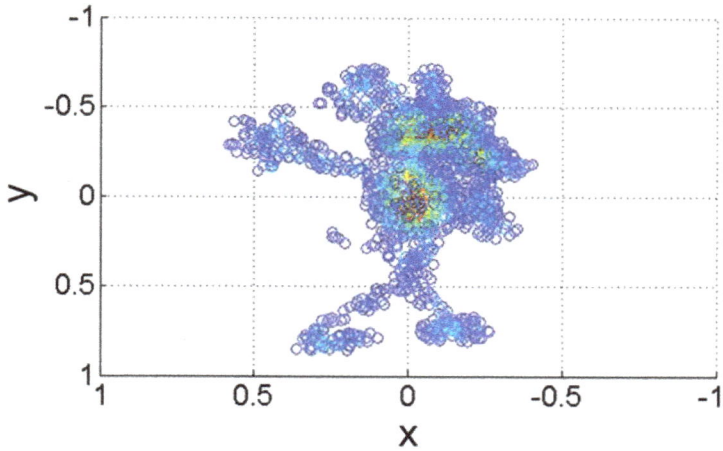

(a)

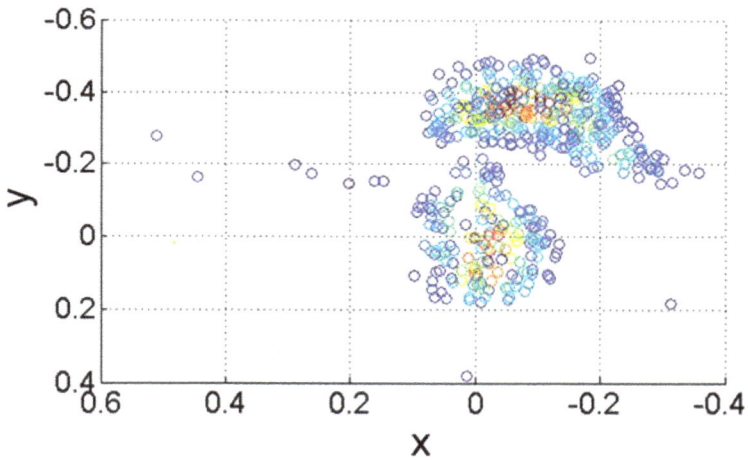

(b)

Figure 1. ISR (implicit shape representation) and WISR (weighted implicit shape representation) of mouse model; (**a**) ISR; (**b**) WISR.

The principal axes are calculated by singular value decomposition. The points p corresponding to the existing $f'(p_i)$ are selected for analyzing the principal axes. The center of gravity of a model is defined as

$$o = \frac{\sum_{i=1}^{N}(f'(p_i) \cdot p_i)}{\sum_{i=1}^{N} f'(p_i)} \tag{5}$$

It is moved to the origin of coordinate to solve the normalization of translation. It represents the weighted average of all points in a model. It is much closer to the center of main body than conventional barycenter. To normalize a model size, a scale factor is defined as follows

$$s = \sqrt[3]{\sum_{i=1}^{N} f'(p_i)}$$ (6)

It is based on the volume of the model and is effective in normalizing the 3D model size. Finally, the 3D model is normalized by achieving scaling, translation, and rotation with respect to the scale factor, center, and principal axes.

4. Panoramic View Generation

Once the shape normalization has been done, one panoramic view will be generated. First, a cylinder is generated around a 3D model as shown in Figure 2a. Its center and axis are the center and the first principal axis of the model. Its radius is defined as $R = 2 \cdot \max\{||o - q||\}$. Its height is the height of the model. We sample the axis of the cylinder with a sample rate F. Each sample point of the axis is a center of a cross section of the cylinder. For each cross section, M rays are emanated from each center to the surface of the cylinder. Thus, the degree between each ray is $2\pi/M$. Each ray may have more than 1 intersection with the surface of the model. The distance $rd \in [0, R]$ from a center to the furthest intersection of the ray is mapped to a value in the range of $[0, 1]$ for representing one pixel in the $F \times M$ range image. After generating the panoramic view, SIFT descriptors are extracted from the panoramic view and stored as the feature of the model. Figure 2b shows the SIFT descriptors of panoramic view-based range image.

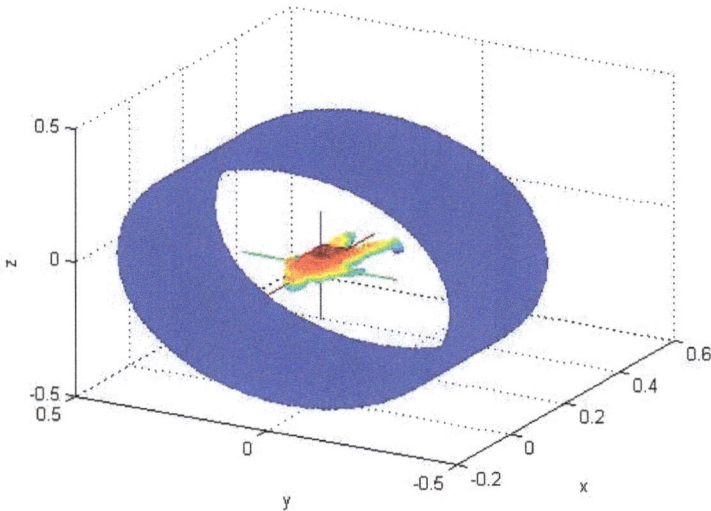

(a)

Figure 2. *Cont.*

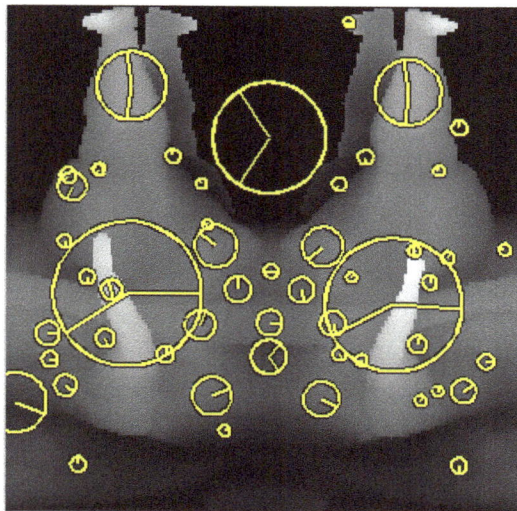

(**b**)

Figure 2. The cylinder around a model and its panoramic view-based range image; (**a**) Cylinder; (**b**) Panoramic view-based range image.

The matching procedure of the SIFT descriptors uses the Euclidean distance as in [16]. Suppose the SIFT descriptor of a query model is $VQ = (vq_1, vq_2, \ldots, vq_n)$ and that of a model in database is $VD = (vd_1, vd_2, \ldots, vd_n)$. The distance D between the two descriptor is given by

$$D = \sqrt{\sum_{i=1}^{n}(vq_i - vd_i)^2},$$ (7)

A keypoint with the least distance value is defined as a matched keypoint. We match the keypoints of the query model to those of the models in the database and obtain the number of matched keypoints. Finally, we identify the model with the maximum number of matched keypoints as the original model of the query model.

5. Experimental Results

In this section, some experimental results about the shape normalizations are shown first. To achieve high precision of 3D model identification, how to accurately normalize the shapes of the models is of great significance in practice. Figure 3a,c are original sumotori and tortoise models. Figure 3b is deformed version of sumotori model by articulating around its joints in different ways. Figure 3d is partially removed version of tortoise model. There is a certain extent of difference between the original models and deformed and removed models. If we extract 6 range images from each view point of six degree of freedom, we can obtain 24 possible poses of a 3D model [8]. We only selected the most representative range image from all possible poses of a model. Figure 4a–l show the range images which have the most representative surface of the models using PCA, ISR, and WISR, respectively. The main body and face in Figure 4b are oblique. Figure 4d shows left side of the model. Figure 4f,h show the range images were viewed obliquely from above. Both Figure 4j,l show their fronts to a view point, which means the deformed and removed models were well normalized using WISR.

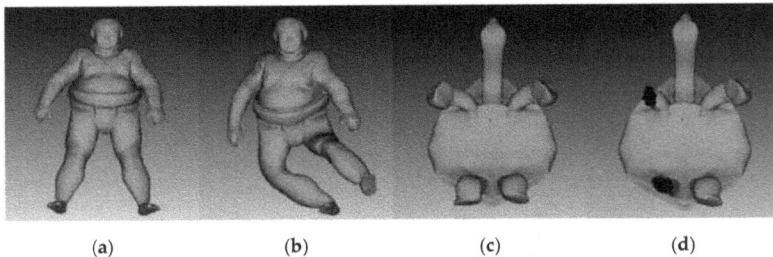

Figure 3. Original, deformed and partially removed 3D models; (a): original sumotori model; (b): deformed sumotori model; (c): original tortoise model; (d): partially removed tortoise model.

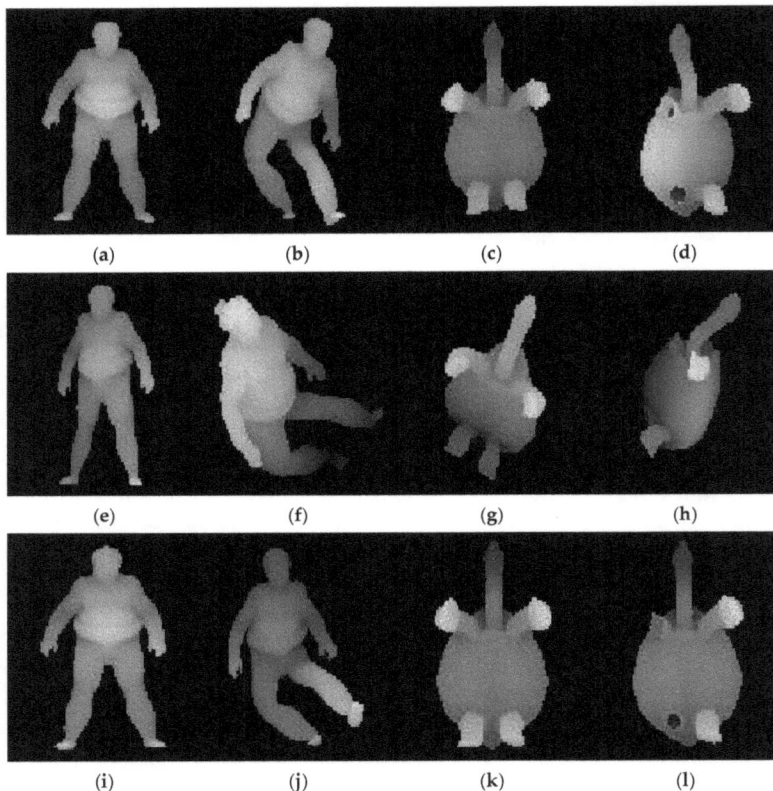

Figure 4. The most representative range images of shape normalized models using PCA (a–d): original and deformed sumotori model, original and partially removed tortoise model; ISR (e–h): original and deformed sumotori model, original and partially removed tortoise model; and WISR (i–l): original and deformed sumotori model, original and partially removed tortoise model.

We evaluated the proposed identification method with 1200 non-rigid 3D models in SHREC 2015 benchmark. The models consist of 24 deformed versions of 50 classes. We selected one model for each class to compose 50 query models. We also experimented with the other 3D model identification methods: combination of PCA and SIFT (PCAS) [9], that of continuous PCA, normal PCA, 2D discrete

Fourier transform, and 2D discrete wavelet transform (CPCA) [10], and that of dodecahedron and SIFT (DODE) [11]. Two types of experiments were performed to evaluate the performances of the methods. First one is to identify the 50 original query models. Then we removed some parts of the models such as arms and legs. Second experiment is to identify the 50 partially removed query models. The percentage of removal ranges from 6.1% to 33.6%. The average percentage is 13.8%. We set the range of the number of clusters from 1 to 10, which means the K is set to 10. Both the sample rate F and the number of rays M are set to be 180. We performed the experiments on an IBM compatible computer with a 3.4 GHz CPU and a 4 GB random-access memory. The average feature size and matching time of the corresponding method for 1200 models are shown in Table 1. Because of using only one range image, the proposed method provides small size of feature and fast matching speed. Figure 5 shows the precision of identification for each method. Although the feature size is greatly reduced, the precision is still greater than those of the other 3 methods even with the removed versions.

Table 1. Average feature size and matching time; PCAS: combination of PCA and SIFT; CPCA: combination of continuous PCA, normal PCA, 2D discrete Fourier transform, and 2D discrete wavelet transform; DODE: combination of dodecahedron and SIFT.

Method	PCAS	CPCA	DODE	Proposed
Size (KB)	19.4	36	110.1	4.1
Time (s)	26.4	80.3	223.5	1.9

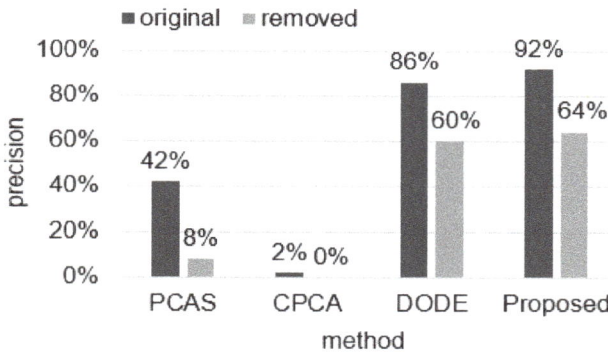

Figure 5. Precision of 3D model identification.

6. Conclusions

In this paper, we have proposed a 3D model identification method, which consists of WISR-based 3D shape normalization and panoramic view for feature extraction. To achieve high precision of 3D model identification with 2D view-based approach, how to accurately normalize the shapes of the models has great significance in practice. The proposed 3D shape normalization clusters random points inside a model and defines the number of nearest neighbors within a specified radius from each cluster center as the weight. The weight is applied to ISR to produce WISR for reducing the influence caused by shape deformation and partial removal. A panoramic view is generated by projecting a 3D model onto the surface of a cylinder for extracting SIFT descriptors. The average feature size and matching time are 4.1 KB and 1.9 s. The precision of identification of original models is 92% and that of removed versions is 64%. The experimental results show the performance of the 3D model identification is significantly improved. In the future work, we will optimize the identification method and increase the precision of the identification.

Acknowledgments: This research project was supported by Ministry of Science, ICT and Future Planning in 2016.

Author Contributions: Both authors contributed to the research work. Both authors designed the new method and planned the experiments. Jongweon Kim led and reviewed the research work. Xun Jin performed the experiments and wrote the paper.

Conflicts of Interest: The authors declare no conflict of interest.

References

1. Ishengoma, F.R.; Mtaho, A.B. 3D Printing Developing Countries Perspectives. *Int. J. Comput. Appl.* **2014**, *104*, 30–34.
2. Harris, A. The Effects of In-home 3D Printing on Product Liability Law. Available online: http://www.sciencepolicyjournal.org/uploads/5/4/3/4/5434385/harris_new_ta1_1.2.2015_lb_mg.pdf (accessed on 15 May 2017).
3. Gupta, D.; Tarlock, M. 3D Printing, Copyright Challenges, and the DMCA. *New Matter* **2013**, *38*.
4. Lee, S.H.; Kwon, S.G.; Lee, E.J.; Moon, K.S.; Hwang, W.J.; Kwon, K.R. Watermarking scheme for copyright protection of 3D animated model. In Proceedings of the IEEE Consumer Communications and Networking Conference (CCNC), Las Vegas, NV, USA, 14–17 January 2012; pp. 1–4.
5. Jain, S.; Mishra, S. Survey Paper on Various 3D View Based Retrieval Methods. *Int. J. Eng. Res. Technol.* **2014**, *3*, 470–473.
6. Liu, Q. A Survey of Recent View-Based 3D Model Retrieval Methods. Available online: https://arxiv.org/abs/1208.3670 (accessed on 15 May 2017).
7. Ali, S.; Tran, T.; Laurendeau, D. A Comparative Survey on 3D Models Retrieval Methods. *REV J. Electron. Commun.* **2013**, *3*. [CrossRef]
8. Daras, P.; Axenopoulos, A. A Compact Multi-View Descript or for 3D Object Retrieval. In Proceedings of the International Workshop on CBMI, Chania, Greece, 3–5 June 2009; pp. 115–119.
9. Ohbuchi, R.; Osada, K.; Furuya, T.; Banno, T. Salient Local Visual Features for Shape-Based 3D Model Retrieval. In Proceedings of the IEEE International Conference on Shape Modeling and Applications (SMI'08), Stony Brook, New York, NY, USA, 4–6 June 2008; pp. 93–102.
10. Papadakis, P.; Pratikakis, I.; Theoharis, T.; Perantonis, S. PANORAMA: A 3D Shape Descriptor Based on Panoramic Views for Unsupervised 3D Object Retrieval. *Int. J. Comput. Vis.* **2010**, *89*, 177–192. [CrossRef]
11. Sfikas, K.; Pratikakis, I.; Theoharis, T. 3D object retrieval via range image queries based on sift descriptors on panoramic views. In Proceedings of the Eurographics Workshop on 3D Object Retrieval (EG3DOR), Cagliari, Italy, 13 May 2012; pp. 9–15.
12. Cortadellas, J.; Amat, J.; Torre, F. Robust normalization of silhouettes for recognition applications. *Pattern Recognit. Lett.* **2004**, *25*, 591–601. [CrossRef]
13. Wang, C.; Liu, Y.S.; Liu, M.; Yong, J.H.; Paul, J.C. Robust shape normalization of 3D articulated volumetric models. *Comput. Aided Des.* **2012**, *44*, 1253–1268. [CrossRef]
14. Vranic, D.; Saupe, D. 3D shape descriptor based on 3D fourier transform. In Proceedings of the EURASIP Conference on Digital Signal Processing for Multimedia Communications and Services, Budapest, Hungary, 11–13 September 2001; pp. 271–274.
15. Sugar, C.A.; James, G.M. Finding the number of clusters in a data set: An information theoretic approach. *J. Am. Stat. Assoc.* **2003**, *98*, 750–763. [CrossRef]
16. Lowe, D.G. Distinctive image features from scale-invariant keypoints. *Int. J. Comput. Vis.* **2004**, *60*, 91–110. [CrossRef]
17. Berretti, S.; Amor, B.B.; Daoudi, M.; Bimbo, A.D. 3D facial expression recognition using SIFT descriptors of automatically detected keypoints. *Vis. Comput.* **2011**, *27*, 1432–2315. [CrossRef]
18. Krizaj, J.; Struc, V.; Pavesic, N. Adaptation of SIFT Features for Robust Face Recognition. *Image Anal. Recognit.* **2010**, *6111*, 394–404.
19. Paquet, E.; Murching, A.; Naveen, T.; Tabatabai, A.; Rioux, M. Description of shape information for 2-D and 3-d objects. *Signal Process. Image Commun.* **2000**, *16*, 103–122. [CrossRef]
20. Tangelder, J.W.H.; Veltkamp, R.C. Polyhedral Model Retrieval using Weighted Point Sets. *Int. J. Image Graph.* **2003**, *3*, 209–229. [CrossRef]

21. Osada, R.; Funkhouser, T.; Chazelle, B.; Dobkin, D. Shape distributions. *ACM Trans. Graph.* **2002**, *21*, 807–832. [CrossRef]

22. Ip, C.Y.; Lapadat, D.; Sieger, L.; Regli, W.C. Using Shape Distributions to Compare Solid Models. In Proceedings of the Seventh ACM Symposium on Solid Modeling and Applications, Saarbrücken, Germany, 17–21 June 2002; pp. 273–280.

23. Godil, A.; Dutagaci, H.; Bustos, B.; Choi, S.; Dong, S.; Furuya, T.; Li, H.; Link, N.; Moriyama, A.; Meruane, R.; et al. SHREC'15: Range Scans based 3D Shape Retrieval. In Proceedings of the Eurographics Workshop on 3D Object Retrieval, Zurich, Switzerland, 2–3 May 2015.

24. Lian, Z.; Zhang, J.; Choi, S.; ElNaghy, H.; El-Sana, J.; Furuya, T.; Giachetti, A.; Guler, R.A.; Lai, L.; Li, C.; et al. SHREC'15 Track: Non-rigid 3D Shape Retrieval. In Proceedings of the Eurographics Workshop on 3D Object Retrieval, Zurich, Switzerland, 2–3 May 2015.

25. Ohkita, Y.; Ohishi, Y.; Furuya, T.; Ohbuchi, R. Non-rigid 3D Model Retrieval Using Set of Local Statistical Features. In Proceedings of the IEEE International Conference on Multimedia and Expo Workshops, Melbourne, Australia, 9–13 July 2012; pp. 593–598.

26. Zhang, Y.; Jiang, F.; Rho, S.; Liu, S.; Zhao, D.; Ji, R. 3D object retrieval with multi-feature collaboration and bipartite graph matching. *Neurocomputing* **2016**, *195*, 40–49. [CrossRef]

27. Wang, D.; Wang, B.; Zhao, S.; Yao, H.; Liu, H. View-based 3D object retrieval with discriminative views. *Neurocomputing* **2017**, *252*, 58–66. [CrossRef]

28. Kashif, M.; Deserno, T.M.; Haak, D.; Jonas, S. Feature description with SIFT, SURF, BRIEF, BRISK, or FREAK? A general question answered for bone age assessment. *Comput. Biol. Med.* **2016**, *68*, 67–75. [CrossRef] [PubMed]

29. Loncomilla, P.; Ruiz-del-Solar, J.; Martinez, L. Object recognition using local invariant features for robotic applications: A survey. *Pattern Recognit.* **2016**, *60*, 499–514. [CrossRef]

applied
sciences

MDPI

Article

Artificial Flora (AF) Optimization Algorithm

Long Cheng [1,2,*] [ID], Xue-han Wu [1] and Yan Wang [1]

[1]   Department of Computer and Communication Engineering, Northeastern University,
     Qinhuangdao 066004, Hebei Province, China; xhwu820@outlook.com (X.W.); ywang8510@gmail.com (Y.W.)
[2]   School of Information Science and Engineering, Northeastern University,
     Shenyang 110819, Liaoning Province, China
*   Correspondence author: chenglong8501@gmail.com; Tel.: +86-189-313-4611

Received: 9 January 2018; Accepted: 17 February 2018; Published: 26 February 2018

Featured Application: The proposed algorithm can be used in unconstrained multivariate function optimization problems, multi-objective optimization problems and combinatorial optimization problems.

Abstract: Inspired by the process of migration and reproduction of flora, this paper proposes a novel artificial flora (AF) algorithm. This algorithm can be used to solve some complex, non-linear, discrete optimization problems. Although a plant cannot move, it can spread seeds within a certain range to let offspring to find the most suitable environment. The stochastic process is easy to copy, and the spreading space is vast; therefore, it is suitable for applying in intelligent optimization algorithm. First, the algorithm randomly generates the original plant, including its position and the propagation distance. Then, the position and the propagation distance of the original plant as parameters are substituted in the propagation function to generate offspring plants. Finally, the optimal offspring is selected as a new original plant through the selection function. The previous original plant becomes the former plant. The iteration continues until we find out optimal solution. In this paper, six classical evaluation functions are used as the benchmark functions. The simulation results show that proposed algorithm has high accuracy and stability compared with the classical particle swarm optimization and artificial bee colony algorithm.

Keywords: Swarm intelligence algorithm; artificial flora (AF) algorithm; bionic intelligent algorithm; particle swarm optimization; artificial bee colony algorithm

1. Introduction

In science and engineering, there are cases in which a search for the optimal solution in a large and complex space is required [1]. Traditional optimization algorithms, such as Newton's method and the gradient descent method [2], can solve the simple and continuous differentiable function [3]. For complex, nonlinear, non-convex or discrete optimization problems, traditional optimization algorithms have a hard time finding a solution [4,5]. Using a swarm intelligence algorithm, such as the particle swarm optimization (PSO) algorithm [6] and artificial bee colony (ABC) algorithm [7], can find a more satisfactory solution.

A swarm intelligence optimization algorithm is based on the interaction and cooperation between individuals in a group of organisms [8,9]. The behavior and intelligence of each individual is simple and limited, but the swarm will produce inestimable overall capacity by interaction and cooperation [10]. Every individual in the swarm intelligent algorithm must be processed artificially. The individuals do not have the volume and mass of the actual creatures, and the behavioral pattern is processed by humans in order to solve problems when necessary. The algorithm takes all the possible solution sets of the problem as the solution space. Then, it starts with a subset of possible solutions for the problem.

After that, some operations are applied to this subset to create a new solution set. Gradually, the population will approach to the optimal solution or approximate optimal solution. In this evolutionary process, the algorithm does not need any information about the question to be solved, such as gradient, except for the objective function [11]. The optimal solution can be found whether the search space is continuously derivable or not. The swarm intelligence algorithm has characteristics of self-organization, robustness, coordination, simplicity, distribution and extensibility. Therefore, the swarm intelligence optimization algorithms are widely used in parameter estimation [12], automatic control [13], machine manufacturing [14], pattern recognition [15], transportation engineering [16], and so on. The most widely used intelligence algorithms include the genetic algorithm (GA) [17,18], particle swarm optimization (PSO) algorithm [19], artificial bee colony (ABC) algorithm [20], ant colony optimization (ACO) [21], artificial fish swarm algorithm (AFSA) [22], firefly algorithm (FA) [23], Krill Herd algorithm (KHA) [24], and the flower pollination algorithm (FPA) [25]. In the 1960s, Holland proposed the genetic algorithm (GA) [26]. GA is based on Darwin's theory of evolution and Mendel's genetic theory. GA initialize a set of solution, known as group, and every member of the group is a solution to the problem, called chromosomes. The main operation of GA is selection, crossover, and mutation operations. Crossover and mutation operations generate the next generation of chromosomes. It selects a certain number of individuals from the previous generation and current generations according to their fitness. They then continue to evolve until they converge to the best chromosome [27]. In [28], the Spatially Structured Genetic Algorithm (SSGA) is proposed. The populationin SSGA is spatially distributed with respect to some discrete topology. This gives a computationally cheap method of picking a level of tradeoff between having heterogeneous crossover and preservation of population diversity [29]. In order to realize the twin goals of maintaining diversity in the population and sustaining the convergence capacity of the GA, Srinivas recommend the use of adaptive probabilities of crossover and mutation [30].

In 1995, Kennedy and Eberhart proposed the particle swarm optimization (PSO) algorithm [31]. The algorithm was inspired by the flight behavior of birds. Birds are lined up regularly during migration, and every bird changes position and direction continually and keeps a certain distance from the others. Each bird has its own best position, and the birds can adjust their speed and position according to individual and overall information to keep the individual flight optimal. The whole population remains optimal based on individual performance. The algorithm has the characteristics of being simple, highly efficient, and producing fast convergence, but for a complex multimodal problem, it is easy to get into a local optimal solution, and the search precision is low [32]. In order to prevent premature convergence of the PSO algorithm, Suganthanintroduced a neighborhood operator to ensure the diversity of population [33]. Parsopulos introduced a sequential modification to the object function in the neighborhood of each local minimum found [34]. The particles are additionally repelled from these local minimums so that the global minimum will be found by the swarm. In [35], a dual-PSO system was proposed. This system can improve search efficiency.

In 2005, Karaboga proposed the artificial bee colony (ABC) algorithm based on the feeding behavior of bees [36]. This algorithm becomes a hot research topic because of its easy implementation, simple calculation, fewer control parameters, and robustness. The bee is a typical social insect, and the behavior of a single bee is extremely simple in the swarm. However, the whole bee colony shows complex intelligent behavior through the division and cooperation of the bees with different roles. However, the ABC algorithm has some disadvantages [37]: for example, its search speed is slow, and its population diversity will decrease when approaching the global optimal solution. It results in the local optimal. Dongli proposed a modified ABC algorithm for numerical optimization problems [38]. A set of benchmark problems are used to test its performance, and the result shows that the performance is improved. Zhong proposed an improved ABC algorithm to improve the global search ability of the ABC [39]. Rajasekhar investigated an improved version of the ABC algorithm with mutation based on Levy probability distributions [40].

This paper proposed a new intelligent algorithm called the artificial flora (AF) algorithm. It was inspired by the reproduction and the migration of flora. A plant cannot move but can spread seeds to let the flora move to the most suitable environment. Original plants spread seeds in a certain way, and the propagation distance is actually learning from the previous original plants. Whether the seeds can survive or not is related to environmental fitness. If a seed, also called offspring plant, cannot adapt to the environment, it will die. If a seed survives, it will become original plants and spread seeds. By using the special behavior of plants, the artificial flora algorithm updates the solution with the migration of flora.

The main contributions of this paper are given as follows:

1. AF is multi-parent techniques, the movement in AF is related to the past two generation plants. So, it can balance more updating information. This can help algorithm avoid running into the local extremum.
2. AF algorithm selects the alive offspring plants as new original plants each iteration. It can take the local optimal position as the center to explore around space. It can converge to optimal point rapidly.
3. Original plants can spread seeds to any place within their propagation range. This guarantees the local search capability of the algorithm. The classical optimization problem is an important application of the AF algorithm. Function optimization is a direct way to verify intelligent algorithm performance. In this paper, we successfully apply it to unconstrained multivariate function optimization problems. We try to apply it to multi-objective, combinatorial, and more complex problems. In addition, a lot of practical problems, such as wireless sensor network optimization and parameter estimation, can be converted to optimization problems, and we can use AF to find a satisfactory solution.

The rest of this paper is organized as follows. Section 2 describes the principle of the artificial flora (AF) algorithm. Section 3 use six benchmark functions to test the efficiency and stability of artificial flora algorithm and compare it with the PSO and ABC algorithms. The conclusions are presented in Section 4.

2. Artificial Flora Algorithm

2.1. Biological Fundamentals

Plants have a variety of modes to spread seeds. Seed dispersal can be divided into autochory and allochory. Autochory refers to plants that spread by themselves, and allochory means the plants spread through external forces. For example, the mechanical propagation is autochory, and biological propagation, anemochory, and hydrochory are all allochory. Autochory provides the conditions for plants to migrate to a more suitable environment autonomously. For example, sorrels, impatiens, and melons can spread seeds by this way. When a sorrel is ripe, its fruits will be loculicidal, and the shells will curl up to pop the seeds. The fruits of the impatiens will burst open and spread its seeds around. When a melon reaches a certain maturity, the seeds will be squirted out along with mucus from the top of the melon. The distance can be 5 m. On the other hand, allochory provides the conditions for plants to migrate to farther and uncharted regions. For instance, the spread direction and distance of seeds are determined by the wind in anemochory as the wind speed and direction changes. These modes of propagation extend the scope of exploration of flora and reduce the possibility of extinction of flora.

Because of climate change, severe natural environment, or competition, the distribution area of flora can be expanded, reduced, or migrated. As flora migrates to new environment, the individual in the flora will evolve as well. Therefore, the migration of flora can change distribution area and induce the evolution, extinction, and rebirth of flora. A plant cannot move and has no intelligence, but flora can find the best place to live by spreading seeds and reproducing.

In the migration and reproduction of flora, the original plant scatters seeds around randomly within a certain distance. The survival probability of a seed is different due to the external environment.

In a suitable environment, a plant survives and spreads seeds around after being ripe. In harsh environments, there is a probability that flora will evolve to adapt to the environment or that become extinct in the region. Before the flora in a region is completely extinct, allochory sows potential probability that the flora may multiply in other areas. The seeds may be taken to any new area where the flora resumes reproduction. Through multi-generational propagation, the flora will migrate to a most suitable area. Under the mechanism of migration and reproduction, the flora completes the task of finding the optimal growth environment through the evolution, extinction, and rebirth of flora.

2.2. Artificial Flora Algorithm Theory

The artificial floras algorithm consists of four basic elements: original plant, offspring plant, plant location, and propagation distance. Original plants refer to the plants that are ready to spread seeds. Offspring plants are the seeds of original plants, and they cannot spread seeds in that moment. Plant location is the location of a plant. Propagation distance refers to how far a seed can spread. There are three major behavioral patterns: evolution behavior, spreading behavior, and select behavior [41–43]. Evolution behavior means there is a probability that the plant will evolve to adapt to the environment behavior [44–46]. Spreading behavior refers to the movement of seeds, and seeds can move through autochory or allochory. Select behavior means that flora may survive or become extinct due to the environment.

The aforementioned social behaviors can be simplified by some idealized rules as follows:

Rule 1: Because of a sudden change in the environment or some kind of artificial action, a species may be randomly distributed in a region where there is no such species and then become the most primitive original plant.

Rule 2: Plants will evolve to adapt to the new environment as the environment changes. Therefore, the propagation distance of offspring plants is not a complete inheritance to the parent plant but rather evolves on the basis of the distance of the previous generation of plants. In addition, in the ideal case, the offspring can only learn from the nearest two generations.

Rule 3: In the ideal case, when the original plant spreads seeds around autonomously, the range is a circle whose radius is the maximum propagation distance. Offspring plants can be distributed anywhere in the circle (include the circumference).

Rule 4: Environmental factors such as climate and temperature vary from one position to another, so plants have different probability of survival. The probability of survival is related to the fitness of plant in the position, fitness refers to how well plants can adapt to the environment. That is, fitness is the survival probability of a plant in the position. The higher the fitness, the greater the probability of survival is. However, inter-specific competition may cause plant with high fitness to die.

Rule 5: The further the distance from the original plants, the lower the probability of survival because the difference between the current environment and the previous environment will be greater as the offspring plan farther from the original plant in the same generation.

Rule 6: When seeds spread by an external way, the spread distance cannot exceed the maximum limit area because of constraints such as the range of animal activity.

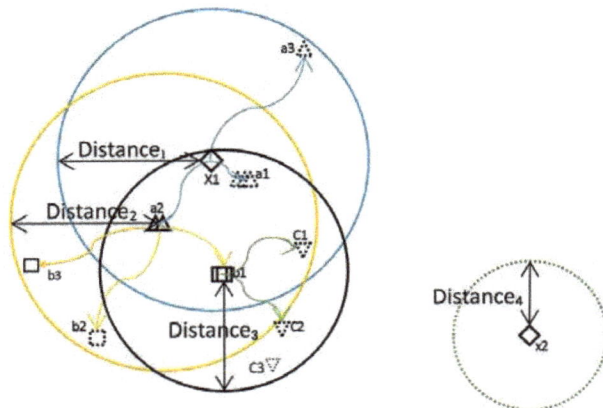

Figure 1. The process of migration and reproduction.

Figure 1 illustrates the process of migration and reproduction. The details are as follows:

1. According to **Rule 1**, there was no such species in the region, due to sudden environmental changes or some kind of artificial action, original plants were spread over a random location in the region, as the ◇(x1) shows in Figure 1.

2. According to **Rule 3**, original plants spread seeds in the propagation range. In Figure 1, Distance₁ is the propagation distance of ◇(x1), offspring can be located in anywhere within the blue circle, and the offspring is shown as △ (a1,a2,a3) in Figure 1.

3. The number of △ stand for the fitness. The higher the number, the higher the offspring's fitness. It can be seen from the Figure 1 that if the offspring is closer to the original plant, the fitness is higher: fitness(a1) > fitness(a2) > fitness(a3). This matches **Rule 5**.

4. According to **Rule 4**, only some of the offspring plant survive because the fitness is different. As shown in Figure 1, the solid line indicates a living plant and the dotted line indicates that the plant is not living. Due to competition and other reasons, the offspring a1 with highest fitness did not survive, but a2 with the fitness less than a1 is alive and becomes a new original plant.

5. The new original plant spread seeds around, as □(b1,b2,b3) shown in Figure 1. It can be seen that b1 and b3 are alive, but b2 does not survive. Then select one plant between b1 and b2 randomly to become latest original plant, and b1 is selected as shown in Figure 1.

6. Distance₂and Distance₃ are the propagation distance of △ (a2) and □(b1), respectively. According to **Rule2**, Distance₂ evolves based on Distance₁, and Distance₃ is learning from Distance₂ and Distance₁. If b1 spreads seeds, the distance of b1's offspring is based on Distance₂ and Distance₃.

7. Plants are constantly spreading seeds around and causing flora to migrate so that flora can find the best area to live.

8. If all the offspring plants do not survive, as ▽ (c1,c2,c3) shown in Figure 1, a new original plant can be randomly generated in the region by allochory.

2.2.1. Evolution Behavior

The original plant spread seeds around in a circle with radius which is propagation distance. The propagation distance is evolved from the propagation distances of the parent plant and grandparent plant.

$$d_j = d_{1j} \times rand(0,1) \times c_1 + d_{2j} \times rand(0,1) \times c_2 \tag{1}$$

where d_{1j} is the propagation distance of grandparent plant, d_{2j} is the propagation distance of parent plant, c_1 and c_2 are the learning coefficient, and $rand(0,1)$ denotes the independent uniformly distributed number in $(0,1)$.

The new grandparent propagation distance is

$$d'_{1j} = d_{2j} \tag{2}$$

The new parent propagation distance is the standard deviation between the positions of the original plant and offspring plant.

$$d'_{2j} = \sqrt{\frac{\sum\limits_{i=1}^{N} (P_{i,j} - P'_{i,j})^2}{N}} \tag{3}$$

2.2.2. Spreading Behavior

First, the artificial flora algorithm randomly generated the original flora with N solutions, which is that there are N plants in the flora. The position of the original plants are expressed by the matrix $P_{i,j}$ where i is the dimension and j is the number of plant in the flora.

$$P_{i,j} = rand(0, 1) \times d \times 2 - d \tag{4}$$

where, d is the maximum limit area and $rand(0,1)$ is an array of random numbers that are uniformly distributed between $(0,1)$.

The position of the offspring plant is generated according to the propagation function as follows:

$$P'_{i,j\times m} = D_{i,j\times m} + P_{i,j} \tag{5}$$

where, m is the number of seeds that one plant can propagate, $P'_{i,j\times m}$ stand for the position of offspring plant, $P_{i,j}$ is the position of the original plant, and $D_{i,j\times m}$ is a random number with the Gaussian distribution with mean 0 and variance d_j. If no offspring plant survives, then a new original plant is generated according to Equation (4).

2.2.3. Select Behavior

Whether the offspring plants are alive is determined by survival probability as follows:

$$p = \left| \sqrt{\frac{F(P'_{i,j\times m})}{F_{max}}} \right| \times Q_x^{(j\times m-1)} \tag{6}$$

where $Q_x^{(j\times m-1)}$ is Q_x to the power of $(j \times m - 1)$ and Q_x is the selective probability. This value has to be between 0 and 1. It can be seen that the fitness of an offspring plant that is farther from the original plant is lower. Q_x determines the exploration capability of the algorithm. Q_x should be larger for the problem that is easy to get into local optimal solution. F_{max} is maximum fitness in the flora this generation and $F(P'_{i,j\times m})$ is the fitness of j-th solution.

The fitness equation is an objective function. Then, a roulette wheel selection method is used to decide if the offspring plant is alive or not. The roulette wheel selection method is also called proportion select method [47]. Its basic purpose is to "accept according probability"; that is to say there are several alternatives and each has its own potential score. However, selection does not completely rely on the value of the score. Selection is according to the accepting probability. The higher the score, the greater the accepting probability is. Generate a random number r with a $[0,1]$ uniform distribution every time, and offspring plant will be alive if the survival probability P is bigger than r, or it will die. Select N offspring plants among the alive offspring as new original plants and repeat the above behaviors until the accuracy requirement is reached or the maximum number of iterations is achieved.

2.3. The Proposed Algorithm Flow and Complexity Analysis

The basic flowchart of the proposed AF algorithm is shown in Figure 2. The main steps of artificial flora algorithm are as follows:

(1) Initialization according Equation (4), generate N original plants;
(2) Calculate propagation distance according Equation (1), Equation (2) and Equation (3);
(3) Generate offspring plants according Equation (5) and calculate their fitness;
(4) Calculate the survival probability of offspring plants according to Equation (6)—whether the offspring survives or not is decided by the roulette wheel selection method;
(5) If there are plants that survive, randomly select N plants as new original plants. If there are no surviving plant, generate new original plants according to Equation (4);
(6) Record the best solution;
(7) Estimate whether this meets the termination conditions. If so, output the optimal solution, otherwise goto step 2.

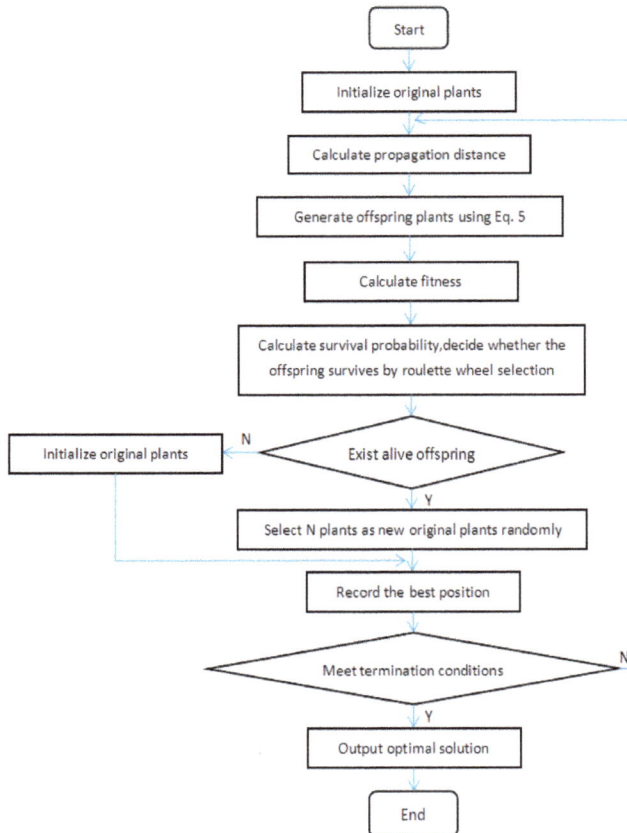

Figure 2. Algorithm flow of artificial flora algorithm.

Based on the aforementioned descriptions, the AF algorithm can be summarized as the pseudo code shown in Table 1.

Table 1. Pseudo code of artificial flora algorithm.

Input: times: Maximum run time
$\qquad$ M: Maximum branching number
$\qquad$ N: Number of original plants
$\qquad$ p: survival probability of offspring plants
$t = 0$; Initialize the population and define the related parameters
Evaluate the N individuals' fitness value, and find the best solution
While ($t <$ times)
$\quad$ For $i = 1:N*M$
$\quad$ New original plants evolve propagation distance (According to Equation (1), Equation (2) and Equation (3))
$\quad\quad$ Original plants spread their offspring (According to Equation (5))
$\quad\quad$ If $rand(0,1) > p$
$\quad\quad\quad$ Offspring plant is alive
$\quad\quad$ Else
$\quad\quad\quad$ Offspring is died
$\quad\quad$ End if
$\quad$ End for
$\quad$ Evaluate new solutions, and select N plants as new original plants randomly.
$\quad$ If the new solutionis better than their previous one, new plant will replace the old one.
$\quad$ Find the current best solution
$\quad$ $t = t + 1$;
End while
Output: Optimal solution

The time complexity of the algorithm can be measured by running time $t(s)$ in order to facilitate the comparison of various algorithms.

$$t(s) = t_A \times A(s) + t_B \times B(s) + \dots + T_P \times P(s) \tag{7}$$

where t_A, t_B, t_P are the time required to perform every operation once and $A(s)$, $B(s)$, $P(s)$ are the number of each operation.

In the artificial flora algorithm, the number of original plants is N, and the maximum branching number M is the number of seeds that one original plant can generate. t_1 is the time to initialize population. t_2 is the time of calculating propagation distance. t_3 is the time to update the plant position. t_4 is the time to calculate the fitness. t_5 is the time to calculate the survival probability. t_6 is the time to decide which plant is alive this generation using roulette wheel selection method. The time complexity analysis of this algorithm is shown in Table 2. Therefore, we can see that the time complexity of artificial flora algorithm is $O(NM)$ in Table 2.

Table 2. The time complexity of artificial flora algorithm.

Operation	Time	Time Complexity
Initialize	$N \times t_1$	$O(N)$
Calculate propagation distance	$2N \times t_2$	$O(N)$
Update the position	$N \times t_3$	$O(N)$
Calculate fitness	$N \times M \times t_4$	$O(N \cdot M)$
Calculate survival probability	$N \times M \times t_5$	$O(N \cdot M)$
Decide alive plant using roulette	$N \times M \times t_6$	$O(N \cdot M)$

3. Validation and Comparison

In this section, we use six benchmark functions [48,49] to test the efficiency and stability of artificial flora algorithm. The definition, bounds, and the optimum values of functions are shown in Table 3. For a two-dimensional condition, the value distributions of these functions are shown in Figures 3–8. It can be seen from the Figures 3 and 4 that Sphere (f_1) and Rosenbrock (f_2) functions are unimodal functions that can be used to test the optimization precision and performance of the algorithm. f_3 to f_6 functions are complex nonlinear multimodal functions. The general algorithm has difficulty finding the global optimal value. Because they have many local extreme points, they can be used to test the global search performance and the ability to avoid prematurity of algorithm.

Table 3. Benchmark functions.

Functions	Expression formula	Bounds	Optimum Value
Sphere	$f_1(x) = \sum_{i=1}^{n} x_i^2$	$[-100,100]$	0
Rosenbrock	$f_2(x) = \sum_{i=1}^{n-1} \left[100(x_{i+1} - x_i^2)^2 + (x_i - 1)^2 \right]$	$[-30,30]$	0
Rastrigin	$f_3(x) = \sum_{i=1}^{n} [x_i^2 - 10\cos(2\pi x_i) + 10]$	$[-5.12,5.12]$	0
Schwefel	$f_4(x) = \sum_{i=1}^{n} \left[-x_i \sin(\sqrt{|x_i|}) \right]$	$[-500,500]$	$-418.9829 \times D$
Griewank	$f_5(x) = \frac{1}{4000} \sum_{i=1}^{n} x_i^2 - \prod_{i=1}^{n} \cos\left(\frac{x_i}{\sqrt{i}}\right) + 1$	$[-600,600]$	0
Ackley	$f_6(x) = -20\exp\left(-0.2\sqrt{\frac{1}{n}\sum_{i=1}^{n} x_i^2}\right) - \exp\left(\frac{1}{n}\sum_{i=1}^{n}\cos(2\pi x_i)\right) + 20 + e$	$[-32,32]$	0

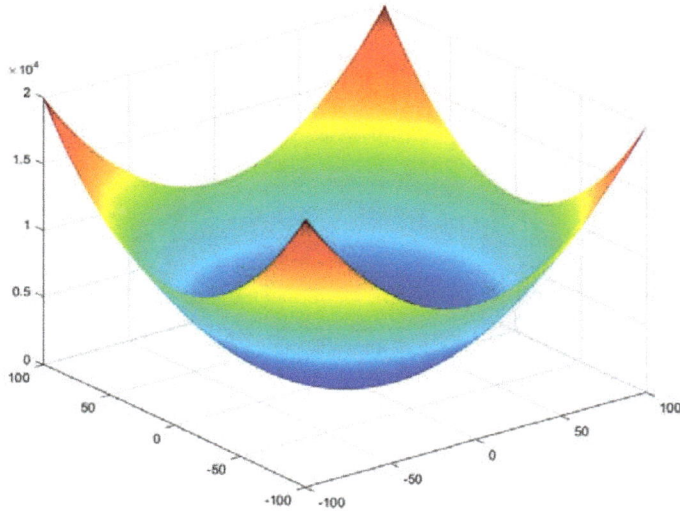

Figure 3. Three-dimensional image of Sphere function (f_1).

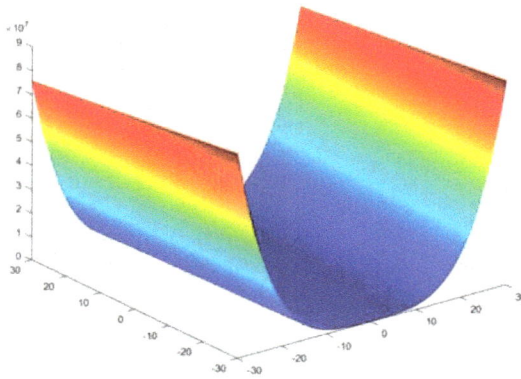

Figure 4. Three-dimensional image of Rosenbrock function (f_2).

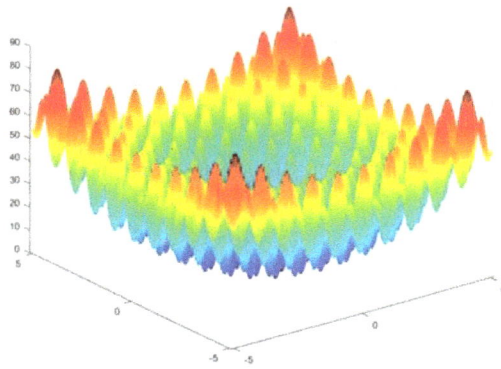

Figure 5. Three-dimensional image of Rastrigin function (f_3).

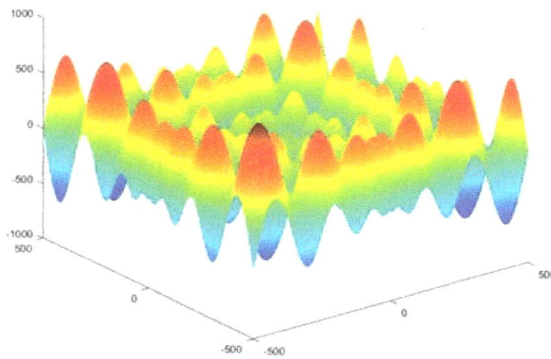

Figure 6. Three-dimensional image of Schwefel function (f_4).

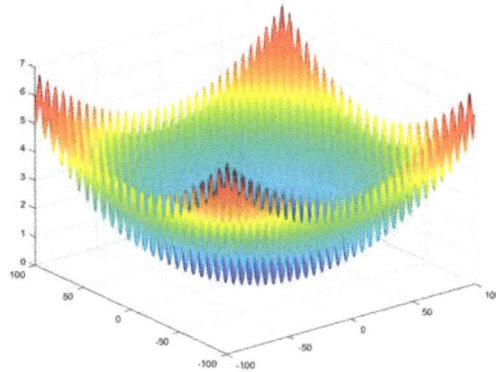

Figure 7. Three-dimensional image of Griewank function (f_5).

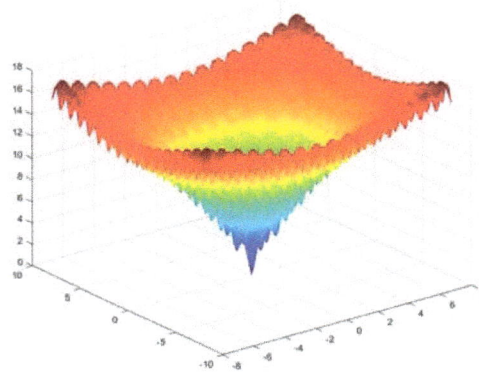

Figure 8. Three-dimensional image of Ackley function (f_6).

The AF, PSO, and ABC are all bio-inspired swarm intelligence optimization algorithms. The PSO and ABC methods are widely used intelligent optimization algorithms. So, we compare the AF algorithm with the PSO [50] and ABC [36] algorithms to prove the advantages of this algorithm. The maximum number of iterations, cycle index, and the running environment are the same. The three algorithms will be iterated 1000 times respectively and run 50 times independently. All the experiments using MATLAB (2012a, MathWorks Company, Natick, MA, USA, 2012) are performed on a computer with Intel(R) Core(TM) i7-7700 CPU @ 3.60GHz and 8.00GB RAM running the Windows 10 operating system. The default parameters are shown in Table 4.

Table 4. The default parameters in particle swarm optimization (PSO), artificial bee colony (ABC), and artificial flora (AF) algorithms.

Algorithm	Parameter Values
PSO	$N = 100, c_1 = c_2 = 1.4962, w = 0.7298$
ABC	$N = 200, \text{limit} = 1000$
AF	$N = 1, M = 100, c_1 = 0.75, c_2 = 1.25$

Tables 5–7 show the statistical results in 20-dimensional space, 50-dimensional space, and 100-dimensional space, respectively. According to the statistical results shown in Tables 5–7 , AF can

find a more satisfactory solution with higher accuracy compare with PSO and ABC. For the unimodal function Sphere, AF can find the globally optimal solution. The accuracy of the solution obtained by AF is improved compare to those obtained by PSO and ABC. For Rosenbrock function, the accuracy of the solution is almost the same between AF and ABC in high dimensions (100-dimensional), and they are all better than PSO. However, the algorithm stability of AF is higher than that of ABC. For multimodal function (Rastrigin and Griewank), AF can steadily converge to the global optimal solution in 20-dimensional and 50-dimensional space, and in 100-dimensional space, AF can find the global optimal solution at best. For Schwefel function, the AF algorithm has better search precision in higher dimensions. In low dimensions, the search precision of the AF algorithm is superior to PSO but slightly worse than ABC. For Ackley function, AF is better than PSO and ABC for finding the global optimal solution.

On the whole, the solution accuracy obtained by the AF algorithm is improved obviously for the unimodal functions and the multimodal functions. It shows that the AF algorithm has strong exploration ability. Also, the stability of AF in these benchmark functions is better than that of PSO and ABC besides the Schwefel function.

Table 5. Comparison of statistical results obtained by AF, PSO, and ABC in 20-dimensional space.

Functions	Algorithm	Best	Mean	Worst	SD	Runtime
Sphere	PSO	0.022229639	10.36862151	110.8350423	21.05011998	0.407360
	ABC	2.22518×10^{-16}	3.03501×10^{-16}	4.3713×10^{-16}	5.35969×10^{-17}	2.988014
	AF	0	0	0	0	2.536061
Rosenbrock	PSO	86.00167369	19,283.23676	222,601.751	43,960.73321	0.578351
	ABC	0.004636871	0.071185731	0.245132443	0.065746751	3.825228
	AF	17.93243086	18.44894891	18.77237391	0.238206854	4.876399
Rastrigin	PSO	60.69461471	124.3756019	261.6735015	43.5954195	0.588299
	ABC	0	1.7053×10^{-14}	5.68434×10^{-14}	1.90442×10^{-14}	3.388325
	AF	0	0	0	0	2.730699
Schwefel	PSO	-1.082×10^{105}	-2.0346×10^{149}	-1.0156×10^{151}	1.4362×10^{150}	1.480785
	ABC	-8379.657745	-8379.656033	-8379.618707	0.007303823	3.462507
	AF	-7510.128926	$-11,279.67966$	$-177,281.186$	25,371.33579	3.144982
Griewank	PSO	0.127645871	0.639982775	1.252113282	0.31200235	1.097885
	ABC	0	7.37654×10^{-14}	2.61158×10^{-12}	3.70604×10^{-13}	6.051243
	AF	0	0	0	0	2.927380
Ackley	PSO	19.99906463	20.04706409	20.46501638	0.103726728	0.949812
	ABC	2.0338×10^{-10}	4.5334×10^{-10}	1.02975×10^{-9}	1.6605×10^{-10}	3.652016
	AF	8.88×10^{-16}	8.88×10^{-16}	8.88×10^{-16}	0	3.023296

Table 6. Comparison of statistical results obtained by AF, PSO, and ABC in 50-dimensional space.

Functions	Algorithm	Best	Mean	Worst	SD	Runtime
Sphere	PSO	13,513.53237	29,913.32912	55,187.50413	9279.053897	0.515428
	ABC	6.73535×10^{-8}	3.56859×10^{-7}	1.17148×10^{-6}	2.37263×10^{-7}	3.548339
	AF	0	4.22551×10^{-32}	2.11276×10^{-30}	2.95786×10^{-31}	3.476036
Rosenbrock	PSO	9,137,632.795	53,765,803.92	313,258,238.9	49,387,420.59	0.707141
	ABC	0.409359085	13.87909385	49.83380808	9.973291581	4.094523
	AF	47.95457	48.50293	48.87977	0.246019	6.674920
Rastrigin	PSO	500.5355119	671.5528998	892.8727757	98.8516628	1.036802
	ABC	0.995796171	3.850881679	7.36921061	1.539235109	3.661335
	AF	0	0	0	0	3.753900
Schwefel	PSO	-1.6819×10^{127}	-5.9384×10^{125}	-2.5216×10^{5}	2.7148×10^{126}	2.672258
	ABC	$-20,111.1655$	$-19,720.51324$	$-19,318.44458$	183.7240198	3.433517
	AF	$-20,680.01223$	$-23,796.53666$	$-93,734.38905$	16,356.3483	4.053411
Griewank	PSO	118.8833865	283.810608	524.5110849	101.3692096	1.609482
	ABC	1.63×10^{-6}	1.29×10^{-3}	3.30×10^{-2}	0.005265446	6.573567
	AF	0	0	0	0	3.564724
Ackley	PSO	20.169350	20.452818	21.151007	0.2030427	1.499010
	ABC	0.003030661	0.009076649	0.033812712	0.005609339	4.315255
	AF	8.88×10^{-16}	8.88×10^{-16}	8.88×10^{-16}	0	5.463588

Table 7. Comparison of statistical results obtained by AF, PSO, and ABC in 100-dimensional space.

Functions	Algorithm	Best	Mean	Worst	SD	Runtime
Sphere	PSO	115,645.5342	195,135.2461	278,094.825	38,558.16575	0.711345
	ABC	0.000594137	0.001826666	0.004501827	0.000839266	3.461872
	AF	0	3.13781×10^{-16}	1.34675×10^{-14}	1.88902×10^{-15}	5.147278
Rosenbrock	PSO	335,003,051.6	886,456,293.7	2,124,907,403	386,634,404.3	1.053024
	ABC	87.31216327	482.9875993	3159.533172	660.8862246	4.249927
	AF	98.16326	98.75210	98.91893	0.143608	9.205695
Rastrigin	PSO	1400.13738	1788.428575	2237.676158	190.5442307	1.711449
	ABC	38.31898075	57.90108742	71.66147576	7.625052886	4.177761
	AF	0	3.55271×10^{-17}	1.77636×10^{-15}	2.4869×10^{-16}	5.526152
Schwefel	PSO	-1.8278×10^{130}	-3.6943×10^{128}	-9.38464×10^{85}	2.5844×10^{129}	4.541757
	ABC	$-36,633.02634$	$-35,865.45846$	$-35,018.41908$	428.4258428	3.776740
	AF	$-42,305.38762$	$-43,259.38057$	$-212,423.8294$	42,713.19955	5.638101
Griewank	PSO	921.4736939	1750.684535	2954.013327	393.6416257	2.117832
	ABC	0.006642796	0.104038042	0.349646578	0.098645373	6.995976
	AF	0	1.71×10^{-11}	4.96314×10^{-10}	7.66992×10^{-11}	5.440354
Ackley	PSO	20.58328517	20.83783825	21.17117933	0.152682198	2.011021
	ABC	2.062017063	2.669238251	3.277291002	0.28375453	4.611272
	AF	8.88×10^{-16}	8.88×10^{-16}	8.88×10^{-16}	0	6.812734

Figures 9–14 show the convergence time of the three algorithms in 50-dimensional space, and Figures 15–20 show the convergence time of the three algorithms in 100-dimensional space.

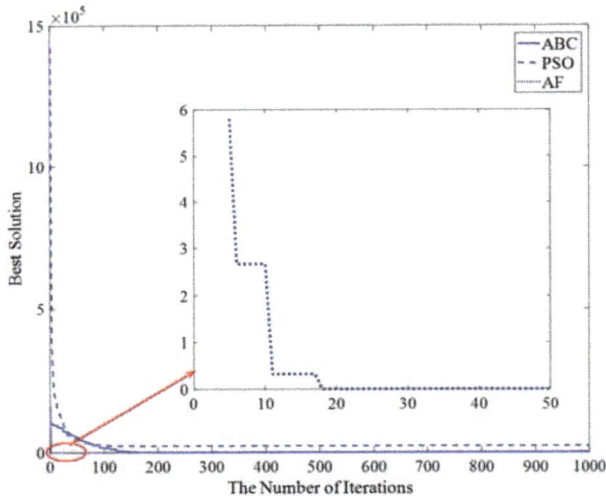

Figure 9. The convergence curve of the three algorithms for Sphere function in 50-dimensional space. PSO: particle swarm optimization algorithm; ABC: artificial bee colony algorithm; AF: artificial flora algorithm.

It can be seen from Figure 9 that the AF algorithm converges very quickly. The rate of convergence of ABC algorithm, PSO algorithm and AF algorithm is slowing down at 120th iteration, 50th iteration, and 15th iteration, respectively. The convergence curves of ABC and PSO intersect at the 50th iteration.

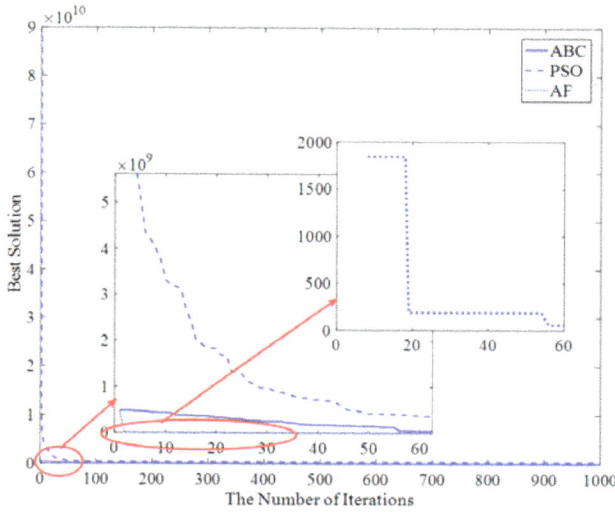

Figure 10. The convergence curve of the three algorithms for Rosenbrock function in 50-dimensional space.

As shown in Figure 10, for Rosenbrock function, the PSO algorithm and ABC algorithm both converge at about 100 iterations, and the AF algorithm converges at about the 55th iteration.

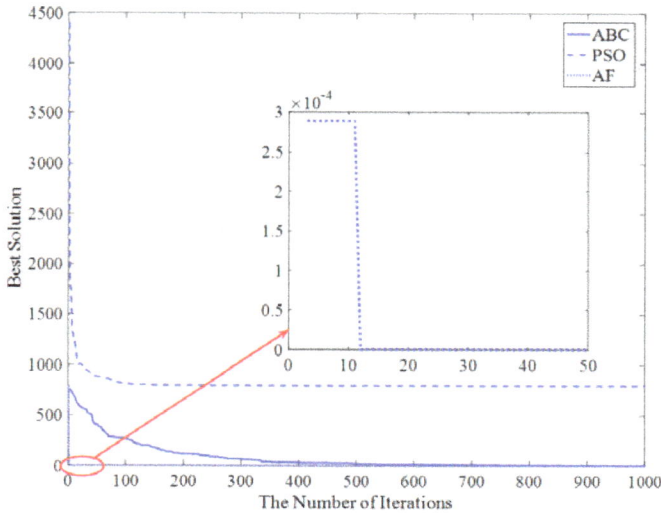

Figure 11. The convergence curve of the three algorithms for Rastrigin function in 50-dimensional space.

Figure 11 illustrates that the convergence rate of the AF algorithm is still better than the other two algorithms for Rastrig in function. The AF algorithm is convergent to a good numerical solution at the 15th iteration. The PSO algorithm converges fast, but it is easily trapped into the local optimal solution. The convergence rate of ABC is slow.

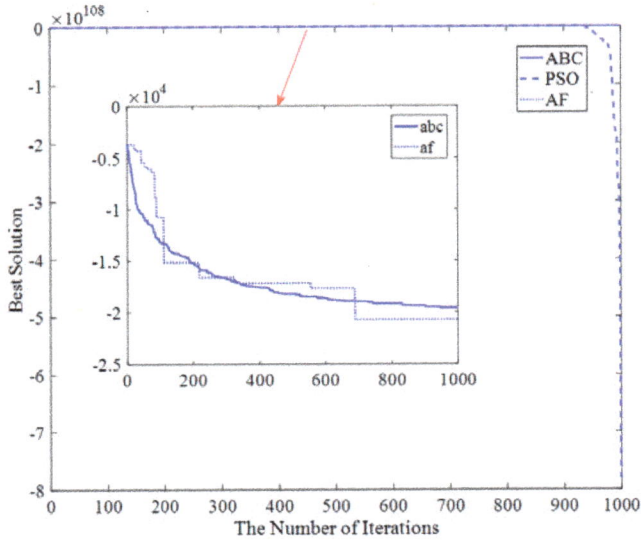

Figure 12. The convergence curve of the three algorithms for Schwefel function in 50-dimensional space.

Schwefel is a typical deceptive function, as shown in Figure 12. The convergence rate of the AF algorithm is similar to that of ABC for Schwefel function.

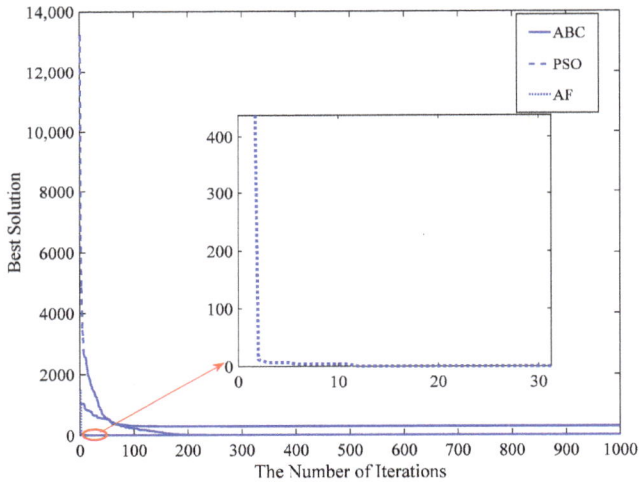

Figure 13. The convergence curve of the three algorithms for Griewank function in 50-dimensional space.

Figure 13 shows that the AF algorithm converges at about the 23rd iteration, and the PSO and ABC algorithms converge at about the 50th iteration and 200th iteration, respectively.

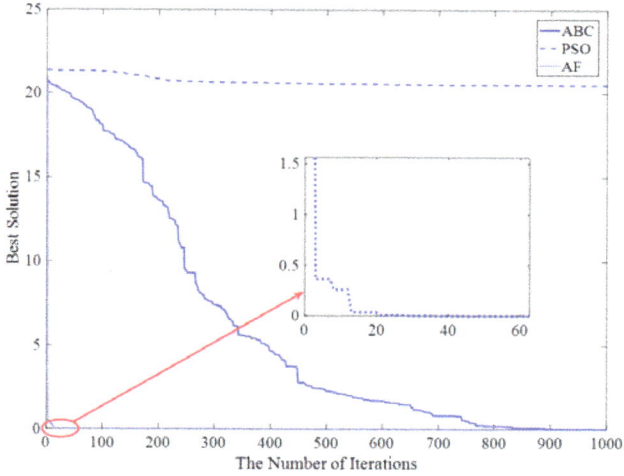

Figure 14. The convergence curve of the three algorithms for Ackley function in 50-dimensional space.

As Figure 14 shows, for Ackley function, the PSO algorithm is easily trapped into a local optimization. The convergence speed of the ABC algorithm is slow. The ABC algorithm converges at about the 900th iteration. However, the AF algorithm can get a convergence solution at only the 40th iteration.

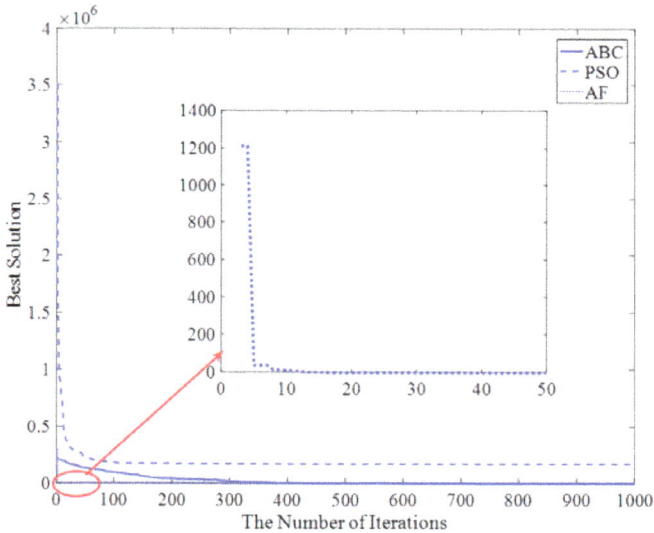

Figure 15. The convergence curve of the three algorithms for Sphere function in 100-dimensional space.

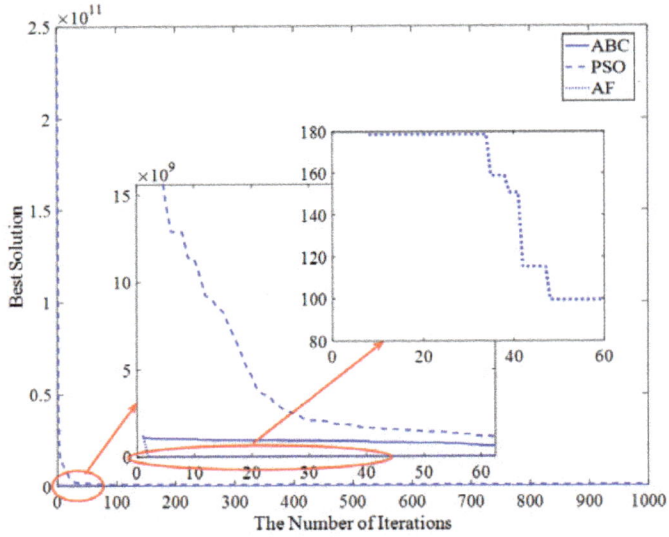

Figure 16. The convergence curve of the three algorithms for Rosenbrock function in 100-dimensional space.

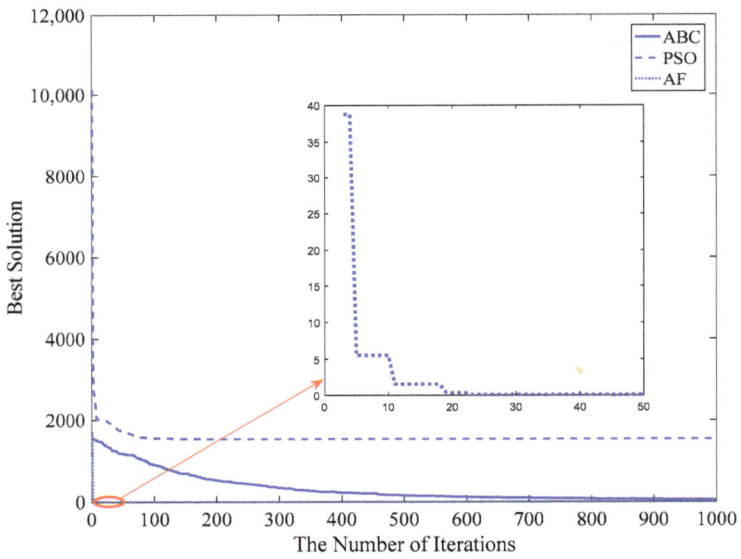

Figure 17. The convergence curve of the three algorithms for Rastrigin function in 100-dimensional space.

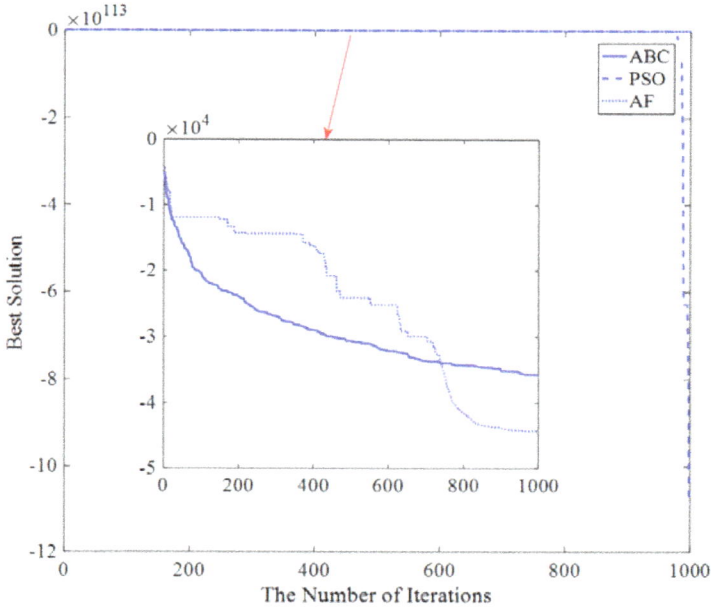

Figure 18. The convergence curve of the three algorithms for Schwefel function in 100-dimensional space.

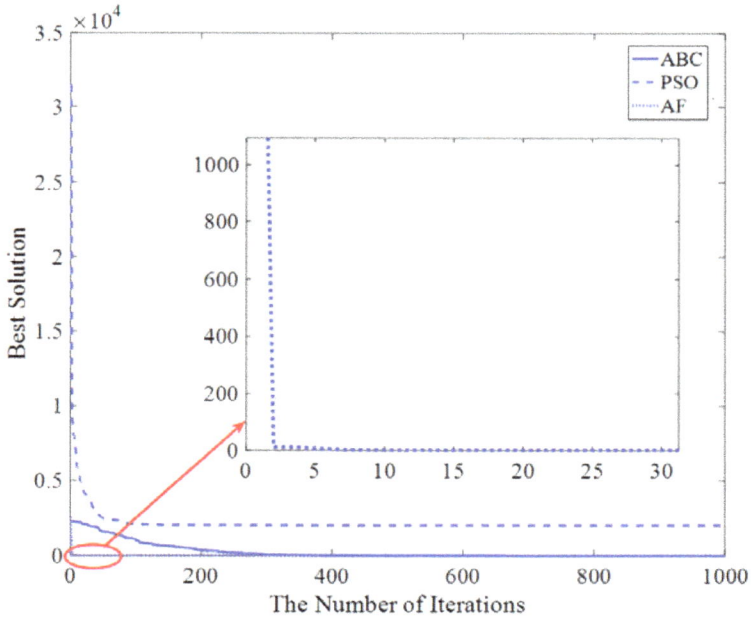

Figure 19. The convergence curve of the three algorithms for Griewank function in 100-dimensional space.

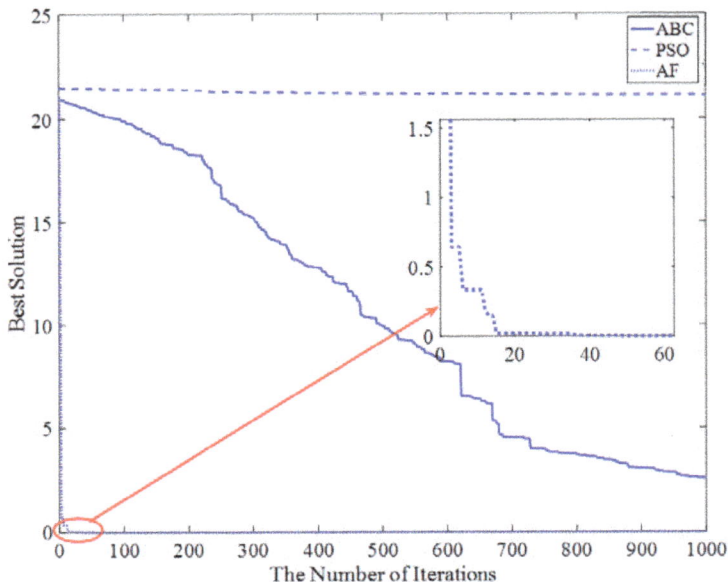

Figure 20. The convergence curve of the three algorithms for Ackley function in 100-dimensional space.

It can be seen from Figures 15–20 that the trend of convergence curves in 100-dimensional space is similar to that in 50-dimensional space.

It can be concluded that the AF algorithm can get a solution with higher accuracy and stability than PSO and ABC according to Tables 5–7 and Figures 9–20. First, since the AF algorithm selects the alive offspring plants as new original plants at each iteration, it can take the local optimal position as the center to explore the surrounding space. It can converge to the optimal point rapidly. Second, original plants can spread seeds to any direction and distance within the propagation range. It guarantees the local search capability of the algorithm. Third, when there is no better offspring plant, in order to explore the possibility that a better solution exists, new original plants will be generated randomly in the function domain. This can help the AF algorithm to skip the local optimum and improve the performance of global searching. Therefore, the AF algorithm has excellent accuracy, stability, and effectiveness.

4. Conclusions

The beautiful posture of birds and the perfect cooperation of a bee colony left an impression on people's minds, so the PSO algorithm and ABC algorithm were proposed. In this paper, the proposed artificial flora algorithm is inspired by the migration and reproduction behavior of flora. There are three main behaviors, including evolution behavior, spreading behavior, and select behavior. In evolution behavior, the propagation distance of offspring plants is evolution based on the propagation distance of parent plant and grandparent plant. The propagation distance is optimized in each generation. Since the propagation distance of offspring plants is not a complete inheritance to the parent plant, there is an opportunity for the algorithm to get out of the local optimal solution. Spreading behavior includes autochory and allochory. Autochory provides the opportunity for the original plant to explore the optimal location around itself. This behavior provides local search capability to the algorithm. Allochory provides opportunity for original plant to explore greater space, and global search capability of the algorithm is obtained from this behavior. According to the natural law of survival of the fittest, the greater the survival probability of a plant with higher fitness, and thus the natural law is called select behavior.

Several simulations have shown the effective performance of the proposed algorithm when compared with PSO and ABC algorithms. The AF algorithm improves the algorithm's ability to find the global optimal solution and accuracy and also speeds up the convergence speed.

In the future, we focus on solving discrete, multi-objective, combinatorial, and more complex problems using the AF algorithm and its variants. For example, we are now trying to apply AF to multi-objective optimization problems. Using the method of generating a mesh, AF can converge to the optimal Pareto front. In addition, a lot of practical problems can be converted to optimization problems, and then we can use AF to find a satisfactory solution. For instance, AF can be used to find a satisfactory solution and can applied to parameter optimization and cluster analysis.

Acknowledgments: This work was supported by the National Natural Science Foundation of China under Grant No. 61403068; Natural Science Foundation of Hebei Province under Grant No. F2015501097 and No. F2016501080; Fundamental Research Funds for the Central Universities of China under Grant No. N130323002, No. N130323004 and N152302001.

Author Contributions: Long Cheng and Xue-han Wu conceived and designed the experiments; Yan Wang performed the experiments; Xue-han Wu and Yan Wang analyzed the data; Long Cheng contributed analysis tools; Long Cheng and Xue-han Wu wrote the paper.

Conflicts of Interest: The authors declare that there is no conflict of interests regarding the publication of this paper.

References

1. Cao, Z.; Wang, L. An effective cooperative coevolution framework integrating global and local search for large scale optimization problems. In Proceedings of the 2015 IEEE Congress on Evolutionary Computation, Sendai, Japan, 25–28 May 2015; pp. 1986–1993.

2. Battiti, R. *First- and Second-Order Methods for Learning: Between Steepest Descent and Newton's Method*; MIT Press: Cambridge, MA, USA, 1992.

3. Liang, X.B.; Wang, J. A recurrent neural network for nonlinear optimization with a continuously differentiable objective function and bound constraints. *IEEE Trans. Neural Netw.* **2000**, *11*, 1251–1262. [PubMed]

4. Li, J.; Fong, S.; Wong, R. Adaptive multi-objective swarm fusion for imbalanced data classification. *Inf. Fusion* **2018**, *39*, 1–24. [CrossRef]

5. Han, G.; Liu, L.; Chan, S.; Yu, R.; Yang, Y. HySense: A Hybrid Mobile CrowdSensing Framework for Sensing Opportunities Compensation under Dynamic Coverage Constraint. *IEEE Commun. Mag.* **2017**, *55*, 93–99. [CrossRef]

6. Navalertporn, T.; Afzulpurkar, N.V. Optimization of tile manufacturing process using particle swarm optimization. *Swarm Evol. Comput.* **2011**, *1*, 97–109. [CrossRef]

7. Pan, Q.; Tasgetiren, M.; Suganthan, P. A discrete artificial bee colony algorithm for the lot-streaming flow shop scheduling problem. *Inf. Sci.* **2011**, *181*, 2455–2468. [CrossRef]

8. Duan, H.; Luo, Q. New progresses in swarm intelligence-based computation. *Int. J. Bio-Inspired Comput.* **2015**, *7*, 26–35. [CrossRef]

9. Tang, Q.; Shen, Y.; Hu, C. Swarm Intelligence: Based Cooperation Optimization of Multi-Modal Functions. *Cogn. Comput.* **2013**, *5*, 48–55. [CrossRef]

10. Demertzis, K.; Iliadis, L. Adaptive elitist differential evolution extreme learning machines on big data: Intelligent recognition of invasive species. In *Advances in Big Data*; Springer International Publishing: Berlin/Heidelberg, Germany, 2016.

11. Du, X.P.; Cheng, L.; Liu, L. A Swarm Intelligence Algorithm for Joint Sparse Recovery. *IEEE Signal Process. Lett.* **2013**, *20*, 611–614.

12. Zaman, F.; Qureshi, I.M.; Munir, F. Four-dimensional parameter estimation of plane waves using swarming intelligence. *Chin. Phys. B* **2014**, *23*, 078402. [CrossRef]

13. Jain, C.; Verma, H.K.; Arya, L.D. A novel statistically tracked particle swarm optimization method for automatic generation control. *J. Mod. Power Syst. Clean Energy* **2014**, *2*, 396–410. [CrossRef]

14. Torabi, A.J.; Er, M.J.; Li, X. A Survey on Artificial Intelligence-Based Modeling Techniques for High Speed Milling Processes. *IEEE Syst. J.* **2015**, *9*, 1069–1080. [CrossRef]
15. Nebti, S.; Boukerram, A. Swarm intelligence inspired classifiers for facial recognition. *Swarm Evol. Comput.* **2017**, *32*, 150–166. [CrossRef]
16. Teodorovic, D. Swarm intelligence systems for transportation engineering: Principles and applications. *Transp. Res. Part C-Emerg. Technol.* **2008**, *16*, 651–667. [CrossRef]
17. Drechsler, R.; Gockel, N. Genetic algorithm for data sequencing. *Electron. Lett.* **1997**, *33*, 843–845. [CrossRef]
18. Jong, E.D.; Watson, R.A.; Pollack, J.B. Reducing Bloat and Promoting Diversity using Multi-Objective Methods. In Proceedings of the Genetic and Evolutionary Computation Conference, San Francisco, CA, USA, 7–11 July 2001; pp. 1–8.
19. Pornsing, C.; Sodhi, M.S.; Lamond, B.F. Novel self-adaptive particle swarm optimization methods. *Soft Comput.* **2016**, *20*, 3579–3593. [CrossRef]
20. Karaboga, D.; Gorkemli, B. A quick artificial bee colony (qABC) algorithm and its performance on optimization problems. *Appl. Soft Comput.* **2014**, *23*, 227–238. [CrossRef]
21. Luh, G.C.; Lin, C.Y. Structural topology optimization using ant colony optimization algorithm. *Appl. Soft Comput.* **2009**, *9*, 1343–1353. [CrossRef]
22. Wang, H.B.; Fan, C.C.; Tu, X.Y. AFSAOCP: A novel artificial fish swarm optimization algorithm aided by ocean current power. *Appl. Intell.* **2016**, *45*, 992–1007. [CrossRef]
23. Wang, H.; Wang, W.; Zhou, X. Firefly algorithm with neighborhood attraction. *Inf. Sci.* **2017**, *382*, 374–387. [CrossRef]
24. Gandomi, A.H.; Talatahari, S.; Tadbiri, F. Krill herd algorithm for optimum design of truss structures. *Int. J. Bio-Inspired Comput.* **2013**, *5*, 281–288. [CrossRef]
25. Yang, X.S. Flower Pollination Algorithm for Global Optimization. In Proceedings of the 11th International Conference on Unconventional Computation and Natural Computation, Orléans, France, 3–7 September 2012; Springer: Berlin/Heidelberg, Germany, 2012; pp. 240–249.
26. Holland, J.H. *Adaptation in Natural and Artificial Systems*; MIT Press: Cambridge, MA, USA, 1992.
27. Dick, G.; Whigham, P. The behaviour of genetic drift in a spatially-structured evolutionary algorithm. In Proceedings of the IEEE Congress on Evolutionary Computation, Edinburgh, UK, 2–5 September 2005; Volume 2, pp. 1855–1860.
28. Ashlock, D.; Smucker, M.; Walker, J. Graph based genetic algorithms. In Proceedings of the Congress on Evolutionary Computation, Washington, DC, USA, 6–9 July 1999; Volume 2, p. 1368.
29. Gasparri, A. A Spatially Structured Genetic Algorithm over Complex Networks for Mobile Robot Localisation. In Proceedings of the IEEE International Conference on Robotics and Automation, Roma, Italy, 10–14 April 2007; pp. 4277–4282.
30. Srinivas, M.; Patnaik, L.M. Adaptive probabilities of crossover and mutation in genetic algorithms. *IEEE Trans. Syst. Man Cybern.* **2002**, *24*, 656–667. [CrossRef]
31. Kennedy, J.; Eberhart, R. Particle swarm optimization. In Proceedings of the IEEE International Conference on Neural Networks, Perth, Australia, 27 November–1 December 1995; IEEE: Middlesex County, NJ, USA, 1995; Volume 4, pp. 1942–1948.
32. Clerc, M.; Kennedy, J. The particle swarm—Explosion, stability, and convergence in a multidimensional complex space. *IEEE Trans. Evol. Comput.* **2002**, *6*, 58–73. [CrossRef]
33. Suganthan, P. Particle swarm optimizer with neighborhood operator. In Proceedings of the IEEE Congress on Evolutionary Computation, Washington, DC, USA, 6–9 July 1999; pp. 1958–1961.
34. Parsopoulos, K.E.; Vrahatis, M.N. On the computation of all global minimizers through particle swarm optimization. *IEEE Trans. Evol. Comput.* **2004**, *8*, 211–224. [CrossRef]
35. Voss, M.S. Principal Component Particle Swarm Optimization (PCPSO). In Proceedings of the IEEE Swarm Intelligence Symposium, Pasadena, CA, USA, 8–10 June 2005; pp. 401–404.
36. Karaboga, D. *An Idea Based on Honey Bee Swarm for Numerical Optimization*; Erciyes University: Kayseri, Turkey, 2005.
37. Alam, M.S.; Kabir, M.W.U.; Islam, M.M. Self-adaptation of mutation step size in Artificial Bee Colony algorithm for continuous function optimization. In Proceedings of the 2013 IEEE International Conference on Computer and Information Technology, Dhaka, Bangladesh, 23–25 December 2011; IEEE: Middlesex County, NJ, USA, 2011; pp. 69–74.

38. Zhang, D.; Guan, X.; Tang, Y. Modified Artificial Bee Colony Algorithms for Numerical Optimization. In Proceedings of the 2011 3rd International Workshop on Intelligent Systems and Applications, Wuhan, China, 28–29 May 2011; pp. 1–4.

39. Zhong, F.; Li, H.; Zhong, S. A modified ABC algorithm based on improved-global-best-guided approach and adaptive-limit strategy for global optimization. *Appl. Soft Comput.* **2016**, *46*, 469–486. [CrossRef]

40. Rajasekhar, A.; Abraham, A.; Pant, M. Levy mutated Artificial Bee Colony algorithm for global optimization. In Proceedings of the 2011 IEEE International Conference on Systems, Man, and Cybernetics, Anchorage, AK, USA, 9–12 October 2011; pp. 655–662.

41. Pagie, L.; Mitchell, M. A comparison of evolutionary and coevolutionary search. *Int. J. Comput. Intell. Appl.* **2002**, *2*, 53–69. [CrossRef]

42. Wiegand, R.P.; Sarma, J. Spatial Embedding and Loss of Gradient in Cooperative Coevolutionary Algorithms. In Proceedings of the International Conference on Parallel Problem Solving from Nature, Berlin, Germany, 22–26 September 1996; Springer: Berlin/Heidelberg, Germany, 2004; pp. 912–921.

43. Rosin, C.D.; Belew, R.K. Methods for Competitive Co-Evolution: Finding Opponents Worth Beating. In Proceedings of the International Conference on Genetic Algorithms, Pittsburgh, PA, USA, 15–19 June 1995; pp. 373–381.

44. Cartlidge, J.P.; Bulloc, S.G. Combating coevolutionary disengagement by reducing parasite virulence. *Evol. Comput.* **2004**, *12*, 193–222. [CrossRef] [PubMed]

45. Williams, N.; Mitchell, M. Investigating the success of spatial coevolution. In Proceedings of the 7th Annual Conference on Genetic And Evolutionary Computation, Washington, DC, USA, 25–29 June 2005; pp. 523–530.

46. Hillis, W.D. Co-evolving Parasites Improve Simulated Evolution as an Optimization Procedure. *Phys. D Nonlinear Phenom.* **1990**, *42*, 228–234. [CrossRef]

47. Ling, S.H.; Leung, F.H.F. An Improved Genetic Algorithm with Average-bound Crossover and Wavelet Mutation Operations. *Soft Comput.* **2007**, *11*, 7–31. [CrossRef]

48. Akay, B.; Karaboga, D. A modified Artificial Bee Colony algorithm for real-parameter optimization. *Inf. Sci.* **2012**, *192*, 120–142. [CrossRef]

49. Meng, X.B.; Gao, X.Z.; Lu, L. A new bio-inspired optimisation algorithm: Bird Swarm Algorithm. *J. Exp. Theor. Artif. Intell.* **2016**, *38*, 673–687. [CrossRef]

50. Shi, Y.; Eberhart, R. A modified particle swarm optimizer. In Proceedings of the 1998 IEEE International Conference on Evolutionary Computation Proceedings, Anchorage, AK, USA, 4–9 May 1998; pp. 69–73.

applied
sciences

MDPI

Article

Parallel Technique for the Metaheuristic Algorithms Using Devoted Local Search and Manipulating the Solutions Space

Dawid Połap [1],*, **Karolina Kęsik** [1], **Marcin Woźniak** [1] and **Robertas Damaševičius** [2]

1   Institute of Mathematics, Silesian University of Technology, Kaszubska 23, 44-100 Gliwice, Poland;
    Karola.Ksk@gmail.com (K.K.); Marcin.Wozniak@polsl.pl (M.W.)
2   Department of Software Engineering, Kaunas University of Technology, Studentu 50, LT-51368,
    Kaunas, Lithuania; Robertas.damasevicius@ktu.lt
*   Correspondence: Dawid.Polap@polsl.pl

Received: 16 December 2017; Accepted: 13 February 2018 ; Published: 16 February 2018

Abstract: The increasing exploration of alternative methods for solving optimization problems causes that parallelization and modification of the existing algorithms are necessary. Obtaining the right solution using the meta-heuristic algorithm may require long operating time or a large number of iterations or individuals in a population. The higher the number, the longer the operation time. In order to minimize not only the time, but also the value of the parameters we suggest three proposition to increase the efficiency of classical methods. The first one is to use the method of searching through the neighborhood in order to minimize the solution space exploration. Moreover, task distribution between threads and CPU cores can affect the speed of the algorithm and therefore make it work more efficiently. The second proposition involves manipulating the solutions space to minimize the number of calculations. In addition, the third proposition is the combination of the previous two. All propositions has been described, tested and analyzed due to the use of various test functions. Experimental research results show that the proposed methodology for parallelization and manipulation of solution space is efficient (increasing the accuracy of solutions and reducing performance time) and it is possible to apply it also to other optimization methods.

Keywords: optimization; meta-heuristic; parallel technique

---

1. Introduction

Computing and operation research demand efficient methods that can increase the precision of calculations. Developments in technology provide new possibilities for faster and more efficient computing. Multi core architectures can support multi threading, where similar tasks can be forwarded to various cores for processing at the same time. This approach speeds up calculations, however it is necessary to implement a devoted methodology. Such a solution can be very useful in practical applications where many operation are made. The main target of these techniques will be, in particular, artificial intelligence (AI). AI provides many possibilities to use the power of modern computing into various applications. [1] presents a survey of modern approaches to multimedia processing. Security and communication aspects for devoted computing systems were presented in [2]. In [3], the authors presented the efficient encryption algorithm based on logistic maps and parallel technique. Moreover, parallel approach found place in medicine, especially in image processing what can be seen in [4] where lung segmentation was presented. The proposed algorithm can be used in medical support system for fast diseases detection. To create the most accurate systems that can prevent people from invisible to the eye, the initial phase of the disease. In [5], the idea of parallel solution to measurements the structural similarity between images based on quality assessment. Similar approach is present in [6], where the authors used artificial intelligence technique for image retrieval from huge medical archives.

All solutions mentioned above presented different approach to parallelization. There are various ideas to parallelize calculations, e.g. by simply performing the same task parallel on all the cores and compare the results after each iteration. Similarly we can repeat only some procedures to increase precision. However most efficient are architecture solutions designed for specific purposes. Methodology that is developed precisely for the computing task can benefit from using multi core architecture.

In recent years, various approaches to optimization problems were solved using parallel processing to increase efficiency. Photosensitive seizures were detected by application of devoted parallel methodology in [7]. The authors of [8] discussed a local search framework developed for multi-commodity flow optimization. A parallel approach to implement algorithms with and without overlapping was presented in [9]. Similarly swarm algorithms are becoming more important for optimization processes and various practical applications. In [10], the author discussed a fusion of swarm methodology with neural networks for dynamic systems simulation and positioning. Parallel implementation of swarm methodology developed for two-sided line balancing problem was discussed in [11]. Massive-passing parallel approach to implement data tests were proposed in [12]. Similarly in [13] research on efficient parallelization of dynamic programming algorithms was discussed. An extensive survey of various approaches to parallelization of algorithms with devoted platforms for classification of biological sequences was presented in [14]. While in [15] the authors discussed constraint solving algorithms in parallel versions.

Again in [16], the authors presented a combination of approximation algorithms and linear relaxation with the classical heuristic algorithm. As a result, a hybrid was obtained, which allowed to reach better results in a much shorter time. Another hybrid was shown in [17], where local search techniques were used. A similar solution has already been used in combination with the genetic algorithm, which is called the Baldwin effect [18,19]. The problem of hybridization is much widely described in [20], where there are two types of combination called collaborative (two techniques work separately and only exchange information) and integrative (one technique is built into the other). Both solutions have their own advantages and the authors pointed out them by showing ten different methodologies. The result of which is obtaining better accuracy of the solution. A particular aspect is to draw attention during modeling this type of combinations to obtain the best features of all combined components. Again in another chapter, two other types of hybridization are presented using the example of a memetic algorithm in the application of character problems. The first one considers branch and bound features within construction-based metaheuristics, and the second one branch and bound derivatives.

In this article, we present an idea for the parallelize optimization technique based on different algorithms. The proposed implementation makes use of multi core architecture by dividing calculations between all the cores, however to make the algorithm more efficient we propose also devoted way of search in the optimization space. From the basic population individuals, we select a group of best adopted ones to forward their positions for a local search in their surrounding. The local search is performed using each core and therefore the methodology benefit from faster processing but also from increased precision of calculations since during parallel mode calculations are based on the best results from each iteration. Moreover, we propose a way to divide the space due to decrease the number of possible moves for individuals in the population. Additionally, we combined both these ideas to one for greater efficiency. Our approach is different from existing one in literature not only by creating hybrids, but by dividing calculations into cores and enabling finding the best areas across the entire space. In practice, the division of space into cores is a new idea that allows not only increasing the accuracy of results but also reducing the performance time.

2. Optimization Problem and the Method of Finding the Optimal Solution

The optimization problem is understood as finding the largest or smallest value of a parameter due to certain conditions. Mathematically, the problem can be defined as follows: Let f be an objective function of n variables x_i where $x = 0, \ldots, n-1$ and $\bar{x} = (x_1, x_2, \ldots, x_n)$ is a point. If the value of the function f at $\bar{x}$ is a global minimum of the function, then $\bar{x}$ is the solution. The problem of finding $\bar{x}$ is called minimization problem [21]. If the value of the function at that point reaches a global minimum, then it is called a minimization problem and it can be described as

$$
\begin{aligned}
&\text{Minimize} && f(\bar{x}) \\
&\text{subject to} && g(\bar{x}) \geq 0 \\
& && L_i \leq x_i \leq R_i \qquad i = 0, 1, \ldots, n-1,
\end{aligned} \tag{1}
$$

where $g(\bar{x})$ is inequality constraint, $\langle L_i, R_i \rangle$ are the boundaries of i-th variable.

For such defined problem, there is a large number of functions for which an optimal solution is hard to locate. The problem is the size of the solution space, or even the number of local extremes where the algorithm can get stacked. Some of these functions are presented in Table 1. One of the most used methods are genetic and heuristic algorithms. As heuristic, we namely algorithms that do not guarantee to find the correct solution (only the approximate) in a finite time.

Table 1. Test functions used in a minimization problem.

Function Name	Function f	Range	f_{min}	Solution $\bar{x}$
Dixon-Price	$f_1(\bar{x}) = (x_1 - 1)^2 + \sum_{i=1}^{n} i \left(2x_i^2 - x_{i-1} \right)^2$	$\langle -10, 10 \rangle$	0	$\left(2^{-\frac{2^1-2}{2^1}}, \ldots, 2^{-\frac{2^n-2}{2^n}} \right)$
Griewank	$f_2(\bar{x}) = \sum_{i=1}^{n} \frac{x_i^2}{4000} - \prod_{i=1}^{n} \cos \left(\frac{x_i}{\sqrt{(i)}} \right) + 1$	$\langle -10, 10 \rangle$	0	$(0, \ldots, 0)$
Rotated Hyper–Ellipsoid	$f_3(\bar{x}) = \sum_{i=1}^{n} \sum_{j=1}^{i} x_j^2$	$\langle -100, 100 \rangle$	0	$(0, \ldots, 0)$
Schwefel	$f_4(\bar{x}) = 418.9829n - \sum_{i=1}^{n} x_i \sin \left(\sqrt{|x_i|} \right)$	$\langle -500, 500 \rangle$	0	$(420.97, \ldots, 420.97)$
Shubert	$f_5(\bar{x}) = \prod_{i=1}^{n} \left(\sum_{i=1}^{5} i \cos((i+1)x_i) \right)$	$\langle -10, 10 \rangle$	-186.7	$(0, \ldots, 0)$
Sphere	$f_6(\bar{x}) = \sum_{i=1}^{n} x_i^2$	$\langle -10, 10 \rangle$	0	$(0, \ldots, 0)$
Sum squares	$f_7(\bar{x}) = \sum_{i=1}^{n} i x_i^2$	$\langle -10, 10 \rangle$	0	$(0, \ldots, 0)$
Styblinski-Tang	$f_8(\bar{x}) = \frac{1}{2} \sum_{i=1}^{n} \left(x_i^4 - 16x_i^2 + 5x_i \right)$	$\langle -10, 10 \rangle$	$-39.2n$	$(-2.9, \ldots, -2.9)$
Rastrigin	$f_9(\bar{x}) = 10n + \sum_{i=1}^{n} \left[x_i^2 - 10 \cos(2\pi x_i) \right]$	$\langle -10, 10 \rangle$	0	$(0, \ldots, 0)$
Zakharov	$f_{10}(\bar{x}) = \sum_{i=1}^{n} x_i^2 + (0.5ix_i)^2 + \left(\sum_{i=1}^{n} 0.5ix_i \right)^4$	$\langle -10, 10 \rangle$	0	$(0, \ldots, 0)$

2.1. Genetic Algorithm

Genetic Algorithms are examples of optimization algorithms inspired by natural selection [22]. It is a model of activities and operations on chromosomes. Algorithm assumes the creation of the beginning set of chromosomes, very often called the population. Each chromosome is presented by a binary code or a real number (more common is the second case, so we assume that). All individuals are created in a random way. Having the population, some operation are made. The first of them is the reproduction which is a process to transfer some individuals to the next operation. The most common way of reproduction is based on the probability of belonging to a particular group. In optimization problem, the group will be created by the best adapted individuals according to fitness function. The probability p_r can be described by the following equation

$$p_r\left(\overline{x_i^t}\right) = \frac{f\left(\overline{x_i^t}\right)}{x_i^t},\tag{2}$$

where $\overline{x_i^t}$ is the i-th individual in t-th iteration. For more randomness, the individual is chosen to reproduction process if it meets the following assumptions

$$P_r\left(\overline{x_{i-1}^t}\right) < \alpha \leq P_r\left(\overline{x_i^t}\right),\tag{3}$$

where $\alpha \in \langle 0,1 \rangle$ is the random value and $P_r(\cdot)$ is the value calculated as

$$P_r\left(\overline{x_i^t}\right) = \sum_{j=1}^{i} p_r\left(\overline{x_j^t}\right).\tag{4}$$

So in this way, the best individuals are selected to be reproduced and it is made by two classic operators known as mutation and crossover. The first of them is understood as the modification of the chromosome by adding random value $\tau \in \langle 0,1 \rangle$ as

$$\overline{x_i^{t+1}} = \overline{x_i^t} + \tau.\tag{5}$$

Of course, not every of them will be mutated – only these that will meet the inequality given as

$$\lambda_i < p_m,\tag{6}$$

where p_m is mutation probability and $\lambda \in \langle 0,1 \rangle$. The second operation, which is crossover is the exchange of the information between two chromosomes x_i and x_{i+1}. They are called parents, and the resulting individuals as childes. The whole process can be presented as

$$\overline{x_i^{t+1}} = \overline{x_i^t} + \tau\left(\overline{x_{i+1}^t} - \overline{x_i^t}\right)\overline{x_i^t},\tag{7}$$

where $\tau \in \langle 0,1 \rangle$.

After using the described operators, all individuals in the population are evaluated by the fitness function $f(\cdot)$ and new population replaces the old one and it is known as succession.

The algorithm is an iterative process, so all operations are repeated until a certain number of iterations are obtained—it is presented in Algorithm 1.

Algorithm 1: Genetic Algorithm

1: Start,

2: Define fitness function $f(\cdot)$,

3: Create an initial population,

4: Evaluate all individuals in the population,

5: Define τ, p_m, α and the number of iteration T,

6: $t := 0$,

7: **while** $t < T$ **do**
8:     Sort individuals according to $f(\cdot)$,

9:     Select best individuals according to Equation (2),

10:     Make a mutation by Equation (5),

11:     Make a crossover using Equation (7),

12:     Evaluate all new individuals in the population,

13:     Replace the worst with new ones,

14:     $t++$,

15: **end while**

16: Return the best chromosome,

17: Stop.

2.2. Artificial Ant Colony Algorithm

Artificial Ant Colony (ACO) is an algorithm inspired by the behavior of ants. At the beginning, the algorithm was designed for discrete problems such as graph [23]. Then, different versions were designed for problems dealing with continuous functions [24]. It is a model of searching for food by ants. If the source of food is found, the ant returns to the nest leaving a pheromone trace that helps to return to the source. Unfortunately, the amount of pheromone is reduced over time due to its evaporation. The ant $\overline{x}^m$ moves towards the selected individual from the population. The probability of selecting the j-th individual in the population is determined as

$$p_j = \frac{(1 + \exp\left(f\left(\overline{x}_j\right)\right))}{\sum\limits_{r=1}^{n}(1 + \exp\left(f(\overline{x}_r)\right))}. \tag{8}$$

Calculating probability, a direction of movement is selected by choosing a colony c as

$$c = \begin{cases} \max\limits_{i=1,2,\dots,n}(p_i), & q \leq q_0 \\ C & q > q_0 \end{cases}, \tag{9}$$

where $q_0 \in \langle 0, 1 \rangle$ is a parameter and q is random value in range $\langle 0, 1 \rangle$ and C is a random ant in population. After choosing the parent colony c, a Gaussian sampling is done. Using the density function, the scattering of pheromones in the entire space is modeled by the following equation

$$g(x_i^m, \mu, \sigma) = \frac{1}{\sigma\sqrt{2\pi}} \exp\left(-\frac{(x_j - \mu)}{2\sigma^2}\right), \tag{10}$$

where x_i^m is the specific coordinate for the m ant $\overline{x^m} = (x_1^m, \ldots, x_n^m)$ and $\mu = x_i^j$ so it is the coordinate for the selected j-th ant, and σ is the mean distance between the coordinate data of a points $\overline{x^m}$ and $\overline{x^j}$ calculated as

$$\sigma = \xi \sum_{r=1}^{n} \frac{|x_r^m - x_r^j|}{k-1}, \tag{11}$$

where ξ is the evaporation rate.

Then, the m ant population is generated in $N(\mu_i, \sigma_i)$, and the worst m individuals are deleted. The more detailed description of ACO algorithm is presented in Algorithm 2.

Algorithm 2: Ant Colony Optimization Algorithm

1: Start,

2: Define fitness function $f(\cdot)$,

3: Create an initial population of ants,

4: Evaluate all individuals in the population,

5: Define ξ, n, m and the number of iteration T,

6: $t := 0$,

7: **while** $t < T$ **do**

8:     **for** each ant **do**

9:         Calculate the probability using Equation (8),

10:         Find the best nest by Equation (9),

11:         Determine Gaussian sampling according to Equation (10),

12:         Create m new solutions and destroy m the worst ones,

13:     **end for**

14:     $t++$,

15: **end while**

16: Sort individuals according to $f(\cdot)$,

17: Return the best ant,

18: Stop.

2.3. Particle Swarm Optimization Algorithm

Particle Swarm Optimization Algorithm (PSOA) [25] is an algorithm inspired by two phenomena—swarm motion particles as well fish nebula. It describes the movement of swarm in the direction of the best individual. Despite targeted movement, the algorithm assumes randomness to increase the ability to change the best individual across the population. In order to model these phenomena, certain assumptions are introduced

- In each iteration, the number of individuals is constant,
- Only the best ones are transferred to the next iteration and the rest are randomly selected.

Each particle moves according to

$$\overline{x_i^{t+1}} = \lfloor \overline{x_i^t} + \mathbf{v_i^t} \rfloor, \tag{12}$$

where $\mathbf{v_i^t}$ is the velocity of the i-th molecule in the t-iteration. The velocity is calculated on the basis of various factors such as the position of the best individuals in current iteration t and labeled as x_{best}^t, which allows them to move in that direction. It is described as

$$\mathbf{v_i^{t+1}} = \mathbf{v_i^t} \cdot \phi_p \cdot \alpha \cdot \left(\overline{x_{best}^t} - \overline{x_i^t} \right) + \phi_s \cdot \beta \cdot \left(\overline{x_{best}^t} - \overline{x_i^t} \right), \tag{13}$$

where $\alpha, \beta \in \langle 0, 1 \rangle$ are the values chosen in random way and ϕ_p, ϕ_s are swarm controlling factors. If $\phi_s > \phi_p$, all particles move in the direction of the best one. In the case when $\phi_s \leq \phi_p$, all individuals move in random way. At the end of the iteration, only the best particles are transferred to the next iteration. The missing particles are added to population at random. The complete algorithm is presented in Algorithm 3.

Algorithm 3: Particle Swarm Optimization Algorithm

1: Start,

2: Define ϕ_p, ϕ_s, *best_ratio*, number of iteration T and n,

3: Define fitness function $f(\cdot)$,

4: Create an initial population,

5: $t := 0$,

6: **while** $t < T$ **do**

7:     Calculate velocity using Equation (13),

8:     Move each individual according to Equation (12),

9:     Sort population according to $f(\cdot)$,

10:     Take *best_ratio* of population to next iteration,

11:     Complete the remainder of the population randomly,

12:     $t++$,

13: **end while**

14: Return the best particle,

15: Stop.

2.4. Firefly Algorithm

Firefly Algorithm is another mathematical model that describes the natural phenomena which is the behavior of fireflies during the searching of a parter [26]. The search is dependent on many factors such as blinking, distance or even perception by other individuals, and this introduces several factors that describes the behavior of that insects and the environment

- ζ – light absorption coefficient,
- κ – coefficient of motion randomness,
- β_{pop} – attractiveness ratio,
- I_{pop} – light intensity.

A firefly moves into the most attractive individuals in the current environment based on the distance and the light intensity of a potential partner. In order to model this behavior, suppose that the distance between two individuals i and j will be be labeled as r_{ij} and it is calculated as

$$r_{ij}^t = \|\overline{x_i^t} - \overline{x_j^t}\| = \sqrt{\sum_{k=1}^N \left(x_{i,k}^t - x_{j,k}^t\right)^2}, \tag{14}$$

where t is the current iteration and $x_{i,k}^t$, $x_{k,j}^t$ – k-th components of the spatial coordinates. Attractiveness between individuals is dependent on this distance – the greater the distance is, they are less attractive to each another. Moreover, the light is absorbed by the air, because of that and simplifying the model, the following assumptions are applied to the model

- Each firefly is unisex,
- The attractiveness is proportional to the brightness, which means that the less attractive firefly will move to more attractive,
- The distance is greater, the attractiveness is lower,
- If there is no attractive partner in the neighborhood, then firefly moves randomly.

Reception of light intensity I_{ij}^t from i by j decreases as the distance r_{ij}^t between them increases. Moreover, the light in nature is absorbed by different media, so attractiveness depends not only on the distance but also on absorption, so light intensity I_{ij}^t is modeled as

$$I_{ij}^t \left(r_{ij}^t\right) = I_{pop} \cdot e^{-\zeta \cdot \left(r_{ij}^t\right)^2}, \tag{15}$$

where ζ is the parameter that describes light absorption mapping natural conditions of nature.

One of the assumption says that the attractiveness β_{ij} is proportional to the brightness (or firefly's lightness) what is defined as

$$\beta_{ij} \left(r_{ij}^t\right) = \beta_{pop} \cdot e^{-\zeta \cdot \left(r_{ij}^t\right)^2}, \tag{16}$$

where β_{pop} is firefly attractiveness coefficient.

The movement of fireflies is primarily dependent on the quality of the neighborhood. The primary equation that describes that movement depends on all dependencies described above what is shown in the following formula

$$x_i^{t+1} = \overline{x_i^t} + \left(\overline{x_j^t} - \overline{x_i^t}\right) \cdot \beta_{ij}^t \left(r_{ij}^t\right) \cdot I_{ij}^t \left(r_{ij}^t\right) + \kappa \cdot e_i, \tag{17}$$

where ζ is light absorption coefficient, κ is coefficient mapping natural randomness of fireflies, e_i is vector defined random change of position. In each iteration, all fireflies move to find the best position according to fitness condition $f(\cdot)$. Described model is presented in Algorithm 4.

Algorithm 4: Firefly Algorithm

Start,

Define all coefficients and the number of iteration T and size of population,

Define fitness function $f(\cdot)$,

Create at initial population,

$t := 0$,

while $t \leq T$ **do**

    Calculate all distances between individuals in whole population according to Equation (14),

    Calculate all light intensity between individuals in whole population according to Equation (15),

    Calculate attractiveness between individuals in whole population according to Equation (16),

    Evaluate and sort population,

    Move each firefly using Equation (17),

    $t++$,

end while

Return the best firefly,

Stop.

2.5. Cuckoo Search Algorithm

Cuckoo Search Algorithm is another metaheuristic algorithm which stands out by gradient free optimization method [27]. It is a model that describes the behavior of cuckoos during the specific nature of breeding. These birds do not take care of theirs own eggs and throw them to other nest. So the algorithm simulates the flight while looking for nests of other birds and laying eggs in there. Of course, there is also need to pay attention to the owner's response. In these model, some assumption must be done

- Cuckoo is identified with the egg,
- Each cuckoo has one egg,
- The nest owner decides to keep or throw the egg out with the probability $1 - \lambda \in \langle 0, 1 \rangle$. If the egg is thrown out, the new cuckoo is replace these one and the position is chosen at random.

At the beginning of the algorithm, an initial population is created in random way. Each cuckoo moves by making a flight which uses the random walk concept. It is modeled as

$$\overline{x_i^{t+1}} = \overline{x_i^t} + \mu \cdot L(\varphi, \rho, \delta), \tag{18}$$

where μ is the length of random walk step with normal distribution $N\left(\frac{\rho}{cuckoos}; 0.1\right)$ and $L(\cdot)$ is Lévy flight defined as

$$L(\varphi, \rho, \delta) = \begin{cases} \sqrt{\frac{\rho}{2\pi}} \dfrac{\exp\left[-\frac{\rho}{2(\varphi-\delta)}\right]}{(\varphi-\delta)^{\frac{3}{2}}}, & 0 < \varphi < \delta < \infty \\ 0, & \text{other} \end{cases}, \tag{19}$$

where φ is the length of the step, δ is the minimum step for random walk and ρ is a scaling parameter.

Once the individuals in the population have completed their movement, decide if the egg stays at the current position should be made. It is a decision-making mechanism by the owner of the nest to which the eggs were thrown. It is modeled as

$$H\left(\overline{x_i^{t+1}}\right) = \begin{cases} 1-\lambda & \text{drop the egg} \\ \lambda & \text{leave the egg} \end{cases}, \tag{20}$$

where $\lambda \in \langle 0,1 \rangle$ is a random value understood as the chance for egg to stay. Whole algorithm is described in Algorithm 5.

Algorithm 5: Cuckoo Search Algorithm

Start,

Define all parameters $\lambda \in \langle 0,1 \rangle$, φ, ρ, δ, *bestratio*, number of *cuckoos* and iterations T,

Define fitness function $f(\cdot)$,

Create an initial population,

t:=0,

while $t < T$ **do**
   Move individuals to another position using Equations (18) and (19),

   According to Equation (20), the nest host decides whether the cuckoo eggs remain,

   Evaluate the whole population,

   Sort the population according to fitness condition,

   $t++$,

end while

Return the best cuckoo,

Stop.

2.6. Wolf Search Algorithm

One of the new heuristic algorithms is Wolf Search Algorithm described for the first time in [28]. In the algorithm, the behavior of wolves during the search for food and avoid other predators is modeled. The model assumes that the wolf can only see in a certain area around himself and he can only move in it. This area is understood as a circle, where the center is the point (wolf) with r radius. The wolf's position is assessed in terms of its adaptability to the function $f(\cdot)$ which values are interpreted as a number of food locations in the circle. There is a situation that the wolf quickly escapes outside this area when another predator is in the vicinity or the amount of food in the area is quite low.

Such a behavior of the wolf while searching for food is modeled for optimization purposes. Let $\overline{x}$ be a particular wolf among the whole population. The actual position of $\overline{x}$ will be designated as $\overline{x}_{actual}$. Wolf moves according to

$$\overline{x}_{new} = \overline{x}_{actual} + \beta_0 \exp\left(-r^2\right)\left(\overline{x}_{neighbor} - \overline{x}_{actual}\right) + \gamma, \tag{21}$$

where β_0 is the ultimate incentive, $\overline{x}_{neighbor}$ is the closest neighbor with higher value of fitness function, γ is random number in $\langle 0,1 \rangle$ and r means the distance between two wolves $\overline{x}_{actual}$ and $\overline{x}_{neighbor}$

calculated as the Euclidean metric already described in Equation (14). Wolf moves by Equation (21), when he spotted a better feeding. Otherwise, the wolf tries to hunt. Hunting of wolves lies in a process of stalking that can be represented into three steps

- initiative stage – wolf moves in the area of his vision and looks for food. This behavior is modeled by changing the position of the wolf in the following way

$$\overline{x}_{new} = \overline{x}_{actual} + \alpha v \gamma, \tag{22}$$

  where v is the velocity of a wolf.
- passive stage – wolf waits for the opportunity to attack on a given position and tries to attack by Equation (21).
- escape – in case of lack of food or the appearance of another predator, the wolf escapes by

$$\overline{x}_{new} = \overline{x}_{actual} + \alpha k \gamma, \tag{23}$$

  where k is the step size.

It is simply model showing the behavior of wolves. In each iteration, wolves search for better food source and in the end, the wolves that is identified with best food source is the result. The full algorithm is presented in Algorithm 6.

Algorithm 6: Wolf Search Algorithm

Start,

Define basic parameters of the algorithm – the number of iterations T, the number of wolves n, radius of view r, step size k, velocity coefficient α and rate of appearance of the enemy p_α,

Generate a population of wolves at random,

$t := 0$,

while $t < T$ **do**

    for each wolf $\overline{x}_{actual}$ in population **do**

        Check the viewing area by Equation (22),

        Calculate the new position $\overline{x}_{new}$ using Equation (21),

        if $d(\overline{x}_{actual}, \overline{x}_{new}) < r \wedge f(\overline{x}_{new}) < f(\overline{x}_{actual})$ **then**

            Move the wolf from $\overline{x}_{actual}$ to $\overline{x}_{new}$,

        end if

        Select the value of the parameter $\beta \in \langle 0, 1 \rangle$ at random,

        if $\beta > p_\alpha$ **then**

            The wolf performs escape by Equation (23),

        end if

    end for

    $t + +$,

end while

Return the fittest wolf $\overline{x}_{global}$ in the population,

Stop.

---

3. Manipulation of Swarms Positions and Space Solution Using Multi-Threaded Techniques

The problem of finding the optimal solution is more difficult if the test function is complicated. As complicated we understand the function of which extremes are hard to locate by classical methods. In this case, the application of meta–heuristic methodology seems to be a good solution. However, in some cases the values of the parameters should be significantly increased like the number of individuals in a population as well as the number of iterations. Increasing the value of these parameters increases the number of performed operations and thus action time. In addition, these algorithms do not guarantee the correct solution. With these problems, the application of these techniques may prove to be very detrimental.

3.1. Proposition I

In order to minimize the amount of computation time, we suggest using automatic parallelization of the algorithms by dividing the population into several groups, which threads are burdened.

From the perspective of nature, individuals analyze the environment and choose the best of them all. In the neighborhood of the best solution, smaller populations called groups may be formed. Suppose that at the beginning of the algorithm, the number of cores pc is detected. In analogy to the original version of the algorithms, an initial population consisting of n individuals is created at random. From this population, pc fittest individuals are chosen. Each individual will be the best adapted solution in the smaller group that will be created under his leadership. The size of the group will be determined as follows

$$n_{group} = \left\lfloor \frac{n}{pc} \right\rfloor. \tag{24}$$

The above equation uses the floor to obtain groups with the same population size for each core. The use of the floor guarantees that, regardless of n, each group will have the same number of individuals, and the sum of all n_{group} will not exceed n.

With the size of the group and their leadership, we can begin to create groups. For every alpha male, we create one thread on which the population consisting of n_{group} individuals is created. Each individual in the group is placed in a random way at a distance of no more than d_{max} from the leader. This distance can be calculated by

$$\begin{cases} \frac{|a-b|}{n} & \text{if} \quad a \neq b \\ \frac{a}{n} & \text{if} \quad a = b \end{cases}, \tag{25}$$

where a, b are the values of the variable's range for the test function.

For each group on a separate thread, all steps from an original algorithms are performed. After completing these steps, pc the best adapted individuals are found as a solution for the optimization problem and selected the best of them. Complete operation of the proposed method is shown in Algorithm 7.

Algorithm 7: Metaheuristic with devoted local search

1: Start,

2: Detect the number of cores pc,

3: Create an initial population at random,

4: Select pc best individuals,

5: Calculate the number of individuals n_{group} in groups using Equation (24),

6: Create pc groups consisting n_{group} individuals based on Equation (25),

7: Put each group on a separate thread,

8: Run chosen metaheuristic with a customized group as a population on each thread,

9: Choose the best individuals from all threads,

10: Stop.

3.2. Proposition II

In the previously proposition, we proposed a technique for putting individuals in a given population on the solution space and assigning them a thread for calculation. Another way to increase the efficiency is to manipulating the solution space in such a way as to limit the possibility of movements in the least favorable areas. Imagine that in the early iterations of the algorithm, the population begins to move in the best areas, i.e., an area where the extreme may potentially occur. Suppose that we have pc processor cores, so pc threads can be created. Our solution space for fitness function f can be presented as

$$a \times b = \langle a_1, a_2 \rangle \times \langle b_1, b_2 \rangle, \tag{26}$$

where a_1, a_2, b_1, b_2 are values that divide the set $\langle a, b \rangle$ into such two subsets $\langle a_1, a_2 \rangle$, $\langle b_1, b_2 \rangle$ that Equation (26) is satisfied and $\times$ means Cartesian product (note that the limit values a_2 and b_2 correspond to a and b). Using that information, we can divide this space into pc smallest intervals as

$$a = \langle a_1, a_2 \rangle = \left\langle a_1, \frac{a_2}{pc} \right\rangle \cup \bigcup_{k=1}^{pc-1} \left\langle \frac{ka_2}{pc}, \frac{a_2}{pc}(k+1) \right\rangle. \tag{27}$$

Taking these small intervals and use them to describe the solution space for function f would be

$$a \times b = \langle a_1, a_2 \rangle \times \langle b_1, b_2 \rangle = \left\langle \left\langle a_1, \frac{a_2}{pc} \right\rangle \cup \bigcup_{k=1}^{pc-1} \left\langle \frac{ka_2}{pc}, \frac{a_2}{pc}(k+1) \right\rangle \times \left\langle \frac{kb_2}{pc}, \frac{b_2}{pc}(k+1) \right\rangle \right\rangle \tag{28}$$

Unfortunately, these formulations give us pc^2 parts of solution space. The reason for that is dividing each side of the interval on pc parts. Having only pc cores, it is necessary to merge some areas to obtain exactly number of pc. To do that, we can describe formula for vertical merge of areas for specific cores—for first one as

$$\left\langle a_1, \frac{a_2}{pc} \right\rangle \times \left\{ \left\langle b_1, \frac{b_2}{pc} \right\rangle, \left\langle \frac{kb_2}{pc}, \frac{b_2}{pc}(k+1) \right\rangle \right\} \qquad \text{for } k \in \{1, pc-1\}, \tag{29}$$

and for each subsequent m core as

$$\left\langle \frac{ma_2}{pc}, \frac{a_2}{pc}(m+1) \right\rangle \times \left\{ \left\langle b_1, \frac{b_2}{pc} \right\rangle, \left\langle \frac{kb_2}{pc}, \frac{b_2}{pc}(k+1) \right\rangle \right\} \qquad \text{for } k \in \{1, pc-1\}. \tag{30}$$

Let us prove, that sum of all these parts are equal to the initial solution space.

Proof. Taking all areas dedicated for first core described in Equation (29), we have

$$\left\langle a_1, \frac{a_2}{pc} \right\rangle \times \bigcup_{k=1}^{pc-1} \left\langle \left\langle b_1, \frac{b_2}{pc} \right\rangle, \left\langle \frac{kb_2}{pc}, \frac{b_2}{pc}(k+1) \right\rangle \right\rangle, \tag{31}$$

the same is done with the rest areas in Equation (30) as

$$\bigcup_{k=1}^{pc-1} \left\langle \frac{ka_2}{pc}, \frac{a_2}{pc}(k+1) \right\rangle \times \bigcup_{k=1}^{pc-1} \left\{ \left\langle b_1, \frac{b_2}{pc} \right\rangle, \left\langle \frac{kb_2}{pc}, \frac{b_2}{pc}(k+1) \right\rangle \right\}. \tag{32}$$

By adding sets obtained above, we have

$$\left\langle a_1, \frac{a_2}{pc} \right\rangle \cup \bigcup_{k=1}^{pc-1} \left\langle \frac{ka_2}{pc}, \frac{a_2}{pc}(k+1) \right\rangle \times \bigcup_{k=1}^{pc-1} \left\langle \left\langle b_1, \frac{b_2}{pc} \right\rangle, \left\langle \frac{kb_2}{pc}, \frac{b_2}{pc}(k+1) \right\rangle \right\rangle, \tag{33}$$
$$= \langle a_1, a_2 \rangle \times \langle b_1, b_2 \rangle = a \times b.$$

□

This gives the pc areas (making the whole solutions space). Now, for each core, $\chi\%n$ of the entire size of the population n is created ($\chi \in \langle 0, 100 \rangle$)—but the individuals are made in the selected area, not in the whole space. After $r = \chi\%t$ of all iteration t, each core k is evaluated as

$$\Phi_k = \alpha \frac{\sum_{i=1}^{r} f(\overline{x}_i)}{n} + \beta f(\overline{x}_{best}), \tag{34}$$

where $\alpha + \beta = 1$ and they are coefficients describing the importance of a given part – the average of all individuals and the best individual on the current thread. We choose the p best areas and repeated the movement of population on each core in the sum of these areas by $(100 - \chi)\%$ of the iteration and $(100 - \chi)\%$ of the individuals. If the case, when individuals leaves the area, he is killed and a new individual is created in his place. After all iteration, the best solution is funded in all populations.

In this proposition, the multi-threading technique has a big role because dividing the space and choosing the best areas does not cost extra time and above all, it allows the placement of most individuals in a smaller area in parallel several times. These actions are described in Algorithm 8

Algorithm 8: Analysis of the solution space for the initial population

---

1: Start,

2: Define the solution space $a \times b$, the size of population n, the number t of iterations and a fitness function f,

3: Detect the number pc of processor cores,

4: Divide and assign the given areas to threads through Equations (29) and (30),

5: **for** each thread **do**

6:     Create a population of $\chi\%n$ individuals at random,

7:     $T := 0$,

8:     **for** $T < \chi\%t$ **do**

9:         Move the individuals in population,

10:         $T++$,

11:     **end for**

12: **end for**

13: Rate populations on each thread and select the best,

14: Define new solution space using the best areas,

15: **for** each thread **do**

16:     Create a population of $(100 - \chi)\%n$ individuals at random,

17:     $T := 0$,

18:     **for** $T < (100 - \chi)\%t$ **do**

19:         Move the individuals in population,

20:         $T++$,

21:     **end for**

22: **end for**

23: Choose and return the best individuals in all populations,

24: Stop.

3.3. Proposition III

Our last proposition is the combination of the above two propositions with some modifications. At first, we dividing solution space according to (29) and (30). Having the number of areas, threads can be created. χ% of all individuals are created in each area for χ%t iterations. The occurring χ for iterations and populations may have different values. To simplify the introduction of a large number of parameters, we assume that they have the same value. At the end, in each population, the best individuals stays, the rest of them is destroyed.

For each survived individual (which are identify with the best solutions), a group is formed exactly like in Section 3.1 but the size of group should not be greater than 50% of all n. Next, all individuals moves for the rest of iterations. In addition, then, the population size is replenished (if the size is smaller than n) in a random way throughout the area.

4. Test Results

All presented propositions have been implemented along with extended versions with the proposed multi–threading technique. All tests were carried out on the six-processor Intel Core i7 6850K clocked at 3.6 GHz.

4.1. The Benchmark Functions

Proposed solutions were tested on different 10 functions described in Table 1. All these functions were given in dimension $D = 100$. The selected functions are the representatives of different types like bowl, plate, valley shaped and with many local minima.

4.2. Experimental Settings

In experiments, we used described version of classical meta–heuristic algorithms. For all tests, we used the same numbers of iterations $t = 100$ and population size of 100 individual and $\chi = 10$. For each test, 100 measurements were taken and averaged. The tests were performed in terms of performance depending on the number of cores and as regards the accuracy of averaged solutions.

The coefficients used by all the algorithm have been selected before the start of operation. The influence of the increase in coefficients values causes the multitude of a given step or displacement of individuals. Therefore, in our considerations we do not analyze the impact of these coefficients on the method and accuracy of the obtained solutions, and each parameter was chosen in a random way in the range $\langle 0.1, 0.4 \rangle$. The obtained values of coefficients were respectively

- Genetic algorithm – $p_m = 0.39$,
- Ant Colony Optimization Algorithm – $\xi = 0.23$, $m = 30$, $q_0 = 0.4$,
- Particle Swarm Optimization Algorithm – $\phi_p = 0.15$, $\phi_s = 0.32$, $best\_ratio = 20$,
- Firefly Algorithm – $\zeta = 0.31$, $\beta_{pop} = 0.28$, $I_{pop=0.18}$
- Cuckoo Search Algorithm – $\lambda = 0.37$, $\delta = 0.12$, $\varphi = 0.33$, $\rho = 0.21$, $bestratio = 20$,
- Wolf Search Algorithm – $k = 0.15$, $\beta_0 = 0.21$, $\alpha = 0.23$.

4.3. Performance Metrics

For the purpose of evaluating algorithms, several basic metrics have been used. The accuracy of the optimization algorithms is evaluated by the average value of the solution obtained from the tests carried out what can be presented as

$$\frac{1}{100} \sum_{i=1}^{100} f(\overline{x}_i), \tag{35}$$

and error calculated as an absolute value between the ideal and obtained solution which is

$$\left| f(\overline{x}_{ideal}) - \frac{1}{100} \sum_{i=1}^{100} f(\overline{x}_i) \right|. \tag{36}$$

The second aspect is parallelization evaluated by two metrics – acceleration Y and efficiency Ψ. Acceleration is the ratio of sequential execution time of the algorithm defined as

$$Y = \frac{\varsigma}{\varphi},$$ (37)

where ς is execution time measured for one processor, and φ is execution time measured for pc processors. The second assessment is made by the following formula

$$\Psi = \frac{Y}{pc}.$$ (38)

In addition, scalability with the number of cores is measured in accordance with Amdahl's law

$$G = \frac{1}{1 - \Theta + \frac{\Theta}{pc}},$$ (39)

where Θ is the proportion of execution time of the proposal to the original versions. For our measurements, Θ was determined as the quotient of the average time for all algorithms for pc cores and the sum of time needed for pc and one processor.

4.4. Results

Firstly, we analyzed the impact of different coefficient values on the algorithms. We noticed that the coefficient values depend on the function itself—the more local extremes, the higher the values should be. This is due to the fact that individuals have to get out in such a minimum location, hence the large values of coefficients can prolong movement in one iteration and allow escape. Such reasoning forced us to depend on the value of coefficients from the pseudorandom generator. This action, combined with averaging the obtained results, enabled to obtain averaged solutions. It was performed for all versions of the algorithms—the original and three proposed modifications in this paper. The obtained solution are presented in Tables 2–5 and errors values are in Tables 6–9. In all cases, the first proposition—the use of devoted local search—reduced the error values in almost every case. Of course, there were cases when the selected algorithms had a minimal difference between the results (see CSA results), although it may be due to bad initial position of individuals. In contrast, the second proposal related to the division of the solution space brought quite a big drop in the value of errors for each case. This points to the fact that the size of the space is very important for metaheuristics—a search of the same area in less time and without necessarily increasing computing needs is a very important issue. The proposed division of space is one of the many cases that can be corrected, but it is one that significantly improves solution for each test function indicates the direction of future research. Moreover, the combination of these two proposition improved the obtained results for many cases, but not for all. GA and PSOA improved solutions for more than 5 cases, when FA improved the score for 9 from 10 benchmark functions. For better visualization the error values, The average error obtained for each version of the algorithm is shown in Figure 1. The graph shows that the error value is the smallest when applying proposition 2 or 3, and 1 has an approximately constant error.

Table 2. Averaged solution values achieved by all original algorithms for each test functions.

Function	GA	PSOA	FA	CSA	WSA	ACO
f_1	0.07593	0.08617	0.26872	0.16432	0.00257	0.00319
f_2	0.12283	0.16489	0.18691	0.1729	0.1275	0.13129
f_3	0.00172	0.27991	0.05206	0.00948	0.00029	0.00192
f_4	0.00506	0.00963	0.00174	0.01354	0.00981	0.00166
f_5	−186.014	−185.831	−185.843	−185.824	−185.805	−185.815
f_6	0.00001	0	0.00001	0.0002	0.00001	0.00001
f_7	0.00105	0.00062	0.66179	0.00035	0.00025	0.00037
f_8	−391.329	−391.58	−391.344	−391.746	−391.598	−391.594
f_9	0.19899	0.07731	0.13266	0.07822	0.1328	0.09898
f_{10}	0.00103	0.00172	0.04368	0.33444	0.00103	0.00098

Table 3. Averaged solution values achieved by all algorithms for each test functions for proposition I.

Function	GA	PSOA	FA	CSA	WSA	ACO
f_1	0.05754	0.02098	0.06574	0.03123	0.16919	0.00317
f_2	0.09337	0.10636	0.08035	0.09318	0.10691	0.08546
f_3	0.00046	0.00019	0.01644	0.15137	0.04208	0.00043
f_4	0.00083	0.00165	0.00203	0.00913	0.0002	0.00035
f_5	−186.918	−187.072	−186.914	−187.967	−187.053	−186.99
f_6	0	0	0	0.00004	0	0.00053
f_7	0.00272	0.00101	0.00023	0.00001	0.00634	0.00053
f_8	−391.783	−391.824	−391.829	−391.919	−391.94	9411-391
f_9	0.1072	0.23339	0.1063	0.98148	0.19899	0.00977
f_{10}	0.00172	0.00006	0.00094	0.01052	0.00109	0.0015

Table 4. Averaged solution values achieved by all algorithms for each test functions for proposition II.

Function	GA	PSOA	FA	CSA	WSA	ACO
f_1	0.03072	0.00027	0.08178	0.00217	0.0039	0.00032
f_2	0.09337	0.07208	0.05691	0.07437	0.10287	0.06821
f_3	0.00001	0	0	0.00006	0.00005	0.00002
f_4	0.00079	0.00083	0.00166	0.00015	0.00011	0.00029
f_5	−186.438	−186.29	−186.597	−186.563	−186.633	−186.694
f_6	0.00001	0	0.00001	0.00003	0	0
f_7	0.00124	0.00023	0.00005	0.00002	0.00013	0.00012
f_8	−391.968	−391.893	−391.9878	−391.983	−391.926	−391.978
f_9	0.01592	0.03343	0.0199	0.00995	0.01	0.00899
f_{10}	0.00314	0	0.00971	0.00117	0.00073	0

Table 5. Averaged solution values achieved by all algorithms for each test functions for proposition III.

Function	GA	PSOA	FA	CSA	WSA	ACO
f_1	0.00892	0.00913	0.00088	0.01001	0.00785	0.00339
f_2	0.06694	0.02898	0.00948	0.01298	0.0238	0.00539
f_3	0	0	0.0001	0.00044	0.00005	0.00001
f_4	0.00218	0.001	0.00012	0.00179	0.00019	0.00049
f_5	−186.692	−186.699	−186.694	−186.698	−186.698	−187.1
f_6	0	0	0	0.00002	0	0
f_7	0.00001	0.00007	0	0	0.00003	0.00008
f_8	−391.893	−391.919	−391.99	−391.999	−391.993	−391.999
f_9	0.00996	0.02995	0.12367	0	0.03033	0.00139
f_{10}	0.00658	0.00023	0.00014	0.01467	0.00022	0

Table 6. Function error values achieved by all original algorithms for each test functions.

Function	GA	PSOA	FA	CSA	WSA	ACO
f_1	−0.07593	−0.08617	−0.26872	−0.16432	−0.00257	−0.00319
f_2	−0.12283	−0.16489	−0.18691	−0.17290	−0.12750	−0.13129
f_3	−0.00172	−0.27991	−0.05206	−0.00948	−0.00029	−0.00192
f_4	−0.00506	−0.00963	−0.00174	−0.01354	−0.00981	−0.00166
f_5	−0.68573	−0.86850	−0.85691	−0.87632	−0.89550	−0.88475
f_6	0	0	−0.00001	−0.00020	0	0
f_7	−0.00106	−0.00062	−0.66179	−0.00035	−0.00025	−0.00037
f_8	−0.67100	−0.41761	−0.65646	−0.25370	−0.40180	−0.40560
f_9	−0.33445	−0.00103	−0.00172	−0.00006	−0.00094	−0.01052
f_{10}	−0.00103	−0.00172	−0.04368	−0.33445	−0.00103	−0.00098

Table 7. Averaged errors values achieved by all algorithms for each test functions for proposition I.

Function	GA	PSOA	FA	CSA	WSA	ACO
f_1	−0.05754	−0.02098	−0.06574	−0.03123	−0.16919	−0.00317
f_2	−0.09337	−0.10636	−0.08035	−0.09318	−0.10690	−0.08546
f_3	−0.00046	−0.00019	−0.01644	−0.15137	−0.04208	−0.00043
f_4	−0.00083	−0.00165	−0.00203	−0.00913	−0.00020	−0.00035
f_5	0.21804	0.37145	0.21421	0.26740	0.35291	0.28987
f_6	0	0	0	−0.00004	0	0
f_7	−0.00272	−0.00101	−0.00023	−0.00001	−0.00634	−0.00053
f_8	−0.21651	−0.17610	−0.17057	−0.08075	−0.06011	−0.05886
f_9	−0.01052	−0.00109	−0.00314	0	−0.00971	−0.00117
f_{10}	−0.00172	−0.00006	−0.00094	−0.01052	−0.00109	−0.00150

Table 8. Averaged errors values achieved by all algorithms for each test functions for proposition II.

Function	GA	PSOA	FA	CSA	WSA	ACO
f_1	−0.03072	−0.00027	−0.08178	−0.00217	−0.00390	−0.00032
f_2	−0.09337	−0.07208	−0.05691	−0.07437	−0.10287	−0.06782
f_3	−0.00001	0	0	−0.00006	−0.00005	−0.00002
f_4	−0.00079	−0.00083	−0.00166	−0.00015	−0.00011	−0.00029
f_5	−0.26173	−0.41035	−0.10293	−0.13672	−0.06741	−0.00622
f_6	0	0	0	−0.00003	0	0
f_7	−0.00124	−0.00023	−0.00005	−0.00002	−0.00013	−0.00012
f_8	−0.03217	−0.10752	−0.01222	−0.01671	−0.07361	−0.02173
f_9	−0.00117	−0.00073	−0.00658	−0.00023	−0.00014	−0.01467
f_{10}	−0.00314	0	−0.00971	−0.00117	−0.00073	0

Table 9. Averaged errors values achieved by all algorithms for each test functions for proposition III.

Function	GA	PSOA	FA	CSA	WSA	ACO
f_1	−0.00892	−0.00913	−0.00088	−0.01001	−0.00785	−0.00339
f_2	−0.06694	−0.02898	−0.00948	−0.01298	−0.02380	−0.00539
f_3	0	0	−0.00010	−0.00044	−0.00005	−0.00001
f_4	−0.00218	−0.00100	−0.00012	−0.00179	−0.00019	−0.00049
f_5	−0.00843	−0.00147	−0.00634	−0.00199	−0.00136	0.400033
f_6	0	0	0	−0.00002	0	0
f_7	−0.00001	−0.00007	0	0	−0.00003	−0.00008
f_8	−0.10710	−0.08110	−0.00981	−0.00009	−0.00710	−0.00009
f_9	−0.01467	−0.00022	0	−0.10287	−0.06782	−0.06694
f_{10}	−0.00658	−0.00023	−0.00014	−0.01467	−0.00022	0

Table 10. Running time values achieved by all algorithms for each test functions for original algorithms.

Function	GA	PSOA	FA	CSA	WSA	ACO
f_1	2006	1821	1648.8	1841	1626.3	1798
f_2	2617	2775	2757	2647	2687	2674
f_3	1151	905	896	898	903	891
f_4	1432	1422	1421	1392	1401	1387
f_5	5421	5500	5458	5240	5521	5341
f_6	651	645	879	664	673	632
f_7	730	720	783	715	706	711
f_8	2818	2756	2929	2749	2755	2765
f_9	801	804	935	798	803	803
f_{10}	2252	2114	2769	2648	2273	2178

Table 11. Running time values achieved by all algorithms for each test functions for proposition I.

Function	GA	PSOA	FA	CSA	WSA	ACO
f_1	1609.2	1784	1820	1802	1589	1673
f_2	2377.7	2409.44	2432.7	2400.3	2382.3	2401
f_3	812.7	822.6	808.2	815.4	806.4	812
f_4	1417	1282.5	1275.3	1286.1	1276.2	1267
f_5	4868.1	4860	4932	4914	4908.6	4912
f_6	591.3	653	601.2	589.5	583.2	592.5
f_7	635.4	633.6	682.6	636.3	586.08	581.4
f_8	2301	2318	2529	2249	2492	2498
f_9	720	702.24	763.6	714.6	732.6	712
f_{10}	2048	2047	2234	2021	2089	2091

Table 12. Running time values achieved by all algorithms for each test functions for proposition II.

Function	GA	PSOA	FA	CSA	WSA	ACO
f_1	1643.4	1584	1622.72	1583.12	1573.44	1602
f_2	2399.4	2280	2583	2349	2482	2403
f_3	789.36	801.68	786.72	762	782.32	773
f_4	1247.84	1291.5	1260.16	1245.2	1249.84	1267
f_5	4785.44	4772.24	4843.52	4762.56	4670.16	4694.95
f_6	571.12	589.6	581.4	583.44	586.08	582.2
f_7	648	583.44	603	586.08	602.8	589.2
f_8	2491	2429	2539	2349	2483	2424
f_9	601.5	728.64	704.88	620.25	724.24	636
f_{10}	2124	2148	2348	2189	2290	2201

Table 13. Running time values achieved by all algorithms for each test functions for proposition III.

Function	GA	PSOA	FA	CSA	WSA	ACO
f_1	1623.6	1349.25	1345.5	1367.25	1335.75	1401
f_2	2418.24	2286.75	2449.8	2399.76	2690.25	2650
f_3	788.48	756	673.5	678	672	673
f_4	1258.4	1060.5	1062.75	1061.25	1060.5	1064
f_5	4094.25	4091.25	4122.75	4001	4104	4005
f_6	483	567.6	488.25	491.25	486	473
f_7	584.32	495.75	545.75	497.25	496.5	491
f_8	2202	2121	2292	2160.75	2176.5	2189
f_9	718.96	601.5	703	597	635	606
f_{10}	2103	2014	2261	2127	2221	2134

We also evaluated individual algorithms by assigning them ranks for each proposal—if the algorithm obtained the most accurate solution for a given function using a particular technique, it received one point. Results are presented in Figure 2, and it is easy to notice that depending on the chosen proposal, another algorithm proved to be the best. It is easy to notice that depending on the chosen proposal, another algorithm proved to be the best. Without any modification the best algorithm was classic version of PSOA and ACO. Adding first proposition the best one were PSOA and FA, CSA, ACO are in the second place equally, and with second proposals, there are the same scores. The third modification allowed CSA and ACO to be the best algorithms. Of course, obtained results depend on the equations of motion, their length and other factors affecting such a large palette of metaheuristic methods. Not only, the accuracy was measured, but the duration of action with using multithreading techniques. Measured time values are presented in Table 4, 10, 11, 12, 13 and on Figure 3. The use of any modification shortens the operating time for almost every case compared to the original versions. What is interesting, first and second proposition shortened time of approximately the same value, when the third obtained the best result in this aspect. To accurately assess the operation time, we used the formulas described in Equations (37) and (38), the obtained results are presented in Table 14. The worst results were achieved for the first modification, than the third one and the second one as the best one in terms of acceleration. Scalability for each proposition (having 6 cores) were approximately successively 1.79, 1.79 and 1.86. To analyze these values, we also calculated the scalability for the 2 and 4 cores which results are presented in Figure 4. Ideal solution would be linear curve, but the more cores are used, the worst scalability is. In the case of the first two proposals, it decreases quite rapidly. However, the scalability of proposition III only minimally decreases after using more than 4 cores. Another aspect is the number of iteration needed for the sequential version to get similar results (approximately) to the presented proposals. The obtained data are presented in Table 15. In the case of 6 cores (for proposition I and II), the number of iteration must be increased by almost 22–26%. Such a large discrepancy is caused by the randomness of the algorithms (for example, the initial distribution of the population). In the case of proposals III, the sequential algorithm needs about 29% more iterations.

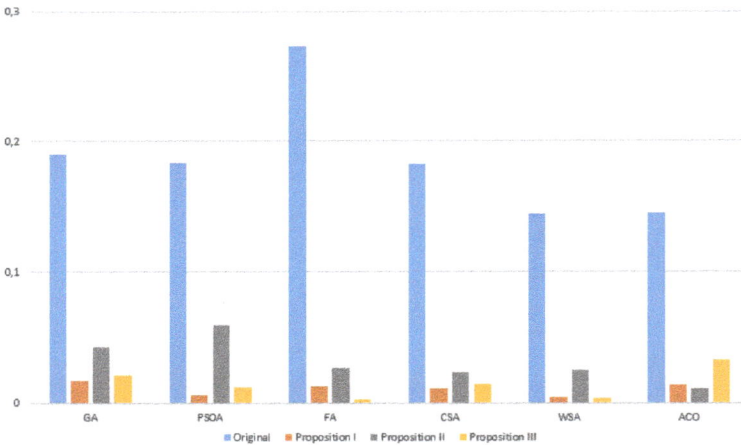

Figure 1. The average error obtained for each version of the algorithm.

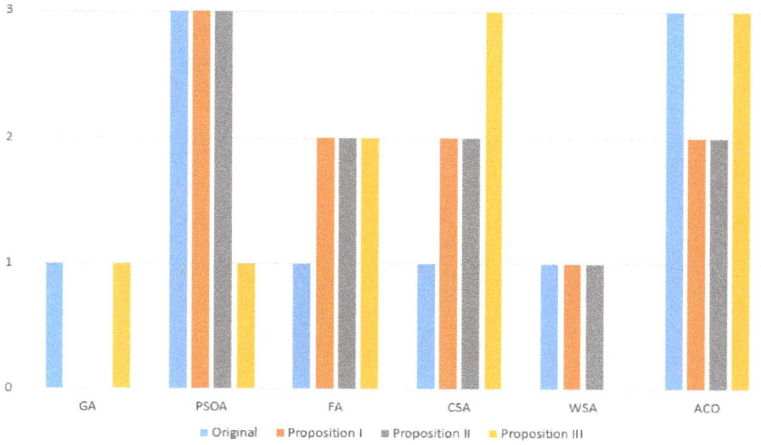

Figure 2. The performance ranking of tested algorithms—the number of times the algorithm ranked first.

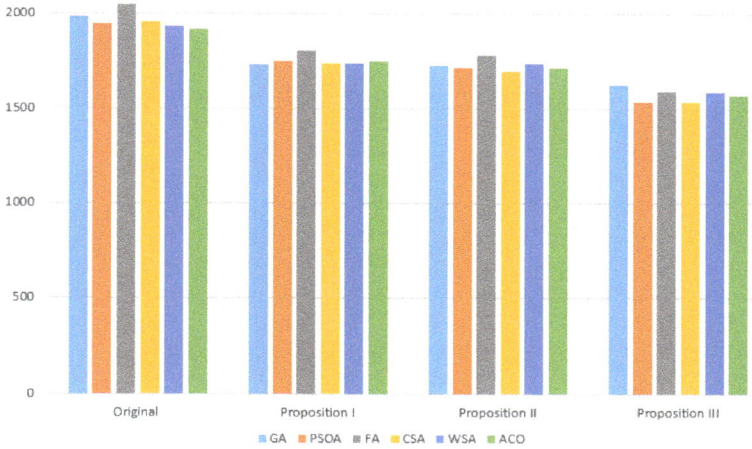

Figure 3. Comparison of the average time needed to find the optimum for 100 individuals during 100 iterations for 100 tests for each algorithm and all tested versions.

Table 14. Obtained results from the use of parallelization for metaheuristic algorithms.

Metric	Proposition I	Proposition II	Proposition III
Y	1.11911	1.13374	1.24793
Φ	0.18652	0.18896	0.20799
G	1.78599	1.79463	1.86089

Table 15. The average amount of additional iterations needed to obtain similar results by a sequential algorithm.

Proposition	GA	PSOA	FA	CSA	WSA	ACO
Proposition I	28	27	29	30	31	28
Proposition II	37	35	35	41	33	32
Proposition III	40	39	43	44	41	39

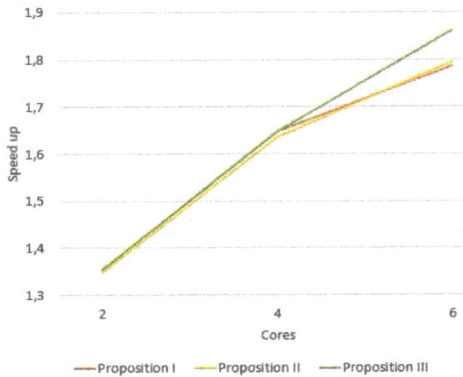

Figure 4. Scalability for each proposition.

A factorial ANOVA test was conducted to compare the main effects of absolute error and running time values among classic meta-heuristic and three proposed techniques. The results was significant both for absolute error ($F(3, 183) = 22.66, p < 0.001$) and running time ($F(3, 183) = 56.60, p < 0.001$). The results of Friedman-Nemenyi tests of ranking further reveal that the performance of Proposition III is the best among all techniques in terms absolute error ($p < 0.001$, critical distance $= 0.66$; tied with Proposition II) and running time ($p < 0.001$, critical distance $= 0.66$). The ranks of the methods within the critical distance are not significantly different (see Figure 5). The results are confirmed by the random permutation test (10000 permutations). Proposition III has lower absolute error than Classic method ($p = 0.88$), Proposition I ($p = 0.78$), and Proposition II ($p = 0.56$). Proposition III has lower running time than Classic method ($p = 0.98$), Proposition I ($p = 0.84$), and Proposition II ($p = 0.88$).

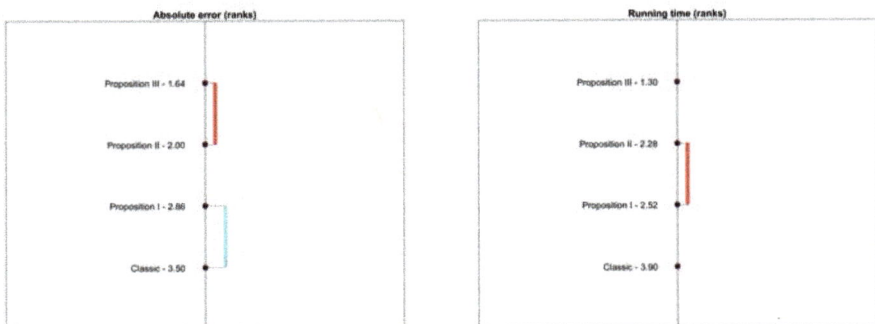

Figure 5. The results of Friedman-Nemenyi tests of ranking.

5. Conclusions

In this paper, we described six, classic meta–heuristic algorithms designed for optimization purposes and proposed three techniques for increasing not only the accuracy, but also the efficiency of the operation. Our ideas were based primarily on the action of multi–threading, which allowed placing individuals of a given population in specific places where an extreme can be located. An additional idea was to divide and manipulate the solutions space, which is interpreted as the natural environment of the individuals in given population. These types of activities have been tested and analyzed in terms of average error for selected functions and the time needed to perform the calculations to find a solution. The obtained results indicated that each proposed modification shortens the time of operation, but not all improve (significantly) the accuracy of the obtained measurements. The high scalability of the proposal indicates that the increasing number of cores speeds up the work of modifications. Moreover, each proposition showed the acceleration of the performance time as well as increasing the accuracy of the obtained solutions regardless of the chosen heuristic algorithm.

While the proposed techniques of parallelization and manipulation of solution space have improved the operation of classical algorithms, they are so flexible that can be streamlined and improved by various ideas. In addition, this can allow to obtain even better results. This paper gives only an example of the parallelization approach. It seems reasonable to divide the search space in such a way that the area given to one particular core will be contained in the next and subsequent one. In addition, a model of communication between populations would be needed to exchange information about unfavorable areas. This would allow them to be removed from space and extended to another area on each core. In practice, this will eliminate unnecessary searches of uninteresting places, and at the same time increase precision (allowing individuals to move around in better places) and reduce computation time due to the reduction of the area on all cores.

Acknowledgments: Authors acknowledge contribution to this project to the Diamond Grant No. 0080/DIA/2016/45 funded by the Polish Ministry of Science and Higher Education and support from Software Engineering Department at Kaunas University of Technology, Lithuania.

Author Contributions: Dawid Połap, Karolina Kęsik, Marcin Woźniak and Robertas Damaševičius designed the methods, performed experiments and wrote the paper.

Conflicts of Interest: The authors declare no conflict of interest.

References

1. Shaoping, L.; Taijiang, M.; Zhang, S. A survey on multiview video synthesis and editing. *Tsinghua Sci. Technol.* **2016**, *21*, 678–695.
2. Hong, Z.; Jingyu, W.; Jie, C.; Shun, Z. Efficient conditional privacy-preserving and authentication scheme for secure service provision in vanet. *Tsinghua Sci. Technol.* **2016**, *21*, 620–629.
3. Rostami, M.; Shahba, A.; Saryazdi, S.; Nezamabadi-pour, H. A novel parallel image encryption with chaotic windows based on logistic map. *Comput. Electr. Eng.* **2017**, *62*, 384–400
4. MY, S.T.; Babu, S. An intelligent system for segmenting lung image using parallel programming. In Proceedings of the International Conference on Data Mining and Advanced Computing (SAPIENCE), Ernakulam, India, 16–18 March 2016; Volume 21, pp. 194–197.
5. Lan, G.; Shen, Y.; Chen, T.; Zhu, H. Parallel implementations of structural similarity based no-reference image quality assessment. *Adv. Eng. Softw.* **2017**, *114*, 372–379.
6. Khatami, A.; Babaie, M.; Khosravi, A.; Tizhoosh, H.R.; Nahavandi, S. Parallel Deep Solutions for Image Retrieval from Imbalanced Medical Imaging Archives. *Appl. Soft Comput.* **2017**, *63*, 197–205.
7. Alzubaidi, M.; Otoom, M.; Al-Tamimi, A.K. Parallel scheme for real-time detection of photosensitive seizures. *Comput. Biol. Med.* **2016**, *70*, 139–147.
8. Munguía, L.; Ahmed, S.; Bader, D.A.; Nemhauser, G.L.; Goel, V.; Shao, Y. A parallel local search framework for the fixed-charge multicommodity network flow problem. *Comput. OR,* **2017**, *77*, 44–57.
9. Gomis, H.M.; Migallón, V.; Penadés, J. Parallel alternating iterative algorithms with and without overlapping on multicore architectures. *Adv. Eng. Softw.* **2016**, *10*, 27–36.

10. Woźniak, M.;Połap, D. Hybrid neuro-heuristic methodology for simulation and control of dynamic systems over time interval. *Neural Netw.* **2017**, *93*, 45–56.

11. Tapkan, P.; Özbakir, L.; Baykasoglu, A. Bee algorithms for parallel two-sided assembly line balancing problem with walking times. *Appl. Soft Comput.* **2016**, *39*, 275–291.

12. Tian, T.; Gong, D. Test data generation for path coverage of message-passing parallel programs based on co-evolutionary genetic algorithms. *Autom. Softw. Eng.* **2016**, *23*, 469–500.

13. Maleki, S.; Musuvathi, M.; Mytkowicz, T. Efficient parallelization using rank convergence in dynamic programming algorithms. *Commun. ACM* **2016**, *59*, 85–92.

14. De Oliveira Sandes, E.F.; Maleki, S.; Musuvathi, M.; Mytkowicz, T. Parallel optimal pairwise biological sequence comparison: Algorithms, platforms, and classification. *ACM Comput. Surv.* **2016**, *48*, 63.

15. Truchet, C.; Arbelaez, A.; Richoux, F.; Codognet, P. Estimating parallel runtimes for randomized algorithms in constraint solving. *J. Heuristics* **2016**, *22*, 613–648.

16. D'Andreagiovanni, F.; Krolikowski, J.; Pulaj, J. A fast hybrid primal heuristic for multiband robust capacitated network design with multiple time periods. *Appl. Soft Comput.* **2015**, *26*, 497–507.

17. Gambardella, L.; Luca, M.; Montemanni, R.; Weyland, D. Coupling ant colony systems with strong local searches. *Eur. J. Oper. Res.* **2012**, *220*, 831–843.

18. Whitlay, D.; Gordon, V.; Mathias, K. Lamarckian evolution, the Baldwin effect and function optimization. In Proceedings of the International Conference on Parallel Problem Solving from Nature, Jerusalem, Israel, 9–14 October 1994; pp. 5–15.

19. Woźniak, M.; Połap, D. On some aspects of genetic and evolutionary methods for optimization purposes. *Int. J. Electr. Telecommun.* **2015**, *61*, 7–16.

20. Blum, C.; Roli, A.; Sampels, M. *Hybrid Metaheuristics: An Emerging Approach to Optimization*; Springer: Berlin/Heidelberg, Germany, 2008.

21. Luenberger, D.G.; Ye, Y. *Linear and Nonlinear Programming*; Springer: Berlin/Heidelberg, Germany, 1984.

22. Lawrence, D. *Handbook of Genetic Algorithms*; Van Nostrand Reinhold: New York, NY, USA, 1991.

23. Dorigo, M.; Gambardella, L.M. Ant colony system: A cooperative learning approach to the traveling salesman problem. *IEEE Trans. Evolut. Comput.* **1997**, *1*, 53–66.

24. Ojha, V.K.; Ajith, A.; Snášel, V. ACO for continuous function optimization: A performance analysis. In Proceedings of the 14th International Conference on Intelligent Systems Design and Applications (ISDA), Okinawa, Japan, 28–30 November 2014; pp. 145–150.

25. Clerc, M. *Particle Swarm Optimization*; John Wiley & Sons: Hoboken, NJ, USA, 2010.

26. Yang, X.-S. Firefly algorithm, stochastic test functions and design optimization. *Int. J. Bio-Inspir. Comput.* **2010**, *2*, 78–84.

27. Yang, X.-S.; Deb, S. Cuckoo search via Lévy flights. In Proceedings of the NaBIC 2009 World Congress on Nature & Biologically Inspired Computing, Coimbatore, India, 9–11 December 2009; pp. 210–214.

28. Rui, T.; Fong, S.; Yang, X.; Deb, S. Wolf search algorithm with ephemeral memory. In Proceedings of the Seventh IEEE International Conference on Digital Information Management (ICDIM), Macau, Macao, 22–24 August 2012; pp. 165–172.

![applied sciences logo]

applied
sciences

MDPI

Article

Event-Driven Sensor Deployment in an Underwater Environment Using a Distributed Hybrid Fish Swarm Optimization Algorithm

Hui Wang [1,2] , Youming Li [1,*], Tingcheng Chang [2], Shengming Chang [1] and Yexian Fan [2]

[1]   Department of Electrical Engineering and Computer Science, Ningbo University, Ningbo 315211, China;
     wangh0802@163.com (H.W.); csm20130504@163.com (S.C.)
[2]   Department of Computer Science Engineering, Ningde Normal University, Ningde 352000, China;
     18250922163@163.com (T.C.); yfan@ndnu.edu.cn (Y.F.)
*   Correspondence: liyouming@nbu.edu.cn; Tel.: +86-152-8030-0017

Received: 4 August 2018; Accepted: 10 September 2018; Published: 13 September 2018

Abstract: In open and complex underwater environments, targets to be monitored are highly dynamic and exhibit great uncertainty. To optimize monitoring target coverage, the development of a method for adjusting sensor positions based on environments and targets is of crucial importance. In this paper, we propose a distributed hybrid fish swarm optimization algorithm (DHFSOA) based on the influence of water flow and the operation of an artificial fish swarm system to improve the coverage efficacy of the event set and to avoid blind movements of sensor nodes. First, by simulating the behavior of foraging fish, sensor nodes autonomously tend to cover events, with congestion control being used to match node distribution density to event distribution density. Second, the construction of an information pool is used to achieve information-sharing between nodes within the network connection range, to increase the nodes' field of vision, and to enhance their global search abilities. Finally, we conduct extensive simulation experiments to evaluate network performance in different deployment environments. The results show that the proposed DHFSOA performs well in terms of coverage efficacy, energy efficiency, and convergence rate of the event set.

Keywords: underwater environment; sensor deployment; event-driven coverage; fish swarm optimization; congestion control

1. Introduction

Underwater acoustic sensor networks (UASNs) are new network systems developed for underwater monitoring. UASNs are composed of numerous sensor nodes with capabilities that include information perception, data storage, data processing, underwater acoustic communication, and more. UASNs have been drawing increasing attention from both governments and research centers due to their extensive use in marine resources surveys, pollution monitoring, aided-navigation, and tactical surveillance. They are a hot topic in the study of sensor networks [1,2].

Recent studies of UASNs have mainly focused on node deployment, location tracking, routing algorithms, energy efficiency strategies, water safety, and other practical aspects. However, the research on node deployment of UASNs (also called coverage control) actually has its shortcomings [3–5]. Node deployment in UASNs has unique challenges which are not found in the deployment of land sensor networks. These include the influence of ocean currents and other factors, the fact that the underwater environments and monitoring targets are more dynamic than their land counterparts, and the challenge that underwater sensor nodes cannot be static and fixed in the monitoring space; instead, network topology must evolve gradually with network operation [6–8]. Therefore, developing a method for adjusting the position of sensor nodes autonomously in response to a changing environment, as well as achieving an effective monitoring system for target waters, are two of the problems researchers face when employing underwater wireless sensor networks.

In recent years, UASN deployment algorithms have mainly included graph-based classes [9], body-centered cubes [10], virtual force classes [11], and group-based intelligent optimization classes [12]. The first three types of redeployment algorithms are relatively complex and thus are not suitable for solving large-scale underwater environment problems. The group-based intelligence optimization algorithm [13], however, can generally determine the optimal solution of a complex optimization problem faster than traditional optimization algorithms [14]. This algorithm is simple to calculate, is neither a centralized nor a global model, and is highly versatile since it utilizes the advantages of group distributed searching. The artificial fish swarm algorithm is an emerging metaheuristic, bionic cluster, intelligent optimization algorithm. Inspired by the operation of the fish swarm system, this paper proposes a distributed hybrid fish swarm optimization algorithm (DHFSOA). The proposed DHFSOA is implemented and its performance is evaluated by simulation.

The following is the general framework of this paper: Section 2 introduces related works; Section 3 defines the underwater sensor deployment problem and its performance metrics; Section 4 presents a detailed introduction to the DHFSOA algorithm; Section 5 consists of a comprehensive evaluation; Section 6 contains our summary and conclusions.

2. Related Works

Swarm Intelligence (SI) is a feature of subjects without intelligence or with simple intelligence exhibiting intelligent behavior through any form of aggregation and collaboration. It is an important branch of artificial intelligence (AI) [15]. Without centralized control and without providing a global model, swarm intelligence provides the basis for finding solutions to complex distributed problems. At present, many research achievements have been made in the field of underwater sensor network coverage control. This section will summarize the coverage control algorithm based on group intelligence optimization.

Iyer [16] proposed an underwater sensor network positioning and deployment scheme based on the genetic algorithm of optimization technology, which determined the fewest number of nodes required to cover an area of interest (AOI). However, this kind of algorithm is obviously easy to fall into local optimum when the network connectivity is not high, and the influence of water flow is not considered. Yiyue [17] proposed an optimal deployment algorithm based on an artificial fish swarm algorithm. This deployment algorithm simulates the preying and following behaviors of artificial fish in order to determine the maximum coverage value. The proposed artificial fish deployment algorithm improves the coverage performance of the common artificial fish algorithm. The inadequacy is that it does not take into account the self-adaptability of the search step size and the information sharing of all nodes in the network, so it is easy to fall into local optimum in the later stage. Dhillon [18] proposed the max average coverage deployment (MACD) algorithm, which uses the grid model to simulate the monitoring area and completes node deployment by utilizing the greedy iterative strategy. The MACD can achieve higher network coverage and connectivity rates, even achieving full network coverage and connectivity. However, since high node density is needed for its successful deployment, this algorithm cannot be applied in situations with sparse underwater sensor network deployment.

In response to the aforementioned shortcomings, Du [19] proposed a particle swarm-inspired underwater sensor self-deployment (PSSD) algorithm that fully utilizes the behavioral characteristics of particle swarms and effectively solves the network coverage problem. However, there exist two obvious disadvantages in this algorithm, one is that it only considers the network coverage of events, and it is difficult to obtain higher network connectivity rates. In addition, since nodes may move blindly when using this algorithm, given their limited energy and the large energy consumption in an underwater environment, underwater nodes will die due to the rapid exhaustion of energy. The other is that the PSSD algorithm was inspired by the classic group intelligence optimization algorithm-particle swarm optimization (PSO). For the traditional optimization algorithm, PSSD is a simple and effective optimization problem, with one obvious drawback, which is the tendency to fall into local extremes [20].

Taking into consideration both the effectiveness and the limitations of the above PSSD algorithm, as well as the non-uniform deployment of underwater monitoring nodes, a distributed hybrid fish swarm optimization algorithm (DHFSOA) is proposed. The DHFSOA provides sensor nodes with an autonomous tendency to cover events by simulating fish foraging behavior and congestion control. Additionally, the concept of an "information pool" is introduced in order to expand the visual range of nodes and avoid blind movements, thus reducing node energy consumption during deployment.

3. Preliminaries

3.1. Description of the Problem

Assume that n underwater sensor nodes are deployed in the monitoring area A and s_i represents the ith node in the network, so that the corresponding sensor node set is $S = \{s_1, s_2, \cdots, s_n\}$. The dynamic point e, which users are interested in, is referred to as an event; thus, in monitoring area A, the event set $E = \{e_i \, | e_i \in A, i = 1, 2, \cdots, m\}$. Assuming that any underwater node has the ability to sense, communicate, and move, $B_j = \left(r_j^s, r_j^c, l_j, P_j\right)$, where r_j^s, r_j^c, l_j, P_j respectively represent the radius of perception, the radius of communication, the maximum moving step length of node s_j, and the current position of the node s_j, and $r_j^s \geq 0$, $r_j^c \geq 0$, and $l_j \geq 0$ $(0 \leq j \leq n)$. In a homogeneous network, all nodes have the same attributes, which are $r_j^s = r^s$, $r_j^c = r^c$, and $l_j = l$ $(0 \leq j \leq n)$. A sensor node can sense an event and communicate with its neighbor nodes to obtain status information (number of events covered) of neighbor nodes. The task of a node is to cover an event, collect information about the event, and maintain connectivity between nodes.

3.2. Coverage Perception Model

It is assumed that in the monitoring area A, the coverage model of each underwater sensor node is a sphere with the sphere's center as the node's coordinates and r_j^s as its radius of perception. The communication range is also a sphere, with radius r_j^c. To ensure the connectivity of the network, the radius of communication is set to be greater than or equal to twice the radius of perception; that is, $r_j^c \geq 2r_j^s$ [21]. Assume the Euclidean distance $d\left(e_i, s_j\right)$ between event e_i and sensor node s_j is

$$d\left(e_i, s_j\right) = \sqrt{\left(x_j - x'_i\right)^2 + \left(y_j - y'_i\right)^2 + \left(z_j - z'_i\right)^2}, \tag{1}$$

where coordinate $\left(x_j, y_j, z_j\right)$ is the coordinate of node s_j and coordinate $\left(x'_j, y'_j, z'_j\right)$ is the coordinate of event e_i. The probability that the defined event e_i is covered by the sensor node s_j is $p\left(e_i, s_j\right)$. A Boolean sensor coverage model is used to simplify the computation, and the probability is a binary function [22]:

$$p\left(e_i, s_j\right) = \begin{cases} 1, & d\left(e_i, s_j\right) \leq r^s, \\ 0, & otherwise. \end{cases} \tag{2}$$

If $d\left(e_i, s_j\right) \leq r^s$, node s_j covers event e_i. In this case $P\left(e_i, s_j\right)$ equals 1; otherwise, it is equal to 0. Similar to the calculation process for a two-dimensional sensor coverage area, the probability that the underwater three-dimensional space event e_i is covered by node set S is $P\left(e_i, S\right)$, where

$$p\left(e_i, S\right) = p\left(e_i, s_1\right) \vee p\left(e_i, s_2\right) \vee \cdots \vee p\left(e_i, s_N\right) = 1 - \prod_{i=1}^{N}\left(1 - p\left(e_i, s_i\right)\right). \tag{3}$$

Definition 1. *According to the preceding analysis, the relative effective coverage degree of event e_i can be described as [19]:*

$$D_A(e_i) = \sum_{s_j \in S} \frac{p(e_i, s_j)}{1 + \sum_{e_i \in E} I(d(e_i, s_j) \leq r^s)}, \tag{4}$$

where $I(\cdot)$ is an indicator function, that is, when the condition $d(e_i, s_j) \leq r^s$ is satisfied, $I(d(e_i, s_j) \leq r^s)$ is equal to 1; otherwise, it is 0. $\sum_{e_i \in E} I(d(e_i, s_j) \leq r^s)$ indicates the number of adjacent events e_i for node s_j.

3.3. Evaluation Standards

In this section, we introduce the coverage efficiency of the event set as well as the network coverage in order to measure the performance of the proposed method.

Definition 2. *Coverage entropy of the event set [19]. This measures the degree of coverage uniformity, and can be calculated as*

$$H_A(E) = \sum_{e_i \in E} D'_A(e_i) \lg \frac{1}{D'_A(e_i)}, \tag{5}$$

where the normalized coverage degree $D'_A(e_i)$ is

$$D'_A(e_i) = \frac{D_A(e_i)}{\sum_{e_j \in E} D_A(e_j)}. \tag{6}$$

It is well known that the coverage entropy of event set $H_A(E)$ reaches its maximum value $\lg m$ only when $D'_A(e_i) = \frac{1}{m}$ (for $i = 1, ..., m$) has equal probability.

Definition 3. *Network coverage C_v is*

$$C_v = \frac{\tilde{t}_e}{t_e}, \tag{7}$$

where $\tilde{t}_e$ is the number of the events covered by nodes and t_e is the total number of the events.

Definition 4. *The coverage efficiency of the event set is [19]*

$$\eta(E) = \alpha \frac{H_A(E)}{\lg m} + \beta \frac{\tilde{n}}{n}, \tag{8}$$

where $\alpha, \beta \in [0, 1]$, $\alpha + \beta = 1$ and $\tilde{n}$ is the number of events covered by nodes.

From Definition 4, we can see that when all nodes cover events, that is, $n = \tilde{n}$, and simultaneously the coverage entropy $H_A(E)$ reaches a maximum value of $\lg m$, $\eta(E)$ will reach its maximum value of 1. Putting it simply, the main goal of underwater node deployment is to place nodes so as to achieve the maximum value of $\eta(E)$.

4. Node Deployment Scheme for UASNs Based on the DHFSOA

The artificial fish swarm algorithm (AFSA) is a heuristic intelligent search algorithm for global optimization. By simulating the preying and survival activities of fish, the AFSA can solve combination optimization problems such as optimal ordering, grouping, or screening of discrete events with a faster convergence speed than previous methods. The fish swarm algorithm and the underwater mobile sensor network are intrinsically related. The sensor node in the sensor network is equivalent to the artificial fish in the AFSA, events are equivalent to food, and the process of the node sensing the event is equivalent to the process of artificial fish searching for food. Therefore, the AFSA has been widely used in underwater mobile sensor networks.

In this study, we propose a DHFSOA and apply it to UASNs. Inspired by the operation of the fish swarm system, the DHFSOA gives the sensor nodes an autonomous tendency to cover events by simulating fish foraging and adjusts the distribution of nodes based on the degree of congestion. Additionally, the concept of an "information pool" is proposed, which expands the node's visual range and accelerates the algorithm's global search capability. Figure 1 is the flow chart of the artificial fish swarm algorithm. Behaviors such as preying, following, and swarming, which occur when fish forage, are the basis for the overall optimization.

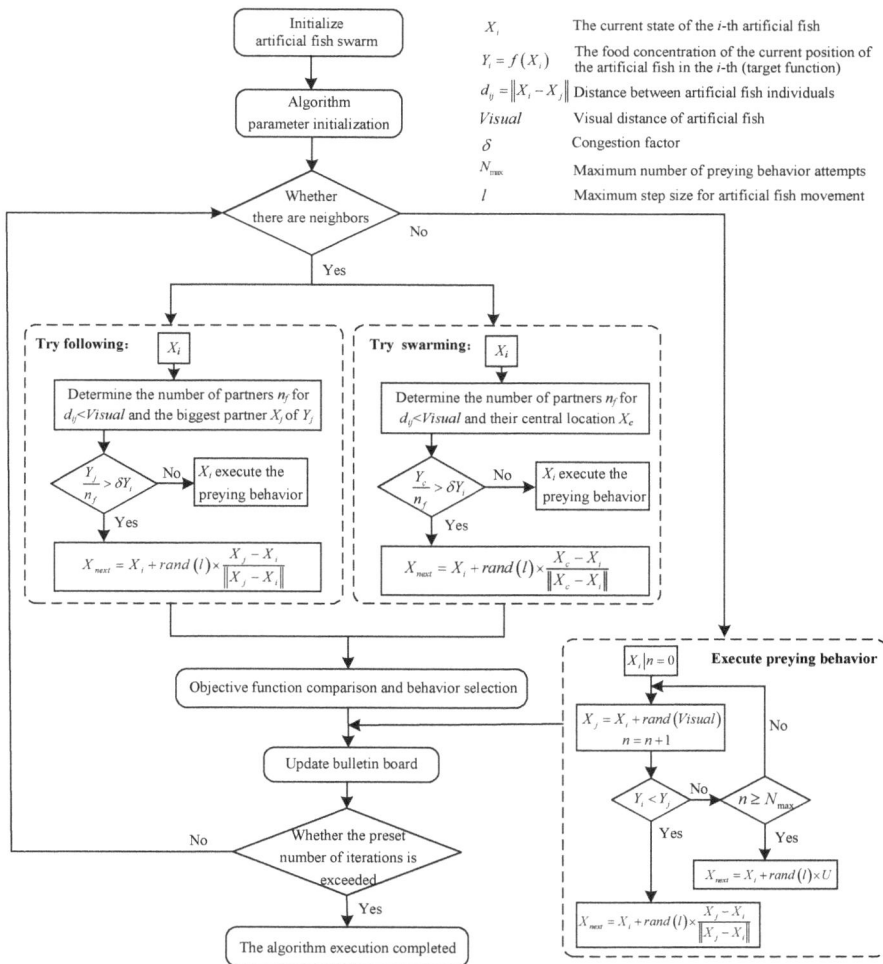

Figure 1. Flow chart of the artificial fish swarm algorithm.

(1) Preying behavior: preying behavior consists of fish randomly swimming in search of food; let the current state of the artificial fish be X_i, randomly select a state X_j within its visual range. When the

maximal value problem is obtained, if $Y_i < Y_j$, then go further in the direction, that is X_{next}; otherwise, re-randomly select the state X_j, judging whether the forward condition is satisfied; after repeatedly trying N_{max} times, if the forward condition is still not satisfied, the step is randomly moved.

(2) Following behavior: following behavior occurs when a fish finds a location with abundant food and other fish quickly follow; suppose the current state of the artificial fish is X_i, the number of partners in the current neighborhood ($d_{ij} < Visual$) is n_f, and the partner with the highest food concentration among the (n_f) partners is X_j (food concentration is Y_j), if $\frac{Y_j}{n_f} > \delta Y_i$, indicating that the state of partner X_j has a higher food concentration and it is not too crowded around, then goes further in the direction of X_j; otherwise, the preying behavior is performed.

(3) Swarming behavior: swarming behavior is the tendency for fish to naturally gather in groups while swimming. Set the number of partners in the current neighborhood ($d_{ij} < Visual$) to be n_f, and the central position status to be X_c. if $\frac{Y_c}{n_f} > \delta Y_i$, indicating that the partner center has more food and the surrounding area is less crowded, moving further toward the partner center position X_c; otherwise, the preying behavior is performed.

Of course, the proposed DSFSOA mainly includes two kinds of behaviors: preying and following. In the following sections, the DHFSOA will be described in detail.

4.1. Construction of the Information Pool

Fish, whether real or artificial, rely on their vision to perceive external conditions, as shown in Figure 2. Here, X_i is the current position of the artificial fish, *Visual* is its visual range, and X_h is the visual position at a particular time. If the concentration of food at the visual position is greater than that of the current position, it is assumed that the fish will proceed towards the visual position, thus arriving at the next position, X_{next}. Otherwise, the artificial fish continues to swim within its visual range. The more the fish swims within its visual range, the more comprehensive the understanding of the state within its visual range will become. This results in a full-scale, stereoscopic perception of the surrounding environment, which aids with corresponding judgments and decisions.

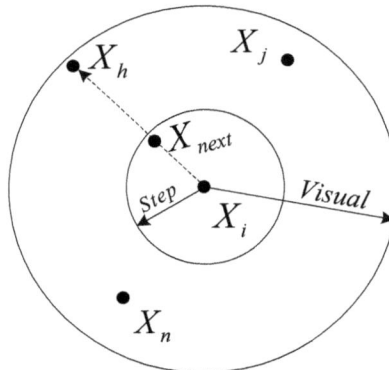

Figure 2. Concept of artificial fish vision.

The sensor node in the DHFSOA is equivalent to the artificial fish in the AFSA, the radius of the communication r^c is equivalent to the visual range of the artificial fish, and the event is equivalent to the food. The process of the mobile node exploring the larger network coverage in the sensor network is similar to the preying and following behaviors of individual artificial fish, and the network coverage of the sensor nodes is analogous to the food concentration in the environment of the artificial fish. However, the traditional artificial fish swarm algorithm cannot be directly applied to the underwater sensor network, mainly due to the fact that sensor nodes have limited amounts of energy. Given this limitation, excessive exploration by sensor nodes within their visual range will lead to their premature death. To enhance the global optimization and neighborhood search capabilities of the artificial fish swarm algorithm, while at the same time avoiding falling into a local optimum, an information pool is introduced here. As shown in Figure 3, it is assumed that there are five nodes in the underwater sensor network $S = \{s_1, \cdots, s_5\}$, and that each node can sense the surrounding events, here the event coverage is defined as the concentration $F = \{f_1, \cdots, f_5\}$. If all other nodes within the radius of communication of a node are referred to as neighbor nodes, then the neighbor nodes of the five nodes s_i ($i = 1, 2, \cdots, 5$) are represented as $g_1 = \{s_2, s_3\}$, $g_2 = \{s_1\}$, $g_3 = \{s_1, s_4\}$, $g_4 = \{s_3\}$, and $g_5 = \{\phi\}$.

The information pool (which can also be thought of as a set) is constructed as follows: each node s_i transmits data (the data mainly consist of the neighbor nodes and the number of coverage events) to each of its neighbor nodes through the network, and each neighbor node then transmits data to neighbor nodes other than the node that sent the data. Continue in this fashion until the data have traversed all the nodes in the connected state. Thus, the information pool in Figure 3 consists of node s_1, s_2, s_3, and s_4, that is, $C_{sum} = \{s_1, s_2, s_3, s_4\}$, and node s_5 is an isolated point. The benefits of the information pool in DSFSOA do not just include an increase in the global search speed of nodes (analogous to fish), but also consist of improvements in network connectivity through collaboration between nodes. As shown in Figure 4, the isolated node s_5 improves its isolated state through the preying behavior, establishes the connectivity between the node s_5 and the network, and expands the amount of information in the information pool, that is, $C_{sum} = \{s_1, s_2, s_3, s_4, s_5\}$, The next step will be to focus on the self-organizing deployment process of nodes. The pseudo-code of the information pool construction algorithm is in Algorithm 1.

Algorithm 1: Construction of the Information Pool (Output Set C_{sum}).

1: $s_i \leftarrow$ a node in monitoring area A;
2: Compute the set formed by node s_j, neighbor of node s_i, $C_i = \{s_j | d(s_i, s_j) \leq r^c\}$;
3: $C_{sum} = C_i \cup \{s_i\}$;
4: $C_{tmp} = C_i$;
5: **while** $(|C_{tmp}| \neq 0)$ **do**
6: $\quad C_k = \overset{|C_{tmp}|}{\underset{j=1}{\cup}} \{s_k | d(s_k, s_j) \leq r^c\}$;
7: $\quad C_{tmp} = C_k - C_{sum}$;
8: $\quad C_{sum} = C_k \cup C_{sum}$;
9: **end while**
10: Output C_{sum};

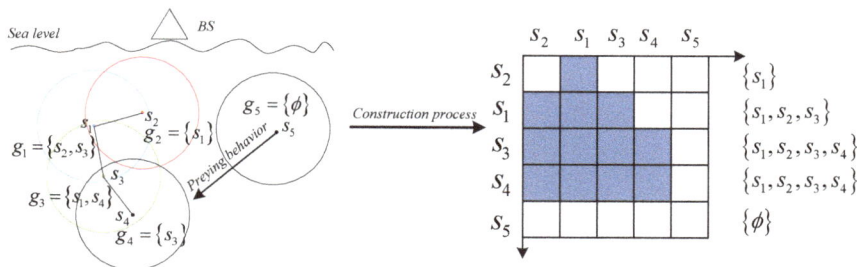

Figure 3. An example of information pool construction (there is an isolated node s_5).

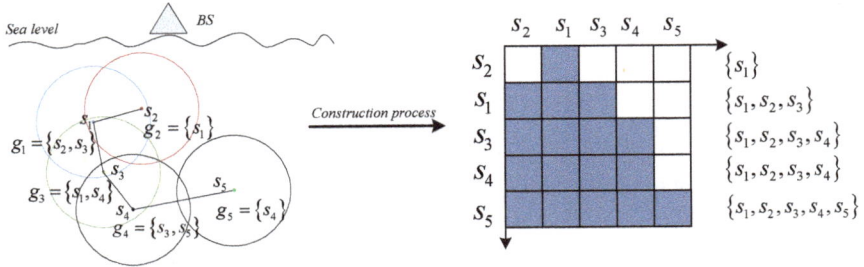

Figure 4. An example of information pool construction (no isolated nodes).

4.2. Description of Artificial Fish Behaviors

The artificial fish swarm optimization algorithm is a centralized, group intelligence search method. Inspired by the operation of the artificial fish swarm system, this paper proposes a distributed and achievable underwater sensor node deployment algorithm, the DHFSOA. The process in which nodes in the sensor network tend to increase network coverage is similar to the preying and following behaviors of artificial fish. Prior to introducing the two behaviors, the following definitions are provided:

Definition 5. *Congestion. The allowed congestion of node s_i in monitoring area A is*

$$\sigma(s_i) = \psi \cdot N_e(s_i),\tag{9}$$

where the constant ψ represents the expected coverage of a single event and $N_e(s_i)$ represents the number of events covered by node s_i, expressed as

$$N_e(s_i) = \sum_{e_j \in E} p(e_j, s_i).\tag{10}$$

Definition 6. *The number of nodes $N_{ne}^s(s_i)$ within the communication range and the number of nodes $N_{co}^s(s_i)$ within the perceived range of the node s_i can be expressed as*

$$N_{ne}^s(s_i) = card(\lambda(s_j)),\tag{11}$$

where $card(\lambda(s_j))$ indicates the number of nodes in the collection $\lambda(s_j)$, $\lambda(s_j) = \{s_j \mid d(s_i, s_j) \le r^c, 1 \le i, j \le n, i \ne j\}$ represents the set of nodes s_j within the communication radius of the node s_i, and $d(s_i, s_j)$ represents the Euclidean distance between node s_i and s_j:

$$N_{co}^s(s_i) = card(\gamma(s_j)),\tag{12}$$

where $\gamma(s_j) = \{s_j \mid d(s_i, s_j) \le r^s, 1 \le i, j \le n, i \ne j\}$ represents the set of nodes s_j within the perceived range of the node s_i

Next, the behavioral description of the artificial fish will be specifically described. n sensor nodes are randomly scattered in the underwater monitoring area A. Node s_i may perform the following operations based on its own status as well as that of its neighbor nodes:

(1) Following behavior: Set the number of partners in the visible domain (radius of communication being r^c) of node s_i as $N_{ne}^s(s_i)$, $N_{ne}^s(s_i) > 0$ and information pool built with the partners as C_{sum}, and determine the optimal node s_{opt} in C_{sum},

$$S_{opt} = \arg\max_{s_k \in C_{sum}} \{ N_{ne}^s (s_k) \}. \tag{13}$$

If node s_i finds more events covered at s_{opt} and s_{opt} is less crowded, i.e., $N_e (s_{opt}) \geq N_e (s_i)$ and $N_{co}^s (s_{opt}) < \sigma (s_{opt})$, then move one step toward the position of partner s_{opt}:

$$X_{next} = X_i + rand (l) \times \frac{X_{opt} - X_i}{\|X_{opt} - X_i\|}, \tag{14}$$

where X_i and X_{opt} represent position vectors of s_i and s_{opt} respectively, and l is the value of the moving step.

(2) Preying behavior: Set the number of partners in the visible domain (radius of communication being r^c) of node s_i as $N_{ne}^s (s_i)$, $N_{ne}^s (s_i) = 0$, which indicates that node s_i is in an isolated state. l is the maximum value of the moving step. Set the current position of node s_i as $\vec{x}_i$, and randomly move to the new position $\vec{x}_j$ within its maximum moving step l:

$$X_{next} = X_i + rand (l) \times \frac{X_i - X_j}{\|X_i - X_j\|}, \tag{15}$$

where $rand(l)$ represents the random value between 0 to l. If $N_e (s_i)$ increases, the preying behavior is successful; if the preying fails, then it randomly reselects a new position. After repeating this process N_{max} times (In general, the value of N_{max} is small, mainly based on our practical experience and repeated experiments [23].), if $N_e (s_i)$ still cannot be increased, then randomly move forward one step:

$$X_{next} = X_i + rand (-l, l) \times U, \tag{16}$$

where U is an arbitrary unit vector, and $rand(-l, l)$ represents a random number between $-l$ and l.

4.3. Description of the DHFSOA

The preceding section describes the process of the sensor nodes simulating the preying and following behaviors of artificial fish. The following analogous behavior can help the sensor node move to an improved state, thus accelerating the convergence of the algorithm. Preying behavior is characterized by the searching activity of the sensor node within the radius of communication r^c, which ensures that the sensor node continues moving towards the optimal state. In addition, in the early stages of algorithm implementation, a larger step size should be adopted. This allows the sensor node to perform a coarse search within a larger range and helps to enhance the global search ability and convergence speed of the algorithm. As the search progresses, the step size is gradually reduced, and the algorithm slowly evolves into a local search. The sensor node eventually locates the area near the optimal position for a precise search, thereby improving the local search capability of the algorithm and the accuracy of the optimization result. Therefore, the step size l of the node is adjusted as follows:

$$l_{Iter} = l_{Iter-1} \times a + l_{min}, \tag{17}$$

$$a = \exp \left(-g \times \left(\frac{Iter}{IterNum} \right)^g \right), \tag{18}$$

where l is the maximum value of the moving step, l_{min} is the minimum value of the moving step, $Iter$ is the current number of iterations, and $IterNum$ is the maximum number of iterations. It is known from Equation (17) that the moving step depends on the value of a, and the value of a is determined by k and g. Figure 5a depicts the relationship between parameter k, g and a when $Iter$ is 20 and $IterNum$ is

50. It is easy to see that the value of a increases as g increases, but decreases as k increases. When k and g are fixed, it is apparent that function $a = f(Iter)$ in Equation (18) is a subtraction function in the interval $[1, IterNum]$. Therefore, the choice of k should be as large as possible, while the choice of g should be as small as possible. $k = 20$ and $g = 5$ are based on our practical experience and repeated experiments. Figure 5b shows the relationship between a and $Iter$ when $k = 20$ and $g = 5$. The DHFSOA algorithm uses the maximum value at the beginning of the search, then gradually reduces it, eventually reaching and maintaining the minimum, which is in line with the original intention of the design. Based on the above description, a complete underwater sensor node placement algorithm inspired by fish swarms is presented in Algorithm 2.

Algorithm 2: DHFSOA Description

1: **Input:** $B_i = \left(r_i^s, r_i^c, l_i, P_i \right)$, $IterNum$;

2: **Output:** P_i^{k+1};

3: $S = \{s_1, s_2, \cdots, s_n\} \leftarrow$ Randomly deploy sensors in UWSNs;

4: **for** $k = 1, 2, \cdots, IterNum$ **do**

5:     $N_e(s_i)$, $i \in [1, n] \leftarrow$ Detect events covered by node s_i;

6:     $N_{co}^s(s_i)$, $i \in [1, n] \leftarrow$ Number of nodes within the node's perceived range;

7:     **if** $N_{ne}^s(s_i) > 0$ **then**

8:         Use Algorithm 1 to get Set C_{sum};

9:         Sort the nodes in Set C_{sum} according to the number of events covered, find Set $\Re$,

            and satisfy $N_e(s_{opt}) \geq N_e(s_i)$ and $N_{co}^s(s_{opt}) < \sigma(s_{opt})$;

10:        $s_{opt} = \arg\max_{s_k \in \Re} \{N_e(s_i)\}$;

11:        Perform following behavior and move closer to node s_{opt};

12:    **else**

13:        **for** $N_{prey} = 1, 2, \cdots, N_{max}$ **do**

14:            Perform preying behavior and randomly move;

15:            **if** $N_e(s'_i) > N_e(s_i)$ **do**

16:                **break;**

17:            **endif**

18:        **endfor**

19:    **end if**

20: **end for**

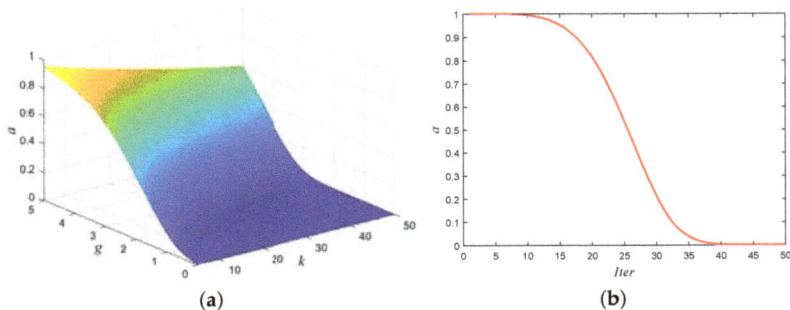

(a)   (b)

Figure 5. Selection of relevant parameters of the moving step in the DSFSOA (distributed hybrid fish swarm optimization algorithm) algorithm. (**a**) the relationship between parameter k, g and a when $Iter$ is 20 and $IterNum$ is 50; (**b**) the relationship between a and $Iter$ when $k = 20$ and $g = 5$.

5. Performance Analysis

To fully verify the performance of the DHFSOA algorithm proposed in this paper, multiple Monte Carlo simulation experiments were implemented in the ocean (3D) node deployment on the Matlab platform(2016b, MathWorks, Natick, MA, USA). The PSSD algorithm is a typical non-uniform deployment algorithm for underwater wireless sensor network nodes. To evaluate the performance of the DHFSOA algorithm, the PSSD algorithm was selected for comparison. Evaluation included simulation, comparison, and analysis of network coverage, coverage efficacy of the event set, and total moving distance of the node. In addition, to eliminate any random effects of individual experiments, the final result was the average of 30 experiments. The parameter settings and experimental parameters of the algorithm are shown in Table 1.

Table 1. Simulation parameters.

Parameter	Value	Parameter	Value
Node's radius of perception r^s	50 m	Maximum number of iterations T_{max}	50
Node's radius of communication r^c	100 m	Constant N_{max}	5
Length of moving step l	15 m	Constant ψ	0.1

5.1. Static Environment Sensor Deployment

Three sets of experiments were implemented in a three-dimensional monitoring area of 200 m × 200 m × 200 m: (1) six sensor nodes and 40 events were unevenly distributed in a T shape; (2) six sensor nodes and 40 events were randomly distributed; and (3) six sensor nodes and 40 events were unevenly distributed in a line.

Figure 6 shows the results of the DSFSOA algorithm for self-organizing deployment of nodes. The light blue sphere represents the three-dimensional sensing range of the sensor node (the red center of the sphere is the position of the node), and the blue star represents the event. It can be seen that the DHFSOA algorithm is capable of achieving a final state in which all events covered by nodes and there is a good match between node distribution density and event distribution density.

The PSSD algorithm and the DHFSOA were used to deploy the sensor nodes. Figure 7 shows the evolution of the total moving distance and event coverage for the two algorithms in the three experiments. It should be noted that the final result for each set of experiments here is the average of 30 experiments. It can be seen in Figure 7a,c,e that the DHFSOA algorithm not only achieved high coverage of the event, but indeed achieved optimal coverage after just a few moves of the node, demonstrating faster convergence speed than the PSSD. More critically, the DHFSOA algorithm overcame the node blindness found in the traditional heuristic random search algorithm, while the PSSD algorithm exhibited significant instability and a poor final result. Figure 7b,d,f, is a comparison of the trend of the total moving distance of the node with the change of the number of iterations of the DSFSOA algorithm and the PSSD. It is clear that the DHFSOA algorithm greatly decreases the total moving distance of nodes during deployment compared with the PSSD algorithm. This is mainly due to the fact that the nodes in the PSSD algorithm make blind movements. The DHFSOA algorithm utilizes information sharing between the nodes based on the information pool. This improves the global sensing ability of the distributed fish swarm algorithm and thus avoids the blind movement of nodes, thereby reducing the total moving distance of nodes during deployment.

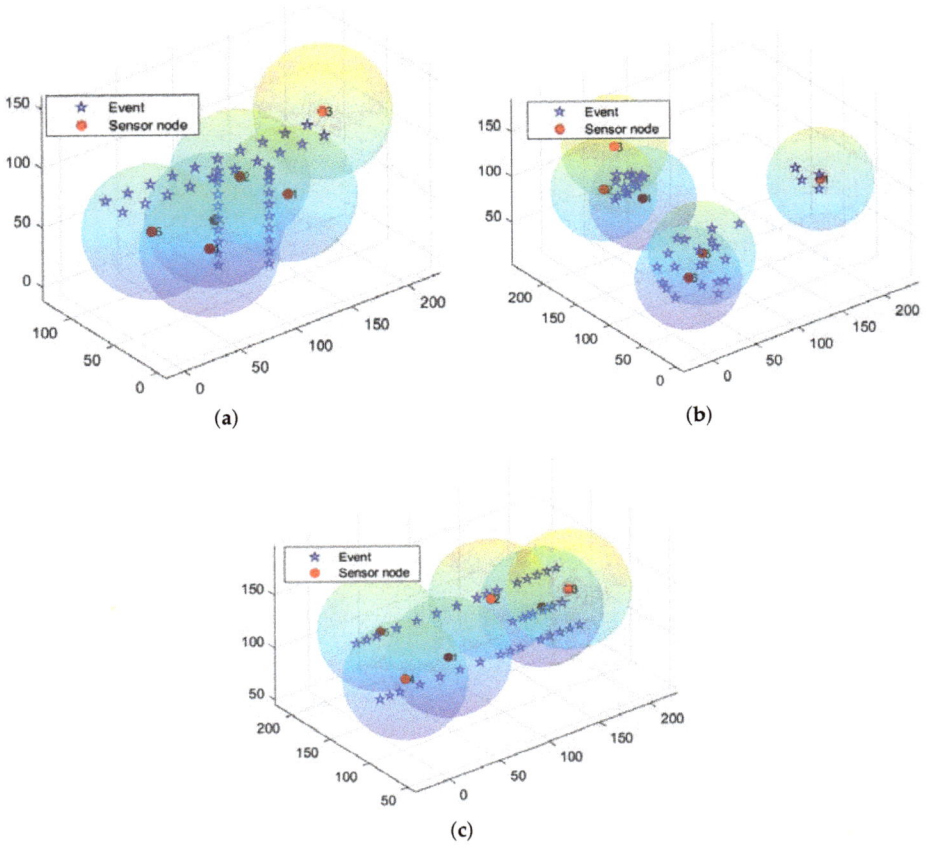

Figure 6. Achievement of self-organized Deployment of Nodes using the DHFSOA. (**a**) events unevenly distributed in a T shape; (**b**) 40 events randomly distributed; (**c**) 40 events unevenly distributed linearly.

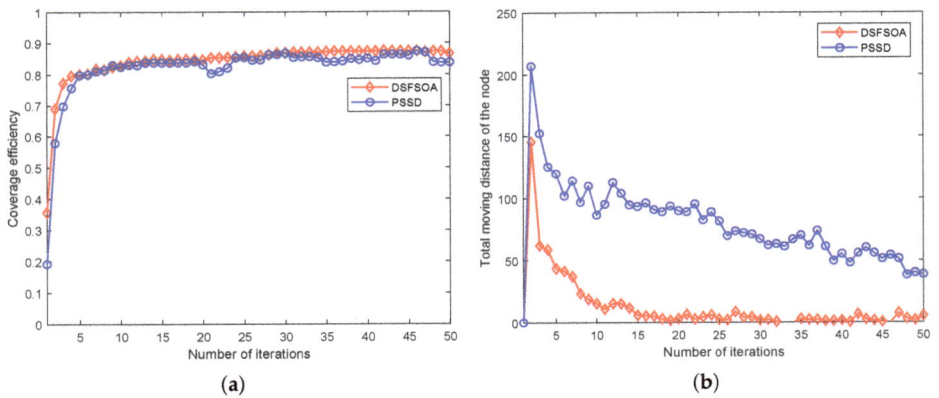

Figure 7. *Cont.*

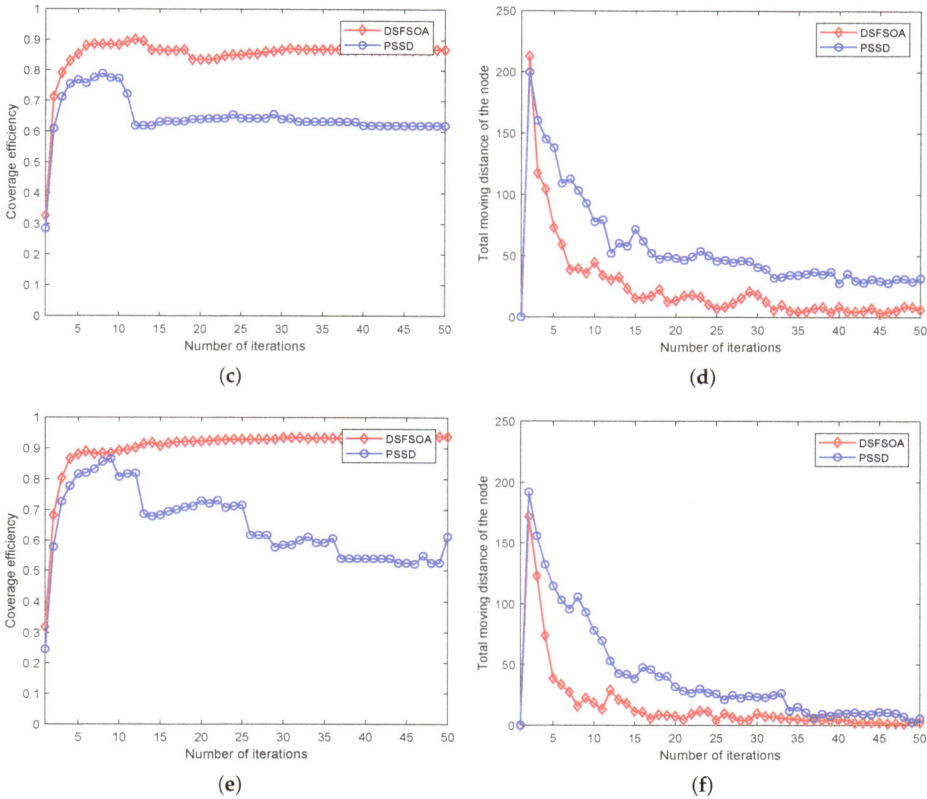

Figure 7. Comparison of the evolution of total moving distance and event coverage of two methods in three sets of experiments. (**a**) Experiment 1: average coverage; (**b**) Experiment 1: total moving distance of nodes; (**c**) Experiment 2: average coverage; (**d**) Experiment 2: total moving distance of nodes; (**e**) Experiment 3: average coverage; (**f**) Experiment 3: total moving distance of nodes.

5.2. Sensor Deployment in a Dynamic Environment

To analyze the reliability and adaptability of the DHFSOA algorithm, this section explores the results of sensor deployment in a non-uniformly covered, dynamic ocean environment. Water flow velocity was generated based on a model presented in a previous study [19,24]; model parameters are listed in Table 2. The update period T for sensors in the DHFSOA was 0.5 s.

For the case in which events take place in a dynamic ocean environment, flowing water will cause their positions to change. The simulation results at four different times are shown in Figure 8a–d. As can be seen in the figures, when events present a linear distribution, underwater nodes also exhibit a linear distribution, and regions with high event densities have more underwater nodes. It can be seen that underwater nodes move with events and always present the same distribution shape. The node covers the events well, and achieves the matching of underwater node density and event density.

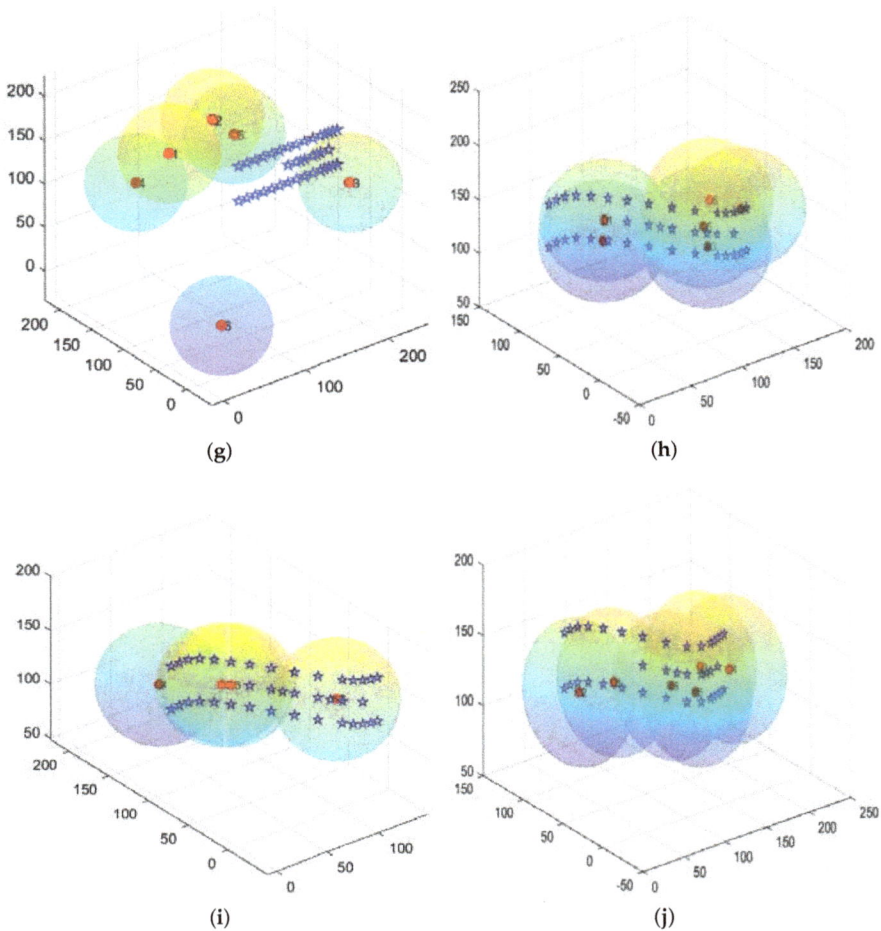

(g)

(h)

(i)

(j)

Figure 8. The distribution of sensor nodes and events at times t_1 to t_4. (**a**) initial time node t_1 and event distribution; (**b**) initial time node t_2 and event distribution; (**c**) initial time node t_3 and event distribution; (**d**) initial time node t_4 and event distribution.

Next, the network operation time was divided into 10 segments. Figures 9 and 10 respectively compare the coverage efficacy of the event set and the evolution of the total moving distance of the nodes during each monitoring period. It can be seen in Figure 8 that the coverage efficacy of the event set is constantly changing with time, and both the DHFSOA and PSSD algorithms maintain good states. The DHFSOA, however, dynamically adjusts quickly and is slightly better than the PSSD algorithm. Figure 9 is a comparison diagram between the PSSD algorithm and the DHFSOA for the changes in total node moving distance during the network running time. It can be seen that, compared with the PSSD, the DHFSOA algorithm greatly reduces the total moving distance of the nodes during the network operation, thus reducing total energy consumption. This allows the nodes to retain more energy, which can be used to participate in other tasks, effectively extending the network life cycle.

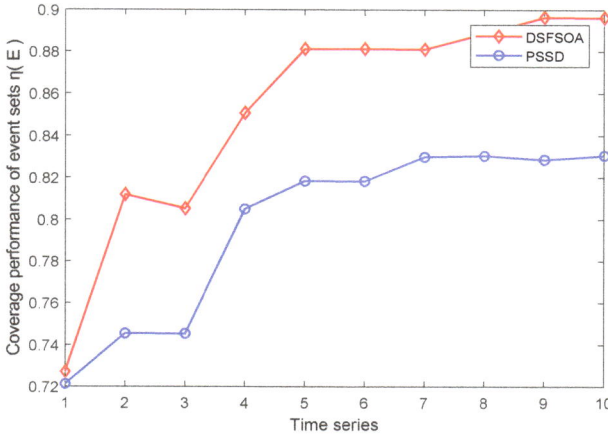

Figure 9. Comparison of the evolution of coverage efficacy at different times.

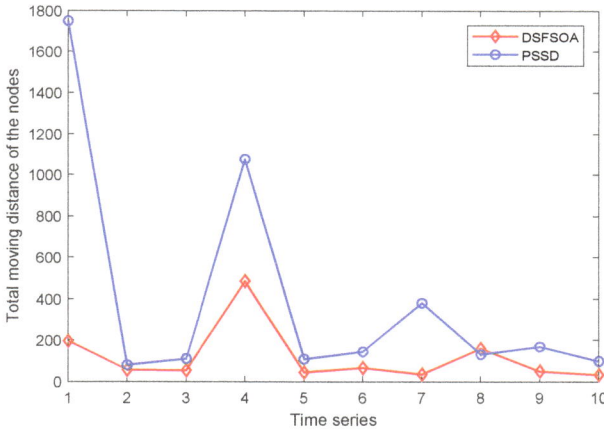

Figure 10. Comparison of the evolution of the total moving distance of nodes at different times.

We can see from the preceding figures that, compared to the PSSD algorithm, the DHFSOA has obvious advantages in terms of network coverage, coverage efficacy of event sets, and total moving distance of nodes. This is due to that fact that, during network operation, the DHFSOA constructs an information pool, expands the nodes' field of vision, enhances information sharing between nodes in the network connectivity state, avoids blind movement of nodes, and retains the global search ability of the traditional fish swarm heuristic algorithm.

Table 2. Parameters of the dynamic ocean environment.

Parameter	The Water Flow Field					Target Number	
	k	c	av	ε	ω	Sensors	Events
Value	$\frac{2\pi}{7.5}$	0.12	1.2	0.3	0.4	6	40

6. Conclusions

This paper has proposed a distributed hybrid fish swarm optimization algorithm (DHFSOA) in order to optimize the deployment of underwater acoustic sensor nodes. The proposed DHFSOA was inspired by the artificial fish swarm operation system designed to simulate the preying, following, and swarming behaviors of fish. Applying these sorts of behaviors to sensor nodes gives them the autonomous tendency and ability to cover events within a monitoring area. Congestion distribution control was used to match node and event distribution densities. In addition, by constructing an information pool, the DHFSOA not only overcame the blindness of the traditional artificial fish swarm heuristic algorithm random search, but also retained the global search ability of the traditional fish swarm heuristic algorithm.

The proposed algorithm was evaluated by running a large number of comparative simulation experiments. Once the static and dynamic environments of the underwater acoustic sensor networks (UASNs) were established, the proposed DHFSOA was used for actual testing. The simulation results showed that the DHFSOA has the following three advantages over the PSSD algorithm: (1) the DHFSOA can maintain higher event coverage and coverage efficacy of event sets; (2) the DHFSOA can avoid blind movement of nodes, thus reducing total node moving distance and thereby reducing total energy consumption during node deployment; and (3) DHFSOA is a distributed algorithm, which shows strong extensibility during node deployment. In our next study, we will improve the proof of DHFSOA convergence and begin experimenting in actual underwater environments.

Author Contributions: H.W. and Y.L. conceived and designed the whole procedure of this paper. T.C. contributed to the introduction and system model sections. S.C. and Y.F. performed and analyzed the computer simulation results.

Funding: This research was supported by the National Natural Science Foundation of China (61571250), the Zhejiang Natural Science Foundation (LY18F010010), the Key Laboratory of Mobile Network Application Technology of Zhejiang Province, the K. C. Wong Magna Fund of Ningbo University, the Youth Project of Ningde Normal University (2017Q105,018Q103), the Teaching Reform Project of the Ningde Normal University (JG20180122), the project of the Education Department of Fujian Province (JT180596) and the project of the Fujian Provincial Natural Science Fund (2017I0016, 2017J01775).

Conflicts of Interest: The authors declare no conflict of interest.

References

1. Akyildiz, I.F.; Pompili, D.; Melodia, T. Underwater acoustic sensor networks: Research challenges. *Ad Hoc Netw.* **2005**, *3*, 257–279. [CrossRef]
2. Chen, K.; Ma, M.; Cheng, E.; Yuan, F.; Su, W. A survey on MAC protocols for underwater wireless sensor networks. *IEEE Commun. Surv. Tutor.* **2014**, *16*, 1433–1447. [CrossRef]
3. Davis, A.; Chang, H. Underwater wireless sensor networks. In Proceedings of the IEEE Oceans 2012, Hampton Road, VA, USA, 14–19 October 2012; pp. 1–5.
4. Berger, C.R.; Zhou, S.L.; Willett, P.; Liu, L.B. Stratification Effect Compensation for Improved Underwater Acoustic Ranging. *IEEE Trans. Signal Process.* **2008**, *56*, 3779–3783. [CrossRef]
5. Wang, C.; Lin, H.; Jiang, H. CANS: A Congestion-Adaptive WSN-Assisted Emergency Navigation Algorithm with Small Stretch. *IEEE Trans. Mob. Comput.* **2016**, *15*, 1077–1089. [CrossRef]
6. Wang, H.; Li, Y.; Chang, T.; Chang, S. An Effective Scheduling Algorithm for Coverage Control in Underwater Acoustic Sensor Network. *Sensors* **2018**, *18*, 2512. [CrossRef] [PubMed]
7. Ian, F. Wireless sensor networks in challenged environments such as underwater and underground. In Proceedings of the 17th ACM International Conference on Modeling, Analysis and Simulation of Wireless and Mobile Systems, New York, NY, USA, 21–26 September 2014; pp. 1–2.
8. Yang, X.; Miao, P.; Gibson, J.; Xie, G.G.; Du, D.Z.; Vasilakos, A.V. Tight performance bounds of multihop fair access for MAC protocols in wireless sensor networks and underwater sensor networks. *IEEE Mob. Comput.* **2011**, *11*, 1538–1554
9. Luo, X.; Feng, L.; Yan, J.; Guan, X. Dynamic Coverage with Wireless Sensor and Actor Networks in Underwater Environment. *IEEE/CAA J. Autom. Sin.* **2015**, *2*, 274–281.

10. Liu, L.F. A deployment algorithm for underwater sensor networks in ocean environment. *J. Circuits Syst. Comput.* **2011**, *20*, 1051–1066. [CrossRef]

11. Abo-Zahhad, M.; Ahmed, S.M.; Sabor, N.; Sasaki, S. Rearrangement of mobile wireless sensor nodes for coverage maximization based on immune node deployment algorithm. *Comput. Electr. Eng.* **2015**, *43*, 76–89. [CrossRef]

12. Hua, C.B.; Wei, Z.; Nan, C.Z. Underwater Acoustic Sensor Networks Deployment Using Improved Self-Organize Map Algorithm. *Cybern. Inf. Technol.* **2014**, *14*, 63–77. [CrossRef]

13. Bonabeau, E.; Dorigo, M.; Theraulaz, G. *Swarm Intelligence: From Natural to Artificial Systems*; Oxford University Press, Inc.: New York, NY, USA, 1999.

14. Liu, X. Sensor deployment of wireless sensor networks based on ant colony optimization with three classes of ant transitions. *IEEE Trans. Commun. Lett.* **2012**, *16*, 1604–1607. [CrossRef]

15. Wang, H.B.; Fan, C.C.; Tu, X.Y. AFSAOCP: A novel artificial fish swarm optimization algorithm aided by ocean current power. *Appl. Intell.* **2016**, *45*, 1–16. [CrossRef]

16. Iyer, S.; Rao, D.V. Genetic algorithm based optimization technique for underwater sensor network positioning and deployment. In Proceedings of the 2015 IEEE Underwater Technology (UT), Chennai, India, 23–25 February 2015; pp. 1–6.

17. Wang, Y.; Liao, H.; Hu, H. Wireless Sensor Network Deployment Using an Optimized Artificial Fish Swarm Algorithm. In Proceedings of the International Conference on Computer Science and Electronics Engineering, Hangzhou, China, 23–25 March 2012; pp. 90–94.

18. Dhillon, S.S.; Chakrabarty, K. Sensor placement for effective coverage and surveillance in distributed sensor networks. In Proceedings of the Wireless Communications and Networking, New Orleans, LA, USA, 16–20 March 2003; pp. 1609–1614.

19. Du, H.; Na, X.; Rong, Z. Particle Swarm Inspired Underwater Sensor Self-Deployment. *Sensors* **2014**, *14*, 15262–15281. [CrossRef] [PubMed]

20. Das, S.; Liu, H.; Nayak, A. A localized algorithm for bi-connectivity of connected mobile robots. *Telecommun. Syst.* **2009**, *40*, 129–140. [CrossRef]

21. Zhang, H.H.; Hou, J.C. Maintaining Sensing Coverage and Connectivity in Large Sensor Networks. *Ad Hoc Sens. Wirel. Netw.* **2005**, *1*, 89–124.

22. Ghosh, A.; Das, S.K. Coverage and connectivity issues in wireless sensor networks: A survey. *Pervasive Mob. Comput.* **2008**, *4*, 303–334. [CrossRef]

23. Neshat, M.; Sepidnam, G.; Sargolzaei, M.; Toosi, A.N. Artificial fish swarm algorithm: A survey of the state-of-the-art, hybridization, combinatorial and indicative applications. *Artif. Intell. Rev.* **2014**, *42*, 965–997. [CrossRef]

24. Caruso, A.; Paparella, F.; Vieira, L.F.M.; Erol, M.; Gerla, M. The Meandering Current Mobility Model and its Impact on Underwater Mobile Sensor Networks. In Proceedings of the IEEE INFOCOM 2008, Phoenix, AZ, USA, 13–18 April 2008; pp. 771–775.

MDPI

St. Alban-Anlage 66

4052 Basel

Switzerland

Tel. +41 61 683 77 34

Fax +41 61 302 89 18

www.mdpi.com

Applied Sciences Editorial Office

E-mail: applsci@mdpi.com

www.mdpi.com/journal/applsci